Major Themes
in the
Reformed Tradition

Major Themes
in the
Reformed Tradition

Edited by

Donald K. McKim

Wipf and Stock Publishers
EUGENE, OREGON

Wipf and Stock Publishers
199 West 8th Avenue, Suite 3
Eugene, Oregon 97401

Major Themes in the Reformed Tradition
By McKim, Donald K.
Copyright© McKim, Donald K.
ISBN: 1-57910-104-6
Publication date: March, 1998
Previously published by Eerdmans, .

To C. Kenneth Hall

A Reformed pastor whose ministry has blessed us
and whose witness to the gospel has blessed the church

Dedicated with appreciation and affection

Contents

THEOLOGICAL INTERACTIONS

Foreword

We have long needed a substantial resource for studying major theological themes in the Reformed tradition. The following essays are collected to meet that need.

The best way to study Reformed theology is to read Reformed writings. To understand these and place them in context, we also have to study the historical developments and expressions of the Reformed tradition. The essays in this volume fall into two categories. Some trace the development of major themes historically through the writings of various Reformed theologians, while others deal with a theological topic from a Reformed perspective. Thus this book has a theological focus with a historical orientation. Both perspectives are needed.

The essays have been grouped into several sections in an attempt to provide some order in the volume, though the order is to some extent artificial. Certainly other sections could have been established, and some of the essays might properly be placed in more than one of the sections that were selected. Nevertheless, the selected categories do provide an indication of some of the important Reformed emphases and prominent theological topics.

It is also apparent that this collection is not comprehensive. Many aspects of Reformed theology and struggles within the Reformed tradition are not represented, and others are underplayed. Candidates for inclusion in the volume grew rapidly from the inception of the project, and there was not nearly room enough for all of them, so regrettably some clusters of concerns are not treated.

The following pieces are primarily historical/theological studies drawn for the most part from previously published sources. I am grateful to authors, editors, and publishers who have granted permission to reprint these pieces. Wherever possible, changes have been made to reflect more inclusive language. I also wish to thank those who wrote new essays for this volume. Throughout, the primary thrust of the pieces is positive; they deal with what the Reformed tradition has to say as an expression of its study of "theology" — study of God. The works do not delve into psychological or sociological analyses of the tradition, nor do they provide detailed descriptions of how the tradition spread historically.

The Reformed tradition has taken shape

locally in thousands of places. It has done so not only through theological writings and the confessions of its churches but also in the lives of Reformed Christians. The primary context of these essays (and essayists) is European and North American. Yet today there are many other areas throughout the world where the Reformed tradition is vibrant. As theological contributions emerge from these contexts, and from heretofore marginalized voices everywhere, from women and nonwhite cultures, it will be important that they take their place in volumes like this.

This book represents for me an ongoing attempt to provide resources for the study of Christian theology. While I have recently tried to tell the story of how foundational doctrines developed early in the church,[1] in this volume, which draws together the work of others, I try to focus directly on developments in Reformed theology.[2]

I am a Reformed theologian by commitment. An important part of that commitment is to acquaint not only scholars but also seminarians, pastors, and laypeople in local churches with this Reformed heritage and legacy. Part of that heritage and legacy involves growth in the Christian faith. Part of that growth involves knowing where the church has been and what it has believed and taught so that we can proceed to listen obediently to the will of God in the present. This book is offered with that aim. Many of the selections are fully documented scholarly articles. Others offerings, written more informally, provide helpful points of departure for group discussion and personal reflection. I could scarcely hope to illuminate the full Reformed tradition in all its diversity in a book of this sort, but I do think these selections make an interesting beginning for such a project.

Others besides the writers have helped me. I would like to thank Prof. Neal Plantinga of Calvin Theological Seminary, who, through Jon Pott, Editor-in-Chief of the William B. Eerdmans Publishing Company, offered significant suggestions to strengthen the range and depth of the book's offerings. Jon Pott himself has been a constant support and has greatly enhanced the scope of the book by his own suggestions. His encouragement and support are a true joy. My wife LindaJo and sons Stephen and Karl also provide true joys for living. Without their love and support, the Reformed tradition would mean less to me, I'm sure.

This book is dedicated to the Rev. Dr. C. Kenneth Hall, Moderator of the 200th General Assembly of the Presbyterian Church (USA). A long-time pastor, Ken has modeled for me the best of the Reformed tradition. His care and friendship have meant much.

DONALD K. MCKIM

NOTES

1. See Donald K. McKim, *Theological Turning Points: Major Issues in Christian Thought* (Atlanta: John Knox, 1988).

2. This has also been my intention in *The Encyclopedia of the Reformed Faith* (Louisville: Westminster/John Knox Press, 1992).

Introduction

The Reformed theological tradition has had a long and important history. International in scope and comprehensive in interest, this tradition has been vitally involved in theological reflection and action since the days of the sixteenth century. At its best, the Reformed tradition has tried to relate theology meaningfully to life. It has sought to combine right thinking about God and God's revelation with right living and the obedient discipleship of Christian living.

The Reformed tradition traces its historical roots to the life and work of John Calvin (1509-1564). The French Reformer who made such an impact on the city of Geneva and the developing Protestant theology of the Reformation has continued to exert an important influence to the current day.[1] The earliest Swiss Protestant Reformer was Ulrich Zwingli (1484-1531). His views developed apart from Calvin's but also had a significant role in the development of Reformed theology. Those who have followed these Swiss reformers and carried on their insights have stressed the need for rigorous intellectual thought as well as faithful Christian devotion. The Reformed

tradition developed throughout Europe and spread to the Americas as a Protestant alternative to Lutheranism and Anabaptism.[2] In its wake, churches, schools, and other institutions developed as Reformed Christians sought to witness to their faith.[3]

Calvin's heavy stress on the need for a coherent theology was a major concern of subsequent Reformed Christians as well. Early indications of this concern are found in the numerous confessions of faith produced by Reformed churches in the sixteenth and seventeenth centuries. The churches worked hard on these formulations of their theological understanding to clarify as much as possible exactly what they believed.[4] The Reformed tradition has produced a number of notable theologians who have contributed significant theological works about virtually every aspect of Christian faith and life.[5] Reformed theologians have written important systematic theologies expounding Christian doctrine and showing the relationships among the various concepts of theology. In the nineteenth-century, Heinrich Heppe gathered together source documents around the different theological doctrines to show what a Reformed dogmatics would look like.[6] In the twentieth century, the works of Karl Barth — especially his *Church Dogmatics* — constitute a vigorous restatement and interpretation of the Reformed faith for the present day.[7] Other major dogmaticians of this century such as Emil Brunner, Otto Weber, Hendrikus Berkhof, and G. C. Berkouwer have also given the Reformed tradition new directions and emphases.

The term *Reformed* arose from the emphasis of the Swiss Reformers on the reform of the church according to the Word of God. During the sixteenth century, the term applied to all Protestant churches, as did the term *evangelical*. But the Swiss Reformers, because of their thorough commitment to Scripture as the source of authority for the church and their emphases on simplicity in worship and discipline both in private and public life, came to be called "Reformed" in a particular way. The desire to reform all life according to the Word of God was a comprehensive commitment and the underlying foundation for those who went on to develop the Reformed theological tradition.[8]

After several centuries, the Reformed tradition continues to unfold. The essays in this volume indicate a number of dimensions with which Reformed theology has dealt. Their purpose is not only to inform and provide theological data but also to show how the Reformed faith can be a vital source of comfort and challenge in today's world as it springs from theological insights and takes shape historically through the lives, thoughts, and actions of Christian believers. As with any tradition, it may be received with gratitude and assessed critically. This book has been assembled for both these purposes. As John Leith has put it,

> the Reformed tradition does not claim to be the only Christian tradition. It does claim to be *one* way the one, holy, catholic, apostolic church has lived, handing on its faith and life to every new generation. It does claim to be an authentic form of the Christian community that has its special strength and also its weaknesses and problems. It intends to be the people of God in all their fullness. On the basis of this claim, it asks for both acceptance and criticism.[9]

SOLI DEO GLORIA!

NOTES

1. On Calvin's theology, see *Readings in Calvin's Theology*, ed. Donald K. McKim (Grand Rapids: Baker Book House, 1984). On his influence, see *John Calvin: His Influence in the Western World*, ed. W. Stanford Reid (Grand Rapids: Zondervan, 1982).

2. For a fine one-volume comparison of the thought of Zwingli, Calvin, Luther, and Menno Simons (the Anabaptist leader), see Timothy George, *Theology of the Reformers* (Nashville: Broadman, 1988).

3. On the spread of the Reformed faith, see John T. McNeill, *The History and Character of Calvinism* (1954; reprint, Oxford: Oxford University Press, 1967), and *International Calvinism 1541-1715*, ed. Menna Prestwich (Oxford: Oxford University Press, 1985).

4. For examples of these confessions, see the following collections: *Reformed Confessions of the Sixteenth Century*, ed. Arthur C. Cochrane (Philadelphia: Westminster Press, 1966); *The Faith of Christendom: A Source Book of Creeds and Confessions*, ed. Brian A. Gerrish

(Cleveland: World Publishing, 1963); *Creeds of the Churches: A Reader in Christian Doctrine from the Bible to the Present*, ed. John H. Leith (Atlanta: John Knox Press, 1973); and the standard work by Philip Schaff, *Creeds of Christendom, with a History and Critical Notes*, 3 vols. (New York: Harper, 1877), which has appeared in several editions.

5. For information on some of these figures, see chapter 4 of John H. Leith's *Introduction to the Reformed Tradition* (Atlanta: John Knox Press, 1977). A valuable bibliographical source for studying Reformed thought is "The Reformed Traditions, 16th-19th Centuries: A Bibliography Selected from the ATLA Religion Database," ed. Thomas J. Davis (Chicago: American Theological Library Association, 1986).

6. See Heppe, *Reformed Dogmatics Set Out and Illustrated from the Sources*, ed. Ernst Bizer, trans. G. T. Thomson (Grand Rapids: Baker Book House, 1978).

7. On Barth and the Reformers, see Eberhard Busch,

Karl Barth: His Life from Letters and Autobiographical Texts, trans. John Bowden (Philadelphia: Fortress, 1976). On Barth's theological influence, see *How Karl Barth Changed My Mind,* ed. Donald K. McKim (Grand Rapids: William B. Eerdmans, 1986).

8. On the term *Reformed,* see Leith, *Introduction to the Reformed Tradition,* p. 34; Jack B. Rogers, *Presby-*

terian Creeds: A Guide to the Book of Confessions (Philadelphia: Westminster Press, 1985), p. 20; and M. Eugene Osterhaven, *The Spirit of the Reformed Tradition* (Grand Rapids: William B. Eerdmans, 1971), pp. 171-78.

9. Leith, *Introduction to the Reformed Tradition,* p. 31.

Acknowledgments

The editor and publisher gratefully acknowledge permission to reprint the following material:

Berkhof, Hendrikus. *Christian Faith: An Introduction to the Study of the Faith*, rev. ed. Grand Rapids: William B. Eerdmans, 1986. Pp. 155-83, 471-94.

Berkouwer, G. C. *Faith and Justification*, trans. Lewis B. Smedes. Grand Rapids: William B. Eerdmans, 1954. Pp. 39-57.

————. *The Sacraments*, trans. Hugo Bekker. Grand Rapids: William B. Eerdmans, 1969. Pp. 134-60.

Bloesch, Donald G. "Process Theology and Reformed Theology." In *Process Theology*, ed. Ronald Nash. Grand Rapids: Baker Book House, 1987. Pp. 35-56.

Boesak, Allan. *Black and Reformed*. Maryknoll, N.Y.: Orbis Books, 1984. Pp. 83-99.

Bromiley, Geoffrey W. *Children of Promise*. Grand Rapids: William B. Eerdmans, 1979. Pp. 27-37, 77-90.

Busch, Eberhard. "Church and Politics in the Reformed Tradition." In *Church, Word and Spirit*, ed. James E. Bradley and Richard A. Muller. Grand Rapids: William B. Eerdmans, 1987. Pp. 163-81.

Buttrick, David. *Homiletic: Moves and Structures*. Philadelphia: Fortress Press, 1987. Pp. 449-59.

Campbell, Cynthia M. "Theologies Written from Feminist Perspectives: An Introductory Study." *Minutes of the 199th General Assembly of the Presbyterian Church (USA)*, Part I, 1987. Pp. 43-51.

Cochrane, Arthur C. "Karl Barth's Doctrine of the Covenant." In *A Covenant Challenge to Our Broken World*, ed. Allen O. Miller. Atlanta: Darby, 1982. Pp. 156-64.

————. "The Mystery of the Continuity of the Church: A Study in Reformed Symbolics." *Journal of Ecumenical Studies* 2 (1965): 81-96.

Dowey, Edward A. Jr. "Confessional Documents as Reformed Hermeneutic." *Journal of Presbyterian History* 61 (Spring 1983): 90-98.

Farley, Benjamin Wirt. *The Providence of God*. Grand Rapids: Baker Book House, 1988. Pp. 229-37.

Gerrish, Brian A. "The Lord's Supper in the

Reformed Confessions." *Theology Today* 23 (1966): 224-43.

Guthrie, Shirley C., "Toward a Theology of Christian Marriage." *Reformed Liturgy and Music* 20 (Summer 1986): 125-28.

Hesselink, I. John. "The Charismatic Movement and the Reformed Tradition." *Reformed Review* 28 (Spring 1975): 147-56.

Klempa, William. "The Covenant in Sixteenth- and Seventeenth-Century Continental and British Reformed Theology." In *A Covenant Challenge to Our Broken World*, ed. Allen O. Miller. Atlanta: Darby, 1982. Pp. 130-47.

Lara-Braud, Jorge. *What Is Liberation Theology?* Atlanta: General Assembly Mission Board of the Presbyterian Church in the United States, 1980. Pp. 36-38.

Leith, John H. *Introduction to the Reformed Tradition.* Atlanta: John Knox Press, 1977. Pp. 67-85.

Little, David. "Reformed Faith and Religious Liberty." *Church and Society* 76 (May-June 1986): 6-28.

McDonald, H. D. *The Atonement of the Death of Christ.* Grand Rapids: Baker Book House, 1985. Pp. 186-94, 208-15, 221-26, 250-57, 278-82, 307-8, 311-16.

McKim, Donald K. "A Reformed Perspective on the Mission of the Church in Society." *Reformed World* 38 (December 1985): 408-21.

McNeill, John T. "The Church in Sixteenth-Century Reformed Theology." *Journal of Religion* 22 (1942): 251-69.

Paul, Robert S. "Presbyterians and Evangelism: Historical Background." *Austin Seminary Bulletin* 100 (April 1985): 15-23.

Plantinga, Alvin C. "The Reformed Objection to Natural Theology." *Proceedings of the American Catholic Philosophical Association* 54 (1980). Reprinted in *Christian Scholar's Review* 11 (1982): 187-98.

Presbyterian Church (USA). "The Confessional Nature of the Church." *Minutes of the 198th General Assembly of the Presbyterian Church (USA)*, Part I, 1986. Pp. 1-6.

———. "The Nature of Revelation in the Christian Tradition from a Reformed Perspective." *Minutes of the 199th General Assembly of the Presbyterian Church (USA)*, Part I, 1987. §§28.149-237.

Shelton, Robert M. "A Theology of the Lord's Supper from the Perspective of the Reformed Tradition." *Reformed Liturgy and Music* 16 (Winter 1982): 3-11.

Smedes, Lewis B. *Union with Christ: A Biblical View of the New Life in Jesus Christ.* Grand Rapids: William B. Eerdmans, 1983. Pp. 55-92.

Winn, Albert Curry, "The Reformed Tradition and Liberation Theology." In *Reformed Faith and Politics*, ed. Ronald H. Stone. Washington: University Press of America, 1983. Pp. 77-91.

Wolterstorff, Nicholas. "Worship and Justice." *Reformed Liturgy and Music* 19 (Spring 1985): 67-71.

Contributors

Berkhof, Hendrikus

Professor of Dogmatics and Biblical Theology Emeritus, University of Leiden, The Netherlands

Berkouwer, G. C.

Professor Emeritus of Systematic Theology, Free University of Amsterdam, The Netherlands

Bloesch, Donald G.

Professor of Theology, University of Dubuque Theological Seminary, Dubuque, Iowa

Boesak, Allan

Director of Foundation for Peace and Justice, Cape Town, South Africa

Bromiley, Geoffrey W.

Senior Professor of Church History and Historical Theology, Emeritus, Fuller Theological Seminary, Pasadena, California

Busch, Eberhard

Professor of Reformed Dogmatics, University of Göttingen, Göttingen, Western Germany

Buttrick, David G.

Professor of Homiletics and Liturgics, The Divinity School, Vanderbilt University, Nashville, Tennessee

Campbell, Cynthia M.

Pastor, First Presbyterian Church, Salina, Kansas

Cochrane, Arthur C.

Emeritus Professor of Systematic Theology, University of Dubuque Theological Seminary, Dubuque, Iowa

Dowey, Edward A. Jr.

Archibald Alexander Professor of the History of Christian Doctrine, Emeritus, Princeton Theological Seminary, Princeton, New Jersey

Farley, Benjamin W.

Eunice Witherspoon Bell Younts and Willie Camp Younts Professor of Bible, Erskine College, Due West, South Carolina

Gerrish, Brian A.

Professor of Historical Theology, University of Chicago Divinity School, Chicago, Illinois

Guthrie, Shirley C. Jr.
William Henry Green Professor of Systematic Theology, Columbia Theological Seminary, Decatur, Georgia

Hesselink, I. John
Albertus C. Van Raalte Professor of Systematic Theology, Western Theological Seminary, Holland, Michigan

Klempa, William
Principal and Professor of Church History, Presbyterian College, Montreal, Quebec, Canada

Lara-Braud, Jorge
Former Professor of Theology and Culture, San Francisco Theological Seminary, San Francisco, California

Leith, John H.
Pemberton Professor of Theology Emeritus, Union Theological Seminary, Richmond, Virginia

McDonald, H. D.
Professor, London Bible College, London, England

McKee, Elsie A.
Archibald Alexander Associate Professor of the History of Worship, Princeton Theological Seminary, Princeton, New Jersey

McKim, Donald K.
Minister, Presbyterian Church (USA), Berwyn, Pennsylvania

McKim, LindaJo H.
Editor, *The Presbyterian Hymnal*, Presbyterian Church (USA), Berwyn, Pennsylvania

McNeill, John T.
Late Professor of Church History, Union Theological Seminary, New York, New York

Paul, Robert S.
Professor of Ecclesiastical History and the History of Christian Thought, Emeritus, Austin Presbyterian Theological Seminary, Austin, Texas

Plantinga, Alvin C.
Professor of Philosophy, University of Notre Dame, South Bend, Indiana

Rogers, Jack B.
Vice President for Southern California and Professor of Theology, San Francisco Theological Seminary, San Anselmo, California

Shelton, Robert M.
Dean and Professor of Worship, Austin Presbyterian Theological Seminary, Austin, Texas

Sell, Alan P. F.
Chair of Christian Thought, University of Calgary, Calgary, Alberta, Canada

Smedes, Lewis B.
Professor of Theology and Ethics, Fuller Theological Seminary, Pasadena, California

Winn, Albert Curry
Former President, Louisville Theological Seminary, Louisville, Kentucky

Wolterstorff, Nicholas
Professor of Philosophical Theology, Yale University, New Haven, Connecticut

FOUNDATIONAL ISSUES

A significant characteristic of Reformed theology and the Reformed tradition has been an emphasis on establishing the bases or foundations on which theological understandings are built. In works of systematic theology this is often seen in "prolegomena" discussions that precede theological exposition. These clarify underlying principles and presuppositions that ground what follows.

The essays in this first part of the volume serve a similar purpose, outlining some of the fundamental ideas on which Reformed theology is constructed. These include discussions of basic motifs of the Reformed tradition, the nature and purpose of confessions of faith, the ways in which God's revelation is understood and the nature of that revelation in Scripture, and the ways in which the tradition has dealt with the issue of natural theology.

John Leith's essay entitled "The Ethos of the Reformed Tradition" identifies nine motifs characteristic of a Reformed style of being Christian. These themes recur throughout the tradition and underlie the ways in which Reformed Christians have understood their specific identity as Reformed believers in Jesus Christ.[1] The implications of many of these motifs are taken up in later essays in this volume. Thus discussions of the guiding lights by which the Reformed faith has done its theology, worshiped, and governed churches through its polity, how it has related to culture and viewed life itself — all these are helpful orientation points from which a study of major themes in the Reformed tradition can begin.

The Reformed tradition has always been a confessional tradition. Confessions of faith have played a major role in defining the tradition and been crucial documents as Reformed churches in their various locales have identified themselves first as members of the church catholic and secondarily as distinctively Reformed bodies. Confessions of faith serve as open, declarative affirmations of what the churches

1

believe to be God's truth and explications of how they currently understand themselves to be bound by the church's earliest confession: "Jesus Christ is Lord." The essay entitled "The Confessional Nature of the Church" explores the nature and purpose of confessions in the Christian tradition and specifically in the Reformed tradition. It also addresses such key issues as the historical limitations of confessions and the authority of confessions for the contemporary church.

Reformed confessions play a crucial role in the life of Reformed churches because they function as guides to the interpretation of Scripture. As Edward Dowey makes clear in his essay "Confessional Documents as Reformed Hermeneutic," confessions have always been understood as "containing biblical teaching in brief form, focused on the essentials, truly stated so as to ward off erroneous construal and heretical distortion." These documents were meant to be "the formal, authoritative interpretation of Scripture in the church, the end product of a churchly hermeneutic." As the church is led by the Holy Spirit, new insights break forth from Scripture, and so new confessional documents are needed.[2]

The church's engagement with Scripture is one aspect of the broader theological issue of God's revelation. "The Nature of Revelation in the Christian Tradition from a Reformed Perspective" deals with various aspects of this complex issue. Revelation is understood as the "self-disclosure of God" which is received in faith as God acting "as the incarnate Lord and Savior in Jesus and as the Holy Spirit inspiring prophets, apostles, and every generation of God's people." Revelation as centered in Jesus Christ and made known through the work of the Holy Spirit is key to the Christian understanding. A central feature of the church's experience of God's revelation is hearing God's voice through the canonical Scriptures. This document focuses on the authority and interpretation of the Bible as theological aspects of how God's revelation has been given and how the church today continues to experience and respond to the Word of God in Scripture.[3]

A historical approach to the issue of biblical authority is found in Jack B. Rogers's "The Authority and Interpretation of the Bible in the Reformed Tradition," a paper prepared for the Biblical Authority Task Force of the United Presbyterian Church in the U.S.A. (now the Presbyterian Church [USA]). This work examines how the authority and interpretation of the Bible have been understood in the Reformed tradition and explains the various approaches that have been prominent in various historical periods. A diversity of expression — which at times erupts into heated conflict on the issue of the nature of Scripture — has been characteristic of the tradition. This is because the question of authority is so important and has far-reaching implications for the church's faith and practice. If Scripture is a primary revelational source for our knowledge of God, the church must come to grips with the nature of this revelation and how God is known through it.[4]

A philosophical orientation to the question of authority and the knowledge of God is found in Alvin Plantinga's essay "The Reformed Objection to Natural Theology." Citing Reformed theologians, including Calvin, who reject attempts to prove or demonstrate the existence of God ("natural theology"), Plantinga argues that the

Reformed objection rests philosophically on the rejection of classical foundational-ism and positively entails that "belief in God can properly be taken as *basic*" to human life.[5]

These essays on foundational issues provide a framework out of which other major themes in the Reformed tradition can emerge. The tradition has centered in theology as reflection and statement of its understanding of God's revelation, and hence "Theological Themes" are prominent. This theology takes shape in the context of the church, which, as the people of God through all the ages, has had many "Ecclesiological Expressions," some of which have focused on the important issues of church and politics and the Reformed faith and religious liberty. Reformed churches have also dealt theologically with the sacraments, and essays in the section entitled "Sacramental Studies" focus on historical and theological themes relating to baptism and the Lord's Supper. These aspects of the church's life are part of the larger "Liturgical Dimensions" of the Reformed faith, including concerns about liturgy, worship, justice, preaching, and marriage. Reformed churches have seen themselves as servants of God, and selections in the "Missiological Motifs" section explore various facets of the church's mission as it lives out its vocation, orders itself through its polity, does evangelism, and ministers to society and culture. Finally, Reformed theology as an ongoing, developing stream of thought is involved in "Theological Interactions" with other contemporary theological movements.

NOTES

1. For a further exposition of basic Reformed thought, see Leith, *The Reformed Imperative: What the Church Has to Say That No One Else Can Say* (Philadelphia: Westminster Press, 1988). Also helpful in outlining a Reformed way of being Christian is I. John Hesselink's *On Being Reformed: Distinctive Characteristics and Common Misunderstandings* (Ann Arbor: Servant Books, 1983).

2. A most helpful contemporary resource on Reformed confessions is *Reformed Witness Today: A Collection of Confessions and Statements of Faith Issued by Reformed Churches,* ed. Lukas Vischer (World Alliance of Churches, 1982). See also the Presbyterian Church (USA) "Brief Statement of Faith."

3. Some guidance through the vast literature on this topic can be found in the selected bibliography in *The Authoritative Word: Essays on the Nature of Scripture,* ed. Donald K. McKim (Grand Rapids: William B. Eerdmans, 1983).

4. Further pictures of the current view of the nature and interpretation of the Bible can be found in Donald K. McKim, *What Christians Believe about the Bible* (Nashville: Thomas Nelson, 1985), and *A Guide to Contemporary Hermeneutics: Major Themes in Biblical Interpretation,* ed. Donald K. McKim (Grand Rapids: William B. Eerdmans, 1986), as well as Jack B. Rogers and Donald K. McKim, *The Authority and Interpretation of the Bible: An Historical Approach* (San Francisco: Harper & Row, 1979).

5. An important debate concerning natural theology in the Reformed tradition took place between Karl Barth and Emil Brunner in 1933. The key documents — Brunner's "Nature and Grace" and Barth's reply, "No!" — can be found in *Natural Theology,* trans. P. Fraenkel (London: Geoffrey Bles, 1946). See also chaps. 2-3 of G. C. Berkouwer, *General Revelation* (Grand Rapids: William B. Eerdmans, 1968).

The Ethos of the Reformed Tradition

John H. Leith

The faith of a people is written in theological books, structured in organizations, and expressed in worship. It is also embodied in style and manner of life. In fact, style of life always betrays basic theological and ethical convictions. "There is an intimate but seldom-seen connection between a person's thought and his style, which Alfred North Whitehead defined as the 'ultimate morality of the mind.' "[1] Hence it is appropriate to place at the beginning of a study of the Reformed tradition an analysis of those motifs that have given a particular style and manner to Reformed theology, worship, polity, culture, and life. Even though life-styles are never pure and never subject to precise definition, certain themes can be specified and substantially verified. At least nine identifiable motifs have significantly shaped the Reformed style of being a Christian.

Reprinted from *Introduction to the Reformed Tradition: A Way of Being the Christian Community,* by John H. Leith. © 1977 John Knox Press. Used by permission of Westminster/John Knox Press.

THE MAJESTY AND THE PRAISE OF GOD

Popular estimates of the Reformed tradition have always identified it with the sovereignty of God and with predestination. This popular estimate has good basis in fact. While efforts to identify Calvinism with a central doctrine from which others are deduced have all failed, a case can be made that the central theme of Calvinist theology, which holds it all together, is the conviction that every human being has every moment to do with the *living* God.

The God with whom humanity has to do is the Creator of heaven and earth who maintains all things in their being and who governs them by his will. God is energy, force, and life. God is purpose, intention, and will. God is the Lord God who "comes with might," "who has measured the waters in the hollow of his hand and marked off the heavens with a span," and before whom "the nations are as nothing" and "are accounted . . . as less than nothing" (Isa. 40:10, 12, 17). This is the Creator God who works mightily in human history to accomplish

JOHN H. LEITH

divine purposes. The chief end of humanity is to glorify God.

H. R. Niebuhr has brought out the peculiar characteristics of this motif by setting it over against another motif that has been widely influential in the Christian community, the vision of God. Thomas Aquinas gave classic statement to this understanding of the Christian life: "man's ultimate felicity consists only in the contemplation of God."[2] The divine attribute that impressed Calvin, H. Richard Niebuhr observed, was not the eternal perfection of goodness, beauty, and truth, but God's forceful reality and power.

> To call the vision man's greatest good is to make contemplation, however prepared for by activity and however issuing in action, the final end of life; to put the sovereignty of God in the first place is to make obedient activity superior to contemplation, however much of *theoria* is necessary to action. The principle of vision suggests that the perfection of the object seen is loved above all else; the principle of the kingdom indicates that the reality and power of the being commanding obedience are primarily regarded. The first term may also be interpreted to mean that the initiative lies with the one who seeks to see while the object is conceived as somehow at rest; and indeed Roman Catholicism has always been inclined toward a Christian or "other-worldly humanism" which believes that man's rational sight is almost, though never quite, sufficient to pierce through to the divine truth. The term "kingdom of God" puts all the emphasis on the divine initiative. The distinction must not be pressed so as to obscure the fundamental agreement between the Christianity of the vision and that of the kingdom. Whether we say *visio dei* or *regnum dei,* "God's first," in Thomas More's phrase. Whether end or beginning be stressed, God remains both end and beginning; whether Christ be called revealer or Lord, he is the mediator; whether one be Greek or Jew, in Christ he is a new creature. Yet it remains true that the differences between the two types of Christianity have been important in the past

and are likely to be so in the future, though in no other way than as complementary views of a reality which refuses to be imprisoned even in the forms of a reason that has been enlightened by revelation.[3]

The consequences of this emphasis on the majesty of God are very vivid in the religious life that flows from it. As Troeltsch points out, the tone of the Christian life is not tied to "the level of self-preservation in the state of grace," and therefore "a constant preoccupation with personal moods and feelings is entirely unnecessary."[4]

> To Calvin the chief point is not the self-centered personal salvation of the creature, and the universality of the Divine Will of Love, but it is the Glory of God, which is equally exalted in the holy activity of the elect and in the futile rage of the reprobate.[5]

The glory of God and God's purposes in the world are more important than the salvation of one's own soul. Personal salvation can be a very selfish act. Berdyaev paints a horrible picture of those who trample over their neighbors in the crush to get through the gates of heaven.[6] Those Calvinists who asked candidates for the ministry if they were willing to be damned for the glory of God were trying to root out the last element of self-seeking in religion. Human beings are religious, the Calvinist asserts, not to satisfy their needs or to give meaning to their lives but because God has created them and called them to God's service. Karl Barth puts it this way:

> It seems to me that if we want to keep the order of the New Testament we must say: God has ordained and chosen them into his temporal and eternal service, and, consequently, into everlasting life. The notion of service should not be missing. In the New Testament, they did not come to the Church merely so that they might be saved and happy, but that they might have the signal privilege of serving the Lord.[7]

Calvin's own life illustrates this point. He

thought he was best equipped by nature and inclination to be a scholar. Yet he gave himself with no self-pity to the demands of church organization, to the challenges of civil and ecclesiastical politics, and to the pastoral care not only of Geneva but also of Reformed Protestantism. When Farel invoked the judgment of God and Bucer reminded him of Jonah, Calvin did not hesitate to accept unpleasant responsibilities. His letter to Farel on his return to Geneva in 1541 reveals the personal dimensions of his theology:

As to my intended course of proceeding, this is my present feeling: had I the choice at my own disposal, nothing would be less agreeable to me than to follow your advice. But when I remember that I am not my own, I offer up my heart, presented as a sacrifice to the Lord. Therefore there is no ground for your apprehension that you will only get fine words. Our friends are in earnest, and promise sincerely. And for myself, I protest that I have no other desire than that, setting aside all consideration of me, they may look only to what is most for the glory of God and the advantage of the Church. Although I am not very ingenious, I would not want pretexts by which I might adroitly slip away, so that I should easily excuse myself in the sight of men, and shew that it was no fault of mine. I am well aware, however, that it is God with whom I have to do, from whose sight such crafty imaginations cannot be withheld. Therefore I submit my will and my affections, subdued and held fast, to the obedience of God.[8]

The emphasis on the majesty and lordship of God has always been a theme of Reformed theology, but there have been variations in the experience. The increasing knowledge and awareness of the physical environment of human existence, as well as changes in the expected forms of Christian experience, led to theological changes. In the time of the Enlightenment and of the Great Awakening, Jonathan Edwards gave expression to the way in which the beauty of God had grasped him, which is different from the experience of Calvin:

The first instance that I remember of that sort of inward, sweet delight in God and divine things that I have lived much in since, was on reading those words, 1 Tim. i:17. *Now unto the King eternal, immortal, invisible, the only wise God, be honor and glory forever and ever, Amen.* . . .

After this my sense of divine things gradually increased, and became more and more lively, and had more of that inward sweetness. The appearance of every thing was altered; there seemed to be, as it were, a calm, sweet cast, or appearance of divine glory, in almost every thing. God's excellency, his wisdom, his purity and love, seemed to appear in every thing; in the sun, and moon, and stars; in the clouds and blue sky; in the grass, flowers, trees; in the water, and all nature; which used greatly to fix my mind. . . . And scarce any thing, among all the works of nature, was so sweet to me as thunder and lightning; formerly, nothing had been so terrible to me. Before, I used to be uncommonly terrified with thunder, and to be struck with terror when I saw a thunder storm rising; but now, on the contrary, it rejoiced me. I felt God, so to speak, at the first appearance of a thunder storm; and used to take the opportunity, at such times, to fix myself in order to view the clouds and see the lightnings play, and hear the majestic and awful voice of God's thunder, which oftentimes was exceedingly entertaining, leading me to sweet contemplations of my great and glorious God.[9]

This emphasis upon God the Creator and Lord gave depth to life. We do not live on the surface of universal history. Human life is not the simple product of history and of natural forces. Personhood is rooted in the will and the intention of God. God thought of every person before he or she was called into being and gave that person individuality, identity, and a name. Human existence is rooted in eternity, and its end is the praise of God. Hence the Christian lives in the quiet confidence that God is greater than all the battalions of earth and that life is at God's disposal. *The Book of Common Prayer* expresses the dialectic of the Christian life, as Calvin understood it, with remarkable clarity: "in the time of prosperity, fill our hearts with thankfulness, and in the day of trouble, suffer not our trust in thee to fail."[10]

THE POLEMIC AGAINST IDOLATRY

More than a century ago Alexander Schweizer observed that Calvinism is distinguished from Lutheranism by its emphasis on the majesty of God and by its assault on all forms of paganism in the medieval church, whereas Lutheranism had been primarily concerned with "judaistic" lapses into salvation by works.[11] Reformed theology has resisted every effort to get control of God, to fasten the infinite and indeterminate God to the finite and the determinate, whether it be in images or the bread and wine of the sacraments or the structures of the church. God is free, and God acts and speaks when and where he chooses.[12]

Calvin never seriously contemplated the possibility of unbelief or no-faith. The human options were exhausted by faith in the living God and idolatry. "God himself is the sole and proper witness of himself."[13] Humanity's responsibility is to listen to the word of God and to correct what one thinks one has heard by continuing to listen. The human starting point is not one's own existence but the will of the Creator or Lord. Therefore every effort to domesticate God, to shape God according to humanity's own understanding of what the Deity should be, to fasten God to some finite and determinate object and thus to control God must be firmly repudiated.

The practical consequence of this polemic against idolatry was an iconoclasm that held in question every human achievement and refused final loyalty to any human being or any

human endeavor. As H. Richard Niebuhr has put it, "the converse of dependence on God is independence of everything less than God."[14] This iconoclasm was not merely negative; it also contributed to the strength of many human endeavors. In his perceptive biography of John Knox, Lord Eustace Percy has written that the best servants of the state are those whose highest loyalty is not to the state but to God.[15] The Reformed polemic against idolatry prevents human endeavors from overreaching themselves, claiming too much for themselves, and thus destroying themselves. Only God is great enough to answer to humanity's highest and total loyalty without destroying the truly human. Every lesser loyalty when made absolute is abortive and destructive.

THE WORKING OUT OF THE DIVINE PURPOSES IN HISTORY

God the Creator and Governor is Lord of history and nature. Paul Lehmann's use of the metaphor "politician" to refer to God is surely in line with early Reformed theology.[16] God is working out a divine purpose in human history. God calls God's people to be the instruments of God's purpose. God's purposes entail more that just the salvation of souls; they also involve the establishment of a holy community and the glorification of God's name through all the earth.

John Calvin stands out in the history of the church as one who was more vividly aware than almost any other of the mighty working of God in human history and of God's call to God's people for service in the world. Christopher Dawson, a Roman Catholic historian of culture, has suggested that

behind Western democracy there lies the spiritual world of Calvinism and the Free Churches, which is . . . completely different in its political and social outlook from the world of Lutheranism, and which has had a far greater influence and closer connexion with what we know as Western civilization without further qualification.

This divergence was only fully manifested in the course of centuries, but it was not simply a result of historical circumstance. It had its root in the very origins of the two confessions and in the personality of their founders. At first sight this may seem difficult to maintain. For there is in the teaching of Calvin the same pessimism with regard to human nature and human will, the same other-worldliness and the same exaltation of divine power and even arbitrariness that is to be found in Luther. Nevertheless, all these conceptions were transformed by the intense spirit of moral activism which characterized Calvin and Calvinism. The genius of Calvin was that of an organizer and legislator, severe, logical, and inflexible in purpose, and consequently it was he and not Luther who inspired Protestantism with the will to dominate the world and to change society and culture. Hence though Calvinism has always been regarded as the antithesis of Catholicism to a far greater extent than Lutheranism, it stands much nearer to Catholicism in its conception of the relation of Church and State and in its assertion of the independence and supremacy of the spiritual power. In this respect it carries on the traditions of medieval Catholicism and of the Gregorian movement of reform to an even greater degree than did the Catholicism of the Counter-Reformation itself.

In an age when the Papacy was dependent on the Hapsburg monarchies and when Catholics accepted the theories of passive obedience and the divine right of kings, the Calvinists asserted the Divine Right of Presbytery and declared that "the Church was the foundation of the world" and that it was the duty of kings to "throw down their crowns before her and lick the dust off her feet." But these theocratic claims were not hierarchic and impersonal as in the medieval Church, they were based on an intense individualism deriving from the certainty of election and the duty of the individual Christian to co-operate in realizing the divine purpose against a sinful and hostile world. Thus

Calvinism is at once aristocratic and democratic; aristocratic in as much as the "saints" were an elect minority chosen from the mass of fallen humanity and infinitely superior to the children of this world; but democratic in that each was directly responsible to God who is no respecter of persons. Calvinism is, in fact, a democracy of saints, elect of God, but also in a sense self-chosen, since it is the conscience of the individual which is the ultimate witness of his election.[17]

Calvin's intention in Geneva was not simply the salvation of souls but a Geneva that was reformed by the Word of God. John Knox in a well-known statement exclaimed, "in other places, I confess Christ to be truly preached; but manners and religion to be so sincerely reformed, I have not yet seen in any other place."[18]

In Scotland and in England the Reformed community sought to build the New Jerusalem. The Puritans who came to New England were not simply seeking freedom to worship God as they liked. They were going on an errand into the wilderness to establish a Christian society and to demonstrate to the decadent society of Europe the possibilities of a Christian community.[19] H. Richard Niebuhr has persuasively argued that this awareness of the powerful activity of God working itself out under the rubrics of the sovereignty of God, the kingdom of Christ, and finally as the coming kingdom is the motif most characteristic of the Christian movement in America.[20]

The Calvinist saint was responsible for the world. The Calvinist was a soldier of the Lord in conquest of the world, the flesh, and the devil, God's elect instrument to fulfill God's purposes. In his study of radical politics, Michael Walzer contends that it did not enter into the thought of Machiavelli or Luther or Bodin "that specially designated and organized bands of men might play a creative part in the political world, destroying the established order and reconstructing society according to the Word of God or the plans of their fellows." He argues that

> it was the Calvinists who first switched the emphasis of political thought from the prince to the saint . . . and then constructed a theoretical justification for independent political action. What Calvinists said of the saint, other men would later say of the citizen: the same sense of civic virtue, of discipline and duty, lies behind the two names. . . .
>
> The saints saw themselves as divine *instruments* and theirs was the politics of wreckers, architects, and builders — hard at work upon the political world. . . . They treated every obstacle as another example of the devil's resourcefulness and they summoned all their energy, imagination, and craft to overcome it.[21]

Calvin, it must be clearly understood, did not think of himself as a "change agent" but as a servant of God. His goal was the kingdom of God, not a human utopia — the glory of God, not humanitarianism — though he did insist that love of neighbor is the truest test of orthodoxy and doctrine. Yet Calvin set in motion movements that did change society because he united his own theology and its peculiar emphases with an awareness of the modern world. W. Fred Graham has put it very well:

> What he did was stand more surely than any other thinker of his time within this new world. . . . He approved of the city and its activities. He was not instinctively disgusted with business and trade, as were medieval churchmen. . . . And he had the sure instinct to perceive the place of religion within this new age, and to curb the worse instincts of the age by the Word of God and godly discipline. . . . Neither Calvin, nor Huguenot, nor Puritan of Old or New England thought for a moment that riches were good or business holy. But they had decided to live in this world, and did their utmost to leash it to the Word of God.[22]

Roland H. Bainton, an astute church historian, has summarized the Calvinist outlook as follows:

> The early Calvinist . . . did not eat his heart out and consume his energies in concern as to his salvation. This point significantly sets off Calvinism alike from Catholicism and Lutheranism. . . .
>
> Their commission was to establish a theocracy in the sense of a Holy Commonwealth, a community in which every member should make the glory of God his sole concern. It was not a community ruled by the Church nor by the clergy nor even in accord with the Bible in any literalist sense, because God is greater than a book even though it contains His Word. The holy community should exhibit that parallelism of church and state which had been the ideal of the Middle Ages and of Luther, but had never been realized and never can be save in a highly select community where the laity and the clergy, the Town Council and the ministers, are all equally imbued with the same high purpose. Calvin came nearer to realizing it than anyone else in the sixteenth century.[23]

The holy community was never realized, however remarkable in any relative judgment some achievements were. Human freedom and proclivity to sin made any achievement partial and precarious. Pietism, the definition of Christian life in terms of personal piety, and evangelism, conceived as plucking individual souls from the burning pit, were sometimes substitutes for the primal vision. In more recent years a pluralistic, secular, mobile society has rightly magnified human freedom in regard to faith and life-style and has made the possibility of the holy community even more remote. Yet the vision lives on in the conviction that the very existence of the Christian community in the larger community does shape history. Moreover, the Christian movement today still has the essential weapons of Calvin's warfare — namely, the power of the preached Word, the strength of a Christian personality, and the testimony of the Christian community's life. These, when undergirded by the power of the Holy Spirit, are not inconsiderable. Furthermore, Reformed Christians in the tradition of the prophets have always believed that God used the Cyruses of the world to do God's will.

Abraham Kuyper (1837-1920), a Dutch Calvinist, gave a distinctive formulation to the vision of the holy community in terms of the principle of sphere sovereignty. This concept continues to be used in fruitful ways, especially by Dutch Calvinists. Kuyper believed intensely that all of life is lived under the sovereignty of God but that different spheres, such as the state, the church, marriage, and education, have an independence from one another. Sphere sovereignty stands in contrast to sphere subsidiarity, which holds that various spheres — the state and science, for example — are subsidiary to the church. The terms of sphere sovereignty allow the sovereignty of God to be realized in a total society without some spheres of the society being subjected to the tyranny of other spheres in hierarchical subordination.[24]

ETHICS: A LIFE OF HOLINESS

John Calvin insisted that Christians should approve their Christianity by a life of holiness. While an exposition of the Ten Commandments was characteristic of most catechisms, the Reformed gave very detailed attention to this exposition in their catechisms and systematic theologies. The polity that American Presbyterianism adopted in 1788 had in its preface the declaration that "truth is in order to goodness."[25] The end of the Christian life, according to Calvin, is to be conformed to the will of God. Therefore, any theology or worship that does not edify must be reexamined.

The Christian life is, on the one hand, justification by grace through faith and, on the other, sanctification. To put it in other words, salvation is both forgiveness and renewal, both God's grace as mercy and God's grace as power. The proper unity of these two aspects of the one experience of salvation is the art of

the Christian life and is never easy to achieve. Some are tempted to overemphasize the experience of forgiveness. The awareness, so vivid to Luther, that we have to be forgiven our best deeds as well as our worst can lead to an indifference to the various levels of goodness and various degrees of sin. Yet on the human level, these differences between forgiven sinners are very significant. Moreover, it is cheap grace that presumes upon forgiveness and refuses to strive to be perfect as the Father in heaven is perfect. Others overemphasize sanctification. They forget that salvation is by grace and not by merit, that humans sin in their best as well as in their worst deed. The Christian life becomes obedience to laws. John Calvin, as Reinhold Niebuhr observed, put these two aspects of salvation together theologically as well as and perhaps better than any other in church history.[26] The Westminster Larger Catechism likewise exercises great care in answer to the question "Wherein do justification and sanctification differ?"

> Although sanctification be inseparably joined with justification, yet they differ, in that, God in justification, imputeth the righteousness of Christ; in sanctification, his Spirit infuseth grace, and enableth to the exercise thereof; in the former, sin is pardoned; in the other, it is subdued; the one doth equally free all believers from the revenging wrath of God, and that perfectly in this life, that they never fall into condemnation; the other is neither equal in all, nor in this life perfect in any, but growing up to perfection.[27]

This is a remarkably balanced statement. In practical life, however, Calvin and the Reformed tradition often failed to maintain the tension and overemphasized sanctification. One result has been legalism, which in the end always lacks grace. Another result has been self-righteousness, especially when sin is reduced to sensuality, which is more manageable than pride or apathy, especially in old age. A third consequence has been obscurantism when the will of God is prematurely identified with some human pattern of conduct. The proper balancing of forgiveness and holiness in Christian life is not simple.

The Reformed community's mistakes have admittedly been on the side of sanctification. This fact must not, however, obscure the strength of the tradition that has insisted that the Christian is not only a forgiven person but an ethical person. This emphasis is reflected in the theology, worship, and polity of the church. It is especially true of the ethos of the church's life. The elect person is called to a life of service and obedience. The forgiven person is summoned to live by the law of God after having heard the comforting words of the liturgy and the declaration of forgiveness. The first use of the law for Calvin was not to bring sinners to repentance or to restrain public behavior but to stimulate and to guide the Christian.[28] Whatever else Reformed Christians may be concerned about, they are concerned about ethics, the law, and morality.[29]

THE LIFE OF THE MIND AS THE SERVICE OF GOD

Zwingli received a first-rate humanist education in preparation for the priesthood. John Calvin also was a humanist and a scholar before he became a Reformer. The humanist tradition of the sixteenth century left an indelible imprint upon the whole future of the Reformed tradition.[30] Wherever the Reformed community went, it established schools alongside the churches, not only to teach the Bible or to teach reading and other skills necessary for studying the Bible but also to teach the whole range of liberal arts in order to liberate the human spirit. Furthermore, Reformed theology has always been careful in the historical study of the sources of the faith, especially the

Bible and the intention of Jesus Christ for the Christian and the church.

The Academy at Geneva was in many ways the crowning achievement of Calvin's work there. Its roots were in the *Institutes* and the church ordinances. In the *Institutes* Calvin wrote that those who have "tasted the liberal arts penetrate with their aid far more deeply into the secrets of the divine wisdom."[31] In the *Ordinances* he declared,

> The office proper to doctors is the instruction of the faithful in true doctrine, in order that the purity of the Gospel be not corrupted either by ignorance or by evil opinions. As things are disposed today, we always include under this title aids and instructions for maintaining the doctrine of God and defending the Church from injury by the fault of pastors and ministers. So to use a more intelligible word, we will call this the order of the schools. . . .
>
> But because it is only possible to profit from such lectures if first one is instructed in the languages and humanities, and also because it is necessary to raise offspring for time to come, in order not to leave the Church deserted to our children, a college should be instituted for instructing children to prepare them for the ministry as well as for civil government.[32]

Thus from the beginning the Reformed sponsored learning as a Christian duty. They placed value on the skills of language, reading, writing, and speaking. They also prized clarity, logic, and precision in mental procedure. They valued the ability to analyze a problem and to formulate an answer. The sermon was an intellectual exercise and a mental discipline that had a significant cultural impact. Yet the Reformed were not intellectualistic. Calvin warned against idle curiosity and speculation. The learning that was joined to piety had a strong pragmatic and utilitarian quality.

The life of the mind as the service of God had special reference to the church. Calvin made knowledge as well as personal commitment a condition for admission to the communion table.[33] He was convinced that Christians should know what they believed and why they believed it. In his letter to Somerset on the reform of the church in England, he left no doubt about the importance of catechetical instruction:

> Believe me, Monseigneur, the Church of God will never preserve itself without a Catechism, for it is like the seed to keep the good grain from dying out, and causing it to multiply from age to age. And therefore, if you desire to build an edifice which shall be of long duration, and which shall not soon fall into decay, make provision for the children being instructed in a good Catechism, which may shew them briefly, and in language level to their tender age, wherein true Christianity consists. This Catechism will serve two purposes, to wit, as an introduction to the whole people, so that every one may profit from what shall be preached, and also to enable them to discern when any presumptuous person puts forward strange doctrine. Indeed, I do not say that it may not be well, and even necessary, to bind down the pastors and curates to a certain written form, as well for the sake of supplementing the ignorance and deficiencies of some, as the better to manifest the conformity and agreement between all the churches; thirdly, to take away all ground of pretense for bringing in any eccentricity or new-fangled doctrine on the part of those who only seek to indulge an idle fancy.[34]

Catechetical instruction simply focused a general passion for knowledge. Solidly written books and pamphlets and learned sermons delivered in plain style without the ostentation of learning were indispensable marks of Reformed churchmanship. As Calvin put it, "the tongue without the mind must be highly displeasing to God."[35]

PREACHING

The Reformation, writes James Nichols, was the greatest revival of preaching in church history.[36] There is good basis for this judgment. The Reformation began in Zurich as Zwingli undertook to preach through the book of Matthew. Preaching was at the very center of the Reformation in Geneva, with sermons scheduled for different hours on Sunday and on most of the days of the week.

In his famous letter to Somerset, Calvin stressed preaching as well as catechetical education. There was too little preaching in England, Calvin feared, and the greater part of that, he chided, was read from a written text.

> Preaching ought not to be lifeless but lively, to teach, to exhort, to reprove. . . . You are also aware, Monseigneur, how he [Paul] speaks of the lively power and energy with which they ought to speak, who would approve themselves as good and faithful ministers of God, who must not make a parade of rhetoric, only to gain esteem for themselves; but that the Spirit of God ought to sound forth by their voice, so as to work with mighty energy.[37]

Even if Calvin himself spent little time on the preparation of particular sermons but drew resources out of his general theological work, and even if he frequently repeated what he had said or written previously, preaching was still a most important part of his life's work. It was the means of grace above all others by which he expected God to transform Geneva. To this end he preached more than three thousand sermons in his fifty-five-year lifetime.[38]

The Reformed community sometimes dared to speak of preaching as the word of God. Bullinger declared in the Second Helvetic Confession that "when this Word of God is now preached in the church by preachers lawfully called, we believe that the very Word of God is preached, and received of the faithful."[39] Yet the Reformed were careful not to bind the Spirit of God to the word in preaching as they believed the Lutherans did. As Bullinger wrote in the *Decades,* a book of sermons, whom he meaneth to bestow knowledge and faith on, to them he sendeth teachers, by the word of God to preach true faith unto them. Not because it lieth in man's power, will, or ministry, to give faith; nor because the outward word spoken by man's mouth is able of itself to bring faith: but the voice of man, and the preaching of God's word, do teach us what true faith is, or what God doth will and command us to believe. For God himself alone, by sending his Holy Spirit into the hearts and minds of men, doth open our hearts, persuade our minds, and cause us with all our heart to believe that which we by his word and teaching have learned to believe.[40]

Calvin sometimes used language that seems to bind the Spirit to the preaching of the word. The minister, he said, is the very mouth of God.[41] Yet he, like Bullinger, knew that preaching is the word of God only in a subordinate sense, and he insisted, as few have, in his exposition of the doctrine of predestination that the Spirit is not bound to preaching. God is still sovereign. Yet this did not diminish Calvin's estimate of preaching as the usual means of God's grace and power. Calvin's position is very well summarized in this statement from the *Institutes:*

> For first, the Lord teaches and instructs us by his Word. Secondly, he confirms it by the sacraments. Finally, he illumines our minds by the light of his Holy Spirit and opens our hearts for the Word and sacraments to enter in, which would otherwise only strike our ears and appear before our eyes, but not at all affect us within.[42]

Puritanism was also a preaching movement. The Puritan, like Calvin, had great confidence in the power of the written and spoken word. Puritans worked to arrive at a style that was appropriate to the preaching of the Word of God. This style, as expounded by the Calvinist theologian William Perkins and as written into the *Westminster Directory of Worship,* was plain, but it was not ineffective or unimaginative. It was designed to be understood and

to move the hearer, which, the evidence indicates, it did in a remarkable way. The reaction against the ornate, witty, rhetorical style of the orthodox Anglican became a mark of the Puritan's conversion.[43] The preaching style of the Puritan was plain and powerful and in the tradition of Calvin. Its influence lingered long in Britain and in the United States, where it was tempered by the frontier revival.

Preaching has also been the great theme of the two best-known Reformed theologians of the twentieth century, Emil Brunner and Karl Barth. Each thought of himself as a preacher, and each wrote his theology for preachers. Brunner preached to large congregations in the Fraumünster in Zurich, and Barth took delight in preaching in the jails.

The Reformed community has always had great confidence — perhaps too great a confidence — in written and spoken words and, in particular, in the power of preaching, when blessed by the Holy Spirit, to change human life and to create a godly public opinion. The demand for simplicity, directness, authenticity, and sincerity that has been emphasized generally in the tradition applies especially to preaching. The Calvinist sermon is not ostentatious or pretentious but plain, rough-hewn, and powerful. In considerable measure, the content, clearly and distinctly presented, is the rhetoric as well as the message. Reinhold Niebuhr, one of the great preachers of the twentieth century, tells in his diary that very soon in his ministry he had to decide if he was going to be a "pretty" preacher. He decided against "pretty" in favor of the rough-hewn and plain-spoken sermons that the Reformed tradition has so much admired.[44]

THE ORGANIZED CHURCH AND PASTORAL CARE

Calvin believed that the organization of the Christian community was critically important for the nurturing of the life of faith and obedience. The human phenomena of church structures and procedures of worship are means of grace and must be appropriate for the work of the Spirit. Hence Calvin and his successors were by no means indifferent to structures. Yet the structures were not important in themselves but as means of grace.

The focus of Calvin's concern with church organization is pastoral care and the "cure of souls." Calvin not only wrote the office of pastor into his church structure but was himself a pastor above all. In the official order for the church's existence in Geneva, he provided for visitation of prisoners and of the sick and for catechetical instruction and examination prior to admission to the Lord's Supper. The confession of sins and the promise of forgiveness of sins, which are in the Sunday liturgy, can also take place in the meeting of Christian with Christian and, in particular, in the pastoral work of the ministers. The deacons were constituted as the church's ministry of compassion to the needy. Yet pastoral care is not only comfort for the bereaved, forgiveness for the guilty, and help for the sick and needy: it is preeminently the renewal of life in the image of Christ. Pastoral care has as its purpose not only the giving of comfort but also the redirection of life.[45] In his voluminous correspondence, Calvin exercised pastoral care all over Europe, not only giving comfort but also calling Christians to the heroic, demanding, and dangerous service of Almighty God.

In a substantial study entitled *Calvin: Director of Souls,* Jean-Daniel Benoit contends that Calvin was first a pastor and then a theologian, or, better, that he was a theologian in order to be a pastor. He also concludes that it was as a pastor rather than as a theologian, church organizer, or powerful personality that Calvin significantly influenced history. For in the care of souls, Calvin was not only concerned for the salvation of the individual but went on to unite this salvation with the advancement of the reign of Jesus Christ.[46]

THE DISCIPLINED LIFE

Personal discipline was a characteristic of the early Protestant reformers of all persuasions, as it is of most persons who accomplish much. Yet even among highly disciplined people, Calvin stands out not only in his personal achievement but also in his insistence that discipline should characterize the Christian life and community. He attempted to make discipline a part of the structure of the organized life of the church, especially in the work of the elders in the consistory or session.[47]

Discipline, as the Reformed tradition has advocated it, can best be understood as the deliberate and economic use of the energies and vitalities of human existence in the pursuit of loyalty to God and the advancement of God's cause in the world. John T. McNeill has suggested that *economy* is a word that is descriptive of the Puritan.[48] It is certainly descriptive of Calvin's personal life and churchmanship. Yet neither Calvin nor the Puritans turned to asceticism in an attempt to escape an evil world. They were ascetic or disciplined only to the extent that they believed in the economical use of a good world. They exulted in the vitality of existence, but they also believed that momentary desires must sometimes be denied for the sake of a later good. Within a disciplined life there is a place for fun and even frivolity, but this place is fitted into a larger order.

German sociologist Max Weber and historian of the social teachings of the churches Ernst Troeltsch were both impressed by Calvinist self-discipline as it applies to work. Troeltsch has written that

> to a people who have been educated on Calvinistic principles the lazy habit of living on an inherited income seems a downright sin; to follow a calling which has no definite end and which yields no material profit seems a foolish waste of time and energy, and failure to make full use of chances of gaining material profit seems like indifference towards God.[49]

Calvin rejected the monastery, but he made the whole world the place of disciplined living and the pursuit of goals that have their end in God and his cause on earth. The discipline of work applied not simply to the productivity of business or labor but also to political and social reform.

The early Calvinist was too reserved to be an exhibitionist in personal feelings or in personal piety. Yet here too Calvin and his followers stood for the discipline of private and public worship. Reformed life can never be reduced to private piety, but it is never without it.[50]

The discipline of the Reformed tradition, especially as illustrated by Calvin and the Puritans, was not regarded as a burden. It was a manner of life that was freely chosen and that they believed to be the means of the joyful and responsible freeing of life's energies and vitalities.

SIMPLICITY

Simplicity is a recurring theme in all of Calvin's writings, and it was a characteristic of his practice.[51] He opposed all redundancy. He was the enemy of the ostentatious, the pompous, the contrived, and of needless spending and consumption, but he also opposed other forms of waste. Simplicity is closely related to Calvin's emphasis on authenticity and sincerity. Every activity or device that covers up reality must be rejected.

Simplicity was a general principle with Calvin. He applied it to liturgy, polity, and style of life. He also applied it to literary style, and this application serves well as an illustration of the way this motif shaped his own life. Early in his professional life, when writing his commentary on Romans (1539), Calvin deliberately set out to write with "lucid brevity," and he did not hesitate to rebuke his elder the distinguished Bucer for being verbose and lacking

in clarity.[52] He deals with style in greater detail in his commentary on 1 Corinthians 1:20. As Calvin understood the situation, Paul's method of preaching was plain, and he objected to "wicked and unfaithful ministers" at Corinth who sought to recommend themselves with a show of words and masks of human wisdom. The simplicity of the gospel was disfigured; the Corinthians themselves "were tickled with a silly fondness for high-sounding style." Hence Calvin speaks approvingly of Paul's "rude, coarse and unpolished style." Yet Calvin does not reject human eloquence. God is its author, and every person ought to rejoice in it, but only as it is used to convey truth and to uncover reality. It must never be an end in itself. Eloquence can get in the way of truth. "In a plain and unpolished manner of address, the majesty of truth might shine more conspicuously." Language is the servant of truth, of reality.

> That eloquence, therefore, is neither to be condemned nor despised, which has no tendency to lead Christians to be taken up with an outward glitter of words, or intoxicate them with empty delight, or tickle their ears with its tinkling sound, or cover over the cross of Christ with its empty show as with a veil; but, on the contrary, tends to call us back to the native simplicity of the gospel, tends to exalt the simple preaching of the cross by voluntarily abasing itself, and, in fine, acts the part of a herald to procure a hearing for those fishermen and illiterate persons, who have nothing to recommend them but the energy of the Spirit.[53]

Simplicity is very close to sincerity. It clears away the ornaments, the ostentations, the contrivances, the pretenses that obscure the real.

There is no one model of the Reformed life-style or personality. Furthermore, the characteristics of the Reformed ethos listed in this discussion are not exclusively Reformed or necessarily even exclusively Christian. Yet they have persistently and frequently characterized the Reformed community. In a variety of patterns they have been embodied in personalities and communities that are Reformed. Furthermore, they have been integrally related to Reformed theologies, polities, and worship.

NOTES

1. Roger Hazelton, *A Theological Approach to Art* (Nashville, Tennessee: Abingdon Press, 1967).

2. Aquinas, *Summa Contra Gentiles,* trans. Vernon J. Bourke (New York: Doubleday, 1956), 3:37, 125.

3. Niebuhr, *The Kingdom of God in America* (New York: Harper & Row, 1937; Harper Torchbook, 1959), pp. 20-21.

4. Ernst Troeltsch, *The Social Teaching of the Christian Churches,* 4 vols., trans. Olive Wyon (New York: Macmillan, 1931), 2: 589.

5. Troeltsch, *The Social Teaching of the Christian Churches,* 2: 583.

6. Nicolas Berdyaev, *The Destiny of Man* (New York: Scribner's, 1937), p. 146.

7. Karl Barth, *The Faith of the Church: A Commentary on the Apostles' Creed according to Calvin's Catechism,* ed. Jean-Louis Leuba, trans. Gabriel Vahanian (New York: Meridian Books, 1958), p. 137.

8. Calvin, letter to Farel, August 1541, in *Letters of John Calvin,* 4 vols., ed. Jules Bonnet, trans. D. Constable and M. R. Gilchrist (1855-58; rpt., New York: B. Franklin, 1974), 1: 280-81.

9. Edwards, *The Works of President Edwards,* 4 vols. (New York: Robert Carter & Brothers, 1879), 1:16-17.

10. "Prayer for Our Country," in *The Book of Common Prayer* (Greenwich: Seabury Press, 1952), p. 36.

11. Schweizer, *Die Glaubenslehre der Evangelischreformierten Kirche dargestellt und aus den Quellen belegt,* vol. 1 (Zurich: Orell, Füssli, 1844-47), p. 45.

12. See John H. Leith, "John Calvin's Polemic against Idolatry," in *Soli Deo Gloria,* ed. J. McDowell Richards (Richmond: John Knox Press, 1968), pp. 111ff.

13. Calvin, *Institutes of the Christian Religion,* Library of Christian Classics, vols. 20-21, ed. John T. McNeill, trans. Ford Lewis Battles (Philadelphia: Westminster Press, 1960), 1.11.1.

14. Niebuhr, *The Kingdom of God in America,* p. 69.

15. Percy, *John Knox* (London: Hodder & Stoughton, 1937).

16. See Lehmann, *Ethics in a Christian Context* (New York: Harper & Row, 1963), p. 85.

17. Dawson, *The Judgment of the Nations* (New York: Sheed & Ward, 1942), pp. 44-46.

18. Knox, in *The Works of John Knox,* ed. David Laing (Edinburgh: Johnstone & Hunter, 1855), 4: 240; spelling changed by author. Cf. *John Knox: A Quatercentenary Reappraisal,* ed. Duncan Shaw (Edinburgh: St. Andrew Press, 1975), p. 26.

19. See Perry Miller, *Errand into the Wilderness* (Cambridge: Belknap Press, 1956), p. 11.

20. Niebuhr, *The Kingdom of God in America.*

21. Walzer, *The Revolution of the Saints: A Study in the Origins of Radical Politics* (Cambridge: Harvard University Press, 1966), pp. 1-3. Walzer also criticizes Calvinism on a number of points, especially for its repressiveness — see pp. 302ff.

22. Graham, *The Constructive Revolutionary: John Calvin and His Socio-Economic Impact* (Richmond: John Knox Press, 1971), p. 198.

23. Bainton, *The Reformation of the Sixteenth Century* (Boston: Beacon Press, 1952), pp. 116-18. John T. McNeill has suggested that Calvinist piety is "not much identified with peculiar words and rites of worship. It is characterized by a combination of God-consciousness with an urgent sense of missions. . . . The Calvinist may not know how it happens; he may be a very simple-minded theologian; but he is conscious that God commands his will and deed as well as his thought and prayer. This is what makes him a reformer and a dangerous character to encounter on moral and political issues. He is a man with a mission to bring to realization the will of God in human society" (*The History and Character of Calvinism* [New York: Oxford University Press, 1954], pp. 436-37).

24. See Gordon Spykman's excellent study "Sphere-Sovereignty in Calvin and the Calvinist Tradition," in *Exploring the Heritage of John Calvin,* ed. David E. Holwerda (Grand Rapids: Baker Book House, 1976), pp. 163-208.

25. "Preliminary Principles," chap. 1 of "The Form of Government, United Presbyterian Church in the United States of America," in *The Constitution of the Presbyterian Church in the United States of America* (Philadelphia: Office of the General Assembly by the Board of Christian Education, 1954).

26. Niebuhr, *The Nature and Destiny of Man,* 2 vols. (New York: Scribner's, 1943), 2: 200.

27. Westminster Larger Catechism, Q. 77, *The Constitution of the Presbyterian Church in the United States of America,* pp. 131-290.

28. See Calvin, *Institutes of the Christian Religion,* 2.7.12.

29. Robert Kingdon has argued that the Calvinist concern with morals was assimilated into the tradition more through the attempt to enforce morality than through theology ("The Control of Morals in Calvin's Geneva," in *The Social History of the Reformation,* ed. Lawrence P. Buck and Jonathan W. Zophy [Columbus: Ohio State University Press, 1972], pp. 3-16). Kingdon's point is well taken, though he underestimates the significance of theology.

30. See Josef Bohatec, *Budé und Calvin* (Fraz: Bohlaus, 1950).

31. Calvin, *Institutes of the Christian Religion,* 1.5.2.

32. Calvin, "Draft Ecclesiastical Ordinances: September and October (1541)," in *Theological Treatises,* Library of Christian Classics, vol. 22, ed. J. K. S. Reid (Philadelphia: Westminster Press, 1954), pp. 62-63.

33. Calvin, "Draft Ecclesiastical Ordinances," p. 63.

34. Calvin, letter to the Protector Somerset, 22 October 1548, *Letters of John Calvin,* 2: 191.

35. Calvin, *Institutes of the Christian Religion,* 3.20.33.

36. Nichols, *Corporate Worship in the Reformed Tradition* (Philadelphia: Westminster Press, 1968), p. 29.

37. Calvin, letter to the Protector Somerset, 22 October 1548, *Letters of John Calvin,* 2: 190.

38. Texts of 1,460 sermons are now available. Records in Geneva indicate that the texts of more than 1,000 sermons have been lost. Hence, 3,000 sermons seems a fair estimate, considering Calvin's ministry in Strasbourg and the possibility of unrecorded sermons. See Bernard Gabnebin, "L'histoire des manuscrits de sermons de Calvin," *Supplementa Calviniana,* vol. 2, ed. Erwin Mulhaupt (Neukirchen Kreis Moers: Neukirchener Verlag, 1961), p. xxviii.

39. The Second Helvetic Confession, chap. 1, in *Creeds of the Churches: A Reader in Christian Doctrine from the Bible to the Present,* ed. John H. Leith (Richmond: John Knox Press, 1973), p. 132.

40. Bullinger, *The Decades of Henry Bullinger,* vol. 1, ed. Thomas Harding (Cambridge: Cambridge University Press, 1849), pp. 84-85.

41. Calvin, sermon on Deuteronomy, in *Ioannis Calvini Opera Quae Supersunt Omnia,* 59 vols. (vols. 29-87

of *Corpus Reformatorum*), ed. Guilelmus Baum, Eduardus Cunitz, and Eduardus Reuss (Brunswick: C. A. Schwetschke, 1863-1900), 25: 713.

42. Calvin, *Institutes of the Christian Religion,* 4.14.8.

43. See John F. Wilson, *Pulpit in Parliament: Puritanism during the English Civil Wars, 1640-1648* (Princeton: Princeton University Press, 1969), pp. 138, 142.

44. Niebuhr, *Leaves from the Notebook of a Tamed Cynic* (Hamden, Conn.: Shoestring Press, 1956), p. 9.

45. See Jean-Daniel Benoit, *Calvin, Directeur d'Ames* (Strasbourg: Editions Oberlin, 1944), p. 11.

46. Benoit, *Calvin, Directeur d'Ames,* p. 11.

47. See Calvin, *Institutes of the Christian Religion,* 4.12.1-15. Cf. "Draft Ecclesiastical Ordinances," p. 70.

48. McNeill, *Modern Christian Movements* (Philadelphia: Westminster Press, 1954), p. 47.

49. Troeltsch, *The Social Teachings of the Christian Churches,* 2: 611.

50. See Calvin, *Institutes of the Christian Religion,* 3.20.19.

51. See Calvin, *Institutes of the Christian Religion,* 4.15.19; 4.14.18; 4.10.14.

52. See Calvin's preface to *Commentary on the Epistle of Paul the Apostle to the Romans,* trans. and ed. John Owen (Grand Rapids: William B. Eerdmans, 1955), pp. xxiii, xxvi.

53. Calvin, on 1 Cor. 1:17, in *Commentary on the Epistles of Paul the Apostle to the Corinthians,* trans. and ed. John Pringle (Grand Rapids: William B. Eerdmans, 1948), p. 77. Cf. Francis M. Higman, *The Style of John Calvin in His French Polemical Treatises* (London: Oxford University Press, 1967), pp. 153ff.

The Confessional Nature of the Church

Presbyterian Church (USA)

I. THE NATURE AND PURPOSE OF CONFESSIONS

29.113 Many people are confused by talk of "confessing," "confessions," and "confessional" churches. Both inside and outside the church confession is ordinarily associated with admission of wrongdoing and guilt: criminals "confess" that they have committed a crime; famous people write "true confessions" about their scandalous lives; persons visit a "confessional" to tell of their sin. In Christian tradition, however, confession has an earlier, positive sense. To confess means openly to affirm, declare, acknowledge or take a stand for what one believes to be true. The truth that is confessed may include the admission of sin and guilt but is more than that. When Christians make a confession, they say, "This is what we most assuredly believe, regardless of what others may believe and regardless of the op-

position, rejection, or persecution that may come to us for taking this stand."

29.114 A distinction must be made between confession as an act of Christian faith and a confession as a document of Christian faith.

29.115 On the one hand, all Christians are by definition people who confess their faith — people who make their own the earliest Christian confession: "Jesus Christ is Lord." The Christian church, called and held together by Jesus Christ himself, lives only through the continual renewal of this fundamental confession of faith that all Christians and Christian bodies make together.

29.116 On the other hand, a confession of faith is an officially adopted statement that spells out a church's understanding of the meaning and implications of the one basic confession of the lordship of Christ. Such statements have not always been called confessions. They have also been called creeds, symbols, formulas, definitions, declarations of faith, statements of belief, articles of faith, and other similar names. All these are different ways of talking about the same thing, though "creed"

Reprinted from Presbyterian Church (USA) document "The Confessional Nature of the Church," 198th General Assembly (1986).

has ordinarily been used for short affirmations of faith, while other names have been used for longer ones.

29.117 While the first and primary meaning of confession as an act of faith must always be kept in mind, this paper will concentrate on the second meaning, confession as an officially adopted church document.

29.118 Presbyterian and Reformed churches are not the only churches with confessional standards. The Roman Catholic, Eastern Orthodox, Lutheran, and to a lesser extent the Anglican, Episcopal, and Methodist churches are also confessional bodies. Even so-called "free" churches that acknowledge only the Bible as their creed have often made semiauthoritative confessions of faith. Most Christian churches officially or informally share the faith of the Apostles' and Nicene Creeds. Therefore what is said in this section about the role of creeds and confessions is applicable not only to Presbyterian and Reformed churches but to the Christian church as a whole. Most of the examples cited come from the Reformed tradition, but similar examples could also be drawn from other traditions.

A. The Three Directions of Confessions of Faith

29.119 A confession of faith may be defined more precisely as a public declaration before God and the world of what a church believes.

29.120 A confession is a public declaration of what a church believes. Individual Christians may and should confess their own personal faith, but a confession of faith is more than a personal affirmation of faith. It is an officially adopted statement of what a community of Christians believe. This communal character of confessions of faith is made explicitly clear in confessions such as the Scots and Second Helvetic Confessions and the Bar-

men Declaration, which speak of what "we" believe. But it is also implicit in such confessions as the Apostles' Creed and Heidelberg Catechism, which speak of what "I" believe, and in other confessions such as Westminster and the Confession of 1967, which speak more objectively. Whatever their form, confessions of faith express what a body of Christians believe in common.

29.121 These affirmations of the church's faith always have three reference points: God, the church itself, and the world. Confessions of faith are first of all the church's solemn and thankful response to God's self-revelation, expressed with a sense of responsibility to be faithful and obedient to God. Secondly, in a confession of faith members of a Christian community seek to make clear to themselves who they are, what they believe, and what they resolve to do. Finally, Christians confess their common faith not only to praise and serve God and not only to establish their self-identity but to speak to the world a unified word that declares who they are and what they stand for and against. Confessions thus have a social and political as well as theological and ecclesiological significance.

B. The Time for Confession

29.122 Throughout the history of the Christian movement, churches have written confessions of faith because they feel that they must do so, not just because they think it would be a good idea. Confessions of faith may result from a sense of urgent need to correct some distortion of the truth and claim of the gospel that threatens the integrity of the church's faith and life from within the church. They may result from some political or cultural movement outside the church that openly attacks or subtly seeks to compromise its commitment to the gospel. Sometimes the urgency to confess comes from the church's conviction that it has a great new insight into the promises and demands of the gospel that is desperately needed by both church and world. Frequently, all three occasions — internal danger, external threat, and great opportunity — are behind the great confessions of the church at the same time. In any case, the church writes confessions of faith when it faces a situation of life or a situation of death so urgent that it cannot remain silent but must speak, even at the cost of its own security, popularity, and success. Or, to put it negatively, when all the church has to say is the restatement of what everyone already knows and believes, or when it has no word to speak other than safe generalities that ignore or cover over the concrete, specific issues of a crisis situation — then it is not the time for confession even though what is confessed might be true in itself.

C. The Content of Confessions of Faith

29.123   At the heart of all confessions is the earliest confession of the New Testament church, "Jesus is Lord." (Strictly speaking, therefore, Christians confess not what but in whom they believe). But the church discovered very early that in order to protect this simple confession from misunderstanding and misuse, it had to talk about the relation between Jesus and the God of Israel, and between Jesus and the Holy Spirit. The earliest christological confession became a trinitarian confession. That led to further reflection on the biblical witness to the reality and work of God the Father, Son, and Holy Spirit in the past, present, and future history of the world in general, in the particular history of the people of God, and in the life of every individual Christian. Moreover, the church could not talk about the "lordship" of Jesus without also talking about the claim the triune God has on the lives of people in their personal and social relationships in the church and in the world. The confession "Jesus is

Lord" necessarily led to the development of a full theology and ethic.

29.124   The length and focus of the church's confessions have varied according to which elements of this developing and expanding faith it has believed should be emphasized to meet the needs and challenges of particular situations.

29.125   Sometimes the situation has called not for a summary of everything Christians believe but for a short pointed confession dealing with one or more specific issues. The Nicene and Chalcedon Creeds, for instance, were the church's response to fundamental heresies in the ancient church concerning the identity of Jesus Christ. The Barmen Declaration was the response of some Reformed and Lutheran churches in Germany to what they believed was the one most critical issue in their situation in 1933, the relation between loyalty to Jesus Christ and loyalty to the state. The Confession of 1967 reformulated important themes of Christian doctrine in confessional literature and showed their social ethical implications.

29.126   Other confessions such as the Apostles' Creed are short summaries of elements of the whole of Christian faith.

29.127   The Lutheran and Reformed confessions of the sixteenth and seventeenth centuries tended to be longer and more comprehensive summaries of faith. In reforming the church, they dealt with the most critical theological and political issues that divided Roman Catholics and Protestants — and Lutheran, Reformed, and Anabaptist Protestants — in the Reformation and post-Reformation period.

29.128   In every time and place the church is called to make the implications of its fundamental confession of the Lordship of Jesus Christ unmistakably clear and relevant. But in order to do that, it has had in every new situation to decide afresh what to say and what to leave unsaid, how much and how little to say, what to emphasize and what for the time being to pass over, which internal and external dangers are critical and which are less critical.

D. The Functions of Confessions

29.129 The shape of confessions has been determined not only by the historical situation in which they were written but also by the uses for which they have been intended.

29.130 1. *Worship.* Like the Apostles' and Nicene Creeds, some creeds and confessions have been used as acts of worship in the church's liturgy. This use is a reminder of the fact that the church's confessions are first of all acts of praise, thanksgiving, and commitment in the presence of God.

29.131 2. *Defense of Orthodoxy.* Most confessions have been intended as polemical defense of true Christian faith and life against perversion from within as well as from attacks from outside the church. They are the church's means of preserving the authenticity and purity of its faith.

29.132 3. *Instruction.* The confessions have been used for the education of leaders and members of the church in the right interpretation of Scripture and church tradition and to guard against the danger of individuals or groups selecting from the Bible or church tradition only that which confirms their personal opinions and desires. Confessions in question-and-answer form (e.g., the Heidelberg and Westminster Catechisms) were written to prepare children and adult converts for baptism and participation in the fellowship of believers.

29.133 4. *Rallying Point in Times of Danger and Persecution.* Confessions have often prepared and strengthened Christians to stand together in faithfulness to the gospel when they have been tempted to surrender to powerful forces of political, racial, social, or economic injustice.

29.134 5. *Church Order and Discipline.* Some churches, such as the Presbyterian Church (USA), have sought to preserve the purity and unity of the church by requiring its ministers and church officers to accept the teachings of its confessions in order to be ordained. The government of these churches is also determined by their confessions of faith.

29.135 Some confessions were originally intended to serve more than one of these purposes. Others have in fact served multiple purposes though their writers may not have foreseen how they would be used.

E. The Historical Limitations of Confessions

29.136 Confessions address the issues, problems, dangers, and opportunities of a given historical situation. But confessions are related to their historical situation also in another way. Even when their writers have believed they were formulating Christian truth valid for all time and places, their work has not only been directed to but limited by their particular time and place. Throughout the history of the church — and also in our time — confessions have been deliberately or unconsciously expressed in the language and thought forms that were commonly accepted when they were written. God's self-revelation in Jesus Christ has sometimes been clarified but also distorted by the language and presuppositions of this or that ancient or current philosophy. The great classical confessions were written before the discoveries of modern science and reflect an outdated understanding of the structure of the world and its natural processes (just as our "modern" confessions will one day seem outdated and "primitive" to a later world). The theology and ethics of confessions of every age are shaped by what seem to be the normative or preferable sexual, familial, social, economic, cultural, and political patterns of a particular period of history. Even those confessions that have sought to be grounded exclusively in biblical revelation have often confused the revelation itself with various historically conditioned thought forms and cultural patterns in which it was received and preserved by people who lived in the ancient Near East. Modern scholarship has shown how extensively earlier confessions of faith saw in Scripture only the confirmation of what they thought they already knew about God, the world, and human life in it (just as future scholarship will reveal how we have done the same thing in our time).

29.137   The confessions of the church, in other words, have indeed interpreted, defended, and preserved biblical Christian truth. They have united the Christian community in its one task of bearing witness to the one Christian confession that Jesus is Lord. But at the same time, despite all good intentions, they have also distorted the truth revealed in Jesus Christ, been unable to grasp parts of the biblical witness to God's presence and work in Christ, and divided the church into churches with conflicting views of what Christian faith and life are all about. Is there any way to distinguish between the truth to which confessions of faith seek to bear witness and their inadequate witness to the truth? Christians in the Presbyterian-Reformed tradition believe they know at least how to go about this task. Their solution will be discussed in the proper place in the following section of this paper.

II. CONFESSIONS OF FAITH IN THE REFORMED TRADITION

29.138   Everything we have said about confessions in general applies also to Reformed confessions. But now we turn to some of the most important characteristics of the Reformed understanding of the nature and purpose of confessions that distinguish it from other confessional traditions and theological movements.

A. The Ecumenical Character of Reformed Churches

29.139   From the very beginning and throughout their history, the Reformed churches have sought to represent the church catholic. Their confessions do not speak only of what Reformed churches or Presbyterians believe but seek to confess what Christians believe. They have not claimed to be the only true church, with a monopoly on Christian faith and life, but have always been open to learn from other churches and traditions and eager to participate in conversations with them that could lead to mutual correction and reconciliation.

29.140   We must not exaggerate this ecumenical openness, of course. Individuals, groups, and whole denominations who claim to be Reformed have sometimes assumed or openly declared that only this or that particular Reformed church is the true church, that all other churches (including other Reformed denominations) are false or at least fatally corrupted, and that conversation with them can only compromise the true understanding of Christian faith and life which is completely, infallibly, and unchangeably contained in this or that particular Reformed confession. But such an attitude is itself un-Reformed and contrary to the very confessional documents used to support it.

29.141   Characteristic of the ecumenicity of the genuine Reformed tradition and its confessions is this statement in the confession of the Synod of Berne in 1528:

But where something is brought before us by our pastors or by others, which brings us closer to Christ, and in accordance with God's word is more conducive to mutual friendship and Christian love than the interpretation now presented, we will gladly accept it and will not limit the course of the Holy Spirit, which does not go backwards towards the flesh but always forward towards the image of Jesus Christ our Lord.

B. Faith and Practice

29.142 It is typical of confessions in the Reformed tradition that they emphasize not only what Christians believe but also how Christians live, not only orthodox Christian faith but also thankful and obedient Christian "practice," not only justification by grace through faith but also sanctification by grace evidenced in "good works." All Christian traditions acknowledge the fact that faith without works is dead. But in Reformed confessions the active Christian life is given special and unique emphasis.

29.143 1. *The Claim of God on All of Life.* Reformed confessional tradition follows Calvin in emphasizing the authority of God over every area of human life: over personal and familial relationships, over the organization and government of the Christian community, and over social, economic, and political "secular" communities as well. Reformed confessions therefore contain both personal and social ethics, a gospel of salvation and a social gospel. (See, for instance, the comprehensive and detailed exposition of the Ten Commandments in the Westminster Larger Catechism.)

29.144 Reformed confessions of different periods differ in their understanding of precisely what God requires. Sometimes they have been too certain that the will of God was identical with the historically and socially conditioned presuppositions of Reformed Christians in a particular time and place. Sometimes they have confused the rule of God in the world with the rule of the church. But however they differ and whatever mistakes they may have made, a consistent theme in Reformed confessions of all periods and places is the responsibility of individual Christians and the Christian church to seek to order all of human life according to the sovereign will of the God who is known in Jesus Christ through Scripture. No room is left for the belief of Christians in some other traditions that there are some areas of individual and social life that are not claimed by God and in which they are excused or prohibited from serving God.

29.145 2. *Grace and Law.* Reformed confessional tradition follows Calvin in believing that because the meaning and purpose of God's sovereign will is made known in Jesus Christ, and because sin separates humanity from God and each other, God's rule over and in the world must be understood as gracious rule exercised for our good. God gives us commands and requirements in order to guide and help us to the achievement of wholeness and happiness in our individual lives and justice, freedom, and peace in human society. The Heidelberg Catechism therefore expresses the theology of all Reformed confessions when it puts its exposition of the law of God under the heading "Thankfulness." The demands of God are understood in the Reformed tradition as the good gift of God to be received with gratitude, exercised for the welfare of all human beings, and obeyed in confidence that God's grace gives us the ability to do what God's law requires. Law, in other words, is a part of the gospel of saving grace, not something opposed to it or some alternative to it.

29.146 This theology of grace and law is one of the most important things that distinguishes the Reformed tradition from other traditions and theologies. (a) It distinguishes Reformed Christians from other Christians who understand obedience to God's commandments as a means of earning or cooperating with the saving grace of God rather than as a thankful response to saving grace already freely given and powerfully at work. (b) It distinguishes Reformed Christians from other Christians who believe that the law of God serves primarily the negative purpose of exposing sin, leading to repentance, and leading to the gospel of God's saving grace rather than the positive purpose of guidance offered by the gospel. (c) It distinguishes Reformed Christians from some other Christians who believe that Christian freedom is freedom from rather than freedom for obedience to the commands of God. (d) It distinguishes Reformed Christians from other Christians for whom obedience to the law is an end in itself rather than a means of loving and serving God and other people. (e) Finally, it distinguishes Reformed Christians from those who use the law of God to justify oppressive "order" in society for the benefit of a few rather than to achieve a free and just society for all.

29.147 One can of course find in the present as well as in the past individuals, groups, and whole denominations of Christians who call themselves Reformed yet understand and use the law of God in all of the un-Reformed ways we have mentioned. But insofar as they do so, they have misunderstood and misused the very theology of grace and law based on God's gracious sovereignty that is one of the most distinctive elements of their own Reformed confessions.

C. The Authority of Confessions in the Reformed Tradition

29.148 The Reformed tradition is unique in its understanding of the authority of its confession. The most revealing clue to this unique understanding is the great number of confessions it has produced. Other Protestant confessional traditions have been content with only a few confessional statements written by a few people within narrow geographical or historical limits. All the Lutheran confessions, for instance, were written by a few Germans in Germany between 1529 and 1580. Authoritative Roman Catholic teaching comes from church councils or from the pope. But from beginning of the Reformation, wherever the Reformed church spread, Reformed Christians made new confessions of their faith, first city by city, then country by country. The confessions of Bern, Basel, Zurich, Geneva, and other Swiss cities were followed by one or more confessions written for Germany, Switzerland, Belgium, Holland, Hungary, and Scotland. The great period of confession writing came to an end for two centuries after the seventeenth century (because under the influence of Protestant orthodoxy the Reformed churches lost sight of the reason for multiple confessions and because the liberal theology that dominated the eighteenth and nineteenth centuries was suspicious of confessional restraint). But the twentieth century has seen a revival of Reformed confessional writing. Reformed churches have participated in the preparation of well over thirty new confessions that have been completed or are in process.

29.149 This multiplicity of confessions, written by many people in many places over such a great span of time, obviously means that the Reformed tradition has never been content to recognize any one confession or collection of confessions as an absolute, infallible statement of the faith of Reformed Christians for all time. In the Reformed tradition confessional statements do have authority as statements of the faith of Reformed Christians at particular times and places, and there is a remarkable consistency in their fundamental content. Some have had convincing power for a long time. Nevertheless, for Reformed Christians all confessional statements have only a provisional, temporary, relative authority.

29.150 Reformed confessions themselves provide three interrelated reasons for this unique attitude toward confessional authority:

29.151 1. Confessions have a *provisional authority* (and are therefore subject to revision and correction) because all confessions are the work of limited, fallible, sinful human beings and churches. In our time we have perhaps become more aware than most of those who wrote and adopted Reformed confessions in the past that even when confessions intend to serve only the revealed truth and will of God, they are also influenced by the sexual, racial, and economic biases and by the scientific and cultural limitations of a particular situation. But from the very beginning and throughout their history, Reformed Christians and their confessions have acknowledged with the Westminster Confession of 1646 that "all synods or councils since the apostles' times, whether general or particular, may err, and many have erred; therefore they are not to be made the rule of faith and practice, but to be used as a help in both" (chaps. XXIII-XXXII).

29.152   2. Confessions have a *temporary authority* (and are therefore subject to revision and correction) because faith in the living God present and at work in the risen Christ through the Holy Spirit means always to be open to hear a new and fresh word from the Lord. As the multiplicity of Reformed confessions indicates, Reformed Christians have never been content to learn only how Christians before them discerned and responded to the word and work of God; they have continually asked in every new time, place, and situation, "What is the living Lord of Scripture saying and doing here and now, and what do we have to say and do to be faithful and obedient in our time?" The Barmen Declaration speaks for the best intentions of the whole Reformed tradition when it says, "Jesus Christ, as he is attested for us in Holy Scripture, is the one Word of God which we have to hear and which we have to trust and obey in life and in death."

29.153   3. Confessions have a *relative authority* (and are therefore subject to revision and correction) because they are subordinate to the higher authority of Scripture, which is the norm for discerning the will and work of God in every time and place. A frequently repeated theme in Reformed confessions is their subjection of their own theological and ethical thought — including their interpretation of Scripture itself — to this higher authority, or to the authority of the Holy Spirit who speaks through it:

We protest that if any man will note in this confession of ours any article or sentence repugnant to God's holy word, that it would please him of his gentleness and for Christian charity's sake to admonish us of the same in writing; and we upon our honor and fidelity, by God's grace do promise unto him satisfaction from the mouth of God, that is, from his holy scriptures, or else reformation of that which he shall prove to be amiss. (Preface to the Scots Confession).

The Supreme Judge, by which all controversies of religion are to be determined, and all decrees of councils, opinions of ancient writers, doctrines of men, and private spirits, are to be examined, and in whose sentence we are to rest, can be no other but the Holy Spirit speaking in the Scriptures. (Westminster Confession, 6.010).

Confessions and declarations are subordinating standards in the church, subject to the authority of Jesus Christ, the Word of God, as the Scriptures bear witness to him. No one type of confession is exclusively valid, no one statement is irreformable. Obedience to Jesus Christ alone identifies the one universal church and supplies the continuity of its tradition. (Preface to the Confession of 1967, 9.03).

29.154   Reformed Christians are put in a difficult position with their self-limiting, self-relativizing confessions. On the one hand they are bound: so long as they are faithful members of a Reformed church, they are not free to interpret Christian faith and life (or even Scripture itself) however seems best to them personally, but are committed to submit themselves to the authority and guidance of the confessional standards of their church. On the other hand they are free: the very confessions to which they are bound allow — require — them to remember the human limitations and fallibility of their church's confessional standards, to be open to hear a new and perhaps different word from the living Lord the standards confess, and to examine critically the church's teachings in the light of further study of Scripture. It is not surprising, then, that Reformed Christians and whole Reformed denominations have sometimes been unable to maintain this balance between authority and freedom. Some have contradicted the very Reformed tradition they confess by claiming for this or that confession the absolute, infallible, unchangeable truth and authority that the Roman Catholic Church has traditionally claimed for its official teaching. Others, while calling themselves Reformed, have acted as if they were members of a nonconfessional "free" church, insisting on their freedom to interpret Scripture for themselves without regard for the guidance and restraint of their church's confessional consensus. Those who choose confessional authority over personal freedom make impossible the continual reformation of the church called for by Re-

formed confessions themselves. They run the risk of idolatrously giving to the church the ultimate authority that belongs alone to the living God we come to know in Jesus Christ through the Bible. On the other hand, those who choose personal freedom over the confessional consensus of the church destroy the church's unity, cut themselves off from the guidance of the church as they interpret Scripture, and run the risk of serving not biblical truth but the personal biases they read into Scripture.

29.155 Difficult as it is to find the way between church authority without personal freedom or personal freedom without church authority, a distinctive mark of the Reformed tradition is the belief that it is only by seeking this difficult way that the church can be a united community of Christians who are both "reformed and always being reformed."

Confessional Documents as Reformed Hermeneutic

Edward A. Dowey Jr.

I. CONFESSIONAL DOCUMENTS AND THE ACT OF CONFESSING

The ecumenical creeds of the early catholic Church and the confessions of classic and modern Protestantism are *documents*. Obviously! We know this from common usage, from the dictionary, and from the constitutions of various church bodies. But documents, even when assent to the content is required by subscription and sealed by ordination, are only part of the church's act of confessing and believing. These documents represent the literary precipitate of the verbal side of confessing, usually formulated under special historical conditions. They are not divine revelation but part of the church's answer to the revelation that has created and renewed the church in history and does so in the present.

Christian confessing has at least three

Reprinted from the *Journal of Presbyterian History* 61 (Spring 1983): 90-98.

aspects. It is verbal, volitional, and personal-communal. (1) There is a content to the Christian faith, expressed most briefly in the earliest confession of the Church: "Jesus Christ is Lord" (Phil. 2:11). Words are needed to understand as well as to communicate and elaborate the meaning of this confession. Hence arose the verbal character of confessing as well as preaching, teaching, theology, doctrine, and dogma. (2) But uttering these words confessionally is never merely verbal. It is at once an act of will, a total commitment that expresses itself in praise and obedience. The term "Lord" makes the confessor a servant, subject, or follower in all possible conditions of life. The one who confesses in these words puts her or his life on the line, as is shown by the language of church history and liturgy in which "martyrs and confessors" are those who sacrificed or were willing to sacrifice their lives for the faith. (3) Confessing is personal-communal, not private or individual. Even when the confessor is physically alone, he or she shares in the community that is created by participation in the Lord's kingdom, both in and beyond the empirical church. Christian confessing always reflects the correlative personal and community dimensions of life in the church.

This threefold character gives rise to certain prominent aberrations in the history and current life of the church. One is confessional-*ism*, the canonization of verbal formulae (sometimes claimed to be infallible) combined with a fixation on doctrinal correctness, usually oriented toward the past and often at the expense of love and faithful obedience. Another aberration so completely emphasizes obedience, departing from old doctrinal formulae and sometimes from any verbal formulae at all, as to become wordless, anonymous action. But love minus confessing words (derived from the Word himself) will finally be cut off from the wellsprings from which it originates. A third aberration is exhibited either in a separated privatism or a formal institutional legalism, whether with reference to words or to deeds.

All this having been said, the confessions and creeds of Christian history still come to us in the first place as documents. They are collectible in large volumes such as Schaff's *Creeds of Christendom* or the more handy form of Leith's *Creeds of the Churches*. Throughout Christian history these documents have been understood as containing biblical teaching in brief form, focused on the essentials, truly stated so as to ward off erroneous construal and heretical distortion. As such these documents were meant to be the formal, authoritative interpretation of Scripture in the church, the end product of a churchly hermeneutic. Both in the patristic period and in the Reformation, rare or difficult biblical materials were to be brought into harmony with the clear and known consensus by a principle designated the "analogy of faith." This proved to be a powerful control on the hermeneutic process. Hence we turn now to formal authority.

II. FORMAL HERMENEUTIC AUTHORITY IN THE REFORMED TRADITION

The Protestant Reformation was at root an event in the realm of hermeneutics. For all the issues of personal and social psychology, economic, political, and cultural change, and ecclesiastical and liturgical practice of the late Middle Ages, the Reformation (Lutheran and Reformed) offered *a corrected interpretation of what the Bible means by grace.* In response to this interpretation, the church confessed anew, and in confessing re-formed itself in words, deeds, and the form of community life. Confessional documents expressing the fresh understanding of grace soon came into being. These documents were to have their influence chiefly as part of the constitutions of the Reformation churches in various lands. The Heidelberg Catechism (1563) is a case in point. It was not only set within the constitution as a criterion of orthodoxy but it provided the structure of theological lectures for the education of ministers, it was divided into fifty-two sections so that each might serve as a sermon subject each week of the year, and it was memorized by all communicants.

Another example from the century after the Reformation is the Westminster Confession and Catechisms. Sydney Ahlstrom calls the Westminster standards "by far the most important confessional witness in American Colonial history. . . . That so many learned and contentious men in an age of so much theological hair-splitting could with so little coercion establish so resounding a consensus on so detailed a doctrinal statement is one of the marvels of the century."[1] Nonetheless, as time went on both in Scottish and American Presbyterianism, formal authority did become coercive. Strict subscription in Scotland forbade "any minister or lay member of the church . . . to speak, write, preach, teach, or print anything whatsoever that would be contrary to, or even inconsistent with, any view contained in the Confession."[2] American Presbyterian subscription was milder and was always limited to the ordained. From the Adopting Act of 1729 to the present, it was not the *ipsissima verba* of the documents but presbytery's often milder judgment of the acceptability of the ordinands' views within the confessional "system of doctrine" that determined who was to be ordained. When this procedure was seen to allow both Old School and New School interpretations, however, a more sinister tack was taken, requiring a more severe adherence among seminary professors. The professor being installed in an Old School Presbyterian seminary, after 1838, was asked to promise *ex animo* "not to inculcate, teach, or insinuate anything which shall appear to me to contradict or contravene, either directly or impliedly, anything taught in the said Confession of Faith, . . . while I shall continue a professor in this Seminary." This reductio ad absurdum of the formal authority of "subordinate" standards survived the reunion of 1869 and remained in effect until twenty-five years ago. (My own refusal to consider teaching at Princeton with the oath in force was the occasion for its removal.) The demonic rigor of this Old School oath was self-defeating, as we shall see below in Section IV, where the confessions themselves are seen to call for the continuing hermeneutic process in the church.

III. THE HERMENEUTIC OF CONFESSING OBEDIENCE

Confessing engages the will. But is there a formal authority for this volitional aspect of confessing comparable to the doctrinal authority just observed? The immediate answer is No. It has not been characteristic of Christian history to produce documents of prescriptive obedience comparable to the Nicene or Chalce-donian theological documents. This may seem strange, given the range of ethical action that across the centuries has variously expressed the will of the church — from early pacifism, through just war for the protection and advance of Christian civilization, to military crusades that were meritorious for salvation; or the shift from family-oriented Christianity to the ascetic, celibate "religious" life; or from accepting to rejecting human slavery and witchcraft. All of these forms of obedience and many more were both the product of and the producers of changes in biblical interpretation, but generally they did not find their way into formal confessional statements.

The Reformed tradition may offer here something of an exception (possibly along with Methodism). Already in early Zurich and Geneva the "third use of the law" and the discipline of the church were used to bend the will of the recalcitrant confessor. When practiced with the cooperation of the state, this produced an ethical impact on society that has been called revolutionary, albeit a "repressive" revolution so far as immediate political liberty was concerned.[3] Martin Bucer's program for the kingdom in England, never enacted, contained essentially the same social control. Analogously, the Westminster Larger Catechism, Questions 91-148, gives an extremely detailed account of what the various commandments of the Decalogue "require" and "forbid" as the Christian's obedience. Generally these teachings belong to individual or personal ethic, although the prescription for the relations among "inferiors, superiors, or equals" is a social dimension of great import. Generally the Larger Catechism was used in America, if at all, to find grounds for the prosecution of ministers caught in egregious immorality. Nonetheless, the personal and social sanctions and prohibitions of nineteenth-century evangelicalism bear a strong resemblance, and not merely by chance, to this Westminster ethic.[4] Subsequently, liberal Protestantism, insofar as it flourished in Presbyterianism in the late nineteenth century and the early twentieth, turned the ethical compass more directly toward social and structural evils, although not away from personal sins and vices. This emphasis was tacitly received and acknowledged within "the broadening church" after the General Assembly deliverance of 1927.[5]

It was with the Confession of 1967 that a strong social-ethical hermeneutic of faithful obedience was introduced into a Reformed confessional document. There was some precedent in the Barmen Declaration of Germany in 1934. But that great confessing document condemns only Nazi impingement on the institutional church. Thus, while rejecting totalitarianism, it does not even mention anti-Semitism or various other social evils of Hitler's Germany.

More directly, the Confession is informed by (1) a reapprehension of the Pauline doctrine of reconciliation under the tutelage of Calvin's *Institutes,* Book III, at a time when (2) twentieth-century Christian pre-understanding *(Vorverständnis)* had already for many years confronted the church with the structural forms of sin in human society. This doctrine of reconciliation overcomes the orthodox dichotomy of justification and sanctification and apprehends with Calvin the inseparability of regeneration and justification, the virtual identity of the terms *justification* and *reconciliation* (*Institutes,* 3.11.4), and the societal import of all this taken together.

It bears repetition that the prominence of reconciliation in the Confession does not mean that the document is to be understood as highlighting a single doctrinal topic among others, any more than in the Reformation itself justification was just one of a list of topics. Luther is said to have called it "the article by which the church stands or falls," and Calvin, "the main hinge on which religion turns." In the Reformation, justification by grace through faith was the fundamental motif decisively af-fecting the import of all confessional words, obedience, and life within the Christian community. It was, in short, the hermeneutical key to faith and life in the sixteenth-century church. And so it is with reconciliation as apprehended in the Confession of 1967.

The word *is* in the first sentence of paragraph 31 offers a succinct way to present the role of reconciliation in the Confession: "To be reconciled to God *is* to be sent into the world as his reconciling community." Calling is sending. As prophets, apostles, and disciples were all called to be sent, so the community created by God's reconciling work *is,* as such, "sent into the world." There is no gap, no option. The church is at once a mission. The structure comes from 2 Corinthians 5:17 through chapter 6, encapsulated as follows: "this community . . . is entrusted with God's message of reconciliation and shares his labor of healing the enmities which separate people from God and from each other."

The societal dimension of the ethic of reconciliation is not constructed in terms of a theory of the state or of economics, a system of discipline, or a prescriptive program for action. Rather its "direction" and "pattern," as befits disciples who follow their Master, is drawn from the life of Jesus (pars. 24 and 32). The Confession points in a direction — a very important word in this document — that is derived from the ministry of Jesus and, like that ministry, drawn by human need. Careful attention should be given to paragraph 43:

> In each time and place there are particular problems and crises through which God calls the church to act. The church, guided by the Spirit, humbled by its own complicity, and instructed by all attainable knowledge, seeks to discern the will of God and learn how to obey in these concrete situations.

These words point the confessional direction for a hermeneutic of faithful obedience. The four paradigms on race, peace, economic life, and sexuality indicate the following of this direction in the contemporary world. They are not exhaustive, but they make the direction unmistakable and concrete. They recognize contemporary (not merely current, or passing) personal and social reality in which the church lives and must enter its confessing obedience — for otherwise it "denies the Lordship of Christ and betrays its calling" (par. 43). The sharp closing words at the end of each of the four paragraphs are meant to serve the function of the anathemas of certain early creeds, defining the church also by negation: in these instances, self-pronounced anathemas.

IV. THE CONTINUING HERMENEUTICAL PROCESS

An insight of Harnack about the history of doctrine is relevant here. Harnack holds that the history of doctrine as authoritatively formulated teaching always fights against the history of theology out of which the formulations actually spring. This is because the church finally claims that its dogmatic decisions are biblical and represent the original truth of revelation, not a historical development. In the Reformed tradition we have already seen this maxim illustrated where formal authority has tried to hold the line against subsequent development. But this is not the whole story, because correctives are built into the confessions themselves.

The Westminster Confession, which we have seen made the subject of some of the most frightening legal restrictions, is known to teach that "all synods and councils since the apostles' times whether general or particular, may err, and many have erred; therefore are not to be made the rule of faith or practice, but to be used as a help in both" (chap. xxi). The preface to the Second Helvetic Confession notes with approval the variety in expression and formu-

lation of doctrine and in rites and ceremonies among the churches stemming from the Reformation. All these are to be allowed within the unity of the fellowship but may be corrected by appeal to Scripture and the "ancient apostolic church." This subordination of churchly documents to Scripture and correction by appeal to Scripture works against overemphasis on formal authority and condemns the very process by which too much is claimed for the confession itself.

More important by far than the formal approach presented above are those provisions in the confessions themselves for the lively process of biblical interpretation in the preaching and teaching of the church. This process continues before, during, and after the preparation of formal documents. The same hermeneutic process that brought on the Reformation continues to modify the Reformed church throughout history. *Semper reformanda!*

Most interesting in this regard is chapter two of the Second Helvetic Confession, entitled "Of Interpreting the Holy Scriptures, and of Fathers, Councils, and Traditions." This remarkable chapter brings into focus both the technical side of exegesis and the movement of the history (fathers, councils, and traditions) in which the church lives as interpreter of Scripture. The need for interpretation is taken as self-evident, along with the need to arbitrate among rival interpretations. The goal is the natural or genuine meaning derived from the Scriptures themselves, expounded and applied to contemporary life. The minister "expounds" and "applies" in order to comfort, strengthen, raise up, rebuke, and the like those in the parish, whether common people or officers of civil government (chap. xviii). And the scope of it all is "the glory of God and man's salvation."

Technical exegetical advice, not at all to be taken for granted in the sixteenth century, is offered by an insistence on understanding according to the genius of the original languages, the context and the historical circumstances, the comparison of like and unlike, clearer and more obscure passages. If this application of the techniques of humanist literary analysis to the text of Scripture seems tame in the twentieth century, it was not so in the sixteenth: the Council of Trent had already canonized the Latin Vulgate and condemned any interpretation "contrary to that sense which Holy Mother Church — whose it is to judge of the true sense and interpretation of the holy Scripture — has held and does hold."

A quite different hermeneutical situation prevails for the church after the scientific and cultural watershed of the eighteenth century. Thus were brought on the efforts in American Presbyterianism to revise the Westminster Confession in the 1890s, the failure of which resulted in the narrowing of the church in the direction of Benjamin Warfield's fundamentalistic orthodoxy. But in the middle of the 1920s a truce was struck. The "broadening" church would stay together, but at the expense of being a vigorously confessing church.

Fortunately, however, the continuing hermeneutic process in the context of teaching and preaching was to show new life, fructified in part by Neo-Reformation thought from the continent and in part by a growing social conscience. One evidence was the appearance of the magnificent Faith and Life Curriculum for church schools, a Christ-centered and covenant-oriented educational instrument. Under the rubric of confessional obedience in a changing social scene came the numerous activities of "Social Education and Action" — which functioned along with the curriculum in preparing the way (without intending it) for a coming new confession of faith.

In the Confession of 1967, several brief paragraphs entitled "The Bible" respond at long last to the cultural change of three centuries in which the modern world was born. The Confession reaffirms the revelation of God in Christ the Word as the Reformation did, over against every human invention and innovation, whether secular or biblicist and fundamentalist. This is a unique achievement among confessional documents to date, and it appears strong enough to lead the church into an unknown future, despite the recent sounds of a frightened and backward-looking bibliolatry.

V. A PRACTICAL CONSIDERATION

Throughout the history of the Reformed tradition, the central place both for the ongoing hermeneutic process urged in the confessions and for the general influence of the confessions in the church has been the pastoral office through preaching, teaching, oversight, and leadership. Correspondingly, it is chiefly the minister of the word, among the other ordained ministries, who is held accountable in the constitutional questions for following the leading and guidance of the confessions of faith. Appropriately, theological education was in the past structured by the theology of the confessions. Rather strongly, thus, I wish to remind those of us that find our calling in theological education that it is scandalous for a faculty member in any discipline in the church's seminaries not to be able to locate his or her work and thought and teaching matter with relation to the confessional teachings. We do not want again the old teaching oath, or any teaching oath at all, and the inevitably stifling conformity it promotes. But neither do we want the chaotic nonconformity of private virtuoso theologies that leave the relation of thought to life in the empirical church to the improvisation of individual ministers. Further, theological education carried out in programs of continuing education or presbytery projects of many types should be oriented by a reasonable awareness of what the church teaches in its confessional and credal literature.

More broadly, it is the educational ministry of the church on all levels that should bear the chief responsibility for a confessionally rooted hermeneutic, worship, and mission. The idiom of the tradition, whether in words or ethic, needs to be exercised in spiritual, biblical, theological, and ethical education.

It would be well, we often think, if one might be just a Christian, and not a Presbyterian, Catholic, or Methodist. But so, it might seem, is the case with language. What if we could avoid German or English and just speak language? But it doesn't work. Esperanto is a wonderful idea, but like Basic English a few years back, it is bereft of the richness of meaning and naturalness of a true language. So a theological Esperanto, or ecumenical Esperanto — for the time being at least — leaves us far from the concrete reality in which we live and speak. The idiom of the Reformed tradition, when fully understood, is the ground and motive both for ecumenical awareness and progress and for other kinds of reform and advance. The promising idiom of our tradition is not abandonment but reform, as new light breaks forth from Scripture and illuminates new situations in our culture and environment and in the world church. So the confession arises out of the hermeneutic process that advances — in words, in obedience, and in churchly militance — under the guidance of the Word and the Spirit.

NOTES

1. Ahlstrom, *A Religious History of the American People* (New Haven: Yale University Press, 1972), p. 94.

2. L. J. Trinterud, *The Making of an American Tradition: A Re-Examination of Colonial Presbyterianism* (Philadelphia: Westminster Press, 1949), p. 39.

3. See Michael Walzer, *The Revolution of the Saints: A Study in the Origins of Radical Politics* (Cambridge: Harvard University Press, 1965).

4. Cf. Ahlstrom, *A Religious History of the American People,* and Robert Handy, *A Christian America: Protestant Hopes and Historical Realities* (New York: Oxford University Press, 1971).

5. See Lefferts A. Loetscher, *The Broadening Church: A Study of Theological Issues in the Presbyterian Church since 1869* (Philadelphia: University of Pennsylvania Press, 1957).

The Nature of Revelation in the Christian Tradition from a Reformed Perspective

Presbyterian Church (USA)

I. GENERAL CONSIDERATIONS ON THE NATURE OF REVELATION

28.149 The nature of revelation will not be summed up in a definition here, but study of the topic may begin with some reflections on (A) the source and content of revelation, and its relation to (B) faith, to (C) language, to (D) experience, and to (E) reason, as well as (F) its ongoing dynamism in history.

28.150 A. *Revelation Is Self-disclosure of God*

28.151 Revelation is self-disclosure of God. Thus God is both its source and its content. Because God is the author and end, and judge and redeemer, of all creation, revelation also illumines our understanding of ourselves and of all other creatures. But it is first and foremost the revealer that is known in it.

28.152 All knowledge of God comes ultimately from God, and thus could be seen in some way as a self-disclosure of God. But in this document "revelation" will be understood as signifying, more precisely, divine self-disclosure that is analogous to the way human persons disclose themselves to one another by words and particular deeds. People are disclosed to each other in their characteristic behavior. Such encounters give knowledge, though not total knowledge, of the self of the other person. In the same way, God's self is disclosed in God's dealing with human beings, but God is still more than what is revealed. Reformed views of revelation have emphasized that God's self-disclosure gives knowledge of God's will or disposition toward us, and not only (or even primarily) of God's inner nature, which remains mysterious and veiled

Reprinted from Presbyterian Church (USA) document "The Nature of Revelation in the Christian Tradition from a Reformed Perspective," 199th General Assembly (1987).

in its revealedness. Through God's self-disclosing activity we learn God's purposes and precepts for our lives, God's judgments, and above all God's promises of grace. So understood, revelation is personal meeting of God with human beings, the experience of which can be reported in language. It is given to bring us, both corporately and individually, into relationship with God, and to open to us a way of life, of reconciliation, peace, and joy, of worship and service, love and justice.

28.153 B. *Revelation and Faith*

28.154 Revelation is received by faith. Revelation and the faith that receives it cannot be understood in isolation from each other.

28.155 Faith is a response of the whole person, mind and body, involving intellect, imagination, emotions, and will. The Reformed tradition has emphasized both faith's dimension of confident trust and its dimension of knowledge. Christian faith has historically been articulated in creeds, but they by no means exhaust even the intellectual aspect of faith. Whether one really understands what has been revealed is shown at least as much by one's ability to relate it to social relationships and the issues of daily life as by one's theological statements. One of the most important ways in which revelation is grasped is through an intuitive and comprehensive sense of the meaning of the gospel, including a feeling for the relative importance of various aspects, implications, and expressions of the gospel.

28.156 C. *Is Revelation "Propositional"?*

28.157 Faith has always sought expression in statements believed to be true. When the church seeks to communicate its faith in preaching and teaching, to celebrate it in worship, to share it in openly faithful life together, and to apply it in Christian ethical reflection and practice, it is driven to try to state what has been revealed. The relation of revelation to these statements or "propositions" has been a subject of intensive reexamination, and controversy, in recent theology. Earlier Christian

thought, speaking of "revealed truths," tended to identify what is revealed with propositions. On this view, which is still held by many in the church, what has been revealed is that certain statements are true. Reformed Christians have found these statements primarily or exclusively in the Bible — for instance, that "God was in Christ reconciling the world to himself" (2 Cor. 5:19). Christians in some other traditions have identified revelation also with certain statements in church pronouncements and especially in the historic creeds — for instance, that Jesus Christ is "very God of very God, begotten not made, being of one substance with the Father."

28.158 Other Christians, however, in the Reformed and in other traditions, now believe that such statements are not themselves identical with the content of revelation, but rather represent an (always imperfect) attempt to express something more primary. Some identify this primary content of revelation with historic or present acts of God; others identify it with nonpropositional modes of religious awareness. The recent discussion suggests that statements about God are one among a number of forms in which our understanding of revelation may be expressed, others being poetic and artistic images and concrete forms of obedient action. Whether or not the content of revelation should be identified with propositions, the difference between statements that are faithful to the gospel and hence to be accepted as true, and those that are not, remains crucial for the life of the church.

28.159 D. *Revelation and Experience*

28.160 Revelation is received in experience. Sometimes "experience" means subjective feelings; sometimes it means certain kinds of evidence. Without excluding either of these, "experience" is used here to refer, more broadly, to human life perceived with some awareness of our own identity. It is in and through experience in this sense that God's personal address to us is recognized and appropriated. For many people, experience of the new life that God gives in Jesus Christ is the principal ground on which the Christian revelation is accepted.

28.161 Experience has cognitive aspects, but it does not have to be primarily intellectual. Often experience of God takes place largely on other levels, as when one is lifted out of oneself by sacred music or art, or when one speaks in tongues, or when one feels the divine love among people assembled for prayer, or when one is aware of God's presence in a way that transcends both thought and feeling. Among the other sorts of experience through which revelation may be received are hearing or reading the story of Jesus, imaging parts of it in meditation, listening to a sermon, forming a significant relationship, grieving over a loss, engaging in controversial action in support of one's convictions, and wrestling (perhaps in prayer) with one's own doubts. Some of these experiences have an intellectual aspect, which may be either subordinate or dominant. But the revelation that may be received in them is not limited by what we can say about it — both because we are sometimes aware of things that we are unable to put into words and because our views of God, of the world, and of ourselves may be transformed in an experience more deeply than we know.

28.162 Experience always has an individual dimension, but it also has a social dimension. Experience is communicated socially by both verbal and nonverbal forms of expression. Thus communities have common or shared experiences, which are an important resource for the understanding of revelation (as discussed more fully in sect. VII.C., below). The social dimension is essential to Christian experience as such; for a Christian experience is by definition one that is shaped by the gospel of Jesus Christ, and therefore by certain historic events that come within the individual's experience only through a social process of recording, interpreting, living out, and communicating in a people of God (as will be discussed more fully below).

28.163 Individual experience is tested as it is shared in the community of God's people. This is not to say that majority approval is the final authority. Today, as in biblical times, an individual's experience may contain a prophetic apprehension of something God is saying that the majority refuse to hear. However, intensity of subjective conviction is also not proof that a belief is from God. In the end individuals cannot escape the responsibility of making up their own minds about religious issues. But such decisions can be made more responsibly after ideas have been tried in the fire of debate and after one has paid attention to the experience of other people.

28.164   E. *Revelation and Reason*

28.165 Revelation is often contrasted with reason as a source of knowledge of God. This is legitimate to the extent that revelation tells us things that we could not have figured out for ourselves if God had not acted in special ways to reveal them. It is a mistake, however, to suppose that belief in revelation must be irrational or that reason and ordinary sources of knowledge cannot play any part in our knowledge of what has been revealed. For example, sources of knowledge from outside the Bible are important precisely in receiving, understanding, and interpreting God's Word in the Scriptures. Without at least a basic knowledge of nature, history, and languages, and without some explicit or implicit principles of logic and interpretation, we would not be able to understand anything at all from the Bible; and knowledge from all of these sources rightly and inevitably influences what we take God to be saying to us there. Likewise, a faith formed by the Bible interacts with other sources of knowledge of the world as it is today to yield further beliefs about what God is doing and calling us to do. For such faith, science is a study of God's ways of creating and governing the world.

28.166 F. *Revelation Is a Continuing Process*

28.167 Revelation is a continuing process. It includes historical events, such as the deliverance of Israel from bondage in Egypt and the crucifixion and resurrection of Jesus; interpretations of those events by prophets and apostles; formation of traditions of wisdom and worship; the telling and retelling, writing and editing of these things by those who shaped and wrote the Holy Scriptures; the gradual selection and acceptance of the canonical Scriptures in the Christian community; the reading of the Bible and preaching based on it; the understanding of the gospel received by Christian individuals and communities under the illuminating work of the Holy Spirit and the transformation of their lives in conformity with it; and the interaction of the historic understanding of the gospel with the ever new needs and experiences of human beings.

28.168 This process counts as revelation because God is active in it and personally encountered in it. Specifically, as Christians, we see God acting to effect revelation as the incarnate Lord and Savior in Jesus and as the Holy Spirit inspiring prophets, apostles, and every generation of God's people.

28.169 The term "process" here is not meant to suggest a purely natural or sociologically necessary evolution of religion. For the most essential thing in revelation is the free activity of God. In a sense, indeed, that activity is the revelation. But since we never encounter the divine self-disclosing activity in complete separation from human response to it, it is appropriate to speak of revelation more broadly as a process in which God's action and human response both play a part.

28.170 The term "continuing," likewise, is not meant to suggest a never-ending progress in which everything that has already been revealed is merely provisional or destined to be superseded. The process of revelation continues because the knowledge of God in any generation involves a fresh and living contact with God. But this fresh contact is based on the permanent authority of revelation that has already occurred.

II. REVELATION AND THE NATURE OF GOD

28.171 As God is both the author and the principal content of revelation, the nature of revelation is determined by the nature of God. The Christian revelation is of a Trinity — Father, Son, and Holy Spirit, three persons in one God — and is centered in the incarnation of the second of these persons. All three persons share, equally and indivisibly, the same nature, which includes the following characteristics that are important for an understanding of revelation.

28.172 A. *God Is Love*

28.173 Both the content and the manner of God's self-revelation are shaped by the divine love. At the very center of revelation is God's declaration of love for us and promise of salvation from sin and death. And one of the chief gifts of divine grace is that it is constantly at work to enlarge our knowledge of God and enrich its effect in our individual and corporate lives. God's love is also rich in forgiveness. We therefore do not need to be anxious about the errors that doubtless affect various aspects of our own thinking about God, nor do we need to be hostile toward those who may disagree with us about religious issues, as if God would not love those who make theological mistakes. We are invited to a faith that trusts in grace, rather than in any rightness of our own, with regard to beliefs as well as behavior.

28.174 B. *God Is Holy*

28.175 Glorious to a degree that we cannot comprehend (and will not comprehend even as far as we can), the holy God cannot be completely known by us. Unveiled in revelation, God remains veiled in the mystery of holiness. The limitation of our knowledge of God is due partly to our creatureliness (i.e., to the vast difference between us and the divine being) and partly to our sin, which pervades and distorts all our thinking and doing, including our response to revelation. In spite of this we do receive the gift of God's self-revelation. We are not able to identify any point at which we know that our vision is in no way clouded or curtailed or perverted by creatureliness and sin. Nevertheless, we believe that what has been revealed to us corresponds authentically to the reality of the holy God and especially to God's will toward us.

28.176   C. *God Is Sovereign*

28.177   God rules not only over the universe in general but also over the process of revelation in particular. There is no point at which God turns over control of the process to us, leaving it to us to extract theological truths from an inert deposit of revelation that has been left in our hands. Our own free response affects all our faith and knowledge of God, but the Holy Spirit is active at every step of the process of our reception of God's revelation. Those who honor the divine sovereignty will expect always to be surprised by the revelation of God's judgment and mercy.

III. THE GOD OF CREATION AND OF ISRAEL

28.178   A single action can be rich in self-disclosure, as all great dramatists know. But if we are really to know other people, they must disclose themselves to us in a variety of ways and contexts in an ongoing relationship. The Christian revelation has that shape. It takes place in a world that declares God's glory as creator (Ps. 19:1-4; Rom. 1:20), and it comprises a centuries-long history of interactions of God with an identifiable community, a people of God. The story begins with the creation of the universe (Gen. 1–2), enters history with God's calling a family of Hebrews from Ur and Haran to the land of Canaan, and includes the deliverance of Israel from slavery in Egypt, the giving of the law at Sinai, the experiences of reliance on God in nation-building and wrestling with God in tragedy, repentance, and new hope, and the widening prophetic vision of God's justice and concern for the poor. In the process God is revealed as an identifiable personal being with a name (YHWH)[1], with relationships and covenant commitments to particular people, and with a character of holiness, justice, and mercy. It is as one already known in this way that God is revealed in the New Testament; and of course it is still primarily on this basis that God is known and worshiped in Judaism.

IV. JESUS CHRIST, THE WORD MADE FLESH

28.179   "The Word became flesh and dwelt among us, full of grace and truth; we have beheld his glory, glory as of the only Son from the Father" (John 1:14). The very person of Jesus Christ is Word of God — divine purpose and speech addressed to us. The life and death and resurrection of Jesus of Nazareth, truly God and truly human, are for Christians the most important self-disclosure of God. The centrality of Christ in a Christian understanding of revelation has been a major theme of Reformed theology of the nineteenth and twentieth centuries — and not only of Reformed theology. The Confession of 1967 (9.27) declares that "the one sufficient revelation of God is Jesus Christ, the Word of God incarnate." The Second Vatican Council, likewise, in its Dogmatic Constitution on Divine Revelation (sect. II), refers to Christ as "himself both the mediator and the sum total of Revelation."

28.180   A. *Christ the Center of Revelation*

28.181   Many different ideas have been used to express the primacy of Jesus Christ in revelation. The one that will be chiefly explored here is that Jesus is the central revelation of God. This means that all other apparent revelation must be tested by its ability to take its place in an understanding and a life organized around him as its center.

28.182   One of the most fundamental ideas put forward in this study document is that the primary criterion of revelation is to be found by organizing it around its center rather than by concentrating on defining its boundaries. This is not a device for avoiding or stopping the debates that are inevitable in a living religious tradition. To say the criterion is in Christ as the center is not to say that we find there an uncontroversial christological thesis or doctrine. It is rather to look toward a single person, Jesus, whom Christians have always understood in differing ways but who remains the same person that all Christians seek to follow. It is thus not retiring with relief from the controversial fringes but directing our attention to the right common reference point.

28.183   To speak of Christ as the central revelation of God is not to say that God has acted in a self-revealing way only in Jesus of Nazareth, in Palestine approximately two thousand years ago. It is not to exclude the possibility or the actuality of revelation in other events and to people in other times and places. The prophets of Israel and the apostles and saints of the Christian church can be seen as participating in revelation as witnesses and interpreters of Christ. But even that does not exhaust the possibilities of a Christ-centered view of revelation. There can be, and have been, revelations of God that have no explicit reference to Christ. For instance, the word of God to Isaiah (5:16), that it is in justice that the holy God is holy, did not need a context of messianic belief in order to be received by the prophet and his hearers as authentic revelation of God.

28.184   To speak of Christ as the central revelation of God is to say, however, that all revelation of God must be understood in the light of Christ and that nothing is to be accepted as revelation that cannot be so understood. All God's dealings with humanity form one single story with Jesus at its center. Christ's centrality is a permanent centrality. As the one who will come again to judge the world, Jesus is the end of history as well as its center. Revelation is a continuing process in which God sometimes surprises us with new disclosures of the divine purpose in new situations; but God's revelation in Jesus will never be superseded, surpassed, made obsolete, or dislodged from its position of centrality.

28.185   B. *A Trinitarian Conception of Revelation*

28.186   The centrality of Christ finds its context in a trinitarian theology of revelation. We see in Jesus the incarnation of an eternal divine Person who prays to Another as Father and promises another as Paraclete (advocate and source of encouragement). The Trinity is a Trinity of persons, not of aspects or functions of God; and they are undivided in will and in their effects in our lives. But it is sometimes primarily one person of the Trinity that is disclosed, or at any rate effectively apprehended, in a particular event of revelation. Only the second person of the Trinity is incarnate in Jesus. It is the third person, the Holy Spirit, that prays in us. And surely God is revealed, in creation and in the law and the prophets and the worship of Israel, as the one whom Jesus called "Father" before there is any clear conception of an eternal Son of God.

V. THE WORK OF THE HOLY SPIRIT IN REVELATION

28.187   The Reformed tradition has always emphasized that we could not hear the voice of God or receive any revelation of God if the Holy Spirit did not continually speak in our hearts and by the mouth of other children of God. This work of the Spirit has been understood in the closest connection with the Holy Scriptures.

28.188   A. *The Inspiration of Scripture*

28.189   To affirm the inspiration of Scripture[2] is to say that the Holy Spirit guided the authors so that their human words might be used as a vehicle of God's self-revelation. It is not necessarily to commit oneself to a particular theory as to the way in which God guided the authors or the extent or respects in which they were preserved from error.

28.190   Inspiration is the work of the Holy Spirit in the whole process of revelation. It is a mistake to focus exclusively on the inspiration of the authors of Scripture, as if that were the chief act of God's self-disclosure. That supreme act of revelation (as stated in sect. IV above) is found in the incarnation — in the ministry and death and resurrection of Jesus. And the inspiration of the biblical authors is only a part of an ongoing activity of the Holy Spirit by which God is made known. The Holy Spirit has guided not only the authors in writing the Holy Scriptures but also the church in receiving and interpreting them. "The Holy Scriptures are to be read . . . ," the Westminster Larger Catechism (Q. 157) states, "with a firm persuasion that they are the very Word of God, and that he only can enable us to understand them."

28.191   This point is of the utmost importance for the acknowledgment of the divine sovereignty over the whole process of God's self-revelation. To say that the Holy Spirit speaks to us in the Bible is not to claim that the Spirit spoke once to the authors and then left the text at our disposal. If that were so, then we would control the hearing of God's word by our scholarship, hermeneutical principles, intuitions, reasonings, and decisions; and the price of our control would be that we would have a dead voice of God. But "the word of God is living and active" (Heb. 4:12). In fact we hear a living voice of God in the Scriptures, and that means that we must turn to them in the expectation that we too will be moved by the Holy Spirit in ways that we could not have predicted.

28.192   B. *The Testimony of the Holy Spirit to the Scriptures*

28.193   There are several points at which the Reformed tradition has particularly emphasized the continued work of the Holy Spirit in making God known. One is the testimony of the Spirit by which the Scriptures are recognized as the word of God. As the Westminster Larger Catechism (Q. 4) puts it, "the Spirit of God, bearing witness by and with the Scriptures in the heart of man, is alone able fully to persuade it that they are the very word of God." It is not necessary to understand this as testimony in which the Holy Spirit speaks primarily about the Scriptures, telling us that precisely these books are inspired. The appeal to the testimony of the Spirit in this context is quite plainly an appeal to a form of Christian experience, and it is more consonant with Christian experience to say that in and through the Scriptures the Holy Spirit speaks to us primarily not about the Scriptures themselves but about Christ, addressing to us the promises and commandments of God concerning the world, the church and us individually. "We call the books of the Bible 'Holy Scripture' because of the continuous experience of the Church that God by the Holy Spirit confronts us and communicates with us through them."[3] In this the Spirit does not so much assert as demonstrate that the Scriptures are the word of God, because we hear the voice of God in them. And this testimony looks to the future at least as much as to the past, imparting to us not so much a theory about the composition of the biblical books as a faith and expectation that we will hear God speaking in them again if we turn to them with penitent and seeking hearts that are open to God and our neighbors.

28.194   C. *The Preaching of the Word of God*

28.195   Another point at which the Reformed tradition has particularly emphasized that in the doctrine of the word of God we have to do with a living voice of God that speaks now, and not with a dead voice that spoke only in the past, is in its teaching regarding preaching. "The preaching of the Word of God is the Word of God," as the Second Helvetic Confession (chap. 1, 5.004) states. In this statement it is of course assumed that the preaching of the word of God is based on Scripture. But the words of the preaching that are quoted or paraphrased from Scripture are not the only part of it that are claimed to be the Word of God. The words of the preacher rightly interpreting what God is saying through the Scriptures, and applying the message to the condition and situation of the hearers and their world, are comprehended in the identification of the preaching of the Word of God as a form of the Word of God. This identification would be impossible apart from the faith that the Holy Spirit continues to inspire and guide the people of God when they offer themselves for the service of the gospel. This faith is confirmed by the experience of Reformed Christians that

> the Spirit of God maketh the reading, *but especially the preaching* of the Word, an effectual means of enlightening, convincing, and humbling sinners, of driving them out of themselves, and drawing them unto Christ, of conforming them to his image, and subduing them to his will; of strengthening them against temptations and corruptions; of building them up in grace, and establishing their hearts in holiness and comfort through faith unto salvation.[4]

28.196   D. *Deeds and Words*

28.197   The Holy Spirit fills deeds as well as words with the power of God's self-revelation. Deeds of Christian love, for example, are at least as important as verbal statements in communicating God's love to most people. This is not to say that such deeds of love are meant by their human agents to be symbolic communications of divine revelation. They may certainly be performed against a background of awareness of their relevance to Christian witness, but their character as acts of love, of affection and service to a fellow creature, is easily damaged by trying too directly to make a religious point.

28.198   But the Holy Spirit also makes use of actions in which it is a primary intention of the human agent to communicate a revelation from God. This is true of enacted prophecies found in the Bible (as in Isa. 20 and Jer. 27:1-15). It is also true of the action of martyrs intending to bear witness in their suffering to the truth of God. In our own time many Christians have felt called not only to state what they believe God is saying about such matters as peace and racial justice but also to express it in symbolic action — often of protest, and sometimes even of civil disobedience. In such actions the Holy Spirit may be at work to make God and God's will known.

28.199   Skepticism or cynicism about religious statements may lead some Christians to hope that words might be largely, if not entirely, replaced by deeds in the constitution and communication of Christian faith. For the Reformed tradition, however, it is only in connection with words that deeds can convey God's truth with any clarity. This is most explicit in Reformed teaching on the sacraments. The sacrament is an event of communication that is partially nonverbal, involving physical objects and actions as signs. In it we meet God and experience the grace of God in ways that exclusively verbal communication would not make possible for us. But the sacraments would not be what they are, and could not be experienced as the confirmations of divine love that they are, without the word of Scripture and preaching that accompanies and interprets them.

28.200   E. *Prayer*

28.201   Many Christians, if asked where they meet God personally, will think first of experiences of worship, and especially of prayer. In prayer it is our privilege to come before God and speak to God as person to person, and it is possible in this way to come to a fuller personal knowledge of God. In prayer, also, we ask for God's will for our lives to be made known to us, and Christians are often convinced that in prayer they have in fact received guidance from God. Paul testifies that the Holy Spirit takes an active part in this process, praying with us, interceding for us, and helping us in our prayer (Rom. 8:15-27). This is a part of the process of God's self-disclosure. It is not meant to be an invitation to unbridled subjectivity, however. Christian prayer grows out of a knowledge of Jesus Christ grounded in the Scriptures, and what we think we learn in prayer must be tested against that same source. It would also be a mistake to think that because we pray our convictions are clothed with some authority in relation to other people.

28.202   F. *New Revelations from the Holy Spirit*

28.203   As the Holy Spirit continues to guide us into all the truth (John 16:13), the question arises whether individual Christians or groups of Christians today may receive new revelations through the Spirit. Many Christians find it natural to speak of having received personal revelations. This way of speaking can be accepted in the sense that individual Christians and groups of Christians can rightly become convinced that they have heard God speaking to them about some issue or situation in their lives. This conviction can rightly serve as a ground for belief in what they have heard God saying. Such revelations will normally arise out of an understanding of the gospel, if not from the words of Scripture themselves, and must be tested by the Christian and the church against God's supreme revelation in Jesus

Christ as communicated in the Bible. For the Spirit by whom we seek to be guided is the Spirit of Christ. In some cases God may be heard speaking about things that directly concern only one person, or a few people. But no revelation is essentially private; all belong in principle to the whole people of God, and new revelation of this sort contributes its bit to the formation of the Christian tradition which has for Reformed Christians a subordinate authority in the church.

28.204   A concrete example may be illuminating here. The Presbyterian Church (USA) ordains women to the ministry of the Word and sacraments [*sic*] — something which churches generally used not to do, and which some still do not do. We would not do this if we were not convinced that it is in harmony with the message of the New Testament. But in all probability we also would not have done it were it not for women who became convinced that the Holy Spirit was calling them individually to this ministry. Such an individual call, in the nature of the case, cannot be deduced from more general principles of Christian doctrine. Women who have pioneered in this area have had to trust in their conviction of God's guidance in standing up to strong opposition. Their experience has now entered into the corporate experience or tradition of the Presbyterian Church (USA) in such a way that it is convinced of God's guidance in ordaining women to the ministry of the word and sacraments [*sic*].

VI. THE AUTHORITY OF THE SCRIPTURES

28.205   A. *The Bible as Word of God*
It is a central feature of the church's experience of revelation that we hear the voice of the living God speaking to us in the canonical books of Scripture. It is a major and valid con-

cern of many Presbyterians that this should be clearly affirmed; and the church (virtually the whole church) has traditionally affirmed it by referring to the Bible as the word of God.

28.206 This way of speaking is used in the Scriptures themselves, but less comprehensively, for the most part, than we are accustomed to use it. In the Bible, "word of God" or "word of the Lord [YHWH]" most often refers to specific prophetic oracles, which make up only a fraction of the biblical text. But the more comprehensive use of "the word of God" as a characterization of the Bible as a whole has long been established in the church, and particularly in the Reformed tradition. Indeed, the classic Reformed confessions make little or no use of the word "revelation," and what they have to say about the doctrine of revelation is found mainly under the heading of "the word of God."

28.207 The appropriateness of this terminology is now widely debated, however, and it has a less dominant role in the most recent confessional documents of the Presbyterian Church (USA). The Confession of 1967 uses the idea of the Bible as word of God only alongside another idea of the Bible as witness — "unique and authoritative witness," "the witness without parallel" — to Christ (9.27). Both the Confession of 1967 and the Brief Statement of Belief adopted by the 102nd General Assembly of the Presbyterian Church in the United States in 1962 discuss these issues about Scripture in the context of a wider doctrine of "revelation." This change in the formulation of Reformed confessional documents reflects the importance of revelation in twentieth-century theology, both in the Reformed tradition and in other branches of the Christian church.

28.208 To speak of the Bible as "the word of God (written)" is certainly to use a metaphor. It is to take language as a metaphor for the process of revelation, for God does not literally speak (or write) in the same sense as

we do. This is not to say that the Bible is not really the word of God. Statements using metaphor are often true, and the metaphor can help to make them understood. If we say, for example, "The Lord is my shepherd . . . ; he makes me lie down in green pastures" (Ps. 23:1-2), we are stating something true about God's care for us, even though we are not literally sheep and do not eat grass. And this metaphor expresses the truth with a vividness and force not likely to be reproduced by a more literal paraphrase.

28.209 The metaphor in which the Bible is spoken of as "the word of God" has its limitations. One is that it focuses attention on the intellectual aspect of revelation, and (among the modes of sensation) primarily on hearing. Reformed Christians are not likely to want to give up their emphasis on hearing and understanding, but accepting alongside the image of "word" other metaphors for revelation — metaphors of appearing, seeing, tasting, touching — which are also found in the Bible and Christian tradition, may help in appreciating and appropriating the nonintellectual and nonauditory aspects of revelation and of worship that are present in biblical religion (as in virtually all religion). An important point of contact in the Reformed tradition for this understanding is the sacraments, in which God's self-revelation is received not in separation from the word but also under such visible and tangible symbols and images as that of "bread of life."

28.210 A serious concern about the use of the metaphor "word of God" for the Bible is that to some it suggests an image of the Deity dictating the sacred text word for word to its human authors. This imagery has indeed played a certain role in Christian thought, but it allows far too little role in the process for the humanity of the authors. It also makes it more difficult to acknowledge and deal in an open way with certain problems that arise from the biblical text. The treasure of revelation comes in earthen vessels, and it is a barrier to many outside the church and a source of real pain to many Christians that parts of the Bible appear to contain such things as injunctions to genocide, calm acceptance of slavery, and gender-exclusive language and other expressions of a culture oppressive to women. In dealing with such facts it is especially important to be able to acknowledge the human limitations and cultural and historical situation of the authors — and to recognize that no human language can perfectly describe God's being, intention, and action in its fullness.

28.211 The principal reason for continuing to call the Bible "the word of God (written)" is the importance of affirming without embarrassment the reality of our meeting with God in the Scriptures. Given the historic role of this metaphor in the discourse and even the liturgy of the Reformed tradition, to abandon it could easily be interpreted as a retreat from the conviction that God's self-revelation has come to us and will come to us through these writings. The other metaphor which is used in the Confession of 1967 for the role of the Scriptures in the process of revelation, that they witness (with unique authority) to the Word of God incarnate (9.27), appropriately expresses the subordination of the Scriptures to Christ, but it has its own limitations. In particular, an exclusive reliance on it might suggest, wrongly, that we are related to revelation only by hearing at second or third hand (see further sect. VI.D., below).

28.212 Those who speak of the Scriptures as the word of God need not deny that, as the Confession of 1967 declares, they are "the words of men, conditioned by the language, thought forms, and literary fashions of the places and times at which they were written" and "reflect views of life, history, and the cosmos which were then current" (9.29). That God speaks to us in and through the Bible is the common experience of Christians; how this can be is in part a mystery (as it is mysterious

in general that a holy and infinite God can be revealed to us finite and sinful creatures), and Presbyterians have held and continue to hold diverse theories about it. To affirm that the Bible is the word of God is not to commit oneself to any one of those theories. In particular, it is not necessarily to commit oneself to the view that the sacred text is "inerrant," that what the biblical authors intended to say is identical with what God is saying to us, or that we must not disagree, for example, with Paul about anything.

28.213 It is significant that the church has generally spoken of the Bible as the word of God (in the singular) rather than as the words of God. This may help to avoid interpreting the metaphor in terms of word for word dictation. It also is consonant with the conviction that God speaks to us in the Bible as a whole which is centered in Jesus Christ, and it suggests that receiving revelation through the Bible is not a matter of picking out certain parts of Scripture as authentic words of God and discarding the rest but rather of seeking to hear God speaking in each part rightly related to the whole.

28.214   B. *The Uniqueness of the Bible's Authority*

28.215 It is a central teaching of the Reformed tradition that the Bible is uniquely authoritative as a medium of revelation — and particularly that more recent expressions of a tradition of the church cannot have a similar status. This has sometimes been understood as meaning that the writers of Scripture were inspired as no other have been.[5] The account of the role of Christ and the Holy Spirit given above, however, implies that the uniqueness of the biblical authors is not to be found in their inspiration, which they share with later generations of Christians. The New Testament seems to expect that the fullness of the gift of the Holy Spirit given at Pentecost will continue until the return of Christ at the end of the age. It does not restrict inspiration to the apostles, nor does it predict an irreversible loss or diminution of the gift of the Spirit in postapostolic generations.

28.216 The authority of the Scriptures and the uniqueness of the biblical writers are derived from the centrality of the Word made flesh in the process of revelation. Jesus Christ is the supreme revelation of God, but he reveals God in a context, and that context is constituted in part by other divine revelatory activity. Jesus comes to a people that remembers historic events and prophetic words in which God's gracious love and judgment, the divine compassion and zeal for justice, have been revealed to them — a people that has learned in prayer and psalm and sacred liturgy to acknowledge the majesty and generosity of God. All of this (and therefore the Old Testament) belongs to the Christian revelation. And God's act of self-revelation in Christ is completed by its reception, for a successful act of communication requires a hearer as well as a speaker. For this reason the faith and testimonies of the apostles belong also to the event of revelation. The writings of the New Testament are the authentic record of apostolic testimony and of what the apostolic church understood to have been communicated to it. The canonical New Testament as the church has accepted it, as a whole, comes as close as we can reasonably expect to the way Jesus was seen by the first generation of those who understood him. It also contains their irreplaceable testimony to his resurrection. No later writings or teachings, however inspired, can stand in these relations to the revelation of God in Jesus. Because the revelation in Jesus is the standard by which Christians must test all other claims and appearances of inspiration, the Holy Scriptures have a uniquely authoritative role. The supremacy of the Bible over other documents of Christian tradition corresponds to the permanent centrality of Jesus Christ. It is an expression of the fact that the revelation in Jesus is not to be superseded and will not come to mean something entirely different from what it meant to those who first met the incarnate Word of God.

28.217   C. *The Bible and History*

28.218   As the authority of the Bible is founded in its relation to certain historical events, the question of the historical accuracy of biblical narrative is of great importance for the understanding of revelation. The affirmation that the Bible is the word of God, or "the witness without parallel" to God's self-revelation, surely claims that the most centrally important things it tells us about God are true. Among these are that Jesus proclaimed the reign of God, offered forgiveness to sinners, died, and was raised again from the dead. It is therefore important to the authority of the Bible that those events really happened. It does not follow, however, that all of the narratives in the Bible must be historically accurate in every respect. The reliability of the Bible as a witness and vehicle of divine revelation addressed to us and our world does not depend, for example, on the accuracy of statistics about the size of armies in the book of Chronicles, or even on the chronological relation of the crucifixion of Jesus to the Passover. These are clear cases in which historical accuracy is and is not important to the role of the Bible as word of God. Some cases are more controversial. It does not belong to a doctrine of revelation to make a much more precise determination of where the line is to be drawn between the accuracy that is and that is not theologically crucial. Detailed decisions in these matters must draw on all the resources of faithful and responsible biblical study and systematic theology, relying on the guidance of the Holy Spirit.

28.219   D. *The Canonical Text as Place of Revelation*

28.220   The canonical text of the Bible as we have it, in its original languages and responsible translations, is our appointed meeting place with God, where we expect in faith that God will speak to us. It is a witness to mighty acts of God, but it is also more than a witness in relation to revelation. The Bible itself is a place of revelation — *a* place, not *the* place, for this status belongs also, for example, to historic events that are attested by the Scriptures. There is an inevitable tension between past and present in the Christian understanding of revelation, and it is not to be resolved by downgrading the Bible as we have it to the status of data for the scholarly reconstruction of a past revelation — whether that be the lost original manuscripts of the Scriptures or the historic events attested by them. Hearing the living voice of God in the Bible does not depend on any such reconstructions, though it may sometimes be aided by them. Although the unique authority of the Scriptures is founded in their relation to certain historic acts of God, we have in many cases no way of knowing with certainty how those events would have appeared to us children of the twentieth century had we been there. In humble faith that God's Word has not returned empty (Isa. 55:11), but that the revelation has been received and understood by witnesses appointed to receive it and inspired to understand it, we must attend to what those closer to the events have written about how they appeared to them and what they meant to them. Faith in the Holy Spirit's guidance and illumination both of our own understanding and the understanding of the biblical writers should be one reason for rejecting excessive anxiety about the historical accuracy of details of biblical narrative.

28.221 Given the holistic and christo-centric view of revelation in the Bible that has been proposed here, some disagreements among the various branches of the Christian church about precisely which scriptures are canonical need not be regarded as crucial. For instance, the exclusion of the book of Revelation from the canon of the Nestorian churches, and the difference between the larger Greek canon of the Old Testament used by most of the Gentile Christian churches in the early centuries and still accepted by the Roman Catholic and Eastern Orthodox churches, and the narrower Hebrew canon favored by Judaism and most Protestant churches, do not imply major differences in understanding of God's self-revelation. This is not, of course, to admit as acceptable the radical abbreviation of the Bible by Marcion[6] or other conceivable extremes of enlargement or contraction of the canon.

VII. THE INTERPRETATION OF SCRIPTURE

28.222 A recent General Assembly document wisely remarks that the issue of biblical interpretation may be "more basic and pressing" than that of biblical authority, because "the use of Holy Scripture is more important than debates about its authority," and "it may not even be necessary to achieve theoretical agreement about Scripture's authority, before reaching consensus about principles which guide its interpretation."[7] By the same token, those aspects of the nature of revelation that have a direct bearing on the way in which Scripture is understood have a special importance for the life of the church. The task of this section is to relate the interpretation of Scripture to the understanding of revelation. . . .

28.223 A. *The Letter and the Spirit*

28.224 Expectation of hearing the voice of God through the Bible calls for a serious and disciplined attention to the letter of Scripture. Careful interpretation must begin with study of the "plain sense" of each text, though it must also go on to relate that sense to the Bible as a whole, to the history of the people of God as we understand it from the Scriptures and from other evidence, and to issues of systematic theology and present-day application. The plain sense is what the normal reader at the time of writing or of final formation of the text would have understood the passage to mean. This is apprehended largely through grammatical and other linguistic knowledge, and partly through historical-critical study. In the context of preaching and Bible study people sometimes hear the word of God through allegory, typology, and other imaginative or speculative interpretations. The Bible itself furnishes examples of very free interpretation of Scripture (for instance, in Gal. 4:21-31). But such imaginative interpretation can hardly claim to be an apprehension of biblical revelation except insofar as it is consistent with an understanding that is rooted ultimately in the plain sense of the texts.

28.225   Closely linked today to the study of the plain sense of the Scriptures are the methods of historical criticism. The development of modern historical scholarship has had an incalculable influence on the development of Christian thought in the last two hundred years. Historical-critical methods have shed new light on virtually every part and every aspect of the Bible. By providing a fuller and more accurate understanding of the original historical contexts of the scriptural texts,[8] these methods have helped us to understand how God spoke in those texts to the people who first received them. By bringing to light new alternatives for interpretation and a new wealth of meanings rooted in the original historical context,[9] they have both complicated the interpreter's task and enriched it with new possibilities. Many Christians have found historical criticism disturbing to their faith, and Christians have good reason to examine methodologies of secular origin to make sure that something contrary to the gospel is not being smuggled in as an unexamined presupposition. At the same time, many Christians scholars, convinced of the fundamental soundness of methods of historical criticism, are compelled, both by honesty and by faith in the historical actuality of God's self-disclosing activity, to claim the opportunity that these methods offer of getting closer to the acts of God in the history of Israel, of Jesus, and of the New Testament church. And while the results of these

studies may disturb some of the preconceptions that we bring to the reading of the Bible, it is also true that these preconceptions may need to be disturbed if we are to hear the voice of God and not just our own voice or the voice of a familiar religious milieu.

28.226   The study of the letter, however, cannot give us hearing of the voice of God without the continuing help of the Spirit. "We call the books of the Bible 'Holy Scripture' because of the continuous experience of the Church that God by the Holy Spirit confronts us and communicates with us through them," as the 1983 position statement "Presbyterian Understanding and Use of Holy Scripture" states. The most important interpretive question about the Bible, therefore, is what God is saying to us now in it. Questions about what Jeremiah and Paul and the other biblical authors meant to say are important, but the ultimate goal is to hear what God is saying to us, and the attainment of that goal depends primarily on the guidance of the Holy Spirit and our receptivity to the message of the gospel rather than on the correctness of our methods.

28.227   Openness to the Spirit in the interpretation of Scripture precludes a clear-cut method for the resolution of controversies. The idea of a method by which agreement can be coerced, typically by rational argument from authoritative sources, is perennially seductive. Experience indicates, however, that this idea spawns disputes; it does not resolve them.

28.228   B. *The Rule of Faith*

28.229   At the same time, there must be (as the Reformed tradition has always insisted) a check on subjective and arbitrary interpretations of Scripture. This is provided, first and foremost, and ultimately through the Scriptures themselves, by what has been called "the rule of faith," which might also be referred to simply as "the gospel." These terms refer to the core of God's message to us in Jesus Christ. It is communicated in propositions or statements and expressed by various summaries of the faith that are found in the New Testament and the creeds of the church. But it is not to be identified with any list of propositions. When Paul speaks in his letters of "the gospel," he refers to a content which he can express in many ways; the primary form of its appropriation is clearly an understanding which is able to choose expressions that are appropriate to the occasion, to recognize statements and actions that agree and that disagree with the gospel, and to weigh considerations according to the importance that they have for the gospel. Such an understanding can and should be aided by scholarship, but it is not essentially a scholarly accomplishment. All Christians are called to attain it, and acceptable interpretations of what God is saying to us in and through the Scriptures must be found in agreement with it. At the same time we must always be open to the possibility that our understanding of the gospel should be corrected in the light of a new interpretation.

28.230   C. *Inclusive Christian Community the Context for Interpretation*

28.231   Another important check on subjectivity is provided by the fact that the Bible is to be studied in the context of the Christian community, where we have to listen seriously to the interpretations of other Christians and expect to hear God's word through them.[10] The community that provides this context is the whole people of God. The methods of philological and historical research in the hands of biblical scholars and ministers of the Word often shed great light on the meaning of the Scriptures, and God uses them in speaking to us. The Reformed tradition has rightly emphasized the value of these tools of study. But the understanding of what God is saying to us through the Scriptures is not the exclusive province of specialized scholarship. The main themes of the gospel are accessible to the ordinary reader of any responsible translation. The most important equipment for the hearing of the Word of God is usually a sense for those

themes and an ability to recognize their centrality. This equipment is received through the guidance of the Holy Spirit in studying the Scriptures in a context of Christian community.

28.232   It is particularly important to see the context of interpretation as being ecumenical in the sense of being inclusive of all the diversity of traditions and experiences that are represented in the church of Jesus Christ. Differences of gender, race, ethnicity, and culture are as important as denominational differences to this ecumenical diversity. Who we are is determined in large part by the experiences that we have and have not had, and in turn enlarges or limits what we hear of God's word and how we respond to it. The significance of the biblical texts for the original authors and readers or hearers depended in part on experiences of theirs that were presupposed. Some of these are universal human experiences that all of us share, some of them are probably beyond any possibility of our recovering, and some are shared by some but not all people today. It is a common observation that the experience of serious illness or bereavement, for example, may open one's eyes for new insight into the Scriptures and into God's working in one's life.

28.233   This is true not only of such individual experiences but also of the social and political experiences of communities. New experience of relations between the sexes, or between races, or among other social groups, may lead to new understanding of God's demand for justice. Many Christians, as poor or exiles, as immigrants in strange lands, as citizens trying to act responsibly in their own land, as women or racial or ethnic minorities, or as subjects of colonial power, have shared with the peoples whose story is told in the Bible the experiences of oppression, struggle, and liberation, of homelessness and pilgrimage, of political responsibility and powerlessness in the context of nationhood. Insights into God's word that are important to the church come to us through such experiences.

28.234   The inclusiveness of ecumenical Christian community does not blot out all differences of viewpoint. We are called to try to understand and appreciate each other's insights. But it is still to be expected that people whose experience of life has been different — for example, people of different sexes or of different cultural backgrounds — will experience and understand God somewhat differently and interpret the Scriptures somewhat differently.

28.235   D. *The Development of Christian Conscience*

28.236   It is a well-known historical fact that Christian conscience and social awareness have changed in the course of centuries. We find in the Bible, for example, no explicit condemnation of the institution of slavery, but Christians today are in virtually universal agreement that slavery is intrinsically an offense against human dignity and against God. This development is a part of the process of revelation, unfolding the implicit significance of the Exodus and of our liberation in Christ. Here, as everywhere in the understanding of revelation, Jesus Christ is the supreme criterion, but interpretation of Christ's significance

must draw on the whole range of human experience, so far as it is accessible to us. Ideas of secular origin about such matters as human dignity and the nature of justice have influenced Christian conscience and should influence it when the Holy Spirit leads us to see them as in conformity with Christ. Christians are not to be confined to the social consciousness of the biblical writers, which (like all human awareness) was in some ways limited.

28.237   Experience of signs of the work of the Holy Spirit often plays an important part in such changes. One of the most important changes in the conscience of the New Testament church was that by which Gentiles were admitted to full Christian fellowship. Both in Acts (10:47 and 11:15-18) and Galatians (3:2-5) the experienced receiving of the Holy Spirit by Gentiles is presented as a principal justification for this development. Similarly, if most Presbyterians now accept the possibility of remarriage for divorced persons, although there are biblical passages that could be interpreted in a contrary sense, this is surely due in part to experience that suggests that many new marriages of divorced persons have been blessed by God with gifts of growth in Christ.

NOTES

1. By the time that vowels were added to the text of the Hebrew Bible, this name was no longer pronounced, for reverential reasons, but another term (commonly "the Lord") was substituted in reading aloud and in translations. The name is thought to have been pronounced "Yahweh."

2. Cf. 2 Tim. 3:16 and 2 Pet. 1:21.

3. "Presbyterian Understanding and Use of Holy Scripture" (1983).

4. Westminster Larger Catechism, Q. 155; italics added.

5. See the Westminster Confession, chap. 1, sect. 3, 6.003.

6. In the second century Marcion founded a Christian sect that rejected the Old Testament and limited the New to the letters of Paul and an expurgated version of the

Gospel according to Luke. His aim was to sever Christianity from its Jewish roots and even from the doctrine of the creation of the world by a good God.

7. "Presbyterian Understanding and Use of the Holy Scripture" (1983).

8. For instance, by situating Isaiah 40–55 in the Babylonian captivity at the time of Cyrus, and the book of Daniel in the resistance to Hellenistic persecution of Judaism in the second century B.C.

9. For instance, the great variety of christological ideas in the New Testament — some of them quite different from those that have usually been developed in systematic theology.

10. See 2 Pet. 1:20 and the Second Helvetic Confession, chap. 2, 5.010.

The Authority and Interpretation of the Bible in the Reformed Tradition

Jack B. Rogers

INTRODUCTION

One of the most important and least-known facts of American church history is that when Archibald Alexander formed the curriculum of Princeton Seminary in 1812, he chose as the textbook in systematic theology the *Institutio Theologiae Elencticae* of Francis Turretin. Sixty years later, in 1872, Charles Hodge's famous *Systematic Theology* replaced Turretin's Latin tome as the text but continued Turretin's theological method until 1929. For over one hundred years, professors at Princeton vowed to "receive and subscribe" the Westminster Confession of Faith and Catechisms. They thought of themselves as followers of Calvin.

But in actuality, they believed and taught a theological method regarding the authority and interpretation of the Bible rooted in a post-Reformation scholasticism, almost the exact opposite of Calvin's own approach. More importantly, certain features of the central church tradition regarding the authority and interpretation of Scripture that had been retained from the early church down through the Reformation were lost in the post-Reformation reaction to the rise of scientific criticism of the Bible.

This peculiar twist of American history — that Turretin rather than Calvin molded the nineteenth-century Presbyterian understanding of the authority and interpretation of the Bible — has served to distort our view of both the central Christian tradition and especially of its Reformed branch. We need to step back and reflect briefly on the central Christian tradition regarding Scripture and how it was carried on in that theological tradition of the Reformation known as Reformed (Calvinist as opposed to Lutheran or Anabaptist).

The argument in this essay is developed and documented extensively in Jack B. Rogers and Donald K. McKim, *The Authority and Interpretation of the Bible: An Historical Approach* (San Francisco: Harper & Row, 1979).

51

I. COMMON FOUNDATIONS
IN THE EARLY CHURCH

Early Christians had to cope with a dual environment. They accepted the Hebrew Scriptures as authoritative, but they had to interpret them to teach that Jesus was the Messiah. A naive literalism was rejected while the spiritual meaning was retained. At the same time they had to communicate their faith in a way compatible with the Greek culture in which most Christians lived. That meant using the categories of Greek philosophy.

Christian teachers struggled for balance between these twin forces. They fought against attacks from without and excesses from within caused by literalism and legalism on the one side and spiritualism and sectarianism on the other side. Literalists (Jews, Gnostics, Marcionites) posed the heaviest threat in the early church. Accordingly, the dominant Platonic philosophy, which stressed a spiritual perspective, became an ally. Plato taught that all persons had within them knowledge of the great unchanging ideas or ideals, such as truth, beauty, and justice. Such apologists as Clement of Alexandria and Origen made use of and to some extent were molded by this philosophical medium. Platonism, modified by biblical meanings, afforded a framework in which theology could be communicated in their culture.

Theologians of the early church shared a fund of common concepts which formed the foundation of a Christian acceptance and interpretation of the Bible. Scripture — Old and New Testament alike — was completely authoritative. The Bible was accepted in faith by the working of the Holy Spirit in human hearts. Faith that Scripture was authoritative freed Christians to proceed to a scholarly understanding of it using the tools and techniques available to them. "Faith leads to understanding" was both a theological method and a call to Christian maturity. The theology that

resulted was viewed as primarily a practical rather than a theoretical discipline. Its purpose, like that of Scripture, was to instruct people concerning God's salvation and guide them in living the life of faith. The Bible was not to be used as a book of science; its focus was rather on that saving wholeness which encompassed love of God and love of neighbor as well. Awareness of that goal also yielded principles of interpretation.

The early theologians affirmed God's accommodated style of communication. The incarnation modeled God's willingness to humble God's self in seeking to bring persons salvation. Christians likened God's speaking in Scripture to that of a parent or teacher who condescended to think in the concepts and speak the language of children for their benefit. The notion of accommodation enabled theologians to exegete Scripture in a way that upheld God's worthiness and accepted human limitations.

Interpreters of the Bible shared the common tradition of typology inherited from rabbinic Judaism. Promises in the Old Testament were linked historically to fulfillments in the New. Beyond that, two divergent methods of interpretation developed. The principal one was allegory, flowing from the Platonic center in Alexandria. It sought spiritual meanings to solve the problems posed by literalism. Augustine exemplified this approach and passed it on to the Middle Ages. The lesser-known school of interpretation was the grammatical-historical one situated in the more Aristotelian center at Antioch. It reacted against allegorism and sought the natural meaning of the author in its historical context. Chrysostom commended this method by his use of it in preaching. The Protestant Reformers followed Augustine's theological ·method, but they focused on Chrysostom as their exegetical mentor.

Despite differences in their method of biblical interpretation, Augustine and Chrysostom exemplified the consensus of the early church regarding the Bible. Their common rhetorical training helped them to separate the depth of truth contained in Scripture from its lowly accommodated style. They sought the intention of the author and the meaning of his thought. Error was a matter of deliberate deception from which the Bible was free. Human limitations of thought and speech reflected in the biblical writings were matters for scholarly study.

Augustine's understanding of the authority of Scripture flowed from his general method: "I believe in order to understand." Scripture was completely authoritative for Augustine. The Holy Spirit had inspired the original writers and illumined present-day readers. For Augustine, the Bible was not a textbook of science but the Book of Life, written in the language of life. When Felix the Manichean claimed that the Holy Spirit had revealed to Manicheus the orbits of the heavenly bodies, Augustine replied that God desired us to become Christians, not astronomers.[1] The style of God's condescension or accommodation in the Bible was as apparent to Augustine as it had been to Origen and Chrysostom. As Calvin noted, "Augustine . . . skillfully expresses this idea: we can safely follow Scripture, which proceeds at the pace of a mother stooping to her child, so to speak, so as not to leave us behind in our weakness."[2]

Augustine was quite conscious of the human character of the biblical material. He declared concerning the differences in the evangelists' reports in the four gospels that "the truth is in no wise violated if the same events are narrated in different ways with different words."[3] A rhetorician such as Augustine knew that truth could be conveyed in a great variety of words, even those which technically could not be harmonized. "In any man's words," he wrote, "the thing which we ought narrowly to regard is only the writer's thought which was meant to be expressed, and to which the words ought to be subservient."[4]

II. DIFFERENCES IN METHOD AT THE MIDDLE AGES

The common foundations on which an understanding of the authority and interpretation of the Bible rested in the early church were decisively divided at the Middle Ages. The Augustinian tradition, rooted in neo-Platonism, was carried on down to the twelfth century. Its chief exponents where John Scotus Erigena and Anselm of Canterbury. They maintained the theological method expressed in the motto "I believe in order that I may understand." Even in their work, a subtle shift of accent occurred as the emphasis moved from believing to understanding.

In the early Scholastic period of the twelfth century, a decisive reversal of theological priorities occurred. Beginning with Peter Abelard, theological method was predicated on Aristotelian logic. The motto of this approach was "I know in order that I may believe." The rediscovery of the metaphysical works of Aristotle stimulated the sweep of rationalism into theology. By the thirteenth century, Scholasticism entered what is now known as its classical period. Albertus Magnus attempted to make all of the Aristotelian corpus known by making a theological commentary on it. Thomas Aquinas produced the *Summa Theologiae,* which gave comprehensive and systematic expression to medieval Scholasticism. As Scholasticism developed, philosophy was given priority over theology. Reason was used to prepare people for faith. Authority shifted from the Scriptures received in faith through the work of the Holy Spirit to proofs for the existence of God developed by rational speculation. Theology was transformed from a practical discipline expounding the saving message of Scripture and giving guidance in the Christian life to a theoretical science. Theology became the queen of the sciences with the right to critique other areas of knowledge from her own theoretical viewpoint. The early church concept of accommodation was replaced by the philosophical concept of analogy. Scripture was no longer the focus of research, looked upon as human language and thought forms by which God as our parent had graciously condescended to communicate to children. God's mind was now understood to be expressed in the orderly processes of nature. By reasoning from God's effects in the world back to a First Cause or by constructing the logical opposite of human qualities and assigning them to God, it was assumed that God's existence and something of the divine attributes could be known. The accent in theology had moved from exegesis of the biblical text to philosophical speculation. Nonetheless, one benefit was a return to the grammatical-historical interpretation of Scripture, which was more scientifically controllable than the allegorical search for spiritual senses.

Franciscan theology continued the neo-Platonic–Augustinian tradition through medieval Scholasticism in opposition to the Aristotelian innovations of the Dominicans. Duns Scotus and William of Occam denied that the truth of Christianity could be rationally demonstrated. The will, rather than the intellect, was given primacy in human actions. Theology again was understood as a practical, not a theoretical, discipline. Authority was to be found in Scripture and in the church, not in the demonstrations of reason.

The most extreme reaction to Scholasticism was expressed in monastic theology. The monks, led by Bernard of Clairvaux, distrusted all academic approaches to theology and developed the mystical tradition. Bernard's theological method was expressed in the notion "I believe in order to experience." Monastic theology called for faith alone and contended that the result of devotional reading of Scripture and prayer should be the experience of union with God. Mysticism skipped the step of studying the human context of the biblical writings and stressed instead the stimulation of subjec-

tive feelings by what was presumed to be the "spiritual" sense of Scripture.

III. THE CONCENTRATION ON FUNCTION AT THE REFORMATION

Luther and Calvin both returned to the Augustinian Anselmian theological method that faith leads to understanding. They were trained in and used the tools of scholarly study developed by the Christian humanism of the Renaissance.

A. Luther

Luther was an Augustinian monk. He was nurtured in the older neo-Platonic milieu which put faith before reason. Luther declared, "Isaiah VII makes reason subject to faith, when it says: 'except ye believe, ye shall not have understanding or reason.'"[5] Luther's training in the "new" thought of Occam gave him a philosophical rationale to support his orientation. Luther rejected nominalist theology, especially in its emphasis on free will, but he shared its anti-Aristotelian attitude.

The imperfect form of the Bible was no problem to Luther. God had condescended or accommodated God's self to human means in communicating his saving message. When Luther said that in Scripture "there is no falsehood," he was speaking not about technical accuracy but the ability of the Word to work righteousness in us.[6]

B. Calvin

Calvin was trained in that branch of Renaissance learning which we know as Christian humanism. He began with the study of Latin and the liberal arts. His father directed him first to theology and then to law. A distinctive mark of Christian humanism which Calvin imbibed was an emphasis on the rhetorical tradition. This tradition from Cicero through Augustine emphasized rhetoric (eloquence) over dialectics (logic). The concern was to make the given truth persuasive rather than to seek to find God at the end of a series of syllogisms. Theology was not *scientia* (science) as in the Middle Ages but *sapientia* (wisdom) taken directly from the pages of Scripture. The laws of Aristotelian logic were not allowed to take precedence over the teachings of Scripture.

Calvin positioned himself squarely in the rhetorical tradition. Plato was the best of the Greek philosophers and the most often cited by Calvin with favor. Calvin called Cicero "the first pillar of Roman philosophy and literature."[7] He quoted Augustine by far the most among the Church Fathers, and his basic theological method followed Augustine's "faith leads to understanding" pattern.

Calvin believed that everyone had an inborn knowledge of God, similar to Plato's innate ideas (*Inst.*, 1.3.1, 3; 1.6.1). However, everyone suppressed this knowledge sinfully, and so no valid "natural theology" could result (*Inst.*, 1.4.1, 2, 4). Although humankind was responsible for this sinful suppression of the truth, God gave "another and better help" properly to direct us to God our Creator: Holy Scripture. Whereas the innate knowledge was blurred and unclear, the revelation in the Bible was sharp and vivid. Scripture thus functioned like "spectacles . . . gathering up the otherwise confused knowledge of God in our minds, [which] having dispersed our dullness, clearly shows us the true God" (*Inst.*, 1.6.1; cf. 1.14.1). The knowledge of God to which persons then came, based on the Bible, was not a theoretical but a practical kind that which led to reverence, worship, and right living.

But how could people know that the Bible was authoritative? Calvin felt that even to ask such a question was to "mock the Holy Spirit"

(*Inst.*, 1.7.1). Asking "Who can convince us that these writings came from God?" was like asking "Whence will we learn to distinguish light from darkness, white from black, sweet from bitter?" (*Inst.*, 1.7.2). The answer for Calvin was self-evident: the Bible was a self-authenticating book.

According to Calvin, the persuasion that God is the author of Scripture was established in us by the internal testimony of the Holy Spirit. Calvin declared, "we ought to seek our conviction in a higher place than human reasons, judgments, or conjectures, that is, in the secret testimony of the Spirit" (*Inst.*, 1.7.4). Human testimonies to the Bible's authority were not in vain *if* "as secondary aids to our feebleness, they follow that chief and highest testimony," the Holy Spirit (*Inst.*, 1.8.13). But Calvin held that we may not begin with evidences or reasoned arguments. He stated quite explicitly that "those who wish to prove to unbelievers that Scripture is the Word of God are acting foolishly, for only by faith can this be known" (*Inst.*, 1.8.13).

Calvin strove for the Augustinian middle way regarding the authority of Scripture. He rejected on the one hand the rationalistic Scholasticism that demanded proofs for the existence of God and the truth of the Bible prior to faith in Christ and Scripture, and he rejected with equal firmness the spiritualistic sectarians who claimed leadings of the Spirit apart from Scripture. The Holy Spirit, for Calvin, "has not the task of inventing new and unheard-of revelations, or of forging a new kind of doctrine, to lead us away from the received doctrine of the gospel, but of sealing our minds with that very doctrine which is commended by the gospel" (*Inst.*, 1.9.1).

Neither was the Bible intended to teach us about science according to Calvin. In his commentary on Genesis, Calvin faced the issue of the relationship between the science of his day and the Bible. Astronomers had proved that Saturn was really a greater light than the moon, spoken of in the Bible as one of the two great lights. Calvin commented, "Moses wrote in popular style things which, without instruction, all ordinary persons, endued with common sense are able to understand; but astronomers investigate with great labor whatever the sagacity of the human mind can comprehend.... Nor did Moses truly wish to withdraw us from this pursuit . . . but had he spoken in things generally unknown, the uneducated might have pleaded in excuse that such subjects were beyond their capacity."[8]

The goal or object of Scripture for Calvin was to point persons to Jesus Christ, in whom is salvation. "We do not deny that believers embrace and grasp the Word of God in every respect; but we point out the promise of mercy as the proper goal of faith" (*Inst.*, 3.2.29). God's revelation of himself in Christ was the model of his method of communicating with us. Calvin declared that "in Christ God so to speak makes himself little, in order to lower himself to our capacity."[9] This incarnational style of communication was evident in the language used in the Bible. Calvin said that God "lisps" in speaking to us as a nursemaid does in addressing children. "Thus such forms of speaking do not so much express clearly what God is like as accommodate the knowledge of him to our slight capacity" (*Inst.*, 1.13.1). Calvin affirmed that the language of the Bible was often crude and unrefined. He noted an inaccuracy in Paul's quotation of Psalm 51:4 in Romans 3:4 and drew the general conclusion "that, in quoting Scripture the apostles often used freer language than the original, since they were content if what they quoted applied to their subject, and therefore they were not over-careful in their use of words."[10] Similarly, in his commentary on Hebrews 10:6, Calvin affirmed that the saving purpose of the biblical message could come through what we consider an imperfect form of words: "they [the apostles] were not overscrupulous in quoting words provided that they did not misuse Scripture for

their convenience. We must always look at the purpose for which quotations are made . . . but as far as the words are concerned, as in other things which are not relevant to the present purpose, they allow themselves some indulgence."[11]

The authority of Scripture, for Calvin, was found not in its style but in its saving content, not in its human forms but in its divine functions. Preaching by limited human messengers was another evidence of God's accommodation, according to Calvin. The limitations of the preacher's words were no hindrance to communication of the divine content. Preaching of the Word of God *was* the Word of God for Calvin.

Because Calvin was assured by the Holy Spirit of the authority of Scripture, he was free to examine its human forms with the tools of scholarship. Whereas Augustine was Calvin's model for theology, John Chrysostom was Calvin's mentor in exegesis. Calvin preferred the grammatical-historical method as the best way to get at the "natural and obvious" sense of Scripture. This did not imply literalism to Calvin. He rejected a narrow literalism (which he called "syllable-snatching") on the grounds that it resulted in legalism (*Inst.*, 4.17.14; cf. 4.17.23). Calvin desired to examine the circumstances and culture in which any part of the biblical message was set. "There are many statements in Scripture the meaning of which depends upon their context," he wrote (4.16.23; cf. 4.15.18). He always looked beyond the bare words to the intention of the author in interpreting Scripture, even with respect to the Decalogue.

Calvin had two requirements for excellence in exegesis: *brevitas* (he warned against the sort of lengthy commentary that could only exhaust the reader) and *facilitas* (he advocated passing over discussions of other commentators to come directly to the meaning of the text). He was equally opposed to allegorical spiritualism and rationalistic literalism. He branded allegory "a most disastrous error."[12] He also opposed the Aristotelian rationalistic exegesis developing among some of the Reformers (e.g., Melanchthon, Bullinger, and Bucer). He feared that Melanchthon's method, for example, could lead to an arbitrary choice of topics not based on the text but imposed on it.

A recent scholarly biographer of Calvin, T. H. L. Parker, aptly summarizes Calvin's views on the authority and interpretation of Scripture as follows: "The creatureliness of the Bible is no hindrance to hearing God's Word but rather the completely necessary condition. . . . For, according to Calvin's concept of accommodation, God genuinely speaks to man in such a way that he is comprehensible to him."[13]

C. The Reformed Confessions

During the sixteenth century, as the Reformation came to various parts of Europe, local communities, from cities to nations, drew up their own confessions of faith. These statements generally had a threefold purpose: to show the biblical character of their doctrinal affirmations, to demonstrate continuity with the ancient creedal forms of unity — the Apostles' and Nicene Creeds especially, and to clarify the distinctive emphases that set the various confessional groups off from Roman Catholicism and other Protestant groups.

Bullinger, the author of the Second Helvetic Confession, reflected the spirit of the Reformed statements regarding Scripture in his *Summa:* "We know very well that the Scripture is not called the Word of God because of the human voice, the ink and paper, or the printed letters (which all can be comprehended by the flesh), but because the meaning, which speaks through the human voice or is written with pen and ink on paper, is not originally from men, but is God's word, will and meaning."[14]

IV. THE CONCERN FOR FORM IN THE POST-REFORMATION PERIOD

A. The Shift in the Second Generation of Reformers

Calvin died in 1564. By that time the Roman Catholic Counter-Reformation had consolidated and focused its strength in rejection of Protestant doctrines at the Council of Trent (1545-1563). In response, the second generation of Reformers tried to prove the authority of the Bible, using the same Aristotelian-Thomistic arguments that Roman Catholics had used to prove the authority of the church. This second generation of Reformers was by then also fighting the extreme rationalism of Faustus Socinus and the Unitarians. Because Socinus claimed that reason did not lead to traditional trinitarian doctrines, the second-generation Reformers became all the more attached to a "natural theology" and tried to defend their doctrines by reason as well as Scripture.

Melanchthon, the successor of Luther, and Beza, the successor of Calvin, both endeavored to systematize the work of their masters by casting it in an Aristotelian mold. Thus a period of Protestant Scholasticism was launched in the immediate post-Reformation period. This Protestant Scholasticism rejected the Augustinian approach of faith, especially in regard to the Bible, and reverted to the Thomistic rationalism of the Reformers' medieval opponents. Two aspects of the central Christian tradition were weakened in this process. Theology was turned more toward an abstract, speculative, technical science and away from its practical and moral methodology. Further, and even more far-reaching in its consequences, the concept of accommodation was discarded. Theologians now unashamedly contended that they thought God's thoughts because the human mind was fitted to think in God's ways. Precision had replaced piety as the goal of theology.

On the Reformed side, Theodore Beza took on the mantle of Calvin. During Calvin's lifetime they had complemented one another. Now, in the post-Reformation polemical situation, Beza tended to rigidify and scholasticize many of Calvin's positions. Beza, Ursinus, Zanchius, and Peter Martyr Vermigli were transitional figures who tended to follow Calvin in their pastoral and exegetical work but who in their more "scientific" and polemical writing moved in the Aristotelian scholastic direction. Those who followed them in the seventeenth century increasingly adopted the Scholastic mold.

B. Francis Turretin

Reformed Scholasticism reached its full flowering in the theology of Francis Turretin, who held the chair of theology in Geneva one hundred years after Calvin's death. Turretin chose the theological method of Thomas Aquinas's *Summa* as the pattern for his own theology. In developing his doctrine of Scripture, Turretin quoted 175 authorities but did not mention Calvin.[15] Scripture was the formal principle on which Turretin founded a scientific systematic theology. The authority of Scripture was predicated on the claim that the Bible contained inerrant words. Turretin adduced external and internal arguments to prove that the biblical writers had not erred in the slightest particular. No trace of Calvin's concept of accommodation is to be found in Turretin's work. Not just the content but the form of the Bible is asserted to be supernatural. Accordingly, Turretin was intensely concerned over the present state of the biblical text. He omitted reference to the internal witness of the Holy Spirit in developing the authority of Scripture but invoked the Holy Spirit to guarantee an authentic canon and a reliable edition of Scripture. This led Turretin to the extreme of claiming inspiration for the (nonexistent) vowel points in the original Hebrew

manuscripts. Turretin's style of Reformed Scholasticism was embodied in the Helvetic Consensus Formula in 1675, which declared that textual criticism of the Old Testament would subject faith in Scripture to "perilous hazard."[16]

Reformed Scholasticism was a mind-set which in a period of defensive reaction made significant changes in the doctrine of Scripture utilized by Calvin. Reason was given priority over faith. Scripture came to be treated as a compendium of propositions from which logical deductions could be drawn.

V. FROM CALVINISM TO SCHOLASTICISM IN GREAT BRITAIN

The English Reformation underwent a development quite distinct from that on the Continent. Civil war retarded the incursion of the new science and philosophy and thus also slowed the Scholastic reaction to them until after the mid-seventeenth century. Puritanism in England also drew on native resources of Augustinian anti-Aristotelianism. This neo-Platonic philosophical orientation was supported in the seventeenth century by the simplified logic of French Protestant philosopher Peter Ramus.

The Westminster Divines, meeting from 1642 to 1649, carried on the Augustinian middle way in theological method, holding that faith leads to understanding. They maintained that the authority of Scripture resides in its central saving message and is affirmed by the inner witness of the Holy Spirit. The purpose of the Bible is to join persons to Jesus Christ, not to judge matters of science. This central saving message can be known by anyone who reads the Bible or hears the gospel preached. Matters of controversy in religion are to be dealt with by scholarship. The historical setting and cultural context of the biblical message are important in understanding the difficult passages. They preferred the grammatical-historical method of exegesis. The Westminster Divines fought the excesses of Anglo-Catholic rationalists on the one side, and spiritualistic sectarians on the other. They endorsed the Reformation assertion that the Word and the Spirit always work together.

John Owen was a transitional figure who illustrated the move toward scholasticism soon after the Westminster Assembly. In reaction to biblical criticism, he contended that the Hebrew original of the Old Testament had been verbally inspired down to the (nonexistent) vowel points. A similar scholasticizing occurred in Scotland through an anonymous commentary on the Westminster Confession of Faith.

After the restoration of Charles II in 1660, the Royal Society was founded. It became a means of introducing the new science and philosophy in England. Its members were clergymen and scientists who separated religion and science into separate spheres. Gradually reason was given priority over faith even in religious matters. Isaac Newton stood as the final flowering of this trend, introducing mechanical laws governing the universe but holding to his belief in God. John Locke applied empirical methods to philosophy, hoping to find certain knowledge based on sense experience alone. For him, as well, reason became the judge of what was appropriate in religion. Theologians adopted a mechanistic, mechanical model by which the Bible was to be judged. Scripture's message had to accord with Lockean reason, and Scripture's language had to conform to Newtonian notions of perfection. Many followed the lure of the new science into Deism. By the end of the eighteenth century, David Hume had followed Locke's lead to the conclusion of skepticism.

Thomas Reid founded a school of Scottish Common Sense philosophy which sought to answer Hume while remaining solely empirical in method. Reid assumed a simple Aristotelian realism and accepted as normative Bacon's naive method of scientific induction. Reid claimed that the mind directly encountered objects in nature. His assurance that this was so was provided by an intuitive judgment of the mind.

Scottish Realism dominated the academic philosophy taught in American colleges during their first half-century. It was brought to Princeton by John Witherspoon in 1768 when he became president of the College of New Jersey. Witherspoon's Scottish Realism laid the foundation for the theories of biblical interpretation developed in the late nineteenth and early twentieth centuries at Princeton Seminary.

VI. THE NINETEENTH-CENTURY PRINCETON THEOLOGY: REFORMED SCHOLASTICISM IN AMERICA

The two streams that carried Reformed theology to the New World both bore currents of Scholasticism. The conservative form of New England Congregationalism carried the tradition of John Owen and its concern for a rational defense of the faith. Scotch-Irish immigration brought another stream strongly influenced by Scottish Realism. They had in common the spirit of the eighteenth century, the belief that Christianity must be harmonized with scientific reason.

The Presbyterian Church had no center of theological training until the founding of Princeton Seminary in 1812. Until that time it was customary for young men to study with pastors in preparation for ordination examination by the presbytery. One such student was Archibald Alexander, born in 1772 of Scotch-Irish parents. In preparation for ordination, he studied Jonathan Edwards, John Owen, John Witherspoon's *Lectures on Moral Philosophy,* and Francis Turretin's *Loci* in a Latin compendium. In 1812, Alexander was named the first professor at Princeton Seminary and given the task of planning the curriculum. He centered that course of study in the works of Francis Turretin and Scottish Common Sense philosophy. Alexander intended that the Seminary should train men to refute Deism (which was in decline) and resist biblical criticism (which was in the ascendancy).

The *Institutio Theologiae Elencticae* of Francis Turretin was the principal textbook in systematic theology at Princeton Seminary for sixty years, from its founding in 1812 until Charles Hodge's *Systematic Theology* replaced it in 1872. Hodge was completely committed to Turretin's system and to the epistemology of Scottish Realism. His *Systematic Theology* therefore made that same post-Reformation Scholastic theology available in English. Succeeding generations of professors at Princeton vowed "to receive and subscribe" to the Westminster Confession of Faith and Catechism. But the terms used in the Confession's chapter on Scripture were defined by concepts taken from Turretin's *Institutio.* Reid's Scottish Common Sense philosophy was thought to be a sufficient guide in interpreting the Bible. Thus, a post-Reformation Scholasticism with a Scottish flavor was taught as the theology of Calvin and Westminster for over one hundred years, until the reorganization of Princeton Seminary in 1929.

The authority of Scripture was to be found in its form of inerrant words according to the nineteenth-century Princeton theology. There was an increasing rigidification from one theologian to his successor through the years. But in keeping with their roots in Turretin, each of them postulated the inerrancy of the Bible in all things. Archibald Alexander wrote that if the evangelists had fallen into mistakes of minor importance, it would be impossible to demonstrate that they wrote anything by inspiration.[17] Hodge declared that the inspiration of the Bible extended not only to moral and religious truth

but to "statements of facts, whether scientific, historical, or geographical."[18]

No trace of the concept of accommodation held by Origen, Chrysostom, Augustine, and Calvin appears in Hodge's work. Buoyed with confidence by Scottish Realism, he asserted that "we are certain . . . that our ideas of God, founded on the testimony of His Word, correspond to what He really is, and constitute true knowledge."[19] Statements in the Bible were treated in the same fashion as objects in nature: it was assumed that the mind came into direct contact with the thing itself.

By the time of Charles Hodge's son, A. A. Hodge, the sciences were no longer supporting Princeton theories of biblical inerrancy. A. A. Hodge rested his case on external evidence but shifted the object of inerrancy to the original (lost) autographs of the biblical text. When B. B. Warfield succeeded A. A. Hodge, he completed the shift in theological method from induction to deduction. Apologetics was now the primary task in a time when the Princeton theories were coming under increasing attack from within the church. Warfield no longer acknowledged the philosophical and theological sources of the Princeton theology in Scottish Realism and Turretin. He identified the Princeton position with the Bible itself and claimed that the church had always held to the Princeton particularities.

A. A. Hodge and B. B. Warfield developed the doctrine of the inerrancy of the Bible as a defensive, apologetic tool. They contributed an article on biblical inspiration to a series in the *Presbyterian Review* dealing with biblical criticism in which Hodge stated that

> the historical faith of the church has always been, that all the affirmations of Scripture of all kinds whether of spiritual doctrine or duty, or of physical or historical fact, or of psychological or philosophical principle, are without error, when the *ipsissima verba* of the original autographs are ascertained and interpreted in their natural and intended sense.[20]

In his part of the article, Warfield averred that one proven error would destroy the Bible's claim to inspiration. But he added that no error could be proved unless it could be shown to be in the original text of the Bible. Since the original manuscripts were all lost, Warfield seemed to have an unassailable apologetic stance.

There was no carefully developed hermeneutic in the writings of the Princeton theologians. They accepted Turretin's theology as the framework into which all theological facts must necessarily fit. Then they proceeded with utter confidence to investigate the Bible's facts like Baconian inductive scientists. Scottish Realists assumed that God had made the natural world orderly and constant and therefore that error could not arise in the observation of facts. Hodge applied that same naive inductive method to theology. He affirmed that God "gives us in the Bible truths which, properly understood and arranged, constitute the science of theology. As the facts of nature are all related and determined by physical laws, so the facts of the Bible are all related and determined by the nature of God and of his creatures."[21]

The Princeton theologians had no interpretive principles by which to distinguish between God's revealed purposes and the cultural context in which human persons applied those divine purposes. Charles Hodge, for example, failed to distinguish between the Pauline thrust against slavery and its restricted application in Roman society. Both before and after the Civil War, Hodge contended that slave-holding was not necessarily a sin, and he opposed abolitionism; at the same time, he abhorred the evils of slavery and urged that those evils be ameliorated.[22]

The Princeton theologians denied that there could be any legitimate development of doctrine. They claimed an identity of their views with those of Westminster, Calvin, Augustine, and Paul. They insisted that neither culture nor context needed to be taken into account in the application of what they took to be universal theological norms. Their pride in an unbending consistency led to Charles Hodge's remark at the celebration of his fiftieth year as professor at Princeton that

> Drs. Alexander and Miller were not speculative men. They were not given to new methods or new theories. They were content with the faith once delivered to the saints. I am not afraid to say that a new idea never originated in this Seminary. Their theological method was very simple. The Bible is the word of God. That is to be assumed or proved. If granted; then it follows, that what the Bible says, God says. That ends the matter.[23]

Thus the inductive method of treating biblical statements like objects in nature was compatible with a system of theology like that of Turretin. Orthodoxy was assured. And it was assumed that the facts of the Bible and the facts of nature could never conflict. When scientists offered views at variance with those of the Princeton theologians, the Princeton men always charged that the scientists were offering speculative theories and not plain facts properly organized.

Despite the intended uniformity of thought among the Princeton theologians, significant changes were made in successive generations. Archibald Alexander began with religious experience and used reason and evidence to confirm it. Charles Hodge continued to honor religious experience as a valid basis for personal religion. He preferred the internal evidence which the Bible presented to the reader over external evidences of its authority, but in the classroom and in writing Hodge asserted that theology was a science and stressed objective proofs of the Bible's divinity. A. A. Hodge and B. B. Warfield increasingly shunned religious experience as a source of knowledge and claimed complete scientific objectivity for their theology.

VII. THE PRINCETON THEOLOGY AND TWENTIETH-CENTURY CONTROVERSY

It was inevitable that the Princeton theology would conflict with the rising tide of biblical criticism in the nineteenth century. The critics assumed the opposite of the Princeton theologians — namely, that patterns of thinking varied with historical periods and cultures. The ancient and Near Eastern worldviews and languages of the Bible were being shown to be quite different from that of nineteenth-century American culture.

The prime antagonist of the Princeton theologians was Professor Charles Augustus Briggs of Union Seminary. Briggs was professor of Old Testament at Union Seminary in New York. He introduced the views of German higher criticism into the Presbyterian Church. He was also a collector and student of the writings of the Westminster Divines. Briggs openly attacked the Princeton theology for departing from Reformation theology and supplanting the theology of the Westminster Confession with the post-Reformation Scholasticism of Turretin's *Institutio*. Warfield attempted to refute Briggs but did not join the historical argument. Warfield simply assumed that Charles Hodge's *Systematic Theology* was a normative example of "all Reformed Systems."[24]

Despite the fact that Briggs was historically correct, Warfield's views prevailed in the Presbyterian Church. The majority of ministers and, through them, members had been trained in the Princeton theology which Warfield defended. In 1891 Briggs was charged with heresy for, among other things, denying the inerrancy of the Bible. After lengthy litigation, the General Assembly of the Presbyterian Church in 1893 suspended Briggs from the ministry. Furthermore, it adopted a statement that the original Scriptures of the Old and New Testaments were without error and went on to assert that this view "has always been the belief of the Church."[25] Thus, the position of the Hodge-Warfield article of 1881 was erroneously read back into the confessional history of the denomination. Similar heresy trials with similar results took place in other denominations in America and Great Britain during this period.

The General Assembly's decision of 1893 was not unanimously accepted. Tensions over the question of the inerrancy of Scripture marked the next three decades in the Presbyterian Church. In 1910 the General Assembly adopted five points that all ordination candidates had to affirm as "essential and necessary doctrines." The first of these points was the inerrancy of the Bible.[26] In 1923 J. Gresham Machen, a Princeton professor, issued a book entitled *Christianity and Liberalism* in which he denied that liberals had the right to be called Christians. On the other hand, in 1924, thirteen percent of the ministers of the Presbyterian Church signed the "Auburn Affirmation," which stated that the doctrine of inerrancy "intended to enhance the authority of the Scriptures, in fact, impaired their supreme authority for faith and life."[27] In 1925 the General Assembly appointed a special theological commission to deal with these sharply contrasting positions. In 1927 the commission issued a report declaring that no one, not even the General Assembly, had the constitutional power to issue binding definitions of "essential and necessary doctrines."[28]

Presbyterians were spared the full consequences of their lack of confessional guidance by the rise to dominance of Neo-Orthodoxy in the thirties, forties, and fifties. The theology of Karl Barth provided a core of consensus in the Presbyterian Church that guided the teaching, preaching, and even church school curriculum of the denomination. Conservatives, who still held to the old Princeton position, rejected Barth as simply another and more dangerous form of liberalism and ignored denominational literature. After a 1958 merger of the Presbyterian Church U.S.A. with the smaller and more conservative United Presbyterian Church in North America, a move to create a new confessional position was launched. A committee headed by new Princeton professor Edward A. Dowey proposed assembling a Book of Confessions, adding some sixteenth-century Reformed documents to Westminster, and drawing up a new, contemporary confession of faith. Upon completion, this latter document was called the Confession of 1967. Conservatives deplored the new confession's statement on the Bible. Two conservative organizations were created — one lay (the Presbyterian Lay Committee) and one largely clergy (Presbyterians United for Biblical Confession) — and they fought the new confessional stance. The clerical group took credit for helping to amend the Confession of 1967 statement on the Bible by adding the phrase "the Word of God written." After Presbyteries approved the confessional revision, Dowey commented,

> Now we can look forward. Writing the confession, studying it, and moving through the slow work of adoption were laborious processes. But they made us talk together, even fight together for the first time in decades about what we believe and what we must do. We discovered that the bitterness of the 1920s is practically gone. Fundamentalism is as dead as the merely social gospel.[29]

Unfortunately for the denomination, subsequent events failed to confirm Dowey's optimistic assessment. Neither fundamentalism nor the Social Gospel was dead, and in the sixties and seventies both showed renewed vitality. Significant discussion of confessional matters nearly ceased soon after the acceptance of the Confession of 1967. Rarely was *The Book of Confessions* invoked in denominational literature or public controversy in the church. In the sixties, concern for particular social problems made theology issue-oriented.

In the seventies, liberation theology offered a framework through which social concerns could be dealt with theologically in the Presbyterian Church. Among professional theologians, the Neo-Orthodox consensus was declared dead by the mid-sixties. Process theology, with its concern to correlate theology with modern science and human experience, began to rise to prominence. Theological seminaries gave consideration to this methodology, and process thought was used as a resource in discussion of denominational problems.

In the seventies, the United Presbyterian Church was rent by disagreement over social issues and the effects of bureaucratic reorganization. Ironically, the Confession of 1967 was blamed for the restructuring and retreat from social involvement by former denominational bureaucrat John R. Fry in *The Trivialization of the United Presbyterian Church,* published in 1975. Fry contended that the choice of "reconciliation" as the central theme of the Confession of 1967 was a response to the call of timid liberals for peace at any price rather than theological confrontation of issues.[30] Fry's thesis was not widely accepted in the denomination. It was, nevertheless, symptomatic of the lack of a confessional consensus in the UPCUSA. Later events of the seventies evidenced the lack of any working agreement on theological method or biblical interpretation in the denomination. Controversies over ordination of women and the ordination of homosexuals found church members in opposition to one another still holding to positions very similar to those of the fundamentalist-modernist controversy of the early decades of the century. Documents prepared in studying ordination of homosexuals identified four methods of biblical interpretation being used in the church. They corresponded to Old Princeton theology, Barthian theology, liberation theology, and process methodologies.

In 1978 two different task force reports to the denomination declared that the basic problem in the church was a lack of consensus on theological method and interpretation of the Bible. The Task Force on Theological Reflection reported to the General Assembly Mission Council that no theological consensus existed in the church and that church members felt that the situation was "one of tension and inability to respond to or deal with pressing questions and issues." But the report went on to say that seeking immediately to re-establish a consensus was "both unnecessary and impossible."[31] A second group, the Committee on Pluralism, formed two years earlier to study the sources of conflict in the church, offered its conclusions to the Advisory Council on Discipleship and Worship. The report asserted that

> of all the factors that contribute to divisiveness within our denomination, none is as pervasive or fundamental as the question of how the Scriptures are to be interpreted. . . . Widely differing views on the ways the Old and New Testaments are accepted, interpreted, and applied were repeatedly cited to us by lay people, clergy, and theologians as the most prevalent cause of conflict within our denomination today. . . . It is our opinion that until our denomination examines this problem, we will continue to be impeded in our mission and ministry, or we will spiral into a destructive schism.[32]

Commissioners to the 1978 General Assembly of the United Presbyterian Church repeatedly expressed concern that there was no identifiable confessional position in the church. The phrase "the center of the church has collapsed" (attributed to President James McCord of Princeton Seminary) was often cited. Delegates desired guidance in the effort to restore a confessional centrist position. The Assembly ultimately adopted the following recommendations:

> C,1: That the General Assembly authorize the Advisory Council on Discipleship and Worship to engage in a study on the diverse ways of understanding biblical authority and interpreting the Scripture, which are now prevalent in our denomination; that components of the study include an exploration of our theological heritage in the Reformed Tradition and an analysis of the confessional standards that guide our interpretation of Scripture; and that a result be recommended guidelines for a positive and not a restrictive use of Scripture in theological controversies.

> C,2: That the Advisory Council on Discipleship and Worship make an interim report . . . to the 192nd General Assembly (1980) and final report with recommendations to the 193rd General Assembly (1981).

> C,3: That the Advisory Council, to accomplish this study, assemble a theologically balanced task force of the most competent church leaders, lay and clergy, who will have the authority to draw upon the expertise of biblical scholars and interpretation of literature from inside and outside the denomination.[33]

NOTES

1. *Proceedings with Felix the Manichee,* 1.10, cited by A. D. R. Polman in *The Word of God According to St. Augustine,* trans. A. J. Pomerans (Grand Rapids: William B. Eerdmans, 1961), p. 59.

2. John Calvin, *Institutes of the Christian Religion,* Library of Christian Classics, vols. 20-21, ed. John T. McNeill, trans. Ford Lewis Battles (Philadelphia: Westminster Press, 1960), 3.21.4. Subsequent references to the *Institutes* will be made parenthetically in the text.

3. Augustine, *The Harmony of the Gospels,* 2.12.28, cited by Augustin Bea in *The Study of the Synoptic Gospels,* ed. Joseph A. Fitzmyer (New York: Harper & Row, 1965), p. 55n.1.

4. Augustine, *The Harmony of the Gospels,* 2.28.67, cited by Bea in *The Study of the Synoptic Gospels,* p. 69.

5. Luther, "The Papacy at Rome," cited in *A Compend of Luther's Theology,* ed. Hugh T. Kerr (Philadelphia: Westminster Press, 1966), p. 4.

6. Luther, cited by Raymond Larry Shelton in "Martin Luther's Concept of Biblical Interpretation in Historical Perspective" (Ph.D. diss., Fuller Theological Seminary, 1974), p. 179.

7. Calvin, *Commentary on Seneca's De Clementia,* cited by Ford Lewis Battles in "The Sources of Calvin's Seneca Commentary," in *John Calvin,* ed. G. E. Duffield (Appleford: Sutton Courtenay Press, 1966), p. 49.

8. Calvin, *Commentary on Genesis* 1:16.

9. *Commentary on 1 Peter* 1:20, cited by Ford Lewis Battles in "God Was Accommodating Himself to Human Capacity," *Interpretation* 31 (January 1977): 38.

10. Calvin, *Commentary on Romans* 3:4.

11. Calvin, *Commentary on Hebrews* 10:6.

12. Calvin, *Commentary on 2 Corinthians* 3:6.

13. Parker, *John Calvin: A Biography* (Philadelphia: Westminster Press, 1975), p. 77.

14. Bullinger, cited by Edward A. Dowey in *A Commentary on the Confession of 1967 and an Introduction to "The Book of Confessions"* (Philadelphia: Westminster Press, 1968), pp. 204-5.

15. See Leon McDill Allison, "The Doctrine of Scripture in the Theology of John Calvin and Francis Turretin" (Th.M. thesis, Princeton Theological Seminary, 1968), p. 92.

16. For the text of the Helvetic Consensus Formula, see *Creeds of the Churches: A Reader in Christian Doctrine from the Bible to the Present,* ed. John H. Leith (Richmond: John Knox Press, 1973), pp. 308-23.

17. Alexander, *Evidences of the Authenticity, Inspiration and Canonical Authority of the Holy Scriptures* (Philadelphia: Presbyterian Board of Publications, 1836), p. 229.

18. Hodge, *Systematic Theology,* 3 vols. (New York: Scribner's, 1871), 1: 163.

19. Hodge, *Systematic Theology,* 1: 134.

20. Hodge and Warfield, "Inspiration," *Presbyterian Review* 2 (April 1881): 238.

21. Hodge, *Systematic Theology,* 1: 3.

22. See Hodge, "The Princeton Review on the State of the Country and of the Church," *Biblical Repertory and Princeton Review* 38 (1865): 637. This passage is cited by William S. Barker in "The Social Views of Charles Hodge (1797-1878): A Study in Nineteenth Century Calvinism and Conservatism," *Presbyterion: Covenant Seminary Review* 1 (Spring 1975): 5; see p. 22 for Barker's evaluation.

23. Hodge, cited by A. A. Hodge in *The Life of Charles Hodge* (New York: Scribner's, 1880), p. 521. A recently (1977) created organization called the International Council on Biblical Inerrancy uses Hodge's exact language as one of its slogans: "What the Bible says, God says," adding the phrase "through human agents and without error." See James Montgomery Boice, "Biblical Inerrancy — The Debate Is Not Over," *Evangelical Newsletter,* 14 July 1978, p. 4.

24. Warfield, *The Westminster Assembly and Its Work* (New York: Oxford University Press, 1931), p. 213.

25. Cited by Max Gray Rogers in "Charles Augustus Briggs: Heresy at Union," *American Religious Heretics,* ed. George H. Shriver (Nashville: Abingdon Press, 1966), p. 138. Cf. Lefferts A. Loetscher, *The Broadening Church* (Philadelphia: University of Pennsylvania Press, 1954), p. 61.

26. See Loetscher, *The Broadening Church,* p. 98.

27. See *The Presbyterian Enterprise,* ed. Maurice Armstrong et al. (Philadelphia: Westminster Press, 1956), p. 286.

28. Loetscher, *The Broadening Church,* pp. 134-35.

29. Dowey, "Now We Can Look Forward," *Presbyterian Life,* 1 April 1967, p. 24.

30. Fry, *The Trivialization of the United Presbyterian Church* (New York: Harper & Row, 1975), p. 3.

31. *Blue Book, 190th General Assembly (1978) of the United Presbyterian Church in the United States of America* (New York: Office of the General Assembly, 1978), C-49 and C-50.

32. *Blue Book,* E-10.

33. *Minutes of the General Assembly of the United Presbyterian Church in the United States of America,* part 1: *Journal* (New York: Office of the General Assembly, 1978), p. 40. A continuation of this study of biblical authority and interpretation will be found in Jack Rogers and Donald McKim's essay "Pluralism and Policy in Presbyterian Views of Scripture," in *The Confessional Mosaic: Presbyterians and Twentieth-Century Theology,* ed. Milton J. Coalter, John M. Mulder, and Louis B. Weeks (Louisville: Westminster/John Knox Press, 1990), pp. 37-58.

The Reformed Objection
to Natural Theology

Alvin C. Plantinga

Suppose we think of natural theology as the attempt to prove or demonstrate the existence of God. This enterprise has a long and impressive history — a history stretching back to the dawn of Christendom and boasting among its adherents many of the truly great thinkers of the Western world. Chief among these is Thomas Aquinas, whose work, I think, is the natural starting point for Christian philosophical reflection, Protestant as well as Catholic. Here we Protestants must be, in Ralph McInerny's immortal phrase, Peeping Thomists. Recently — since the time of Kant, perhaps — the tradition of natural theology has not been as overwhelming as it once was: yet it continues to have able defenders both within and without officially Catholic philosophy.[1]

Many Christians, however, have been less than totally impressed. In particular, Reformed or Calvinist theologians have for the most part taken a dim view of this enterprise. A few Reformed thinkers (e.g., B. B. Warfield)[2] endorse the theistic proofs, but for the most part the Reformed attitude has ranged from indifference, through suspicion and hostility, to outright accusations of blasphemy. This stance is initially puzzling. It looks a little like the attitude some Christians adopt toward faith healing: it can't be done, and even if it could, it shouldn't be. What exactly, or even approximately, do these sons and daughters of the Reformation have against proving the existence of God? What *could* they have against it? What could be less objectionable to any but the most obdurate atheist?

This selection was originally delivered as an address to the American Catholic Philosophical Association in April 1980 and subsequently appeared in the *Proceedings of the ACPA* 54 (1980); this text is reprinted from *Christian Scholar's Review* 11 (1982): 187-98.

I.

Let's begin with the nineteenth-century Dutch theologian Herman Bavinck:

Scripture urges us to behold heaven and earth, birds and flowers and lilies, in order that we may see and recognize God in them. "Lift up your eyes on high, and see who hath created these." Is. 40:26. Scripture does not reason in the abstract. It does not make God the conclusion of a syllogism, leaving it to us whether we think the argument holds or not. But it speaks with authority. Both theologically and religiously it proceeds from God as the starting point.[3]

We receive the impression that belief in the existence of God is based entirely upon these proofs. But indeed that would be "a wretched faith, which, before it invokes God, must first prove his existence." The contrary, however, is the truth. . . . Of the existence of self, of the world round about us, of logical and moral laws, etc., we are so deeply convinced because of the indelible impressions which all these things make upon our consciousness that we need no arguments or demonstration. Spontaneously, altogether involuntarily: without any constraint or coercion, we accept that existence. Now the same is true in regard to the existence of God. The so-called proofs are by no means the final grounds of our most certain conviction that God exists: This certainty is established only by faith; i.e., by the spontaneous testimony which forces itself upon us from every side.[4]

According to Bavinck, then, a Christian's belief in the existence of God is not based upon proofs or arguments. By "argument" here, I think he means arguments in the style of natural theology — the sort given by Aquinas and Scotus and later by Descartes, Leibniz, Clarke, and others. And what he means to say, I think, is the Christians don't *need* such arguments. Don't need them for what?

Here I think Bavinck means to hold two things. First, arguments or proofs are not, in general, the source of the believer's confidence in God. Typically the believer does not believe in God on the basis of arguments; nor does one believe such truths as, for example, that God has

created the world on the basis of arguments. Second, argument is not needed for *rational justification;* believers are entirely within their epistemic right in believing that God has created the world, even if they have no argument at all for that conclusion. Believers don't need natural theology in order to achieve rationality or epistemic propriety in believing; their belief in God can be perfectly rational even if they know of no cogent argument, deductive or inductive, for the existence of God — indeed, even if there *isn't* any such argument.

Bavinck has three further points. First, he means to add, I think, that we *cannot* come to the knowledge of God on the basis of argument: the arguments of natural theology just don't work. (And he follows this passage with a more or less traditional attempt to refute the theistic proofs, including an endorsement of some of Kant's fashionable confusions about the ontological argument.) Second, Scripture "proceeds from God as the starting point," and so should the believer. There is nothing by way of proofs or arguments for God's existence in the Bible; that is simply presupposed. The same should be true of the Christian believer then; one should *start* from belief in God rather than from the premises of some argument the conclusion of which is that God exists. What is it that makes those premises a better starting point anyway? And third, Bavinck points out that belief in God relevantly resembles belief in the existence of the self and of the external world — and, we might add, belief in other minds and the past. In none of these areas do we typically *have* proof or arguments, or *need* proofs or arguments.

According to John Calvin, who is as good a Calvinist as any, God has implanted in us all an innate tendency, or nisus, or disposition to believe in God:

There is within the human mind, and indeed by natural instinct, an awareness of divinity. This we take to be beyond controversy. To prevent anyone from taking refuge in the pretense of ignorance, God himself has implanted in all men a certain understanding of his divine majesty. Ever renewing its memory, he repeatedly sheds fresh drops. Since, therefore, men one and all perceive that there is a God and that he is their Maker, they are condemned by their own testimony because they have failed to honor him and to consecrate their lives to his will. If ignorance of God is to be looked for anywhere, surely one is most likely to find an example of it among the more backward folk and those more remote from civilization. Yet there is, as the eminent pagan says, no nation so barbarous, no people so savage, that they have not a deep-seated conviction that there is a God. . . . So deeply does the common conception occupy the minds of all, so tenaciously does it inhere in the hearts of all! Therefore, since from the beginning of the world there has been no region, no city, in short, no household, that could do without religion, there lies in this a tacit confession of a sense of deity inscribed in the hearts of all.[5]

Indeed, the perversity of the impious, who though they struggle furiously are unable to extricate themselves from the fear of God, is abundant testimony that this conviction, namely, that there is some God, is naturally inborn in all, and is fixed deep within, as it were in the very marrow. . . . From this we conclude that it is not a doctrine that must first be learned in school, but one which each of us is master from his mother's womb and which nature itself permits no one to forget. (*Inst.*, 1.3.3)

Calvin's claim, then, is that God has created us in such a way that we have a strong propensity or inclination toward belief in God. This tendency has been in part overlaid or suppressed by sin. Were it not for the existence of sin in the world, human beings would believe in God to the same degree and with the same natural spontaneity that we believe in the existence of other persons, an external world, or the past. This is the natural human condition; it is because of our presently unnatural sinful condition that many

of us find belief in God difficult or absurd. The fact is, Calvin thinks, one who doesn't believe in God is in an epistemically substandard position — rather like a man who doesn't believe that his wife exists, or thinks she is like a cleverly constructed robot and has no thoughts, feelings, or consciousness.

Although this disposition to believe in God is partially suppressed, it is nonetheless universally present. And it is triggered or actuated by widely realized conditions:

> lest anyone, then, be excluded from access to happiness, he not only sowed in men's minds that seed of religion of which we have spoken, but revealed himself and daily discloses himself in the whole workmanship of the universe. As a consequence, men cannot open their eyes without being compelled to see him. (*Inst.*, 1.5.1)

Like Kant, Calvin is especially impressed in this connection by the marvelous compages of the starry heavens above:

> even the common folk and the most untutored, who have been taught only by the aid of the eyes, cannot be unaware of the excellence of divine art, for it reveals itself in this innumerable and yet distinct and well-ordered variety of the heavenly host. (*Inst.*, 1.5.2)

And Calvin's claim is that one who accedes to this tendency and in these circumstances accepts the belief that God has created the world — perhaps upon beholding the starry heavens or the splendid majesty of the mountains or the intricate, articulate beauty of a tiny flower — is entirely within one's epistemic rights in so doing. It isn't that such a person is justified or rational in so believing by virtue of having an implicit argument — some version of the teleological argument, say. No, one doesn't need any argument for justification or rationality. One's belief need not be based on any other propositions at all; under these conditions one is perfectly rational in accepting belief in God in the utter absence of any argument, deductive or inductive. Indeed, a person in these conditions, says Calvin, *knows* that God exists, has knowledge of God's existence, apart from any argument at all.

Elsewhere Calvin speaks of "arguments from reason," or rational arguments:

> the prophets and apostles do not boast either of their keenness or of anything that obtains credit for them as they speak; nor do they dwell upon rational proofs. Rather, they bring forward God's holy name, that by it the whole world may be brought into obedience to him. Now we ought to see how apparent it is not only by plausible opinion but by clear truth that they do not call upon God's name heedlessly or falsely. If we desire to provide in the best way for our consciences — that they may not be perpetually beset by the instability of doubt or vacillation, and that they may not also boggle at the smallest quibbles — we ought to seek our conviction in a higher place than human reasons, judgments, or conjectures, that is, in the secret testimony of the Spirit. (*Inst.*, 1.7.4)

Here the subject for discussion is not belief in the existence of God but belief that God is the author of the Scriptures; I think it is clear, however, that Calvin would say the same thing about belief in God's existence. Christians don't *need* natural theology, either as the source of their confidence or to justify their belief. Furthermore, Christians *ought* not to believe on the basis of argument; if they do, their faith is likely to be unstable and wavering. From Calvin's point of view, believing in the existence of God on the basis of rational argument is like believing in the existence of your spouse on the basis of the analogical argument for other minds — whimsical at best and not at all likely to delight the person concerned.

II. FOUNDATIONALISM

We could look further into the precise forms taken by the Reformed objection to natural theology. Time is short, however, and what I shall do instead is tell you what I think underlies these objections, inchoate and unfocused as they are. The Reformers meant to say, fundamentally, that belief in God can properly be taken as *basic.* That is, we are entirely within our epistemic rights, entirely rational, in believing in God, even if we have no argument for this belief and do not believe it on the basis of any other beliefs we hold. And in taking belief in God as properly basic, the Reformers were implicitly rejecting a whole picture or way of looking at knowledge and rational belief — call it *classical foundationalism.* This picture has been enormously popular ever since the days of Plato and Aristotle; it remains the dominant way of thinking about knowledge, justification, belief, faith, and allied topics. Although it has been thus dominant, Reformed theologians and thinkers have, I believe, meant to reject it. What they say here tends to be inchoate and not well articulated; nevertheless, the fact is they meant to reject classical foundationalism. But how shall we characterize the view rejected? The first thing to see is that foundationalism is a *normative* view. It aims to lay down conditions that must be met by anyone whose system of beliefs is *rational* — and here "rational" is to be understood normatively. According to the foundationalist, there is a right way and a wrong way with respect to belief. People have responsibilities, duties, and obligations with respect to their believings just as with respect to their (other) actions. Perhaps this sort of obligation is really a special case of a more general moral obligation; or perhaps, on the other hand, it is *sui generis.* In any event, there are such obligations: to conform to them is to be rational, and to go against them is to be irrational. To be rational, then, is to exercise one's epistemic powers *properly* — to exercise them in such a way as to go contrary to none of the norms for such exercise.

Foundationalism, therefore, is in part a normative thesis. I think we can understand this thesis more fully if we introduce the idea of a *noetic structure*. A person's noetic structure is the set of propositions that person believes together with certain epistemic relations that hold among the person and these propositions. Thus some of my beliefs may be *based on* other things I believe; it may be that there are a pair of propositions A and B such that I believe A *on the basis of B*. Although this relation isn't easy to characterize in a revealing and nontrivial fashion, it is nonetheless familiar. I believe that the word "umbrageous" is spelled u-m-b-r-a-g-e-o-u-s: this belief is based on another belief of mine, the belief that that's how the dictionary says it's spelled. I believe that $72 \times 71 = 5112$. This belief is based upon several other beliefs I hold — such beliefs as that $1 \times 72 = 72$, $7 \times 2 = 14$, $7 \times 7 = 49$, $49 + 1 = 50$, and others. Some of my beliefs, however, I accept but don't accept on the basis of any other beliefs. I believe that $2 + 1 = 3$, for example, and don't believe it on the basis of other propositions. I also believe that I am seated at my desk and that there is a mild pain in my right knee. These too are basic for me: I don't believe them on the basis of any other propositions.

An account of my noetic structure, then, would include a specification of which of my beliefs are basic and which are nonbasic. Of course it is abstractly possible that *none* of my beliefs is basic; perhaps I hold just three beliefs — A, B, and C — and believe each of them on the basis of the other two. We might think this improper or irrational, but that is not to say it couldn't be done. And it is also possible that *all* of my beliefs are basic; perhaps I believe a lot of propositions but don't believe any of them on the basis of any others. In the typical case, however, a noetic structure will include both basic and nonbasic beliefs.

Second, an account of a noetic structure will include what we might call an index of degree of belief. I hold some of my beliefs much more firmly than others. I believe both that $2 + 1 = 3$ and that London, England, is north of Saskatoon, Saskatchewan; but I believe the former more resolutely than the latter. Here we might make use of the personalist interpretation of probability theory;[6] think of an index of degree of belief as a function $Ps(A)$ from the set of propositions a person S believes or disbelieves into the real numbers between 0 and 1. $Ps(A) = n$, then, records something like the degree to which S believes A, or the strength of his belief that A. $Ps(A) = 1$ proclaims S's utter and abandoned commitment to A; $Ps(A) = 0$ records a similar commitment to not-A; $Ps(A) = .5$ means that S, like Buridan's ass, is suspended in equilibrium between A and not-A. We could then go on to consider whether the personalist is right in holding that a rational noetic structure conforms to the Calculus of Probability.[7]

Third, a somewhat vaguer notion: an account of S's noetic structure would include something like an index of *depth of ingression*. Some of my beliefs are, we might say, on the periphery of my noetic structure. I accept them, and may even accept them quite firmly, but if I were to give them up, not much else in my noetic structure would have to change. I believe there are some large boulders on the top of the Grand Teton. If I come to give up this belief, however (say by climbing it and not finding any), that change wouldn't have extensive reverberations throughout the rest of my noetic structure; it could be accommodated with minimal alteration elsewhere. So its depth of ingression into my noetic structure isn't great. On the other hand, if I were to come to believe that there simply is no such thing as the Grand Teton, or no mountains at all, or no such thing as the state of Wyoming, that would have much greater reverberations. And if, *per impossible*, I were to come to think there hadn't been much of a past (that the world was created just five minutes ago, complete with all its apparent memories and traces of the past), or that there weren't any other persons, that would have even greater reverberations; these beliefs of mine have great depth of ingression into my noetic structure.

Now, classical foundationalism is best construed, I think, as a thesis about *rational* noetic structures. A noetic structure is rational if it could be the noetic structure of a person who was completely rational. To be completely rational, as I am here using the term, is not to believe only what is true, or to believe all the logical consequences of what one believes, or to believe all necessary truths with equal firmness, or to be uninfluenced by emotion; it is, instead, to do the right thing with respect to one's believings. As we have seen, the foundationalist holds that there are responsibilities and duties that pertain to believings as well as to actions, or other actions; these responsibilities accrue to us just by virtue of our having the sorts of noetic capabilities we do have. There are norms or standards for beliefs. To criticize a person as irrational, then, is to criticize the person for failing to fulfill these duties or responsibilities, or for failing to conform to the relevant norms or standards. From this point of view, a rational person is one whose believings meet the appropriate standards. To draw the ethical analogy, the irrational is the impermissible; the rational is the permissible.

A rational noetic structure, then, is one that could be the noetic structure of a perfectly rational person. And classical foundationalism is, in part, a thesis about such noetic structures. Foundationalists note, first of all, that some of our beliefs are based upon others. They immediately add that a belief can't properly be accepted on the basis of just *any* other belief; in a rational noetic structure, A will be accepted on the basis of B only if B *supports* A or is a member of a set of beliefs that together support A. It isn't clear just what this "supports" relation is; different foundationalists propose different candidates. One candidate, for example,

is *entailment;* A supports B only if B is entailed by A, or perhaps is self-evidently entailed by A, or perhaps follows from A by an argument in which each step is a self-evident entailment. Another and more permissive candidate is probability; perhaps A supports B if B is likely or probable with respect to A. And of course there are other candidates.

More important for present purposes, however, is the following claim: in a rational noetic structure, there will be some beliefs that are not based upon others — call these its *foundations.* If every belief in a rational noetic structure were based upon other beliefs, the structure in question would contain infinitely many beliefs. However things may stand for more powerful intellects — angelic intellects, perhaps — human beings aren't capable of believing infinitely many propositions. Among other things, one presumably doesn't believe a proposition one has never heard of, and no one has had time, these busy days, to have heard of infinitely many propositions. So every rational noetic structure has a foundation.

Suppose we say that *weak* foundationalism is the view (1) that every rational noetic structure has a foundation and (2) that in a rational noetic structure, nonbasic belief is proportional in strength to support from the foundations. When I say Reformed thinkers have meant to reject foundationalism, I do not mean to say that they intended to reject weak foundationalism. On the contrary; the thought of many of them tends to support or endorse weak foundationalism. What then do they mean to reject? Here we meet a further and fundamental feature of classic varieties of foundationalism: they all lay down certain conditions of proper or rational basicality. From the foundationalist point of view, not just any kind of belief can be found in the foundations of a rational noetic structure; a belief, to be properly basic (i.e., basic in a rational noetic structure), must meet certain conditions. It is plausible to see Thomas Aquinas, for example, as holding that a proposition is properly basic for a person only if it is self-evident to that person (such that one's understanding or grasping it is sufficient for one's seeing it to be true) or "evident to the senses," as he put it. By this latter term I think he meant to refer to propositions the truth or falsehood of which we can determine by looking or listening or employing some other sense — such propositions as

(1) There is a tree before me
(2) I am wearing shoes

and

(3) That tree's leaves are yellow.

Many foundationalists have insisted that propositions basic in a rational noetic structure must be *certain* in some important sense. Thus it is plausible to see Descartes as holding that the foundations of a rational noetic structure don't include such propositions as (1)-(3) but more cautious claims — claims about one's own mental life, for example:

(4) It seems to me that I see a tree
(5) I seem to see something green

or, as Professor Chisholm puts it,

(6) I am appeared greenly to.

Propositions of this latter sort seem to enjoy a kind of immunity from error not enjoyed by those of the former. I could be mistaken in thinking I see a pink rat; perhaps I am hallucinating or the victim of an illusion. But it is at the least very much harder to see that I could be mistaken in believing that I *seem* to see a pink rat, in believing that I am appeared pinkly (or pink ratly) to. Suppose we say that a proposition with respect to which I enjoy this sort of immunity from error is *incorrigible* for me; then perhaps Descartes means to hold that a proposition is properly basic for *S* only if it is either self-evident or incorrigible for *S*.

Aquinas and Descartes, we might say, are

strong foundationalists; they accept weak foundationalism and add some conditions for proper basicality. Ancient and medieval foundationalists tended to hold that a proposition is properly basic for a person only if it is either self-evident or evident to the senses; modern foundationalists — Descartes, Locke, Leibniz, and the like — have tended to hold that a proposition is properly basic for *S* only if it is either self-evident or incorrigible for *S*. Of course this is a historical generalization and is thus subject to contradiction by scholars, such being the penalty for historical generalization; but perhaps it is worth the risk. And now suppose we say that *classical foundationalism* is the disjunction of ancient and medieval with modern foundationalism.

III. THE REFORMED REJECTION OF CLASSICAL FOUNDATIONALISM

These Reformed thinkers, I believe, are best understood as rejecting classical foundationalism.[8] They were inclined to accept weak foundationalism, I think, but they were completely at odds with the idea that the foundations of a rational noetic structure can at most include propositions that are self-evident or evident to the senses or incorrigible. In particular, they were prepared to insist that a rational noetic structure can include belief in God as basic. As Bavinck put it, "Scripture . . . does not make God the conclusion of a syllogism, leaving it to us whether we think the argument holds or not. But it speaks with authority." Both theologically and religiously, it proceeds from God as the starting point (see note 3 above). And of course Bavinck means to say that we must emulate Scripture here.

In the passages I quoted earlier, Calvin claims the believer doesn't need argument — doesn't need it, among other things, for epistemic respectability. We may understand him as holding, I think, that a rational noetic structure may perfectly well contain belief in God among its foundations. Indeed, he means to go further, and in two separate directions. In the first place, he thinks a Christian *ought* not believe in God on the basis of other propositions; a proper and well-formed Christian noetic structure will *in fact* have belief in God among its foundations. And in the second place, Calvin claims that a person who takes belief in God as basic can nonetheless *know* that God exists. Calvin holds that one can *rationally accept* belief in God as basic; he also claims that one can *know* that God exists even if one has no argument, even if one does not believe on the basis of other propositions. A weak foundationalist is likely to hold that some properly basic beliefs are such that anyone who accepts them, *knows* them. More exactly this view likely holds that among the beliefs properly basic for a person *S,* some are such that if *S* accepts them, *S* knows them. A weak foundationalist could go on to say that *other* properly basic beliefs can't be known, if taken as basic, but only rationally believed — and one might think of the existence of God as a case in point. Calvin will have none of this; as he sees it, one needs no arguments to know that God exists.

Among the central contentions of these Reformed thinkers, therefore, are the claims that belief in God is properly basic and the view that one who takes belief in God as basic can also *know* that God exists.

IV. THE GREAT PUMPKIN OBJECTION

Now, I enthusiastically concur in these contentions of Reformed epistemology, and by way of conclusion I want to defend them against a popular objection. It is tempting to raise the following sort of question. If belief in God is

properly basic, why can't just any belief be properly basic? Couldn't we say the same for any bizarre aberration we can think of? What about voodoo or astrology? What about the belief that the Great Pumpkin returns every Halloween? Could I properly take *that* as basic? And if I can't, why can I properly take belief in God as basic? Suppose I believe that if I flap my arms with sufficient vigor, I can take off and fly about the room; could I defend myself against the charge of irrationality by claiming this belief is basic? If we say that belief in God is properly basic, won't we be committed to holding that just anything, or nearly anything, can properly be taken as basic, thus throwing wide the gates to irrationalism and superstition?

Certainly not. What might lead us to think that Reformed epistemologists are in this kind of trouble? The fact that they reject the criteria for proper basicality purveyed by the classical foundationalist? But why should *that* be thought to commit them to such tolerance of irrationality? Consider an analogy. In the palmy days of positivism, the positivists went about confidently wielding their verifiability criterion and declaring meaningless much that was obviously meaningful. Now suppose I rejected a formulation of that criterion — the one to be found in the second edition of A. J. Ayer's *Language, Truth and Logic,* for example. Would that mean I was committed to holding that

(7) 'Twas brillig; and the slithy toves did gyre and gymble in the wabe,

contrary to appearances, makes good sense? Of course not. But then the same goes for the Reformed epistemologist; the fact that one rejects the criteria of classical foundationalism does not mean that one is committed to supposing that just anything is properly basic.

But what then is the problem? Is it that the Reformed epistemologist not only rejects those criteria for proper basicality but seems in no hurry to produce what is taken to be a better substitute? If one has no such criterion, how can one fairly reject belief in the Great Pumpkin as properly basic?

This objection betrays an important misconception. How *do* we rightly arrive at or develop criteria for meaningfulness or justified belief or proper basicality? Where do they come from? Must one have such a criterion before one can sensibly make any judgments — positive or negative — about proper basicality? Surely not. Suppose I don't know of a satisfactory substitute for the criteria proposed by classical foundationalism; I am nevertheless entirely within my rights in holding that certain propositions are not properly basic in certain conditions. Some propositions seem self-evident when in fact they are not; that is the lesson of some of the Russell Paradoxes.[9] Nevertheless, it would be irrational to take as basic the denial of a proposition that seems self-evident to you. Similarly, suppose it seems to you that you see a tree; you would then be irrational in taking as basic the proposition that you don't see a tree or that there aren't any trees. In the same way, even if I don't know of some illuminating criterion of meaning, I can quite properly declare (7) meaningless, even if I don't have a successful substitute for the positivist's verifiability criterion.

And this raises an important question — one Roderick Chisholm has taught us to ask.[10] What is the status of criteria for meaningfulness, or proper basicality, or justified belief? These are typically universal statements. The modern foundationalist's criterion for proper basicality, for example, is doubly universal:

(8) For any proposition *A* and person *S, A* is properly basic for *S* if and only if *A* is incorrigible for *S* or self-evident to *S*.

But how does one know a thing like that? Where does it come from? (8) certainly isn't self-evident or just obviously true. But if it isn't, how does one arrive at it? What sorts of arguments would be appropriate? Of course I might find (8) so appealing that I simply take it to be true, neither offering argument for it, nor accepting it on the basis of other things I believe. If I do so, however, my noetic structure will be self-referentially incoherent. (8) itself is neither self-evident nor incorrigible; hence, if classical foundationalists accept (8) as basic, they violate the condition of proper basicality they themselves lay down in accepting it. On the other hand, perhaps a philosopher might have some argument for it from premises that are self-evident; it is exceedingly hard to see, however, what such arguments might be like. And until the philosopher has produced such arguments, what shall the rest of us do — we who do not find (8) at all obvious or compelling? How could the philosopher use (8) to show us that belief in God, for example, is not properly basic? Why should we believe (8) or even pay it any attention?

The fact is, I think, that neither (8) nor any other revealing, necessary, and sufficient condition for proper basicality follows from obviously self-evident premises by obviously acceptable arguments. And hence the proper way to arrive at such a criterion is, broadly speaking, *inductive.* We must assemble examples of beliefs and conditions such that the former are obviously properly basic in the latter, and examples of beliefs and conditions such that the former are obviously not properly basic in the latter. We must then frame hypotheses as to the necessary and sufficient conditions of proper basicality and test these hypotheses by reference to those examples. Under the right conditions, for example, it is clearly rational to believe that you see a human person before you — a being who has thoughts and feelings, who knows and believes things, who makes decisions and acts. It is clear, furthermore, that you are under no obligation to reason to this belief from others you hold; under those conditions, that belief is properly basic for you. But then (8) must be mistaken; the belief in question, under those circumstances, is properly basic, though neither self-evident nor incorrigible for you. Similarly, you may seem to remember that you had breakfast this morning, and perhaps you know of no reason to suppose your memory is playing you tricks. If so, you are entirely justified in taking that belief as basic. Of course it isn't properly basic on the criteria offered by classical foundationalists, but that fact counts not against you but against those criteria.

Accordingly, criteria for proper basicality must be reached from below rather than above; they should not be presented as *obiter dicta* but argued to and tested by a relevant set of examples. But there is no reason to assume in advance that everyone will agree on the examples. Christians will of course suppose that belief in God is entirely proper and rational; if they don't accept this belief on the basis of other propositions, they will conclude that it is basic for them, and quite properly so. Followers of Bertrand Russell and Madalyn Murray O'Hair may disagree, but how is that relevant? Must my criteria, or those of the Christian community, conform to their examples? Surely not. The Christian community is responsible to *its* set of examples, not theirs.

Accordingly, Reformed epistemologists can properly hold that belief in the Great Pumpkin is not properly basic, even though they hold that belief in God is properly basic and even if they have no full-fledged criterion of proper basicality. Of course we are committed to supposing that there is a relevant *difference* between belief in God and belief in the Great Pumpkin if we hold that the former but not the latter is properly basic. But this should be no great embarrassment; there are plenty of candidates. Thus the Reformed epistemologist may concur with Calvin in holding that God has implanted in us a natural tendency to see God's hand in the world around us; the same cannot be said for the Great Pumpkin, there being no Great Pumpkin and no natural tendency to accept beliefs about the Great Pumpkin.

By way of conclusion, then: the Reformed objection to natural theology, unformed and inchoate as it is, may best be seen as a rejection of classical foundationalism. As Reformed thinkers see things, being self-evident, or incorrigible, or evident to the senses is not a necessary condition of proper basicality. They go on to add that belief in God is properly basic. They are not thereby committed, even in the absence of a general criterion of proper basicality, to suppose that just any or nearly any belief — belief in the Great Pumpkin, for example — is properly basic. As everyone should, Reformed thinkers begin with examples, and they may take belief in the Great Pumpkin as a paradigm of irrational basic belief.

NOTES

1. See, for example, James Ross, *Philosophical Theology* (Indianapolis: Bobbs-Merrill, 1969); and Richard Swinburne, *The Existence of God* (Oxford: Clarendon Press, 1979).

2. See Warfield, "God," in *Studies in Theology* (New York: Oxford University Press, 1932), pp. 110-11.

3. Bavinck, *The Doctrine of God*, trans. William Hendriksen (Grand Rapids: William B. Eerdmans, 1951). This is a translation of vol. 2 of Bavinck's *Gereformeerde Dogmatiek* (Kampen: Kok, 1918), p. 76.

4. Bavinck, *The Doctrine of God*, p. 78.

5. Calvin, *Institutes of the Christian Religion*, Library of Christian Classics, vols. 20-21, ed. John T. McNeill, trans. Ford Lewis Battles (Philadelphia: Westminster Press,

1960), 1.3.1. Subsequent references to this work will be made parenthetically in the text.

6. On this, see, for example, Richard Jeffrey, *The Logic of Decision* (New York: McGraw-Hill, 1965).

7. On this, see my paper "The Probabilistic Argument from Evil," *Philosophical Studies* 30 (1979): 21.

8. Here I think they were entirely correct; both ancient and modern foundationalism are self-referentially incoherent. See my paper "Is Belief in God Rational?" in *Rationality and Religious Belief*, ed. C. Delaney (South Bend, Ind.: University of Notre Dame Press, 1979), p. 26.

9. See "Is Belief in God Rational?" p. 22.

10. Chisholm, *The Problem of the Criterion* (Milwaukee: Marquette University Press, 1973).

THEOLOGICAL THEMES

Historically, the Reformed tradition has given sustained attention to theology. Church confessions, theological writings, and the basic conviction that "the knowledge of God is the service of God" have kept theology at the forefront of emphasis for Reformed churches throughout the world. The essays in the following section provide capsule resources of historical and theological developments of major Christian doctrines. In some of these developments, Reformed perspectives have been distinctive and unique. In all of them, Reformed theologians have sought to ground their theological understandings in Scripture and in obedience to the living Lord encountered in Jesus Christ through the witness of the Holy Spirit.

Hendrikus Berkhof discusses the doctrine of creation and the world as created by God in his essay "God as Creator and the World as Createdness." Berkhof explores what it means for our knowledge of God that God is related to the world as Creator according to Christian faith. He then asks what this means for the human understanding of the world. His concluding eleven points spell this out with special clarity.

God's relationship with the people of God is also of the essence for the Reformed understanding of providence. Benjamin Farley's essay "The Providence of God in Reformed Perspective" (the final chapter of his book *The Providence of God*) summarizes his study of this doctrine, a "central tenet of Reformed theology." God's providential activity in maintaining creation, providing order, and sustaining and directing life toward God's ultimate purposes has been a powerful theological theme for Reformed Christians, inducing praise and spurring them to action.

The Reformed tradition has also specially emphasized the doctrine of the covenant. Two essays trace the important developments in covenant theology in earlier centuries and contemporary times. William Klempa's "The Concept of the Covenant in Sixteenth- and Seventeenth-Century Continental and British Reformed

Theology" explores theological thought on the covenant from its biblical origins through church history with a focus on the significant notion of covenant or federal theology developed by post-Reformation theologians. Klempa notes both difficulties and positive contributions of covenant theology. In the twentieth century, the doctrine of the covenant has been significantly recast by the Swiss Reformed theologian Karl Barth. In an essay entitled "Karl Barth's Doctrine of the Covenant," Arthur Cochrane points out the distinctive aspects of Barth's view.

God's purposes for salvation are seen through the atonement of Jesus Christ. In an essay entitled "Models of the Atonement in Reformed Theology," H. D. McDonald explores some aspects of Christ's atoning death. The different images for atonement stressed by Reformed thinkers from Zwingli to G. C. Berkouwer in the present day show that in Reformed thought, as in Christian theology generally, there is no one standard, authoritative view or model of the atoning death of Jesus Christ. The diversity of theological images reflects the panoply of biblical pictures of what the death of Christ means and how it relates to views of both God and humanity.

Justification has been another prominent theme among the Protestant Reformers, Reformed theologians included. It was an issue of crucial importance at the time of the Reformation in the struggles of the Reformers against Roman Catholic teachings. Justification by faith as an outgrowth of the work of Christ in the atonement was a major description of the nature of Christian salvation in the sixteenth century, and remains so today. In "Justification by Faith in the Reformed Confessions," G. C. Berkouwer surveys Reformed thought and examines how Reformed documents have defined and distinguished justification by faith from other aspects and views of salvation.

Though often overlooked as a theological topic, "union with Christ" is a crucial concept which speaks in the strongest ways of how believers are joined to Jesus Christ, the source and sustainer of salvation. Lewis Smedes's essay "Being in Christ" explores this important New Testament theme with a helpful analysis.

A Reformed perspective on the ongoing aspects of the Christian existence can be found in Hendrikus Berkhof's essay "The Christian Life: Perseverance and Renewal." Berkhof captures the essence of the struggles of believers against sin, the growth of faith, God's preservation of believers (divine election viewed from human perspective), and the complete renewal of life in conformity with Christ in the future consummation (eschatology).

These theological themes set forth some of the essential aspects of Reformed theology as they have been diversely expressed through the history of the Reformed tradition and as they are formulated and discussed today.

God as Creator and
the World as Createdness

Hendrikus Berkhof

I. GOD AS CREATOR

The God we meet in the revelation to Israel
and in Christ is the Creator of the world.
To some this confession sounds self-evident,
to others blasphemous. To many it sounds self-
evident because the world of God and the gods
as the expression of the absolute as such transcends our reality and is the ground of that
reality; the terms "God" and "ground of the
world" are thus identical. This identification
causes no difficulty as long as one can think
of the Godhead as being just as ambiguous and
capricious as the world it has produced. This
becomes quite different if one's experience of
God and that of the world clash with each
other. That has happened in Israel and it continues in the Christian faith. God as holy love
with God's acts and promises did not agree

with what the world was like. For the most part
the world does not reflect God's love but
clashes with it. Revelation, therefore, holds the
promise of rescue, of deliverance from existence as we know it. This, of course, makes it
far from obvious to say that the revelational
God of holy love is also the Creator of the
world.

Yet it is being said and it must be said.
Though the God we meet in revelation is in
conflict with the world, this is so in such a way
that it is clear that it is God's own world, and
in fact that God clashes with it precisely because it is God's own creation. The rescue
which God seeks is not a deliverance out of
this existence, not a writing off of the world,
but the deliverance of this world and of this
existence. Salvation means purifying this
world and raising it to a higher level, not denying and rejecting it.

It is clear that this identification of Creator
and Redeemer evokes great tensions for faith
and great problems for the intellect. It is just
as clear that if we were to drop this identifica-

Reprinted from *Christian Faith*, rev. ed., trans. Sierd
Woudstra (Grand Rapids: William B. Eerdmans,
1986), pp. 155-83.

tion, we would create much greater tensions and problems, or, putting it more correctly, it would mean that we would deny the essence of the redemptive encounter itself and would thus abandon the Christian faith. But belief in the Creator is certainly far from self-evident. As the term itself implies, it is a matter of belief. "I believe in God the Father, the creator of heaven and earth." As with the entire content of the Christian faith, so here, it is a confession that conflicts with what is daily experienced. We insist that this world of sin, suffering, and death is created by the Father of Jesus Christ. With that insistence, the Christian faith takes over again the belief in the self-evident character of creation as this is found in religion, though now it is made non-self-evident by revelation, so that it can be incorporated, corrected, into the context of a new redemptive faith.

God is thus (also) Creator. We ask what knowing this means for our knowledge of God. And the answer must be that in holy love God has decided to live with a reality outside God's self, a reality that as created is of a totally different order. It has pleased God to make this reality share in the glory and love of God's own being. The act of creation is an act of condescension. The creative act thus bears the same stamp we discovered in the revelational encounter as originating in the very being of God. To create means that God stoops down, that God limits God's self, that God provides living and breathing space for the other, which as such is imperfect and will even be rebellious.

We said that God decided this, that God wanted it. Between God and creation lies a decision of the will. God's will is not something arbitrary; it is the expression of God's being as holy love. But as the will of God it is at the same time irreducible. "For thou didst create all things, and by thy will they existed and were created" (Rev. 4:11) — that is the hymn of praise sung by faith; yet at the same time it is a hard problem for the mind. Here

we stand before a wall. Existence cannot be traced back further. From our perspective it rests on contingency and not on necessity. We cannot make transparent why there is something and not nothing.

But this stumbling block for the mind becomes much greater yet when we are faced not only with something irreducible but with an irreducible break, a discontinuity in existence, a jump of the infinite into the finite. The created world is an imperfect world, a reality happening in time. It comes from the perfect and eternal God. How can we ever trace back to God that which is temporal and imperfect? True, we can say that God is "above" the world and eternally existed "before" it, but the above-and-under, the before-and-after are also created by God. We can think only in the categories of space and time, which entails that we cannot comprehend what it means that God is the ground of our existence. We cannot penetrate this mystery; we can only make it our starting point. "The existence of a creation cannot at all be grasped by the intellect . . . nor has any person been able to think of creation in this way" (Fichte).

For that reason, thinkers (including religious thinkers) have through the centuries tried to get away from the unthinkable idea of creation. Instead of conceiving of the relationship between Creator and creation as discontinuous and dualistic, they have tried to see it as continuous and monistic, as a relation of essence and appearance, of ground and development, of a river and its source, and in terms of evolution, emanation, correlation, or polarization. The result is that creation is regarded as eternal and coexisting with God. Mindful of the "in the beginning" with which the Bible begins, the church has on the whole fiercely opposed these ideas. There is, however, more to it, something that has not always been realized. If Creator and creation are to be thought of as being involved together in one process, then the possibility of facing each other in a personal relationship is excluded. For a personal relationship is based on discontinuity. A God who forms a continuous and coexisting unity with the world cannot as a person and with a divine will stand opposite the world and the other. And humanity is then not God's partner but only his product. One who takes a starting point in the revelational encounter by which the Christian faith orients itself cannot think otherwise about the world and its origin than in terms of creation, person, will, leap, and duality. If we fail to do that, we saw off the very branch on which we sit. The idea of creation is indeed at the limit of our thinking, but only if we willingly accept this limit as an intellectual crux will we be able to make a new start, will we be able to do justice to the secularity of the world, the personality of humans, and to God as the God of the encounter and the covenant. Then we shall no longer try to avoid whatever other breaks and discontinuities we may find in our reality and in God's association with us. Moreover, this makes clear the meaning of the two statements that Christian thought has always conjoined to its confession of God as Creator and strongly emphasized — namely, that God created the world through the Word and that God created it out of nothing.

The assertion that God created the world *through the Word* is based on a number of biblical passages, and the purpose behind the assertion is to bring out, through the identification of the Word with the eternal Son, the connection between creation and re-creation. We are meant to realize also that especially in the Old Testament the Word is *the* means by which God brings about and maintains the revelational encounter. By repeatedly and emphatically saying that that whole created reality came into being through this speaking of God, one confesses that the world is meant for the encounter and communication. By also saying that the world was created *out of nothing*, one confesses that in this encounter God and humans do not come from two different directions and meet each other as equal conversational partners but that our partnership in the encounter (and thus the encounter itself) is based on and depends on God's initiative and on nothing else. If this were not the case, if our existence depended on other elements besides God, there would be other gods and powers that we would have to fear. Therefore we may not with a show of profundity explain the expression "out of nothing" as if God, for example, might have created us out of "the Nothing," out of some dark and chaotic power that keeps threatening our life. Out of nothing means simply not out of anything. The world has one ground: the will of God, who is holy love.

For that reason the confession of our creation, both in the Bible and in the church's hymns, so often takes the form of a hymn of praise. If created reality, which can enrapture but also frighten us, has its sole source of being in the initiative of the Father of Jesus Christ, then, in spite of everything, it must be a good thing. Creation is good because the Creator is good.

II. THE WORLD AS CREATEDNESS

First we considered what it means for our knowledge of God that God is related to the world as its Creator. Now we ask what this means for our knowledge of the world. For centuries this was hardly a question, because the answer seemed readily available. The authority of Scripture was taken to mean that whatever the Bible says about the creation of the world — and of course especially in Genesis 1 and 2 — is divinely given information about the origin and existence of the world, information essentially similar to the results of natural science or philosophical convictions. Hence, under the heading of creation, many dogmatics offered all kinds of information about stars and animals, angels and humans, body and soul, the origin of the soul, and similar subjects.

That tradition has now come to an end. Successively it has been undermined by the Reformation, the historical-critical study of the Bible, and modern science; Kant's philosophical dualism contributed much to this process. In our century the tradition has entirely collapsed.

If it is true that faith is not able to make independent statements about the origin and structure of the world, can it then say anything of significance about our reality? Does it have to content itself with the confession that God created this reality, without adding to it some pronouncement about this reality itself? But putting it this way would be to suggest a wrong alternative. Indeed, an enormous reduction has (rightly) taken place that has excised all sorts of (pseudo-)information. What remained was the confession of the relationship that the Father of Jesus Christ has with the world as its Creator. But in speaking of this relationship, which is of fundamental significance for the world, we assume a certain amount of basic information. The contrast is not "information or no information" but "information from the center of the faith or from other sources."

The Christian understanding of redemption entails a number of things concerning the knowledge we have of the world.

1. The createdness of this world implies that it and everything in it is structurally good and important. Nothing is evil, nothing is disguised, nothing is inferior.

2. Createdness not only means that everything is good but also and for that reason that nothing is absolute. Nothing is less than a creature of God, but nothing is more than a creature of God either. The world has no pivot in itself — not in matter that is eternal, not in the course of nature, not in a world-soul, not in an absolute spirit. The world is not divine, and when it is treated as such, it needs to be de-deified from the perspective of the belief in creation.

3. The createdness of the world implies the fundamental unity of the world. More basic than the diversity of nations, races, and cultures is their unity. And more basic than the difference in matter and spirit, body and soul, nature and existence, is their oneness.

4. Createdness implies parts, plurality, and variety — variety that is real. If the world had its ground in itself, the variations, being only surface phenomena, could be reduced to that ground. But creation means that all phenomena are irreducible, because the world has its ground outside itself in its Creator. Everything forms a unity, but within that unity everything also has its own place and character: spirit is not "really" matter, a plant is not an animal, an animal not a plant. The variety is just as real as the unity, and the unity exists precisely as the composite of the diverse parts.

5. The fact that the world is created by the God of holy love, who is faithful amid changeableness, means that it is dependable. It is not a haunted house or a bizarre fairy tale. We can depend on it. We can orient ourselves in it, feel secure in it, and make plans for its and our future. Its habitability depends on its knowability, and this knowability is that of a universe governed by law.

6. The fact that the world is created by the God of holy love, who is changeable in faithfulness and who works toward God's goal in ever new ways, means that it is also open to surprises and changes. It is not a haunted house, but it is not a bunker either. Creation by *this* God entails not only natural causality but also the possibility of miracle.

7. The fact that the world is created by the God of revelation also decides the purpose of existence. To begin with, it tells us that the world was purposely made. It is not a chance result of a blind process of accidental evolutionary happenings. That belief is a return to the passive resignation of the nature religions

which regard the chaos as the final secret of the cosmos. One who believes that the world was intended by God will say, in the first place, that reality has its purpose in itself. God created it for the sake of creating it, in order that it might exist and develop. Next we should recall that this Creator has begun a history with humanity — in fact, that God has elected to meet us humans as a human, because God has a further purpose with us. We begin our realization of that purpose whenever we no longer seek only ourselves, but seek our purpose in fellowship with and obedience to God. Those who let themselves be guided by that purpose, however, experience the guidance of a God whose purpose is precisely humanity and its salvation. Putting all these successive points of view on one denominator, we can say that the purpose of the world is the kingdom of God as the full realization of human existence through fellowship with God.

8. These last points brought us close to making a statement about created reality in its relation to salvation. Now we will have to say that if this world is the handiwork of Israel's God, the Father of Jesus Christ, it must bear the imprint of the holy love of this God and must be intended for the loving encounter with God. The historical-critical investigation of the biblical traditions of creation has made us aware of how often these traditions look upon creation as the first in the series of God's redemptive deeds and how they describe it as analogous to it. This means for us as New Testament believers that we confess our belief in creation with an eye to Christ. We believe that from the appearance of Christ we can learn the final purpose of creation.

9. If Christ with his life and his surrender of that life, with his resurrection and exaltation, is the firstfruits of a new humanity, the pattern of existence for which creation is intended, then the question must arise to what extent this purpose is written into the structures of creation and can be learned from them. In any

case, it implies that two fundamental statements have been made about creation: on the one hand, the confession concerning its goodness, which we dealt with above and which was presupposed in the preceding discussion, and on the other hand its provisional and unfinished state. In the eyes of faith, creation, in the combination and the tension of goodness and provisionalness, is itself a witness to its christological-eschatological purpose. But exactly this second element was until very recently almost completely ignored in the study of the faith. For everything that lies at the basis of that statement, especially the presence of suffering and death in God's good creation, and furthermore the catastrophes and the struggle for life in nature — all those things dogmatics treated for centuries under the rubric of "the consequence of sin." It was assumed as a matter of course that the good creation corresponded to the static Greek ideal of perfection, which does not accommodate such dissonant features. Whatever was unharmonious had to be ascribed to the great disruption of sin. From that viewpoint it was natural to think that all this was a punishment in which humanity had to acquiesce.

Today we know that this representation of the facts is untenable if for no other reason than that struggle, suffering, death, and natural catastrophes were already a fact millions of years before humanity appeared on the scene. We also know that these negative phenomena are not purely negative, because they hang inseparably together with the positive good of the continuation of life. Through the food chain, animals that devour each other maintain a biological equilibrium the disruption of which would turn the earth into a desert, a jungle, or a slaughterhouse. We know, too, that humanity, biologically considered, is a highly complex animal and that pain and calamities, suffering and death, are integral aspects of created existence. This holds even for phenomena that at first sight appear clearly connected with sin — we think of the disposition toward aggressiveness, inherited from the animal world, which we must learn to control and yet which we can never do entirely without as a stimulus for the development of life.

As humans we stand in dual relation to this negative side of creation: on the one hand we accept it as an integral part of existence; on the other hand we experience it as an abnormality and rebel against it. This is seen in our medical, hygienic, and social care activities and in our unceasing attempts to ward off natural calamities, crop failures, epidemic diseases, and the like.

Human beings do not acquiesce in existence as it is, and in that respect we differ radically from the nonhuman creation (insofar as we can understand it). As the only creature that is in principle dissatisfied, the human being rebels against existing reality and presupposes the existence of another kind of reality; we dream of this other reality but never experience it. We are created with what can alternately be called nostalgia, rebellion, longing, idealism, illusion, and utopia. We cannot just be what we are. We run ahead of ourselves. One can also say that humanity "is" precisely that which humanity is not (yet). Our authentic existence lies above and ahead of us — as a promise or as a mirage? Faith says: as a promise. The creation is meant to be elevated, to become a world that is centered upon and that serves a radically new form of humanity, in conformity to the image of the glorified Christ. The believer knows of this secret and therefore will be found not in the company of those who like to acquiesce in the present world but among those who actively long for another world.

With that we acknowledge that the world contains a tragic element. It is incomplete, unfinished, defective. True, there is much happiness, but even that is not without the awareness of its imperfection. There is much sorrow for which no one can be blamed. There is much

suffering that no one can remove. We know that all this is part of God's good creation, yet we also know that it will be eradicated from the new world as it is re-created in Christ. Therefore, we can acquiesce in it if necessary, and wherever possible fight against it. What we cannot do is explain it. Why has God (provisionally) wanted something that nevertheless (ultimately) God does not want? The only answer we can give is no answer: apparently it was never God's purpose to call into existence a ready-made and complete world. God evidently wants creation to go through a history of resistance and struggle, of suffering and dying. If this is the will of the God whom we have come to know as holy love, we may believe that someday it will become clear that all the pains of the childbirth and growth of this world cannot be compared with the glorious outcome.

10. With regard to the doctrine of creation, the historical-critical study of the Bible and the hermeneutics based on it has, quantitatively, taken away much information, but qualitatively it has given back much more (see under 8). One important insight derived from this investigation has already been mentioned but requires further consideration. The conceptions of creation in the Old and New Testaments, the fruit of extrapolations to the beginning of experiences with God in redemptive history, are all, quite naturally, expressed in terms of contemporary conceptions of nature and the origin and existence of the world. An early account speaks in terms of a struggle between Yahweh and the Leviathan. A later account speaks in terms of the creation and watering of the world desert. Still later came talk of a creation out of nothing of progressively higher forms of existence by the creative word. And in the Hellenic period there arose talk of a creation through the logos and a creation of "powers" or "elements of the world." It is senseless and impossible to harmonize all these representations. In fact, their multiplicity challenges following

generations to articulate afresh the belief in creation in terms of their own views of the universe.

For our age, that task entails articulating the belief in creation in terms of the evolutionary view of the universe. That seemed impossible in the previous century, because Christian thinking was still attached to the (one-sidedly understood) creation account of Genesis 1 and because traditional deterministic Darwinism seemed to exclude the idea of creation. Both mutually impeding presuppositions have now fallen away. Contrary to the universal law of entropy, on our planet the evolutionary process has again and again lifted existing forms of reality over their own thresholds and led to results of the greatest improbability: a marvelous and capricious process that has nothing of a determined course about it but that should to the contrary be termed *évolution créatrice*.

Connecting the Christian belief in creation with this worldview is certainly no more difficult than connecting it with the ancient Babylonian or the Aristotelian-Ptolemaic worldview. In fact, we must even say that it is easier to link it to the notion of evolution than to the static Ptolemaic worldview. After all, the doctrine of evolution makes a great historical process of what we call nature, a process leading to the phenomenon of humanity, and so continuing in humanity, leading in a new way toward a new and open future. In the Bible, creation and history are similarly connected. In Genesis 1, creation is set forth as a historical process taking six days — we would say taking the form of an evolutionary process — and so prefigures the history of redemption, which reaches toward the eschatological future. This does not entail the obliteration of the difference between belief in creation and the theory of evolution. The creation faith contains as such no information about the manner in which God called the world into existence. And, conversely, the theory of evolution has no answer

to the question of the sense and purpose of that turbulent process which billions of years ago likely began with a massive, chaotic gas cloud. The believer who accepts the evolutionary view regards it as the description of the phenomenal exterior of the creation event — for the time being, for later it may turn out that we need other models to speak about the origin of the universe. The vocabulary of the creation faith can as such be connected with all kinds of scientific vocabularies which can underline, concretize, and illustrate it; but what this faith speaks of remains independent of all these modes of expression.

11. Most handbooks on dogmatics include a section on angels in their discussion of creation. The Bible speaks repeatedly of such "ministering spirits," sinless inhabitants of a world in which spirit is not hampered by matter but uses it freely, without limitations; at the same time they are creatures who, in spite of and with their senses of a higher order, serve the cause of the redemption, protection, and direction of earthly humanity. What can one say about these beings in a study of the faith? Faith is based on the encounters of God and man within the context of our earthly reality. Humans may make the discovery that in special cases God uses the mediation of extraterrestrial beings for such encounters. One who cannot speak from experience about such mediation does well to refrain from passing judgment on the credibility of those who maintain that they do know such experiences. But one cannot be expected to develop a doctrine of angels, an angelology. By far the great majority of systematic theologians of our time are not ready for that. From that it by no means follows that they are on the wrong track. For no matter how often the Bible may speak of incidental appearances of angels, there is hardly any reflection on it, and one finds no basic outlines of an angelology.

Nevertheless, the accounts of angels are based on a threefold assumption that is certainly closely related to the Israelite-Christian faith. The appearances of angels give expression to the belief that (1) God's world, including those beings who are consciously subject to God, is far richer than what can be seen on our planet; (2) outside this provisional and alienated world there are other realities that already now are fully and perfectly filled with God's glory; and (3) these worlds do not look down with contempt on our darkened planet but possess a genuine willingness to be used in the service of God's love for humans to help our world reach its destination. It is worth considering whether the belief in the "eternally rich God" does not point us in the direction of this threefold insight, even though we know that nothing can be proven here. Those who are convinced that human beings are the only rational creatures in the universe and that God has nowhere yet reached God's ultimate goal will attach a narrowness and importance to the redemptive events on earth that is in conflict with the bright and wide expanse of sky under which these events take place. A generation like ours that assumes (without proof) in its theories and science fiction literature the existence of conscious beings on other planets who are interested in this earth can hardly find the belief in angels strange. But theology can do more than suggest such lofty, faraway, and yet helpful nearby beings.

It is customary also to speak about heaven in connection with the angels. In the Bible the word has three distinct yet confluent meanings: (1) the visible starry firmament; (2) a higher created reality, inaccessible to human observation, where God is praised and served; and (3) the sphere, the space of God's being itself. In the context of our subject, our concern is with the second meaning, for it seems to coincide with the significance of the angels. Up to a point this is indeed so. But the concept of heaven includes more. The word *heaven* belongs to the figurative language of the faith, to a language that, precise though it may be, points to real though shadowy distances that loom up when we encounter God. The earth is not alone. It exists as the opposite of a higher created reality where God's will is continuously and perfectly done. This reality is not only the counterpart of the earth but also the partner that surrounds it with blessings and the end for which it is intended. Not that the earthly life, as that which is inferior and no longer useful, will be cast off; it will be made heavenly, glorified. The goal is: "Thy will be done, on earth as it is in heaven." Everything that serves that purpose may be called "heavenly." Christ comes from heaven, we receive a heavenly calling, heavenly gifts, and a heavenly blessing, and we expect a heavenly inheritance, a heavenly city, and a heavenly country. Faith looks beyond, and its horizon is wider than our world in its present state. Hence we conceive of the angels as residing in that heavenly world, yet that world itself is more comprehensive. It is also the exemplar and emblem of the earthly creation. Salvation means that heaven is active in penetrating the earth. That belief is the opposite of world flight. Speaking about heaven, we say that our world still exists in a lower stage of development and that we expect that God's work on earth will lift the earth to a higher level of existence, in harmony and fellowship with a mode of existence that is fully permeated with God, of which we surmise that for a long time already it is blessingly and invitingly embracing us.

The Providence of God in Reformed Perspective

Benjamin Wirt Farley

The Reformed doctrine of the providence of God emphasizes that the triune God, in goodness and power, preserves, accompanies, and directs the universe. This work of preservation, accompaniment, and direction pertains to the entire universe — physical and human — and excludes no facet of God's work.

The doctrine of providence constitutes a central tenet of Reformed theology and belongs to the essence of the biblical message. To that extent, it is held and expounded as a doctrine of the church's faith, based on divine revelation, and must be energetically preached as part of God's Word.

Furthermore, it is derived theologically from an exploration of the biblical text in a manner that always seeks to make the church's hermeneutical principles subservient to Scripture first, guided specifically by the Old Testament, Pauline, Augustinian, and Calvinist

awareness of the primacy of election in God's relationship with this world. For this reason, modern proponents of a Reformed perspective (e.g., Brunner and Barth) have rightly argued that the older orthodox interest in the divine decrees and predestination plays an important hermeneutical role in enlarging our understanding of the providence of God. This is seen in the realization that, ultimately, providence is a function of divine election that in turn constitutes the presupposition on which providence rests.

In accordance with Reformed practice, the doctrine of the providence of God has traditionally been treated under three headings: *conservatio, concursus,* and *gubernatio.*

First, God's providential activity in the world may be understood as a work of *conservatio, sustentatio,* or *preservatio.* God continues to see that creation is maintained, that order prevails, that life is sustained through, in, and above the species' divinely bestowed powers of self-propagation and survival. In particular, God may be said to preserve the

Reprinted from *The Providence of God* (Grand Rapids: Baker Book House, 1988), pp. 229-37.

physical universe and all its creatures directly, humankind and God's covenant people in particular. For Louis Berkhof this means not only that all created things owe their full powers to God but also that they possess real efficiency as secondary causes. For Brunner *preservatio* means that God has given the world of nature its constancy and order, through which God continues to be revealed as "Creator-Spirit." Hence, nature can never stand as an independent phenomenon apart from God.

Second, closely associated with God's work of *conservatio* is God's *concursus*. Berkhof defines *concursus* as "the co-operation of the divine power with all subordinate powers, according to the pre-established laws of their operation, causing them to act and to act precisely as they do."[1] *Concursus*, states Berkhof, reminds us that although the powers of nature do not work by themselves (echoes of Calvin), yet secondary causes are real. Brunner prefers not to pursue *concursus;* he labels it off limits as the "danger zone" of theological investigation. Yet Barth praises the doctrine for its attempt to deal justly with "the problem of a co-existence and antithesis of the divine and creaturely action which should correspond with the testimony of Scripture."[2] Consequently, Barth develops his doctrine of *concursus* in a manner similar to Aquinas's concept of God as total cause.

Third, God's providential activity includes the work of guiding and steering humankind and history toward a *telos* that God both wills and controls. This means, according to Brunner, that the natural-historical nexus of occurrence cannot be understood in itself.[3] Barth asserts that "God has an aim for the creature when He preserves and accompanies it . . . and . . . as Ruler guides it towards this *telos*."[4]

The Graeco-Roman world developed a number of views regarding necessity and freedom — doctrines of "providence," as its philosophers referred to the matter. The classical world's concept of God, or the logos, and the relationship of this logos to the world, tended to take three distinct forms. According to Stoic principles, nature was the manifestation of the logos, and hence nature and history were interpreted as results of the sequential cause-and-effect occurrences of the logos within the natural-historical nexus (as illustrated by Chrysippus and Cicero). According to Aristotelian principles, the divine-world order was a harmony of eternal entities responding in eros to a *primus actus* which motivated all entities toward their respective realizations. According to Platonic and neo-Platonic principles, the world order is the result of a descent or emanation from the realm of perfection to imperfection or nonbeing and then ascent again to perfection.

The idea of the providence of God developed through the patristic period as the Church Fathers variously modified, rejected, and incorporated aspects of the classical understanding of providence. This was the case even with Augustine, whose overall doctrine is most compatible with a Reformed perspective.

During the Scholastic era, individuals such Proclus, Dionysius, Boethius, Erigena, and Anselm continued to build on neo-Platonism until the rediscovery of Aristotle and the medieval philosophy of Aquinas, Scotus, and Occam. Especially worthy of note in this regard are Aquinas's and Occam's attempts to articulate a clear doctrine of *concursus* in which God acts as total cause while not acting coercively on secondary causes.

Later, Luther and Zwingli adopted classical concepts of immutability, tending to interject elements of determinism into their doctrines of God's providence. Calvin took an approach that not only avoided this binding reductionism and allowed him to argue for God's dynamic accompaniment and guidance of all creatures but also permitted him to preserve the reality and efficiency of secondary causes.

During the orthodox period, Reformed positions tended both to incorporate varying degrees of determinism (Zanchi, Beza, Turretin, and Westminster) and to emphasize the role of secondary causes and their freedom to act as such (Bullinger, Zanchi, Beza, Wollebius, Dort, and, again, Turretin). Throughout this period, the divine decrees were inched forward as a hermeneutical principle, thus acknowledging grace (or predestination and election) as an essential presupposition for an understanding of divine activity.

Also during the period of orthodoxy, a fledgling scientific and philosophical worldview began to replace Calvin's sense of God's dynamic guidance of creation with a mechanical view of the universe and with increasing skepticism about God's reality or presence in that universe.

Subsequently, various modern theologians have attempted to explain the realm of history as the arena within which God operates as an active agent. There has arisen, in particular, an insistence that nature and history form an "unbroken web" in which all cause-and-effect occurrences are tightly interconnected. Modern theologians have also insisted that God's providential activity must not be viewed as an activity that comes into history from without, as if God were an alien force in the universe and its natural-historical nexus. Etienne Gilson has reinterpreted Aquinas's concept of God as total cause in a manner that supports a Reformed allegiance to *concursus* and the efficiency of secondary causes.

PENULTIMATE CONSIDERATIONS

Before drawing any final conclusions, there are appropriate penultimate statements to be made. These have to do with the wider boundaries within which the doctrine of the providence of God is set, as well as with the doctrine's purpose.

First, our knowledge of God ultimately depends on what God chooses to disclose of God's self. Our understanding of both God and God's relationship with the world hinges on what God decides is most proper for us to know. Calvin referred to this as "accommodation." It is how God spoke to Job out of the whirlwind (Job 38–41).

Because God is ineffable — "for my thoughts are not your thoughts, neither are your ways my ways" (Isa. 55:8) — both God's aseity and *modus operandi* are for God alone to know and enjoy. We can only respond to God insofar as God gives of God's self to us to be known and insofar as God provides us with the means for knowing God. This God has done (1) by creating us in God's image and endowing us with rationality, accountability, and an awareness of God's existence; (2) in God's self-disclosures to the central figures of the *Heilsgeschichte* story; and (3) through God's gracious election, which is behind all calling to effectual faith.

God's ineffability remains. Nevertheless, the triune God's self-revelation and love for the world — expressed especially in the life, death, and resurrection of Jesus Christ — more than assures God's people that they can live with God's ineffability.

Second, the problem of verifying the divine presence and fathoming its *modus operandi* is inseparable from God's aseity and the mystery of faith itself. The fact that humankind can never penetrate the how of God's operation within God's universe — other than through the phenomena of secondary causes — in no way detracts from the reality of God or from the realization that God has acted marvelously or was "in Christ . . . reconciling the world to himself" (2 Cor. 5:19).

Science and modern philosophy emphasize the necessity of verification. This is absolutely essential in that context: if statements are to be valued as meaningful, then data must be cited in support of their claims. However, the whole phenomenon of faith transcends this data-hungry preoccupation of our time, and so too does the aseity of God. This is not to say that religious experience and revelation do not constitute forms of data. The matter, however, is more complex.

A God that was not ineffable, a God that was entirely knowable as an object, a thing, or a datum, would not be the God of Scripture. The God of Scripture refuses to be identified with any "fact" of creation other than as its Creator. Indeed, faith itself is possible only because God refuses to be identified with any "object" per se. To do so would be to rob humanity of completing its own joy, save in the response of faith, which God elicits and makes possible. The only exception to this identification is the mystery of the God-Man: the logos becomes flesh, and yet in such a way as both to require and invite faith.

Scripture abounds with divinely called servants of God who witness that God *has* acted and *is* acting in the natural-historical nexus. In general, God allows them to see that God acts as Creator, Judge, and Redeemer within the human arena. *How* God so acts often escapes them; *that* God acts in these ways they cannot deny. Nonetheless, the "thatness" of God's providential activity can be theologically and philosophically pursued, defended, and explored, as the history of Christian thought and Western philosophy amply illustrates — from Paul's admiration of "his invisible nature" (Rom. 1:20) to Hartshorne's reflections on God's "dipolar modes" and activity of "making things make themselves" out of the profundity of divine love.[5]

Third, the providence of God requires history to look beyond its nexuses for ultimate meaning. In the final analysis, the purpose of the doctrine of providence, as it is derived from revelation, is both to remind and to assure us that the meaning of history is incomplete apart from the will and goal of God. History rests in God's hands, as does the deeper meaning of every human life. The whole natural-historical nexus functions according to God's "rules." It is open to God's presence, God's mystery, and God's goodness. In the end, God's way will endure, and all "who are called according to his purpose" (Rom. 8:28) will endure with God; and, along the way, nothing can separate them "from the love of God in Christ Jesus" (Rom. 8:39).

Fourth, for Calvin especially, as well as for Augustine and Luther, the doctrine of the providence of God possesses pragmatic urgency. It is meant to edify the church. Its purpose is to call men and women of faith to serve in the world in trust and joy, knowing that the ways of God endure and can transform society and the cities of humankind — even within the limits of a fallen humanity. This is where the emphasis ought to be — not on *how* or *why*. It is enough to know that God loves and provides for each of God's children here and now and calls upon each person to act justly and with mercy toward his or her neighbor. On this side of the infinite — short of "our heavenly existence," as Calvin would have put it — the Scriptures tell us that we are part of a process that God loves and guides and will one day redeem and complete in accordance with God's own good wishes.

CONCLUSIONS

We are now prepared to draw this project to a close. There are many facets that could be emphasized, but the following seem sufficient.

First, the sovereignty of God is simply indispensable to a doctrine of providence. This recognition is both biblically required and theologically defensible. As God says to Cyrus:

I surname you, though you do not know me.
I am the LORD, and there is no other,
    besides me there is no God; . . .
I form light and create darkness,

I make weal and create woe,
I am the LORD, who do all these things.

Isaiah 45:4-5, 7

The Reformed tradition cherishes the concept of the sovereignty of God. It does so not because it wishes to veil itself behind any misconceptions of divine power ("for my power is made perfect in weakness" [2 Cor. 12:9]) but because it knows that the God of the universe is without rival. Hence, whatever processes exist, whatever forms and laws there are, whatever powers and order there may be, all are willed, allowed, anticipated, bestowed, and conferred by God.

At the same time, the doctrine of the sovereignty of God includes the concept of secondary causes and their efficient role in the universe. What Scripture makes clear, and what theological reflection attempts to fathom, is the realization that God chooses, for reasons purely of God's own, to limit God's self in the exercise of power toward creatures. Hence, although it is philosophically correct to argue that God alone is the total cause of all contingent occurrences and concurrently operates within their own operations and powers, nevertheless, every entity enjoys a reality apart from God, as well as a capacity for "partial self-determination." Thus, every entity experiences its own existence, and does so within a context in which it functions as a cause and effect. As E. L. Mascall suggests, "God is not the only cause, though he is the only ultimate one."[6] Or as Calvin argues in his *Treatise against the Libertines* (especially chap. 14), God is not the unqualified cause of all causes.

Furthermore, God has freely willed this order or process and both preserves and works immediately within it. As Mascall states, God "maintains the order which is discernible in the universe not by annihilating the causal relationship of beings toward one another, but by preserving it."[7] Or in a more Calvinist tone, we

are not to conceive of these conferred orders or powers as functioning in some abstract, mechanical, independent, or naturalistic sense.[8] Rather, God is always and everywhere present, "diligently" and "energetically" achieving God's good pleasure in, with, through, and, when necessary, in spite of the intended efficiency of secondary causes ("as for you, you meant evil against me; but God meant it for good" [Gen. 50:20]).

Hence, we can concur with Gilkey that though we may be partially self-determined, we are never partially indebted to God. Every creature's "destiny" and "freedom" are given to it by God alone; yet, because God limits God's self, every creature participates in and determines its own "destiny" and "freedom" as well as participates in and influences the "destiny" and "freedom" (or lack of it) of others.

God has freely willed this process. Its origins lie in God; its past, present, and future are possible only because of God; and God directs, participates in, and transcends it at every moment of its being.

Second, the Reformed tradition acknowledges that God's power, goodness, and the reality of evil are real and indisputable. In a profound sense, the central concepts here are those Augustine expounded: the immutability of God, the mutability of finitude, and the depth and mystery of God's wisdom, justice, and mercy. When these concepts are kept subservient to a biblical understanding of God, then they have the power to contribute to our understanding of God's relationship to the world.

More specifically, in the Augustinian tradition, where the divine is understood as immutable goodness, the meaning of finitude becomes clear. At best, finitude can never be more — and never less — than a mutable good (Gen. 1:1–2:3). This insight has the power to guide us through all the conundrums of theodicy.

God alone is God. God alone is immutably good and perfect. Had God created an immutable, perfect world, then God would have done nothing other than replicate God's self, which would have been absurd. Thus God chose to create a mutably good world, not an immutably perfect one. As such, it would have the freedom to exist apart from God as well as possess the possibility to respond to God and be fulfilled in God, by virtue of God's love for it and his creative presence within it.

Hence, the universe, as we know it today, is a fitting "creation" of God's handiwork and will. Its very mutable form accounts for the possibility of natural "disharmony." Moreover, God's will to create a being for responsible and independent existence both accounts for and allows for the possibility of moral evil while not requiring its necessity. Hence the powers of death and hell are real, along with the bondage of the will. Yet, all the more thereby, owing to God's immutable goodness, does the need for redemption, incarnation, atonement, and eschatological action become apparent and — because of God's activity in history — each a reality in turn.

A Reformed theology does not have to argue that this is the best of all possible worlds. God could have chosen to create some other world than God did. However, in God's wisdom and goodness, God chose to create the one we know. Therefore, to long for a perfect and immutable world is to long for deification (a longing somewhat akin to that of the early Church Fathers). Certainly this is a longing that would undermine our created mutability, which God found pleasing and "very good" (Gen. 1).

Hence God made us mutably good. God created us as creatures whom God loves, sustains, accompanies, and guides toward the highest possible fulfillment of our creatureliness in Jesus Christ. Why long for more? Why settle for less?

In the final analysis, is this not what the Reformed doctrine of the decrees is about? *The mystery of our human existence is a function of the gracious decree of God.* The true peace and wisdom of God is the grace and courage to accept the world as we find it (the courage to be) and to live boldly in it, in obedience to God's redemptive love in Christ Jesus.

Third, all God's purposes will be achieved. What God has willed to come to pass will be accomplished. From Genesis to Revelation, this is the unremitting note of Scripture. God will not — indeed, cannot — be thwarted by any process God has created or allowed to come to pass. Every process and every event will yield the *telos* God has envisioned since eternity.

Creation itself will participate in the "glory" and "liberty" to be revealed to the children of God (Rom. 8:19-22). As for all who love God, "who are called according to his purpose" (Rom. 8:28), nothing "in all creation" can separate them from his love in Christ Jesus, which will triumph in the end (Rom. 8:39).

Above all, central to the most secret counsels of God's will is the role Christ plays in the *telos* God has planned for the world. Christ is "the plan for the fullness of time" in whom all things are to be united (Eph. 1:10); he is the "eternal purpose" (Eph. 3:11); he is the secret power "in," "through," and "for" whom all things were created (Col. 1:16).

There is no doubt in the biblical writers' minds. All who belong to God will be with him. This is a high and holy mystery, and only the profoundest metaphors of eschatological longing can fathom the depth of the final satisfaction (John 14:1-3; Rev. 21:1-8, 22-27; 22:3-5). There in the end time, in the consummation, in his presence, we shall see God face to face (Matt. 5:8; 1 John 3:2); we shall know as we are known (1 Cor. 13:12); God, who confronts the soul with the searching imperative "Seek ye my face" (Ps. 27:8), will finally be revealed in the splendor of divine glory.

That glory will be experienced by the saints. Death will be swallowed up in victory. This is more than symbolic language. It points to a metaphysical reality, grounded in God, which gives our life both now and to come its ultimate sense of purpose. Therefore we can live in the present with vitality, hope, and courage, knowing that we belong to God and to each other, now and for all time.

"Therefore, my beloved brethren, be steadfast, immovable, always abounding in the work of the Lord, knowing that in the Lord your labor is not in vain" (1 Cor. 15:58).

NOTES

1. Berkhof, *Systematic Theology,* 4th ed. (Grand Rapids: William B. Eerdmans, 1949), p. 171.

2. Barth, *Church Dogmatics,* 4 vols., ed. Geoffrey W. Bromiley and Thomas F. Torrance (Edinburgh: T. & T. Clark, 1935-1969), III/3: 96.

3. Brunner, *The Christian Doctrine of Creation and Redemption,* Dogmatics Series, vol. 2, trans. Olive Wyon (Philadelphia: Westminster Press, 1979), p. 176.

4. Barth, *Church Dogmatics,* III/3: 155.

5. See Hartshorne, *Omnipotence and Other Theological Mistakes* (Albany: Albany State University of New York, 1984), pp. 46, 73.

6. Mascall, *He Who Is: A Study in Traditional Theism* (London: Longmans, Green, 1943), p. 123.

7. Mascall, *He Who Is,* p. 123.

8. See Calvin, *Institutes of the Christian Religion,* Library of Christian Classics, vols. 20-21, ed. John T. McNeill, trans. Ford Lewis Battles (Philadelphia: Westminster Press, 1960), 1.16.3.

The Concept of the Covenant in Sixteenth- and Seventeenth-Century Continental and British Reformed Theology

William Klempa

The most influential development in Reformed thought after Calvin's death was the theology of the covenant. This theology developed gradually in the Reformed churches in Switzerland, Germany, Holland, Scotland, and England in the sixteenth century and came to its major flowering in the seventeenth century. It was given systematic and classical form in the theological work of John Coccejus (1603-1669), particularly in his *Summa doctrinae de foedere et testamento Dei* (1648), and in the work of Herman Witsius (1638-1708), whose book *De oeconomia foederum Dei cum hominibus* (1677) was translated into English in 1837 and became a standard source for the knowledge of covenant theology in its later and more developed form.[1]

Covenant or federal theology, as it was sometimes called, made the concept of the covenant the generative and organizing principle of a system of divinity. It sought to understand the whole history of salvation and divine-human relationships in terms of a bond or agreement between God and humankind, first in a covenant of works and then, after that failed, in a covenant of grace. In its developed form, covenant theology represented a significant reaction against a mechanical version of the Calvinistic doctrine of predestination. Instead of locating the work of salvation solely in the divine decree, covenant theology sought to provide a distinctly biblical and dynamic understanding of God's dealings with humanity in successive stages of human history, thus furnishing a formula for the Christian interpretation of history.

While the source of covenant theology is unquestionably the biblical revelation, covenant theology was suggested and influenced by the development of political and juridical theory,

Reprinted from *A Covenant Challenge to Our Broken World*, ed. Allen O. Miller (Atlanta: Darby, 1982), pp. 130-47.

particularly the idea of contract law.[2] Thomas Hobbes (1588-1679) in his *Leviathan* traced the existence of society and the nation of rights and duties to a covenant in which there was a transition from a state of war to a state of peaceful coexistence. The Dutch lawyer and theologian Hugo Grotius (1583-1645) and the first German professor of natural and international law, Samuel Pufendorf (1632-1694), used the covenant idea as a basis on which to build their systems of public law and the rights and duties of nations.[3] In an age in which the affairs of church and state overlapped, particularly in Britain, the popularity of the covenant idea and the strong hold it had on the minds and the imaginations of the people became evident in a profusion of individually sworn covenants and the signing of such religious and political agreements as the National Covenant in 1638, the Solemn League and Covenant in 1643, and the application of the name "covenanters" to those who rejected the idea of the divine right of kings and opposed the absolution that crushed the political and religious liberties of the Scottish people. The history of Scotland in the seventeenth century centered on the covenant idea.

Covenant theology became the ruling orthodoxy of the Reformed churches in the seventeenth century. A mild form of the federal theology was given confessional status in chapter 7 of the *Westminster Confession of Faith* (1647), which draws a distinction between two covenants of God with humanity — the covenant of works made with Adam and his posterity on the condition of perfect obedience and the covenant of grace made in Christ with believers, offering the gift of salvation on the condition of faith in him.[4] In the eighteenth century the Bremen theologian F. A. Lampe (1683-1729) made use of the federal scheme and secured its acceptance among the German Pietists.[5] The "salvation history" school of Erlangen, and particularly J. C. K. von Hofmann, were strongly influenced by it, and thus indirectly covenant theology had an

impact on the philosophy of German Idealism and by this route on the Marxist view of history.[6] It is not without significance that Jürgen Moltmann, whose philosophical mentors are Hegel and Ernst Bloch, speaks appreciatively in his *Theology of Hope* of covenant theology as "the start of a new eschatological way of thinking, which called to life the feeling for history."[7] In the period immediately before Moltmann, the theology of Karl Barth displays remarkable similarities to the covenant theology of John Coccejus, though not without corrections of some important emphases.[8]

Of comparable importance is the contribution of covenant theology in the social and political realm. Its influence on political and juridical theory has already been alluded to. Through the Puritan movement in both England and later in America, covenant theology contributed to the development of democracy. In fact, H. Richard Niebuhr viewed it as a formative influence in American democracy and as a basis of world community because of its important insight that "the world has this fundamental moral structure of a covenant society and that what is possible and required in the political realm is the affirmation and reaffirmation of man's responsibility as a promise-maker, promise-keeper, a covenanter in universal community."[9]

It is my aim in this paper to explore the origins and the development of covenant theology, to assess its place in theological history, and to indicate something of its abiding significance.

BIBLICAL ORIGINS

Few words are as important in the Scriptures as the word *covenant,* and few words are as complex and difficult to understand. Some older and even more recent studies tend to treat covenant as a uniform concept throughout the Old Testament. Most contemporary scholars are agreed, however, that there are many different forms of covenant in the Bible and that these different forms imply different meanings.[10]

By and large these different forms and meanings were not always recognized by theologians before the advent of modern critical study of the Bible. But what earlier theologians could not fail to notice was the pervasiveness and importance of the covenant idea in the Bible. Inevitably, a number of them in the Reformation and post-Reformation period — a time of renewed intensive study of the Bible — constructed their dogmatic systems upon it.

The Hebrew word *berith*, translated "covenant," occurs first in the story of Noah when God established a covenant with Noah and his family and every living creature to save them from the flood (Gen. 9:8-17). This covenant, entered into with all humanity and every living creature, is followed by a different covenant, a more particular one made with Abraham and his descendants (Gen. 15:18). According to the author of Exodus 2:24, it is this covenant with Abraham, Isaac, and Jacob that God remembered when Israel was in bondage in Egypt. After the Exodus, God made a covenant with Moses and the people of Israel, and "the words of the covenant" were set forth in "the ten commandments" (Exod. 34:28). The Old Testament writers also speak of covenants between certain individuals — for example, a covenant of peace between Laban and Jacob (Gen. 31:43-54) and a covenant of friendship between David and Jonathan (1 Sam. 18:1-4). Marriage is referred to as a covenant (Mal. 2:14). Moreover, in the course of Israel's history, the covenant is renewed by Joshua on Ebal and Gerizim (Josh. 8:30), by Josiah in Jerusalem (2 Kings 23), and by Ezra and Nehemiah (Neh. 8).

Jeremiah speaks of a new covenant that God would establish with Israel (Jer. 31:31-33) in which the outward law would be written inwardly on the people's hearts. Among the later prophets, Ezekiel expressed a similar hope for the future (Ezek. 34:25; 37:26) and

Deutero-Isaiah looked forward to the extension of the covenant to other nations (Isa. 42:6; 49:8).

The New Testament writers identify this covenant with the one established in Christ, which is contrasted with the Mosaic law, characterized as the former or old covenant (Gal. 4:24; Heb. 8:8-13). It is asserted that the new covenant is superior to the temporary and imperfect "first covenant" (Heb. 8:7–9:1). The new covenant is symbolized in the cup that Jesus gave to his disciples at the Last Supper (Mark 14:24; 1 Cor. 11:25). In Romans 11:27, a reference to the covenant from Isaiah becomes the basis for the hope of the eventual salvation of Israel.

USE OF THE COVENANT NOTION IN PATRISTIC AND MEDIEVAL THEOLOGY

In view of the prevalence of the covenant notion in the Bible, it is all the more surprising that prior to the sixteenth century the idea of the covenant did not figure prominently in theological works. Irenaeus did make some use of it, speaking in one place of God giving four principal covenants to the human race: "one, under Adam; the second, under Noah; the third, under Moses; and the fourth under Christ."[11] What is noteworthy is Irenaeus's extension of the covenant idea backward to include the pre-Mosaic period. In this respect, Irenaeus is typical of the development of later covenant theology.

Augustine and later medieval theologians did not make much use of the covenant idea apart from employing it to speak of the relation between the Old and New Testaments. Toward the end of the medieval period, Gabriel Biel (1420-1495), provost of the house of the Brethren of the Common Life, related the idea of the covenant to justification. He spoke of justification taking place through the sacrament not as a result of merit but *ex pacto divino* (through divine covenant).[12] Through the theology of Biel and the piety of the Brethren of the Common Life, which provided an intellectual milieu for the spiritual development of both Erasmus and Luther, the covenant idea appears to have gained currency during the pre-Reformation and Reformation periods.[13]

THE USE OF THE COVENANT IDEA BY THE PROTESTANT REFORMERS

The Rhineland Reformers were the first to make full use of the covenant idea. Their covenant theology represented an advance on medieval Scholasticism in that they tried to understand the work and Word of God dynamically as a historical event unfolding from creation to the day of judgment rather than statically as a system of self-evident truths. Oecolampadius (1482-1531), the Basel Reformer, argued that the eternal covenant of God with humanity was the law of love that was inscribed on the human heart at creation and was later expounded by the written law of the Bible.[14] Wolfgang Capito (1478-1541), the Strassburg Reformer, made use of the covenant idea in his commentaries.

Ulrich Zwingli (1484-1531) employed the covenant concept in his theology chiefly as a way of defending the practice of infant baptism. The Anabaptists, against whom he argued, liked to call themselves *Bundesgenossen* (covenant members). They regarded their believers' baptism as belonging to the covenant of grace and the practice of infant baptism as belonging to the Abrahamic covenant. Zwingli opposed their views by affirming the unity of the two covenants. God made a covenant with Adam, then with Noah for the whole human race, and then with Abraham for the people of Israel. But it was always the one covenant ex-

tending from creation to the end of the world, a covenant of grace. Therefore, if children were included in the Abrahamic covenant by being circumcised, are not the children of Christians placed at an intolerable disadvantage if they are not baptized?[15]

Beginning with Heinrich Bullinger (1504-1575), the covenant became increasingly important in Reformed thought. Bullinger took over the covenantal aspect of Zwingli's thought and broadened it. He published the first specific treatise on the covenant, *De Testamento sive foedere Dei,* in 1534. In *The Decades* (1550), Bullinger defines God's covenant as follows:

> God, in making of leagues, as he doth in all things else, applieth himself to our capacities, and imitateth the order which men use in making confederacies. . . . And therefore, when God's mind was to declare the favour and good-will that he bare to mankind, . . . it pleased him to make a league or covenant with mankind.[16]

In this same sermon, Bullinger states that God "did not first begin the league with Abraham, but did renew to him the covenant. . . . For he did first of all make it with Adam, the first father of us all, immediately upon his transgression."[17] This view was to play an important role in later covenant theology. Barth has pointed out that for both Zwingli and Bullinger the covenant had a universal character. From the very first it was open to the whole human race, not in the sense that all were automatically members of it but in the sense that it was made for all and applies to all and that it is the destiny of all humankind to become members of it. In the later development of covenant theology, this universalism, Barth says, was quickly obscured if not obliterated.[18]

Zwingli and Bullinger spoke of one covenant of grace, as did John Calvin (1509-1564). According to Calvin, the covenant God made with Abraham, Isaac, and Jacob was already the *foedus evangelii* of which Christ was not only the fulfillment but the eternal basis. The distinction between the old and new covenants relates not to the substance but only to the mode of administration.[19] Although we must distinguish between law and gospel, we must not imagine that the gospel has "succeeded the whole Law in such a sense as to introduce a different method of salvation. It rather confirms the Law, and proves that everything which is promised is fulfilled. What was shadow, it has made substance."[20] Calvin's discussion of the covenant displays something of the living dynamism of history. E. Harris Harbison has said that Calvin took Luther's sense of history and transformed it into a sense of destiny.[21] He united creation and redemption in a special way by seeing the kingdom of God as the special end of creation.[22] Unfortunately, at this point as at others, his theology was compromised by the *decretum absolutum* of double predestination.

Following Zwingli, Bullinger, and Calvin, the covenant became a prominent feature of the theological-exegetical works of Wolfgang Musculus (1497-1563) of Augsburg and Bern, Martin Bucer (1491-1551) and Peter Martyr (1499-1562) of Strassburg, and Andrew Hyperius (1511-1564). Yet the two most influential theologians with regard to covenant theology in this period were Caspar Olevianus (1536-1587) and Zacharius Ursinus (1534-1583), the authors of the Heidelberg Catechism.

In his *Summa doctrinae de foedere,* Coccejus expressly refers to Olevianus as a forerunner of the covenant theology. His main work was *De substantia foederis gratuiti* (1585), in which he gave the covenant idea structural significance and made a comprehensive scheme under which the whole content of Christian faith and practice could be brought. Yet, like Calvin but unlike later covenant theologians, Olevianus recognized in principle only a single covenant, the covenant of grace.

The elements of later covenant theology are found quite clearly in the work of Ursinus.

In his *Summa Theologiae* (1584), he speaks of a covenant of nature that was made with humanity at creation, promising eternal life upon obedience and eternal punishment upon disobedience. Ursinus distinguished this covenant of nature from the covenant of grace, in which the gift of eternal life is promised on the condition of faith in Christ. Franz Gomarus (1563-1641) thought along similar lines. In his *Oratio de foedere Dei* (1594) he speaks of two covenants, a natural covenant and a supernatural covenant, which were founded at the same time and run concurrently and everywhere merge into each other. Apparently it was Polanus who rendered the dubious service of replacing the concept of *foedus naturale* with that of *foedus operum.*[23]

SUMMARY

These main features of covenant theology began to have considerable vogue among Continental Reformed theologians during the 1580s and 1590s. Although it is not altogether clear how the idea of a covenant of works emerged, since it lacked a solid biblical basis, it would appear that the idea of a covenant was carried back to the state of Adam in paradise from the analogy of a covenant of grace. It proved to be a serviceable concept, not only theologically as an organizing principle but also socially and politically. The idea of a covenant of works provided a theological basis "for a moral, civil, and religious obligation binding upon all men, elect or non-elect, regenerate or unregenerate, professedly Christian or pagan."[24] Eventually the natural law of the covenant of works and the natural law of the state were identified, providing a theological foundation for the state contract theory. But as Leonard Trinterud has observed in his important discussion of the origins of Puritanism, the practical applications of this view were not fully exploited on the Continent.[25] It remained for the Puritan theologians to work this out more fully.

COVENANT THEOLOGY IN ENGLAND AND SCOTLAND

In addition to the covenant theology on the Continent, there was a corresponding development on the other side of the English Channel. During the reign of Edward VI, a number of Rhineland Reformers — Peter Martyr, Martin Bucer, Tremellius, and others — came to England. Drawing on the work of Ursinus, Olevianus, and others, these theologians promoted the covenant view. Nor was the theological traffic all one way: English and Scottish writers profoundly influenced the development of covenant theology on the Continent.[26]

The idea of the covenant was known to Chaucer and Caxton[27] and appeared in 1549 in the English marriage service, where it still remains. According to Leonard Trinterud, it was William Tyndale (1494-1536) who first began to make use of the covenant concept as an interpretative principle for the understanding of Scripture.[28] Tyndale singled out the promise of God as the central message of Scripture. He maintained that this promise constitutes a covenant by which certain blessings are offered to humankind on the condition that they keep God's law. The covenant was first made with Adam after the fall, and people now reenter it at baptism. Trinterud holds that Tyndale regarded the covenant as conditional upon human obedience, but it is probably more accurate to say that God's promise involves certain conditions and is not nullified when those conditions are not met.

There were English treatises on the covenant by Dudley Fenner in 1583 and by William Perkins in 1590, in which a distinction was drawn between a covenant of works and a covenant of grace. The earliest Scottish monograph on the covenant, *Some Questions about the Covenant of God*, was published in 1596 by Robert Rollock (1555-1598), principal of the University of Edinburgh. In his *Treatise on Effectual Calling* (1597), Rollock asserts that "all the word of God appertains to some covenant; for God speaks nothing to man without the covenant."[29] Rollock was one of the first to speak of a "covenant of works" and to distinguish this covenant from the covenant of grace:

> The covenant of God generally is a promise under some one certain condition. And it is twofold: the first is the covenant of works; the second is the covenant of grace. . . . The covenant of works, which may also be called a legal or natural covenant, is founded in nature. . . . Therefore the ground of the covenant of works was not Christ, but the nature of man in the first creation holy and perfect endued also with the knowledge of the law.[30]

Here we have a fully developed form of federal theology.

A number of English monographs were published on the covenant during the first half of the seventeenth century, including John Preston's *Covenant or the Saints' Portion* in 1629, George Downame's *Covenant of Grace* in 1631, and Edward Leigh's *Treatise of the Divine Promises . . . the Bundle and Body of all the Promises* in 1633.

William Ames (1576-1633) gave the idea of the covenant systematic form in his *Medulla Theologiae* (1923), translated as *The Marrow of Sacred Divinity* (1642). Ames had to leave his position at Cambridge because he refused to wear a surplice. He fled to Holland and from 1622 to 1632 served as professor of theology at the University of Franeker, where Coccejus was his student. Ames was the chief theological mentor of the New England Puritans.[31] He distinguished two covenants: a covenant of works established with Adam in paradise and the covenant of grace made with the redeemed through Christ. He divided the covenant of grace into several periods: under the Old Testament, the periods from Adam to Abraham, from Abraham to Moses, and from Moses to Christ; and under the New Testament, the period from Christ to the end of the world and the period of the eternal reign of the saints in heaven. These ideas became the basis of the federal scheme.

It would appear that there was nothing in the mild form of covenant theology in the Westminster Confession of Faith (1647) that had not already been put forward by the English Puritan and Scottish writers. In 1645, during the time the Westminster Assembly was meeting, John Ball published *A Treatise of the Covenant of Grace,* in which he spoke of a number of covenants: the covenant of God made with Adam in the state of innocence; the covenant of promise made with Adam upon his fall; the covenant of grace first with Abraham, then with Moses, David, and Israel after the Babylonian captivity; and finally the covenant of the New Testament established through Christ. This book was given commendatory notices by Edward Reynolds, Danile Cawdry, and Edmund Calamy, all members of the Assembly.[32]

Covenant was frequently discussed in the latter half of the seventeenth century by Puritan divines including the great Puritan theologians Richard Baxter (1615-1691) and John Owen (1616-1683). Both Baxter and Owen distinguished a covenant of redemption between the Father and Son from a covenant of grace made by the Father with the elect in Christ. Over against the stricter predestinarians who denied the conditionality of the covenant, Baxter and Owen insisted on what they called its true conditionality. In other words, as William Adams Brown has observed, "while they held that the redeemed were enabled to fulfill their part only through the grace which Christ had merited for them, yet they believed in preaching as though all depended upon the action of human will.[33]

For the Puritans the covenant was the very essence of God's created order. They drew on the covenant or contract idea in maintaining that every person had certain inalienable natural political rights that could never be contracted away. They argued for separation of church and state in the interests of freedom and conscience. Although Puritanism failed in its attempt to reconstruct the English nation, its achievement was considerable. As Leonard Trinterud has said,

> responsible parliamentary government, the beginnings of the distinction between, and separation of, church and state, the gaining of at least a measure of religious tolerance, the striking of some balance between the duties and rights of the individual over against the group, the sense of public morality, the religious tone of the nation as a whole, . . . were the concrete result of the Puritan movement. Wherever one examines the theoretical and constitutional basis of these achievements the covenant-contract theory is everywhere present, explicitly or implicitly.[34]

THE FEDERAL THEOLOGY OF COCCEJUS AND WITSIUS

According to Barth, John Coccejus "represents the Federal theology in a form which is not only the most perfect, but also the ripest and strongest and most impressive."[35] Coccejus studied Hebrew under Matthias Martinus and theology under William Ames. After teaching at Bremen, where he was born, and at Franeker, he became a professor of theology at Leyden from 1650 to 1669. His work led to a revitalization of biblical studies and dogmatic theology in the Reformed churches. He gave the notion of the covenant a systematic development that raised it to a place of importance in theology.

Coccejus wanted to develop a biblical-theological dogmatics more closely related to the life of faith than the speculative theological systems of his day. To guard against the danger of speaking about God in the abstract or of deducing the whole of theology from the eternal decrees, Coccejus turned to the covenant concept, in which he found a way of speaking of God always in relation to humanity and a way of giving God's dealings with the creation a dynamic interpretation. According to Coccejus, the various divisions of Scripture and the history of God's dealing with humanity are given in the successive phases of the covenant of God. "Christian doctrine," Coccejus said, "is wholly drawn together into one stream with this particular point as a centre."

The main work in which Coccejus sets forth his system is his *Summa doctrinae de foedere et testamento Dei* (1648). After a discussion of the meaning of the word *foedus,* or "covenant," he defines it as "nothing other than a divine declaration of the method of perceiving the love of God and of obtaining union and communion with Him."[36] God's covenant differs from human covenants in that "men make covenants for mutual benefits, God makes His covenant for His own benefit" (*Summa,* I, 5). It is always God who initiates the covenant, and it is primarily a one-way covenant. Yet it is not God alone who prescribes and promises something to humanity; humanity also passes over into God's covenant. God always looks for a response, and so the covenant becomes mutual when humanity by God's grace binds itself to accept its provisions.

In line with the development of the double-covenant scheme in Continental, English, and Scottish theology, Coccejus distinguishes two covenants: a covenant of works and a covenant of grace. The covenant of works rests on the law of nature. Through the covenant of works, eternal life is offered on the condition of perfect obedience. This covenant is made with Adam for himself and all his descendants. Christ alone is not included in this covenant (*Summa,* II, 46). Coccejus finds proof

for the existence of the covenant of works (1) in the human conscience, which approves God's law and strives after what is praiseworthy; (2) in the human will, which seeks the true good and longs after life eternal; and (3) in all the benefits bestowed by God on humanity by which he excites them and in a manner pledges himself to them (*Summa,* 1, 8-9).

According to Coccejus, then, Scripture presents two methods of attaining righteousness and hence complete human happiness, clearly indicating the distinction between works and faith. When humanity is obedient and faithful, God offers it eternal life through the covenant of works. When it has fallen, God seeks to redeem it through the covenant of grace.

The covenant of works was abrogated in a fivefold manner: (1) by sin, when Adam did what was forbidden and thereby forfeited eternal life; (2) by the institution of the covenant of grace, by which God found a way of restoring humanity in accordance with his goodness and righteousness, demanding faith alone; (3) by the promulgation of the covenant of grace in the Old Testament prefiguring the redemption in Christ — in the writing of the law on human hearts by the Spirit, in the freeing of consciences by the forgiveness of sins, and the planting of the church among the Gentiles; (4) by what Coccejus calls the death of the body — that is, the battle of spirit against flesh in the regenerate; and (5) by what Coccejus calls the reawakening of the body, which will be fully accomplished at the time of the promised eschatological redemption and consummation.[37]

The abrogation of the covenant of works leads to the covenant of grace. For Coccejus the covenant of grace has an essentially universal basis. God, he says, resolved "to employ an ineffable kindness and longsuffering towards the entire human race" (*Summa,* IV, 74).[38] Coccejus describes the covenant of grace as an event that occurs in the Godhead itself — a pact between God the Father and God the

Son to redeem humankind. The work of salvation is the historical execution of this pact between the two divine partners — that is, God with God.

Since Coccejus sees in the covenant of God successive stages of development, the system of covenants becomes in his hands a philosophy of history. According to Coccejus, Scripture enshrines a series of covenants between God and humanity through which salvation unfolds from a preexisting divine counsel through a covenant of works and its abrogation. The eternal purposes of God take into account human disobedience and provide a means of salvation in the face of human unfaithfulness in the covenant of works. When the covenant of works is violated by disobedience, an alternative way of salvation is established in the covenant of grace. The climax of the series of covenants takes place in a future consummation, giving the system an eschatological character.

Coccejus became the leader of an extremely influential school of thought in Reformed theology. This school included such theologians as Franz Burmann (1628-1679), W. Momma, J. van der Waeyen, and Hermann Witsius (1638-1708).

The work of Witsius deserves special mention. His *Oeconomia foederum Dei cum hominibus* (1677) is important because it became a theological textbook both in Britain and in America. After an initial discussion of the covenant in general, in which he defines it as "an agreement between God and man, about the way of obtaining consummate happiness; including a combination of eternal destruction,"[39] Witsius proceeds to employ the double-covenant scheme. "In Scripture," he says, "we find two covenants of God with man: the Covenant of Works, otherwise called the Covenant of Nature, or the Legal; and the Covenant of Grace."[40] He sees certain similarities and also certain differences between the two covenants. The similarities are that the

contracting parties are the same in both; there is the same promise of eternal life; both demand perfect obedience to the law; and both have the same end — the "glory of the unspotted goodness of God." They are different in that (1) God relates himself to humanity in the first as lawgiver and in the second as infinitely merciful; (2) in the covenant of works there is no mediator, whereas in the covenant of grace there is a mediator — Christ; (3) in the covenant of works the condition of perfect obedience is required of humanity, whereas in the covenant of grace it is performed by the mediator; (4) works are required in the first and faith in the second; (5) the covenant of works is conditional, whereas the covenant of grace is based on the absolute promises of God; and (6) the special end of the covenant of works is the manifestation of God's justice and holiness, whereas the special end of the covenant of grace is "the praise of the glory of his grace."[41]

Although Witsius acknowledges that the covenant of works comes first, he holds the covenant of grace to be superior. He states that in the covenant of grace, "the way is pointed out to a Paradise far preferable to the earthly, and to a more certain and stable felicity than that from which Adam fell."[42] Like Coccejus, Witsius distinguishes between the covenant of redemption made by the Father with the Son and the covenant of grace made by God with the elect. With the work of Witsius, the covenant theology reached its full development, and what followed added nothing in principle to what had come before.

Treatises continued to be written on the subject of the covenant. In Scotland, Thomas Boston (1676-1732) began to feel uneasy about the subtle kind of legalism that had crept into Scottish preaching, which he traced to the notion of the conditionality of the covenant of grace in covenant theology. Boston came across a book entitled *The Marrow of Modern Divinity*, written in 1645 by Edward Fisher. The central theme of the book was the distinction between legal repentance and evangelical repentance; Fisher followed Calvin in arguing that forgiveness leads to true repentance. Legal repentance appeals to the false motives of fear of hell and hope of heaven. Evangelical repentance, the preaching of Christ and his cross, appeals to the motives of gratitude and joy.[43] James Hog had the book printed, and it led to the Marrow Controversy, which resulted in the secession of Ralph and Ebenzer Erskine, James Hog, Ralph Wardlaw, and others from the Church of Scotland. Boston's *View of the Covenant of Grace* was published posthumously by his son. On the Continent, François Turretin (1623-1687) gave the covenant idea a large place in his theology and with his system it passed to America, where it reappeared in the federalism of the Princeton theologians Charles and A. A. Hodge.

NEGATIVE ASPECTS OF COVENANT THEOLOGY

It now remains for us to consider a number of difficulties and also some positive contributions of covenant theology. On the negative side the following difficulties can be noted.

First, the double-covenant scheme lacks a solid biblical basis. Covenant theologians have appealed to Hosea 6:7 ("they like Adam have transgressed the covenant; there have they dealt treacherously against me") as proof of an original covenant of works contracted with Adam. Although the Masoretic text may be translated in several ways (e.g., "like Adam," "like human beings"), most scholars are of the opinion that Adam here is a place name, the well-known ford of the Jordan (cf. Josh. 3:16). Other passages appealed to (e.g., Rom. 3:27, which speaks of a law of works and the law of faith, Gal. 2:16, Rom. 8:3) involve a reading of the law back to the act of creation rather than connecting it with the law given at Sinai.

The lack of a solid biblical basis for the covenant of works was commented upon early by such critics as C. Vitringa. Although he acknowledged that the state of Adam in paradise can *sano sensu* be called a covenant, still "the Bible makes no mention of covenant; on the contrary, this notion is clearly presented to us, that God as absolute and natural Lord of man has treated him as subject, of whose affection and obedience he desired to make trial. And it really seems that the notion of a covenant pertains to the economy of grace; both Scripture and reason favoring this view."[44] More decisively, historical criticism has challenged this kind of thinking. We know now that the two creation stories in Genesis 1 and 2 are intended as a preamble to the story of God's dealings with Israel. As Hendrikus Berkhof has pointed out recently, "this noncontrasting but introductory relation of creation to salvation is found in all biblical designs of creation, including those in the NT."[45] The purpose of the creation stories is not to describe a different way of salvation but to serve as a preamble and pointer to the story of God's gracious salvation of humanity.

A second and even greater difficulty is the notion that God deals with humanity in two distinct ways: first, on the basis of works, offering salvation on the condition of obedience, and second, when the first way fails, on the basis of grace, offering salvation freely to those who believe. This difficulty is compounded by the fact that federal theology, the covenant of grace, is presented in an essentially negative way. Although it includes the whole history of redemption, it is regarded as merely one of the five abrogations of the covenant of works. The covenant of grace turns out to be a subsequent and secondary arrangement rather than the first, essential, and only way in which God relates himself to humanity.

Spanheim, Maresius, and others criticized Coccejus for introducing an element of change into the unchangeableness of the divine counsel.[46] Unquestionably, federal theology suffers from the appearance of setting forth two ways of salvation — one without Christ and the other through him — thus disturbing the unity of God's activity in relation to humanity. It can be said partly in defense of covenant theology that it did look upon the covenant of works which embraced the natural moral law and the primitive condition as being imperfect in many respects. In his extremely helpful discussion of covenant theology, Karl Barth sees a certain vacillation on the part of Coccejus at this point. According to Barth, Coccejus was so impressed with the uniqueness of the covenant of grace that again and again he seemed to speak of it as "a *Prius* and not a *Posterius.*" He did this, Barth says, because "for him the new thing in the New Testament is the oldest thing of all, that which goes back to the very beginning."[47] Still, we have to ask why the covenant theologians put the covenant of works first and made it the framework and the standard reference for the covenant of grace. In doing so they made the grace of God a secondary and expedient thing after the obvious failure of the first way of salvation.

Third, the idea of an intertrinitarian pact between God the Father and God the Son is open to serious criticism. Barth has raised the following question about such a pact:

> Can we really think of the first and second persons of the triune Godhead as two divine subjects and therefore as two legal subjects who can have dealings and enter into obligations one with another? This is mythology, for which there is no place in a right understanding of the doctrine of the Trinity as the doctrine of three modes of being of the one God, which is how it was understood and presented in Reformed orthodoxy itself. God is one God. . . . We do not regard the divine persons of the Father and the Son as partners in this contract, but the one God — Father, Son and Holy Spirit — as the one partner, and the reality of man as distinct from God as the other.[48]

The idea of an intertrinitarian pact opens up the possibility of a dualism in the Godhead, of a will of God the Father that is different from the will of God the Son, so that an agreement has to be reached, a contract negotiated, in order to accomplish the work of salvation.

Fourth, there is a tendency in federal theology to confuse the idea of covenant with the idea of contract from which it was in part derived. The two are different. Covenant always implies unlimited commitment; contract implies limited commitment. Covenant is an unconditional binding of one person to another (as in marriage) without primary attention to certain advantages; contract is entered into for the sake of mutual advantages. H. Richard Niebuhr has argued that in later religious and social history the covenant idea degenerated into the limited contract idea.[49] God was regarded as a being who had contracted to do certain things for God's people on the condition that they performed certain reciprocal duties rather than as a being who accepted the obligation to keep the covenant no matter what the cost might be. Similarly, civil or political society was viewed as being based on a limited contract into which citizens entered for limited purposes and which they might reject if they did not gain from it benefits they had been promised. Marriage could also be regarded as a contract entered into for the sake of gaining certain advantages rather than as a covenant of unlimited commitment.

In an article entitled "Covenant or Contract?" James B. Torrance has argued that covenant theology turned covenant into contract and made God's grace conditional upon human obedience. This thesis requires some qualification, since Reformed theologians such as Coccejus always insisted that God's covenant is one-sided. According to Coccejus, the human partner is taken up into communion with God by means of the covenant and is enabled to respond to God's demand only by God's grace. In this respect, Coccejus is faithful to the fundamental idea in Reformation theology that the individual is dependent on God in all things. Other covenant theologians are not always as careful. Witsius, for example, speaks of the covenant as a contract, a bargain, a "mutual agreement between parties with respect to something," and this way of looking at the matter colors his whole system.

When the covenant of works becomes the standard of reference for the covenant of grace, there is always a tendency for covenant to take on the meaning of contract and to lose its original meaning of God's unconditional binding of God's self to the human partner. "The original meaning of *berith*," Martin Buber reminds us, "is not 'contract' or 'agreement'; that is, no conditions were originally stipulated therein, nor did any require to be stipulated — not a contract but an assumption into a life-relationship."[50] The shift from covenant to contract led to a legalism in preaching, notably in Scottish preaching in the eighteenth century. It was against this legalism — making repentance, faith, and holiness the conditions of the covenant — that the Marrow men protested. This protest was renewed in the nineteenth century in the theology of John McLeod Campbell.

POSITIVE ASPECTS OF COVENANT THEOLOGY

On the positive side, the following contributions of covenant theology should be noted.

In the first place, covenant theology sought to base itself on the revelation of God in Scripture. It adopted the covenant idea as central because it believed that it was central in Scripture. While there are those who object to the singling out of any one motif in Scripture and attempting to make it normative for other motifs, it is definitely the task of systematic theology to search out those generative ideas or horizons of thought that enable the unity within the diversity of the biblical witnesses to the one

God to come to expression. The primary question is not whether a particular theology is selective with regard to its organizing principle — of course it will be selective — but rather how adequate that principle is in integrating the broadest range of data.[51] Despite all its faults, covenant theology chose a central biblical idea by which to organize the biblical data and to communicate the Christian faith to an age in which the covenant was as pervasive and important an idea as the concept of evolution was in the nineteenth century and possibly the idea of hope is today. Through the use of the covenant concept, Reformed theologians were able to interpret the history of salvation in a dynamic way. According to William Robertson Smith, federal theology was "the most important attempt, in the older Protestant theology, to do justice to the historical development of revelation."[52]

Second, covenant theology broke the rule of Aristotelian Scholasticism in Protestant theology. Both Luther and Calvin were anti-Scholastic, but shortly after Calvin's death a crust of Scholasticism formed over both Lutheran and Reformed theology. The tendency in Reformed theology was not only to allow the doctrine of predestination to assume too abstract a form but also to allow it to occupy too prominent a place in this form. This led in time to a concentration on the divine decree to the neglect of the actual fulfillment of that plan in the history of salvation in time. Covenant theology sought to bring Reformed theology down from the heights of metaphysical speculation to a living connection with history, the history of salvation.[53] It did this with a measure of success and helped Reformed theology to break out of the rigid scheme of the predestinarian position. J. A. Dorner has observed that Coccejus "sowed the seeds of opinion which of themselves involved the disuse of the predestinarian system and necessarily smoothed down its austerity. So purifying a progress was a lasting gain."[54]

Third, covenant theology represented a

move in the direction of a more inclusive and universal understanding of God's work of salvation. This is evident in a number of ways. Coccejus rejected an original decree of reprobation. In his system, the covenant of works is represented as having a universal character, and, as we have already noted, the covenant of grace has an essentially universal basis. Moreover, Coccejus held that Israel has a call to salvation independent of the church, a call that remains to the end.[55]

Fourth, on the whole, covenant theology gave the covenant an evangelical interpretation and practical application. It tried to hold together the sovereignty of God and human responsibility, the rightful claims of God and human freedom. Though sometimes artificial in its account of the relation between God and humanity, especially in its idea of a covenant of works, it made God's covenant the basis of Christian assurance and hope. Nowhere is this more evident than in these words which Oliver Cromwell asked Fleetwood to pass on to his daughter:

> Bid her be cheerful, and rejoice in the Lord once and again; *if she knows the Covenant,* she cannot but do so. For that transaction is without her; sure and steadfast, between the Father and the Mediator in His blood. . . . And thus we have peace and safety, and apprehension of love, from a Father in covenant, — who cannot deny Himself. And truly in this is all my salvation: and this helps me to bear my great burdens.[56]

NOTES

1. The work was translated by William Crookshank as *The Economy of the Covenants between God and Man* (London: T. Gegg & Son), 1837.

2. See H. Richard Niebuhr, "The Idea of Covenant and American Democracy," *Church History* 23 (1954): 130.

3. Hugo Grotius is known for his many and political works, among which *The Right of War and Peace* is the most important. Pufendorf's book is *Of the Laws of Nature and Nations* (1672; E.T., 1710).

4. Earlier, the Irish Articles of 1615 had made use of the covenant scheme. According to A. F. Mitchell, the Westminster Confession of Faith may be traced to the Irish Articles, which are believed to have been prepared by Archbishop Ussher when he was Professor of Divinity in Trinity College, Dublin. See Mitchell, *The Westminster Assembly* (London: James Nisbet, 1883), pp. 372-73.

5. See Karl Barth, *Church Dogmatics*, 4 vols., ed. Geoffrey W. Bromiley and Thomas F. Torrance (Edinburgh: T. &T. Clark, 1936-69), IV/1: 55.

6. See G. Schrenk, *Gottesreich und Bund im alteren Protestantismus* (Darmstadt: Wissenschaftliche Buchgesellschaft, 1967). See also Barth, *Church Dogmatics*, IV/1: 55.

7. Moltmann, *Theology of Hope,* trans. James W. Leitch (New York: Harper & Row, 1967), p. 70.

8. Barth writes, "we are following an important insight of J. Coccejus (*S. Theol.* 1662, c. 37,2) when we trace back the concept of predestination to the biblical concept of the covenant or testament" (*Church Dogmatics*, II/2: 102), and "the merit of Coccejus consists primarily in that he reunites two things which would never have been sep-arated if the Bible had been studied properly: the eternal election of grace and the eternal decree of salvation" (*Church Dogmatics*, II/2: 114-15). Barth states that Coccejus did not exploit this identity as he might have, and yet his discovery was like "a light shining above the doctrine of this particular school, but not interpenetrating it in such a way as to mark off its outlines clearly and effectively from those of the older Calvinistic teaching held by the orthodox dogmaticians of the Reformed Church" (p. 115). See also the *Church Dogmatics,* IV/1: 54-66.

9. Niebuhr, "The Idea of Covenant and American Democracy," p. 135.

10. See D. J. McCarthy, *Old Testament Covenant: A Survey of Current Opinions* (Richmond: John Knox Press, 1972), p. 4.

11. Irenaeus, *Against Heresies*, 3.11.8, in *The Ante-Nicene Fathers*, ed. A. C. Coxe (Buffalo: Christian Literature Publishing, 1887), p. 429.

12. See Heiko A. Oberman, *The Harvest of Medieval Theology: Gabriel Biel and Later Medieval Nominalism* (Cambridge: Harvard University Press, 1963), pp. 148, 189-90.

13. John W. Beardslee III, "Reformed Covenant Theology: Historical Reflections" (unpublished paper), p. 3.

14. See Leonard J. Trinterud, "The Origins of Puritanism," *Church History* 20 (1951): 41.

15. Schrenk, *Gottesreich und Bund im alteren Protestantismus*, pp. 37-39.

16. *The Decades of Henry Bullinger*, vol. 3, ed. Thomas Harding (Cambridge: Cambridge University Press, 1850), p. 169.

17. *The Decades of Henry Bullinger,* 3: 169.

18. Barth, *Church Dogmatics,* IV/1: 57.

19. Calvin, *Institutes of the Christian Religion,* Library of Christian Classics, vols. 20-21, ed. John T. McNeill, trans. Ford Lewis Battles (Philadelphia: Westminster Press, 1960), 2.10.2.

20. Calvin, *Institutes of the Christian Religion,* 3.9.4.

21. See Harbison, "Calvin's Sense of History," in *Christianity and History* (Princeton: Princeton University Press, 1964), pp. 282ff. Harbison cites Calvin's statement that God is "not such as is imagined by sophists, vain, idle and almost asleep, but vigilant, efficacious, operative and engaged in continual action . . . a power constantly exerted on every distinct and particular movement."

22. See Calvin, *Geneva Catechism in the School of Faith,* ed. Thomas F. Torrance (London: James Clarke, 1959).

23. See Barth, *Church Dogmatics,* IV/1: 59.

24. Trinterud, "The Origins of Puritanism," p. 48.

25. See Trinterud, "The Origins of Puritanism," p. 48.

26. A. F. Mitchell mentions the influence of Ames on Coccejus. In his preface to the *Summa doct. de foed.,* Coccejus mentions his debt to Olevianus but neglects to speak of his debt to Ames. Mitchell complains that "had the Dutch writers really preceded the English these resemblances would no doubt have been confidently appealed to as proof that the English had borrowed from or followed in the wake of the Dutch" (*The Westminster Assembly,* p. 378).

27. See G. D. Henderson, "The Idea of the Covenant in Scotland," in *The Burning Bush* (Edinburgh: St. Andrew Press, 1957), p. 63.

28. Trinterud, "The Origins of Puritanism," pp. 39ff.

29. *Selected Works of Robert Rollock,* vol. 1, ed. William M. Gunn (Edinburgh: Woodrow Society, 1849), p. 33.

30. *Selected Works of Robert Rollock,* 1: 34.

31. See Sydney Ahlstrom, *A Religious History of the American People* (New Haven: Yale University Press, 1972), p. 131.

32. See Mitchell, *The Westminster Assembly,* p. 377.

33. Brown, "Covenant Theology," in *Encyclopedia of Religion in Ethics,* vol. 4, ed. J. Hastings (Edinburgh: T. & T. Clark, 1811), pp. 221-22.

34. "The Origins of Puritanism," pp. 44-45.

35. Barth, *Church Dogmatics,* IV/1: 60.

36. Coccejus, *Summa doctrinae de foedere et testamento Dei* (Amsterdam: Apud Johannum a Someren, 1672), I, 5. Subsequent references to this work will be made parenthetically in the text.

37. See Barth, *Church Dogmatics,* IV/1: 59-60.

38. As cited by Heinrich Heppe in *Reformed Dogmatics,* ed. Ernst Bizer, trans. G.T. Thomson (London: George Allen & Unwin, 1950), p. 371.

39. Witsius, *De oeconomia foederum Dei cum hominibus* (1677), I, ix.

40. Witsius, *De oeconomia foederum Dei cum hominibus,* I, xv.

41. Witsius, *De oeconomia foederum Dei cum hominibus,* I, xv.

42. Witsius, *De oeconomia foederum Dei cum hominibus,* II, iv.

43. See James B. Torrance, "Covenant or Contract?" *Scottish Journal of Theology* 23 (1970): 59.

44. Vitringa, cited by G. P. Fisher in *Discussions in History and Theology* (New York: Scribners, 1880), p. 377.

45. Berkhof, *The Christian Faith* (Grand Rapids: William B. Eerdmans, 1979), p. 167.

46. See J. A. Dorner, *History of Protestant Theology,* vol. 2, trans. G. Robson and S. Taylor (Edinburgh: T. & T. Clark, 1871), 39.

47. Barth, *Church Dogmatics,* IV/1: 61.

48. Barth, *Church Dogmatics,* IV/1: 65.

49. Niebuhr, "The Idea of Covenant and American Democracy," p. 134.

50. Buber, cited by Torrance, "Covenant or Contract?" p. 53.

51. See Christopher Morse, *The Logic of Promise in Moltmann's Theology* (Philadelphia: Fortress Press, 1979), p. ix.

52. Smith, *The Prophets of Israel* (London: Adam & Charles Black, 1895), p. 375.

53. On this, see T. M. Lindsay, "The Covenant Theology," *British and Foreign Evangelical Review* 28 (1879): 534-35.

54. Dorner, *History of Protestant Theology,* p. 43.

55. See Jürgen Moltmann, *The Church in the Power of the Spirit* (New York: Harper & Row, 1977), p. 138.

56. Cromwell, cited by T. M. Lindsay in "The Covenant Theology," p. 521.

Karl Barth's Doctrine of the Covenant

Arthur C. Cochrane

I. AN EVERLASTING COVENANT

God's one covenant of grace in Jesus Christ is the underlying and unifying theme of the *Church Dogmatics*, for Barth believes that it is the underlying and unifying theme of Holy Scripture. Not that there are not various promulgations and administrations of covenants in both the Old and New Testaments. Yet they are all related to the one covenant of grace. The covenant is the presupposition of God's work of reconciliation of the world in Jesus Christ, and reconciliation is the fulfillment of the covenant. It is fulfilled in the justification, sanctification, and calling of sinful and fallen humankind in the death and resurrection of Jesus Christ. Although the covenant has been fulfilled once and for all in the death of God's Son and manifested to the apostles during the forty days following his resurrection, it will be redemptively manifested in the final parousia, when everyone will see and confess that Jesus Christ is Lord, to the glory of God the Father (Phil. 2:11). The ultimate fulfillment of the covenant will occur when the holy city, the new Jerusalem, comes down out of heaven from God and God will dwell with humans and they shall be his people; God will be with them and be their God, and there shall be no more death, pain, or mourning (Rev. 21:1-4).

At the beginning and end of Scripture, the covenant is seen as God's covenant with humankind, all men and women in every age and clime. Yet the partner of God is not "man" as an idea, nor "humanity," but the one man Jesus and the "people represented" in him. "Only secondarily, and for His sake, is it 'man' and 'humanity' and the whole remaining cosmos."[1]

The covenant that God initiates consists of two inseparable parts: election as the sum of the gospel, and the divine commandment. "The one elected finds a Master and Lord. Grace does not will only to be received and known. . . . It wills also to rule. . . . There is no grace without the lordship and claim of grace. There is no dogmatics which is not also and necessarily ethics" (*CD*, II/2: 12). Since

Reprinted from *A Covenant Challenge to Our Broken World*, ed. Allen O. Miller (Atlanta: Darby, 1982), pp. 156-64.

we have to do with the gospel insofar as it has always the form of the law, the law of the covenanting God has nothing in common with a perverted "law of works" or of "sin and death" or with a so-called covenant of works. On the contrary, the commandment of God the Creator and Reconciler is holy, just, and good, sweeter than the honeycomb because its ground and content is Christ and because, in contrast to all other laws, it frees men and women for obedience.

Included in the covenant with and election of humanity in Jesus Christ is the special covenant with and election of the one community composed of Israel and the church. It is a mediating and representative community in that it has to bear witness to Jesus Christ and call the whole world to faith in him. There is no independent covenant or election of either Israel or the church apart from him. To claim such would be either Jewish or ecclesiastical fantasy and arrogance. "What is elected in Jesus Christ (His 'body') is the community which has the twofold form of Israel and the Church. . . . We cannot, therefore, call the Jews the 'rejected' and the Church the 'elected community' " (CD, II/2: 199). We cannot claim that the church has superseded Israel as the covenant people of God. We cannot say that Israel is no longer God's chosen people because they do not believe that Jesus of Nazareth is their Messiah, the King of the Jews. "Has God rejected his people? By no means! . . . God has not rejected his people whom he foreknew. . . . Have they stumbled so as to fall? By no means! . . . As regards the gospel they are enemies of God, for your sake [the sake of Gentiles]; but as regards election they are beloved for the sake of their forefathers. For the gifts and the call of God are irrevocable" (Rom. 11:1, 2, 11, 28, 29).

God's covenant with the twelve tribes of Israel and their descendants is an "everlasting covenant" (Gen. 17:7, 13, 19; 2 Sam. 23:5, 1 Chron. 16:17; Ps. 105:8-10; Isa. 55:3; 61:8;

Jer. 32:40). Even though Israel is punished for repeatedly breaking the covenant, God promises, "I will remember my covenant with you in the days of your youth, and I will establish with you an everlasting covenant . . . and you shall know that I am the LORD . . . when I forgive you all that you have done" (Ezek. 16:60, 62-63; cf. 37:26). Nowhere in the New Testament is it ever suggested that God has abrogated the covenant with Israel because of its unbelief and hardness of heart. On the contrary, the birth of Jesus means that the Lord God of Israel "has visited and redeemed his people . . . to remember his holy covenant, the oath which he swore to our father Abraham" (Luke 1:68, 72-73). To Israelites after the flesh belong the covenants (Rom. 9:4).

To be sure, Israel is not the church, and the church is not Israel. Israel bears witness to humanity's turning toward humanity (both Jews and Gentiles!). "The antithesis between the two cannot be formulated in exclusive terms. Behind and above the human obduracy characteristic of the Israelite form of the community there stands the divine rejection, but there stands also God's election in which He has determined Himself to take upon Himself the rejection. And behind and above the divine calling characteristic of the Church form of the community there stands indeed the divine election, but for the same reason there stands also the rejection that God has taken upon himself" (CD, II/2: 200). Therein is to be seen their differentiation, but also their indissoluble unity.

The notion that the church has superseded and replaced Israel as God's covenant people is the theological root of anti-Semitism, or rather anti-Jewishness. It is the darkest blot on the long history of Christendom. In part it has its roots in the covenantal theology of our Reformed churches. This error has to be openly confessed and repudiated.

For those who have eyes to see, the existence of Jews in the state of Israel and in the Dispersion is the one natural proof of God's faithfulness to his covenant. Woe to those who do not respect the right of the state of Israel to exist! Yet Israel does not have this right at the expense of the right of the Palestinians to a homeland of their own. For God is also the God of Ishmael and Esau.

II. RECONCILIATION AS THE FULFILLMENT OF THE COVENANT

If God's covenant with Israel is eternal, if it has not been abrogated or replaced, we now ask in what sense the New Testament (in keeping with the promises of the Old Testament) speaks of it as a "new" and "better" covenant. It is new and better in both a christological and pneumatological sense. It is new and better in that the original purpose of the covenant with Israel has now been fulfilled in Christ and in the outpouring of the Holy Spirit.

It is not like the covenant God made with the fathers, which the people of Israel did not continue to keep but broke. It is this disobedience that God will no longer tolerate in the last days. The covenant is new in that now God "will forgive their iniquity and will remember their sin no more" (Jer. 31:34; Heb. 6:12; 10:17). As the Lord's Supper reminds us, the new covenant is in Christ's blood, "which is poured out for many for the forgiveness of sins" (Matt. 26:28) and which "cleanses us from all sin" (1 John 1:7). What is envisaged by Jeremiah and Isaiah is the salvation of all Israel by the Deliverer who will come out of Zion and will banish ungodliness from Jacob, "and this will be my covenant with them when I take away their sins" (Rom. 11:27). What is foreseen is a once-and-for-all redemption "from the transgressions under the first covenant" (Heb. 9:15) not through "the blood of goats and calves but [Christ's] own blood, thus securing an eternal redemption" (Heb. 9:12). Thus "Christ is the mediator of a new

covenant," of which the first was only a shadow — "for a will [*diatheke* — "covenant" or "testament"] takes effect only at death, since it is not in force as long as the one who made it is alive" (9:15, 17). This is the new perfected covenant God has made with all Israel, which is remembered and proclaimed by apostolic preaching and the Lord's Supper — "to the Jew first and also to the Greek" (Rom. 1:16).

"Also to the Greek." The covenant in Christ's blood is new in that the Gentiles are now in the covenant that God fulfilled with Israel. We should observe first that the inclusion of the Gentiles was the original intention and purpose of the covenant made with Israel. This promise is contained in the covenant that God made with Abraham and his descendants: "in you all the families of the earth will be blessed" (Gen. 12:3). Moreover, Isaiah brings out the fact that Israel has been elected and called to fulfill a mission — namely, to be a light to the Gentiles (Isa. 49:6), "a light to the nations" (Isa. 42:6; cf. Luke 2:32; Acts 13:47; 26:23). In the last days, the redemptive will of God will be declared to all humanity. Not only that, but the last day, which is the redemption of Israel, will also be the day of judgment and redemption for the nations (Isa. 2:2-4; 25:6-8; Mic. 4:1-4). In Isaiah 19:24-25 a historical situation is merged into a vision of events in the last days. "In that day Israel will be third with Egypt and with Assyria, a blessing in the midst of the earth, whom the LORD of hosts has blessed, saying, 'Blessed be Egypt my people, and Assyria the work of my hands, and Israel my heritage.'"

The new covenant in Christ's blood in which Gentiles are now included is not a separate covenant God has made with Gentiles or with Gentile Christians. On the contrary, the way to the universality of the covenant is through the particularity of the one covenant of grace with Israel. This is made clear in Paul's letter to the Ephesians. We who are Gentiles are to remember that at one time we were separated from Christ, Israel's Messiah, alienated from the commonwealth of Israel, and strangers to the covenants of promise. But now in Christ Jesus we who were afar off have been brought near in the blood of Christ (Eph. 2:11-13). Let it be observed that the "now," the new time, occurred not when Gentiles came to believe but in the event of Christ's death itself. Christ has broken down the dividing wall of hostility between Jews and Gentiles. He has created one new person in place of two. He has reconciled both Jew and Gentile to God in one body *through the cross* (Eph. 2:14-16). So we Gentiles are now no longer strangers and sojourners but members of the household of God. We emphasize that this *has* taken place in the shedding of Christ's blood and is a true and valid reality whether Jews and Gentiles, Jews and Arabs believe it or not. The cross of Christ is not merely an ideal, principle, or potentiality that subsequently has to be realized by faith. It is a finished work of God for all humankind. The proclamation of the good news calls for faith, but it does not depend upon our faith. The grace apprehended by faith is just the reconciling work of God already accomplished for the whole human race in the death of Christ.

The breaking down of the wall of hostility between Jews and Gentiles in the cross of Christ is the paradigm of the overcoming of all sorts of alienation and hostility between men and women, young and old, races and nations (cf. Gal. 3:28). The church is called to proclaim reconciliation as the fulfillment of the covenant in Christ in the teeth of all empirical evidence to the contrary. It is to address its message to concrete situations of alienation and hostility.

III. THE OUTPOURING OF THE SPIRIT AS THE FULFILLMENT OF THE COVENANT

We turn now to another dimension of God's covenant of grace with Israel and the church.

We are asking about the reality and possibility of the existence of God's people in the midst of the nations of the world. We are asking about the possibility of its faith, love, and hope, about the possibility of its bearing witness to the reconciliation of the world accomplished in the death and resurrection of Jesus Christ. We are asking about what might be called the subjective reality and possibility of reconciliation — about reconciliation being not only *pro nobis,* yes *pro mundo,* but *in nobis.* The answer to this set of questions is that the covenant of grace God made with Israel is fulfilled in the outpouring of the Holy Spirit upon all flesh — Jews and Gentiles (Acts 2:17).

In Ezekiel 11:19-20 we read, "and I will give them one heart, and put a new spirit within them; I will take the stony heart out of their flesh and give them a heart of flesh, that they may walk in my statutes and keep my ordinances and obey them; and they shall be my people, and I will be their God" (cf. 36:26-27). Jeremiah expresses it somewhat differently: "Behold, the days are coming, says the LORD, when I will make a new covenant with the house of Israel and the house of Judah, not like the covenant which I made with their fathers when I took them by the hand to bring them out of the land of Egypt, my covenant which they broke, though I was their husband, says the LORD. But this is the covenant which I will make with the house of Israel after those days, says the LORD: I will put my law within them, and I will write it upon their hearts; and I will be their God, and they shall be my people. And no longer shall each man teach his neighbor and each his brother, saying, 'Know the LORD,' for they shall all know me, from the least of them to the greatest, says the LORD" (31:31-34; cf. 32:39-40; Heb. 8:9-12). According to the prophecy of Joel 2:28-29, the Spirit will be given not only to Jews but "to all flesh" — that is, to Gentiles also. And according to Luke the prophecy was fulfilled on the day of Pentecost: "and in the last days it shall be, God declares, that I will pour out my Spirit upon all flesh; and your sons and daughters shall prophesy, and your young men shall see visions, and your old men shall dream dreams; yea, and on my menservants and my maidservants in those days I will pour out my Spirit; and they shall prophesy" (Acts 2:17-18; cf. 2:1-21).

In 2 Corinthians 3:6 Paul declares that God "has qualified us to be ministers of a new covenant, not in a written code but in the Spirit; for the written code kills, but the Spirit gives life." In this light Paul goes on to argue that a veil lies over the minds of the Israelites whenever Moses is read — the letter of the law of the old covenant. But "only through Christ is [the veil] taken away. . . . When a man turns to the Lord the veil is removed. Now the Lord is the Spirit, and where the Spirit of the Lord is, there is freedom" (2 Cor. 3:14, 16-17). The covenant is fulfilled in two great names: Jesus Christ and the Holy Spirit. For Christ is the bearer and dispenser of the Spirit.

Where the Spirit is, there is freedom to hear, trust, and obey Jesus Christ as the one Word of God, freedom to confess and bear witness to him. Paul contrasts the Jew who is one only outwardly with the Jew who is one inwardly "by the circumcision that is of the heart, in the Spirit and not in the letter" (Rom. 2:29; cf. Deut. 30:6) and with the Gentiles who have come to faith in Christ and who apart from the law do by nature the works of the law and who show that the work of the law (not the νόμος but the ἔργον τοῦ νόμου) is written in their hearts (Rom. 2:14-16).

Elsewhere in the New Testament it is explained how an individual (whether a Jew or a Gentile) becomes a member of the covenant people through the outpouring of the Holy Spirit. It is not like Israel, which is constituted by a succession of natural and physical generations. An individual becomes a Christian and thereby a member of the body of Christ, the church, by a second and new generation and birth, which is in sharp contrast to one's natural genesis.

His natural origin in the procreative will of his human father is absolutely superseded and transcended (Jn. 1:13). "That which is born of flesh is flesh" (Jn. 3:6). The Christian, however, comes into being in a very different way, of incorruptible not corruptible seed (I Peter 1:23). Thus the question of Nicodemus (Jn. 3:4) how a grown man can return to his mother's womb and be born again is quite pointless. Not *as* a child, but *like* a child (Mk. 10:15), beginning from the very beginning, as is proper to ἀρτιγέννητα βρέφη (I Peter 2:2), a man comes to see the kingdom of God, receive it, enter into it. For this he must be born ἄνωθεν, not on the horizontal plane of the sequence of generations, but on the vertical plane of direct divine fatherhood (Jn. 3:3). . . . To love God and to believe in Him he must be born of God (Jn. 1:13; I Jn. 4:7; 5:1). . . . They are thus born of the Spirit, who as πνεῦμα ζωοποιοῦν (Jn. 6:63, I Cor. 15:45) blows where He wills (Jn. 3:8). (*CD*, IV/4: 9)

Barth's doctrine of the church and of the life of a Christian in the *Church Dogmatics*, volume 4, parts 1-4, may be seen as an account of the unfolding of the work of the Spirit in fulfillment of God's covenant of grace. It may be summed up as follows: by the awakening, quickening, and illuminating power of the Holy Spirit, the church comes to know its being as the body of Christ and is gathered, built up, and sent forth in mission for the world, and certain individuals are made free for faith, love, and hope in Jesus Christ.

The church, therefore, is not an outgrowth of a historical process or of natural procreation. An infant does not become a Christian by virtue of being born to a believing parent. Nor should it be baptized as a sign that it is a child of the covenant. Nor does a person become a Christian by means of baptism with water. Finally, a person does not become a Christian by means of a religious or moral experience. He or she is born again on Golgotha and apprehends it by faith through the Holy Spirit.

Under the old covenant, the Spirit was

given to judges, priests, kings, and prophets to teach and rule God's people. But according to the prophecy of Joel fulfilled at Pentecost, the Spirit was given to the whole Christian community. No longer is there a division between clergy and laity, between the *ecclesia docens* and the *ecclesia audiens,* between a hierarchical episcopate and the so-called faithful, between men ordained to preach and teach and women who are to keep silent at all times, or between those who by ordination are somehow qualified to administer the "sacraments" and those who passively receive them. To be sure, there is a diversity of the gifts of the Spirit, but all are for the common good of the body, of which there are many members, and "for the work of ministry." The priesthood of all believers should be implemented more fully than has been done even in our Reformed churches.

Since the church and its members are made free by the Holy Spirit to obey Christ's commands to preach the gospel to all nations and to eat and drink in remembrance of Christ and to proclaim his death for all people, the Lord's Supper, like the sermon, is as open to all people as "the outstretched arms of Christ on the cross" (Moltmann).

"Christ appeared once and perfected and fulfilled fellowship with God by a unique sacrifice. A sharp distinction is drawn between it and all" (Kraus). Preaching, baptism, and the Lord's Supper are therefore not extensions, repetitions, or realizations of the incarnation, death, and resurrection of Jesus Christ but testimonies through the power of the Spirit to the fulfillment of the covenant of grace in God's exclusive work of reconciliation in Christ.

IV. ISRAEL'S UNBELIEF AND THE CHURCH'S FAITH

We have seen that the covenant with Israel is an everlasting covenant and that in spite of

their unbelief, Abraham's descendants remain God's chosen people. We have also seen that the church form of the one elect community is composed of a small number of Jews and a large number of Gentiles who by the Holy Spirit have come to faith but that Israel as a whole has persisted in unbelief. Why is this? Was not the Spirit promised to Israel and is not the freedom to believe promised to Jews? Yes, indeed! Paul and all other Jews who believe in Jesus Christ are proof that God's promise of the Spirit was not in vain. How, then, are we to explain the "mystery" that "a hardening has come upon part of Israel"? How is it that though their election stands firm, they live as those rejected? How is it that they are called "vessels of wrath" in contrast to "the vessels of mercy"? Is there injustice with God? Is God arbitrary and capricious? These are questions that Paul wrestles with in Romans 9–11.

God is not unrighteous. It is not a question of an eternal and absolute double predestination by a secret decree (Calvin). It is a question of God's will to show his power and wrath to manifest, *to make known* the riches of his glory and mercy, *to show* the kindness and severity of God (severity to those who have fallen, kindness to those who continue in his kindness by faith), and *to proclaim* his name in all the earth (Rom. 9:17, 22-23; 11:22). The twofold witness of Israel and the church is that God has imprisoned (συνέκλεισεν) all — both Jews and Gentiles — in disobedience in order that they may obtain mercy (11:32). As the Creator of a humankind that has sinned and fallen away, God has the right to make this provisional distinction between vessels of mercy and wrath (Rom. 9:19-24).

But this divine decision is no cause or ground for Christians to be proud and boastful with respect to Jews. For it is through the trespass of the Jews that salvation has come to the Gentiles. Their rejection is the reconciliation of the world (Rom. 11:18-20, 11, 15). The church is to remember that it does not support

Israel, the root, but that Israel supports the church (Rom. 11:18). Christians are to stand in awe because they stand fast only by faith (Rom. 11:20). "If God did not spare the natural branches, neither will he spare you" (11:21; cf. John 15:1-11, concerning the true vine and the branches). Moreover, in the end time the roles of Israel and the church will be reversed: "Just as you were once disobedient to God but now have received mercy because of their disobedience, so they have now been disobedient in order that by the mercy shown to you they also may receive mercy" (Rom. 11:30-31).

V. CREATION AND COVENANT

Barth teaches that creation and covenant, though distinguishable, are inseparable. Creation is the external presupposition of the covenant, and the covenant is the internal presupposition of creation (*CD*, III/1, §41; cf. III/1: 27). The same is true of the doctrine of providence, or God's preservation and government of the cosmos. A doctrine of the covenant is incomplete without the doctrines of creation and providence. Thus Barth interprets Genesis 1 and 2 as setting forth twofold presuppositions. As Calvin taught, God created heaven and earth to be "the theatre of God's glory." Barth explains that God willed that there would be a time and place in which humanity could live as God's covenant partner — that is, in a vertical relationship with God and in a horizontal relationship with fellow human beings. Humanity is created in the image of God, male and female, in a cohumanity that reflects the covenant of grace between Yahweh and Israel, Christ and the church, which is representative of God's covenant with all humankind.

The creation is good because it is a fit state for the history of God's covenant with Israel and the church, and the covenant is the inner meaning of world history. We affirm the same thing when

we confess that God created all things in and by Christ (John 1:3; Col. 1:16-17; Heb. 1:2). Moreover, in spite of humanity's sin and fall, God preserves the human race. Here we think of the everlasting covenant God made with Noah and "every living creature of all flesh that is upon the earth" (Gen. 9:1-17; cf. 8:20-22). The Noahic covenant is often referred to as a covenant of preservation in contrast to the covenant with Abraham, which is referred to as a covenant of grace and salvation. But as Barth observes, although it certainly has to do with the preservation of the human race, it is not an abstract preservation but a preservation in the face of and in spite of humanity's sin and apostasy. For both before and after the flood, "the imagination of man's heart is evil from his youth" (Gen. 8:21; 6:5). Humankind is preserved with a view to one who is to come to take away their sin.

> Therefore the Noahic covenant . . . is already a covenant of grace in the twofold sense of the concept of grace: the free and utterly unmerited self-obligation of God to the human race which had completely fallen away from Him, but which as such is still pledged to Him (as is shown by the sacrifice of Noah in Gen. 8:20 and the divine direction in Gen. 9:1f.); and as the sign of the longsuffering of God obviously also the promise of the future divine coming which will far transcend the mere preserving of the race. (*CD*, IV/1: 26-34)

VI. THE COMMANDMENT OF GOD THE CREATOR AND RECONCILER

We have already noted that according to Barth the covenant consists of dogmatics and ethics, the gospel and the law, and that these are inseparable. Accordingly, the doctrine of God's gracious election is followed by the doctrine of God's commandment as God's claim, decision, and judgment upon humanity. Following three volumes in the *Dogmatics* on the doctrine of creation, there is a fourth on a special ethics under the rubric "The Commandment of God the Creator." To the consternation of many of Barth's readers, he indicated his intention to append to his doctrine of reconciliation a fourth volume on special ethics as the commandment of God the Reconciler. (As it turned out, he managed to publish only the fragment on baptism before he died.) What bothered Barth's critics was his proposal to consider Christ's commandments to preach, baptize, eat and drink, and pray as ethical demands calling for a free human response to the grace of reconciliation in a manner controverting the time-honored view that the church can and should perform divine-human works as vehicles and means of saving grace. But surely Barth's proposal is quite consistent with his dogmatics: he is asserting that reconciliation as the fulfillment of the covenant is exclusively the work of God in Jesus Christ and the Holy Spirit. Humanity is not saved by Christ and the Spirit *plus* the church's ministry. Humanity does not cooperate with God in his creation, reconciliation, and redemption. In the covenant of grace, humanity is a co-worker with God but not a co-creator and co-redeemer. It is by grace alone that humans are co-workers. Humanity's work consists in the obedience of faith to the divine command. Broadly speaking, it consists solely in his witness in response to the one grace of creation and reconciliation in Christ and the Spirit.

Nevertheless, despite the unity of God's command as Creator, Reconciler, and Redeemer, there is a special command of the Creator. Definite, concrete, and vertical commands are given in a horizontal context in which God's command and humanity's act have continuity and constancy. Barth prefers to speak of "contexts" or "spheres" gleaned from God's Word rather than of "orders" (Brunner) or "mandates" (Bonhoeffer) of creation. By considering these spheres, special ethics establishes approximations and directives of command and conduct (*CD*, II/4: 27-31). Accord-

ingly, Barth expounds the command of God as Creator as a command of freedom in four anthropological areas: freedom before God (*CD*, III/2, §53), freedom in fellowship (*CD*, III/2, §54), freedom for life (*CD*, III/2, §55), and freedom in limitation (*CD*, III/2, §56).

Under the heading of the creature's relationship to God, Barth expounds (1) the holy day, (2) confession, and (3) prayer. Under the heading of humanity's co-humanity, he deals with (1) man and woman, (2) parents and children, and (3) near and distant neighbors. Under the heading of humankind's freedom to live he discusses (1) respect for life, (2) the protection of life, and (3) the active life. Under the heading of freedom in limitation, he takes up (1) the unique opportunity, (2) vocation, and (3) honor.

Under the heading of freedom in community, Barth discusses the relationship of male and female in general, then marriage, celibacy, polygamy, divorce, patriarchalism, feminism, adultery, fornication and homosexuality, the relationship of parents and children in the family, and relationships to one's countrymen and to other nations. Under the heading of freedom for life, Barth deals with reverence for plant, animal, and cosmic life (ecology). In regard to human life, he addresses questions of physical and mental health care, the service of doctors and medicine, faith healing and prayer, the role of wages, hours, housing, working conditions, recreation, sport, and technology. Concerning the protecting of life, he considers murder, suicide, abortion, euthanasia, self-defense, capital punishment, treason, tyrannicide, war, conscription, conscientious objection, and pacifism. Under the heading of the active life, he deals with the nature of work, first in the Christian community and then in society. Since God has created humans to work with and for their fellow human beings, Barth is able to make an incisive criticism of capitalism, but he is also critical of state communism, under which injustice and suppression of human freedoms are perpetuated in another form.[2]

POSTSCRIPT

In the foregoing I have provided only a broad outline of the commandment of the Lord of the covenant and the conduct of God's covenant partner. Space did not permit consideration of the many ethical issues Barth discusses. It is my hope that Barth's corrective to Reformed covenantal theology of the sixteenth and seventeenth centuries will help us to arrive at a proper biblical approach to concrete issues facing the church and society in our day.[3]

NOTES

1. Karl Barth, *Church Dogmatics*, 4 vols., ed. Geoffrey W. Bromiley and Thomas F. Torrance (Edinburgh: T. & T. Clark, 1936-69), II/2: 8.

2. For Barth's critique of capitalism, see *CD*, III/4: 534-45.

3. Barth gives an excursus on the concept of covenant in the history of Reformed theology in *CD*, IV/1: 54-66.

Models of the Atonement in Reformed Theology

H. D. McDonald

THE DEMAND OF JUSTICE

Ulrich Zwingli

Zwingli was a leader of reform independent of Luther. His center was among the Swiss, where his voice was early heard declaring the gospel of justification by faith. He later became acquainted with Luther, and some of his declarations are clearly influenced by the German Reformer. Zwingli's basic idea of God is that of his absolute sovereignty, an almost arbitrary view of sovereignty after the fashion of Peter Damian's "On Sovereignty." For Zwingli it was more a philosophical than a religious concept, the result of reflection rather than of experience, as in the case of Augustine. God is free to do what God wills, and having the power to do what God wills, God has

elected to salvation whom God would. The election of God is free and unmerited — for God chose us before the foundation of the world. In spite of his assertion of God's freedom, Zwingli was still an advocate of the penal theory of the atonement. So free is God that God is bound by no necessity. Could he not therefore will to forgive humanity's sin without exacting a penalty? Zwingli does not face that difficulty. He proceeds rather to affirm that Christ in his death bore the penalty due to the sin of God's elect people. Christ was a "victim making satisfaction forever for the sins of the faithful." By his death, Christ "expiated our crimes," being made "a sacrifice to satisfy the divine justice." "He offered himself to the Father for us to placate his eternal justice." In what he has to say about the work of Christ, Zwingli faithfully reproduces the Reformers' view of the cross and justification by faith.[1] But it almost seems that his own view of the divine omnipotence, which he makes no effort to coordinate with the doctrine of Christ's work, was taken over from Luther.

Reprinted from *The Atonement of the Death of Christ* (Grand Rapids: Baker Book House, 1985), pp. 186-93; 208-15; 307-8; 311-16.

John Calvin

Calvin's intellectual and spiritual qualities far outclassed those of Zwingli, and they united to give shape to Reformed theology. Calvin's Christian commitment was closer to that of Luther than that of Zwingli, while his emphasis on the divine sovereignty, which was for the father of the Swiss Reformation a philosophical concept, was for Calvin a religious experience. No other Christian theologian or leader, except perhaps Luther, has been the subject of so much investigation. Every single aspect of his theology has been canvassed again and again. No history of Christian thought has any claim to attention that does not give Calvin's ideas appropriate space. His understanding of the atonement continues to be influential and has been restated repeatedly in numerous theologies as a viable view of Christ's work. Statements of Calvin's atonement doctrine appear in many church confessions, theological journals, and university dissertations. Here, however, we will refer directly to the primary source, Calvin's own *Institutes of the Christian Religion*.

The section of the *Institutes* in which Calvin deals with the subject of Christ's atoning work is preceded by one in which he presents Christ in his offices of prophet, king, and priest. Jansen has sought to subsume an exposition of Calvin's atonement doctrine under this trio of designations.[2] However, we prefer to regard these as qualifying Christ for his saving work; Calvin writes, "the office of Redeemer was assigned to him in order that he might be our Savior."[3] In this context, the references are not unique to Calvin. Peter Mogila, the metropolitan of Kiev, "repeated the idea of prophet, priest and king all in one. It was a perfectly orthodox idea, having had one of its expressions in Eusebius; but it had not really become a topic of Christian dogmatics until the *Institutes* of John Calvin, whence it came into the doctrinal works of various denominations."[4]

For Calvin the three offices coalesce in Christ's person as Redeemer. He is prophet: "The purpose of this prophetical dignity in Christ is to teach us, that in the doctrine which he delivered is substantially included a wisdom which is perfect in all its parts" (2.15.2). He is king, "the Father having appointed him over us for the express purpose of exercising his government through him" (2.15.2). He is priest: "the end and use of Christ's priesthood is that as Mediator, free from all taint he may by his holiness procure favor of God for us" (2.15.6).

With this threefold office secured, Calvin sets out in the next chapter "to consider in what way we obtain salvation from him" (2.16.1). He begins this consideration by stating that God's wrath is real, and there is a sense in which it can be rightly said that he "was our enemy until he was reconciled to us by Christ." On two counts humanity needs a Mediator. On the one hand, after Adam's fall, "no knowledge of God was effectual without" such. And, on the other hand, God was the enemy of humans until they were restored in favor by the death of Christ (Rom. 5:10); they were cursed until their iniquity was expiated by the sacrifice of Christ (Gal. 3:10, 13). Calvin does not, however, think of God's anger as vindictive. He insists that his love was in it. "Accordingly, God the Father, by his love, prevents and anticipates our reconciliation in Christ" (2.16.3). It is, in fact, "because he loves us that he afterwards reconciles us to himself" (2.16.2). So does he quote approvingly a long passage from Augustine: "Incomprehensible and immutable is the love of God. For it was not after we were reconciled to him by the blood of his Son that he began to love us, but he loved us before the foundation of the world, that with his only-begotten Son we too might be sons of God before we were anything at all. . . . He had his love towards us even when, exercising enmity towards him, we were the workers of iniquity. Accordingly, in a manner wondrous and divine, he loved even when he hated us" (2.16.4). He himself later quotes John 3:16 with the comment, "we see that the first place is assigned to the love of God as the chief cause or origin [of our salvation], and that faith in Christ follows as the second and more appropriate cause" (2.17.2).

The divine punishment and wrath Christ took upon himself. He "interposed, took the punishment upon himself, and bore what by the just judgment of God was impending over sinners" (2.16.2). What did it take for Christ to abolish sin and remove the enmity between God and us? It took "the whole course of his obedience" (see Rom. 5:19). "From the moment when he assumed the form of a servant, he began, in order to redeem us, to pay the price of deliverance." But "particularly and especially to the death of Christ" does Scripture refer "the mode of salvation." " 'He was numbered with the transgressors' (Isa. 53:12; Mark 15:28). Why was this so? That he might bear the character of a sinner, not of a just or innocent person, inasmuch as he met death on account not of innocence, but of sin" (2.16.5). By Pilate he was condemned and yet declared without fault. Such was the manner of his death at the hands of humans. It was a parable and a fact regarding his death in relation to God. He died as one guilty. The "guilt which made us liable to punishment was transferred to the head of the Son of God." But he was nevertheless himself without sin. God cannot love sin, and his love of the Son never ceased. He bore the divine anger to the utmost, yet God was not angry with him. "How could he be angry with the beloved Son, with whom his soul was well pleased?" (2.16.11). What we perceive, then, is "Christ representing the character of a sinner and a criminal while, at the same time, his innocence shines forth, and it becomes manifest that he suffers for another's and not for his own crime" (2.16.6).

Not only sin's guilt and penalty, but the very curse of sin he took upon himself. The "whole curse, which on account of our iniquities awaited us, or rather lay upon us, [was] transferred to him." Thus was he in his death "bearing, by substitution, the curse due to sin" (2.16.6). On him as "a propitiatory victim for sin" was our guilt and penalty laid, and no longer imputed to us; thus did he make "a full expiation." "Christ in his death, was offered to the Father as a propitiatory victim; that, expiation being made by his sacrifice, we might cease to tremble at the divine wrath." He was not himself overwhelmed by the curse he endured, "but rather by the enduring of it he repressed, broke and annihilated all its force" (2.16.6).

To make his exposition complete, Calvin, following the articles of the Apostles' Creed, insists that attention must be given not only to the fact of Christ's crucifixion but also to the clause *was dead and buried,* for thus did he "substitute himself in order to pay the price of our redemption" (2.16.6). Nor must we "omit the descent into hell," for he had "to feel the full weight of the Divine vengeance." "There is nothing strange in its being said that he descended into hell, seeing he endured the death which is inflicted on the wicked by an angry God" (2.16.10). Calvin does not overlook the importance of the resurrection, for by it is the victory over death assured: "by his death sin was taken away, by his resurrection righteousness was renewed and restored" (2.16.13).

"Our salvation," Calvin then declares, "may be thus divided between the death and the resurrection of Christ: by the former, sin is abolished and death annihilated; by the latter, righteousness was restored and life revived, the power and efficiency of the former being still bestowed upon us by means of the latter" (2.16.13). All things that belong to our salvation are, then, to be found in Christ: without him, nothing; with him, everything. There is

strength in his government; purity in his conception; indulgence in his nativity in which he was made like us in all respects, in order that he might learn to sympathize with us; if we seek redemption, we will find it in his passion; acquittal in his condemnation; remission of the curse in his cross; satisfaction in his sacrifice; purification in his blood; reconciliation in his descent into hell; mortification of the flesh in his sepulchre; newness of life in his resurrection; immortality also in his resurrection; the inheritance of a celestial kingdom in his entrance into heaven; protection, security, and the abundant supply of all blessings, in his kingdom; secure anticipation of judgment in the power of judging committed to him. In fine, since in him all kinds of blessings are treasured up, let us draw a full supply from him, and none from any other quarter. (2.16.19)

Both Luther and Calvin were at one in emphasizing the justice and love of God for sinners. On the one hand there is the wrath of God upon sin, and on the other is the grace of God in providing an atonement, and both unite in Christ's redeeming work. They regarded love as belonging to God's essence, while wrath is his "alien work," expressed only because of sin. Pure and undeserved mercy is the fountainhead of God's saving action and the whole actuating motive of the atonement. But it belongs to Calvin to have given to the penal substitutionary doctrine of the atonement a compelling statement. His account brings into review those considerations that are necessary for any acceptable theory. He underlines the seriousness of sin as demanding punishment. He does not conceive of God dealing arbitrarily with humanity. He gives full weight to the dignity of the moral law and rightly stresses that the atonement effects God's relation to us.

Subsequent controversies between the Lutheran and Reformed branches of the Reformation concerned two main issues. The first had to do with the ground of the atonement. While Calvin shows that Scripture focuses the atonement more particularly in the death of Christ, he nevertheless stresses "the whole course of Christ's obedience," with the resurrection and ascension involved in the saving act. But later theologians, especially those following Anselm, drew a distinction between Christ's active and passive obedience. By his active obedience, it was maintained, he obeyed the divine law, and as a result of that obedience he could impute to the believer his own righteousness. By his passive obedience he endured the penalty of sin, taking on himself its punishment and thus satisfying the retributive righteousness of God.

On the whole the Lutheran theologians refused to allow the distinction. The Augsburg Confession and the Formula of Concord make no reference to it. The latter says, "that righteousness which is imputed to faith, or the believer, of mere grace, is the *obedience, suffering,* and *resurrection* of Christ by which he satisfied the law for us and expiated our sins." Later Lutheran theologians argued that since Christ was himself the Lord of the law, he was not bound by obedience to it. The Reformed theologians, on the other hand, considered that Christ, by virtue of his human existence, was bound to keep the law, but they insisted that no absolute separation could be made between his life and death to apportion his saving work altogether to the latter. The life of Christ was truly involved in the vicarious work. Thus could Francis Turretin declare that Christ's satisfaction must not be restricted to his passion but must be "extended to the active obedience whereby he perfectly fulfilled the law in his whole life."[5]

The second controversy concerned the extent of the atonement. The Lutherans, partly under the influence of Melanchthon, maintained that Christ died for all, although the benefits of the cross are restricted to those who actually believe. The Reformed theologians insisted upon a limited atonement: Christ died for the elect only. This seemed to them a logical outcome not only of the doctrine of election but also of the penal theory of the atonement.

For if Christ took on the penalty of all, then justice requires that all be pardoned.

Both Luther and Calvin coordinated the two principles of love and justice in the atonement. And as long as they were thus coordinated, an acceptable penal substitutionary doctrine could be elaborated. But in its development, the principle of love came to be subordinated to that of justice, and the theory left itself open to criticism. Thus, for example, Turretin and Quenstedt at an earlier date and Shedd and the Hodges at a later date elevated the principle of justice and worked out the penal theory in virtual exclusive relation thereto.

Francis Turretin

Turretin begins his consideration of the atonement by presenting various proofs for its absolute necessity. He specifies the need of humanity, the sanction of the law, and the preaching of the gospel which "announces the violent and painful death of the Mediator and Surety on the cross" (p. 27). But he puts first, as the most cogent, "the vindicatory justice of God." Such an attribute is "natural and necessary" to God. "This avenging justice belongs to God as judge, and he can no more dispense with it than he can cease to be judge or deny himself. . . . This justice is the constant will of punishing sinners, which in God cannot be inefficient, and his majesty is supreme and his power infinite. And hence the infliction of punishment upon the transgressor or his surety is inevitable" (p. 25).

With this promise, Turretin sets out to establish the penal doctrine of the atonement as satisfying the divine justice. He adduces the biblical passages that relate our redemption to the price of Christ's blood to show "that a satisfaction in its true and proper sense has been made, since price always has reference to distributive justice" (p. 33). Christ bore our

sins and our sins were laid on him: "none of these could be said, unless Christ took upon himself and suffered the punishment of sin" (p. 39). Thus does Turretin regard Christ's punishment as an act of justice. Punishment, he argues, must necessarily be inflicted impersonally on every sin, but not at once personally on every sinner. For in a singular act God has exempted from such punishment those for whom a substitute has been found. Since Christ was made a curse and made sin for us, Turretin asks, "Is it not most evident that there was a real substitution of Christ in our room; and that in consequence of this substitution, a real satisfaction, expiation or atonement has been made, and that this is the doctrine taught by these Scriptural phrases?" (p. 43). Christ has paid the full price of our redemption by experiencing in himself, for us, the wrath of God, the curse of the law, and the penalties of hell. And God's approval of his Son's person and vindication of his work declare that his atoning deed is perfect and complete. "Unless Christ has satisfied to the uttermost, can we believe that God the judge, whose inexorable justice demands full payment, would have freed him, and exalted him to the supreme glory, which was the reward of his sufferings?" (p. 71).

Quenstedt likewise declares that "the form, or formal reason, of the satisfaction rendered by [Christ] consists in that most exact and sufficient payment of all those things which we owed. For our debt, which Christ our Mediator freely took to himself, and which was imputed to him by the divine judgment, he, in time, fully paid" (De Christi Offico, 1.38).

W. G. T. Shedd

Shedd is emphatic that "the eternal Judge may or may not exercise mercy, but he must exercise justice." The divine wrath is a necessity of God's pure essence in its antagonism against evil, whereas his love or benevolence, by contrast, issues from his voluntary disposition. It is therefore primarily in relation to God's justice that the atonement must be expounded. Thus, in his *Dogmatic Theology* Shedd represents the atonement of Christ as vicarious: "the satisfaction of justice intended and accomplished by it is for others, not for himself."[6] In Shedd's reckoning, *"Vicariousness implies substitution"* (p. 382). He distinguishes sharply between personal and vicarious atonement and says that the former, in contrast with the latter, is made by the offending party and is incompatible with mercy. "Vicarious atonement in the Christian system is made by the *offended* party" — by God, against whom sin is committed. It was God who made atonement, because no creature could perform so high a task. And although the essence of God is incapable of suffering by any external means, for "nothing in the created universe can make God feel pain or misery," yet "it does not follow that God cannot *himself* do an act which he feels to be a sacrifice of feeling and affection" (p. 382). In giving up his Son to humiliation and death, God was not unaffected by the act.

Atonement is necessary to forgiveness and is thus "objective in its essential nature" (p. 393). Also were the sufferings of Christ *"penal* in their nature and intent." They met the demands of justice and the reality of God's wrath. "They were judicial infliction voluntarily endured by Christ, for the purpose of satisfying the claims of law due from man; and this *purpose* makes them penal" (p. 457). Shedd, in fact, equates atonement and punishment as "kindred in meaning. Both denote judicial suffering" (p. 458). And Christ's sufferings are of "infinite value." "In the substitute, the amount is fully equal to that of the original penalty. The worth of any suffering is determined by the *total subject* who suffers, not by the particular nature in the subject which is the seat of the suffering" (p. 459).

THE POTENCY OF DIVINE ACTION

Friedrich Schleiermacher

Schleiermacher has been universally recognized as pioneering the modern era of theology. He is, says R. S. Franks, "deservedly called the father of modern theology."[7] He it was, agrees Emil Brunner, "who blazed the trail for the theological thought of the nineteenth century."[8] His *Christliche Glaube* (*The Christian Faith*, 1821) is a full-scale systematic theology which, according to H. R. Mackintosh, "next to the *Institutes* of Calvin, . . . is the most influential dogmatic work to which evangelical Protestantism can point, and it has helped to teach theology to more than three generations."[9] These, and many like enthusiastic verdicts, compel that some reference to his views cannot be passed over in any historical account of the atonement.

Schleiermacher first established a hearing for himself by the publication of his *Reden (Speeches)* in 1799, which comprise a series of addresses on religion "to its Cultured Despisers." In these Schleiermacher sought to call people to a religious view of the world by awakening those religious feelings they would surely find within themselves. It was Schleiermacher's basic thesis that an awareness of the spiritual nature of reality is native to the human spirit. Thus did he renounce the intellectualism of the Enlightenment and contend instead for the feelings as the organ of religious apprehension. His total rejection of the use of reason and the place of knowledge in religion pervades the speeches. Dogmas and propositions, he asserts, have no home therein, and ideas and principles are all foreign. Religion, in a word, is a matter of the heart, not of the head; of the feelings, not of the mind. Schleiermacher consequently conceives of religion as the soul's direct contact with the divine. It is an immediate, self-conscious awareness of one's unity with, and dependence on, the divinity which is at the heart of things. For all existence is instinct with the divine. In Schleiermacher, then, romanticism comes into top gear and finds expression in terms of "theological" pantheism, of which the absolute idealism of Hegel, whom Schleiermacher was instrumental in bringing to the new University of Berlin where he was himself professor of theology, was the philosophical counterpart.

For Schleiermacher, then, God is near, is here, is everywhere. He is within us — within all of us. We have used the pronoun *he*, but we are hardly sure of its correctness in reference to Schleiermacher's God. For him God is hardly personal, cannot really be contemplated objectively, and is seemingly not to be disassociated from the pious feelings of the "spirituality" of reality. Thus for Schleiermacher doctrines about God are one and the same with descriptions of one's native religious feelings. In the thought of Schleiermacher, God appears more as an all-pervasive Absolute than as a personal being.

In this context of ideas the speeches announce humanity's redemption as the stimulation of his feeling of awareness of all finite things in and through the Infinite and all temporal things in and through the Eternal. Herein is the essence of religion and the purpose, the hope, and the desire of all religion that make for its fundamental oneness despite its manifold expressions. And the Redeemer figure in any religion is he who was first and foremost in its bringing about in humans their consciousness of absolute dependence on that divinity which shapes our ends. Thus Christ is not the only redeemer of humanity but also the *primus inter pares*, the "sublime" and "most glorious of all that have yet appeared." He is, indeed, the highest representative of religious piety, the archetype of the truly religious person.

Against this background and with these convictions, Schleiermacher approached his systematic presentation in *The Christian Faith.* For him the method of a Christian dogmatic is

the summation of religious feelings, and its content the idea of redemption as the governing thought of its every subject. On the first of these features he is emphatic that "Christian doctrines are accounts of the Christian religious affections set forth in speech."[10] As in the speeches, so here: it is the feelings that are regarded as the way and ground of humanity's religious relation to God. The basis of all religion is neither knowledge nor will but specifically that continuum of feeling, that intuitive awareness that is called self-consciousness. The method of a dogmatic is to appeal to experience first and to Scripture last. Of the religious awareness both Scripture and ecclesiastical dogma are alike formulations, only the doctrine of Scripture is more poetical and rhetorical, while dogmatic theology is more didactic and scientific. By the descriptive analysis of experience, Schleiermacher believes that he not only holds the key to an understanding of religion qua religion but that he also possesses the sole criterion to assess past creedal statements and the means by which to make Christian faith acceptable to modern persons. Therefore, he affirms, "in our exposition all doctrines properly so called must be extracted from the Christian religious self-consciousness, i.e., the inward experience of Christian people" (p. 265).

The distinctive mark of Christianity, that which sets it apart from and elevates it above all other expressions of the religious spirit, is its emphasis on humanity's redemption and its relation to Jesus of Nazareth. But why the need for such redemption? And how does Jesus come into the experience of it? For answers to these questions we must seek Schleiermacher's views of sin and Christ's saving work.

It may be asserted right away that Schleiermacher's doctrine of sin has the merit of being eminently clear but the demerit of being preeminently shallow. Sin in the individual, according to Schleiermacher, is at once a personal and corporate act. We are conscious of sin "partly as having its source in ourselves, partly as having its source outside our own being" (p. 283).

Regarding sin as a personal act, Schleiermacher finds the cause for its presence in the individual in the conflict between spirit and flesh. Spirit, for Schleiermacher, is conceived to be an inherent God-consciousness native to every person, whereas flesh is the animal side of human nature. When awakened, this God-consciousness comes into conflict with humanity's lower nature. By reason of human development, however, the flesh has the start, so that the spirit enters the battle under heavy handicaps. In the ensuing struggle the spirit seeks to control the flesh, while the flesh resists being controlled by the spirit. This conflict between the existing flesh and the awakened God-consciousness, according to Schleiermacher, is a fact of universal experience: "in each individual the flesh manifests itself as a reality before the spirit comes to be such, the result being, that, as soon as the spirit enters the sphere of consciousness (and it is involved in the original perfection of man that the independent activity of the flesh cannot of itself prevent the ingress of the spirit), resistance takes place, i.e., we become conscious also of sin as the God-consciousness awakes within us" (p. 274). Sin is then the self-activity of the sense-life which is not yet controlled by the spirit. It is present in human life in the measure in which that life has not yet attained spirit; sin is "an arrestation of the determinative power of the spirit, due to the independence of the sensuous functions." Thus does the awareness of sin arise in relation to the God-consciousness. "We are conscious of sin as the power and work of a time when the disposition to the God-consciousness had not yet actively emerged in us" (p. 273).

Sin does, however, Schleiermacher allows, have a radical influence on humans. As a personal, deliberate, self-chosen act, it disturbs human nature and produces in humans the inability for goodness that is their need for

"redemption." But this does not prevent Mackintosh from declaring that Schleiermacher "seems on the brink of defining sin as the relic of the brute in man, and therefore no more than something 'not yet' spiritualized."[11] The logical result of such a view of sin is that it can be overcome by ignoring the activities of the sense-life. Evil must disappear in proportion as the God-consciousness increases.

Yet Schleiermacher affirms his belief in the doctrine of original sin by his statement that in all people actual sin is its consequence (pp. 281ff.). Original sin exists prior to any action of the individual's own and has its origin outside the person. There is nonetheless no creative relation between the primal sin of our first parents and our own. Sin arose in Adam from the conditions of his human existence, but it did not effect any change in his fundamental nature. The sin of our first parents was, in truth, but "a single and trivial event" (pp. 291, 302). Yet, like a pebble that causes ripples on the pond, so did the first sin introduce a disturbing element into human conditions, which every new individual's sinful acts only serve to widen and increase. Original sin thus exists as "the corporate act of the human race" (p. 300). It is "in each the work of all, and in all the work of each, . . . for the sinfulness of each points to the sinfulness of all alike in space and time, and also goes to condition that totality both around him and after him" (p. 288).

Thus sin exists as, so to speak, the social context within which individuals begin the unequal struggle to free their God-consciousness from the hindrances of their lower nature. "There is a common life of sin, due to the interaction of individuals one upon another, and transmitted as a social tradition from the past."[12] As with original sin, so it is with personal guilt of everyone who shares in it: "it is best represented as the corporate act and the corporate guilt of the human race, and . . . the recognition of it as such is likewise recognition of the universal need of redemption" (p. 285).

But how is this redemption made available to humanity in Christian faith? The question opens up a consideration of Christ's work as Redeemer of humanity. Schleiermacher is, of course, committed to the proposition that in the Christian faith the human sinful condition is answered by Christ. Accordingly his view of Christ's person and work is matched by his view of human sin and need. Sin exists for humans rather than for God. It neither calls out God's wrath nor causes God to withhold active love. Yet God appoints that men and women should have a consciousness of it so as to feel their need of redemption. God works in us the sense of sin and guilt to spur us on to the pursuit of the good, although for God neither sin nor guilt has real existence. Such a view of humanity's sin in relation to God does not require for human redemption a person of Christ essentially divine nor a work of Christ absolutely atoning. Thus does Schleiermacher regard Christ as the one historic person in whom God chose to be present in fullest measure and in whom the God-consciousness was uppermost from the first and so remained. "The Redeemer, then, is like all men in virtue of the identity of human nature, but distinguished from them all by the constant potency of his God-consciousness, which was a veritable existence of God in Him" (p. 385).

It is this "potency of his God-consciousness" that Christ communicates to humans, and therein is their redemption. "The Redeemer assumes believers into the power of his God-consciousness, and this is His redemptive activity" (p. 425). Further on Schleiermacher says, "the Redeemer assumes the believers into the fellowship of his unclouded blessedness, and this is His reconciliating activity" (p. 431). For Schleiermacher, then, the work of Christ is his redeeming and reconciling activity. The redeeming aspect comes first as the calling into action, under the stimulus of Christ's absolute God-consciousness, of our own God-consciousness. His activity as Redeemer is thus the energizing action of his own unclouded

God-consciousness. It is through his redeeming activity that there is reconciliation. As the God-consciousness is stimulated by the living interests of Christ, there is born in us the feeling of our reconciliation with God despite our sin. "Hence, just as the redemptive activity of Christ brings about for all believers a corporate activity corresponding to the being of God in Christ, so the reconciling element, that is, the blessedness of the being of God in Him, brings about for all believers, as for each separately, a corporate feeling of blessedness" (p. 433).

Schleiermacher goes on to work out the threefold offices of Christ — the prophetic, the priestly, and the kingly — which had become popular in Protestant theology. Throughout all his exposition he remains true to his fundamental thesis that Christ's significance for humans is that of the source of their spiritual life, bringing about in them the triumph of spirit over flesh through the energy of his own dominant God-awareness. But what part does the cross play in this scheme for humanity's redemption and reconciliation? The true answer is, not much. In his exposition of both these doctrines, the sufferings of Christ have no mention. Schleiermacher seems studiously to avoid reference to the word *atonement*. In fact, he emphatically characterizes as "magical" the views that make the forgiveness of sins "to depend upon the punishment which Christ suffered," and the blessedness of humans be seen "as a reward which God offers to Christ for the suffering of that punishment" (p. 435). Yet he grants that some connection between the forgiveness of sins and the sufferings of Christ cannot be denied. They can, indeed, be regarded as vicarious in that they result from his sympathy with sinners and are a consequence of his entry into the human situation, wherein he shared with humanity in the nexus of social evils due to humanity's choosing to live after the flesh and not after the spirit. Thus while Christ's sufferings and death are in no way penal, nor do they provide in any sense an objective expiation, they are necessary so as to initiate humankind into the utmost possibility of sympathy. Without the sufferings and death, no assumption into the vital fellowship with Christ that makes redemption and reconciliation intelligible would have been possible. His sufferings had their climax in sympathy. And, considered historically, his death was the natural conclusion of his mission. But both his sufferings and death, when considered morally and ethically, exhibit the steadfastness of Christ's God-consciousness over against sin. Spiritually they reveal his complete entry into sympathy with erring humanity. Thus Christ is for us not truly a vicarious satisfaction but a vicarious representative.

Here is a subjective view of the work of Christ that fails altogether to accord to his death any objective significance for humanity's salvation. Schleiermacher reverses the proper order of the relationship between redemption and reconciliation so as to make humanity's restoration dependent on renewal. "If therefore," he says, "we think of the activity of the Redeemer as an influence upon the individual, we can only allow the reconciling moment to follow, and out of, the redeeming moment." This is certainly the relationship if the work of Christ is read in terms of influence. And on this point Schleiermacher is emphatic: he teaches that "the spontaneity of the new corporate life" has "its relation to the Redeemer" in virtue of its susceptibility to his influence (see pp. 477-78). He has maintained that Christ fulfilled God's will by the flowering in him of the absolute potency of his God-consciousness. But he forbids us saying that he fulfilled the divine will in our place, much less that in our stead he bore the judgment of God on our sins. Christ's chief work was to inspire in humans the desire and effort to fulfill God's will. Thus does Christ's redeeming work consist in administering a tonic to the spiritually enfeebled rather than, as the New Testament teaches, making an atonement for the sinfully helpless.

The idea of the work of Christ as the stimulation of the God-consciousness in hu-manity by the potency of his own absolute God-awareness has the result that "the nearer the Christian comes to this state the more unnecessary does Christ become to him. If he is really taken up into the absolutely potent God-consciousness, then he becomes an ideal (archetype) like Christ and needs Christ no longer."[13] Besides, since sin has no effect on God, the question of Christ's work in removing sin's guilt does not arise. Schleiermacher has in fact little to say regarding the forgiveness of sins, and for him the reality of guilt consequent upon the recognition that sin is against God is nonexistent. Moreover, he dismisses the wrath of God as an "obscure illusion." The result is that justification becomes for Schleiermacher but another way of declaring for the subjective echo within us of the beginnings of redemption. It is one and the same as the regenerative change to be detected in ourselves by the impartation to us of Christ's own God-consciousness. Schleiermacher's idea of reconciliation is not therefore concerned with the removal of the consciousness of guilt but with the removal of the sense of evil around and within us. In the end, the view of Christ's work presented by Schleiermacher is quite other than that given to us in the New Testament. There the cross is central in the gospel of redemption. There is revealed Christ, Son of man and Son of God, suffering for human sin and bearing the load of human guilt. There from Golgotha's hill is heard the voice of God speaking his word of forgiveness to humanity.

CONTEMPORARY VIEWS

Karl Barth

Nothing need be said here about the tremendous influence of Barth on recent theology. His multivolumed *Church Dogmatics* is witness enough to the breadth and depth of his thought. Not least among his contributions has been his refocusing theology on God rather than on humans. Volume 4 of his *Church Dogmatics,* entitled *The Doctrine of Reconciliation,* shows how profoundly he conceived of Christ's work as God's act for humanity's salvation. Yet he does not propound any specific doctrine of the atonement. For Barth, God's acts are so superlatively divine as to put them beyond the neat formulations of human reasoning. Thus is the atonement at once mystery and miracle. Yet there is "in the temporal happening of atonement God's eternal covenant with man, His eternal choice of this creature, His eternal faithfulness to Himself and to it."[14]

Barth stresses that the whole event of Christ constitutes the atonement: the history of Jesus Christ is the history of atonement. "Jesus Christ exists in the totality of His work as the Mediator. He alone is the One who fulfils it, but He does completely fulfil it" (IV/1: 124). Therefore we have peace with God on the sole basis of the grace of God as "the coming of God to man which is grounded only in itself and can be known only by itself, the taking place of the atonement willed and accomplished by Him." Thus "the atonement made in Jesus Christ will be seen to be wholly an act of the grace of God and therefore an act of sovereignty which cannot be understood in all its profundity except from the fact that God is this God and a God of this kind." Since it is such an act of the divine sovereignty, "we are forbidden to try to deduce it from anything else or to deduce anything else from it. But above all we are commanded to accept and acknowledge it in all its inconceivability as something that has happened, taking it strictly as it is without thinking round it or over it" (IV/1: 80-81). At the same time, the cross is so central for Barth in the Christian message that everything else shines in its light and is illuminated by it.

While Barth has eschewed attempts to set forth a logical and coherent theory of the atonement, he does stress some aspects of what was accomplished by God's atoning act in Christ. He gives special emphasis to the idea of Christ's victory over the demonic adversaries of humanity, both personal and cosmic.[15] And throughout he shows affinities with Anselm's satisfaction view: Christ bore the penalty of humanity's sin in his total selfhood, human and divine; both concur to make effective Christ's work. There is a judicial note in the statement that "He has therefore suffered for all men what they had to suffer: their end as evil-doers; their overthrow as the enemies of God; their extirpation in virtue of the superiority of the divine right over their wrong" (IV/1: 552-53). Barth can declare also that Jesus Christ "has not only borne man's enmity against God's grace, revealing it in all its depth. He has borne the far greater burden, the righteous wrath of God against those who are enemies of His grace, the wrath which must fall on us" (II/1: 152). "In His own Word made flesh, God hears that satisfaction has been done to His righteousness, that the consequences of human sin have been borne and expiated, and therefore that they have been taken away from man — the man for whose sake Jesus Christ intervened" (II/1: 403).

G. C. Berkouwer

Berkouwer's *The Work of Christ* is, like other volumes in his Studies in Dogmatics series, a vigorous defense of the historic Reformed doctrine in relation to recent and contemporary criticism and contrary ideas. Three basic presuppositions for his understanding of the redeeming activity of Christ are secured at the beginning. First, there is recognition of a variety of emphases on the subject of Christ's work in the several New Testament books. At the same time it is insisted that "in this variation there is the harmony of one, multilateral work."[16] Historical theologies Berkouwer judges to have failed insofar as they have given exclusive stress to one aspect of Christ's rich and many-sided mediatorial act. Yet he will not himself be so much biblicistic that he must neglect the light the church has accumulated on the subject over past ages.

Berkouwer's second presupposition is that the fullest account must be given to the interrelation of Christ's person and work. It is impossible, he declares categorically, to separate his person and his work. Indeed, to mention his name is in the same breath to mention his work. For theology and for proclamation, the two cannot be finally separated. All Christ's gifts are one in himself. "No more than the object may be an abstract ontological interest in Christ's person, may his work, his Word, his influence, as such, be the source of any truly Christian faith" (p. 20).

The third basic premise of Berkouwer's teaching on the work of Christ is his insistence on the soteriological purpose of the incarnation. He vigorously defends the hamartiologic or hamartiocentric conception — that it was only because of sin that the Word became flesh. The idea that the incarnation would have taken place even if there had been no fall of humanity must give to the atonement a mere post hoc aspect, having only a contingent and relative relation to human sin. Berkouwer contends rather for the exclusively soteriological framework of Christ's coming into the world. The upshot of the view that there would have been an incarnation of God in Christ even had humanity not sinned has led to a "mankind christology" and to the deification of humanity characteristic or Enlightenment-oriented theologies. Rightly to conceive of the incarnation is to see it "not as a thing by itself; it preaches not the *elevatio* of human nature but its *deliverance* and *restoration* by him whom the Father had sent" (p. 29). The Christmas event is no mere "Immanuel idea"; it is associated from the first with the salvation of God. The Messiah "being sent and his coming are unto *salvation and deliverance*" (p. 30).

Berkouwer affirms later that those who isolate the incarnation not only make Christ's redemptive work a mere incidental reaction in the midst of the course of history but go on to declare the event itself a "natural" affair. They thus denude Bethlehem of its wonder and its mystery and deny Christ's miraculous birth, and the depth of its mystery is lost to the natural person in the poverty of the occasion. Yet God's "activity is so evident [to faith's apprehension] in the birth of Christ that it surpasses every human standard; every human construction is overtaken by the testimony concerning what took place here (Luke 2:15)." "Faith alone is able to understand the miracle, not as an incidental and miraculous 'appearance' but as incarnation, as the beginning of a way (cf. Luke 1:76)" (p. 94). For "Christ's birth is entirely unique; it is the *mystery* of the incarnation" (p. 133). Thus "Immanuel's coming is integral to the prospect of salvation" (pp. 33-34).

His coming was a real condescension, a humiliation to the darkness and suffering of the cross that was to issue in his exaltation, which together are uniquely connected in the redemptive act. "Not selected parts of Christ's life but the totality of his humiliation and exaltation is incorporated and passed on in the *kerygma.*" The whole succession of events from the cradle to the throne determines the caesura of Christ's work. "In this caesura salvation becomes historical reality for all times" (p. 39). And this humiliation and this exaltation are themselves, as surely and certainly as is the cross, historical realities and not just associated mythologies. The exaltation follows the humiliation and is intimately connected with it. Thus "Christ's exaltation cannot be understood apart from his work 'for us.' The exaltation is also soteriological" (p. 56).

Noting the dangers of the application of the concept of office to Christ's work — schematization and scholasticism, and removing Christ to a distance from us — Berkouwer thinks nevertheless that his threefold office of prophet, priest, and king is not inappropriate. "His office does not conflict with the *personal* qualities of his life's work. He himself is the living reality *in* the fulfilment of his office" (p. 59). Therefore, "Christology does not speak of the threefold office because it wishes to force the work of Christ into a special scheme, but because of the testimony of Scripture" (p. 65). To separate sharply, however, the offices, and to make one the major if not indeed the exclusive feature of Christ's work, is to give both his person and his work a false perspective. In fact, any one office itself loses its real significance when separated from its integral relationship in its essential threefoldness. "The reality of this *munus triplex* is based on the Father's commission to the mediatorial task, and this task is by no means terminated with Christ's exaltation, according to Scripture" (p. 76).

The Apostles' Creed follows the affirmation of Christ's conception by the Holy Spirit with reference to the fact that he suffered. This allusion, Berkouwer declares, is intended to focus on what Christ suffered as having a significance other than that he participated in the general suffering of humanity, or that in his case it was a fate altogether undeserved, he being innocent himself of any punishable offense. In harmony with Scripture, however, Berkouwer affirms that though Christ was himself personally sinless, yet he did in himself bear humanity's guilt. On this account he suffered and "therein and thereby God's wrath and condemnation descended upon him who, although innocent, but as the Mediator and the Lamb of God, was burdened with our guilt and thus condemned" (p. 139). The sufferings he endured were certainly brought about by humans, but their inner and divine purpose was realized in God's action for humanity. Therein lies the mystery of the cross. In his sufferings Jesus was fully aware of "God's activity in and through the suffering which men inflict upon

him" (p. 143). And such sufferings were unto the full measure of God's utmost judgment upon sin — to the last agony of death and the final reality of hell, and to a real God-forsakeness, "by which he as the Mediator bore the guilt of sin." Thus were his sufferings specifically substitutionary (p. 178; cf. pp. 289, 302ff.).

In the concluding section of his book, under the heading "Aspects of the Work of Christ," Berkouwer tries, he says, "to catch some glimpses of the light which Scripture sheds on Christ's work by discussing its teaching under the following headings: (a) Reconciliation; (b) Sacrifice; (c) Obedience; (d) Victory" (p. 254).

He gives the largest space by far to the concept of reconciliation, in an effort to clarify its several overtones and rebut its weakened connotation in some contemporary theologies. For himself, "access and boldness, peace and trust are of the essence of the *katallagē*" (p. 255). Since, however, the reconciliation has its initiative with God, it was not effected to bring about in him a change of mind occasioned by the Son's intervention. At the same time Christ's reconciling work has reference to the wrath of God, but not in any patripassian sense. It is not a case of God, so to speak, expressing revulsion against sin and internally overcoming anger at its sheer awfulness: the wrath of God against sin was real indeed, and was given objective expression in the cross of Christ. There is no sharp dilemma between salvation as God's initiative and the "placating" of God's wrath in the suffering of Christ. That is to say, there is no ultimate antagonism between God's love, which is the cause of humanity's reconciliation, and the cross, in which God's righteous anger against human sin is satisfied. These realities, seemingly contradictory, have their ultimate resolution in the unfathomable mystery of God. Yet this final fact of mystery illumines in some measure our reconciliation to God in the deed of the cross.

The mystery of reconciliation is such that we cannot approach it by saying that God's justice was satisfied *beforehand* in order that the doors of grace might be opened; rather, there is a mysterious harmony between God's love *from eternity* and Christ, whom he appointed as the means of reconciliation. . . . In the cross of Christ God's justice and love are *simultaneously* revealed, so that we can speak of his love only in connection with this reality of the cross. For this reason we speak of a mystery: not a mystery in general, but the mystery of reconciliation. (Pp. 277-78)

Giving less space to the concepts of sacrifice, obedience, and victory as biblical aspects of the one many-sided work of Christ, Berkouwer wants each to be taken in a literal and not in a metaphorical sense. He denies, for example, that the sacrifice idea is a mere analogy to the idea of self-surrender. In line with the epistle to the Hebrews, he insists that "this High Priest does not have to offer for himself first; the power of his sacrifice is manifest in the fact that he truly bears and consequently puts away sin" (p. 299). Although the New Testament statements concerning Christ's sacrifice do not furnish a systematic exposition of his work, as is the case for all the other aspects, "there is nevertheless harmony in the one, central message concerning the sacrifice 'for us' wherein he bears our sins as the Substitute. Thereby Christ has revealed historically the meaning and joy of the entire Old Testament sacrificial cult, so that his sacrifice provides salvation for all time" (p. 302).

Allied to the idea of sacrifice is, then, that of substitution. it is not a case here of either/or but of both/and. As it is with Christ's sacrifice on our behalf, so it is with his substitution in our stead: "the doctrine of substitution is based squarely on the teaching of Scripture" (p. 309).

Berkouwer's understanding of Christ's obedience (Phil. 2:8; Heb. 5:8; cf. Rom. 5:19) is a no less scriptural view of his work. Christ's

life, first and last, from its beginning through to its ending, was an act of loving submission to his Father's will in fulfillment of the divine work he had come to do. "Christ's obedience comprises not simply a part of his life, but the totality of his Messianic work" (p. 316). Berkouwer allows the distinction between Christ's active and passive obedience — not as two distinct and separate types but in the sense suggested by Bavinck, whom he quotes: "the active obedience is not an outward addition to the passive, nor vice versa. Not one single act and not one single incident in the life or suffering of Christ can be said to belong exclusively to the one or the other" (p. 321). Neither will Berkouwer have either aspect denied, although he is sensitive that in maintaining the distinction there is danger of dividing Christ's work into two "parts" (p. 327).

The concluding fourteen pages of Berkouwer's book consider the work of Christ under the aspect of victory. He allows that there are passages of Scripture that support Aulén's presentation of the work of Christ in the terms of *Christus Victor,* but he maintains that Aulén's exclusive use of this category gives a limited and less profound picture of Christ's work in that "the *Christus Victor* theme carries with it the temptation to secularize Christ's triumph by lifting it out of its rich scriptural contexts" (p. 339). Nevertheless, there is a truth in the view: "his power and victory are unique because they are the victorious power of reconciliation and mercy in the way of his suffering and death" (p. 335). Because "Christ's triumph is wholly unique, so, too, is the believer's victory" (p. 341).

There is no doubt about the strength of Berkouwer's doctrine of the work of Christ. In the fullness of all that Christ came to accomplish, there is an abundant salvation open to all who in faith apprehend his saving benefits. Berkouwer has well stated the "thatness" of Christ's redeeming action; of the "howness" he is less clear. To his credit it should be remembered that he eschewed the idea that the work of Christ can be given formal statement. He declares besides on not a few occasions that there is final mystery in the incarnation and the cross. His many digressions to tilt at opposing views tend to blur the clarity of his own positive exposition. It is not always easy to follow his path through the jungle.

NOTES

1. See "The Clarity and Certainty of the Word of God," "On the Lord's Supper," "The Forgiveness of Sins," and "Faith and Works" in Zwingli's *Exposition of Faith.*

2. See John F. Jansen, *Calvin's Doctrine of the Work of Christ* (London: J. Clarke, 1956).

3. Calvin, *Institutes of the Christian Religion,* 2 vols., trans. Henry Beveridge (Edinburgh: Calvin Translation Society, 1854), 2.16.5. Subsequent references to this work will be made parenthetically in the text.

4. Jaroslav Pelikan, *The Christian Tradition: A History of the Development of Doctrine,* 5 vols. (Chicago: University of Chicago Press, 1971-89), 2: 293.

5. Turretin, *Institutio Theologiae Elencticae* L.14, Q.13. His full statement on the work of Christ can be found in *Turretin on the Atonement of Christ,* trans. J. R. Willson (Grand Rapids: Baker Book House, 1978). Subsequent references to this work will be made parenthetically in the text.

6. Shedd, *Dogmatic Theology,* 3 vols. (New York: Scribner's, 1888-94), 2: 378. Subsequent references to this work will be made parenthetically in the text.

7. Franks, *The Work of Christ: A Historical Study of Christian Doctrine* (New York: Nelson, 1962), p. 533.

8. Brunner, *The Mediator: A Study of the Central Doctrine of the Christian Faith,* trans. Olive Wyon (New York: Macmillan, 1934), p. 47.

9. Mackintosh, *Types of Modern Theology: Schleiermacher to Barth* (New York: Scribner's, 1958), p. 60.

10. Schleiermacher, *The Christian Faith,* ed. H. R. Mackintosh and J. S. Stewart (Edinburgh: T. & T. Clark, 1928), p. 76. Subsequent references to this text will be made parenthetically in the text.

11. Mackintosh, *Types of Modern Theology,* p. 83.

12. Franks, *Work of Christ,* p. 537.

13. Brunner, *The Mediator,* p. 92.

14. Barth, *Church Dogmatics,* 4 vols., ed. Geoffrey W. Bromiley and Thomas F. Torrance (Edinburgh: T. & T. Clark, 1936-69), IV/1: 80. Subsequent references to this text will be made parenthetically in the text.

15. On this, see Donald G. Bloesch, *Jesus Is Victor! Karl Barth's Doctrine of Salvation* (Nashville: Abingdon Press, 1967), pp. 24ff., 41ff.

16. Berkouwer, *The Work of Christ,* Studies in Dogmatics, trans. Cornelius Lambregste (Grand Rapids: William B. Eerdmans, 1965), p. 12. Subsequent references to this text will be made parenthetically in the text.

Justification by Faith in the Reformed Confessions

G. C. Berkouwer

As we turn to our subject, we are conscious of entering a field on which theologians have engaged each other in dispute almost perpetually since the early days of the church. The struggles with Pelagianism and semi-Pelagianism, with Rome and the Remonstrants are all concerned with the relation between faith and justification. Strange, though, that so much hostility should be kindled at this point. Surely here we could expect, at least among those who accept the authority of Scripture over their thought and confession, a universal and profound accord. For the Scriptures speak about justification through faith with the utmost clarity: "being therefore justified by faith, we have peace with God through our Lord Jesus Christ" (Rom. 5:1). And again, "we reckon therefore that a man is justified by faith apart from the works of the law" (Rom. 3:28).

Further reflection, however, suggests that even where the phrase *justified by faith* is not rejected in so many words, it has been given interpretations that were sure to be contested. An example of this is the attitude of the Roman Church toward *sola fide* and *sola gratia*. The Roman Church, claims one of its theologians, accepts both of these as unreservedly as did Paul and the Reformers.[1] Such a claim prods us on to a more careful study of the relationship between faith and justification as understood in various quarters, especially since Roman Catholic theologians today are insisting with more than usual persistency that the religious motive of the Reformation is fully honored by the Roman Church. This, they say, is the gratifying part of the drama of the great schism. Of course, they recognize differences; the Roman view is often presented as somewhat more complicated, while that of Protestantism is set up as the product of oversimplification. But, at any rate, it is suggested that Rome and the Reformation had more in common than both realized.

Reprinted from *Faith and Justification*, trans. Lewis B. Smedes (Grand Rapids: William B. Eerdmans, 1954), pp. 39-57.

Given this situation, it will be most useful if we begin by surveying the fields where the struggle over *sola fide* has, for the most part, been waged. We shall address ourselves, to this end, to a few of the confessions of the churches of the Reformation. Needless to say, this does not mean that the confessions are absolutely decisive. They themselves arise from the conviction that we can and may speak only as we put ourselves under the yoke of Scripture. Our reflection, too, and for the same reason, must proceed in the train of Scripture. But we can hardly circumvent that bitterest of all struggles for a pure understanding of the gospel, the Reformation of the sixteenth century. It was then as at no other time that justification through faith was trumpeted as the article with which the church stands or falls. *Sola fide* was not presented as a discrete aspect or section of the confession. It embraced the whole gospel. And this conviction is reflected in a number of Reformed and Lutheran confessions.

* * * * *

The Heidelberg Catechism, after it has presented the Apostles' Creed, asks what the *profit* of all this really is. It had already turned this keen, practical edge to each of the various individual articles: Christ's holy conception and birth (Q. 36), his sacrifice (Q. 43), his resurrection (Q. 45) and ascension (Q. 49), and the glorification of our Head, the Christ (Q. 51). It asked, furthermore, about the *comfort* of the doctrine of the resurrection of the body (Q. 57) and Christ's return (Q. 52). In concrete fashion, thus, the significance to the believer of God's mystery of salvation in Jesus Christ was brought to the foreground.

Finally, in Lord's Day 23, the question is put: "But what does it profit you now that you *believe all this?*" The answer, which is related to the whole of faith and its content, is: "That I am righteous in Christ before God, and an heir to eternal life." Faith has intense relevance

to this "profit," this benefit with which the Catechism is so warmly concerned. Faith is not a reasonable acceptance of certain truths, after which it can be set aside for the immediate practical affairs of the day. Through faith humans participate in reality — a comforting reality, to be sure — and in a perspective of an eternal future.

The phrase *in Christ* is included in the declaration of personal justification. We are, as it were, conducted into a court of law to hear a merciful declaration of pardon. But the answer displays to us the unique character of this declaration. The accusation was not without grounds; it was secured by incontrovertible facts. The offense that had to be judged was the reality of great sin against God. And this was not something brought up out of a hazy past; the accused is still set for a plunge into the worst of evil. This is all so irrefutable that the sinner can do nothing but admit the justness of the charge.

There would seem to be no possibility of acquittal. But there is an unparalleled counterbalance to the reality of guilt. Christ Jesus is confessed: he has satisfied; he makes good the righteousness, justice, and holiness; and he is the cause of the pardon. He is the surprise of God's unexpected salvation from the just accusation that still is being brought against us. The impossible has here become undoubted reality. The result is an electrifying and truly incomparable judgment of pardon. The doors swing open; the soft lights of the new freedom are shed over our whole future — we are heirs of eternal life.

It is in this connection that faith is mentioned, qualified by the word *alone:* justification is through faith alone. We are now miles away from a cooperation between divine salvation and the human work of faith. For this faith is directed exclusively to Christ, in the recognition that his righteousness and his acts alone could create the amazing situation in which a person can say: "God, without any merit of mine, of mere grace, grants and imputes to me the perfect satisfaction, righteousness, and holiness of Christ, as if I had never had nor committed any sin, and myself had accomplished all the obedience which Christ has rendered for me" (Lord's Day 23). Notice the phrase *as if*. It suggests, perhaps, that we are being told of a fiction, an illusion, a pretense. It recalls the so-called "As if" philosophy of Hans Vaihinger, who tried to demonstrate the great significance of the fictitious for the various sciences.

But this "as if" of the Catechism has to do with far more than a fiction. There is, indeed, an element of analogy, for we have not in reality performed this obedience. We have certainly sinned and are certainly sinners. We were in fact disobedient and slaves of sin. But the creative force of Christ's righteousness is so good and so tender and so miraculous that the new situation can be sketched in terms like the Catechism's "as if." The reality of our performance is not commensurate with the "as if" of the Catechism, and yet we are faced with the immeasurable blessing of Christ's work which is valid for eternity at God's judgment seat. Jesus Christ is the secret of the "as if."

He is its content. Therefore it is an accurate formulation of the message of divine justification. It finds its counterpart in Scripture: "Come now, and let us reason together, saith Jehovah: though your sins be as scarlet, they shall be white as snow; though they be red like crimson, they shall be as wool" (Isa. 1:18). "I, even I, am he that blotteth out thy transgressions for mine own sake; and I will not remember thy sins" (Isa. 43:25). "I have blotted out, as a thick cloud, thy transgressions, and, as a cloud, thy sins: return unto me; for I have redeemed thee" (Isa. 44:22). "Who is a God like unto thee, that pardoneth iniquity, and passeth over the transgression of the remnant of his heritage? He retaineth not his anger for ever, because he delighteth in lovingkindness. He will again have compassion upon us; he will

tread our iniquities under foot; and thou wilt cast all their sins into the depths of the sea" (Mic. 7:18, 19).

There is a striking commentary on the *quasi* of Lord's Day 23 in Zechariah 3, where Joshua the high priest, with Satan at his right hand, stands before the face of the angel of the Lord. Joshua, accused by Satan, wears a filthy robe, yet the accuser is turned away. "And Jehovah said unto Satan, Jehovah rebuke thee, O Satan; Salem rebuke thee: is not this a brand plucked out of the fire?" (Zech. 3:2). But there is a difference in Lord's Day 23; here the accuser is not Satan but our own conscience. The "as if" for this reason gets a unique color; it stands in bold relief against the drabness of our own stained conscience and confessed guilt.

Everything is really said in an unobtrusive phrase, *in Christ*. The possibility and reality of justification are concentrated in this one phrase. This appears most clearly in the manner in which faith is approached. It is not added as a second, independent ingredient which makes its own contribution to justification in Christ. On the contrary, faith does nothing but accept, or come to rest in the sovereignty of his benefit. Further, to ward off any misunderstanding, Lord's Day 23 declares, with a touch of emphasis, that we are not acceptable to God because of the worthiness of our faith. Grace is exclusively and totally God's; therefore, says the Catechism, we can do nothing else but accept it through faith (Q. 61). To walk the way of faith is simply to admit that Christ is the Way. These are the accents of the Reformation. Every conceivable fancy of merit in any human quality, position, or activity that might have been viewed as a cooperating cause of our justification before God is excluded. *Sola fide* and *sola gratia:* it is plain that they mean the same thing.

Christ is the one light that burns here. Faith sees nothing except in this Light. And this is the miracle of faith as the gift of God.

* * * * *

Though justification through faith gets special attention in Lord's Day 23, the same faith-reality is described elsewhere in the Catechism. This is most striking in Lord's Day 22, where the forgiveness of sins is discussed in terms similar to those used in the description of justification by faith — satisfaction made by Christ, the gift of Christ's righteousness, the escape from God's judgment in spite of the sinful condition against which we are engaged in a lifelong struggle. In other connections, too, we catch glimpses of the richness of salvation: payment for our sins, redemption from the lordship of Satan, and the assurance of eternal life (Q. 1); the ingrafting through faith and by mere grace of all God's benefits (Q. 20); the reception of the Savior with a true faith (Q. 30); membership in Christ through faith (Q. 32); becoming a possession of Christ (Q. 1, 34); the covering of our sins before God's face (Q. 36); participation through faith in Christ and all his benefits (Q. 53); implanting in Christ through true faith (Q. 64); confidence in the forgiveness of sins (Q. 81); acceptance of the promise of the gospel with a true faith (Q. 84) without merit on our part and merely out of grace (Q. 86). These are pillars of the Christian faith; together they form a colonnade about the correlation between faith and salvation.

The Belgic Confession draws the same lines. Jesus Christ is the point from which all rays extend. This is especially apparent in Articles 22 and 23. Faith is not a second factor in justification, we are told. It plays its role in justification by embracing Christ and all his merits, seeking nothing outside of him. Referring to Romans 3:28, the Confession says, "therefore we justly say with Paul, that *we are justified by faith alone,* or *by faith apart from works*" (Art. 22). This is particularly striking since the confessors knew quite well that the phrase *justified by faith alone* appears nowhere in Paul. They had been reminded of this time and again by Rome. Exegetical or grammatical

error is improbable. Their formulation was determined by the conviction that, along with the way of the law, all ways other than faith ran to dead ends. Through this fact the only way, the way of faith, became the more clear. *Sola fide,* as it is used in this passage, is completely identified with the Pauline doctrine that salvation is "apart from the works of the law." This is to be understood, as it is in Lord's Day 23, as meaning that faith is not an independent meritorious act accepted by God as good enough for him. It is a total commitment to the one Way, Christ. Really it is not faith itself that justifies; faith is only an instrument with which we embrace Christ, who is our justification.

We shall have to return to the idea of faith as an instrument somewhat later. But even here the intent of the term is clear: the radical amputation of all prestige from faith. Faith is not a human act that complements God's act of grace — not according to the Belgic Confession. Faith holds us in fellowship with him who is our justification. And his merits, "which have become ours, are more than sufficient to acquit us of our sins" (Art. 22). This is the theme of the psalm that the church's theology has on its lips. Our justification lies in free forgiveness (Art. 23). The obedience of the crucified Christ — this is the *alpha* and *omega* of our justification. He covers our disobedience with his obedience, our unrighteousness with his righteousness. He gives us courage, frees us from the torments of a guilty conscience, dissolves our dread of standing alone before God. The justified person need not be like Adam when confronted by God. Our courage takes the place of Adam's terror. It is the "as if" of the Catechism that changes things so radically. And this "as if" agrees with Article 23 of the Belgic Confession: "and, verily, if we should appear before God, relying on ourselves or on any other creature, though ever so little, we should, alas! be consumed. And therefore everyone must pray with David: O Jehovah, enter not into judgment with thy servant; for in thy sight no living person is righteous" — a remarkable and meaningful conclusion to an article on justification through faith alone.

* * * * *

Although the Canons of Dort do not speak very extensively about justification by faith, in what they do say it is clear that Christ is the total substance of our justification. This is the relation between faith and salvation in Christ taught by Dort: "But such as receive it and embrace Jesus as Savior by a true and living faith are by him delivered from the wrath of God and from destruction, and have the gift of eternal life conferred upon them" (I, 4). We hear again the same theme that we heard in the Catechism and the Belgic Confession: pure grace, Christ as the foundation of our salvation (I, 7). Salvation is, of course, viewed in the light of election. That election occurs on the basis of foreseen faith or of the obedience of faith is repudiated (I, 9). To say that faith is a condition of salvation is an "injurious error," which renders impotent the pleasure of God and the merits of Christ; through it "men are drawn away by useless questions from the truth of gracious justification and from the simplicity of Scripture" (I, Rejection of errors 3). Election is the fountain of all saving good (I, 9). Believers are given over to Christ gifted with true faith, justified, and made holy. Salvation comes forth from unmerited election (I, 17). The Canons' sharp protest against the Remonstrants demonstrates how the priority of grace is firmly grasped and how the confessors were in no spirit for concessions. They were unable to be conciliated by the Arminian concession that the foreseen faith on the basis of which we are justified was a gift of grace, nor by the statement that God "chose out of all possible conditions (among which are also the works of the law), or out of the whole order of things, the act of faith which from its very nature is undeserving and which offers only incomplete

obedience, as a condition of salvation" (I, Rejection of Errors 3). This was unacceptable precisely because it made faith a condition, chosen from all possible conditions, actually putting faith and the law on the same level, though one is accepted by God and the other not.

The Canons are not remarkable for subtlety. They simply permeate themselves with the all-sufficiency of the Savior. For this reason humility and confession of guilt characterize much of them. As much as grace is praised, so much is the worth and merit of human work abjured. This is what was missing in the Remonstrant thesis that election waited on foreseen faith, conversion, sanctification, and godliness, so that the complete and decisive election was reserved for the person who was "more worth than he who is not chosen." The Scripture knows of no such comparative worthiness, as the theologians of Dort realized, quoting Paul: "but if it is by grace, it is no more of works" (Rom. 11:6).

A single theme plays through all three documents, the Belgic Confession, the Heidelberg Catechism, and the Canons of Dort: the theme of *sola fide*. And this is the heart of the Reformed confession. The various and varied expressions are religiously simple and transparent. The theologians understood that justification through faith alone was the confession preeminent, the confession sine qua non.

* * * * *

Was there a common Reformation confession on this important point? Were the Lutheran and Calvinistic Reformation united in this profound confession of divine grace? It has been said more than once that there was not only a confessional and dogmatic divergence but a deep religious cleavage between the two. Schneckenburger, in his comparative study of the Calvinistic and Lutheran movements, saw a radical difference not only in christology and sacraments but in the doctrine of justification as well. The Lutheran construction of the doctrine was alleged to have been more sharp in its antithesis with Rome. The Lutheran doctrine was more "synthetic," the Reformed more "analytical," with the *sola fide–sola gratia* getting much more play in the Lutheran than in the Reformed confession.[2] Schneckenburger's argument has not, however, stood the test of comparative readings in the two confessional groups. His error arose mostly from reading into the Reformed confessions the arguments of certain later Reformed theologians. A brief excursion into a few Lutheran confessions will reveal that Schneckenburger's thesis holds no water, that in the crucial points there is a profound correspondence between the Reformed confessions and the Lutheran.

We may note first the Augsburg Confession, in which the Reformed conviction on justification is very lucidly expressed. The idea of merit is wholly disowned, as is the possibility of facing God with one's own powers, merits, or good works (Art. IV). In the articles in which the new obedience, faith, and good works are discussed in defense against the charge that good works were prohibited by the Lutheran doctrine, the necessity of good works is stated in such a way as to insist that we do them but not that we may be justified by the doing of them (Arts. XX and VI). The Augsburg Confession polemicizes against Rome's doctrine of free will and the ability to please God apart from grace and the help and work of the Holy Spirit. Rome, we read, says less than formerly about alms, pilgrimages, fasting, and the like (Art. XX) and now proclaims the necessity of faith, "on which in previous times she was practically silent." Rome says now that a person is not justified by works alone but that one is justified by faith and works. The Augsburg Confession rejects this new construction just as finally as it did the former one.

Whoever considers oneself able to earn redemption in one way or another denies Christ

and seeks a way of salvation that is condemned by the gospel (Art. XX). *Sola fide* is proclaimed in place of all doctrines of works (Art. IV). God imputes righteousness to this faith (Art. IV). If we have done everything, we are still unprofitable servants. In all this, the confession is conscious of proposing no new doctrine, but only of translating the gospel. Thus, it cites Ambrose as saying that whoever believes in Christ is saved, not through works but only through faith apart from merits (Art. VI).

The background of this confession is the Pauline message, along with the words of Christ about the unprofitable servants and his insistence that "without me, ye can do nothing" (Art. XX). We read of the imputation of righteousness in Romans 3 and 4 (Art. IV), of the relation of the natural man to the Spirit of God in 1 Corinthians 2:14, of the only Mediator in 1 Timothy 2:5, of faith as the gift of God in Ephesians 2:8, and of justification through faith in Romans 5:1 (Art. XVIII). This doctrine is a message of reassurance and comfort to the conscience terrorized by its inability to come to rest through its works. The Augsburg Confession is so convinced that it only translates the gospel, that it considers any charge of heresy against itself a violation of Christian love and unity.

Sola fide comes again into prominence in the second part of the Confession, the section dealing with various abuses. For instance, in the article on distinctions in foods it is said that when humans must earn grace through such human institutions, the doctrine of grace and faith is maligned — regardless of how preeminently faith is held above other works. Recalling Paul's struggle against human traditions, the Confession teaches that "we are not made holy by our works, but rather through faith in Christ alone, a doctrine that has almost disappeared."

This theme, then, is the same in Lutheran and Reformed confessions, and displays the existence of a profound Reformation unity. Calvin's agreement with the Augsburg Confession underscores this early concord.[3]

* * * * *

What has been said of the Augsburg Confession holds no less for the Apology for the Confessio Augustana, in which a defense is made against fierce Roman criticism. The doctrine of justification through faith alone is indicated as the highest and most important article of the faith, and as the key to all the doors of Scripture.[4] The critics are accused of a total ignorance of what faith, grace, and righteousness mean. They have robbed human consciences of the treasure of the knowledge of Christ, and it is therefore the more necessary to establish the doctrine of justification in the Apology (p. 87).

The teaching of justification in the Apology has been the subject of a good many debates since the appearance of the document, debates that arise from differences in interpretation of certain articles. The discussions have to do with the relation of this confession to the teaching of Luther himself. The most important question was whether in writing the Apology Melanchthon did not introduce a new view of justification. It is claimed that this new element was the cause of later erroneous developments concerning the forensic character of justification.[6] Melanchthon, not Luther, is said to have become the molder of popular opinion on the doctrine. The forensic or declarative emphasis in Melanchthon is distinguished from the more ethical construal of Luther. It was especially in his contention with Osiander, it is said, that Melanchthon moved away from Luther. Here he began to wrap the relation between justification and sanctification in a blanket of fog, up out of which the later discussions about analytical and synthetic justification were to loom.

These discussions have been, until the present day, generally unfruitful, in our opinion, a misfortune occasioned in part by the tendency to take the terms of the Apology as fixed scientific phraseology.[7] It is encouraging, therefore, that later Lutheran theologians, such as Elert, have emphasized the religious character of forensic justification as it is perceived in Luther as well as in the Apology.[8] In the Apology, as appears convincingly from a close study, there was no devaluation of the renewal of humanity (which is usually discussed side by side with justification). There was, however, an earnest attempt to dig into divine grace, the deepest ground of justification.

We are criticized, says the Apology, because we teach that the believer receives forgiveness of sins through Christ only by faith, apart from any subjective merit (p. 87). The Apology delivers the countercharge that the critics have put Christ in darkness, have buried him anew, so that we cannot recognize him any longer as the only Mediator. For they deny that we receive forgiveness of our sins from him only through grace and without merit, and dream that we are able to merit forgiveness through good works and obedience to the law (p. 90). They do not understand how sinful our heart is and do not know that we forget all merit and all work when our heart feels the wrath of God or when our conscience is full of dread (p. 90). The devotion of the Apology is to the radical Pauline antithesis between justification through faith and the righteousness of works (p. 94).

This becomes yet more clear in the section on justifying faith. The uniqueness of this faith is, in various ways, the most discernible in its gravitation toward its object and content. Faith is the kind of divine service that is poured out and given to me, in contrast to that in which I do the libations. The promise is received through faith; all worthiness and merit are disclaimed, and grace and mercy receive all the praise — for grace is received without merit (p. 96).

A remarkable parallel with Lord's Day 23 of the Heidelberg Catechism occurs here: faith does not justify as though it were in itself a noble work; it justifies only in that through it the promise of grace is accepted (p. 96). Reject *sola fide,* and you must tear pages from Paul's testimony, the Apology reminds us, including those that indicate that we are saved by grace through faith, and that not of ourselves, for it is the gift of God — "not of works, that no man should glory" (p. 100). Herein is the exclusiveness of grace confessed. *Sola fide* is not an exclusive hobby that prohibits recognition of other truths. It does not exclude evangelization and the sacrament; it excludes only our own merits. At this point there is an extensive explanation of why we are saved through faith and not through love or good works. Love and works are not disqualified; love must follow faith. However, we are not to build our confidence on love, as though for its sake and through it we should expect to receive forgiveness of sins and redemption from God (p. 108).

Love is distinguished from faith, for *sola fide* points to the divine-transcendent character of redemption in Christ, to *his* work and *his* love as the only grounds for our salvation. This explains the keen-edged protest against Rome's devaluation of faith to a preparation for justification, to an intellectual assent, to a thing yet to take its form from love and good works. Faith gets a more central position in the Reformation than it can possibly have in the Roman Catholic faith; it is a total commitment to God's mercy which encounters us in Christ.

Whoever seeks to understand *sola fide,* writes Melanchthon elsewhere, must realize that "we have only divine mercy, and not human merit, to thank for our justification."[9] In the same treatise, he follows his discussion of justification with the claim that the activity of faith, the works of faith, are to be understood in Paul's sense, that faith works through love. Melanchthon does not sever the bond of faith and love, not even in reaction to Rome's appeal to Galatians 5:6. But within the activity of faith, the critical, evangelical function of *sola fide* remains perfectly intact.

* * * * *

From this all but complete review of the Confession and the Apology, we have been able to catch an inkling of the force of the Reformation antithesis between faith and works. We can follow the same lines in other Lutheran confessions, in the Smalkald Articles and Luther's Catechism, until, at last, the Lutheran doctrine of justification is given its final formulation in the Formula of Concord. Again in this larger document, faith is sketched as an instrument and means "whereby we lay hold on Christ the Savior, and so in Christ lay hold on that righteousness which is able to stand before the judgment of God" (p. 528).[10] The terminology of the Formula of Concord is more fixed and rigid than that of the Apology, and differences of interpretation are hardly possible. Justification is taught as being a pardon for sins (p. 529) in order to maintain the forensic character of the doctrine. The more precise formulation does not bring about a lesser appreciation for moral renovation and good works, but it does fix the relation between justification and sanctification. It refutes the proposition "that faith bestows salvation upon us for the reason that the renewal which consists in love towards God and our neighbor, commences in us through faith" (p. 530).[11] Justification and sanctification are cleanly distinguished, and justification is described as a divine judgment upon the sinner (p. 613). Faith corresponds to this justification; it accepts this divine judgment of grace, and therewith it disavows all meritorial claims.

Sola fide!

This brief confessional review will have given the wrong impression if it suggests that all subsequent development of the doctrine of justification has continued to translate the gospel with similar faithfulness. In Melanchthon's *Loci* of 1559 there is a perceptible shift from the original confession: the Word of God, the Holy Spirit, and the nonresistant human will are now set side by side — enough to remind us that *sola fide* is not a sort of trademark that guarantees the purity of scriptural thought! On the other hand, it is quite untrue to say that the tendency toward a forensic or juridical justification during the period leading up to the Formula of Concord was an about-face from Luther's more ethical teaching.[12] The forensic justification of the Formula of Concord is not a slip into the net of a scholastic, intellectual order of salvation; it is the end result of a desire to keep the *sola fide* and keep it pure. Elert has said quite correctly that forensic justification implicitly held an antithesis to the scholastic idea of justification and that declarative justification was only another facet of the righteousness of faith.[13] This was the uniting truth of the sixteenth century. All differences, some of which were not unimportant, within the Reformation stood in the shadow of this transcending verity.

For this reason, too, it is impossible to characterize the Lutheran and Calvinistic confessions as being respectively anthropocentric and theocentric. This dilemma has bothered us too long, as has that other false antithesis — soteriological and theological. If we say that the Lutheran confessions underline the comfort of justification to the restless conscience and then interpret that as a tendency toward anthropocentricism, we have missed the real point of the confessions. We should be doing the same thing as is done when the allegedly more theological Belgic Confession is contrasted with the Heidelberg Catechism, in which "my only comfort" is the ruling motif. The Catechism is then supposedly soteriological and the Belgic Confession theological, with the implicit suggestion that *soteriological* is the same as *anthropocentric*. This is also implied in the irresponsible oversimplification which says that the Lutheran Reformation is characterized by its *sola fide* and the Calvinistic by its *Soli Deo Gloria*. This is in the light of Scripture a completely false antithesis. We must get at the

meaning and intent of *sola fide* and *Soli Deo Gloria*. The Lutheran *sola fide* is essentially directed to the glory of God in God's mercy and grace, just as it is in the Calvinistic confessions, and the Calvinistic *Soli Deo Gloria* is not and ought never to be abstracted from this same mercy and grace. Out of their essential contexts the phrases become irreligious bromides.

Paul thought he was giving glory to God by persecuting the church (see also John 6:2). The phrase *Soli Deo Gloria* was, as it were, emblazoned across the life and work of Ignatius Loyola, founder of the Jesuits. In his *Exercitia spiritualia* he says repeatedly that humanity is created to praise God, to honor God always and serve God only. It was not for nothing that Loyola was said to have been obsessed with obedience. Nothing, says Loyola, may motivate humans nor guide them other than the service and praise of God; humans must be a staff in the divine hands. It is hardly surprising that the Jesuits honored humility as the noblest of all virtues. This should warn us against making *Soli Deo Gloria* an abstract, fine phrase, a neat and formal measure of judgment. In contrast, *sola fide* and *Soli Deo Gloria* were significantly united in the life of Abraham. They were, indeed, one. "He wavered not through unbelief, but waxed strong through faith, giving glory to God" (Rom. 4:20).

In faith God is honored. This is why the Catechism is indeed soteriological but not anthropocentric. For between the comfort of *sola fide* and the objectivity of *Soli Deo Gloria* there is a beautiful correspondence. They belong together.

The Reformed confession of *sola fide* is a warning sign along the path of church history. The phrase carries no guarantee against the deceits of the human heart. No formula is a security for the glory of God. *Sola fide* makes sense only in the act of true faith. But the confessions of the Reformation are plain. They tell of grace without the works of the law; they witness against the glory, the elevation, and the trustworthiness of humanity. They whisper of the comfort of God's redemption, but in such a way as to suggest the danger of making humanity's comfort the *alpha* and *omega* of Christianity. The warning is needed, for we would undoubtedly enjoy making of the doctrine of justification a projection of our own wishes and desires, a postulate of our own distress. But *sola fide* points the other way, toward God's elective love in Jesus Christ, who takes priority over all human desires. This is why *sola fide* is theocentric, and *therefore* soteriological. For the grace of God *that bringeth salvation* has appeared to all persons (Tit. 2:11). This description of grace concludes with the expectation of the *glorious* appearance of our *great God* and Savior Jesus Christ (Tit. 2:13).

Sola fide!
Soli Deo Gloria!

NOTES

1. W. H. van der Pol, *Het Christelijk dilemma* (1948), p. 75 (ET: *The Christian Dilemma*, 1952).

2. M. Schneckenburger, *Vergleichende Darstellung des lutherischen und reformierten Lehrbegriffs*, 2 vols. (1855), 2: 31.

3. Calvin's attitude toward the Augsburg Confession proves how keenly he appreciated the religious depth of the Lutheran Reformation. Consider the famous statement Calvin made about Luther: "Though he call me a devil, I shall honor him as one of the foremost of God's servants" (cf. K. Holl *Calvinstudien*, pp. 79, 115). Holl writes that the Lutheran doctrine of justification forms the heart of Calvin's *Institutes* (*Calvinstudien,* p. 116). He calls Calvin "a Lutheran from the very beginning" and says that Calvin was always conscious of being "heir to Luther." This is indeed true as far as the doctrine of justification is concerned. Luther, before Calvin, preached from the rooftops the sovereign grace of God. If certain specifically Calvinistic doctrines are mentioned in opposition to this, let it be remembered that everything doctrinally specific has its right to existence only if it is a pure translation of the gospel.

5. See the version of the Apology in J. T. Müller, *Bekenntnisschriften der evangelisch-lutherischen Kirche,* 12th ed. (1928), p. 87. Subsequent references to this work will be made parenthetically in the text.

6. Cf. K. Holl, *Die Rechtfertigungslehre im Licht der Geschichte des Protestantismus,* vol. 3 (1928), pp. 525ff.

7. The debate is focused particularly on Art. 72, and then especially on the words *ex iniustos justos effici seu regenerari* and *justos pronuntiari seu reputari.* See J. Kunze, *Die Rechtfertigungslehre in der Apologie* (1908); and Herman Bavinck, *Gereformeerde Dogmatik,* vol. 4.

8. See W. Elert, *Der Christliche Glaube* (1940).

9. Melanchthon, *Grundbegriffe der Glaubenslehre (Loci communes),* F. Schad edition (1931), p. 162.

10. Translation from Schaff, *The Creeds of Christendom,* vol. 3 (1877), p. 116.

11. Translation from Schaff, *The Creeds of Christendom,* 3: 120.

12. See W. Elert, *Morphologie des Luthertums,* vol. 1 (1931), p. 88.

13. Elert, *Morphologie des Luthertums,* p. 93.

Being in Christ

Lewis B. Smedes

I. FOCUSING ON PAUL

A. *Life Outside of Christ*

One way to find out what a French person is like is to watch how he or she looks at the rest of the world. One way to tell what life in Christ is like is to see how a person in Christ looks at life outside of Christ. Paul's observations of life outside of Christ are kaleidoscopic — they come in many shapes and colors, and they keep moving. Sometimes he catches the personal contradictions of that life. Sometimes he is more impressed with the superhuman powers that control and confine personal life. His vocabulary is often like a foreign language to us. We cannot possibly enter into all the complexities of interpretation that have kept scholars preoccupied in recent years, but perhaps we can grasp enough of Paul's general outlook to cast some light on the new life in Christ.

Reprinted from *Union with Christ*, 2nd rev. ed. (Grand Rapids: William B. Eerdmans, 1983), pp. 67-92.

Paul's favorite words for life outside of Christ are *flesh, law, sin,* and *death.* But these are intertwined and interdependent. Together they are the verbal net in which Paul catches the futility and hopelessness of life without Christ.

1. Life in the Flesh. Anyone demanding a clear and simple definition of "flesh" as Paul uses the word is doomed to disappointment. Yet the word appears everywhere. The apostle never bothers with precise definitions of it, but it is not hard to make a rough working distinction. Paul's "flesh" has two dimensions: (1) flesh is weak, created human existence, to be accepted in humility and lived in gratitude; (2) flesh is life in sin, opposed to Christ and to the Spirit of Christ; it is a life in which it is *impossible* to please God. Let us take a longer look at each.

Flesh as Weakness. A fleshly person is one who can be vexed by a thorn and who, paradoxically, finds strength in accepting it in grace (2 Cor. 12:7-9). The fleshly person gets sick and dies (Gal. 4:13; 1 Cor. 15:50). Abraham was a man of flesh (Rom. 4:1), and so was

Jesus (Rom. 1:3; 9:5). The Christian lives a life of faith "in the flesh" (Gal. 2:20), and while it is not as appealing as being "with Christ" (Phil. 1:22, 23), it does offer an opportunity to demonstrate the life of Christ even in so earthen a vessel (2 Cor. 4:11).

Flesh stands for humanity. It means people whose existence needs a continuous inbreathing of God; the moment God takes breath away, flesh collapses. As flesh, we are always on the edge of nothingness; to know this, and to know it well, is to know oneself and, almost, to know God. But to say that God's creature of flesh always needs God is not to say that being flesh is bad.

Flesh as Sin. As we have seen, being "in the flesh" is not necessarily opposed to being "in Christ." But Paul also puts being "in the flesh" in the same category as being on the wrong side. Being "in the flesh" here is far more than regrettable: it is a fatal identification with evil. In the first place, "those who are in the flesh cannot please God" (Rom. 8:8). No Hebrew of the old covenant would have dreamed of saying this: to him humanity *was* flesh, and the way to please God was to face up to it. So, being "*in* the flesh" cannot mean here the same thing as *being* flesh. "In the flesh" means "outside of Christ."

When one is "in the flesh" one lives "according to the flesh" (Rom. 8:5, 7) and sets one's "mind" on the flesh (Rom. 8:5). And when this happens, one's life bears fruit that is not only different from but incompatible with the fruits of the Spirit (Gal. 5:16ff.). But why? Why does the flesh war against the Spirit; why are "the desires of the flesh against the Spirit" (Gal. 5:17)? Why is the person who "lives according to the flesh" fated to die (Rom. 8:13)?

Obviously, a new dimension is introduced into the life of the flesh. Pious persons once admitted and were glad that they were flesh, for this meant that they threw themselves into the hands of God. Now persons of flesh are sinful, condemned, and doomed because they are opposed to God. Being "in the flesh" now means that one puts total stock in the flesh, making it an "ultimate concern," one's chief interest. Being "in the flesh" betrays where one's heart is, where one's hope and trust are planted. The world *flesh,* therefore, has come to stand for the sinful environment in which one is willingly located and by which one identifies oneself. It is an environment dominated and characterized by the powers of evil. "Flesh" epitomizes the character of life in the unredeemed world; it is an epigram for life outside of and hostile to Christ.

2. Life under the Law. The law appears on the scene as another competitor to Jesus Christ (Gal. 5:4). Paul's fundamental thesis about the law is that its time had come to an end, for Christ is the end of the law (Rom. 10:4). To be under the law is to opt for the "old things" that passed away when everything became new in Christ (2 Cor. 5:17), and this state has the same ultimate frustrations and fatality as life "in the flesh."

Paul's attitude toward the law, like his feelings about everything, was deeply prejudiced by his life stance within the new Christian reality. He was not much interested in anything in the abstract; what he wanted to know, as the decisive factor, was the bearing a thing had on life in Christ. This is why he was concerned not only with the *what* of a thing but with the *how* as well. In the case of the law, what he faulted was not its content but the *function* it had within the religious community, for its function settled the question of how it bore on people's relationship to God. Anything — even the holy law of God — that got in the way of grace was judged as a threat to salvation in Christ.

Obviously Paul's basic attitude toward the law is positive. This is not surprising: the God of Jesus Christ is the God of creation and the covenant *and* the law. As far as its content is concerned, the law is "holy and just and good"

(Rom. 7:12). Who would expect the apostle to believe anything else? Christ is the end of the law in this sense; he is the one person whose life was all the law meant human life to be. And the Spirit's function within us is to enable us, too, to fulfill the genuine demands of the law (Rom. 8:4). *What* the law is, *what* the law reveals, *what* the law demands are unassailable from the vantage point of Jesus Christ.

The *content* of the law gets unconditional assent. But the use people make of the law is another matter. Here things become more complex. There is an important distinction within the function of the law. We can talk about its legitimate and intended function on the one hand and its illegitimate and distorted function on the other. We can talk about the function that God meant it to have and the function that people invested it with.

Let us take, first, its *intended* positive function. Was the law ever meant to be a means to save oneself? Paul says that the law itself witnessed to the free gift of grace (Rom. 3:21). The beginnings of the decalogue proclaim that Israel's identity as the people of the law rested in God's mighty act of redemption from Egypt: "I am Jehovah thy God, who brought thee out of the land of Egypt." As such the law was a promise: it functioned as a harbinger, a pointer to the reality of divine grace. This is why David and the congregation could sing of their *love for the law*. As long as the law functioned as a promise or a witness of better things to come, it had to be accepted as a conditional good, but when the reality came, this function was no longer necessary.

But there is also a useful negative function of the law. The law exposes acts of sin for what they are — rebellion against a living God. The law pins sinners down, nails them at every corner; it sweeps the whole of life into its net and brands every infraction a culpable act of rebellion (Rom. 7:7-9). As it prohibits immoral and hostile acts, it reveals their true context. At the same time it shows that everyone living under the law is under a curse: we are condemned (Gal. 3:10). And this is a good and necessary function.

Accepting at full value Paul's positive attitude toward the law, we do an abrupt about-face to hear Paul's indictment of the law. Looked at from within Christ, the law is a bad thing. It is a prison, the dank dungeon of spiritual bondage (Gal. 3:22-23). It is the jailor as well, the one who keeps people in chains (Rom. 7:6). The law is a domineering, restrictive guardian or pedagogue who keeps a child too long from the freedom of the mature (Gal. 3:24). It makes sin the worse (Rom. 7:13) and can even be branded as the power behind sin (1 Cor. 15:56). In fact, the law destroys the souls of people (2 Cor. 3:6). No wonder Paul says to people who want to find salvation in the law, "You are severed from Christ" (Gal. 5:4). The law is not merely a good thing now outmoded; it is a monster.

In this sense, Christ is the destroyer of the law. He "canceled the bond which stood against us with its legal demands; this he set aside, nailing it to the cross" (Col. 2:14). His crucifixion of the law was of a piece with his defeat of the "principalities and powers" (Col. 2:15). The law had become a tool of the enemy; one of God's great goods had been stolen by the enemy and used to destroy God's creatures.

The law became a destructive power because of its alliance with the flesh. When the law came, the "flesh" made the law an instrument of self-righteousness. The law became part of a religious system that fostered humanity's sense of self-sufficiency. It became party to humanity's monstrous delusion.

This was the Judaistic religious system that Paul recognized as the enemy of Christ. The law had been turned inside out: rather than a witness to humanity's need of being saved, it had become a technique to save oneself. The inner meaning of the law had been forgotten; the letter alone was left when the spiritual content of love was ignored. This is the character of life outside of Christ. Although Paul has the Judaistic distortions before him,[1] the situation is parallel to every religious system in which people in weakness pretend to be people in strength, in which people in need of grace pretend to be people without need of grace. Paul sees the world outside of Christ as controlled and dominated by this alliance of moral law (or religious law) and flesh. The moral and religious life of all people is bound to and structured by this fatal alliance.

The law teamed with flesh produces sin, and sin ends in death. This is the fatality of the alliance. Flesh plus law equals death because flesh plus law leaves men in sin. This is why Paul talks about "the law of sin and death" (Rom. 8:2).

3. Life in Sin. Sin, for Paul, is personal hostility toward and flight from a personal God (Col. 1:21). And it is judged and forgiven on a decisively personal level. There is no escaping the fact that for Paul every person, privately and personally, is responsible for sin. To be "in sin" is to be a voluntary sinner.

But the sinfulness of the human situation betrays the fact that all persons are somehow *bound* to sin. In one sense, God has allowed us to bind ourselves to sin: God gave humanity over to a "reprobate mind" (Rom. 1) and "consigned all things to sin" (Gal. 3:22). This could mean that God assigned us to the situation to which we willingly assigned ourselves. In any case, God considers humans to be embedded in a situation that is sinful. Therewith, sin dominates us. It dominates our minds (Rom. 1:21), our wills (Rom. 7:15-20), and our bodies (Rom. 7:24). We are controlled by a force that Paul telescoped into the word *sin*.

To be "in sin" is to be dominated by sin. Sin is a despot (Rom. 5:21). It "entered" the world and achieved mastery over humans (Rom. 6:6, 11ff.). The person is sin is the person "sold under sin" (Rom. 7:14). People living under the control of sin are, therefore, "in sin."

Sin was not introduced by the fateful alliance between the flesh and the law. "Sin indeed was in the world before the law was given" (Rom. 5:13). But the collusion of flesh with law intensified and deepened the hopelessness of the sinful situation.

All of Paul's ways of summarizing the human predicament point to the same situation. When he says "being in the flesh" is hostile to being "in the Spirit," or that being "under the law" is incompatible with being "under grace," or that being "in sin" is impossible while one is "in Christ," he is pointing to the same situation. The tragic alliance of these three powers creates the human situation as it is controlled, betrayed, and doomed by the "powers of darkness" behind the scenes.

B. The New Creature in Christ

"Therefore, if any one is in Christ, he is a new creation; the old has passed away, behold, the new has come" (2 Cor. 5:17). This is by all reckoning the best known of the "in Christ" passages and without doubt among the most central.

The classic passage on the new creature in Christ begins with a "therefore," and this word points back to the crucifixion. The event that changed things for people is the death of Jesus. The place where the "old things passed away" and the new came into being is Calvary, back there in history now gone by. "He died for all, that those who live [having once died] might live no longer for themselves but for him who for their sake died and was raised" (2 Cor. 5:15). The crucial moment is a moment in past history. The crucial category is an event.

Reconciliation is firmly planted in this historical event. God reconciled us to God's self by means of a particular occurrence at a particular place during three particular hours that could have been measured on anyone's clock. Reconciliation brings together people who had been estranged. In this case, it brings a world of people back into partnership with the God from whom they had been alienated. This is how it happens that they become new creatures, and it comes about because "hostility was brought to an end" at the cross.

We are not groping in a world of ideas about initiation into the divine-human life of a universal Spirit. We are in a set of historical events. Jesus did something that changed things between God and us. It is true that some translations of verse 16 can mislead us: "wherefore henceforth know we no man after the flesh: yea, though we have known Christ after the flesh, yet now henceforth know we *him* no more." Readers have been known to jump on the last part of this sentence as disclaiming an interest in the historical Jesus, but such a move is precipitate. The RSV provides this discerning translation: "though we once regarded Jesus from a human point of view, we regard him thus no longer." Paul is not dissociating his gospel from the earthly Jesus; he is dissociating himself from earthly judgments about Jesus.

The measure that Paul takes of Jesus is not by ordinary canons. This is why he says he does not regard Jesus any longer "after the flesh." People whose wisdom was limited to the "flesh" or "the world" judged Jesus to be deserving of hammer and nails.

Paul knows that when Jesus died, the world was won to God. Paul's vision of reconciliation is not cabined by a narrow theology that counts as gospel only the possibility of individuals escaping hell. The entire world that God made, the world that people led away from God's love, the world that God kept on loving, the world to which God gave God's Son — this is the world reconciled through Christ. Nothing less than the panoramic vision of a world re-created will capture Paul's vision of reconciliation.

What, then, is the new creature?

Paul speaks in the indicative mood. He is not urging people to *become* new creatures. Nor is he, expressly at any rate, telling us what they *may become* in some distant and perhaps remote future. He does not urge us to put aside the old and work ourselves into the new life. He appears to be stating a bald fact about the *present* state of the person in Christ. And it must be noted that he seems quite unconcerned about what could only have been perfectly obvious to him — the fact that even he had not shed his "old nature" and become wholly new. He retained in himself more than a few embers of sin. Yet he states with utter surety that the person in Christ *is* a new creation.

Where is the new creation? May we look for it in the changed moral life of individual Christians? There, too, of course, but not primarily there. The new exists wherever Christ is known, confessed, and served as the Lord of life. The new exists wherever people are in fact reconciled to God. May we insist, as Neugebauer and most interpreters do, that the new creation is the church?[2] I think we may. If I understand this thesis, it suggests that anyone who is genuinely part of the community where the reconciliation of Christ is preached and lived is part of that new movement in history called the new creation.

The new creation takes the form now of a community aware of the new reality. And this means that Paul is saying something like this: if anyone is reconciled to God within the community of Christ, one is by that token in Christ. What is helpful about this interpretation is the reminder that the new creature is social, just as the old creature is. The person in Christ is never there by himself or herself; being in Christ is always an existence in communion.

What Paul is stressing is the existence of a new creation through reconciliation. The old order is doomed and as good as dead. "With the old order passed away, the new has taken its place. That these two should co-exist in one sphere is impossible. When the new arrives, the old must be disrobed of power."[3] Paul is proclaiming this as a cosmic fait accompli. As Geerhardus Vos said, "there has been created a totally new environment, or, more accurately stated, a totally new world. . . . The whole surrounding world has assumed a new aspect and a new complexion."[4] The creative center is the cross. The dominant person is Christ. The arena is history. The Christian is a person in the new world.

All this points us in the direction of the historical cross, an event, as the determining factor: it points us to history. Albert Schweitzer was right: "like a lighthouse that throws its beam upon the ocean of the eternal, the Pauline mysticism stands firm, based upon the firm foundation of the historical manifestation of Jesus Christ."[5] The most famous of the "in Christ" passages is rooted in the nonmystical world of Pontius Pilate, Roman soldiers, public executions, and garden tombs.

Since being "in Christ" is not an escape from history but a participation in the new reality in history, the person in Christ is in agony. For while being "in Christ" involves the relocation within a whole new order of existence in history, one can find little in actual history that lives up to the radical righteousness and love that is true of the new creation. The "old things" have not all passed away. The "new" has come only ambiguously at best. And the saints on earth cry even more agonizingly than the saints under the altar: "How long, O Lord?" (Rev. 6:9-10).

If being "in Christ" were a mystical or idealistic experience of the soul or mind within the life of divinity beyond history, we could escape the agony. Were it an existentialist category of personal decision, we would not be bothered by the apparent contradiction between the "new thing" in Christ and the actual existence around us of the "old things." But if the "god of this age" has been defeated, if "old things have passed away and the new has come," we are in agony. But it is the agony of one who believes that the root of things has

really changed and is going to change; only the person who knows in faith that something has happened and is going to happen is likely to cry "how long?"

C. Freedom in Christ

Scholars have sometimes seen two minds in Paul struggling for possession of his theology — the prophetic mind and the mystical. The prophetic mind was the Hebrew in Paul. The mystical mind was the Greek. According to the prophetic mind, God was the holy and just Judge who pardoned us. According to the mystical mind, God was the One who shared God's life in Christ with us. The prophetic mind proclaimed justification by faith. The mystical mind offered union with Christ through the Spirit. The prophetic mind preached forgiveness through the atonement made at the cross. The mystical mind offered new experience through the Christ who had become Spirit. The prophetic mind said that Christ was "for us." The mystical mind said that we are "in Christ." And for many scholars it has been a fascinating game to prove that one mind or the other was at work in a given instance, or that both were reconciled into a synthesis.[6]

No single sentence shows that Christ "for us" is not in tension with our being "in Christ" more clearly than does the famous opening verse of Romans 8: "There is therefore no condemnation for those who are in Christ Jesus." Here we have the language of the courtroom ("no condemnation") combined with the language of mysticism ("in Christ"). But what is the relationship between these two factors? Perhaps we will find the crucial clue in our answer to this question: What lies behind the "therefore"?

The preceding chapter (Rom. 7) is primarily a picture of human history under the lordship of the "powers of darkness." Humans here are under the control of a situation beyond their undoing. They are "sold under sin" (7:14). There is a "law of sin" (7:23) to which a person "in the flesh" is captive. This "law" — or prevailing power — dominates, frustrates, and dooms human life. We are shackled to the situation. This is why Paul ends his description of the futility and bondage of life with a desperate "Who will deliver me?"[7]

The anguish is answered by God in action. Paul's song is "Thanks be to God through Jesus Christ our Lord" (7:25). More specifically, the situation has changed and humanity is released from the "law of sin." "For God has done what the law, weakened by the flesh, could not do: sending his own Son in the likeness of sinful flesh, and for sin, he condemned sin in the flesh" (8:3). This is the action that changed the old situation into the new one. When Paul says that Christ "condemned sin," he is not talking about so weak a thing as moral disapproval. We would expect Christ to disapprove of sin. Everyone agrees that it is better to be good than to be bad. Everyone in deepest conscience approves the good, even "delights in the law of God" (7:22). When Christ "condemned sin," he doomed sin as a power, disarmed and dethroned it as the prevailing force in the new age and sentenced it effectively to exile.

But the effect of the cross is far more than negative; it introduced the new age of the Spirit. In Romans 8 Paul goes on to depict life in the new situation in terms of the Spirit, mentioning the Spirit some twenty times. Here we must recall that in the new covenant of freedom the "Lord is the Spirit."

Thus, when Paul describes the new situation as governed by the "law of the Spirit," he is also saying that the new situation is the historical scene of the lordship of Jesus Christ. The "law of the Spirit" dominates the new situation as the "law of sin" dominated the old. The "law of the Spirit of life in Christ Jesus" has set us free. Now the Spirit dominates even as the Spirit liberates; the Spirit leads even as the Spirit sets us free; and the Spirit enables us

to "fulfill the just requirements of the law" even as the Spirit liberates us from the "condemnation" of the law and sin.

Clearly freedom in Christ does not retire us from obedience to the moral law. Christ does not make the law an obsolete vestige of a more primitive religious age; what he does do is change our way of looking at the law. Once, in our stupidity, we thought that with the help of the law we could conquer the moral life, but we were weak, and the law was unable to protect our flanks. But Christ created a new alliance; now we are under him as Lord, with the Spirit enabling us to "fulfill the just requirement of the law."

Now the whole face of the law is changed. Now the law looks like the living Christ, who himself fulfilled the demands of the law. The content of the law is the same — the life of total love — but the function is quite different. Now the law means the service of Christ who set us free, and obedience is a matter of being "led by the Spirit." The law is now the way of life within the lordship of Christ. That person is free, indeed, whose life is "in the Spirit" and not "in the flesh." We are free *from* something so that we can be free *for* something: we are liberated from condemnation so that we can freely serve in the Spirit.

So we have in Romans 7 and Romans 8 two basic divisions in human history. The first is tragically guilt-ridden; the second is joyfully guilt-free. The first is an alliance between humans in their weakness and the law in its impotence; the second is an alliance between humans in their weakness and the Spirit in the Spirit's power. The first is bondage to sin; the second is freedom in service. The first stands condemned; the second stands liberated from condemnation. The first ends in death; the second ends in life.

Who is the person "in Christ"? It is the person who has been brought into the new life situation of the Spirit, who has been liberated from the "law of sin and death" and given a permanent home in which the "law of the Spirit of life" is in force. It is a person in the new situation within human history, in which Christ is Lord and the Lord is Spirit. Being "in Christ" means being within the dominion of Christ, under Christ's lordship as it is made good on earth by the Spirit.

Surely the theology of Christ "for us" cannot be in tension with the theology of existence "in Christ." Paul is not of two minds. Only if we let ourselves think of Christ "for us" in a purely personal and juridical way and then let ourselves think of being *in Christ* in a purely personal and mystical way — only if we *let* them be at odds will they be at odds at all.

To be "in Christ" is to be part of the new community in which the Spirit of holiness and life is the dominant power and guiding norm. Christ's creative, life-giving, and life-styling action is the way Jesus Christ exercises his lordship. It is the way of love and peace and assurance. And from this new situation, nothing can separate us, nothing at all, for it is the situation in which we are kept by "the love of God in Christ Jesus our Lord" (8:39). And to be there, where he is, is to be "in Christ."

D. In Christ and in Adam

Christ and Adam represent the beginnings of two conflicting histories of humanity. Each in his way is so crucial to human destiny that Paul finds it meaningful to say that people are "in Adam" just as he says they are "in Christ": "for as in Adam all die, so also in Christ shall all be made alive" (1 Cor. 15:22). We die "in Adam" and are alive "in Christ." As members of the old, sinful humanity, we are in Adam. As members of the new, forgiven humanity, we are in Christ.

How does life "in Adam" help us understand how we are "in Christ"? Paul looks at everything from his vantage point in Christ. This was true of the law, and it is true of Adam.

When he says that we are "in Christ" as we are "in Adam," he brings in the parallel because he first sees man as in Christ. Says Berkouwer, "Adam stands in the light of Christ. Christ is the center and theme of the whole argument. Adam only stands for the darkness into which *this* light has dawned."[8] Barth says the same: "Paul does not go to Adam to see how he is connected with Christ; he goes to Christ to see how *He* is connected with Adam."[9]

This is clearly the case. Yet Paul must have assumed that the analogy would make sense to his readers; he must have assumed that the story of being "in Adam" would be familiar to them. So, while Barth is right in warning us against explaining the "in Christ" doctrine by means of your own theory of the unity of the human race in Adam, this should not keep us from asking what *Paul* had in mind with his "in Adam." Nor should it prevent us from asking what light the analogy sheds on the reality of our new existence "in Christ."

The comparison is this: one person brought death to all and another person brought life to all. The first Adam brought death. The last Adam — the final or "eschatonic" Adam — brought life. How did the final Adam bring life? Paul gives a double answer. The final Adam brings life by the *event* of his own resurrection. And he brings it by the fact that he became *the life-giving Spirit*. By his resurrection he overcame the power of death. In becoming the life-giving Spirit, he became the creator of new life. Each of these is indispensable. If Christ were not risen, the message of hope would be false (1 Cor. 15:14). If Christ were not the life-giving Spirit, there would be no possibility of our overcoming mortality.

Adam, too, was decisive in his effect on humanity's history by virtue of an *event*. This we learn from Romans 5. He brought death into history by his *act* of disobedience. By "one man's disobedience many were made sinners" (Rom. 5:19). And sin results in death.

The parallel between Adam and Christ,

then, is focused on the decisive *events* in which each was the central figure. Adam is not the first person because he was first on the scene. He is not the originator of the old because he was the first psychic or biological person. Paul's interest here is not cultural or biological; his interest is theological. Adam is first in the significance of what he *did in response to God's demands*. And Christ is final in the same sense.

So in one respect Adam and Christ are parallel, though opposite in their significance. In another respect, they are not parallel: "the first man Adam became a living being, while the last Adam became *a life-giving Spirit*" (1 Cor. 15:45). Paul tells us here that we cannot judge the possibilities of the future by the psycho-biological nature of Adam; for now, in the new situation, we have an association with another kind of being. Jesus Christ is the life-giving *Spirit*. The only criterion for measuring our new possibilities is the power of Christ as Spirit.

The parallel between our being "in Adam" and our being "in Christ" must be understood, then, in terms of the stories of their decisive actions. Adam by his act gave history a destiny. Christ by his act gave history a new destiny. To be in the situation each key person created is to be "in" that person.

We have said enough, I think, to show that the parallel between Adam and Christ — and our existence in each — is a matter of the historical consequences of their actions for the rest of the human race. We are not dealing with a mystical identity with them personally. Nor is it a case of being germinally present in Adam's sperm or physically present in the human nature of Jesus. Rather, we are dealing with the fact that what Adam *did* and Christ *did* had a chain of consequences that radically affects the situation in and under which other persons live. If any theory about the mystical unity or the biological unity of the human race helps to underscore this reality, it may be use-ful, but it can in no way be the key to the reality at stake here. To be in Adam is to be a member of the human race whose life and history are basically affected by what Adam did. We see this because we know that to be in Christ is to be a member of the new race of persons whose life and history are basically determined by his redemptive acts of death and resurrection.

E. Elect in Christ

> Blessed be the God and Father of our Lord Jesus Christ, who has blessed us in Christ with every spiritual blessing in the heavenly places, even as he chose us in him before the foundation of the world, that we should be holy and blameless before him. (Eph. 1:3-4)

No other sentence that Paul wrote carries more mystery into our union with Christ than this doxology. And the doxology can easily be spoiled by trading the mystery for a crisp formula. The Christian faith is better off when it bows before the mystery of antecedent love than when it carries off the prize of a precise formula. Still, the words are in front of us, and words are meant to help our understanding as well as to kindle our devotion.

What does the doctrine of election tell us about our life in Christ? This is the reverse of the question that one ordinarily asks of this text: what does the fact that we are chosen in Christ tell us about the doctrine of election? But the two questions are interwoven. And, in a sense, we are forced to ask them both at the same time. For each question, if asked separately, implies that we already have the answer to the other. So we had better ask again about "*election* in Christ" and also ask if it illumines the reality of our *being* in Christ.[10]

First we must observe that Paul sings his song to electing love from within the reality of life in Christ. He begins from where we are — in Christ. We are, he says, blessed in Christ and present with Christ "in heavenly places" (1:3).

"Heavenly places" points to the new creation that is really but not comprehensively present. So it is the language of hope: the "heavenly places" point ahead to a future reality — the reality of "all things" united in Christ. The surprising fact is that we are already included in the new reality.

Only a sense of wonder and the experience of surprise inspire songs. A person is not moved to sing by commonplaces. The inevitability of a syllogism does not inspire a doxology. We sing when we wonder; our songs are born of mystery. And the wonder here is that people *like us* are "in the heavenly places with Christ." How does one account for this reality, this "being in Christ"? There is no accounting for it. There is no *reason* in heaven or earth why we should be so blessed.

It is a gift. Paul ran from Christ; Christ pursued and overtook him. Paul resisted Christ; Christ disarmed him. Paul persecuted Christ; Christ converted him. Paul was an alien; Christ made him a member of the family. Paul was an enemy; Christ made him a friend. Paul was "in the flesh"; Christ set him "in the Spirit." Paul was under the law; Christ set him in grace. Paul was dead; Christ made him alive to God. How does one give reasons for this? He does not give reasons; he sings: "blessed be God who blessed us . . . even as he chose us in him."

The reason for saying this is to remind us that Paul is not philosophizing about the eternal plan of an absolute Deity. He is stricken by grace, overwhelmed by love, and he sings. What he says of election in Christ is a song, a confession, a hymn of wonder. Love is not a *reason;* it is a mystery to sing about.

We must now turn to the fact that our election was *in Christ* from before the worlds were made. This means that Christ, *too,* was elect. And to say this is only to repeat what the New Testament says again and again. Jesus' death was predestined (Acts 2:23; 4:28). "This is my Son, my chosen," Luke reports the Father as saying (Luke 9:35). God loved him before

the world was founded (John 17:24). He is the Lamb of God, elect to be slain for humanity's atonement (1 Pet. 1:20). And like Melchizedek he was a priest with no earthly antecedents to account for him (Heb. 7:16). Moreover, he was *appointed* "the heir of all things, through whom [God] also created the world" (Heb. 1:2).

He was elect as the *concrete* individual doing the specific task that he was chosen to do. But we must also note that his election was not only as the *concrete* individual Jesus Christ; he was also elect as the *comprehensive* Christ. Paul is always concerned with Jesus in his total significance, in his grand context.

The context is, first of all, the election of Israel. Israel is God's chosen; out of all the nations of the earth, this nation was God's unique concern. "You only have I chosen out of all the families of the earth," says Jehovah (Amos 3:2). Israel may have distorted and twisted the meaning of its own election, but it could not undo the fact of it.

The essential meaning of Israel's election is: God and God's people in vital community. Community is the purpose or end of election. But it crystallizes the meaning as well as the goal: "I will be their God, and they shall be my *people*" (Jer. 31:33). Jeremiah's conviction is echoed by prophet after prophet, and it is echoed in new forms in the New Testament until, in the vision of the Apocalypse, John hears the great voice from the throne crying, "Behold, the dwelling of God is with men. He will dwell with them, and they shall be his *people,* and God himself will be with them" (Rev. 21:3).

Israel was elect as Jehovah's servant for the blessing of the nations.[11] Jesus is the culmination of Israel's election, for he is the "suffering servant of Jehovah" for the salvation of the world. His cross and resurrection are what Israel's election was all about. He established a covenant "in his blood" that cannot fail. And the core of his covenant is the same as the core of Israel's covenant — God and humanity in reconciled partnership (Isa. 42:1).

This thought must be brought back to our election in Christ; God's election is God's "plan for the fulness of time, *to unite all things in him*" (Eph. 1:10). Christ was elect as the Christ "to reconcile to himself all things, whether on earth or in heaven, making peace by the blood of the cross" (Col. 1:20). He is elect as the one in whom a new creation is brought into being through the reconciliation of humanity with God at the cross. He is elect as head of his body, the church, which is the harbinger of the coming new creation. This is the comprehensive sense in which we must think of the election of Jesus Christ. Christ the concrete individual, the One for others, is elect. But *his election, like Israel's, and with Israel's, is the decision of God to create a new world of people in partnership with God. When we think of election, we must think of God's comprehensive decision to have a "new creation."*

Thus, when we think of ourselves as elect in Christ, we must think of ourselves as elect in the *comprehensive* Christ. When Paul says "Christ," he includes his universal goal and its universal achievement. We are in God's decision to unite "all things" in Christ. The Christ of the cross is God's elect Christ. So is the Christ within whom all things are created. And we are elect within that concrete and comprehensive Christ.

If we reflect on our "election in Christ" in this way, we will be spared from the frightening abstractions that have so often plagued the doctrine of election.[12] We will never think of election as a grace-less, love-less decree to select some individuals for heaven and to reject other individuals for hell. The election in Christ is not a matter of numbers. Paul is talking, as we said, as a person dumbfounded that *he* and *we* were included in God's election. He is singing of the mercy of God that included us; he is not speculating on why certain others are not included.

We are elect *in* Christ. How hard it is to *say* what this means! Christ and Christians, the Lord and the Lord's subjects, the King and the kingdom, the Reconciler and the reconciled, the Leader and the followers, the Head and the body are elect together. Bavinck says, "the community and Christ are together in the one decision; they are, as one community, the elect."[13] Perhaps this is what we should be content to say. God wanted a new creation with people in it who were God's people, and *this* was God's election. God elected a kingdom *with* a King, a body *with* a Head, a people *with* a Leader, a universe *with* a Lord, and sinners *with* a Savior. He elected us in the comprehensive Christ, the Christ who was — in faith — first defined as "Lord of All."

Being chosen in Christ means that we can no more be the object of God's agapic desire apart from Christ than a fraction can exist without an integer, a part without a whole. He is the circle in which we are included. He unites the whole of which we are individually parts. He is the elect Head of whom we are the body. To confess that we are chosen is, then, to confess that our new being is in Christ fundamentally and eternally, and that is to say that we are included in the new creation in Christ only through God's agapic, free decision of love. To make the discovery that one is in Christ is, at the same time and with the same wonder, to confess that one is in Christ because God in love freely desired a new creation in Christ.

What, then, does election by God's free agapic decision tell us of union with Christ? It tells us that the new order begun at the cross and resurrection, which sweeps into the here and now under God's lordship and in the power of God's Spirit, and which will culminate in a new earth where all things are reconciled, is rooted, not in time present, but in God's own eternal desire in love to give God's own self in partnership with humanity and to restore a situation where we will be "God's people" and God will be "our God" and Christ shall be all in all.

II. SUMMARY

We have walked a long and arduous mile in search of what Paul means by the expression "in Christ." We have seen enough to provide the category in which Paul thought when he said "in Christ." The category is history. A new historical situation was created for humanity by Christ. To be in that situation, which began at Calvary and climaxes in the "new earth" to come, is to be "in Christ." We have seen that being "in Christ" is not primarily a subjective moral experience, nor a mystical experience, but existence within a radically new situation in the continuing turmoil of human history.

We can summarize some of the main thoughts of this chapter as follows:

1. Central to understanding how we are "in Christ" are the cross and resurrection. It was in his death and resurrection that Christ began a new history with a new destiny for all who are incorporated in his new order.
2. The new situation gets its character and style from the controlling and liberating Spirit, who is Christ in action as Lord on earth. This is why being "in the Spirit" is the same as being "in Christ."
3. The new situation is so inclusive of life in all its dimensions that it can be called a "new creation." While it will not be complete until the fullness of time, the new creation is already present because the Spirit of the Lord is here and at work in the whole of life.
4. The unity of persons "in Christ" is analogous to their unity "in Adam" because both Christ and Adam began an order of life by their decisions and actions.
5. Life "outside of Christ" is life "in the flesh," "under the law," and "in sin." These words — *flesh, law,* and *sin* — crystallize the whole of history under the moral and spiritual influence of evil. As *they* represent the sole dynamic of the historical order outside of Christ, so the name *Christ* represents the whole new reality governed by Christ as Lord.
6. Divine election is God's decision to recreate the world in Christ. It is God's loving decision to establish, dominate, and realize a new creation that has Christ as the center.

Being "in Christ" means being part of a program as broad as the universe. The new creation is not merely the renewal of individuals, though this must be given its due. The familiar text about being "new creatures in Christ" should not be waved too easily as a slogan for what happens "in me" when I am converted. The design of Christ's new creation is far too grand, too inclusive to be restricted to what happens inside my soul. No nook or cranny of history is too small for its purpose, no cultural potential too large for its embrace. Being in Christ, we are part of a new movement by his grace, a movement rolling on toward the new heaven and new earth where all things are made right and where he is all in all.

NOTES

1. It has been shown that the Judaism of Paul's day was a much more complex system than we are led to suspect by Paul's indictment of it. There was always present within Judaism some sense that forgiveness is necessary and that the written law is not sufficient. W. D. Davies gives a rather sympathetic account of Judaism in *Paul and Rabbinic Judaism* (London: S.P.C.K., 1955), pp. 321ff. The Qumran community and its use of the law present a picture less legalistic than the Judaism that Paul knew. But Paul was not making fine distinctions.

2. Fritz Neugebauer, *In Christus* (Göttingen: Vandenhoeck & Ruprecht, 1958), p. 112.

3. Seesemann, "πάλαι κτλ.," in *Theological Dictionary of the New Testament*, 10 vols., ed. G. Kittel and G. Friedrich (Grand Rapids: William B. Eerdmans, 1964-76), 5: 719-20.

4. Vos, *The Pauline Eschatology* (Grand Rapids: William B. Eerdmans, 1952), p. 47.

5. Schweitzer, *The Mysticism of Paul the Apostle*, trans. William Montgomery (New York: Macmillan, 1955), p. 379.

6. Neugebauer presents a lucid summary of several attempts to work with Paul in this manner (*In Christus*, pp. 9ff.). Davies dispels quite effectively the notion of a Hebrew-Greek dichotomy in Paul (*Paul and Rabbinic Judaism*, p. 320).

7. Romans 7 is *not* a picture of the twisting and turning of the person in Christ as one who wrestles against one "old nature." It is a profile of life in the old order. Paul is not describing his personal experience but the experience common to the native of the old order. This does not apply to every verse in Romans 7, the most obvious exception being verse 25. If the reader is interested in exegetical roll calls, I may say that I am here following Bultmann (*Theology of the New Testament*, vol. 1, trans. Kendrick Grobel [New York: Scribner's, 1951], pp. 244ff., 266, et al.) and Ridderbos (*Aan de Romeinen* [Kampen: J. H. Kok, 1959], pp. 142ff.). For a creative presentation of a *via media*, see A. Bandstra, *The Law and the Elements of the World* (Kampen: J. H. Kok, 1964), pp. 138ff.

8. G. C. Berkouwer, *Sin*, Studies in Dogmatics, trans. Philip C. Holtrop (Grand Rapids: William B. Eerdmans, 1971), pp. 509-10.

9. Barth, *Christ and Adam: Man and Humanity in Romans 5*, trans. T. A. Smail (New York: Collier Books, 1962), p. 60.

10. Albert Schweizer firmly believed that the nature of our union with Christ was explained by Paul's doctrine of election. "Once it is perceived that we have to start from the conception of the predestined solidarity of the Elect with one another and with the Messiah," he writes, "the mystical body of Christ is at once explained" (*The Mysticism of Paul the Apostle*, p. 117). This is too large a claim, it seems to me, but it does have point. Taken in its whole breadth, to include the goal of election as well as the fact of it, to include God's purpose to unite all things in Christ by means of his resurrection, it does tell us something truly significant about union with Christ. But Schweitzer's entire book is weakened, in my judgment, by the fact that he finds in the "pre-ordained solidarity" of the Messiah and his people the key to understanding Paul's "mysticism." There is too much of real history, including our experience and discovery of God in history, to make *pre*-ordination the key to Paul.

11. Of course, Israel's election was a privilege as well as a summons to service. Israel's was the law, the oracles, and the covenant, "and of their race, according to the flesh, is the Christ" (Rom. 9:5). And who is to say that it will not have a time and place in the election of God again? "As regards the gospel they are the enemies of God, for your sake; but as regards election they are beloved for the sake of their forefathers. For the gifts and the call of God are irrevocable" (Rom. 11:28-29). Who can tell what that "irrevocable" call may yet mean in history? After all, they became enemies of God for *our sake*.

12. Berkouwer suggests that Ephesians 1:4 is the text that, more than any other, keeps us from "abstractions and determinism in which the traits of the living God, the Father of Jesus Christ, are obscured by the hiddenness and the menace of inscrutable fate" (*Divine Election*, Studies in Dogmatics, trans. Hugo Bekker [Grand Rapids: William B. Eerdmans, 1960], pp. 153-54).

13. H. Bavinck, *Gereformeerde Dogmatiek*, vol. 2 (Kampen: J. H. Kok, 1911), p. 421.

The Christian Life:
Perseverance and Renewal

Hendrikus Berkhof

I. PERSEVERANCE

The more that believers, prompted by their security in God, venture into the life of new obedience, the more they need, as they struggle along, the certainty that God's faithfulness and Christ's substitution will carry them through. Justification tells us that we stand on an unshakable foundation on which we can always fall back. But who guarantees that we, as we struggle and stumble along, and even suffer defeats, will not slide off this foundation? The more we fight, the more we sense how fearfully great the resistance in our heart is to surrendering ourselves to God and remaining faithful in the struggle. Then the question concerning certainty and security arises anew — this time as a question regarding not the foundation but the horizon. The question is not

"Am I really a sinner received in grace?" but "Will this adoption be permanent and show its effects in my life?" Who can guarantee that? And we might also ask who, without such a certainty, can avoid succumbing to despair and keep up the courage to continue to fight.

These questions bring us to the doctrine that is known in church history as *the perseverance of the saints.* It is a doctrine that articulates a fundamental insight. Paul, whose epistle to the Romans is entirely devoted to the renewal of humanity, starts with justification (chaps. 1–5), speaks next about struggle and progress (chaps. 6–8), and concludes the train of thought of the first half of his epistle by affirming his conviction that believers will persevere and overcome (8:28-39). It could not be otherwise: our wavering faithfulness is upheld on all sides by God's unwavering faithfulness. This faithfulness is not dependent on our faith; rather, our faith depends on this faithfulness of God. "For I am sure that nothing will be able to separate us from the love of God in Christ Jesus our Lord" (Rom. 8:39).

Reprinted from *Christian Faith*, rev. ed., trans. Sierd Woudstra (Grand Rapids: William B. Eerdmans, 1986), pp. 471-94.

Believers may and dare to believe that they will persevere in that faith and that nothing will snatch them out of God's hand. Nevertheless, here again we come across what we have noticed so often in questions about the faith — namely, that its systematic reflection poses great intellectual problems. I cannot imagine that believers would doubt their perseverance on the mistaken assumption that ultimately it would depend on them; were that the case, ultimately all of salvation would be dependent on them, and that would mean that it would no longer be a matter of saving grace freely given. Yet I cannot imagine either that believers would dare to assert with a quiet and unruffled confidence that they will persevere in the faith throughout their lives; such an assertion would border on recklessness and be as much at variance with the faith as the fear that they would not make it. The same Paul who wrote Romans 8 issued many exhortations to struggle on, lest we lose the victory and find ourselves disqualified in the end.

Those who intellectually detach themselves from the faith (a danger particularly for students of theology) feel themselves compelled to choose whether God guarantees the faith and to that end manipulates humans, or whether humans, on account of the decisive character of our cooperation, are totally dependent on the power and permanence of our own faith. God and humanity are not locked in a competitive struggle, however, and do not limit each other in this way. Rather, they meet each other in a covenant in which God elicits human responsibility and cooperation and at the same time helps us in our weaknesses. God's faithfulness also consists in the fact that God creates and seeks our faithfulness and realizes God's faithfulness in and through our faithfulness and so causes it to triumph. We do not persevere, but God perseveres, by constantly calling us, disturbing us, inspiring us. So we learn to persevere and receive the assurance that "he who began a good work in you will bring it to completion at the day of Jesus Christ" (Phil. 1:6).

In the Bible, especially the New Testament, we regularly find this witness of certainty and perseverance, as the manifestation not of human steadfastness but of divine faithfulness. In the discussion of the perseverance of the saints, its defenders always point to Luke 22:32; John 6:37, 40; 10:27; Romans 8:29-30, 34, 39; Philippians 1:6; 1 John 2:19; 3:9; and to the Johannine concept of "remain" (menein). Those who are opposed, however, point to all those passages that warn believers against a possible falling away or that presuppose such a possibility, such as Ezekiel 18:24; Romans 11:20; 1 Corinthians 9:27; 10:12; 2 Corinthians 13:5ff.; Galatians 5:4; Hebrews 6:4-8; 10:26-31; 2 Peter 2:18-22. They also point to such apostate Christians as Alexander and Hymenaeus and Demas (1 Tim. 1:20; 2 Tim. 4:10; cf. 1 Tim. 4:1). David's and Peter's deep falls also come up in this respect, although their lives could also be used as evidence by the supporters of the doctrine of perseverance.

Augustine, a thinker with a passionate concern for God's work of renewal in humans, deals specifically with perseverance in De dono perseverantiae (429). His starting point is that though believers can lapse totaliter, they cannot not lapse finaliter. In a fine way of getting at the subject, he deals with perseverance first of all as the presupposition of the six petitions of the Lord's Prayer (chaps. 2–7).

But it was not until the Reformation that these questions received broad and thorough attention. Soon significant differences announced themselves. The Lutherans put the main emphasis on the assurance implicit in justification, leaving the struggle in sanctification largely in the shadows; consequently, they felt far less the need for the assurance afforded by the doctrine of perseverance. In contrast, Bucer, emphasizing much more the progress in the renewal process, wrote of perseverance as based on the "divine seed" that the Holy Spirit plants in believers already at their birth as a religious potential (cf. 1 John 3:9). Calvin dissented; he did not believe in such an innate goodness. He asserted that the elect "do not differ at all from others except that they are protected by God's special mercy from rushing headlong into the final ruin of death" (Inst., 2.24.10). He wrote a balanced, careful, and pastoral presentation of perseverance (see especially Inst., 2.2.15-28, 38-39 and 2.24.6-7), in which he tries to provide a basis for certainty (certitudo) while warning against false security (securitas). Nevertheless, he could not prevent the rise, since Beza, of a rationalistic systematization. The Remonstrants came to doubt perseverance and eventually even denied it. In the alternative they proposed, they came close to the Roman Catholic dialectic of cooperation plus "assistance of divine grace." The Synod of Dort (1619), mainly by going back to Calvin's position, stood in a strong position against this dubious Arminian standpoint.

Pastoral concerns, too, played a role in the differences. The Lutherans and the Remonstrants feared that the doctrine of perseverance would make people careless and indifferent. Calvin sought to comfort the fearful with it — a comfort that according to the Lutherans was fully offered in the doctrine of justification. A fine dogma-historical and dogmatic discussion of this theme, in the spirit of Calvin, is offered by G. C. Berkouwer in *Faith and Perseverance* (E.T. 1958) and by J. Moltmann in *Prädestination und Perseveranz* (1961). In both one can also read about the controversy since 1561 between the Lutheran Marbach and the Reformed Zanchius, which led to a sharper demarcation of the positions. Berkouwer contends that perseverance is a confession of *faith*, one that is possible only through listening to the scriptural admonitions and the contemplation of one's own ups and downs. "Apart from faith nothing can be said here, but all thought will entangle itself in contradiction" (p. 106).

This is the place to say something about the concept of the *ordo salutis* as this is current in Reformed dogmatics. On the basis of Romans 8:29-30 (sometimes Acts 26:17-18 is cited as well), attempts were made to introduce a kind of sequence in the renewal process, e.g. faith-justification-calling-illumination-regeneration-mystical union-renewal (so H. Schmid, *Dogmatik*, pars. 41-48), or calling-justification-sanctification-perseverance (so Bavinck, *Gereformeerde Dogmatiek*, IV). That easily led to "categorization," thereby turning the way of salvation into a psychological process. Already the aorists used by Paul, even for designating *future* "phases" (*edoxasen*), prove that that was not what he had in mind; he was concerned with the unity of the aspects in the process of renewal as they exist in God's eternal gracious purpose for humankind. But precisely that unity means that in the study of the faith various aspects must be distinguished. Aspects are logical distinctions; they do not suggest a chronological sequence, let alone a psychologically observable evolutionary process. Yet renewal means participation in a way of God through history, and such a way has at least a logical before and after. Barth, looking to Hollaz, is too negative on this point (*Church Dogmatics*, IV/3: 505-7), although he also gives evidence that he needs a kind of logical order (*Church Dogmatics*, IV/1-3). Misuse should warn us, but it does not abolish its use. A. König offers a correction and renewal as well (*Heil en heilsweg* [1983]).

Meanwhile, in our study of the concept of perseverance we have come in the vicinity of another concept closely tied in with it, one that through the centuries has received much theological attention — namely, election. It is correct to say that what is called "perseverance" from the human perspective is from God's point of view "election." But this is also a term with which we cross the boundaries of the renewal process and its difficulties. For "election" is not only the final resting place of the heart in the ups and downs of the spiritual struggle; it is also the basic word, which is as comprehensive as salvation itself, because it characterizes the totality of God's dealing with God's people, God's church, God's world. Everywhere we meet a God who takes the initiative for and often against humanity in order to establish a saving fellowship and carries it through despite our opposition and apathy. God supports us despite ourselves. That is how we came to know God in the way of Israel, in the life of Jesus, in the working of the Spirit, in the upbuilding of the church, and as God calls, blesses, and equips people. And we shall get to know God fully when, despite all our resistance, God makes all things new.

My favorite term to designate God's fellowship with us has been *covenant*. But I have also regularly pointed out that this differs from a human covenant in which the two partners are equal. That difference is expressed in the word *election*. We are elected to this strange covenant in which the One not only calls the other, challenges and involves the the other, but also precedes, supports, and cares for the other, because the Faithfulness of the One is ultimately not dependent on the faithfulness or unfaithfulness of the other.

This makes it understandable that there are people for whom election is the center and foundation of their faith and their reflection on the faith. But in this study of the faith I do not follow them. The reason is that the confession of election is rooted in a covenant fellowship that is not comprehensively characterized by the word *election.* For this word only states what God does. It expresses the unilateral initiative by which God makes specific people and groups the objects of God's grace and calling. In election, Israel, the church, or humanity is only object. In the covenant, on the other hand, humanity is given a subjective standing. The covenant also involves humans in their responsibility, their guilt, their conversion, their obedience. All that is not contained in the word *election,* yet it is only those who know of all that and who are burdened by their own failures as covenant partners who can and may fall back on the one-sided Faithfulness by which they know themselves to be upheld. Election is the first word in God's activity and the last in the confession of believers. It marks the horizon that surrounds and makes the covenant arena possible.

Lifting the word out of the covenant context from which it arises causes accidents, as has been abundantly demonstrated in church history. When election is made into an isolated subject, is one-sidedly applied to the individual and his or her eternal destiny, and when it is no longer confessed but intellectually analyzed, it evokes a series of questions that are absolutely unanswerable, because they are out of the covenant order — questions such as "Why, years ago, was only Israel chosen?" "Why is Christ our Savior and not some other savior figure?" "Why is the church sometimes spread all over the world and then again a diminishing minority?" "Why have many never heard the gospel?" "Why do some hearers believe and many others do not?" With those questions we no longer take our stand on this side of the covenant fellowship but on the side of God and eternity. That is not our side; therefore we are unable to ask the right questions, and we receive no answers. The penalty is a fatal choice: *either* we have to believe in a God who is arbitrary and fickle, *or* in a God who is powerless and thus totally dependent on the initiative of humans themselves.

The mystery of election, far from detracting from whatever is to be said about the actions and the failures of the human covenant partner (free will, resistance, conversion, obedience), presupposes and establishes it. How? That we do not know; we are not God and therefore do not know how it is possible that God's divine sovereignty does not detract from our human freedom but instead evokes it and makes it possible. We do not fathom *how* it can be done, but we do experience and confess *that* it happens.

Purposely we discuss the word *election* at the end of this section which is full of our human responsibility, a responsibility that again and again proves too much for our limited strength. What keeps us from despairing is the certainty that we persevere because God in God's election perseveres with us. But it is to be remembered that this comfort is only for those who keep struggling.

For an extensive survey of the concept and the words for *election* in the Bible, see the *Theological Dictionary of the New Testament,* vol. 4, *s.v. legō (eklegomai, eklogē, eklektos).* In the Old Testament the concept is in turn applied to the people of Israel, the patriarchs, kings, priests, the remnant, and the servant of the Lord. Here the focus is on election to the service of God and in God to the people, the neighbor, and the world. In the New Testament the concept is in turn applied to Christ, the apostles, sinners and outcasts, the church, and the individual. Here the main focus is election unto children of God and to eternal salvation (which includes election to service; see Eph. 1:12; 1 Pet. 2:9). I mentioned already how Paul in Rom. 1–8 structures the process of renewal, culminating in the perseverance of the saints. In integral relation to it, Paul mentions election (8:28-30), which then in 9–11 he extends beyond the boundaries of the church and the individual to apply it to Israel and the nations of the world.

As a fundamental term, *election* can come up for discussion with a variety of subjects: in connection with God's counsel and good pleasure; in connection with sin that makes it impossible for us to save ourselves; in connection with Christ, the chosen One, in whom we are chosen; in connection with the Spirit, who alone can create faith; in connection with the chosen church; and in connection with the individual who within the church ventures to believe in his or her personal election. Always, however, election stands in the context of doxology and gratitude.

Not until Augustine did election become a permanent theme in the history of the church. In his thought this doctrine is closely interwoven with the doctrine of original sin and humanity's inability to save itself. It is noteworthy, too, that the above-mentioned *De dono perseverantiae* forms the second half of a tract of which the first half is entitled *De praedestinatione sanctorum* (428). The history of the doctrine of predestination is described in many handbooks and monographs. Here I mention only some of the highlights. Luther, who in his *On the Bondage of the Will* challenged Erasmus, boldly presented predestination from the perspective of God's total sovereignty as this is implied in God's existence. But later he did not repeat those thoughts. Predestination was given a secondary importance; Lutheranism did not really need the doctrine, for the same reason that it could virtually do without the doctrine of perseverance. Calvin and Calvinism moved in an opposite direction. Initially the doctrine was not much emphasized. In the first edition of the *Institutes* (1536) and in the Catechism of Geneva (1542) it is only incidentally mentioned, in connection with the doctrine of the church (viewing the church, in Augustinian fashion, as the *numerus praedestinorum*). In the final edition of the *Institutes* (1559) it is taken up in the context of the conclusion of the renewal process (3.21-24) in much more detail and with a polemic thrust. Next to beautiful pastoral passages (for Calvin predestination was on the one hand a humiliation and on the other a comfort), we come across this statement: "since election itself could not stand except as set over against reprobation . . . those whom God passes over, he condemns. . . . From this it follows that God's secret plan is the cause of hardening" (*Inst.*, 3.23.1). Thus election threatens to become an abstract principle and God an arbitrary God — which leads Calvin, convinced of his faithfulness to Scripture at this point, to make the following painful statement: "the decree is dreadful indeed, I confess" (*Inst.*, 3.23.7).

At this point emerges what is called "supralapsarianism," the doctrine according to which God already in the decree of creation, irrespective of sin, differentiated between elect and nonelect. Yet in the Heidelberg Catechism, election is mentioned only in passing, in connection with the church (answer 54). And the Calvin-inspired Gallican Confession (1559) and the similar Belgic Confession (1561) turned away from Calvin's strict logic to follow the infralapsarian line, according to which God in just judgment "leaves" people, because of their sin, in the perdition to which they have condemned themselves, while saving others

from it solely out of grace. The Canons of Dort speak in similar vein about predestination (I, 6). But there was something inconsistent about this whole approach. Hence Calvin's successor, Beza, developed the supralapsarianistic doctrine, making it into a system. This detached predestination from the doctrine of renewal and put it back in the doctrine of God, the *locus de decretis Dei*. Many regarded this consistent system as deterministic and rejected it. Remonstrantism countered it with the doctrine that God does not elect *to* faith but *on account of* faith, but again this placed the ultimate decision in the hands of humanity. Generally, Reformed Protestantism has opted for the infralapsarian position and accepted its weaknesses and consequences along with it. Evaluating these controversies with the advantage of historical distance, I must say again that those who grapple with this issue felt that they were faced with choosing between God and humanity as the subject and that they lacked the theological categories with which to grasp the uniqueness of the biblical-covenantal (intersubjective) mode of speaking. That is not to say that it is easier for us to solve the problems they faced, only that we who view them from the perspective of different intellectual categories are better able to see how insoluble they are: we are more aware of our limitations in formulating theological concepts. Two worthwhile attempts at reformulating the classical problems and placing them in a biblical framework are J. G. Woelderink's *De uitverkiezing* (1951) and G. C. Berkouwer's *Divine Election* (E.T., 1960). These publications stress the pastoral tenor of election and oppose an extrapolation that turns it into a deterministic doctrine. Another attempt (polemic in design) at restructuring the doctrine of election along more biblical lines is James Daane's *The Freedom of God: A Study of Election and Pulpit* (1973).

Going the other way, Barth has tried to break through the classical impasse in the *Church Dogmatics*, II/2. Handling election as a basic term, he treats it as comprehensively and supralapsarianistically as Beza — with this great difference, that he knows of no double predestination, because election in Christ is solely and totally a matter of grace. "The doctrine of election is the sum of the Gospel," he writes (*Church Dogmatics*, II/2: 3). But then many questions arise, particularly in reference to the force of humanity's "No." Is human resistance still taken seriously here? Barth has not convinced me that we should make election the basic theological term. See also K. Schwarzwäller, *Das Gotteslob der angefochtenen Gemeinde* (1970), who, however, goes back to Luther's *On the Bondage of the Will*. An extensive and thoughtful discussion of the classical questions is offered by Weber, *Grundlagen der Dogmatik*, vol. 2 (1962), pp. 458-562. Unlike him, however,

I have preferred to include wherever relevant the discussion of the elective dimension of all God's work, using a terminology that fits the particular topics, and to place the explicit formulation of the concept of election at the end of my discussion of humanity's renewal (just as Calvin did in *Inst.,* III).

II. THE COMPLETED RENEWAL

Whatever progress and improvement there might be in the believer's life, the ultimate goal of the renewal, conformity with Christ, still lies far ahead of us — so far that it may seem unattainable to us, due to our own sin as well as to our being a part of a world that is subject to sin, misery, and death. In this respect, particularly death is the power robbing us of the hope that total renewal might be within our reach. And not just the death that comes prematurely, but every death. Precisely the "normal" death makes us aware that this life is meant to be finite. Indeed, until the very last moment, we may develop more of our inherent potential, and in general it is true that each phase of our lives expresses in its own way the inexhaustible mystery of human nature, of what it means to be "human." That implies, however, that it is incorrect to speak of an evolution in one's personal life; what may be done is to speak of the kind of progress in which we continually make discoveries, which, however, tend to displace earlier ones. When people die at an advanced age, we usually have a feeling that they had reached the end of their potentialities, or even — considering modern medicine — that they outlived their potentialities. That, however, is particularly the experience that goes with our modern Western civilization. Before our time and around us, millions of people, perhaps the majority, have died too early, because famine, illness, war, and natural catastrophes prematurely cut off their potentialities. But close to us, too, every day thousands are dying, whose lives, due to circumstances beyond their control, illness or whatever, never came to real fruition. Further pondering this, one could ask whether anyone ever realizes more than a fraction of his or her potential. So death always evokes in us contradictory feelings; it is necessary and good for people as well as for the history in which they play their role (how else would subsequent generations get their opportunity?), yet all the time it also cuts short possibilities by withholding from people and their history the realization of these possibilities. Out of an indestructible longing for much more of a realization than this earthly life offers, humankind's hopes and beliefs have therefore through the ages reached beyond death. But is that anything more than wishful thinking?

I am not suggesting that we should not be able to obtain new insights about death by looking at it from the perspective of entirely different areas of human experience. Such is certainly the case when we look at death from the viewpoint of the Christian faith. We have been placed on a new way, the way of God's covenant faithfulness, a way that begins with Israel and on which we meet God as the God who with all God's heart works for lost humankind, who therefore in Jesus creates a new human existence that through death attains to resurrection and glorification, and who in Jesus is at work with the Spirit to involve people in that new way of life. This salvation is so great that it cannot possibly be realized within the confines of the present provisional and sinful existence that is now our lot. Therefore death cannot be the end of God's way. This becomes especially clear from the theme of this chapter: if the Spirit wins people for God and imparts to them in struggle and pushing forward a renewal that is no more than very fragmentary, then God will have to finish beyond death what is started here — or death would be more powerful than God and thus the real god and the ultimate, chill mystery of human life. On the ground of this alternative or, rather, in virtue of the encounter with this faithful God, the Christian believes in what is called, in traditional terms, a "life after death": we believe in the completion of the renewal.

The Christian church is thus not basing this expectation on, for example, scientific discoveries or occult experiences. The church does not even appeal to the widespread feeling that somehow this fragmentary human life must be able to come to full unfolding after death; as such that feeling could very well be "wishful thinking" or rash self-affirmation. Faith is not confirmed by this feeling; on the contrary, this feeling is confirmed by faith or, better stated, by God who is moved by our frustrations and our groaning (Rom. 8:18-22).

Meanwhile, we are not to think of this hope in the face of death as a more or less rational inference, nor as a more or less irrational leap. It is not the case that the believers on their way of renewal suddenly happen on the wall of death and then, those cliffs notwithstanding, continue to believe in the completion of their renewal. Death is not a surprise event but one that, in other forms, believers have met often on the way of renewal. Death is included in the renewal process as a fermenting element. Four times so far we have come across it: (1) in Jesus' death as the necessary consequence of his obedience, a death that became the doorway to his exaltation; (2) in our dying to ourselves as the other side of our justification; (3) in the dying we experience as we meet the hostility of the world; and (4) in death in the form of our constant self-denial in the renewal process. In all these forms of death a dissolution of the human self occurs, which will at the moment or in retrospect prove to be the other side of liberation and renewal. Hence the believer knows that on the path God travels with God's people, death and renewal do not exclude but rather include each other. The natural death that comes to all individuals as a biological necessity does indeed seem entirely different from

the preceding forms of death, but in Christ's death the two have been linked to each other. What is established between them is the link between creation and redemption. As concerns its provisional character, creation is meant to be dissolved. Humanity's created nature is such that we can reach our destination only through the dissolution of our selfhood. Our sin is that we refuse this self-surrender and in self-affirmation resist death. So long as we do that, we are bound to experience death as a defeat — a defeat that, from the perspective of faith, is "the reward of sin." But through our participation in salvation, we come to understand death in relation to its divinely designed purpose — not only as the confirmation of the provisionality of this earthly existence but also as its abolition and therewith as the gateway to the perfection of this life.

It remains difficult to tie this faith in with our negative experience of dying and death. After all, the principle of life that integrated and animated the organism is completely gone. Humanity that was taken up into a covenant with God apparently or seemingly no longer exists. However, God, who entered into this relationship with humanity, is still there. With the "guarantee" of God's Spirit, God ensures this relationship, and thereby the person with whom God entered into covenant will persist in his or her new life. More we cannot and need not know on this point.

It is unusual to discuss already in this context what is called "personal eschatology"; normally this is done at the end, as an aspect of eschatology. The major concern is then the consummation of the world and of history, while the destiny of the individual after his or her death remains a more or less unrelated subject alongside of it. Then we get this question: Where "is" humanity in the interval between death and the consummation of the world? When the question concerning an intermediate state is formulated like that, faith has no way of giving an answer, because we transpose our personal life to a strange context, lifting it out of its primary context, this earthly life in which our faith, hope, and love are no more than fragmentary, clamoring for perfection. In reaction against an individualistic eschatology, we are today in danger of forgetting that the core of all expectation and the climax of God's covenantal saving work is the perfection of *persons*. The tendency not so long ago to relate the consummation primarily to the future structures of society remains below the level of the Christian expectation. It makes those who have died before "fertilizer on the fields of the future."

In the course of the seventies (the "Me" generation), the interest within and outside the church shifted (again) to the personal "hereafter," now reinforced (scientifically or not) by testimonies of past-life and near-death experiences. Because of that the modern idea that our self is totally dependent on the body and therefore simultaneously dies with it is not as firm as it used to be. That can be a gain. The fact is, however, that the testimonies of reincarnation point neither to a heightening of humanness and of communion with God nor to greater insight into the human situation; they only satisfy the desire for repetition, the hope that this life can be perpetuated. But this life is unrepeatable, and that should be taken seriously. The fact is that in our consciousness there is no recollection of earlier lives. Near-death experiences are common, but they happen on this side of death. They point to an enlargement of the human consciousness, and no one knows how much truth there is in them relative to the hereafter. Both experiences involve a "self," but seldom if at all is there any indication of a personal relationship with God associated with them.

Theology has also become newly interested in what may await the individual after death. In *Death and Eternal Life* (1976), J. Hick tries to relate the Christian expectation of the future with that of Buddhism and Hinduism by means of the idea that the individual is perfected only by surrendering to the vastness of the totality. He thinks of many vertical reincarnations of the one earthly life. For a summary, see chapter 5 of his *Centre of Christianity* (2nd ed., 1977). In addition to this book, with its universal-religious and speculative-synthetic method, is H. Küng's *Eternal Life?* (E.T., 1984), which is based exclusively on the resurrection of Jesus and is much more reserved in its statements. But because Küng conceives of Jesus' resurrection as a form of immortally going-to-heaven, he detaches the personal expectation of the future from the history of humankind and its future in the kingdom of God.

Inevitably the question arises of why the Old Testament says so little about humanity's personal future. One can refer to Isaiah 26:19 and Daniel 12:2, and possibly to Psalms 16:9-11; 49:16; and 73:25-26. Very likely all these statements are from a rather late phase of Old Testament covenant history. At first the individual person was only a part of the nation as a totality, and only gradually did the person become detached from it. Until the New Testament era, the promises concerning the individual person remained a matter of dispute (Matt. 22:23; Acts 23:8); the decisive answer was given only in Jesus' resurrection (1 Cor. 15:12-22). The protracted silence of the Old Testament serves as a warning not to think of the otherworldly perfection of the individual as God's sole purpose; God is also concerned about the present, society, the world, and its structures.

However, anyone who after Jesus' resurrection would still regard the perfection of the person as *quantité négligeable* should note how in Matthew 22:29, 33; 1 Corinthians 15:34; and Philippians 1:6 this perfection is directly related to God's own reality and nature: the living God requires the living partner.

In the New Testament, the words *zōē* and *thanatos* have more than one level of meaning; see *TDNT, s.v.* Hence it is customary in the study of the faith to distinguish between spiritual, temporal, and eternal death. The distinctions we are required to make here are so much one subject in the Bible that in such passages as Genesis 2:17; 3:19; and Romans 5:12-21; 6:23, the biological normality of "ordinary" death is ignored. 1 Corinthians 15:45-49 shows, however, that Paul was aware of a death that occurs apart from sin. But in the context of sinful humanity's concrete life and death, this is an abstraction devoid of essential significance; only in the context of faith is it reasonable to make such distinctions. (The statement in Rom. 6:23 about death as the wages of sin is, in light of 6:15-22, to be regarded as a phase that by faith we have left behind us.)

A much-discussed problem is that of the continuity and discontinuity between our earthly life and the life that awaits us. Already Paul grappled with it and used the metaphor of the seed and the full-grown plant (1 Cor. 15:35-38). On account of God's faithfulness also in and beyond death, the continuity must have the first and the last word in our faith and in our thinking. It is indeed only by virtue of that faithfulness that God graciously bridges the rupture of death. For centuries, church and theology have sought the anthropological correlate of this faithfulness in a Platonically conceived "immortal soul" that naturally survives purely physical death. That is definitely not the view the New Testament takes; on the contrary, it asserts that only God possesses immortality (1 Tim. 6:16) and that in the resurrection we will be *clothed* with immortality (1 Cor. 15:53). In reaction, many in our century have denied every anthropological continuity. But that detracts from the covenant relationship: God's faithfulness holds on to us even in death and guarantees our identity even in discontinuity. From the perspective of this side of death we are unable, however, to determine what that identity is. Bavinck writes: "What that is we do not know and can never find out" (*Gereformeerde Dogmatiek*, IV, no. 573). But God guarantees that I, or my "self" (whatever that may be), will be kept and renewed.

Yet lately thinkers have again begun to take their starting point in an anthropological continuity. One of these is Karl Rahner, who sees death primarily as an act of the immortal person by which he or she brings himself or herself to maturation. This view is widespread among present-day Roman Catholic theologians, but is attacked by Schillebeeckx (in *Tijdschrift voor theologie* [1970], pp. 418ff.), among others. It misjudges the hard discontinuity of death and ascribes to human beings at this point a self-determination that they do not possess. Later Rahner became more "dialectic."

The relation of continuity and discontinuity is a very precise one; it will not do to play off the one against the other or to detract from the one at the expense of the other. The continuity of the Spirit's work from beginning to end requires the radical demolition of so much, of everything in our life that is opposed to God's total claim upon us.

Only now, finally, can we raise the main question of this section: What can we know by faith about the content of the perfection on the other side of the boundary of death? We can say this much: the knowledge is limited to what we, in virtue of the coherence between this side and the other side, can derive or surmise from our experience of the faith. We know that Christ's Spirit, who here takes possession of people and partially transforms them, on the other side completes that process in the sense that we, to use some New Testament terminology, "will be with Christ," "will be made like his image," so that "God may be all in all." But all of this lies so far beyond our present experience, is so far beyond our faith experience, and is so unimaginable, that we are inclined to think of it as being the product of an instantaneous re-creative act of God, that from death humanity suddenly awakes to a totally changed life. But then we detract from the close tie between life on both sides of the death crisis. The New Testament also speaks about the completion as "fruit," "harvest," and "wages" of the sowing and struggling in this life.

That tie has first of all a negative consequence: on the other side, in the light of the all-exposing light of God's presence, we shall become aware of our culpable failure with respect to God's covenant faithfulness as we never did or could within the confines of our earthly existence. Death does not instantaneously and automatically transfer us into the consummation. The connection with our former life is first of all expressed in what the Christian faith calls "the judgment." There can be no deep and joyful awareness of the renewal without an equally deep sense of obstruction. The radical renewal does not im-*media*-tely follow upon our earthly life: it is mediated by the judgment that bridges the chasm. Only by way of an exposure that puts us utterly to shame can we, as people with an *earlier* existence and with an earlier existence in which we were *different*, receive the renewal as God's marvelous gift.

But if that is so, we can hardly stop at this negative mediation. In the judgment we are shown how great is the distance that separates us from the goal and that must still be bridged. Will that distance suddenly, as if by magic, by bridged by a re-creative act of God? Or is there on the other side of death something like purification and maturing? Will we on the other side be required to lose ourselves in still more and new processes of death, in order to become completely ourselves relative to God? On this point we can do nothing else than ask questions. But these are questions that must be raised if we are serious about the tie between life here and beyond. If renewal here is no magical metamorphosis — and nowhere in creation do we observe such a discontinuous transformation — then we may not and should not expect it for the future. What awaits us beyond death may rather prove to be a continuing road, albeit on a higher level and with the goal more clearly in view.

Considering this idea may also keep us from viewing the consummation first of all as a fulfillment of our own earthly desires. It is not a matter of safety but of sanctity. Only through radical surgery are we made ready for a world in which God is all in all and in which God, as our God, satisfies all the desires that have been created in us.

There is thus a goal that by virtue of God's intention is going to be reached. Its content can be variously described. In the New Testament and in church history we find many descriptions: "vision of God," "eternal rest," "being with Christ," and so on. I prefer to speak of "conformity with Christ," for reasons I have given elsewhere. In the current context, this description has the advantage of clearly maintaining the connection with Christ's earthly work and that of the Spirit. It also has an advantage over the rhetoric of "vision" and "rest" in that it lacks the overtones of individualism and passivism. If we are to resemble Christ, then we, like him, must be totally oriented toward God and the neighbor. Such conformity is possible only in fellowship. Hence the New Testament portrays the consummation as the consummated covenant communion of God in Christ with those who have become conformed to Christ's image — as a banquet, a city, a celebrating multitude. The idea of the vision of God and of resting are each implicitly included in this larger concept.

It remains yet to refer to the practical import of this belief in the consummation. Only the outsider will think that this faith deprives our earthly life of its importance. The opposite is true: this perspective lends an eternal importance to our earthly life. For judgment and consummation tell us how seriously God takes this life and how great a responsibility God has given us in this life. At the same time, this seriousness does not crush us, because God guarantees its consummation. And because this earthly life is not a goal but a road, we need not demand and expect everything from it. So the expectation of consummation liberates us *from* our passion for happiness now and *unto* the free service of God and humanity.

On the method of eschatology that extrapolates from what already happens here and now, see K. Rahner, "The Hermeneutics of Eschatological Assertions," in *Theological Investigations*, IV (E.T. 1966), pp. 323-46; and H. Berkhof, *Well-Founded Hope* (1969), pp. 16-21 and *passim.*

The New Testament sees a close connection between life on this side and on the other side of the death line: the latter is the consequence, the fruit, and the reward of the former. Note the use of such words and images as prize, crown, fruit, harvest, seed and full-grown plant, sowing and harvesting (see, e.g., Matt. 13:24-30; Mark 4:1-9; John 12:24-25; 1 Cor. 15:35-53; Gal. 5:8-9). Especially characteristic in this connection is the use of the concept "wages." This term was taken away from the Jewish moralism of the time and filled with an opposite content (see Matt. 20:1-16). Wages is now no longer the correlate of merit but of the expectation that grace has awakened in the heart. The faithful suffering on this side, the struggle and perseverance, will on the other side of the death line prove not to have been in vain, will be fulfilled and crowned by God. There will be rewarded what is faithfully professed here.

The concept of judgment is used above in one specific sense — namely, as the judgment of the works done by believers in their earthly life (see Rom. 14:10-12; 1 Cor. 3:10-15; 2 Cor. 5:10; Gal. 6:8-9). In Protestant theology, this viewpoint is almost completely pushed aside by the accent on grace. In Roman Catholic piety it is (or used to be) very prominent in connection with the veneration of saints and purgatory. The Roman Catholic Church assumes correctly that believers differ greatly in regard to their progress and fruitfulness. In Roman Catholicism a saint is one who has performed perfect or even supererogatory good works *(opera supererogatoria);* such a person can by his or her works and intercession plead the cause of weaker believers on earth. We do not know, however, what God's standards are, nor whether even one lives up to them. This doctrine is particularly unacceptable because of its moralistic framework. According to the New Testament proclamation of judgment, we are each of us personally responsible for our lives and should have the desire to make sure that in the judgment our life will prove to have answered as much as possible to God's purpose (see Gal. 6:1-10), because the coming perfection will be connected with the measure of our success and failure in this life. While not making the ethical caliber of our deeds here a condition for salvation, these acts do become extremely important, since they co-determine how God will give us his salvation.

So the idea of a judgment according to one's deeds leads of itself to the consideration of a process of purification, called purgatory in the Roman Catholic tradition. The Reformation broke with this doctrine because of its moralistic conception of salvation and its detrimental effect on the practice of piety (indulgences, intercessory prayers, and masses for the dead). It postulated a sudden, radical transformation after the judgment, usually without giving it further theological reflection and without connecting it with the struggle for sanctification on earth. Meanwhile, Roman Catholic thinking has also become much more reserved. Rahner has put forth the idea of "ripening" *(ausreifen)* ("The Life of the Dead," in *Theological Investigations,* IV [E.T. 1966], pp. 347-54). He develops this idea in connection with his dubious view of death, but that connection does not take away its value. The Roman Catholic appeal to 1 Corinthians 3:15 as "proof" for a phase of purification is farfetched, yet that statement does suggest that Paul thought of more than an abrupt re-creation of humanity, that salvation is accompanied by a painful journey toward awareness of one's failures on earth. The difficulties here are more an open question for theological reflection than a subject for back-and-forth theological denunciation. The matter of making inferences from faith about what lies beyond death is fraught with far too many difficulties. One can state

with Bavinck that "after death there is no more sanctification, one enters upon a state of complete sanctity . . . for death is the greatest leap someone can make, a sudden transposition of the believer into Christ's presence, and thereby a complete destruction of the outward man and a complete renewal of the inner man" (*Gereformeerde Dogmatiek,* IV, no. 650, under 4). But one can also ask with G. J. Heering, "Does this change instantaneously, when God shows mercy to the repentant soul and takes it to himself? . . . Life is called a training school, but perhaps there is a higher training school above" (*De menselijke ziel* [1955], pp. 190, 192).

It is striking that in the divergent traditions of the New Testament, the content of the consummation is preferably and very soberly and concentratedly designated "being with Christ" (Luke 23:43; John 14:2-3; 17:24; 2 Cor. 5:8; Phil. 1:23; 1 Thess. 4:14, 17; cf. Rev. 14:13). Next to this, the content is often called "seeing God." The image of rest, which has become even more popular, is marginal in the New Testament (Heb. 4:8-11; Rev. 14:13), which in any event contains nothing that would suggest that this rest is a blessed idleness. For the pros and cons of the various images and concepts, see H. Berkhof, *A Well-founded Hope,* pp. 53-57.

ECCLESIOLOGICAL EXPRESSIONS

The concept of the church is a central theme in the Reformed tradition. In Reformed views, the church is the people of God, who are called by God through the Holy Spirit as they confess Jesus Christ as Lord and Savior. The essays in this section express the essence of Reformed thinking about the nature of the church and of how the church relates to the political structures of its society, especially in regard to the vital issue of religious liberty.

John T. McNeill's historical/theological essay "The Church in Sixteenth-Century Reformed Theology" surveys formative Reformed thought about many aspects of the nature and function of the church.

Since the church is elected and called to live in the present world, no survey of ecclesiology can omit a consideration of how the church is situated in history in the political contexts in which it finds itself. In "Church and Politics in the Reformed Tradition," Eberhard Busch studies the relation of church and state as set forth especially by Zwingli and Calvin. While the cultures of the Reformers differ in many ways from our own, Busch finds important insights in the Reformers' views in this area — the implications of which they did not always apply to their own specific situations.

In a similar way, though with a special focus on religious freedom, David Little in "Reformed Faith and Religious Liberty" surveys two basic attitudes evident in the Reformed tradition — on the one hand, an affirmation of the importance of a firm line of separation between church and state, and on the other hand an affirmation of the importance of a religious foundation for the civil order, and hence the importance of positive, cooperative relations between church and state. Little explores ways in which the strain between these two basic attitudes has been resolved throughout the Reformed tradition.

167

The essays in this section remind us that while there are deep and mysterious theological dimensions to the doctrine of the church, they are expressed historically in the arenas in which the visible church lives, works, and ministers. And while we can distinguish between the mysteries of the church and its practical ministries for the purposes of theological study, in a more profound and practical sense, these two aspects can never ultimately be separated.

The Church in Sixteenth-Century Reformed Theology

John T. McNeill

The founders of Protestantism were intent not only upon a revival of personal piety; it was their aim also to reshape the corporate forms of religion. They did not go about converting individuals to the Protestant faith only to leave them in a state of lonely detachment; they labored to rebuild the church and felt themselves highly called to be the agents of its restoration. It was their unfaltering belief that the holy catholic church had been instituted by God for the nurture and fellowship of souls and that outside of it there is "no ordinary possibility of salvation." Accordingly, the theologians of the Reformation laid emphasis upon the nature and function of the church and sought to understand and explain it. Ecclesiology is a prominent and an essential part of their theology.

In recent generations this emphasis has been lost. Before the rise of the ecumenical

Reprinted from *Journal of Religion* 22 (1942): 251-69.

movement in the present century, few concerned themselves with the doctrine of the church. In general, only perfunctory statements in theological handbooks reminded ministerial students that the church had once been an object of thought and the subject of explicit teaching. Ministers were content to serve churches without comprehending the church. That stage is ended, and rethinking the church has in the past decade become a leading interest of the Christian mind.

It is natural that in any Protestant attempt to find an acceptable view of the church our first resort should be to the writings of the sixteenth-century Reformers. We may not rest content with what they say, but we must *know* what they say. Further, this knowledge will not help much if it is confined to a few special students. It is important that the rank and file of ministers should have it and impart it to their people. This does not mean that the Reformers should become oracles from whose utterances there can be no dissent. None of them would have desired that. But in a field that they explored and in which we are less familiar and can scarcely hope to attain to a comparable expertness, we may profit immeasurably by their aid. Indeed, we should be wise to regard an intimate understanding of their teaching on the church as a prime requirement in the equipment of Protestant leaders today. It could hardly fail to invigorate all Protestantism and to prove a stimulus to Christianity at large.

Prior to World War II, theologians and historians on the continent of Europe were, with increasing zest and attention to detail, examining the ecclesiology of the Reformers. We are concerned here not with these discussions but with a limited part of the source material to which they refer. The ecclesiology of early Protestantism is to be sought in a body of theological writing that is, of course, far too extensive to be examined in so brief a study as that here proposed. The substance of this paper is derived from utterances of accredited leaders of the Reformed branch of Protestantism and, within that field, is restricted to the more characteristic passages in the works of Zwingli, Bullinger, Calvin, and Zanchi.

I.

In the thought of the Reformation theologians, Lutheran and Reformed alike, as also in that of Augustine, the concept of the church moves within an ellipse of which the foci are heavenly perfection and human imperfection. No writer better illustrates this statement than Zwingli. In his treatment of the church he creates in his reader's mind a vivid awareness of its double aspect as the holy and ideal society of the truly faithful and the mundane and defective organization of the professed Christians.[1]

In the *First Zurich Disputation* (1523), Zwingli affirms that the true church is not earthly but spiritual, "the spotless bride of Jesus Christ governed and refreshed by the spirit of God."[2] In his *Treatise on True and False Religion* (1525), he treats the church of Christ and stresses the point that the church is not the hierarchy but the Christian people.[3] In this work he incorporates his *Reply to Emser* (1524).[4] Here he refers to the Hebrew and Septuagint words for "congregation" or "assemblage"[5] and states: "In like manner in the New Testament also we find that the word 'ecclesia' is used for all those who have named the name of Christ and who walk and live within the company of Christians, even though in reality they are not very faithful." And again: "Here we learn that the whole multitude of Christians that counts itself faithful is called one faithful people, one Church, and also is not yet the Church undefiled; for it has many blemishes, at some of which it is not foreign to Christ to wink." Beside the defective, empiric body of professors of the faith, Zwingli places what he calls "a second kind of Church" that consists of those truly faithful and is "a glorious and noble Church, the spouse of Christ, without any spot or wrinkle." It is an error to charge that this unblemished church is like Plato's *Republic*,[6] since it has also real existence in those who are built upon the rock of belief in Christ as the crucified Son of God. It "refuses to be so restricted as to contain within it only a few members who arrogate this honor to themselves; but, spreading throughout the whole world, it receives members everywhere; and the vaster and wider it is, the more beautiful also it is." In contrast to "the church of the pontiffs," this church "rests on the Word of God alone" and therefore cannot err. The number of those who are its members "is veiled from men's eyes."

Individual churches have disciplinary authority over their members, "but all these churches are one Church, Christ's spouse, which the Greeks call catholic and we call universal."[7] The argument of this treatise is summed up in the concluding paragraphs, as follows:

The Church that embraces those also who falsely assume the name of Christ is not the spouse of Christ, and there is no mention of it in the creed.

The Church that with firm faith rests upon Christ, the son of God, is the catholic church, the communion of saints, which we confess in the creed, having neither spot nor wrinkle. For Christ has washed it with His blood, that it may be His glorious spouse.

This Church — early in the words of Peter (I Pet. 4:3) — walks not for the rest of its life in the way of the Gentiles; for it is on its guard against sin, in which it beforetime lay dead. And since its way is polluted as long as it walks in the flesh, it has need of repentance and of expiation through Christ, its head.

This Church is known only to God; for man looks on the outward appearance, but God on the heart (I Sam. 16:7).

The Church of the pontiffs, which declares its own word, is the church of our enemy, i.e., the devil, who in the silence of the night sows tares (Mt. 13:24-30). And the sheep that hear this church are not sheep of Christ; for Christ's sheep hear not the voice of strangers (Jn. 10:5). Behold the infallible judgment of God's word!

The Church that is the spouse of Christ judges both the shepherd and His word. Therefore the pontiffs are not the lords or judges of the church, but are its ministers; it belongs entirely to the church to cast them out, together with their word, provided it is their own and not Christ's word that they declare.

The individual church also rejects the shameless, and receives again into favor the penitent; but only by virtue of the fact that it is a member of Christ's church.[8]

In 1530 Zwingli presented a statement of his beliefs to Charles V — *Fidei ratio* ("An Account of the Faith"). In Section VI of this short confession, he distinguishes the various meanings of the word *church* in the Scriptures. There are principally three. It is used (1) of that church of the elect alone which is known only to God, (2) of the universal perceptible church

(universalis sensibilis ecclesia) of nominal or professing Christians (who, however, are sometimes called the "elect" as in 1 Pet. 1:1-2), and (3) of every particular congregation of this universal and visible church. The latter, while it maintains the true confession, is one everywhere and includes baptized children.[9]

Zwingli's *Short and Clear Exposition of the Christian Faith,* addressed to Francis I in 1531,[10] contains (chap. 6) a brief statement on the church. Here his thought revolves around the words *invisible* and *visible* and the relation of church and state. The members of the invisible church of believers are known to God and themselves alone. The visible church is not that of Rome but of all baptized Christians. Since some of these are rebellious and traitorous members indifferent to church censures, there is need of a temporal government to restrain such sinners. In the following chapter, Zwingli affirms that government is as necessary as preaching in the church and that in fact it cannot exist without the civil government.

II.

Bullinger follows and at points expands Zwingli's teaching on the church. In his *Decades* (1549-51), Bullinger, citing Cyprian, Augustine, Gregory the Great, Paschasius, Leo the Great, and Thomas Aquinas for the omission of the word *in* in the credal statement "I believe in the holy catholic church," interprets the clause to mean that "we must acknowledge and confess the Holy Catholic Church but not believe in the Holy Catholic Church."[11] The church of Christ "stretcheth out itself through the compass of the world and into all ages, and doth contain all the faithful from the first Adam even unto the very last saint." All particular churches being

as it were members of one body under the only head, Christ (for Christ alone is the head of his church, not only triumphant but militant also) do make one only Catholic Church. In this church are all the faithful dispersed throughout the whole compass of the earth, and they also that at this time live in heaven, as many, I say, as are already saved, or shall even until the end of the world be born and be saved, are one body, having gotten fellowship and participation with God and a mutual communion among themselves.

Bullinger's *Fifth Decade* (1551) constitutes an extended treatise on the church. The first sermon is entitled "The Catholic Church" and contains the principal elements of his ecclesiology. He describes the church as "the whole company and multitude of the faithful" in heaven and on earth agreeing in faith and sacraments and united "as it were in one house and fellowship." "This church is usually called catholic, that is to say, universal. For she bringeth forth her branches in all places of the wide world, in all times of all ages; and generally doth comprehend all the faithful of the whole world." Bullinger distinguishes between the triumphant and the militant church. The latter, fighting against sin in the world, may be thought of in two ways: (1) as the "lively members" of the inward and invisible church of God, which we profess in the creed, and (2) as the "outward and visible church" of the professors of the true religion, some of whom are unfaithful.

Another telling sentence may here be quoted, since it has many parallels in the works of the Reformers:

But the Catholic Church of God doth abide with us continually from age to age from the beginning, and is at this time dispersed throughout the whole world, both visibly and invisibly: and the Lord's people and God's house shall continue upon earth unto the world's end . . . for the testimonies of the ancient prophets do record that the church is perpetual.

Many subordinate aspects of the doctrine are touched upon in this sermon. It closes with a section devoted to the subject of church power — the power to ordain ministers, to teach true doctrine, to bind and loose, to administer the sacraments, and to judge of doctrines. Bullinger here drafts an outline of the doctrine of church power as it was to be elaborated in later Reformed theology.

Like the other Reformers, Bullinger lays emphasis upon the love that binds the members of the church into one close-knit fellowship, focusing on New Testament passages concerning charity or love. "Neither do we separate love from faith," he writes.

The only mark of the Church next after faith is love, a bond most firmly knitting all the members together. . . . For inasmuch as Christ, the king, the head and high bishop of the Catholic Church, enduing us all with one and the same Spirit, hath made us all his members, the sons of God, brethren and fellow heirs, whom undoubtedly he loveth tenderly; every faithful man cannot choose but with fervent love embrace the members and fellow heirs of their king, their head and their high bishop.

In the second sermon, "Of the Unity of the Church," Bullinger warns against schism for diversity of opinions not affecting fundamental doctrine, for the offenses of ministers, for diversity of ceremonies, and for the evil behavior of private members, but justifies departure from the alleged church in which the inward and outward works of the true church are absent. He emphasizes in this connection the sole headship of Christ in his church.[12]

In his *Instruction to Bavarian Protestants* (1559), Bullinger answers a series of questions with a treatment of the marks of the true church, the Word and sacraments. He asserts that the universal church is not confined with respect to place and that there there is no salvation outside of it. Bullinger here recognizes the sacraments as marks of the true church that are commanded by the Lord.[13] He discredits the claims based on episcopal succession and declares that the Roman Church under the pope is not the universal catholic church but entirely unlike its apostolic original, since the marks of the true church are no longer to be found in it.[14] In answer to the question of where the true universal church has hitherto been,[15] he points to the Greek and Eastern churches and to the believers separated from Rome under Turkish and other oppressors. There is no salvation outside of the Christian church, but this cannot be said of the Roman Church. Bullinger encourages the hope of the salvation of "our forefathers," who suffered constraint and distress under that Church because they held the fundamentals of Christianity. "Some there were who preached salvation in Christ from God's Word, though in many cases such persons were put to death: Thus even in the midst of the papal church the Lord called out his own." To show the church's hidden survival, Bullinger cites the stock passage of Elijah and the seven thousand in Israel. Repudiating the charge of schism, he remarks,

> We must inquire what is that true unity which none may sever. As there is only one God, one world, one Son [of God] etc., so there is only one divine truth, only one true Christian faith, and only one universal Christian Church in which all believers hearken and adhere to the divine truth alone, love the one true God with all their heart and soul and strength, worship and invoke and reverence Him alone.[16]

III.

Calvin's teaching on the church is characteristically lucid and comprehensive. So greatly was he preoccupied with this topic that if we are to know the range of his thought upon it, we must consult most of his works. But in certain passages he has given utterance with special care to the main elements in his doctrine. Many have attempted to trace the development of Calvin's conception of the church with reference to the influence of predecessors and associates. This subject has its own importance but must here be excluded. Our present purpose will be served if we rely chiefly upon that ample statement of his mature thought on "the Church its Government, Orders and Powers" which extends through nineteen of the twenty chapters of Book IV of the 1559 edition of the *Institutes*.

Calvin identifies, as does Luther, the expressions "catholic church" and "communion of saints" in the Apostles' Creed. Recognizing the late date of the addition of the clause "communion of saints" to the Creed, he nevertheless says it "ought not to be neglected because it excellently expresses the character of the Church, as though it had been said that the saints are united in the fellowship of Christ on this condition that whatever benefits God confers upon them, they should mutually communicate to each other." In addition to "communio sanctorum" Calvin had earlier (1536) used the expressions "numerus electorum" (or "praedestinatorum") and "coetus fidelium" as equivalents of "ecclesia." These phrases indicate his view that, on the one hand, the church is provided with members by divine predestination and that, on the other, it is an assembly or fellowship in which the members mutually communicate their blessings. Calvin would prefer to say with Augustine "I believe the catholic church" rather than "I believe *in* the catholic church," yet he expressly regards the church as an object of faith that Christians ought to dwell upon in their thoughts.[17] We are to believe in its existence and divine preservation even when, as in the time of Elijah, it lacks outward manifestation.[18]

In accord with Zwingli's distinction between the church of the professed Christians and the true Spouse of Christ, "the number of whose members is veiled from human eyes," Calvin distinguishes the two senses contained in Scripture uses of the word *church*. In one sense it comprises the church as God sees it, consisting only of those "who by adoption and grace are the children of God and by the sanctification of the Spirit true members of Christ." In another scriptural sense, the word designates "the whole multitude dispersed throughout the world who profess to worship one God and Jesus Christ," partake of the two sacraments, and conform outwardly to the church. This visible church contains numerous hypocrites, but Calvin affirms the necessity of fellowship with it: "As it is necessary, therefore, to believe that Church which is invisible to us and known to God alone, so this church, which is visible to men, we are commanded to honor, and to maintain communion with it" (*Inst.*, 4.1.7).

The very word *communion* conveys the greatest comfort *(consolatio)*, since it brings realization of a partnership in the graces conferred by God upon the members of the church (*Inst.*, 4.1.3). Conversely, Calvin insistently stresses the sinfulness of schism. "For so highly does the Lord esteem the communion of his Church, that he considers everyone as a traitor and apostate from religion, who perversely withdraws himself from any Christian society which preserves the true ministry of the word and sacraments." Calvin's argument here leads to the emphatic statement that "departure from the Church is a renunciation of God and Christ" (*Inst.*, 4.1.10).[19] Although the visible church is by definition imperfect, yet that true visible church which is recognized by the proper signs or marks possesses divinely sanctioned authority and commands obedience. In consideration of Calvin's zeal for the unity of the visible church, it may be appropriate here to quote the concluding sentence of his *Reply to Sadoleto* (1539):

> The Lord grant, Sadoleto, that you and all your party may at length perceive that the only true bond of ecclesiastical unity would exist if Christ the Lord who hath reconciled us to God the Father, were to gather us out of our present dispersion into the fellowship of his body, that so, through his one Word and Spirit, we might join together with one heart and one soul.

The church, moreover, as mother of the faithful, fulfills a unique and indispensable function in the work of salvation, of which Calvin speaks with enthusiasm. "We may know from the title of Mother how useful and even necessary it is to know her; since there is no other way of entrance into life, unless we are conceived in her, born of her, nourished at her breast, and continually preserved under her care and government" (*Inst.*, 4.1.4). The edification of the faithful proceeds "under the education of the church" (*Inst.*, 4.1.5).

How, then, is the true visible church to be recognized? "Wherever we find the word of God purely preached and heard, and the sacraments administered according to the institution of Christ, there, it is not to be doubted, is the Church of God" (*Inst.*, 4.1.9). Again, "where the Word is heard with reverence and the sacraments are not neglected, then we discover, while that is the case, an appearance of the Church which is liable to no suspicion" (*Inst.*, 4.1.10). It is such a church that is entitled to our unqualified attachment. It is to be noted that in Calvin's true church the word is not only preached but reverently heard. Casual sermons to unbelievers do not constitute a church; nor can it consist of the clergy alone. To pretend to the name of "church" without the word and sacraments is a "delusive pretension" (4.1.11).

Yet Calvin would not fix orthodoxy rigidly at all points. There exists the category of nonessentials. Diversity of opinion respecting nonessential points of doctrine[20] ought not to be a cause of discord between churches. So prone are we to ignorance that trivial differences ought not to be made a pretext for abandoning the church. And "in bearing with imperfections of life we ought to carry out indulgence a great deal further." It is vain to expect the church on earth to be completely purified. Paul did not

separate himself from the Corinthians but acknowledged them "as a Church of Christ and
a society of saints," even though they were
involved in contention, cupidity, and litigation
and some of them "ridiculed the doctrine of the
resurrection" (*Inst.,* 4.1.13-14). To condemn
wickedness in church members is one thing; to
renounce church membership on account of it
is another. The church, not the individual, has
authority to excommunicate. A strong passage
from Cyprian is quoted in support of this view.
The church is holy in the sense that it daily
advances toward holiness: it has not arrived at
perfection. A holy church of aspirants toward
perfect holiness has existed from the beginning
of the world and will abide "to the consummation of all things" (*Inst.,* 4.1.17, 19). Had these
generous passages been appreciated by the
more censorious followers of Calvin, the history of the Reformed churches might have been
happier than it has been.

Calvin notes that in the Creed "communion of saints" is immediately followed by
"forgiveness of sins," wherein God's grace is
constantly exerted toward the members of the
communion. He gives somewhat extended
treatment to this topic, condemning the error
of Novatianist and Anabaptist rigorists, who
alike affirm postbaptismal perfection. When
the saints pray "forgive us our debts," they
confess themselves still sinners and seek the
continual mercy of God (*Inst.,* 4.1.20-29).

Calvin equally rejects Roman Catholic
claims that the papal church is the true and the
only true church. That church has, he affirms,
departed from the word and introduced impure
and idolatrous worship. "The communion of
the Church was not instituted as a bond to
confine us in idolatry, impiety, ignorance of
God and other evils" (*Inst.,* 4.2.2). Departure
from the church of Rome is not, therefore, an
act of schism but a spiritual necessity. He concludes the chapter on this topic with a section
in which he states that "while we refuse . . . to
allow the Papists the title of the Church,

without any qualification or distinction, we do
not deny that there are churches among them."
But he indicates that these latter are profaned
and dejected under papal despotism (*Inst.,*
4.2.12).[21]

In later chapters on the ministry, power,
and discipline of the church, Calvin elucidates
his position, especially in relation to the
Roman claims, with extensive references to
ecclesiastical history and literature. He devotes
a weighty chapter (4.12) to the corrective discipline of the church, which he holds to be of
prime necessity, as the sinews or ligaments that
connect the members of the body. By discipline, "those who have previously fallen may
be chastised in mercy, and with the gentleness
of the spirit of Christianity." He distinguishes
the treatment of private offenses from that of
public and notorious offenses and between
slight delinquencies, for which admonition and
reproof are sufficient, and grave crimes, such
as adultery, theft, robbery, sedition, and per-
jury, for which offenders should be excommunicated.

This discipline is necessary, first, to avoid
profanation of the sacred mystery of the Lord's
Supper and the scandal of acknowledging the
profane as members of the church. Second, it
provides a protection against the corruption of
the good by association with the wicked. Third,
its object toward offenders is that through
shame they may be led to repentance (*Inst.,*
4.12.5). The disciplinary jurisdiction of the
church extends over all, princes as well as ple-
beians, since to Christ "the sceptres and di-
adems of kings" are properly subject (*Inst.,*
4.12.7). Here again Calvin refers to the importance of tempering severity with gentleness.
"The design of excommunication is that the
sinner be brought to repentance." Citing Cyprian, Chrysostom, and Augustine, Calvin rejects the idea of long years of penance if the
sinner gives to the church the testimony of his
repentance and by so doing obliterates the
scandal of his offense (*Inst.,* 4.12.8). Even

those who remain obstinate are not to be "condemned to eternal death" by the church, which cannot prescribe limits to the mercy of God (*Inst.*, 4.12.9). All excommunicated individuals are to be treated as candidates for restoration to communion (*Inst.*, 4.12.10).

IV.

Girolamo Zanchi (Hieronymus Zanchius, 1516-90), a learned Italian who taught at Strasbourg and Heidelberg, was highly influential among Reformed theologians after the death of Calvin. As a result of his controversy with rigid Lutherans at Strasbourg, he signed with explanations the Augsburg Confession and in this concession was able to claim — as he explained (1563) in a letter to Grindal (later Archbishop of Canterbury) — the favorable judgment of Calvin. While perhaps more conciliatory than most Reformed theologians, he was really a follower of Calvin; his works can best be read as a reaffirmation of Calvinist doctrine and, at the same time, as an introduction to the Scholastic era of Reformed theology.

In a book on the doctrines of the Christian religion, Zanchi provides a point-by-point exposition of the doctrine of the church.[22] In a section on the church of Christ in general, he writes,

> by the name "Church of Christ" we understand a certain number and assembly (*coetum*) known to God, of the elect and predestinate both of angels and of men. [These compose an eternal fellowship] but also in time [its members are] called forth by the Holy Spirit from the number of the others and joined to Christ as their head, and are therefore truly saints. [The church exists] from the foundation of the world to these times, and will be continued to the end of the world, indeed to all eternity. [It is] partly with Christ triumphant in the heavens,

partly still on earth warring for Christ with various enemies, preaching and hearing the word of the Gospel, administering and partaking of the sacraments, taking care to do the commands of Christ both publicly and privately.

This true church consists of the elect only: hypocrites are in it but not of it.

Zanchi views the church in its threefold character as one, catholic, and holy. He expounds the doctrine of the church's unity.[23] It always was, and is, one body, of which Christ is made head by the Father, and one spirit by which the members are joined to the head. It has one faith, one salvation, one inheritance in the heavens. The church before the coming of Christ is identified with "that which now is and will be to the end of the world." It is one with respect to times, places, and persons, and so "we say it is one communion of all saints, and we hold it established by holy writ that those who perpetually secede from it do not belong to this one body." The church is also, in the next place, holy. Zanchi asserts the sole headship of Christ and the holiness of the church from its most holy, sanctifying head. Again he affirms that it is "truly catholic, that is universal," because the head of it is catholic and eternal, and the members are joined to him through all times and places, from all races and nations.

Zanchi has a careful discussion of the church militant which is "fighting [*pugnans*] on earth with flesh and blood, with the world and the devil." Called out of all nations, numbering some hypocrites, who are like the tares and the foolish virgins, and composed of many particular churches, the church militant nevertheless partakes of the characteristics of the whole church as previously described: it is one, catholic, apostolic, and holy. It is one because it was always, and is now, being gathered to Christ by the same Spirit, and the faith of all is one. It is catholic because it is extended to all times and places and is made up of all kinds of persons and peoples. It is apostolic because it is founded upon the foundation that the apostles laid and it relies upon the apostolic teaching of the prophets. Finally, it is holy — not that it is sinless, but, because it is implanted in Christ and endowed with perpetual repentance and faith, no sins are imputed to it; instead the holiness of Christ is imputed to it, and it is said to be the spotless bride of Christ.

On the marks by which the true church may be known, Zanchi has nothing peculiar, except perhaps an unusual explicitness of language, to differentiate him from other Reformed theologians. The pure doctrine of the gospel is preached, heard, "and alone admitted": the last phrase is an addition to Calvin's formula, though consistent with Calvin's exposition. Discipline, exercised from charity, proceeds by public and private admonition, correction, and, in extreme cases, excommunication. Apostolic succession is, for Zanchi (who was on friendly terms with Anglican bishops), succession in apostolic doctrine. "The habit does not make the monk," nor do bishops make the church. Through a series of numbered distinctions, Zanchi upholds the doctrine of unity while guarding the purity of doctrine. As not every kind of consensus makes a church, so not every kind of dissent destroys it, but only that which concerns fundamentals of the Apostles' Creed. The peace of the church is not to be broken on account of every sort of difference in doctrine or ceremonies.[24] Even more than the unity of the particular church is that of the whole catholic church to be striven for. But secession from the church of Rome is, by reason of that church's apostasy, not a departure from the unity of the body of Christ. There can be no holiness and no salvation outside the catholic church of faith, but this character is not attached to specified persons and places.

In his *Commentary on Ephesians* Zanchi expounds the church once more as one, holy, and catholic.[25] It consists not of one (Jewish) race but of the children of God from all peoples, nations, and races. He also dwells upon the notion of the church as the spouse of Christ and the object of his redemptive love. It is beloved from all eternity by Christ as God, and in time by Christ as human, and thus "with a two-fold love, divine and human, each most sincere, mighty, perfect, constant and enduring." For this church of elect believers, "he gave himself."

V.

These characteristic passages offer some indication of the elements that entered into the Reformers' exposition of the doctrine of the church. They held in common a high conception of the church as the divinely ordained agency through which souls are "revivified" and sanctified. The church is the holy spouse of Christ and likewise, as Calvin said, mother of those to whom God is a Father. They all distinguished its aspect of heavenly perfection and its aspect of earthly imperfection — the church as invisible and as visible. In variant terms they tried to clarify this difficult but necessary distinction. In common with the Lutheran theologians, they denied that the invisible church is an imaginary entity, a mere spiritual Republic of Plato. We may perhaps distinguish three considerations that led them to apply to the church the word *invisible:* (1) the number of those within the true church is veiled from human eyes, and its extent and limits are unknown to all but God; (2) the true church cannot as a whole assemble in one place where it may be observed; and (3) in times of religious depression, as in the days of Elijah and the late medieval period, the true church is driven almost to invisibility, while that which humans account the church is so corrupted as not to merit the designation. In such times, says Calvin, God preserves his church *in latebris,* in concealment (*Inst.,* 4.1.2). In this sense, mere invisibility is abnormal and undesirable, and the task of church reform is to make manifest the hidden church of God.

Both as invisible and as visible, the true church is "one, holy, and catholic." It is uniformly affirmed that the visible church is itself catholic and ecumenical. Spread abroad throughout the earth, it professes a common faith and cherishes a common fellowship. The head, Christ, being one, the body cannot be a plurality. Its catholicity and unity depend upon the Christocracy, and this headship excludes human headship. Thus far the visible church shares the character of the invisible and perfect church. The former, we may say, is penetrated by the latter. But the visible church is defective: it attracts some hypocrites. We are not to be too impatient with its imperfections, and it is a grievous sin to depart from the church so long as it retains the marks of its reality as a church.

Possessing these marks — the true word preached and heard, the true sacraments administered according to Christ's institution — and equipped by discipline to maintain the sanctity of the fellowship and to bring offenders to repentance, it commands our unreserved loyalty. Moreover, by divine appointment the visible church possesses powers inseparable from it, principally the power to determine doctrine in accordance with scriptural truth and the power to exercise censures and restore the penitent to communion.

Finally this visible catholic church is of perpetual duration in the mundane scene. It is not a transient phenomenon of history or a frail institution whose continuity depends on a favorable political environment. It survives all assaults and tumults to provide a fellowship of the children of God and dynamically to serve the cause of the kingdom of God in the world, unto the end of the earthly drama.

NOTES

1. See A. Baur, *Zwinglis Theologie: Ihr Werden und ihr System,* 2 vols. (Halle: Niemeyer, 1889), 1: 210ff., 467ff., 542; 2: 255ff., 767; P. Wernle, *Der evangelische Glaube,* vol. 2: *Zwingli* (Tübingen, 1919), pp. 193ff.

2. *Huldreich Zwinglis sämtliche Werke,* 12 vols. (= *Corpus Reformatorum,* vols. 88ff.), 1: 538.

3. "Ecclesia enim coetus est, concio, populus universus, collecta simul universa multitudo. . . . Ficus ergo ficus adpellent et ecclesiam sinant 'concionem' significare. . . . populum, concionem et coetum Christi" (*Zwinglis Werke,* 3: 741-42).

4. *Zwinglis Werke,* 3: 252ff., 743ff.

5. עֵדָה, קָהָל, συναγωγή, ἐκκλησία.

6. Cf. R. Staehelin, *Huldreich Zwingli, sein Leben und Wirken,* vol. 2 (Basel, 1897), p. 207: "Als die Stiftung Christi ist sie aber andererseits auch nicht ein blosses Ideal nach der weise des platonischen Staates."

7. *Zwinglis Werke,* 3: 257-58, 261-62; *The Latin Works of Huldreich Zwingli, Translated for the Late Samuel Macauley Jackson,* vol. 3, ed. C. N. Heller (Philadelphia, 1929), pp. 371, 374-75.

8. *Zwinglis Werke,* 3: 267-68; *Latin Works of Zwingli,* 3: 381-82.

9. E. F. K. Müller, *Die Bekenntnisschriften der Reformierten Kirche* (Leipzig, 1903), pp. 84ff. (E.T., *Huldreich Zwingli,* 2d ed., trans. S. M. Jackson [New York, 1900], pp. 463ff.).

10. *Christianae fidei a Huldrycho Zvinglio praedicatae brevis et clara expositio,* in *Huldreich Zwinglii opera completa,* 8 vols., ed. Melchior Schuler and Johann Schulthess (Zurich: Friedrich Schulthess, 1828-36], 4: 42-78; E.T. by W. J. Hinke in *Latin Works of Zwingli,* 2: 235-93. Cf. *Zwinglis Theologie,* 2: 760ff.

11. *The Decades of Henry Bullinger . . . ,* 4 vols., ed. Thomas Harding (Cambridge: Cambridge University Press, 1849-52), 1: 161.

12. *The Decades of Henry Bullinger,* 4: 67, 86-87.

13. Bullinger, *Anleitung für die, so wegen unsers Herrn Jesu Christi und seines heiligen Evangeliums ihres Glaubens halben erforscht und mit allerlei Fragen versucht werden* (1559), in *Heinrich Bullinger: Leben und ausgewälte Schriften,* ed. C. Pestalozzi (Elberfeld, 1858), pp. 526ff.

14. *Bullinger: Leben und ausgewälte Schriften,* pp. 529ff.

15. *Bullinger: Leben und ausgewälte Schriften,* pp. 531ff.

16. *Bullinger: Leben und ausgewälte Schriften,* pp. 533ff.

17. "Eo quod in fide sita est . . . cogitandam esse." The passages cited are from *Institutes of the Christian Religion,* trans. John Allen (Philadelphia: Westminster Press, 1936), 4.1.1-3. Subsequent references to this work will be made parenthetically in the text.

18. "Sciamus . . . Deumque mirabiliter ecclesiam suam quasi in latebris servare" (*Inst.,* 4.1.2).

19. "Unde sequitur, discessionem ab ecclesia, Dei et Christi abnegationem esse." Calvin also refers to this act as "criminal," "an atrocious crime," and "sacrilegious perfidy."

20. "Dissensionem de rebus non ita necessariis" (*Inst.,* 4.1.12). Calvin cites the question of the immediate passage of the soul to heaven at death.

21. Cf. 4.6-7 and elsewhere.

22. Zanchi, *De Religione christiana fides* (Neustadt, [1585]). The following notes are on chaps. 23 and 24. Chapter 25, "On the Government and Ministry of the Church Miiltant," is omitted from consideration here. Two translations of this work — *H. Zanchius — His Confession of Christian Religion* (Cambridge, 1599) and R. Winterton's later rendering, *The Whole Body of the Christian Religion* (London, 1659) — helped to extend Zanchi's influence among English readers.

23. Zanchi, *De religione . . .* , pp. 140-41.

24. Zanchi, in a letter to Queen Elizabeth dated 10 September 1571, which was suppressed by his friend Grindal's wish, and in a letter to Jewel written a week earlier, takes exception to certain Anglican usages but in a moderate spirit. To Jewel, indeed, he writes in favor of obeying, under protest, the rules regarding vestments, since they are really "res sua natura adiaphoras."

25. *Hieron. Zanchii in D. Pauli Epistolam ad Ephesios Commentarius* (Neustadt, 1600), pp. 193-94, 286, 527ff.

Church and Politics in the Reformed Tradition

Eberhard Busch

As a pastor in the Reformed Church in the Swiss Canton of Aargau, I am committed to a church order in the first paragraph of which Jesus Christ is called the "Lord and hope" of our church. Its commission is "to live according to the Gospel and to declare to all people the sovereignty of God." According to this, to live *from* the gospel means to live *according to* the gospel, and this means to witness to "the sovereignty of God" to all people. Although it comes a paragraph later, this statement belongs unconditionally to this witness: "the congregation and its members are called by the love of Jesus Christ to work for the solution of political, economic and social questions of the day. They are to intercede particularly on behalf of the weak and disadvantaged for justice and truthfulness in all areas."

The binding declaration that in the obser-

vation of its spiritual commission the church also bears a social responsibility, and that in so doing it is not meddling in someone else's business, I perceive to be a fruit of the Reformed tradition. Now, even with such a paragraph, our church has hardly arrived at the kingdom of God. Indeed, as we shall see, I believe our Reformed tradition is encumbered with a rather heavy mortgage. Nonetheless, that such a paragraph is found in our church order, and that again and again it plays a genuine role — in discussions on the military and peace, on the banking and financial system, and on the problem of asylum and development, for example — I see as a sign of the liveliness of the Reformed tradition.

If one should ask what has kept this tradition alive all these centuries, I would point not last to the custom in our worship of singing, with a certain partiality, the psalms which yet today make up the first section of our hymnal. Through them runs a certain unmistakably characteristic tone — a tone of militance toward the mighty and also of solidarity with

Reprinted from *Church, Word and Spirit*, ed. James E. Bradley and Richard A. Muller (Grand Rapids: William B. Eerdmans, 1987), pp. 163-81.

those suffering injustice — and in that tone a conviction that faith in God and the well-being of the people in justice have a great deal to do with one another. In fact, the tone is so loud in the hymnal that it has etched its mark in the Reformed Church, even its church order — a tone often covered over but never completely drowned out. As we examine the character of the Reformed tradition through its theological foundations in Ulrich Zwingli and John Calvin, we should keep in mind that their understanding in this matter remained alive and was renewed in spite of all opposing and contradictory developments because in its core it was nourished continually by the hymns of praise and confession in the gathered congregation. We will examine this understanding in four sections, from both its bright and dark sides.

THE DISTINCTION BETWEEN PROCLAMATION AND POLITICS

As is well known, Luther emphasized in "On Temporal Authority" (1523) that the tasks of the church and state are of two types and that they are to be distinguished from each other and may not be mixed. Later he failed to see this same point in Zwingli and accused him of being a man seduced by "a devilish rogue," a man who had meddled "seditiously in temporal government."[1] His charge, however, is not at all correct, because in fact such a thing was possible neither in Zurich nor in Geneva at the time.[2] More importantly, in 1523, a few weeks after Luther's publication, Zwingli published his own work on the same question, "On Divine and Human Righteousness [Gerechtigkeit]," in which "divine righteousness" refers to the content of the church's proclamation, God's gracious activity, and "human righteousness" (or justice) is that of the earthly state. In this work he stresses the differences between the two tasks in such a way that one

immediately suspects his dependence on Luther,[3] inasmuch as he suggests that the tasks are as different as heaven and earth.[4] But Calvin, too, said at the very beginning of his chapter "On Civil Government" in the *Institutes* that "Christ's spiritual kingdom and the civil order are two completely different things" and that "we may not — as people commonly do — unwisely mix these two together."[5]

The distinction between church and state in all three Reformers is based upon their total separation from the Roman Church of the day, for they intended to rebuke it for the assumption of worldly power by its clergy. The distinction reached its highest point in the church's repudiation of mixing its spiritual task with the use of power and force in its own spiritual realm. Calvin's statement in a letter of 1562 is characteristic: it would be a "betrayal of God" were he not to warn against a preacher becoming a soldier, "and it is even much worse when he, hardly down from the pulpit, reaches for his weapon."[6]

One must consider that the reformer's insistence on this distinction was also a reaction to the dramatic changes in the social environment of the day. The political authorities, moreover, had emancipated themselves from the church, but in such a way that they intentionally adapted what had been papal-episcopal laws to the exercise of political power.[7] With their distinction between church and state, the Reformers approved of this as appropriate, but it was not a process that they were responsible for setting into motion, as has been suggested occasionally. We see, in fact, that they reversed the emphasis completely — just as bishops were not to be worldly princes, so temporal rulers should not go too far and extend their rule into the church. This concern was the actual occasion for Luther's "On Temporal Authority," a significant part of which was made up of his warnings against it.[8] Zwingli likewise warned against the "Obere" (authorities) who "lay their violent hand on the Word of God."[9] In Calvin, the second-generation Reformer, this warning received even greater urgency, as after the deaths of Luther and Zwingli he saw state-church governments established in the territories in which they had been influential.[10]

One must add that this distinction between church and state in both Zwingli and Luther is connected with a sort of self-defense on the part of the Reformation — but not yet against the "Schwärmer," as is often assumed.[11] Their movement had not actually begun until after these two works were written; indeed, the radicals may have actually been provoked by the doctrines represented in these works. Zwingli saw his reforming activities attacked in influential Catholic circles which characterized his "Lutheran doctrine as the root of all disobedience against the authorities."[12] With the intent of moving the state to attack the Reformation, they charged that the Reformation would destroy the state. This accusation put Zwingli, and Luther as well, in the delicate position of proving that one may preach the word of God as long as one does not teach rebellion against the authorities. In this situation the distinction between church and state received an apologetic interpretation: in effect it was suggested that the Reformation was merely spiritual and did not enter into the domain of the state, though from the standpoint of faith it could recognize the state as legitimate per se.

For their defense against the charge of destroying the state, Zwingli and Calvin stressed as strongly as Luther the Christian's duty to obey state officials regardless of their worthiness to be obeyed.[13] In their overzealousness to refute the accusation of their opponents, the Reformers certainly overstated this side of the argument. This occurred especially in their quickness to distance themselves from the Schwärmer, whom the Reformers understood to be denying that a true Christian still needs a state authority (a thesis that Luther and

Zwingli affirmed in principle).[14] They did this to defend themselves against the Schwärmer's argument that the state is to be rejected because of its profane nature, especially because it is established by force. Over against this, the distinction between church and state signified that each realm has the right to exist and that the state, too, is established by God and thus also is to be respected by Christians.[15] According to Calvin, the Schwärmer reject not only "the authorities but push God aside as well."[16] As a result, the Reformed theologians emphasized the state's right to use force and the Christian's duty to obey even an "un-Christian" government — emphasized it to the point that they came into conflict with other of their own principles. They resolutely redirected the charge (which was not very applicable to the Schwärmer) of "destroying the state" with consequences not only deadly for the Schwärmer but also troublesome for their own theory and praxis.

Although the Reformation distinction between church and state is embedded in this problem, it should be noted nonetheless that the aversion to mixing the spiritual and worldly, the presumption of the church's own particular duty in the recognition of the state's particular task, is an important and indispensable Protestant characteristic. The Reformers distinguished between the two even though they presumed (often incorrectly) that they were dealing with a "Christian government." We need not regret their distinction today even though we are no longer capable of these presuppositions. This distinction basically means that the church would be unfaithful to itself and its task were it to understand itself as state and that the state would be unfaithful to itself were it to see itself as church. However close these relations may be in specific situations, they are meaningful only so long as church remains church and state remains state. More pointedly, this distinction means that the church can recognize the task of the state as meaningful and that it cannot be indifferent to whether the state does its task more or less well. The church can do nothing better, indeed can do nothing else, than remain alert and live and act according to its own "law."

The Reformed theologian Karl Barth affirmed the meaning of this distinction for our time as well. The state "must renounce itself if it wishes to be the Church, and the Church, for its task's sake, cannot wish it to cease being the State. It [the State] cannot be the true Church. It could, if it dared such madness, only become a false Church. And all the more must the Church renounce itself should it want to become the State. . . . It cannot be the true State, it can only become a State of clergy . . . with a bad conscience because of their neglected duty."[17]

In this first section I have deliberately presented the common Reformation view first. I wish to understand the differences between the Lutheran and Reformed views as differences within this commonality. I also wish to plead thereby for "tolerance" within the churches of the Reformation as it hardly has been practiced since Luther's time — tolerance not in the sense that these differences are to be considered of no consequence but rather in the sense that the Reformed deviation from Luther will not be seen prematurely as a fall from the heights of the Reformation.

THE RELATION BETWEEN CHURCH AND STATE

The thesis that the tasks of the church and state are to be distinguished but not separated leads us closer to the particular Reformed accent here. The thesis is expressed in the title of Zwingli's work "On Divine and Human Righteousness," with the significant subtitle "How They Relate to One Another." Even if the two "righteousnesses" are different, as different as heaven and earth, that with which they are concerned can be designated by the *same* concept — "righteousness." Thus they "are related." Calvin, too, continues in the abovementioned chapter on civil government, "as we have just now pointed out that the temporal government is distinct from the spiritual Kingdom of Christ, we must also know that they do not stand in contradiction" — at least not fundamentally.[18]

In order to evaluate the particular Reformed emphasis, it is good to cite Gottfried Locher's insightful observation that on the whole Zwingli — and this applied to Calvin as well — took a different approach from that of Luther. Zwingli was similar to Luther in his aversion to Judaism, legalism, and works-righteousness, but at the same time and perhaps even more rigorously, he reacted against the danger of secularism.[19] Thus both Zwingli and Calvin stressed not only the justification of the sinner by grace but also the sanctification of the person by God. They thought more in Old Testament terms than Luther, which in this case meant they were always wary of the other great danger with which particularly the Old Testament struggled — peace with false gods. From the outset they thought more in social terms than Luther, reasoning not so much along the lines of "How do *I* find . . . ," but rather "How does my *people* have a gracious God?"

This emphasis worked itself out in their understanding of the relation of the church to the state. In his approach to matters of law, Luther was prepared to leave the state to the caprice of human reason. One must say that in his skepticism toward all human possibilities he showed great indifference to the question of how the worldly nature played itself out in state. For him it was enough that the church limit itself to its own task — to proclaim grace to sinners and thereby to comfort those who are oppressed by the laws of the state — in order that at the same time it might appeal to the conscience of the princes who are also Christians.[20]

Zwingli and Calvin, on the other hand, were always distrustful of a state left to determine itself by its own laws — or at least they were distrustful of the sanctification of Christians who were indifferent to the political structure of human society. They held that there can be no occasion for indifference, because there is a *relation* between church and state. Calling special attention to this relation was all the more important to the Reformed thinkers since the emancipation of the state from the church was precisely the political process occurring at that time. It would be approved by the Reformed, but they would not let the matter rest with their approval. Rather, basic to this relation is the fact that it is not the "church" but the *Lord* proclaimed in the church who has a "relation" with the state. God is present, of course, even in the state where God is not proclaimed: God is the Lord even over this territory.

Luther said this as well, but he emphasized that God's presence there is *completely different* from God's presence in the spiritual arena. The Reformers did not dispute this, but they emphasized more that there is *no other one* than God who is proclaimed in the church. The "doctrine of civil government" is, particularly in Calvin, not so clearly "established by the royal office of Christ," as Wilhelm Niesel claims.[21] Calvin speaks not, like Luther, of the God who governs and is "hidden" beneath the law but often abstractly of the reigning "providence of God."[22] Moreover, like Luther, he can separate "Christ's spiritual kingdom" in the church from the state.[23] The connection between this and his assertion that worldly government is "an image of the royal rule of our Lord Jesus Christ" is not so clear.[24] Calvin can say further that, even before his appearance, Christ, as "eternal King," possessed "all power in heaven and on earth" to rule over all earthly rulers or, if they opposed him, to depose them.[25] Because of the unclear relation between the rule of Christ and the providence of

God, it appears that his talk of "Christ" in this connection tends toward the abstraction of his central revelation; Christ appears sooner as the personified "content" of that freely reigning providence — and perhaps at bottom here lies the root of the weakness of Calvin's perspective. Nonetheless, it is clearly his intent to say that the God who is believed in the church is also the Lord of the political realm.

God is particularly present there in the fact that the simple existence of the state can be recognized by Christians as a gift and order of God. Thus Zwingli and Calvin, like Luther, said that the government rests upon divine "ordinance."[26] For them, as in Romans 13, government is "God's servant" — indeed, as Calvin so boldly put it, God's minister.[27] The Reformed theologians' emphasis was different, however, and in fact constituted their most decisive departure from Luther. To oversimplify, Luther tended toward the idea that the government is God's servant *because and insofar as* it is the *government.* Zwingli and Calvin, on the other hand, tended toward the idea that the government is true government *when and insofar as* it is *God's servant.* Thus the Reformers refused to identify a government directly and automatically with God's will, "as if God had made over his right to mortal men, giving them the rule over mankind! Or as if earthly power were diminished when it is subjected to its Author!"[28] Thus even if the state rests upon a divine order, it never takes the place of God. Here Calvin corrects a misunderstanding of his view of "government" as God's minister with the critique that it robs "God of his glory" when it wants "so much to take his place" that it demands blind obedience.[29] Having ordained the government, God remains Lord over this ordinance. In any case, government remains "in subjection" to God. Obedience to God and obedience to a temporal government always remain two different things, and obedience to the government always takes second place to obedience to God.

If there is no other Lord who reigns in the political world than the One to whom the church bears witness, then God is in any case *the Lord* here as much as there — the Lord who, in Calvin's bold words, possesses "the government of the world" and indeed has "absolute monarchy in the world."[30]

This viewpoint was at the core of Karl Barth's thought in 1933-1934 in the German "Kirchenkampf" dispute with a Lutheran tradition that equated Hitler's state with "God's servant." Barth asserted the viewpoint already formulated by Calvin: "The Lord is King of all kings who, when he has opened his sacred mouth, must alone be heard; next to him we are Subject to those who are in authority over us, but only in him. If they command anything against him, let it go unheeded, it matters not."[31] One can compare as well a sentence from the Dutch Reformed Confession of 1949: "Obedience to the authority of government finds its basis and its limits in obedience to the authority of the Word of God."[32] The classic Bible verse to which the Reformed appeal here is Acts 5:29, "one should obey God rather than persons!"[33] Luther, too, cites this verse in his work on government.[34] But if it remains unclear just what this means for the Christian, the Reformed appeal to the word gives more concretely the possibility of examining whether a temporal government is fulfilling its own office.[35]

Indeed, this viewpoint offers the possibility of seeing that the state is always (not *only,* as Luther saw it) threatened from *below* by the people in that they ignore the divine ordinance of the government; and it also makes it possible to see that the state is also threatened from *above* by those who hold government office in that they demand absolute obedience and thereby transgress against the One through whom their office is established in the first place. Chaos, the prevention of which is (according to Luther) the good and divine reason for establishing temporal government, can thus come even from within the government. Calvin expressly said that it was for this reason that he purposed to develop his doctrine of the state: he stood against the double danger of rebellion against the government by the people and the misuse of power against the people by the government.[36] Thus for him any talk of the duty of the "subjects" cannot be meaningful unless one at the same time speaks of the duty of the "authorities" to care for the welfare of all.[37] Zwingli took aim at rebellion from below even earlier, in "Who Gives Cause for Rebellion" ("The Troublemakers," 1524), but he attacked more energetically rebellion from above, by the mighty who are quick to call others rebels even though they themselves are rebels. They are the ones who give occasion for rebellion "from below."[38]

Now certainly Luther was not blind on this point. In "On Temporal Authority" he complains about the wickedness of the rulers who "do and command only what they want," who "are commonly the greatest fools and worst scoundrels on earth; thus one should always expect the worst from them and must expect little good of them."[39] But it remains a mystery why this complaint is a cry of caution without consequence in Luther; it never led to constructive, concrete criticism of the deplorable state of affairs among the authorities. It is indeed a mystery how he could expect these "fools and scoundrels" to do what, according to him, they were supposed to do (in that they are in fact the authorities) — namely, protect the good from the evil.[40]

Luther obviously intended to give the matter no further thought, because precisely here he rather abstractly assigned the categories of "law and gospel" to the categories of "state and church." In asserting that the state represents the law, he drained the concept of "law" of so much of its basic meaning in Scripture as to render it basically just a wrath that terrifies people. The state *is* a category of wrath, and thus for Luther the sword is its *essential* mark — which in a sense implies that it does stray far from serving its purpose even when it is bad. Its subjects must understand and endure it as God's wrathful judgment upon them as sinners, which should draw them to the comfort of the gospel which the church has to proclaim.

Even though the Reformers said this at times as well,[41] their situation was different. They enjoyed the possibility of making concrete criticisms of governmental misuse of power. This possibility also included for them the task of pointing out positively what the task of worldly government is, the mark against which its work must be measured. They had considered the best forms of government — monarchy, aristocracy, and democracy.[42] They preferred a mixture of the last two and were thus in favor of a form of representative democracy. None of these forms was without danger, which is why for them the question of the *form* of government was secondary to the *content* of a political system, however it might be organized.

In determining the task of the state by its content, however, they were prevented from simply dividing "law and gospel" into "state and church" because they were unwilling either to separate so widely the law and gospel as testified to in Scripture or to conceive of them as almost opposite expressions of God's will. They too understood the law as the power of wrath insofar as it was isolated from the gospel,[43] but with God the two belong together: God's law and gospel, God's righteousness and grace. Thus Zwingli summed up the message of God's grace and commandments in the concept "righteousness." The church cannot simply delegate the notion of law to the state; its proclamation must include both law and gospel, since both are forms of God's righteous grace.

If the two may not be separated in the church's proclamation, how then can the content of the worldly government's task be determined? Here we encounter a major difficulty

in the Reformers' theology in which, with disastrous results, they achieved no clarity. Their answer to the question naturally was that a state is humanly righteous when "its laws conform to the divine will."[44] But how does temporal government know this divine will? And how may this divine will be binding for the state, which indeed is not the church and is composed of the unfaithful as well as the faithful? Calvin emphasized that by the will of God he did not mean the Mosaic law exactly as found in the Bible but rather an "ethical law," a "lasting rule of love" upon which even the law of Moses based itself as upon the "eternal standard of righteousness," and which allows for the "freedom" to establish itself in laws formulated differently.[45] But this does not remove the difficulty. Either the "divine will," that ethical law to which the laws of the state are to conform themselves, is determined by revelation — in which case the government must at least be bound by the word proclaimed in church and to that degree be Christian — or, if one wishes to avoid this, one must make the "will" of God one with the *lex naturalis* that is already to be found in the human heart, as Zwingli and Calvin actually suggested.[46] Quite contrary to their intent, however, this means that this element and the gospel are hopelessly separated.

It appears that both Calvin and Zwingli swung back and forth uncertainly between these two possibilities. They could not work their way out of this dilemma to the satisfactory conclusion that Christianity can do no more than participate in the political process, that it must not seek to impose itself prescriptively on a secular government. It is not impossible that, given the circumstances at that time, both theologians actually meant to promote the idea of simple participation in the political process. In any case, they assumed that not only believers but unbelievers as well lived in the state. Their goal in advocating that the laws of the state be conformed to the divine will was not expressly that the state be "Christian" but rather that it be a *human* state in caring for a life worthy of humanity. Both Reformers understood that the state is clearly not the church in that its task is the protection of life and community, whether its citizens are believers or not. And insofar as the state provides for this, its actions, while not identical to the righteousness and will of God proclaimed in the church, are nonetheless in conformity with them — the essence of that righteousness and will being that God desires not the death of sinners but their repentance and well-being (Ezek. 33:11). Christians recognize a state as just to the extent that it meets this requirement.

This means two things. First, the Christian cannot be indifferent to the manner in which the state and the "authorities" govern. Constant work and cooperation for *improvement* are possible and necessary so that the laws of the state become "more in conformity" with the will of God.[47] As Karl Barth said in 1946, the state is "capable of conformity" and "in need of conformity" in relation to the kingdom of God proclaimed in the church.[48] Second, in this way a truly *positive* determination of the task of the state was possible for the Reformers. The state is in essence not at all an order to impose punishment and violence. Calvin said against this that *kindness* is the first gift of the princes.[49] And above all, the primary task of a temporal government is to attend to the preservation of life and community — Zwingli held that it was to ensure "righteousness and peace,"[50] a formulation used in the Barmen Declaration.[51] Or, as Calvin said, its task is to provide for "welfare and the common peace,"[52] to see that "humanity remains in existence among people."[53]

What Luther considered decisive, Zwingli and Calvin did not even deem important: the state's protection of the good from the evil. Rather, their first criterion for the humanness of the state was its protection of the weak from the strong.[54] "True righteousness consists in mercy toward the weak and needy."[55] For them

the first mark of the state is not the sword. To be sure, it bears the sword — they never disputed this — but it bears it more as merely an accessory. In 1933 a group of leading German theologians in the Lutheran tradition said (in rather macabre fashion in light of the state's proceedings against the Jews) that "the State has to judge, the Church has to save."[56] This would have been unthinkable for Zwingli and Calvin. In one sense it entailed too high an estimation of the church — suggesting that it is the one that "saves" (this is especially so in the case of the Jews, where it never even made an attempt). In another sense it entailed too low an estimation of the state — suggesting that it is not to save at all. Its essence is not the sword: mere power does not make a true state; might does not make right. The authorities, rather, have the right to use force only in a certain function — to provide for "justice and peace" and to protect those suffering violence. The use of civil power must always be tested against this end. Otherwise the state will come to be run by violence, which is also a concern of the Reformed tradition.

THE CHURCH'S OFFICE OF WATCHKEEPER OVER THE STATE

Zwingli himself occasionally called his preaching office a "watchkeeper's office." More frequently he linked it to the service of a "prophet."[57] Both expressions call to mind the Old Testament prophets in their watchfulness against godlessness and unrighteousness in the life of the people. Calvin readily called preachers shepherds, "pastores," but he also said, using an expression from Ezekiel, that they "are placed in the Church as watchmen."[58] Thus for Calvin this dimension also belongs to the church's duty of proclamation.

What does it mean that the ecclesiastical office of watchkeeper belongs to the Reformed tradition? By the office of watchkeeper I do not intend to replace the biblical sermon with a political speech. Neither Zwingli nor Calvin ever forgot the difference between church and state. For them, direct involvement in politics did not belong in the pulpit but rather in the appropriate political arena. Zwingli was somewhat active in politics, but only in his roles as a member of the Zurich Council and as a representative on the civic commission, in which contexts he spoke as just one voice among others. Calvin was not a member of the municipal government, and in many cases he found that he was unable to stem its (in his opinion too strong) influence on the church. Nevertheless, through the power of his personality he was able to exercise some degree of influence on the state as a citizen.[59] While the Reformers considered it possible for a Christian to participate in politics, they certainly did not as yet see with the necessary clarity the difference between the realm of the state and that of the church as Karl Barth did in this century. In Barth's view, Christians can participate at the political level but must do so *"anonymously"* —that is, they must not claim to act in the name of Christianity but rather must translate their Christian motives into commonly comprehensible arguments.[60]

In any case, the Reformers had already emphasized that one can participate as a Christian in arenas other than the church. They held, for example, that a Christian can, if necessary, mix in politics by refusing to participate in an unjust government. Indeed, from the very beginning, the doctrine that a government that has become pure tyranny can be "dismissed by God" belongs to the Reformed tradition.[61] As we have already seen, the doctrine in this tradition made it possible for the Reformers to assume that there can be not only a "revolt" from below, by the people against the government, but also a revolt from above, by the government against the people — both of which they viewed as disobedience against God. Nonethe-

less, Zwingli and Calvin had considered that there might be circumstances and ways in which such an extreme measure as the removal of a government could be accomplished legitimately, without new injustice thereby arising but rather so that justice would replace injustice.

A Christian can become involved politically in this or that matter, but that is not yet the church's office of watchkeeper. This office belongs immediately to the church's witness itself, in contrast to individual political activity, which is not *directly* a matter of the church's testimony. Zwingli answered the question (and Calvin thought no differently) of what the church of Christ is by saying that it is "the one who hears his Word!"[62] To the question of what the kingdom of God is, he said, "it is nothing other than the Word of God."[63] And to the question of what the preacher should proclaim, he answered, "nothing other than the Word of God."[64] The proclamation of and witness to this word of God is the whole task of the church, besides which it has no other. Here we can answer the question of how the church can influence the state so that its laws conform more to the will of God in the way the Reformed theologians intended: it can do so by nothing other than preaching the word of God. We can expand on Zwingli's points: not only in the sermon, but whenever the church speaks and acts *as* church, it must bear witness only to the word of God.

Of course the Reformers were convinced that if one only applied and proclaimed the unqualified word of God in church according to the whole of Scripture, it would also have a political effect. Indeed, this effect will be, in a certain sense, in the best interests of the state; but in certain circumstances it will be quite different from what politicians would desire from the church. Calvin speaks clearly of how politicians and often tyrants desire a religious inauguration so that their "work may have a pious appearance" and so that they may erect temples to themselves. Of course if "one asks what they mean by this, the answer comes: We do this to the glory of God! But in this they seek only their own fame."[65] "Even though they thus despise God in their pride, they still use religion to strengthen their power and . . . to keep their people duty-bound [to them]." Indeed, they do not deny God but "shut God up in heaven" and desire that God will not "meddle in people's affairs."[66] Calvin saw, moreover, that it is precisely the bad rulers who readily surround themselves with flatterers and find many who will dance "to the King's pipes" and agree "with great applause."[67]

Insofar as God and God's word are always obeyed first and foremost, the duty of the preachers cannot be that of the flatterer or the one who delivers the higher sanction that problematic political programs may seek. Their obedience to God must be a clear protest against this; it must automatically create a critical distance and especially destroy the desired false religion. This preaching must be a witness to God, who, by no means "shut up in heaven," indeed "mixes in people's affairs."

Even beyond this, since God and God's word as found in Scripture are first and always obediently applied in the church, one will not only refuse to submit to the misuse of power, one obviously will have to speak out against injustice against the oppressed and against the causes of injustice and strife. It was along these lines of the Reformed tradition that Karl Barth asked in Berlin in October 1933, "What does the Church say to what is going on in the concentration camps? Or to the treatment of the Jews? Or to all that is done in the name of eugenics? Or to the absolute claim of the State?" Then came the decisive sentence: "whoever has to proclaim the Word of God must say to such proceedings what the Word of God says."[68] It is characteristic of the Reformed style of confession to speak so "abruptly" (H. Gollwitzer) from the word of God to a concrete political problem. Behind this stands the conviction that where nothing but the word of God is proclaimed, one will have to address concrete injustice and real threats because the word of God *itself* addresses them. A bit later Barth reproached the church for remaining silent in the face of all manner of injustice "which the Old Testament prophets surely would have addressed."[69] The reference to the Old Testament is characteristic, as the Reformed frequently used it in their criticism of abuses. Calvin diligently compiled verses precisely from this section of the Bible and held them up before the princes: Do not oppress strangers, widows, and orphans! Do justice to the needy! Save the least out of the hand of the oppressor! Hear the small as well as the great![70]

Thus in its origins the word of God in Scripture had to with with earthly justice in the state. Again, if this "earthly justice" has to do with the enhancement of human life, it is acting in conformity with divine justice as preached in the church, in which God desires not the death of the sinner but that the sinner may live. One who witnesses to this divine righteousness in a sermon should remember that it always has something to do, directly or indirectly, with earthly justice. Indeed, if the word of God is truly proclaimed, the word of God will itself ensure that it has an effect in the area of earthly justice. For, as Zwingli says, this word of God is "so powerful that from that very hour all things will conform to it or . . . be formed by it."[71] This means that the conformity of earthly justice with divine righteousness actually is taken care of by God's word itself — if only it is preached according to all of Scripture.

But whoever does this and does not cease to say to earthly injustice "what the Word of God says" will find anything but "conformity," or agreement. Rather, says Zwingli, they will be sent out by Jesus as sheep among wolves.[72] They will encounter outright opposition or at least the attitude that although they should indeed preach, they should preach "no further than the authorities will allow." The powerful ask immediately "What does that have to do with the gospel?" Indeed, says Zwingli, "the demons spoke thus from the possessed man: Jesus, what have we to do with you!"[73] Thus one may not give in to this expectation in the church. Calvin also was of the opinion "that we cannot follow God's command without danger to our lives" and that one ruins everything through "cowardice and timidity" and hence must rather "go out and meet death unafraid than disobey."[74]

This is precisely the office of watchkeeper in the Reformers' theology: to be undaunted, to speak the truth according to God's word straightforwardly and plainly, and thus also to call injustice by name without fear of being accused of being a rebel, as Zwingli said.[75] After Zwingli's death, when the young Heinrich Bullinger assumed his position, the city council sought to forbid him in the future from mixing in worldly things. He answered that he would not be forbidden to preach what Scripture had to say, for God's word "would also have its discord."[76] Shortly thereafter the Council of Bern made similar demands of its pastors, to which one of the most beautiful Reformed Confessions, the Synod of Bern, responded, "Because the truth (always also) bites and is sharp," the pastors should spare no one the divine word, "please or displease whomever it will." Even if the authorities should thereby believe themselves unjustly criticized, the pastors should say of themselves, "better a slanderer whom the authorities can charge with being untruthful than a friend who says yes to everything. For the latter lulls them into a false security, while the former keeps them alert so that they behave all the more uprightly."[77] This is the language of a church in which the office of proclamation discharges the prophetic office of watchkeeper and is not the sacral lackey of the government.

Nevertheless, even when the church speaks to the state in its office of watchkeeper, it must remain clear that it does not thereby cease to be church or somehow put itself in the place of the state. Rather it is the point of this office that the church thereby presses the state to be a *true* state.

THE STATE'S OFFICE OF WATCHKEEPER OVER THE CHURCH?

Now we come to the truly problematic aspect of the old Reformed view of the relation of church and state. We must add immediately that the problems with this view are not recent but have deep roots that have borne such questionable fruit that the other, good elements have been overshadowed and historically without much influence. This problematic aspect is the Reformers' recognition of something like an office of watchkeeper in the state over the church.

First of all, this is not at all to suggest that the temporal government may, by the power of its office, meddle in the spiritual task of the church. Governmental figures may properly be involved in the church only to the extent that they are members of the Christian community as well as members of the government. The contention that members of the government are *praecipua membra* (special members) of the church with special claims to authority in it (as not only the Lutheran but also the Reformed theologians allowed)[78] finds no support in the Bible. James 2:2ff. tells us that the wealthy person in the congregation deserves no special treatment relative to other members, and surely this must apply to persons with civil authority as well. Nevertheless, as Christians alongside others, they ought equally to be able to participate in ecclesiastical matters.

But in the writings of the Reformers we have a different matter: it is suggested that politicians — not as church members but as *repre-*

sentatives of the state — are to see that the church fulfills its spiritual task. Just as the church, in exercising its office of watchkeeper, may not take the place of the state but has as its goal that the state be a proper state, so the state may not in its office make itself into the church but must — and this is emphasized by Zwingli and Calvin as well as by Luther[79] — give full freedom to the proclamation of the church and thus in its role toward the church have as its only goal that the church be true church.

This definition shows that the Reformers held that church and state in fact must seek in their own interest the well-being of the other. Zwingli's frequent remark that there can be no better government than one under which God's word is proclaimed most clearly in the church[80] was easily misunderstood to imply that the church was to supply the grease for a smoothly functioning state. Yet the deepest meaning of the statement is that it is also in the best interests of the state when the church does earnestly what the state cannot and may not do, and thus it should desire this and support the church in it. Surely behind this stands the thought of a mutual interdependence — the church depending on the state for the protection of life, and the state relying on the church to tell *why* this life is to be protected.

If one keeps firmly in mind the difference between church and state stressed by the Reformers, one will be able to affirm these thoughts but refine the conclusion. It is proper for the true state, as evidence of its having been instituted by God, to give freedom to the church in its task and testimony. But we must take into account that the state — even when it calls itself "Christian" — can always grant this freedom for reasons that are completely different from those the church has for exercising it. Thus one must formulate this concern rigorously, as Karl Barth did over against Hitler's state in 1933. In his words, the church "is the natural border of very . . . State," and it is thus "for the good of the people, for *that*

good which neither State nor Church can create, but which the Church is called to proclaim."[81] The true state requires limits to which it can consent, so that it will not itself become an "institution of salvation" and an idol — and thus a totalitarian state. But it is only in faith and *in* the church that one knows about *this* meaning of the self-limitation of the state. Thus the church should expect from the state only that it will limit itself to its task and thereby allow freedom for the church. No matter how foreign the state's motives for doing this may be to the concerns of the church, in doing this the state in fact does what it ought to do in seeing that the church is true church.

The Reformed theologians consciously went further in defining the state's concern for the church — apparently because they presupposed a Christian government. One should not rush to say that in their day this presupposition was correct, while today we can no longer assume such a thing. Even at that time their assumption was highly questionable and was the starting point for an ominous meddling of the state in the church. What led them astray was not the idea that the worldly government was in fact "Christian" but rather that as true government it is *necessarily* Christian. They were unable to draw a second conclusion from the thought, in itself correct, that earthly justice must use "divine righteousness" as its standard. This is one more area in which the Reformers did not take seriously the distinction between church and state; they did not appreciate the fact that "divine righteousness" can influence the formation of "earthly justice" in only very *indirect* ways and can be applied anonymously in the state. Rather, they postulated that in order to act correctly, the authorities must have a *direct* knowledge of God's will and righteousness. By the force of this idea they also ascribed to the authorities the competence to see that the church says of the will of God what they need to know of it in order to be able to act correctly.

On this basis Zwingli developed the idea that for its own sake the true state should desire the existence of the church. In fact, his conclusions entail that the entire supervision of the church be entrusted to the state.[82] Thus he handed over to the Zurich Council complete rights over the church — the use of church property, the installation and removal of pastors, the exclusion of certain people from the Lord's Supper, supervision of the pastors and their sermons, the right to carry out or prevent reforms, and so on. In this Zwingli had overlooked the fact that already before the Reformation the Council had begun to assume not only the worldly but also the ecclesiastical rights of the bishop — and not out of pure delight in the gospel but rather out of clear interest in power. Thus Zwingli, with the permission of the state, approved of its systematic progress "to make the clergy subject to the State."[83] How could the clergy resist after the external law of the church was handed over to the state? Calvin rightly took Zwingli's solution to task, saying that here Protestant doctrine was "subject not only to the power, but even to the mere gesture of a few men — theologically uneducated ones at that: one must speak or be silent according to how they wave their finger."[84]

Here Calvin was not afraid without reason. This danger was not yet acute in Zwingli himself — he was too mighty a prophetic watchkeeper for that — but it did become acute in the territories where his thought was influential in the following centuries. The clergy were made subject to the interest of the state and for centuries had to take an oath on their spiritual office, first strictly to obey the government and second also to preach the word of God.[85] The Reformed church put up with this huge demand, which stood the concerns of the Reformers on their head. In fact, around 1830 the church submitted when a (by that time) secularized government forbade the use of the Heidelberg Catechism.[86]

With Calvin circumstances were a bit different, but not so different that he could prevent a similar development, despite his criticism of Zwingli and despite his success in securing for the church its own spiritual leadership and organization. Indeed, against the hand of the state, which in his case as well was grabbing strongly at the church, he could not achieve all he had in mind.[87] But his creation for the church of its own leadership was impressive in comparison not only with Zwingli but also with the Lutheran territories where the leadership of the church was handed over to the "sovereign state government of the Church" (the authorities). Calvin believed that representatives of the offices of the church should lead the church according to the model of early Christianity (pastors, teachers, deacons, and elders — this last office, of course, being where the political leadership also sat in church leadership). With this, Calvin paved the way for the important understanding Karl Barth introduced into proposition three of the Barmen Declaration in 1934: that the church may not be left to the state even in its outward form of organization but rather must be structured according to its own nature.[88] Otherwise it will be robbed of its power to confess *to* the state — and, if necessary, *against* it — and it will become to the contrary a structure easily manipulated by state and society.

Nevertheless, Calvin was not only unable to avert this danger but helped increase it. This resulted precisely from the conclusion he drew from the thought that (as he formulated it) the advancement of God's glory and the humaneness of humanity belong inseparably together, and the keeping of the second table of the Ten Commandments in the state is impossible without the keeping of the first table as well. If Calvin held, with Zwingli, that the authorities did not have to exercise the organizational leadership of the church, he also held that as the political power they had the right and duty to enforce the observance of the first table —

and this not only formally for the freedom of the church but also materially for the institution and preservation of true worship and the abolition of false worship.[89] John Knox then included his belief that rulers are "appointed not only for civil government but also to maintain true religion and to suppress all idolatry and superstition" in the Scots Confession.[90] The danger of this statement is evident in its immediate implication (even when it is limited by the qualification that the authorities fulfill their office properly): "therefore . . . those who resist the supreme powers . . . are resisting God's ordinance."

Barth observed correctly that "spiritual corruption must be overcome by spiritual and not by political power. If the Church fails to recognize this, who can save it, what reforms could be demanded of it one day with political power?"[91] It came to demands soon enough in Geneva, where already in 1537, at Calvin's instigation, the police wanted to force all inhabitants to swear by his Reformed confession of faith.[92] Calvin's complete lack of comprehension of Bullinger's and Capito's criticisms of the proceedings shows that the development was not a mere coincidence but rather was clearly the consequence of this thinking. This then validated in rather infamous fashion the trial of the antitrinitarian Servetus and a series of similar incidents.[93]

The problem with Calvin's thinking on this point is that it can lead to even greater demands. Once the state is granted the right to mix with political power in the spiritual realm, how can the church protect itself if authorities who no longer see themselves as Christian choose to hang onto this right? Further, what if Calvin's grounding of the state's authority on the doctrine of providence is completely separated from its already loose ties to the doctrine of the reign of Christ? Further still, what if Calvin's favorite verse, Daniel 2:21, that the Lord establishes and deposes kings,[94] were to be put into the framework of a general doctrine

of providence in history? As long as "the Lord" does not depose the authorities, must not any capricious act toward the church by a long-secularized worldly government be accepted as God-given? It was not coincidental that later forms of Calvinism granted themselves a "legitimacy" over against the government.[95]

This was particularly the case in German-speaking Switzerland, as evidenced in the principle that the secularized government expressed in 1800: the state protects the church with the qualification that no Christian avoids "his civil duty on the pretext of religion."[96] Here the favorite words of the old Reformed theologians were twisted into an opposite meaning — it is no longer "one should obey God rather than persons" but rather one should first obey the state (or else the social customs) and then, as far as there is agreement, God as well. This not only strips the Christian faith of any social and political influence but reduces it to a "religion" that can take up no more than a corner of life, compared with the vastly greater reach of the state. Of course things did not get as bad as all that. Nevertheless, in most cases the observation of the church's prophetic office of watchkeeper was the exception in the Reformed territories. Moreover, in most cases much of what was crucial in the Reformed doctrine of church and state went awry and failed to develop. Under the circumstances, the paragraph in the church order cited at the beginning of this paper is indeed Reformed, but nonetheless, it is a miracle. Its implications are now in a long-term struggle with the just-mentioned Swiss Reformed mentality.

It was indeed an indirect result of Calvin's thought that the way was paved for a consciousness of freedom in other areas influenced by him and that resistance movements against the capricious use of force developed in Holland, France, and Scotland.[97] Barth was right when he observed in Calvin what, *mutatis mutandis,* applies to Zwingli as well: "his political attitude is distinguished by the same light, but also by the same shadows, which are characteristic of his theology."[98] Calvin's and Zwingli's important discovery of the church's "prophetic office of watchkeeper" over injustice by the state was moved into the shadows by Calvin and Zwingli themselves. They allowed the primary obedience of the Christian to God, which is the basis of the office of watchkeeper, to be limited by granting the state the right to supervise this obedience. The light in this matter will shine only when this shadow with which they have burdened their understanding is removed. Their light will shine only when we subject their concession of a limitation of Christian obedience to God by an order of the state to a thoroughgoing criticism. Only then will the closing statement in Calvin's chapter on temporal government (and indeed in the *Institutes* in general) have real meaning. Christ has bought and redeemed us at such a great price "that we should not enslave ourselves to the evil desires of humanity, and much less should we submit to godlessness. Glory be to God!"[99]

NOTES

1. Luther, *An den Rath zu Münster,* vom 21. December 1532, in *Erlangen Ausgabe* (1826ff.), 54.346.

2. See Ulrich Gäbler, *Huldrych Zwingli. Eine Einführung in sein Leben und Werk* (Munich: C. H. Beck, 1983), p. 18; William F. Dankbaar, *Calvin. Sein Weg und sein Werk,* 2d ed. (Neukircken: Neukirchener Verlag, 1966), pp. 88ff.

3. See Christof Gestrich, *Zwingli als Theologe. Glaube und Geist Beim Zürcher Reformator* (Zurich: Zwingli-Verlag, 1967).

4. Zwingli, "Von göttlicher und menschlicher Gerechtigkeit," in *Zwingli Hauptschriften,* 8 vols., ed. Fritz Blanke, Oskar Farner, and Rudolf Pfister (Zurich: Zwingli-Verlag, 1948), 7: 56.

5. Calvin, *Institutes,* 4.20.1.

6. Dankbaar, *Calvin,* p. 163.

7. See Gäbler, *Zwingli,* p. 22; Dankbaar, *Calvin,* pp. 88-89.

8. Luther, *Von weltlicher Obrigkeit, wie weit man ihr Gehorsam Schuldig sei,* in *Erlangen Ausgabe,* 22.82f.

9. Zwingli, *Von göttlicher und menschlicher Gerechtigkeit,* p. 75.

10. See Wilhelm Niesel, *Die Theologie Calvins,* 2d ed. (Munich: Christian Kaiser Verlag, 1957), p. 232.

11. See Oskar Farner, *Huldrych Zwingli,* 4 vols. (Zurich: Zwingli-Verlag, 1943-60), 3: 388.

12. Zwingli, *Sämtliche Werke,* vol. 2 (Leipzig, 1908), 437.3.

13. See Zwingli, *Von göttlicher und menschlicher Gerechtigkeit,* p. 74; Calvin, *Institutes,* 4.20.24.

14. Luther, *Von weltlicher Obrigkeit,* pp. 66, 68; Zwingli, *Von göttlicher und menschlicher Gerechtigkeit,* p. 55.

15. Calvin, *Institutes,* 4.20.5; Zwingli, *Von göttlicher und menschlicher Gerechtigkeit,* pp. 74-75.

16. Calvin, *Institutes,* 4.20.7.

17. Barth, *Rechtfertigung und Recht* (Zollikon: Evangelischer Verlag, 1938), p. 31.

18. Calvin, *Institutes,* 4.20.2.

19. See Locher, *Huldrych Zwingli in Neuer Sicht. Zehn Beiträge zur Theologie der Zürcher Reformation* (Zurich/Stuttgart: Zwingli-Verlag, 1969), p. 36.

20. Luther, *Von weltlicher Obrigkeit,* p. 96.

21. See Niesel, *Die Theologie Calvins,* p. 228.

22. See Calvin, *Institutes,* 4.20.6, 30.

23. Calvin, *Institutes,* 4.20.1

24. See Niesel, *Die theologie Calvins,* 228.

25. Calvin, *Ezechiel und Daniel,* in *Auslegung der Heiligen Schrift,* 9 vols., ed. Otto Weber (Neukirchen: Neukirchener Verlag, 1938), 9: 394.

26. Calvin, *Institutes,* 4.20.4; Zwingli, *Von göttlicher und menschlicher Gerechtigkeit,* pp. 74ff.

27. Calvin, *Institutes,* 4.20.4.

28. Calvin, *Ezechiel und Daniel,* p. 385.

29. Calvin, *Ezechiel und Daniel,* pp. 435, 413.

30. Calvin, *Ezechiel und Daniel,* p. 385.

31. Calvin, *Institutes,* 4.20.32.

32. *Lebendiges Bekenntnis. Die "Grundlagen und Perspektiven des Bekennens" der Generalsynode der Niederländischen Reformierten Kirche 1949,* 2d ed., ed. Otto Weber (Neukirchen: Neukirchener Verlag, 1959), p. 62.

33. Calvin, *Institutes,* 4.20.32; Zwingli, *Von göttlicher und menschlicher Gerechtigkeit,* p. 77; Zwingli, *Auslegen und Begründen der Schlussrden,* in *Zwingli Hauptschriften,* 4: 108, 112.

34. Luther, *Von weltlicher Obrigkeit,* p. 101.

35. See note 33.

36. Calvin, *Institutes,* 4.20.1.

37. See Niesel, *Die Theologie Calvins,* p. 241.

38. Zwingli, *Wer Ursache gebe zum Aufruhr,* in *Zwingli Hauptschriften,* 7: 170ff.

39. Luther, *Von weltlicher Obrigkeit,* pp. 62, 89.

40. Luther, *Von weltlicher Obrigkeit,* p. 65.

41. See, e.g., Zwingli, *Auslegen und Begründen,* p. 98.

42. See *Aus Zwinglis Predigten zu Jesaja und Jeremia,* ed. Oskar Farner (Zurich: Verlag Berichthaus, 1957), pp. 269ff.; Calvin, *Institutes,* 4.20.8.

43. Calvin, *Institutes*, 2.7.6-9.

44. Zwingli, *Auslegen und Begründen*, pp. 112ff.

45. Calvin, *Institutes*, 4.20.14.

46. Zwingli, *Auslegen und Begründen*, p. 114; Calvin, *Institutes*, 4.20.16.

47. Zwingli, *Auslegen und Begründen*, pp. 112ff.

48. Karl Barth, *Christengemeinde und Bürgergemeinde* (Stuttgart: Kohlhammer, 1946), pp. 29-30.

49. Calvin, *Institutes*, 4.20.10.

50. See Erik Wolf, "Die Sozialtheologie Zwinglis," in *Festschrift Guido Kisch* (Stuttgart, 1955), p. 188.

51. See Proposition 5 of the Barmen Declaration.

52. Calvin, *Institutes*, 4.20.9.

53. Calvin, *Institutes*, 4.20.3.

54. Zwingli, *Auslegen und Begründen*, p. 112; Calvin, *Institutes*, 4.20.12. Calvin urges the use of force only as the last resort.

55. Calvin, *Ezechiel und Daniel*, p. 437.

56. Kurt Meier, *Kirche und Judentum. Die Haltung der Evangelischen Kirche zur Judenpolitik des Dritten Reiches* (Göttingen: Vandenhoeck & Ruprecht, 1968), p. 83.

57. Zwingli, *Sämtliche Werke*, 2: 313.

58. Calvin, *Institutes*, 4.3.6.

59. See Dankbaar, *Calvin*, p. 98.

60. Barth, *Christengemeinde und Bürgergemeinde*, p. 48.

61. See Zwingli, *Auslegen und Begründen*, p. 136.

62. Farner, *Huldrych Zwingli*, 3: 367.

63. Zwingli, *Sämtliche Werke*, 2: 182.

64. Zwingli, *Der Prediger*, in *Zwingli Hauptschriften*, 1: 187.

65. Calvin, *Ezechiel und Daniel*, p. 405.

66. Niesel, *Die Theologie Calvins*, p. 236.

67. Calvin, *Ezechiel und Daniel*, p. 409.

68. See Hans Prolingheuer, *Der Fall Karl Barth. Chronographie einer Vertreibung, 1934-1935*, 2d ed. (Neukirchen: Neukirchener Verlag, 1984), p. 18; Klaus Scholder, *Die Kirchen und das Dritte Reich*, vol. 1 (Frankfurt: Propyläen, 1977), p. 687.

69. Barth, *Zum Kirchenkampf. Beteiligung, Mahnung, Zuspruch*, Theol. Existenz Heute, N.F. 49 (Munich: Christian Kaiser, 1956), p. 34.

70. Calvin, *Institutes*, 4.20.9.

71. Zwingli, *Der Prediger*, p. 79.

72. Zwingli, *Der Prediger*, p. 231.

73. Zwingli, *Sämtliche Werke*, 2: 494; *Wer Ursach gebe zum Aufruhr*, p. 190.

74. Calvin, *Ezechiel und Daniel*, pp. 368, 459.

75. Zwingli, *Auslegen und Begründen*, p. 109.

76. Farner, *Huldrych Zwingli*, 4: 509.

77. *Der Berner Synodus von 1532*, vol. 1, ed. Gottfried Locher (Neukirchen: Neukirchener Verlag, 1982), pp. 112-13, 120-21.

78. See Alfred Farner, *Die Lehre von Kirche und Staat bei Zwingli* (Tübingen: Mohr, 1930); Dankbaar, *Calvin*, p. 93; Niesel, *Die Theologie Calvins*, p. 232.

79. Luther, *Von weltlicher Obrigkeit*, pp. 82ff.; Niesel, *Die Theologie Calvins*, 232; Zwingli, *Eine freundliche Bitte und Ermahnung, . . . dass man das Heilige Evangelium zu predigen erlaube* (1522).

80. E.g., Zwingli, *Auslegen und Begründen*, pp. 90, 121.

81. Barth, *Theologische Existenz Heute!* (Munich: Christian Kaiser Verlag, 1933), p. 40.

82. See Gäbler, *Zwingli*, p. 89.

83. Gäbler, *Zwingli*, p. 76.

84. *Johannes Calvins Lebenswerk in seinen Briefen*, ed. Rudolf Schwarz (Neukirchen: Neukirchener Verlag, 1961), p. 231.

85. *Neu-verbesserte Predikanten-Ordnung Des sammtlichen Ministerii Der Teutschen Landen Hoch-Loblicher Stadt Bern* (Bern, 1748), p. 121.

86. Jakob Heiz, "Zur 400 jährigen Jubiläumsfeier der Berner Reformation," in *Menschenrat und Gottestat, Geschichte der Berner Reformation*, ed. Ernst Marti (Bern: Büchler, 1927), p. 19.

87. See Dankbaar, *Calvin*, pp. 93, 98.

88. Proposition 3 of the Barmen Declaration reads, "we reject the false teaching that the church may surrender . . . her order . . . to the changes of the political convictions of those currently in power."

89. Calvin, *Institutes*, 4.20.9.

90. Scots Confession, Article 24.

91. Barth, *Gotteserkenntnis und Gottesdienst nach reformatorischer Lehre* (Zollikon: Evangelischer Verlag, 1938), p. 210.

92. See Fritz Blanke, "Calvins Fehler," *Reformatio* 8 (1959): 298ff.

93. See Blanke, "Calvins Fehler," pp. 303ff.

94. Calvin, *Ezechiel und Daniel*, p. 386; *Institutes*, 4.20.26.

95. Otto Weber, "Calvinismus," *Evangelisches Kirchenlexicon*, vol. 1 (Göttingen: Vandenhoeck & Ruprecht, 1956), p. 663.

96. Heiz, "Zur 400 jährigen Jubiläumsfeier," p. 22.

97. See Gerhard Gloede, "Calvin," *Evangelisches Kirchenlexicon*, 1: 656.

98. Karl Barth, "Calvin als Theologe," *Reformatio* 8 (1959): 318.

99. Calvin, *Institutes*, 4.20.32.

Reformed Faith and Religious Liberty

David Little

INTRODUCTION

There exists at the heart of Reformed faith a deep tension in regard to church-state relations and religious liberty. That tension derives from certain theological and ecclesiological themes that pull in different, if not conflicting, directions.

On the one side, the tradition has committed itself consistently to an essential distinction between the "internal forum" of conscience and the "external forum" of civil authority, between the "law of the spirit" and the "law of the sword." Such a conviction implies firm lines of separation between church and state and vigorous respect for the free exercise of conscience in religious belief and practice.

On the other side, the tradition has understood the civil order to need a religious foundation. That conviction favors positive, cooperative relations between church and state,

Reprinted from *Church & Society* (May/June 1986): 6-28.

and calls for civil restriction of religious belief and practice in the interest of maintaining civil order.

The way the strain between these two basic convictions has been variously resolved constitutes an important part of the story of Reformed faith, and more particularly of Presbyterianism, from the sixteenth century to the present.

I. CALVIN AND THE REFORMATION

The rise of the Christian church as a distinct institution entitled to govern the spiritual concerns of mankind in independence of the state may not unreasonably be described as the most revolutionary event in the history of Western Europe, in respect both to politics and political philosophy.[1]

There was nothing very special in the history of Western Christianity about the concern of the Protestant Reformers to work out the correct relations between church and state. The concern was as old as the Christian church itself and in an important sense had been at the heart of Christian cogitation, in its diverse forms, from the beginning of Christianity.

The word in Greek for church — *ekklesia* —means *called out* or *set apart*. It thus presupposed as the foundation of Christian faith an ineradicable distinction between two orders of life, an *inner* and an *outer,* a *spiritual* and a *temporal* sphere. Whatever else it involved, being a Christian meant believing that human beings are in reality subject to two sorts of laws of behavior: one external, imposed, coercive, and governed finally by the *law of the sword;* the other internal, heartfelt, voluntary, and governed finally by the *law of the spirit*.

The opening quotation alludes to a crucial fact about the Christian church in Western civilization. By forming itself into a separate spiritual institution alongside the temporal institution of the state, and by laying claim to its own independent jurisdiction, the church dramatically recast the existing Roman and Judaic understanding of the state, its shape, and its purpose. At the same time, the emergence of the church in the first century A.D. established a central perplexity for all who would come after, including the members of our own age: how to relate the two spheres without compromising or neglecting the distinction between them.

The spiritual leaders of the Protestant Reformation — Martin Luther in Germany, Richard Hooker in England, John Calvin in French Switzerland, and the various left-wing Anabaptists, among others — may usefully be distinguished from medieval Catholics as well as from each other in reference to the way each responded to this central perplexity. If medieval Catholics espoused a relatively static hierarchical solution to the relations between the spiritual and temporal orders, Calvin introduced considerable fluidity, if not volatility, into the situation.

In place of the monarchic form of government that had come to dominate Roman Catholicism at the time of the Reformation, Calvin urged a "polyarchic" model, "a system compounded of aristocracy and democracy" that was, he believed, more appropriate to governing the spiritual order (and eventually the civil order as well). A proper officer of the church is "not so much higher in honor and dignity over his colleagues" as one who simply has certain *functions* that have been decreed "by the general voice." The central emphasis is on the voluntary, consensual participation in the determination of church affairs by all Christians.

That emphasis, in turn, flows from the intensification in Calvin's theology of conscientious spiritual and personal moral responsibility as the fruit of true regeneration and sanctification. To be a Christian is ideally to be part of a community that conducts its affairs according to the voluntary obedience and mutual edification and direction of all its members — a community governed, as Calvin puts it, according to the "administration of the Spirit."

Not that Calvin was anywhere close to being a modern democrat. He was deeply suspicious of what he regarded as the dangers of anarchy implicit in any polity that did not modify the participation of the people. Still, his opposition to monarchy, especially in the church, was consonant with his strong commitment to "participatory Christianity," and that commitment was to have vibrant effects wherever Calvinism spread.

Calvin's response to the perplexity of determining church-state relations is also different, in important ways, from that of such other Reformers as Luther and Hooker. In contrast to the tendency of these men, each in his own special way, to inwardize and spiritualize the Christian life, Calvin gave extensive consideration to the theological significance of church order and the outward "example of life" that Christians are supposed to display. Calvin's characteristic stress on the "third use of the law," for which Luther and Hooker appear to have had no use whatsoever, illustrates the point. The first two uses of the law are to convict people of their sin and to restrain them from outward violations; the third use instructs "believers in whose hearts the Spirit of God already lives and reigns." Calvin's impulse to transform outward behavior according to the law of God was something distinctive among the major Reformers.

Finally, in contrast to what he regarded as the utopian visions of the Anabaptists and their consequent disparagement of "courts, laws, and magistrates," Calvin envisioned a more constructive role for government in the service of God's kingdom, though he was not entirely clear or consistent in stating his views on this subject. Calvin, like many of the Anabaptists, also emphasized the sharp separation between freedom and coercion, between the spirit and the sword. We must appreciate, he writes,

> how great a difference and unlikeness there is between ecclesiastical and civil power. For the church does not have the right of the sword to punish or compel, not the authority to force; not imprisonment, nor the other punishments which the magistrate commonly inflicts. Then, it is not a question of punishing the sinner against his will, but of the sinner professing his repentance in a voluntary chastisement. The two conceptions are very different. The church does not assume what is proper to the magistrate; nor can the magistrate execute what is carried out by the church.[2]

The arm of the state may reach and control the actions of people, which are "outward," but not their inner intentions and motivations, including their attitudes toward God.

> There is a twofold government in man: one aspect is spiritual, whereby the conscience is instructed in piety and reverencing God; the second is political, whereby man is educated for the duties of humanity and citizenship that must be maintained among men. These are usually called the "spiritual" and "temporal" juris-

diction . . . by which is meant that the former sort of government pertains to the life of the soul, while the latter has to do with the concerns of the present life — not only with food and clothing but with laying down laws whereby a man may live his life among men holily, honorably and temperately. For the former resides in the inner mind, while the latter regulates only outward behavior. The one we may call the spiritual kingdom, the other, the political kingdom. Now these two, as we have divided them, must always be examined separately; and while one is being considered, we must call away and turn aside the mind from thinking about the other. There are in man, so to speak, two worlds, over which different kings and different laws have authority. (*Inst.*, 3.19.15)

Calvin's proclivity for dwelling on the importance of Christian liberty, of voluntary, self-directed conduct and thought, rather than upon being forced or goaded into living properly obviously underscores these sentiments. For Calvin, there is much at stake in Christians taking to heart the distinction between the "two worlds, . . . [with their] different kings and different laws."

However, if Calvin says that the two spheres are irreconcilable, that is not all he says. In fact, there is much ambiguity and tension in Calvin's thought on this question; that is part of the abiding volatility of the Calvinist response to the central perplexity of Christian thought and life. Having laid it down in no uncertain terms that the two kingdoms "must always be examined separately; and while one is being considered, we must call away and turn aside the mind from thinking about the other," Calvin proceeds in numerous places to disregard that counsel.

> We must know that [the two kingdoms] are not at variance. For spiritual government, indeed, is already initiating in us upon earth certain beginnings of the Heavenly Kingdom, and in this mortal and fleeting life affords a certain forecast of an immortal and incorruptible

blessedness. Yet civil government has as its appointed end, so long as we live among men, to cherish and protect the outward worship of God, to defend sound doctrine of piety and the position of the church, to adjust our life to the society of men, to form our social behavior to civil righteousness, to reconcile us with one another, and to promote general peace and tranquillity. (*Inst.,* 4.20.2)

In short, the inner tension of Calvinism is produced by the fact that Calvin both disassociates and interconnects the two tables of the Decalogue, the first table concerning worship and the "sound doctrine of piety and the position of the church," and the second concerning "civil righteousness" and the achievement of "general peace and tranquillity."

The conflict here is between two essentially incompatible images of the relation of church and state. One is a uniformist, establishmentarian image in which the state by means of coercion enforces, at least externally, true piety and worship as well as civil righteousness, after the fashion of Calvin's own experiment in sixteenth-century Geneva. On this image, exemplified in much of the Old Testament, proper piety and worship are taken to be indispensable to the cultivation of civic virtue, specifically the restraint of arbitrary violence (murder, theft, libel) such as is proscribed in the second table of the Decalogue.

The other image moves in the opposite direction. It differentiates true piety and worship — "things of the spirit," of the inner life — from social behavior and civic virtue. Since civil offenses themselves involve the use of illicit coercion and the victimization of one human being by another, the state may properly intervene and apply coercion in order to restrain or punish such offenses. But as the inner life — the sphere of mind and heart, of faith and worship — is effectively addressed and transformed only by weapons of the spirit, the spiritual order must at all costs be placed beyond the reach, and must conduct its affairs

independently of, civil "courts, laws and magistrates."

The underlying assumption here is this: with regard to "heavenly things" (pure knowledge of God, the nature of true righteousness, and the mysteries of the heavenly kingdom), "human knowledge wholly fails" (*Inst.,* 2.2.24) and thus requires explicit supernatural assistance. In regard to the conduct of "earthly" affairs (government, household management, mechanical skills, and the liberal arts), on the other hand, "there exist in all men's minds universal impressions of a certain civic fair dealing and order. . . . Some seed of political order has been implanted in all men. And this is ample proof that in the arrangement of this life no man is without the light of reason" (*Inst.,* 2.2.13). Consequently, "men have somewhat more [natural] understanding of the precepts of the Second Table [than the First] because these are more closely concerned with the preservation of civil society among them" (*Inst.,* 2.2.24). In other words, Calvin here attributes to human beings a significant degree of natural moral capability to order their civic lives without requiring any particular religious revelation or guidance. This is the basis in Calvin's thought for the provisional separation of the civil-moral sphere from the religious-spiritual sphere, a separation that would have important consequences in the hands of left-wing Calvinists such as Roger Williams.

Accordingly, while Calvinism unquestionably inspired an impulse toward uniformity and established religion, it simultaneously inspired a countervailing impulse toward dissociating the spiritual from the temporal kingdom and immunizing the one from the other.

This deep-seated ambivalence resulted in an analogously ambivalent attitude toward the conscience and its freedom of operation and expression. If, on the one hand, human laws might prompt conscience toward true piety and worship, on the other hand, they "do not of themselves bind the conscience" (*Inst.,* 4.10.5).

In support of this rather radical doctrine, Calvin invokes

> that common distinction between the earthly forum and the forum of the conscience. While the whole world was shrouded in the deepest darkness of ignorance, this tiny little spark of light remained, that man recognized man's conscience to be higher than all human judgments. Although they afterward indeed cast away what they confessed in one word, God still willed that some testimony of Christian freedom appear even then, to rescue consciences from the tyranny of men. (*Inst.*, 4.10.5)

Like much of the rest of Calvin's thought, this idea of the sovereignty of conscience as over against all human laws was to have most disruptive consequences in some Reformed quarters.

II. POST-REFORMATION DEVELOPMENTS IN SCOTLAND AND FRANCE

Armed with this unstable combination of ideas, it was not surprising that, wherever it went, Calvinism worked a peculiarly destabilizing and renovative effect on political and religious life.

The central theme of the Scottish Reformation under the leadership of John Knox, as well as of the French Huguenot movement, was precisely the attempt "to rescue consciences from the tyranny of men." In Scotland, Knox took Calvin's idea that alien forms of religious belief and practice established by the civil law were a violation of the sovereignty of conscience and as such were in no way binding upon the Christian, and pushed it further than Calvin himself would allow by deducing from it an active and, if need be, violent right of resistance.

In the name of the freedom of Christian conscience, Knox endeavored to reform Scotland along the lines of Calvin's Genevan ideal.

The brand of Scottish Presbyterianism that resulted was a particularly resolute form of the uniformist, establishmentarian side of Reformed faith. The dimension of Calvin's thought that distinguished and separated the spiritual from the temporal realm was systematically minimized in Knox's intrepid campaign to root out with the sword all idolatry and blasphemy. Indeed, in Knox's thought, as in the thought of some other Calvinists, the assault on idolatry became the foundation for political resistance and reform.

> The punishment of such crimes as are idolatry, blasphemy and others that touch the Majesty of God, doth not appertain to kings and chief rulers only, but also to the whole body of that people, and to every member of the same, according to the vocation of every man, and according to that possibility and occasion which God doth minister to revenge the injury done against his glory, what time that impiety is manifestly known.[3]

Two themes are worthy of note here: (1) blasphemy and idolatry are seen as civil crimes to be punished by civil authority, and (2) they are to be punished by "the whole body of the people and to every member of the same" if necessary.

Knox's influence and the circumstances of Scottish political life conspired to produce a persistent policy of religious intolerance. The eminent seventeenth-century Scottish divine Samuel Rutherford, who was to play an important if short-lived role in the religious affairs of England during the English civil war in the 1640s, perpetuated Knox's point of view in two staunch antitolerance treatises, *A Survey of Spiritual Antichrist* and *A Free Disputation against Pretended Liberty of Conscience.* The king was to "take vengeance upon blasphemy, idolatry, [and] professed unbeleefe . . . which are . . . moral ills hindering men as members of the Church in their journey to the life eternal."

Also of interest, however, are the implications of Knox's thought, along with the thought of such other Scottish Presbyterians as George Buchanan and Rutherford, for a doctrine of political obligation. Knox called upon all citizens to accept the consequences of a belief in the sovereignty of conscience by trying — each in their own "inner forum" — the fundamental legitimacy of existing civil law, and, if they adjudged any illegitimate, to consent to replace that tyranny with a government conforming to the dictates of true conscience. Thus the notion of a *covenantal* or *contractual* basis for political obedience emerged. The sovereignty of the "external forum" was finally derived from and subordinate to the sovereignty of the "inner forum."

Although the Huguenots in France initially manifested many of the emphases found in the Scottish Reformation, their attempts to work out a doctrine of church-state relations reveal an even more complex amalgamation of the divergent themes of original Calvinism. The leading Huguenot political tract, *Vindiciae contra Tyrannos* (1574), which is reasonably attributed to Philip Mornay, echoes the same contractual theory of political obligation encountered in the Scottish Reformation. Each citizen was entitled to stand in judgment, finally, upon the authority of existing law. If a given regime departs from God's law, the people are entitled to replace the rulers. The discussion of the fourth question in the *Vindiciae* clearly authenticates, as with Knox, the direct use of force in overthrowing heresy and idolatry.

But in contrast to the rigid uniformity and intolerance of Scottish Reformed ideas, Huguenot thought also reflected that strand in Calvin's theory advocating the sharp separation of the spiritual from the temporal realm. As noted, that strand encouraged restraining the use of force in religious affairs in favor of permitting the free operation of the inner, voluntary characteristics of the religious life. Mor-

nay, for one, came more and more to dwell upon the inappropriateness of mixing the spirit and the sword: "idolatry must be overthrown," he wrote, "by the Word of God, not by the hammer blows of men."[4] He went from place to place reiterating his developing conviction that truth alone dispels error and that to employ coercion in the service of faith only distracts the mind and heart from the true source of religious belief.

III. THE ENGLISH EXPERIENCE IN THE LATE SIXTEENTH AND SEVENTEENTH CENTURIES

From roughly the middle of the sixteenth century, when Calvinism began to have a decisive impact on English life and thought, the conflicting and countervailing tendencies in Calvin's thinking began to express themselves in different and frequently antagonistic religious movements and parties that were, despite their differences, chips off the same block. The "travail of religious liberty" from the mid-sixteenth century onward cannot be understood apart from the multifaceted contribution of Calvinism.

Starting in the 1550s, Reformed Christianity polarized into Presbyterianism on the one side and a "free church" separatist form of Congregationalism on the other. The Presbyterians featured the uniformist, establishmentarian part of Calvin's thought, the part that found such dramatic display in Calvin's own Geneva and in the Scottish Reformation. In contrast, the separatist Congregationalists made much of the Calvinist commitment to the superiority of voluntary and consensual over coerced religious participation.

The antipathy between these two parties persisted well into the civil-war period in the middle of the seventeenth century. For all of that, they both sprang from sources that were perceived with justification as threatening the foundations of existing English society. In 1570 Thomas Cartwright, leader of Elizabethan Presbyterianism, lost his job as professor of theology at Cambridge after attacking the hierarchic and monarchic structure of the Anglican Church, much in the spirit of Calvin's attack on the Roman Catholic hierarchy.

> I would ask if the church be not in as great danger when all is done at the pleasure and lust of one man, and when one carrieth all into error, as when one pulleth one piece with him, another piece, and a third his part also with him. And it is harder to draw many into error than one, or that many should be carried away by their affections than one. . . . (Even though ecclesiastical monarchy might be said at times to keep the peace) yet the peace which is without truth is more execrable than a thousand contentions. For as by strikeing of two flints together there cometh out fire, so it may be that sometimes by contention the truth which is hidden in a dark place may come to light, which by a peace in naughtiness and wickedness, being as it were buried under the ground, doth not appear.[5]

And Cartwright loved to quote fellow Presbyterian Walter Travers: "election[s] made by the people, where everyman gives his voice, are compared by some to a banquet, where everyman brings his dish, which is so much daintier the more there be that come unto it."

The unrelenting emphasis on participatory Christianity by this leader of the Presbyterians included a predictable modification of the "general voice of the people." Like Calvin, Cartwright stressed the special authority of the elders (or presbyters) in the interest of checking and balancing any possible fickleness on the part of the people. Still, there remained the unmistakable marks of a consensual, representative polity, conceived as shaping and running its own affairs independently of civil authority. Such a conception was deeply challenging to Anglican authority.

Finally, although Cartwright and his fellow Presbyterians resolutely excluded any consideration of religious toleration or freedom of conscience as later generations came to understand those ideas, Presbyterians nevertheless furnished some of the premises from which such ideas would eventually follow: "For that which may be conveniently won with a word should not be gotten by the sword; and that which may be gotten to be done with conscience should not be essayed by compulsion."

In fact, it was these very ideas out of which Robert Browne, father of separatist Congregationalism, deduced a more radical lesson. Browne studied under Cartwright at Cambridge and then proceeded to revise Cartwright's thought so as to draw out the radical potentialities contained within it. For one thing, Browne reiterated a consensual or covenantal theory of the church.[6] Next he explored the radical consequences of Cartwright's emphasis on the separation of spirit and sword.

> Yet may [the magistrates] do nothing concerning the Church, but only civilly, and as civil magistrates; that is, they have not that authority over the church, as to be prophets or priests, or spiritual kings, as they are magistrates over the same, but only to rule the commonwealth in all outward justice, to maintain the right welfare and honor thereof with outward power, bodily punishment, and civil forcing of men. . . . But to compel religion, to plant churches by power, and to force submission to ecclesiastical government by law and penalties, belongeth not to them.[7]

This concept of separation provides a crucial basis for the doctrine of religious toleration and freedom that was to come to fruition later in the seventeenth century.

The antagonism between the Presbyterians and the separatist Congregationalists produced by these conflicting applications of Calvin's thought essentially set the terms of debate among Reformed Christians, or Puritans, that dominated affairs during the Puritan Revolution and the Interregnum (1640-1660).

Into the 1640s, the Presbyterians pursued the uniformist side of the Calvinist tradition reinforced by such Scottish Presbyterians as Samuel Rutherford. In the Westminster Assembly (1634-44), which was called by the Parliament to try to resolve the divisions concerning the religious character of England, they proposed a Presbyterian form of church life in place of the existing Anglican system. In the Westminster Confession of 1647, they left no doubt that the proposed arrangement would be backed by civil enforcement, thereby preventing religious pluralism and toleration.

> The civil magistrate may not assume to himself the administration of the Word and Sacraments, or the power of the keys of the Kingdom of Heaven: yet, he has authority, and it is his duty, to take order, that unity and peace be preserved in the church, that the truth of God be kept pure and entire, that all blasphemies and heresies be suppressed, all corruptions and abuses in worship and discipline prevented, or reformed, and all the ordinances of God duly settled, administered, and observed.[8]

But the Presbyterians did not have their way. There would be no replica of the Scottish Reformation in England. Ironically, that was in part because the very ideas the Presbyterians espoused and the practices they engaged in to promote their cause were eventually turned against them and used to produce their defeat. As William Haller eloquently puts it,

> by the end of 1644 the divines of the [Westminster] assembly had failed to silence opposition in the press as completely as they had failed to secure agreement among the members of their own order. . . . The [Presbyterian] preachers had done their pulpit work well, but with practical results that few of them had looked for and many of them deplored. They had sown the word without foreseeing the harvest they had now to reap. They had preached the doctrines of calling and covenant,

evinced by faith, manifested in action, to be crowned by success here or hereafter, and they had thus planted in many minds dreams of new heaven and new earth. But it is one thing to launch people on a quest for the New Jerusalem, quite another to stop them when they have gone far enough. . . . Hence all attempts in 1644 to impose a presbyterian frame upon revolutionary Puritanism served simply to evoke the many-headed hydra of English dissent.[9]

The way was thereby opened for the emergence of the more liberal side of the Reformed tradition, enunciated in the sixteenth century by Robert Browne. With the failure of the Presbyterian alternative, the "independent" and left-wing Puritans began experimenting with quite radical doctrines of liberty of religion and conscience. These were all very much cast in the terms of a voluntary, consensual, covenantal fellowship sharply separated from the engines of civil coercion and intended as a master model for organizing political and other societies. The effects of such thinking on the development of elaborate doctrines of religious liberty, separation of church and state, and freedom of conscience by such figures as John Locke in the late seventeenth century are now clearly established.[10]

IV. THE AMERICAN TRADITION

A. *The Seventeenth Century*

The impact of Reformed Christianity — including the eventual Presbyterian role — on the American struggle for religious liberty can be understood only against the background of the seventeenth-century New England experience. In general, what happened there was simply an extension and replication of the religious conflicts in England that were to an important extent generated by the inner tensions of Calvinism. Although the Presbyterians as such were effectively absent until the eighteenth century from the unfolding drama in America, the uniformist and establishmentarian side of Calvinism was vigorously represented in Massachusetts Bay by the nonseparatist Congregationalists, led by John Cotton.

The opposition, still mostly within the Calvinist fold, was rallied by Roger Williams. Williams laid out in definitive terms the grounds for and the shape of the understanding of religious liberty, freedom of conscience, and the separation of church and state that became foundational for the American tradition.

Cotton leaned toward Calvin's Genevan model as a guide for determining the right relations between church and state. Like Calvin, he meant to distinguish clearly the inward or spiritual from the outward or temporal sphere. For one thing, that entailed stringent limitations on civil as well as ecclesiastical power, as Cotton says in his justly famous summary of the Calvinist attitude toward all institutional power:

> It is necessary, therefore, that all power . . . on earth be limited. Church power or other. . . . It is counted a matter of danger to the State to limit prerogatives; but it is a further danger, not to have them limited. . . . It is therefore for everyman to be studious of the bounds which the Lord has set: and for the people, in whom fundamentally all power lies, to give as much power as God in his word gives to men: And it is meet that magistrates in the commonwealth, and so officers in the Churches should desire to know the utmost bounds of their own power.[11]

Cotton firmly advocated "the simplicity of the Church," which betokens the pure freedom of the inner things of the spirit from external control. He favored freedom of conscience and independent judgment as the logical consequence of Christian liberty. In no way should the civil sword be allowed to persecute conscience. Moreover, he, with Calvin, stressed

the importance, within due limits, of consensual participation by all members — "in whom fundamentally all power lies" — in the conduct of the church's affairs. Such participation, prompted by the Spirit and not by the civil authorities, is itself a manifestation of the crucial separation of church and state.

Nevertheless, Cotton balanced this emphasis with an announced preference for direct civil protection of Reformed religion. He held, again as did Calvin, that the two tables of the Decalogue ought not to be too sharply divorced, for there is a profound connection between true piety and civil virtue. "The establishment of pure religion, in doctrine, worship, and government, according to the word of God, as also the reformation of all corruptions of any of these," directly concerns civil peace and welfare. As with Knox and other right-wing Calvinists, he viewed blasphemy, idolatry, and "professed unbelief" as the first step toward the breakdown of civil order and consequently held that the magistrates are bound by their oath of office to suppress and punish "all corruptions" of "pure religion." Indeed, Cotton held that such corrupting actions were tantamount to "soul-murder," something virtually equivalent to physical murder, and thus liable to the same punishment.

Cotton went so far as to argue that if the state punishes a person for heretical belief, it is not thereby violating freedom of conscience but is, in fact, enforcing it.

> The fundamentals [of true religion] are so clear, that a man cannot but be convinced of the truth of them after two or three admonitions; and that, therefore, such a person as still continues obstinate is condemned of himself. And if he then be punished, he is not punished for his conscience, but for sinning against his own conscience.[12]

Because, on this account, the individual who rejects "the fundamentals" of pure religion is actually acting against conscience rather than "in conscience," that individual must be classified as thoroughly depraved.

> Never look for true dealing from an heretic that lies against the Gospel, and against his own conscience; never believe any doctrine of theirs, for they aim at subverting. If they deal not truly with God, they will not deal truly with man.[13]

The consequence of all this was the imposition of religious qualifications for citizenship and for other civil opportunities on the populace of Massachusetts Bay. The magistrates laid it down in no uncertain terms that "no man shall be admitted to the freedom of this body politic, but such as are members of some of the churches within the limits of the same."

Roger Williams, whose lengthy disputes with Cotton exhibit well the conflicting tendencies of Calvinism, perpetuated and extended the radical "free church" side of the tradition, as exemplified by Robert Browne and later by segments of the left wing of the Puritan Revolution. Although Williams's Reformed credentials have at times been doubted, it is no accident that he was chosen to occupy the place of the American representative upon the monument to Reformed Christianity in Geneva. He was, to be sure, a deviant Calvinist and frequently gave Calvin's doctrines a novel twist. After he was ejected from Massachusetts, he affiliated for a time with the Baptists and then identified himself in quite unconventional ways. Still, the central doctrines of Calvin's theology did constitute his point of reference.

For example, Williams imaginatively turned Calvin's doctrine of predestination against the establishment-minded view of Cotton and his associates. If God were indeed the sole author of election, then there is no need for civil coercion in matters of belief. Coercion is nothing, said Williams, but a distraction from authentic piety.

In fact, the idea of allowing as much room as possible for free, voluntary faith and worship to express itself was the overriding theme of Williams's theology. If there was a danger that the failure to provide civil restraints upon religious belief might lead some astray, there was an even greater danger, to Williams's mind, that the enforcement of orthodoxy might cause pretense, hypocrisy, and deception in matters of belief and worship to prevail.

In arguing his case, Williams simply took up and redeployed some of Calvin's favorite tenets. First, he took what he believed were the consequences of Calvin's contention that the "inner forum" of conscience is both distinguishable from and prior to the external authority of the civil order. To try to convince a person of the truth of something by threatening injury or by imprisoning that person is to make a mistake about how the mind and spirit actually work.

> To batter down idolatry, false worship, heresy, schism, blindness . . . out of the soul and spirit, it is sin, improper, and unsuitable to bring those weapons which are used by persecutors — stocks, whips, prisons, swords. . . . I observe that as civil weapons are improper in this business, and never able to effect aught in the soul, so also . . . they are unnecessary.[14]

To the argument that civil force avails nothing "in the soul," Williams conjoined a second of Calvin's fundamental convictions, that in matters relating to civil order and righteousness, matters touching the second table of the Decalogue, human beings have "somewhat more" natural understanding (or understanding independent of expressly religious instruction). They therefore, it would seem, could be trusted to conduct their civil affairs in relative independence of authorized religious guidance.

> There is a moral virtue, a moral fidelity, ability, and honesty, which other men (beside Church-members) are, by good nature and education, by good laws and good examples nourished and trained up in, that civil places need not

be monopolized into the hands of Church-members (who sometimes are not fitted for them), and all others deprived of their natural and civil rights and liberties.[15]

Without question, Williams radicalized Calvin's teaching at this point. Calvin, Knox, Cartwright, and Cotton had all, in one way or another, given their support to the idea of a "natural" basis among human beings for civil life and moral virtue. At the same time, they modified, if not eclipsed, that idea by pro-pounding in a louder voice the inseparability of public orthodoxy and civil rectitude. Wil-liams directly assailed the claim that attesta-tions of orthodoxy guaranteed social righ-teousness. Against the beliefs of the established church in Massachusetts Bay, he asserted that to confound "the nature of civil and moral goodness with religious [goodness] is as far from goodness as darkness is from light." Moral and civil virtue do not depend upon a prescribed and shared set of religiously based beliefs and values.

Williams underscored this radical convic-tion by unfavorably contrasting the practices of orthodox Christians in England and America with "the Indians wild," whom he had come to know and appreciate in a thoroughly uncon-ventional way. Their record in respect to "moral virtue" was, he claimed, frequently bet-ter than that of the pious colonists.

> If nature's sons both wild and tame
> Humane and courteous be,
> How ill becomes the sons of God
> To want humanity?[16]

It would, incidentally, be a mistake to con-clude from this that Williams held that religion has nothing to do with morality and the civil order. That was not Williams's view at all, nor was it the implication of his view. He simply believed that the connections had to be worked out by each individual, in groups or alone, on the basis of conscientious consideration. Wil-

liams believed that the religiously pluralistic society he founded in Rhode Island in the 1630s was the proper expression in civil insti-tutional terms of the central Christian convic-tion that the only authentic religion is voluntary religion. It so happened that in this regard Christian insight corresponded with the con-clusions of natural reason.

Williams believed that conscience could successfully exercise its sovereign rights only in a society that acknowledged its limitations in regard to religious affairs, that appreciated how unsusceptible to civil control were the affairs of the heart and spirit. Too much sug-gestion of an easy compatibility between re-ligion and the civil order would impede the vitality of religious exploration implied in Wil-liams's vision. It is these views, and others like them — mostly mined from a Calvinist quarry — that provided the basis for both the theory and practice of religious liberty that Williams worked out in Rhode Island against great odds.

B. The Eighteenth Century

Through the seventeenth century in the Amer-ican colonies, Calvinism was represented principally by the New England Congregation-alists and the Baptists in Rhode Island and elsewhere. Because of their small numbers, the Presbyterians did not feature largely in the early American disputes over church-state re-lations.

But at the turn of the century, Presbyteri-ans began to emerge as a prominent Reformed denomination, and that in the midst of a con-troversy over religious liberty. In 1707, Francis Makemie, the "founding father" of Presbyteri-anism, was charged by the pro-Anglican gover-nor of New York with being a "Disturber of Government" for preaching dissenting doc-trines without a license. Makemie was acquitted by the courts, and, according to one contemporary observer, the governor's heavy-handed action "so soured a great many that subscriptions are [growing] to build a Dissenting Meeting House . . . and . . . support will be provided for one of their Ministers."[17]

As the Presbyterians quickly grew to become a leading influence in the middle colonies as well as a burgeoning force in Virginia, they were drawn progressively into the problems of religious liberty. Throughout the eighteenth century, they exhibited something of the ambivalence toward church-state relations that had been characteristic of Calvinism from its beginnings.

The ambivalence appeared dramatically in the struggle among Presbyterians in Virginia over disestablishing religion at the time of the adoption by the Virginia legislature in 1786 of Jefferson's *Statute for Religious Freedom*. Virginia Presbyterians, out of their rude experience as dissenters under an Anglican establishment, had shown initial enthusiasm for Jefferson's proposal to remove all state support for religion.

However, an influential part of the denomination grew reluctant as the time of reckoning approached. Leaders such as Stephen Stanhope Smith (president of Hampden-Sydney Academy and later of Princeton) displayed one side of the Calvinist tradition by resisting any radical separation of church and state. Smith's unrelenting defense of the proposition that the state needs and must provide for some kind of public religion, even while tolerating a diversity of different churches, helped to delay the kind of unified and fervent support for Jefferson's statute that came, as might have been predicted, from the Separate Baptists.

In a characteristic sermon, "Religion Necessary to National Prosperity," Smith gave voice to a theme that the Calvinist tradition would find very hard to live down and a theme that still abides in and out of Calvinist circles.

> Where have we seen a people, under the full influence of religious and moral principle, in the full vigor of frugal and virtuous habits, which has fallen prey to internal disorders, or to foreign domination?
>
> The belief of the principles of religion, and the practice of its duties, under some form which calculated profoundly to impress the public mind with the sentiment of God, and the righteous government of his Providence over human affairs, is essential to the prosperity of nations.
>
> When a nation has abandoned religion, the firmest basis of civil government is dissolved. Voluptuousness and effeminacy, avarice and prodigality, a restless ambition, dark treacheries, and a universal disregard of justice, which are the natural consequences of a general impiety, accumulate every species of misery on a wretched people, forsaken of God, and lost to virtue.[18]

By 1785, however, Virginia Presbyterians gravitated away from Smith's position. For a variety of theological and other reasons, the denomination came to join forces with the Baptists and helped to provide the backing requisite for the final adoption of the statute. A "Memorial" on the subject by the Presbytery of Hanover expressed eloquently what came to be the majority opinion:

> In the enlightened age, and in a land where all, of every denomination are united in the most strenuous efforts to be free, we hope and expect that our representatives will cheerfully concur in removing every species of religious, as well as civil bondage. . . . There is no argument in favor of establishing the Christian religion, but what may be pleaded, with equal propriety, for establishing the tenets of Mahomed by those who believe in the Alcoran. . . . Therefore we ask no ecclesiastical establishments for ourselves; neither can we approve of them when granted to others.[19]

In petitions such as this, Presbyterians were swinging toward the "free-church" side of the Calvinist tradition, toward Williams's liberal interpretation of freedom of conscience and the separation of church and state.

In fact, it is of the greatest significance that Jefferson's *Statute for Religious Freedom,* together with James Madison's *Memorial and Remonstrance against Religious Assessments* (which indirectly supported the statute), drew upon the standard free-church arguments for religious liberty. There is the same concern to draw firm lines between the "internal forum" and the "external forum" and to protect the former from the latter by guaranteeing every individual's natural civil and political rights. There is the same conviction that the law of mind and heart is not the same as the law of prison and sword. There is the same contention that neither true religion nor a just civil order can exist unless each properly respects the independence of the other.

While the personal religious beliefs of Jefferson and Madison were very different from the beliefs of the Presbyterians and Baptists, the strong compatibility of argument among all the principal supporters of the statute should be remembered.

Simultaneously, the Presbyterian synods of New York and Philadelphia appointed a committee to reconsider church organization, including the question of church-state relations. With the help of strong advocates of religious freedom such as John Witherspoon, president of Princeton, the committee proposed revisions in the church order and even more radical alterations of the doctrines of religious uniformity and establishment contained in the Westminster Confession.

After 1789, when these proposals were adopted, the teaching of the church no longer ascribed to the civil magistrate the right to initiate action against heresy or to convene a church synod. Indeed, the church now declared that the magistrate had no authority "in the least, [to] interfere in matters of faith." Its only responsibility, so far as religious faith and practice went, was to protect all religious assemblies from "molestation."

As "God alone is Lord of the conscience," in the words of the preface to the New Form of Government, the church considers "the rights of private judgment in all matters that regard religion as universal and unalienable." No church ought to be "aided by the civil power, further than may be necessary for protection and security, and at the same time may be equal and common to all others."[20]

However, even in face of this unmistakable stride in the direction of free-church Calvinism, the concern for religious uniformity and for civil encouragement of religion that was so much a part of Genevan Calvinism, and of Scottish and English Presbyterianism, did not completely die. For example, with all his devotion to religious liberty and pluralism, John Witherspoon held out for some form of "multiple establishment" to ensure that church bodies not only might be protected against outside interference but also equally and positively assisted by the government in financial and other ways.

Moreover, Witherspoon no doubt reflected widespread Presbyterian sentiment in favor of public support for a form of "common" or "civil" Christianity, whereby civic virtue and some minimal kind of shared religious respect and devotion would be publicly propagated and enforced among all citizens. In short, even though a fundamental redefinition in Presbyterian doctrine concerning civil authority had occurred by the end of the eighteenth century, the key tensions over church-state questions that lay so deep in the Calvinist experience were by no means thoroughly relaxed.

C. The Nineteenth and Twentieth Centuries

Nor were they relaxed in the next two centuries. On one extreme, the Reformed Presbyterians, in the early nineteenth century, thoroughly rejected Jefferson's and Madison's ideas of church-state separation. "There are moral evils essential to the constitution of the United

States," they declared, "which render it necessary to refuse allegiance to the whole system." Reformed Presbyterians particularly objected to the failure of the Constitution to acknowledge the Christian God, and they condemned the requirement, according to Article VI, to admit "pagans" to public office. Members of the church were therefore enjoined from voting, serving on juries, or holding public office lest they suggest approval of the United States Constitution. At the other extreme, the southern Presbyterians, in response to the crisis over slavery, developed a doctrine of the "spirituality of the church" that was simply a radical interpretation of the deep separationist impulse that constituted one side of Calvinism. An influential exponent, the Rev. James H. Thornwell of Columbia Theological Seminary in South Carolina, defended theological indifference to the slavery question on the grounds that the Presbyterian church "is exclusively a spiritual organization and possesses only a spiritual power. Her business was the salvation of men; and she had no mission to care for the things or to become entangled with the kingdoms and policy, of this world."[21] Thereafter, the southern Presbyterian bodies were reluctant, until well into the twentieth century, to issue pronouncements on questions of "worldly" public policy.

The majority of Presbyterians tried, during the nineteenth and the first half of the twentieth centuries, to work out some sort of compromise between the two extremes. Nevertheless, without abjuring the principles of separation laid down in 1789, the balance of sentiment unquestionably tipped toward affirming and, if possible, enforcing by civil means explicitly religious directives.

For example, David Rice, a pioneer minister from Kentucky, was typical of those Presbyterians who believed that the institution of slavery ought to be eliminated as a direct application of God's will. "Human legislatures should remember that they act in subordination to the great Ruler of the universe, [and that

they] have no right to take government out of his hand, nor to enact laws contrary to his."[22]

In the same spirit, New School Presbyterianism — that vigorous and influential response to the evangelicalism of the "Second Great Awakening" in the early decades of the nineteenth century — singled out slavery and the southern defense of the institution during the Civil War as an everlasting affront to the millennial kingdom God was in the process of creating in America. The southern cause, stated George L. Prentiss, a prominent New School minister from New York, was "an anathema such as the Christian church has put upon an open denial of God. It is like atheism and subverts the first principles of our *political worship* as a free order-loving and covenant-keeping people."[23]

For Prentiss, the war was

a true Apocalyptic contest, full of mysterious seals and vials of tribulation; but it is in the hands of Him who in righteousness doth judge and make war. Let us not doubt that in due time he will bring forth judgment unto victory. "Then," to conclude in the glowing words of Milton, ". . . Thou, the eternal and shortly-expected King, shalt open the clouds to judge the several kingdoms of the world, and distributing national honors and regards to religious and just commonwealths, shalt put an end to all earthly tyrannies, proclaiming thy universal and mild monarchy through heaven and earth."[24]

In New School Presbyterianism, the doctrine of the divine mission of America wedded evangelical and millennial fervor to the civil theology that Calvin and many of his followers had constructed out of an Old Testament vision of God's ultimate reign.

Toward the end of the nineteenth century, Presbyterians manifested similar self-assurance regarding the compatibility of God's law, as they understood it, and proper civil order in the controversy over the Mormon practice of polygamy. Expressing the dominant religious spirit of the age, the General Assembly of 1881 found the Mormon teaching on polygamy "all the more detestable because it hides its crime under the garb of religion." In a move reflected in several of the Supreme Court decisions against the Mormons, the intricate question of religious liberty and free exercise was avoided simply by stipulating that any teaching that is "condemned alike by the Church, [and] the State" could not count as bona fide religious teaching in the first place, and therefore was not even eligible for consideration under the First Amendment. There is the strong flavor here of an informal, but no less pervasive, "Protestant Establishment" fully encouraged and supported by a large proportion of Presbyterians.

That *establishment* was also manifested in the successful agitation by Presbyterians (and other Protestants) on behalf of Prohibition and Sabbath observance throughout the nineteenth and early twentieth centuries. There was, from time to time, expression of concern lest the church become too directly entwined with civil affairs by means of direct participation in the political process. Still, on matters as overriding as temperance and Sabbath observance, most Presbyterians showed little reluctance either to urge or to work directly for the passage of legislation to enforce what they regarded as God's indisputable law.

In the light of the increasing religious pluralism in America that followed a period of extensive immigration, the 1909 General Assembly became exercised over the question of whether the United States was losing its identity as a *Christian nation*. In the words of a report to the Assembly, "our continent was not settled by bands of atheists or infidels having no religion, nor by Jews or Mohammedans refusing the name of Christ, but by colonies of Christian people acknowledging Jesus Christ as Lord."[25] Adopting the spirit of the report, the General Assembly went on to call for renewed public support for that tradition.

Something of the same commitment to "Christianizing" the civil order was exhibited up through the first half of the twentieth century in the Social Gospel movement and in the expressions of support for the American effort in the two world wars. Although Presbyterians registered some initial qualms about American participation in the First World War, by 1918 the General Assembly was able to discern the unmistakable religious purpose of the war. It communicated its strong support for the policies of President Wilson:

> In this crucial hour of Christian civilization, the General Assembly of the Presbyterian Church in the United States commends you to the God of all grace; we are confidently relying upon you, as the spokesman for the moral forces of the world, to carry on your gigantic task to righteous consummation.
>
> We believe that, with your superb courage and sublime faith, you will be used as the means of saving to us and to humanity the Christian principles which are the priceless heritage from our fathers.[26]

Until 1963 Presbyterians did not seriously or systematically call into question the tilt toward religious establishment of one kind or another that, with some modification, prevailed in the church throughout the nineteenth and early twentieth centuries. In that year, the General Assembly's pronouncement "Relations between Church and State in the United States of America" represented a strong reaffirmation of the principles of separation that had existed, if ambiguously, in the Calvinist tradition from the beginning.

> Presbyterians said this back in 1789; we say it again today. *American Presbyterians believe in religious liberty.* They do not believe that the state should exercise control over the church. "They do not even wish to see any religious constitution aided by the civil power." Presbyterians fought beside members of other denominations, as well as those who did not make any

religious profession, in the great debates in Virginia, under the leadership of Thomas Jefferson and James Madison. Their overwhelming concern was for a constitution that would forever separate civil authority from the administration of religious institutions.[27]

They believed that a state church was a peril to civil liberty; they also feared that it was dangerous to the purity of religion. "While American Presbyterians share John Calvin's passion for relating faith to life, we have no desire to emulate the pattern of Calvin's Geneva, where civil authority was largely controlled by the churches."[28]

The pronouncement called strongly for the church to witness to and, when necessary, to call into question the state's policies.

> *American Presbyterians believe that God is sovereign over all nations.* It is our conviction that God created the world and established civil authority among men. We firmly believe that the people of the nations forget God at their peril. We are convinced that the faith, the prayers, and the works of the church are necessary for the well-being of our country.[29]

Still, the pronouncement categorically rejects any attempts to give direct civil support and encouragement to religious beliefs.

> The government of our country must be neutral on matters of faith, dogma and indoctrination. This policy of neutrality applies to the claims of the secularist point of view as well as of churches and other religious groupings. Because of this we adhere to the principle of separation of church and state.[30]

V. THE CONTEMPORARY SITUATION

To an important extent, the present-day debates over the relation of religion to the civil order reveal the same tensions that have existed in the Reformed tradition from the beginning.

On the one hand, there is widespread concern, expressed by President Ronald Reagan, Secretary of Education William J. Bennett, and by numerous religious leaders in the land, that America is a religious nation that is losing its bearings through a process of radical secularization. In order to endure, in order to preserve its identity, the nation must return to its Judeo-Christian heritage, must unashamedly espouse and inculcate the fundamental beliefs and values associated with that heritage by means of direct governmental encouragement.

Here are the strong echoes of the one side of Calvinism, the side that favors governmentally supported and encouraged religious belief and practice in the interest of civil harmony and prosperity. This side of the tradition has, as we have seen, expressed itself in a number of ways throughout the years. For Calvin and Knox, for the English Presbyterians and the Massachusetts Bay Congregationalists of the seventeenth century, the strong Calvinist impulse toward ensuring a religious foundation for civil order exhibited itself in the most thoroughgoing form of civilly enforced uniformity.

In the eighteenth, nineteenth, and early twentieth centuries, American Presbyterianism modified and restrained the Genevan model that had so influenced Reformed Christianity. Room was made for religious diversity and liberty. Still, vestiges of that model continued powerfully to motivate Presbyterians in the form of Samuel Stanhope Smith's civilly sustained "principles of religion," or of John Witherspoon's "common" or "civil" Christianity, or of George L. Prentiss's doctrine of the divine mission of America, or of the 1909 General Assembly's image of America as a Christian nation. There can be no question that the American "Protestant Establishment" in the nineteenth and early twentieth centuries was heavily influenced by these and other versions of "civil theology" that are so deeply embedded in Reformed Christianity.

The unflinching and self-confident spirit in which many political and religious leaders currently invoke a common divine center for American political life is in many ways fully consonant with the one side of the Calvinist tradition.

At the same time, the contemporary concern for a new vigilance on behalf of religious liberty and free exercise of religion, fervently expressed in many quarters, and frequently by the same people who advocate a common civil religion, calls to mind the other side of the tradition. Calvin's own unmistakable claims concerning the unalterable difference between the *spiritual* and *temporal* jurisdictions — "the former resides in the inner mind, while the latter regulates only outward behavior" — and the analogous distinction between the "forum of the conscience" and the "earthly forum" laid the groundwork for the radical doctrines of freedom of religion and conscience represented by such "deviant" Calvinists as Robert Browne in the sixteenth century and Roger Williams in the seventeenth. Moreover, it was this side of the tradition that inspired the striking degree of compatibility that was eventually achieved between Virginia Presbyterians and Thomas Jefferson in respect to the *Statute for Religious Freedom* and inspired as well the drastic reformulation of Presbyterian church-state thinking in 1789.

If our historical analysis is correct, then whatever the full explanation of the contemporary controversies over church-state relations may be, Reformed Christians are no strangers to those controversies. As we have seen, their tradition is itself a dramatization of some deep tensions that are very much still with us in both the church and society.

NOTES

1. See George Sabine, *History of Political Theory* (New York: Holt, 1953), pp. 161-62.

2. John Calvin, *Institutes of the Christian Religion*, Library of Christian Classics, vols. 21-22, ed. John T. McNeill, trans. Ford Lewis Battles (Philadelphia: Westminster Press, 1960), 4.11.3. Subsequent references to this work will be made parenthetically in the text.

3. Knox, *Appellation* (Geneva, 1558).

4. C. A. du Mornay, *Du Mornay: A Huguenot Family in the Sixteenth Century*, trans. Lucy Crump (London: G. Rutledge, 1926), p. 172.

5. John Whitgrift and Thomas Cartwright, *Works of Whitgift*, 3 vols. (London, 1851-53), 2: 238.

6. See W. K. Jordon, *Development of Religious Toleration in England*, 4 vols. (London: George Allen & Unwin, 1932), 1: 263-75.

7. Browne, *Reformation without Tarrying for Any*, cited in *Creeds and Platforms of Congregationalism*, ed. W. Walker (Boston: Pilgrim Press, 1960), pp. 12-13.

8. "Westminster Confession," in *Constitution of the Presbyterian Church U.S.A.* (Philadelphia: Westminster Press, 1955), pp. 6-7.

9. Haller, *Liberty and Reformation in the Puritan Revolution* (New York: Columbia University Press, 1955), pp. 141-42.

10. See Roland Bainton, *Travail of Religious Liberty* (Philadelphia: Westminster Press, 1951), chap. 9.

11. Cotton, *An Exposition upon the Thirteenth Chapter of Revelations*, cited in *The Puritans*, 2 vols., ed. Perry Miller (Boston: Beacon Press, 1963), 2: 72.

12. Cotton, cited in *Roger Williams, John Cotton and Religious Freedom*, ed. Irwin H. Polishook (Englewood Cliffs, N.J.: Prentice-Hall, 1967), p. 72.

13. Cotton, cited in *Roger Williams, John Cotton and Religious Freedom*, p. 77.

14. Williams, cited in *Roger Willliams*, ed. Perry Miller (New York: Atheneum, 1962), pp. 131-32.

15. *Complete Writings of Roger Williams*, 7 vols. (New York: Russell & Russell, 1963), 4: 365.

16. *Complete Writings of Roger Williams*, 1: 39.

17. Carl Bridenbaugh, *Mitre and Sceptre* (New York: Oxford University Press, 1962), p. 123.

18. Smith, "Religion Necessary to National Prosperity," cited by Fred J. Hood in "Presbyterianism and the New American Nation, 1783-1826: A Case Study in Religion and National Life" (Ph.D. diss., Princeton University, 1968).

19. "The Presbyterian Church and Our National Foundations," *Sequicentennial Paper No. 1*, ed. Guy S. Klett (N.p.: Publicity Dept. of the General Assembly, n.d.), pp. 14-15; cited by Graydon E. McClellan in "Presbyterian Concepts of Church and State in Historical Perspective," unpublished paper, p. 40.

20. "Preliminary Principles" for "Form of Government," in *Constitution of the Presbyterian Church U.S.A.*, p. 239.

21. Thornwell, cited by Louis Weeks in "Faith and Political Action in American Presbyterianism," in *Reformed Faith and Politics*, ed. Ronald H. Stone (Washington: University Press of America, 1983), p. 107.

22. Rice, cited by Weeks in "Faith and Political Action in American Presbyterianism," p. 105.

23. Prentiss, cited by George M. Marsden in *The Evangelical Mind and the New School Presbyterian Experience* (New Haven: Yale University Press, 1970), p. 207.

24. Prentiss, cited by Marsden in *The Evangelical Mind and the New School Presbyterian Experience*, p. 207.

25. Cited by Weeks in "Faith and Political Action in American Presbyterianism," p. 112.

26. Cited by Weeks in "Faith and Political Action in American Presbyterianism," p. 115.

27. *Relations between Church and State in the United States of America*, Pronouncement by the 175th General Assembly (1963) of the United Presbyterian Church (Philadelphia: Office of the General Assembly, 1963), 3-4.

28. *Relations between Church and State in the United States of America*, p. 4.

29. *Relations between Church and State in the United States of America*, p. 5.

30. *Relations between Church and State in the United States of America*, p. 5.

SACRAMENTAL STUDIES

John Calvin said that the church exists "wherever we see the Word of God purely preached and heard, and the sacraments administered according to Christ's institution." Reformed theology has always given careful attention to the theology of the sacraments — baptism and the Lord's Supper. Sacramental theology is part of what distinguishes the Reformed tradition from other Reformation traditions, especially Lutheranism. Yet within the Reformed tradition itself there have been varying and conflicting understandings of the nature and purpose of the two sacraments. The essays in this section provide discussions of Reformed teachings on baptism and the Lord's Supper.

In "The Sacraments as Signs and Seals," G. C. Berkouwer delves into two key descriptors of sacraments in the Reformed tradition. He explores the meanings of both these concepts as they apply to Reformed understandings of sacraments and focuses especially on how the terms function in relation to Christian baptism.

A biblical-theological study is presented in Geoffrey W. Bromiley's "The Meaning and Scope of Baptism." Bromiley lays out in simple fashion the scriptural warrant and biblical theology of baptism and its relationship to the rest of the Christian life, including "conversion," or the "new birth," and our identification with the death and resurrection of Jesus Christ. He states that "baptism tells us what has been done, what is being done, and what will be done for us, to us, and in us."

Historically and theologically, the Lord's Supper has also provided an arena of disagreement not only within Protestantism generally but within the Reformed faith specifically. A measure of the differing views here is indicated by Brian Gerrish in "The Lord's Supper in the Reformed Confessions." Gerrish identifies three different types of eucharistic theology in the body of Reformed confessional writings. This discovery calls for more careful study of the eucharistic theologies of those who

215

wrote these confessions and raises the contemporary question of what views about the Lord's Supper are held by Reformed Christians today.

In "A Theology of the Lord's Supper from the Perspective of the Reformed Tradition," Robert Shelton complements these historical studies with a discussion of the real or true presence of Jesus Christ in the Supper, the affinity between the symbols and the reality, the nourishing and sustaining of the Christian life, and the corporate nature of the sacrament. All these issues are central to what the church is in fact doing when it celebrates the Lord's Supper.

Sacramental issues have been the focal point of much debate and divisiveness within the holy catholic church through the centuries. These studies from within the Reformed tradition provide not only an acquaintance with the particular emphases of this theological stream but also point beyond these particular communions to the communion of the saints in the church universal and the sacramental realities that unite all Christians in the bonds of love and faith.

The Sacraments as Signs and Seals

G. C. Berkouwer

Reformed theology speaks of the sacraments as signs and seals. This designation can be understood only against the background of the distinction between Word and sacrament. The sacraments are signs and seals, with the Word, of the promise of God; as the Heidelberg Catechism formulates it, "the sacraments are ... appointed of God ... that He may the more fully declare and seal to us the promise of the gospel" (Q. 66). It is striking in how many different ways the Reformed sacramental doctrine speaks of the significance and intent of the sacraments. We read, for example, that they have been designed to direct our faith to Christ's sacrifice and that the Holy Spirit assures us by the sacraments that the whole of our salvation stands in that sacrifice (Q. 67). In Article 33 of the Belgic Confession we hear of the sealing of God's promises and of the sacraments as pledges of God's benevolence and grace toward us and as "visible signs and

seals," while Article 34 says that the sacrament of baptism serves us as a testimony that God will be our God forever, and that God wants to make something clear to us with it — namely, that which the sacrament indicates.

In all these definitions, the element of comfort and certainty comes clearly to the fore, as it does also in the form for baptism. The dipping in or sprinkling with water teaches us something. The impurity of our souls is signified so that we may be admonished. We also hear of witnessing and sealing. It is said that the Father witnesses and seals, that the Son seals, and that the Holy Spirit assures us, while the word addressed to the parents mentions God's ordinance in baptism to seal for us and our children God's covenant. In the prayer, the sealing and confirmation are mentioned as cause for gratefulness in connection with God's acceptance of us as God's children.

It is clear that in all these modes of expression no sharp and consciously scientific distinctions are intended that as such could be handled in dogmatic reflection. Their focus, however, is uniformly the certainty of believers, toward which baptism is directed. They

Reprinted from *The Sacraments*, trans. Hugo Bekker (Grand Rapids: William B. Eerdmans, 1969), pp. 134-60.

receive assurance of salvation and rest in the fullness of the Lord's promises. This is already true in Calvin, who points emphatically to the nature of the sacraments when he says that the purpose of the sacrament is one of "confirming and sealing the promise itself, and of making it more evident to us and in a sense ratifying it." It is not so much the strengthening of God's Word as the strengthening of our faith in that Word.[1]

The sacraments are testimonies of the grace of God and "are like seals of the good will that he feels toward us, which by attesting that good will to us, sustain, nourish, confirm, and increase our faith" (*Inst.*, 4.14.7). In that, says Calvin, consists the office of the sacraments. All these motifs occur often throughout the Reformed tradition on the sacraments. They could be summarized in the definition that the sacraments are signs and seals of God's promises in order to strengthen our faith (cf. *Inst.*, 4.14.9).

This does not mean that these signs and seals can in themselves perform the miracle of strengthening our faith. They cannot be detached from the power of God and from the working of the Spirit, who convinces us *in* the sacrament. The administration of the sacraments does not fulfill its function with regard to our salvation unless the Spirit as "teacher" sends his power, the Spirit "by whose power alone our hearts are penetrated and affections moved and our souls opened for the sacraments to enter in" (*Inst.*, 4.14.9). If it were not for this working of the Spirit, says Calvin, the sacraments would have no effect on us. When Calvin says that he wants to make a distinction and "distribution" between the Spirit and the sacrament, he means that the working of the sacrament cannot be explained or demonstrated by "natural" evidence, for only the operation of the Spirit can fill the sacraments with power (*Inst.*, 4.14.9).

The various Reformed definitions of the sacraments show that their doctrine cannot be described adequately as "symbolic," even though many have done so. In the Reformed view, the sacraments are not simply illustrations and depictions but signs *and seals* of God's promise. The Heidelberg Catechism shows that clearly when it says that God wants "to assure us by this divine pledge and sign that we are spiritually cleansed from our sins as really as we are outwardly washed with water" (Q. 73).

Only if we respect this emphasis can we understand that precisely this designation of the sacraments, as signs and seals, contains a rejection of the symbolic interpretation. It manifests a reaching beyond symbolism and hence is incompatible with the theory of so-called *nuda signa*, as we can clearly discern, for example, in Calvin's struggle against Zwinglian symbolism.[2] Calvin insists here that the *signum* must be connected with the sealing of God's promises.

The words "seal and sign" refer, then, to an act of God: God signifies and seals by God's promise. Nor may the signifying and sealing be separated from each other, for both concern one act of God. It is possible, of course, that individuals in their unbelief may receive the outward sign without desiring or receiving the "truth" of the sacrament, without receiving Christ who is signified by the sacrament, and the Belgic Confession (Art. 35) says that the sacraments are nothing at all without their truth — namely, Christ — but it is clear that this "nothing at all" can never be said of the sacraments as institutions of God, and it is also clear that this phrase points to the uselessness of taking the sacraments without faith. This warning does not reduce the sacraments to *nuda signa*, for whoever does not receive the "truth" of the sacrament has nevertheless been confronted with baptism as sign and seal, and precisely therein lies the basis of the serious sin of misusing the sacraments.

It is probably clear by now that the formula "sign and seal" is of great importance for Reformed sacramental doctrine. Moreover, the addition of "seal" to "sign" is the really significant aspect of this doctrine, for it indicates that the symbol has been taken up into the whole of baptism and that it is undetachably connected with the acts of God. By itself, the sign could be an illustration and nothing more than that; but when the sign has been incorporated into the sealing act of God to strengthen our faith, the sign receives its specific significance, for then it is ordered in sharply defined relations. The sign is an indication in which there is nothing arbitrary because it is founded by the institution of God.

M. H. Bolkestein has suggested that Calvin in his further description of the sacraments went much further than the words *sign* and *seal* admit, and more "than his definition would make us expect."[3] Here Bolkestein confronts us with a very important question — namely, whether the designation "sign and seal" may indeed be called sufficient. Bolkestein's theory is that Calvin's statements involving sign and seal issue largely from his polemics against Rome but that when Calvin turns to argue against Zwingli and the spiritualists, he uses stronger language. There he says that the truth of the sign, that which is signified, cannot be separated from the sacrament. Hence the sacrament is always efficacious.

Now, it is true that such strong statements are common in Calvin and that in many respects they even determine his sacramental doctrine, but that does not mean that Calvin here initiates a second line of thought. Rather, it is precisely herein that Calvin confronts us with the profound meaning of "sign and seal." For the sign and seal cannot exist in themselves, and Calvin sees them in the living and dynamic connection of the acts of God, which involve faith and which grant the gifts of salvation in the true *usus sacramenti*.[4] Hence Calvin's line of opposition against Zwingli is not a second line, nor does it go beyond the limits of the definition of the sacrament; rather, it

belongs undetachably to what he understands by the "sign and seal" of God.

Bolkestein's assertion that the conceptions of sign and seal are very important for Calvin but that they are not sufficient for him is somewhat problematic. For Calvin is not so much concerned with conceptions as with the mystery of the sacraments, and with their reality as it is indicated by the mystery. That, I think, is the reason why Bolkestein is incorrect when he says, "not only with Calvin, but also with those who followed him, we see that the limits of the concepts 'sign' and 'seal' are repeatedly trespassed. It is evident that they are unable to interpret the full context of the sacraments."[5] Such a statement can be maintained only if sign and seal are again detached from the living God. Because Calvin never does that, one can say of him that the sacrament is correctly defined and described by the designation sign and seal, as it is done in Reformed theology and the Reformed confessions. No "plus" is necessary, for it is the act of God toward which faith is directed and to which it adheres in order thus to receive that richness of which Calvin so emphatically speaks.

It is interesting that Bolkestein calls Calvin's two conceptions of the sacrament "symbolic representation" and "effective presentation" respectively. The latter, presumably the "plus" factor, is where Calvin goes beyond the merely "cognitive" aspect of the sacrament, designated by "sign and seal."[6] But that is certainly not the case. For Calvin, the granting of salvation does not come separate from the sign and seal. The hypothesized dualism does not in fact exist. Bolkestein gives the impression that "sign and seal" refer to something merely symbolic, and then he explains that "if the concepts of sign and seal fall under the symbolic representation, the concept of [effective] presentation goes beyond that, and it is precisely this concept that takes us to the heart of the sacrament."[7] I believe that this interpretation devaluates Calvin's use of "sign and seal" to something symbolic in the illustrative sense, and that is impossible for Calvin with respect to "sign," and even more so with respect to "seal." The whole point of "sign and seal" is precisely what Bolkestein calls "presentation," because Calvin does not speak of sign and seal *in abstracto;* he speaks of the signs and seals of faith, which finds rest in them because of what they mean.

It is therefore wrong to say that Calvin trespasses the limits of the concepts sign and seal, and it is also wrong to credit Luther with correcting Calvin by going beyond a merely "cognitive" sacramental doctrine.[8]

Bolkestein rejects the latter view, of course, because he thinks that Calvin holds the "effective presentation" theory. But Calvin does not hold it as a "plus" factor, which goes beyond "sign and seal." Rather, according to Calvin it belongs to the essence of the sacrament that the signs are instrumentally (not abstractly) interpreted in the light of the correlation between faith and sacrament. Calvin has thus arrived at a harmonious concept of the sacraments, although it is not at all a rational systematics in which all elements of the sacrament occupy a logical, evidential place. His mode of speaking — in a harmonious manner — issues from his acknowledging the connection that God himself has laid between sign and that which is signified in the presence of faith.[9]

There is therefore good reason to maintain the designation of the sacraments as signs and seals.[10] That does not mean that a good description of the sacraments guarantees a pure, believing understanding of the sacraments and a good and worthy use of them, but it does make it possible, when teaching the doctrine of the sacraments, to explain what they are. The two words taken together make clear that the sacraments are symbols, but not symbols that stand by themselves.

It can hardly be denied that this designation of the sacraments is linked to the human custom of attaching a seal to a certain docu-ment or that this general custom forms the background for the use of this concept in Scripture. When the sacrament was designated in the church as "seal," it was done to emphasize its trustworthiness. People were confirmed and stimulated by the manner in which Scripture spoke of seal and sealing, and it is hardly surprising that the church started very early to make use of the designation "seal."[11] When we study the concept "seal" and "sealing" in Scripture, we discover that it can be used in a wide and general sense. That general use we find, for instance, in 1 Corinthians 9:2, where Paul writes to the church, "for the seal of mine apostleship are ye in the Lord." The context makes it clear that Paul is speaking of the recognition of his apostleship by the Corinthians. They are the seal in and through their recognition of his apostleship. The word *sphragis* is used in a general sense with a strong accent on the trustworthiness, the authenticity, and the guarantee.[12]

The use of the word *seal* for the sacrament becomes still more meaningful when we remember that Paul connects it specifically with circumcision when he writes that Abraham "received the sign of circumcision, a seal of the righteousness of the faith which he had while he was in uncircumcision" (Rom. 4:11). Here, too, the issue is the sealing, the guarantee regarding the righteousness of faith — which is to say, the righteousness toward which Abraham's faith was directed. In the seal that he received — namely, circumcision — he received "the means of confirmation and of verification."[13] We find a similar use of the word *seal* in John 6:27: "Work not for the food which perisheth, but for the food which abideth unto eternal life, which the Son of man shall give unto you: for him the Father, even God, hath sealed." This is not the sacrament of Christian baptism but a designation of the veracity of Christ's messiahship. In the divine sealing lies the emphatic acknowledgment of Jesus Christ as the Son of God and of his messianic dignity.

According to Grosheide, the form of the verb *to seal* points to a specific act of God; in this connection Grosheide thinks of baptism or of the miracles that Jesus performed as "proof" of his messiahship. It is clear from the New Testament, then, why the Christian church began very early to describe that element of trustworthiness and confirmation with the word *seal.*[14]

That becomes still more evident when we note the manner in which Scripture speaks of "sealing." We think of 2 Corinthians 1:21-22: "now he that establisheth us with you in Christ, and anointed us, is God; who also sealed us, and gave us the earnest of the Spirit in our hearts"; and along with that, Ephesians 1:13-14: "in whom, having also believed, ye were sealed with the Holy Spirit of promise, which is an earnest of our inheritance." And finally Ephesians 4:30: "and grieve not the Holy Spirit of God, in whom ye were sealed unto the day of redemption." It appears here that there is a very close relation between sealing and the gift of the Spirit, who is an earnest of our salvation and inheritance. That is especially clear in 2 Corinthians 1:22, which speaks of an earnest of God's promises (1:20). It is a confirmation *in* the Anointed One, a confirmation by judicial power and guarantee.[15] God gives that in the gift of the Spirit, the seal, the earnest of the inheritance, so that here also the element of certainty and trustworthiness stands in the foreground. "God puts his seal on the believers by giving them the Holy Spirit, through which they are sealed as his children."[16]

And finally, we recall Revelation 7:22ff., where we hear of the angel who has the seal of the living God, and of the number of those who were sealed — 144,000. Those who have the seal are spared in the judgment (Rev. 9:4; cf. 14:1; 22:4); those with the seal of God stand in contrast to those bearing the mark of the beast on their right hand or their forehead (Rev. 13:16-17; 14:11).

The question may be asked whether in these contexts the connection between baptism and seal becomes visible. Grosheide, who maintains that in the New Testament "seal" does not always imply baptism, believes that 2 Corinthians 1:22 does have a connection with baptism. This is not inconsistent, as long as we recognize that "seal" is not yet a technical term designating baptism. It is only a matter of definite contexts, centering on the description of veracity and trustworthiness.

Before we look more closely into the significance of baptism as seal, it is necessary to notice a very special connection that Roman Catholic doctrine finds in texts speaking of sealing and baptism — the well-known doctrine of the *character indelebilis.* This is certainly one of the most remarkable themes in Roman Catholic dogmatics, especially because of the manner in which the givens of Scripture are treated.

According to Rome, the indestructible mark is given with the administration of baptism and also with the administration of confirmation and ordination. It is not the same as an infusion of supernatural grace (which is not *indelebilis*), but something else that cannot be defined so easily. For the indestructibility of this character in baptism, Rome appeals to the texts mentioned: 2 Corinthians 1:22 and Ephesians 1:12 and 4:30. Conclusions drawn from these texts became part of the church's doctrine, especially at Trent, where the anathema is spoken against those who do not accept that in these three sacraments the "character" is stamped into the soul, the spiritual and indestructible sign, from which it follows that they never can be repeated.[17]

It is deduced from these texts that baptism marks the recipient with "a spiritual sign, different from grace" by means of a "spiritual mark imprinted in the soul."[18] The essence of this "character" is indicated in various ways. It is distinguished from supernatural grace because that grace can be lost through mortal sin, something that cannot be said of the "character." It is described as an "ornament of the soul," as a *habitus* or disposition of no small significance, since for the sake of this character, baptism does not have to be repeated even though grace is lost. In the mark lies a certain dedication to the service of the Lord, which is not sanctifying in nature. It is, so to speak, an ontic substratum of grace, something to which grace can always be rejoined. It is acknowledged that the New Testament does not render a clear and independent proof, but it does contain references "which can be explained along the lines of the dogma and by leaning on tradition."[19]

In connection with the textual references cited for this character, it is understandable that there were a number of theologians in the Middle Ages (Alexander of Hales, Bonaventura, A. de Grote) who were of the opinion that the character was grace itself and that thereby believers were distinguished from unbelievers. This is entirely understandable, since Scripture does not speak in the references mentioned of something neutral that abides even if supernatural grace is lost, as a kind of ontic substratum in the soul. Scripture speaks rather, in a decidedly soteriological and comforting context, of a confirmation appealing to the faithfulness of God, who in the Holy Spirit gives the earnest of the inheritance to come. But Rome detaches the character from this soteriological context and thus makes it a habit that can be isolated from salvation and that continues to exist in the soul even if grace is lost.

It is clear that what Scripture says of sealing lies precisely on the plane of everyday speech, in which seal and sealing indicate the guaranteeing, sealing, and assuring of God's promise. But Rome turns it into a "mark" in the soul which does not assume the continuous presence of grace in the soul. It becomes a "spiritual and indelible mark."[20] To be sure this is connected with the meaning of "seal," but only in the sense of a spiritual dignity. It is an evidence of Christ's taking possession "once

for all" of the baptized person, a being-connected-with-Christ, a becoming-like-unto-him.[21] The character thus forms the foundation for sanctifying grace, and so, says Rome, explains the revival of sacramental grace. When, because of a sinful disposition, a person does not receive supernatural grace in baptism, he or she still receives the sacramental sign, the character, which remains active since it is an act of God. When the impediments are removed, the character produces grace.[22]

Although the "character" is esteemed very highly, it evidently has nothing to do with sealing in its comforting aspect. Paul speaks of that as the Yea and Amen of God's promise, as the dwelling in and the earnest of the Holy Spirit, who keeps and safeguards us for the inheritance and seals us "unto the day of redemption" (Eph. 4:30).

The difficulties of this Roman Catholic doctrine of the *character indelebilis* (of which Thomas himself said that the essence of the mark was difficult to define)[23] have sometimes been resolved by assuming that the Holy Spirit is the "character" and that therefore a *qualitas creata* is not the identifying characteristic of the mark. Differences regarding the nature of the mark existed already in Scholasticism.[24] Durandus saw it as nothing but a relation, but generally it was regarded as a reality present in the soul, now and after death. That is a great mystery, according to some even more mysterious than grace itself, "for the latter manifests itself much more in its concrete effects and is also more clearly and decisively described in revelation."[25] In connection with the doctrine of the supernatural, Farine came to see the character as the person of the Holy Spirit, not as quality infused into the soul. It is remarkable that he appeals to the same texts for this view that form the basis for the official doctrine of the character. "It is inconceivable that the existence of a metaphysical-qualitative character [in the sense of Scholasticism] could be derived from the same [texts]."[27]

In order to maintain his own position, Farine points out that especially the seal imprinted on us (2 Cor. 1) is identical with the pledge that is in our hearts — namely, the Holy Spirit. It is not something that is imprinted by the Holy Spirit. "There is no mention whatsoever of such a causality of the Holy Spirit." From there, Farine comes to the conclusion: "The Holy Spirit must therefore be the imprinted, divine seal."[27] He points to a similar criticism based on the normal, scriptural usage of these texts in Scotus and Biel, but he does not accept their conclusion that therefore the doctrine of the "character" is incorrect. In spite of the rejection of this character as a created reality, he contends that we must maintain the doctrine.

Farine is evidently impressed by the urgent significance of the work of the Spirit, of which the New Testament speaks in connection with sealing. But he connects his conclusion (that the seal is the person of the Holy Spirit) with the Roman Catholic doctrine of the character, which is distinguished from grace. That brings him into great difficulties, for according to Trent the character is an indestructible mark, and of course he agrees. He wonders therefore how this can be compatible with his interpretation of the seal as the person of the Holy Spirit. He seeks the solution by supposing that the character comes to everybody but that it is a sign of likeness unto Christ for those who love God. "For the others, however, those who forever have excluded themselves from this communion in love, it is a sign of eternal perdition." In that sense, they participate "in the divine, living Spirit."[28]

The incompatibility between the scriptural light (which connects sealing with the pledge of the Spirit) and the dogmatic church doctrine of the "character" is clearly evident here. The result is that nothing is left of the comfort of the sealing "unto the day of redemption." It is astonishing to be told that the Holy Spirit, who dwells as "character" in the heart, nevertheless provides no divine guarantee to the person who possesses this character. To be sure, Farine speaks of a kind of "guaranteeing," but it is purely a conditional guarantee. "As pledge and indestructible sign, the character lays the foundation for the complete ransom of the full property, for the just as well as for the wicked."[29] So the earnest of the Spirit is detached from perseverance, because it is not grace itself. The sealing retreats behind the conditional promise that is and remains present in the "character" in the "reality" of the Holy Spirit.

We now return to the question how we must understand the sacrament as seal. An answer is possible only if we start from the fact that the sign and the seal may never be separated. Regrettably, they have often been separated: the sign as something external has been contrasted with the seal as something internal. The implication is that one can receive the sign without the truth of the sacrament. This is how Article 35 of the Belgic Confession is sometimes read, when it speaks of the wicked who receive the sacrament but not its truth, not Christ, who is signified by the sacrament. But this is a different situation, which Calvin has so vividly described as the vanity and uselessness of the sacraments when they are involved with unbelief. This does not affect the nature of the sacrament as instituted by God. The distinction between sacramental sign and the truth of the sacrament is quite different from the distinction between sign and seal. To miss this point would lead one to the conclusion that the wicked have the sign of the sacrament but that they have never come into contact with the sacrament as seal. Baptism then becomes a mere appearance, because there is a relation only to the external sign, and this divests the sacrament of its integrity, despite that fact that at first it had been described as sign and seal.

It is understandable that this approach should have been taken more than once, for it is a fact that although the sacraments are instituted only for believers to strengthen their faith, they are at the same time administered in the church of Christ on earth to some who do not believe. To solve this problem, a distinction was made between sign and seal, and the seal and sealing were associated with the work of the "inner Teacher," with the work of the Holy Spirit in the hearts of believers. The definition of the sacraments could then no longer be maintained, with the result that the distinction between the sacrament as sign and as seal contributed to a serious devaluation of the sacrament and its objectivity.

We learn here that the serious problem of the relation between unbelief and the sacrament may never be solved by separating what God has put together. What humanity does in unbelief must not determine our understanding of the sacraments as divine institutions. One can say that although unbelievers receive the sacrament, they do not receive its truth (Jesus Christ), but it cannot be said that unbelievers receive the sign but not the seal,[30] for unbelievers have no right to harm the power and integrity of the sacrament as seal and sign. Both the sign and the seal in the one act of God in the sacrament have bearing on the word of promise; what is abandoned with respect to the seal, then, cannot be retained with respect to the sign. That is why a distinction must never be made between the sacrament as sign and the sacrament as seal for the mere sake of solving a rational difficulty.

Others have found a different solution to the problem. They admit that the sign and the seal cannot be separated, but then they distinguish an "objective" sealing through the sacrament of baptism from a "subjective" sealing by the Holy Spirit. These two "sealings" happen independently of each other and then must somehow be reconnected through a combining of objectivity and subjectivity.

More than once the sealing by the Holy Spirit has been detached in a mystical manner from baptism and given a separate efficacy. In this context, the promise of baptism becomes something "objective" and "external" with a general, impersonal address. The sealing through baptism becomes a general promise that is strengthened and confirmed by the subjective seal of baptism. Behind this interpretation of baptism stands the idea that God's promise is a general promise, valid in itself, implying however an absolute being-directed-toward-us, so that it cannot be understood as a comforting promise either.[31] With that, the divine promise has been undone from its real content, and becomes a general offer of grace.

It is no mystery why this interpretation of baptism should arise. People realize that the promise and baptism have a bearing on faith. Belief is then seen as the subjective factor that individualizes the "general" promise and gives this promise (sealed in baptism) its directedness and its "for us" character. Faith then acquires a constitutive aspect, even a creative one, because this faith *makes* the sealed offer a solace. Through faith, the objective sealing becomes a saving good.

This theory, however, destroys the biblical correlation between faith and promise. Faith is accorded a totally incorrect function. For in the Bible, faith does not make the general promise concrete but rather acknowledges what comes to us in the divine promise as divine comforting. Faith does not possess one single constructive and creative moment; it rests only and exclusively in the reality of the promise. It does not create but rather rests in the promise, and the sealing is connected with precisely this, that the creative character of faith is radically excluded. Our assurance of salvation is surely at stake here, for if our faith must create, it may also fail to create.

We see now that the mystery of the sacramental doctrine lies in this pure relation between faith and sacrament. This has nothing to do with a subjectivizing of the sacrament by virtue of faith, but it indicates the relation that is implied in the purpose of the sacrament. Faith does not compete with the objectivity of the sacrament; it is rather a believing understanding of the meaning of God's word in the sacrament. Unbelief cannot understand this meaning. The question now arises, however, whether outside the true *usus sacramenti* baptism has any meaning at all. Does baptism then become a mere outward act with no significance, an apparent baptism and nothing more.

This matter is extremely important and has played a decisive role in many discussions, so much so that the church has felt it necessary to reject emphatically the idea of false baptism. In the ecclesiastical controversy among the Reformed churches, the synod of Utrecht of 1945 stated that "according to the judgment of the synod, baptism which is administered to those who later in unbelief reject the sacrament may never be designated as false baptism, because baptism, administered in Christ's Church upon God's sovereign command, can never be empty and vain." This thesis was addressed to those who thought the synod favored an interpretation of baptism that logically contradicted the objective structure of the sacrament. It was therefore no accident that at a specific point in the contention "false baptism" was concretely discussed. Nevertheless, this rejection of false baptism has not led to a reconciliation, because critics have argued that the presuppositions logically preclude formal opposition to false baptism. Greijdanus, for instance, has written regarding this thesis against false baptism that there was no reason to argue about the *words* "false baptism," but that the *idea* was actually there in synod's opinion that "baptism is a full baptism with whoever believes; it is not full baptism with whoever does not believe." "Even though one refuses to call the latter false baptism, it is not full baptism; its content is less, different from that of full baptism."[32]

With that, Greijdanus thinks, the objectivity of the sacrament is affected, for then one can begin to construe the sacrament in the light of the contrast between faith and unbelief. And against this view Greijdanus specifically refers to Calvin, who said that baptism remains the water of regeneration even though all the world be unbelieving, as the Lord's Supper remains the distribution of Christ's body and blood even if there be no spark of faith left.

This controversy, which is not at all a new event in dogmatics, has as its background the relation between baptism and the unbeliever, a relation that received much attention long before it sparked a conflict in the Reformed churches. However, in the ecclesiastical conflict the matter was sharply defined, as is shown by Greijdanus when he writes that the distinction between full and nonfull baptism is found neither in the first question regarding baptism nor in the confessional writings, that it is utterly uncalled for, and that the results of this distinction must be called nothing less than disastrous.[33]

It is necessary to see clearly what the problem is here. Perhaps it is correct to say that the whole problem of the sacraments is concentrated in the controversy about false baptism, for if false baptism is admitted, or at any rate a point of view is admitted in which false baptism can be rejected only through inconsistency, one can conclude that the sign, instituted by God, could — within the church — be nothing but an appearance, a meaningless sign, or even a mistake of the church.

That explains why the controversy about false baptism is at the heart of the discussions: it touches fundamentally upon the integrity of the sacrament. It must immediately be added, however, that one must be careful in this analysis, precisely because such serious consequences are involved, the more so when false baptism is rejected with an emphatic appeal to the institution of God. Simplistic solutions, employing distinctions that introduce "rational clarity" and nothing more, contribute nothing. The very fact that Article 35 speaks of "the sacrament, but not the truth of the sacrament" indicates that in Reformed theology and its confession an attempt is made to express the relation between unbelief and sacrament as it affects the church's administration of baptism. Bavinck already touched upon this when he wrote, "of this baptism, Christ is the administrator. And only if he baptizes and gives the signifying matter with the sign, is one truly baptized" — a statement that is echoed in various of Bavinck's other works.[34]

Obviously, everything depends on the meanings of the words here. It is necessary to say this not only about Bavinck but about Greijdanus as well, who before the ecclesiastical struggle over baptism and the covenant made statements much like Bavinck's. A clear example is found in Greijdanus's exegesis of Romans 6, in which he says that Paul speaks here of "baptism as such" and then continues, "not only of water-baptism, but of the full, real baptism, of the spiritual reality with water-baptism as sign and seal."[35] A little further, Greijdanus speaks of "connection and communion with the Lord Jesus Christ as it came about through real baptism and as it is signified and sealed through the baptism by water."

The same thought is developed in his commentary on Galatians. "Baptism is here taken as a whole, not baptism by water alone, without its inner significance, its inner essence, but full baptism, that is, the connection with Christ and its visible revelation in the baptism by water which signifies and seals it."[36] This is the same trend of thought that we found in Bavinck. It is evident that neither Bavinck nor Greijdanus intends to devaluate baptism with water when a distinction is made between water-baptism and real baptism. But of course such a mode of expression opens up the danger of misunderstanding, for the impression may be given that one is trying to devaluate baptism with water after all.

On the other hand, it is also evident that in these commentaries neither Bavinck nor Greijdanus wishes to admit the possibility of false baptism. Rather, both want to express what Article 35 says of the sacrament and the truth of the sacrament. All such statements find their basis in that; all want to allow the fullness of the sacrament in all its connections, especially in the connection between the sign and that which is signified. No one wishes to devaluate the sacrament, as becomes clear when Greijdanus speaks of baptism as such in Romans 6. It is still *possible* to speak of a nonfull baptism, however, because of the mysterious fact that one who does not fully acknowledge the historical word of the covenant and the baptism administered by the church can distort its actual structure, treating water-baptism as if it were independent of belief or unbelief. On the other hand, one can direct an eye toward the connection between the sign and that which is signified and speak, as does Article 35, in terms of a distinction that has nothing to do with a devaluation of the sacrament but only points to the sin of unbelief with respect to the sacraments.

This last point is relevant not only to baptism but also to the Lord's Supper. It is strange that with respect to the nonfull Lord's Supper (received by the unbeliever), one does not feel the same objection as with respect to the nonfull baptism. Nevertheless the problem is the same in principle, and the statement of Article 35 applies to both. We see, then, that there is a danger of quarreling overmuch about words. It may be that the expression "nonfull" baptism is unfortunate because it conveys the impression that one does not respect fully the objectivity of baptism. But it is quite wrong to infer from such expressions as used by Bavinck and Greijdanus that they teach a "false" baptism. The intention of such statements is more decisive than the choice of words.

It is then highly significant when a church with great emphasis rejects "false baptism" in response to the criticism that it has subjectivized the statement, and when it does so with an appeal to the institution of Christ.[37] It is still possible, of course, to charge that this church is really committed to false baptism by the presuppositions of its sacramental doctrine; the Lutherans of the sixteenth century brought such a charge against the Reformed view of the Lord's Supper, on the grounds that it did not do justice to the real presence of Christ. But one can also look upon it in a different manner. It is also possible that one wants to reflect on baptism only within the limits of God's revelation and for that reason one rejects the notion of false baptism a priori.

It is of course true that one's presuppositions about the baptismal sacrament may not contradict that. If the Reformed baptismal doctrine did teach that water baptism could not yet be called full baptism and that we must therefore in some roundabout way come to know whether we belong to God's covenant before we can apply the promise of baptism to ourselves, then baptism would indeed have been devaluated. But this interpretation surely finds no support in Calvin. This leaves Reformed theology with the serious question of how to interpret "full baptism" consistently with the confessional statement that we can receive the sacrament without participating in the truth of it. This question has never been answered satisfactorily.[38] Those who have attempted to formulate an answer have either come back to the well-known distinction between the sacrament and the truth of the sacrament or they have subjectivized baptism by asserting that the giving of the promise is objectively indubitable, while the application of the promise depends on the decision of faith.

If we want to reject this latter formula (as I do), we must admit at the same time that no perfectly rational synthesis can make the objectivity of baptism transparent. Calvin was always aware of this fact and acknowledged it again and again, not in order to flee into a romantic sphere of irrationality, but because he understood that these connections could not be apprehended apart from faith and that a rational synthesis between subjectivity and objectivity would not do. He was not concerned with a

twofold baptism and a twofold Holy Supper in a strange duality that would affect the power and the objective structure of the sacraments. That is why he speaks of *offering (offerre)* with respect to both baptism and the Lord's Supper, because he saw that through the relation between Word and sacrament the integrity of the sacrament is maintained. That is why we cannot speak of a twofold promise, each time with a different content, without violating the integrity of the sacrament and breaking the relation between Word and sacrament. But as long as we hold to the integrity of the sacrament, we can reject emphatically both false baptism and false Holy Supper because they separate what God has united.

Once more, then, the question arises of how it is possible that baptism can be administered to those who later reveal themselves as unbelievers. One should not lightly conclude that the sacrament has no meaning for such people. The sacrament is administered here on earth, where it is impossible to know the human heart fully. This being the case, it is possible to distinguish between that which belongs to the essence and purpose of the sacrament and that which actually occurs in the administration of the sacrament. In this possible relation between unbelief and sacrament, the acts of the church and the sin of humanity lie intertwined, and who would think that we can make transparent what sin has made so opaque? And so, lacking the power of logical synthesis, we must rather approach the problem from the pastoral point of view, remembering always that one must never minimize the objectivity of the sacraments, which is based on the relation between word and sacrament.

It is this theme that leads some people to speak (with no attempt at technical precision) of the relation between unbelief and covenant and baptism. They introduce the notion of covenant-breaking and speak of the urgency with which the covenant promise also comes to those who disdain the covenant of the Lord in unbelief. This attempt to understand the problem is no proof of the weakening of the objectivity of baptism but rather an indication of the fact that the sacrament that was instituted for believers is administered in a world of sin and unbelief.[39]

At this point Calvin's concept of "offering" is relevant, and it leads him in a direction principally different from that of Greijdanus. For Calvin does not want to say that in the giving of the sign, the thing signified is received by all and in that sense the sign and the thing signified are always connected with each other. Greijdanus has objectivized the conjunction between the sign and the thing signified, and in doing so he has given a different "point" to the structure of Article 35 and to the Reformed sacramental doctrine. In this manner he has gained clarity at the cost of Calvin's distinction between offering and giving (and receiving).[40] And we see clearly that the controversy about false baptism remains in every sacramental doctrine and that one can do injustice to the structure of the sacrament with a seemingly clear polemic (full baptism and full Supper).[41]

Closely related to these questions is the problem of whether baptism is a sealing of the promise or a sealing of believers — a problem that has occupied Woelderink and Oorthuys. Woelderink, who calls the Reformed designation of the sacrament as sign and seal "brilliant," adds immediately, "one thing must be remembered. When we are baptized, not we, but the promise of the gospel is sealed."[42] If this had been understood clearly, he says, the doctrine of presumptive regeneration would never have arisen. "For baptism does not seal us as regenerated people, but it seals to us the promise of the Covenant, that promise wherein undoubtedly regeneration is also implied and on the basis of which we may expect the vivifying Spirit with faith and prayer."[43] Woelderink denies that the sacraments are a seal of infused grace.[44]

Oorthuys starts with the same dilemma.[45] He speaks of pietism, which always points out that originally only adults were baptized. Then it was indeed possible to say that believers were sealed, because faith and conversion were evident. But, he thinks, this historical contingency has affected our conception of the essence of baptism leading us to associate sign and seal with what is present in the believer; thus the sealing is no longer applied to the promise of the gospel.[46]

This consideration undoubtedly contains an important element of truth. On this point, Oorthuys attempts to maintain the objectivity of baptism and to seal it against subjectivism. Woelderink and Oorthuys correctly oppose the view that presumptive regeneration forms the basis of baptism in the sense that one can speak of baptism only as a sealing of assumed regeneration. The correlation between faith and the sacrament thus becomes a relation between the sacrament and grace infused beforehand, while baptism would be the objective sign and seal. But this line of thought threatens the promise of baptism by making it contingent on already existing grace. It would evoke a kind of self-analysis altogether different from the biblical mode of self-examination. Such attention to our interior life cannot fail to weaken our attention to the Word. Inward grace becomes the basis for baptism, and when it is assumed not to be present, baptism becomes false baptism pure and simple, because it has been detached from the institution by God and from the promise of God.

But this very real danger cannot be escaped by distinguishing between the sealing of baptism and the sealing of believers by the Holy Spirit. This only raises the problem later on of reconnecting the two elements that were first separated. Moreover, it is a fact that the sealing of the promise functions precisely to seal believers by the Holy Spirit. There is a profound interrelation between the sealing of the promise through baptism and the sealing of

believers, for the believer who uses the sacrament as sign and seal in faith is therein sealed
in the sense that the believer accepts God's
promise to us (sealed in baptism!) and rests
therein. That is why the sealing of believers by
the Holy Spirit is not a separate working of the
Spirit, detached from the sealing of the promise
through baptism, but is one with it. The Spirit
uses the sacraments for the strengthening of
faith, to the end that we gain assurance regarding our personal status and find rest in the
trustworthiness of God. Woelderink's and Oorthuys's trend of thought is a strong reaction
against subjectivism and mysticism, which
make inward grace the basis for a traditionally
accepted but essentially superfluous baptism.
We must agree that such a reaction against the
undermining of baptism is necessary, but it is
nevertheless possible to speak of the sealing of
the believer in baptism in a different manner
than happens in subjectivism.

One can say unhesitatingly that baptism is
the sign and seal of the promise of God and at
the same time that believers are sealed for the
day of redemption in their belief, which rests
on this promise. This sealing is not based on
the fact that interior grace is already present;
rather, we take our rest in the seal of God.
Therein, according to the language of Scripture, believers are sealed, and therein we know
of the safety of our own life. This act of faith
does not render the word of promise unstable;
on the contrary, it acknowledges its stability
and rests in it. That is why there is no contrast
between sealing through baptism and the sealing of believers by the Holy Spirit — in the
way of word and sacrament.

When Oorthuys distinguishes the objective promise from the status of believers in
order to resist subjectivism, and therefore distinguishes the seal of baptism from the "mark
of God on our regenerated state," he has chosen
as his opponent a subjectivistic interpretation
of the relation between baptism and regeneration. He does not fully recognize, however, that

the Reformed confessions speak of the believing use of the sacraments or that they speak of
salvation in its fullness as it comes to believers
through the efficacy of the Spirit. Only here
can the contrasts between baptism and regeneration fade away.[47] And that is the only
way in which we can understand Article 33 of
the Belgic Confession, which says that in the
sacraments we are presented with what God
gives us to understand through God's Word and
what God does in our hearts, confirming in us
the salvation which God imparts to us. This
does not subjectivize the sacraments or violate
their objectivity, but it does reject a view of the
sacraments that objectivizes the promise and
detaches it from its connection with faith.

Knowing oneself to be a child of God is
thus not a work of self-analysis apart from the
sacrament that entails accepting the sacrament
only as an "outward" sign. This symbolic view
stands squarely opposed to the confession of
the sealing by the Holy Spirit, who makes use
of the sign in order to overcome the resistance
of the human heart. Believers are thus truly
sealed in the sacrament. The one work of the
Holy Spirit that leads to the conquest of all
uncertainty stands in an unbreakable and profound relation. Therein, baptism is absolutely
eschatologically directed. To be sure, there is
in baptism, as in the Lord's Supper, the so-
called sign of pledging wherein the believer
confesses his or her belief (I believe; help thou
my unbelief) and is thus distinguished from the
unbeliever through baptism. But this subjective
act is directed toward the objectivity of salvation, and there is therefore never any tension
between the two. The purpose of the sacrament
is the assurance of salvation, stability rather
than instability, proof against doubt, a song of
praise about the trustworthiness of God in contrast with the mendacity of the human heart,
and a guarded inheritance in the midst of the
dangers of this unstable life. Those who do not
understand the ways of God because they remain fixed on the outward sign live only in

their own wisdom. But those who follow God's way will learn increasingly that God uses these pledges of mercy in the weakness of our faith.

Here, through the efficacy of the Spirit, humanity's trust is more and more strengthened, and faith rests in what the Spirit of God has said. In this way, it is also understood why the word of promise can come to us in what is usually called the conditional form. That does not affect the sovereignty and trustworthiness of the promise, but it urgently points out to us that this promise and this confirmation can be understood only in the way of faith. This trustworthiness cannot be seen and acknowledged apart from the way of faith. The marvel of the Spirit makes us understand the promise as a directed promise. It is the faith that has heard it from the Spirit's own mouth. It has nothing to add to this promise, certainly not the application to one's own life, for it was precisely this individual, personal life that was meant and touched by the divine promise. Over against the depersonalization of the sacrament, we must keep our eyes upon the absolute directedness of the promise that in Jesus Christ is Yea and Amen.

In this light one can fully honor the teaching that the sacrament of baptism is never an empty sign but is rather connected with the promise of God in such a manner that the nature of this sacrament can never be affected by its being misused. This is not a matter of objective and subjective factors but of the call to belief which sees in the signs and seals the fullness of salvation signified and sealed and which accepts them as signs and seals of God. The sacrament is not detached from the connections of promise and demand, then, nor abstracted from the living God but is acknowledged in the intention that God has laid in them. That is why baptism stands for us as the sign and seal of the promise of all of salvation. Therein lies the undetachable relation of the baptismal promise with regeneration and the renewal by the Holy Spirit, with justification and sanctification, and, not least (as indicated by Calvin), with the incorporation into Christ's church.

When belief speaks of baptism, it can speak meaningfully and positively of signified and sealed salvation, as the form for baptism does. If these statements and prayers should be detached from the relation between faith and promise, they may lead us to the opinion that the language is too positive, and we may try to counter this positiveness by beginning to speak of the problem of unbelief. But in doing so, we forget that these things are said in the light of the conjunction between the sign and that which is signified, not in the spatial sense but according to the nature and structure of the sacrament. For in this conjunction full justice is done to the call and demand of the promise, but in such a way that the so-called "conditional" does not become a threat, because the voice of God is heard in the promise of the covenant.

Precisely in the way of promise and demand, it becomes clear that we can speak of the unconditional character of God's promise without in any way minimizing the call in the covenant. Those who speak *in abstracto* of the unconditional character of the promise violate the connections between promise and demand and fail to recognize the way in which God leads us to salvation with a promising call and an admonishing voice. But we can also speak in a nonabstract manner of the unconditional character of God's promise if we accept the promise and if this acceptance is not a consequence to our fulfilling the condition but a resting in the covenant which is unshakable. That is possible only in the believing use of the sacraments, in which the believer's perseverance becomes visible. We think of the struggle at Jabbok when Jacob said, "I will not let thee go, except thou bless me" (Gen. 32:26).

This perseverance is nothing but a laudation of God's trustworthiness and the unconditional character of God's mercy. It is the purpose of the sacraments to produce strengthened faith that no longer doubts in unbelief but gives the honor to God (Rom. 4:20). Precisely through this condition, anxiety about the remaining fulfillment of the condition is taken from us, not in superficiality but through trust in God, who will not let go of the works of God's hand.

Baptism, seen in belief, is thus the sign of the incorporation into Christ's church, in holy communion, of true believers in Christ, who expect their salvation in Jesus Christ, being washed with his blood and sanctified and sealed by his Spirit.[48] He is the sign of this transition from the old to the new life which becomes revealed in the church of Christ through his grace.[49] This seclusion does not issue from proud self-exaltations; it can be described only in the categories of the most humble confession: the purification through the blood of Jesus Christ, the regeneration from above that does not issue from our flesh and blood, the communion with the *ecclesia militans* and with the Shepherd of the sheep, as the sheep who hear his voice.[50]

This is nothing else but the miracle of the conjunction. This conjunction can be affected by superficiality and by misappreciation of the Holy Spirit if one wants to rest in the sign without knowing and loving the God of the sign. Then the sacrament becomes an empty and useless figure, because of the unbelief that does not understand the meaning of the sacrament and hence disdains it. One thinks here of Israel when it interpreted circumcision apart from faith and love and when it took the ark as a protecting power in the midst of Shiloh's dissoluteness. In such circumstances the "powerlessness" of circumcision and of the ark

becomes revealed to the Gentiles round about. And then the people can be called an uncircumcised people, and Paul can say, "neither is circumcision anything, nor uncircumcision, but a new creature" (Gal. 6:15).

If we try to draw logical inferences from this statement of Paul, we miss the point of his admonition. But if we understand the urgency of these words, we know that there is also a conjunction between the sign and that which is signified that is no usurpation. To this conjunction we are called in the struggle of life. This is not a theoretical conclusion drawn by the reasoning mind but rather the way of the church in faith and love. In this conjunction, the call of baptism to salvation is not seen as a strange matter, as a mechanical addition to salvation, but as a fulfillment of this richness in the midst of life. Whoever has not seen and accepted the connection between baptism and obedience[51] has not understood the sacrament of baptism, nor the meaning of Romans 6, where Paul lifts the connections between "sacrament" and ethics above all relativizing.[52] For sacrament and remission are undetachably linked with each other, and for that reason also sacrament and confession of sins. That is why the setting apart of the believer through baptism as "the mark of the covenant"[53] is not a false antithesis but a sign and seal of the mercy of God, and baptism is an incorporation into the church of Christ. Here the sealing by the Holy Spirit is seen in its most beautiful form when in the change and instability and the smallness of faith of Christian life the confession is spoken because of God's trustworthiness: "and that I am and ever shall remain a living member of the church."[54]

NOTES

1. See Calvin, *Institutes of the Christian Religion*, Library of Christian Classics, vols. 20-21, ed. John T. McNeill, trans. Ford Lewis Battles (Philadelphia: Westminster Press, 1960), 4.14.3. Subsequent references to this work will be made parenthetically in the text.

2. See, e.g., *Johannis Calvini Opera Selecta*, 5 vols., ed P. Barth, W. Niesel, and D. Scheuner (Munich: Kaiser, 1926-52), 2: 273. Cf. Consensus Tigurinus, *passim*.

3. Bolkestein, "Repraesentatio bij Calvijn," *NedTT* (1952): 572.

4. Cf. Confession, Art. 33.

5. Bolkestein, "Repraesentatio bij Calvijn," p. 278.

6. Bolkestein, "Repraesentatio bij Calvijn," p. 280.

7. Bolkestein, "Repraesentatio bij Calvijn," p. 281.

8. Bolkestein makes this assertion, citing G. C. van Niftrik ("De kinderdoop en Karl Barth," *NedTT*, II, 18ff.) to the effect that the definition of the sacrament as sign and seal is unsatisfactory. However, see Bolkestein's note on Van Niftrik, "Repraesentatio bij Calvijn," p. 181.

9. The problem mentioned by Bolkestein of the "plus" of effective presentation touches the core of the sacramental doctrine. What Bolkestein indicates as a "plus" *(de exhibitio)* is definitely essential in the sacramental doctrine of Calvin and the Reformed, and I reject the view that this is a "plus" consideration that enriches the interpretation of the sacrament as sign and seal.

Another question is the one that Polman posed in connection with Calvin's sacramental doctrine regarding the "temporary definition of the sacrament" *(Onze Ned. Geloofsbelijdenis,* IV, 111-14). Polman is discussing here the manner in which Calvin speaks of the sacrament as coinciding with the visible sign and then again of the signifying matter as incorporated into the definition of the sacrament (p. 114). Polman points to the Confession as parallel, where we sometimes get the impression that the sacrament is only the visible sign, and then again that the outward and the inward action are incorporated into the definition of the sacrament (Art. 35). This, I think, touches on a different problem from the one of the "plus" of Bolkestein. Polman says correctly that regarding the question "whether the sacrament is only a testimony or also an efficacious organ of the Spirit," Calvin adhered to the latter view. That Polman does not intend to introduce a duality with that "also" between testimony and organ is evident from his exegesis of that sacrament at many places. That is why this problem is different from Bolkestein's. See, e.g., Polman, *(Onze Ned. Geloofsbelijdenis,* IV, 135, and especially p. 137, where he says that Calvin "has maintained on the one hand the God-willed conjunction between sign and the thing signified, and between sacrament and the truth, while on the other hand he has not for a moment subjectivized the sacraments from the side of faith."

10. See G. C. van Niftrik, *Kleine Dogmatiek* (1953), p. 280. Cf. W. F. Golterman, "Teken, symbool of chiffre?" *NedTT,* III, 439.

11. "Among the many riddles of the oldest Christian baptismal stories," says Heitmüller, "one of the most enticing is the designation of baptism as *sphragis*" *(N.T. Studien* [1914], p. 40).

12. Grosheide, *Commentaar op 1 Corinthe.*

13. Heitmüller, *N.T. Studien,* p. 46.

14. See Grosheide, *Commentaar op Johannes,* vol. 1, p. 431.

15. Grosheide, *Commentaar op 2 Corinthe,* p. 68.

16. See F. J. Pop, *Commentaar op 2 Corinthe,* p. 45.

17. "S.q.d. in tribus sacramentis, baptismo scilicet, confirmatione et ordine non imprimi characterem in anima,

hoc est signum quoddam spirituale et indelebile, unde ea iterari non possunt, A: S." (Ses. VII Can. 9; Denz. 852).

18. *DTC, s.v.* "Charactère sacramental," p. 1701. Cf. Bavinck, *Gereformeerde Dogmatiek,* 4: 464.

19. Michael Schmaus, *Katholische Dogmatiek,* 5 vols. (Munchen: Hochschulverlag Hueber, 1948-59), IV/1: 38ff., 122ff.; Bartmann, *Dogmatik,* 2: 219ff.; M. J. Lucian Farine, *Der sakramentale Charakter* (1904), p. v.

20. A. Janssens, *Doopsel en vormsel,* Serie Kath. Kerk, 12, p. 61.

21. Janssens, *Doopsel en vormsel,* pp. 62, 63, 65.

22. Janssens, *Doopsel en vormsel,* p. 66.

23. Aquinas, *Summa Theologiae,* III, Q. 63. Cf. Farine, *Der sakramentale Charakter,* p. vi.

24. See Bartmann, *Dogmatik,* 2: 221.

25. Bartmann, *Dogmatik,* 2: 221.

26. Farine, *Der sakramentale Charakter,* p. 41; cf. p. 15.

27. Farine, *Der sakramentale Charakter,* p. 43.

28. Farine, *Der sakramentale Charakter,* p. 59.

29. Farine, *Der sakramentale Charakter,* p. 59.

30. Cf. L. van der Zanden, *De Kinderdoop, Sacrament der gelovigen* (1946), pp. 73ff.

31. Cf. Bavinck's statement regarding this idea in *Gereformeerde Dogmatiek,* 4: 468.

32. S. Greijdanus, "De 16 uitspraken van de synode van Utrecht in Augustus 1945," p. 33. Greijdanus subsequently speaks of two baptisms, a real, full baptism, and an unreal, nonfull baptism. He declares that the thesis against false baptism is directed against the *words* "false baptism" and that the problem proper is left untouched.

33. Greijdanus, "Mijne schorsing door de Generale Synode van de Geref. Kerken in Nederland," p. 13.

34. H. Bavinck, *Gereformeerde Dogmatiek,* 4: 510. Cf., e.g., Bavinck, *Roeping en Wedergeboorte,* p. 184.

35. Greijdanus, *Commentaar op Romeinen,* p. 294.

36. Greijdanus, *Commentaar op Galaten,* p. 250.

37. See my *Gevaren en perspectieven voor ons kerkelijk leven* (1946), pp. 13ff.

38. That becomes evident in Greijdanus when he speaks of the objective basis for faith ("Mijne schorsing door de Generale Synode van de Geref. Kerken in Nederland," p. 17).

39. Cf. Polman, *Onze Ned. Geloofsbelijdenis,* IV, 137.

40. The reference to the "offering" in connection with the objective structure of the sacrament we find not only in Calvin but also in various Helvetian confessions when they speak of the truth and integrity of the sacraments. Cf., e.g., Müller, *Bekenntnisschriften,* Helv. Conf.

41. See, e.g., S. Greijdanus, *Korte bespreking van het Praeadvies van Commissie I,* p. 7.

42. J. G. Woelderink, *Het doopsformulier* (1938), p. 279.

43. Woelderink, *Het doopsformulier,* p. 280.

44. Woelderink, *Het doopsformulier,* pp. 106, 243ff.

45. G. Oorthuys, *De sacramenten,* p. 61; see also G. Oorthuys, *Doopboekje,* p. 148.

46. Oorthuys, *Doopboekje,* pp. 145, 148.

47. It becomes evident that Oorthuys's polemic is incorrect when he represents the point of view that he is criticizing in the following terms: "The apostles did not teach us that baptism seals such powerful effects because those who were baptized were believers and regenerated." This suggests that in the baptism which he opposes, grace would be the starting point of baptism. See for criticism of Oorthuys's view: S. v. d. Linden, *De leer van den Heiligen Geest bij Calvijn* (1943), p. 186.

48. Confession, Art. 27.

49. Cf. *Inst.,* 4.15.1.

50. Confession, Art. 33.

51. Cf. the form for baptism about the admonition and duty to a new obedience.

52. Cf. Hans von Soden, *Sacrament und Ethik bei Paulus,* Marburger Theol. Studien (1931).

53. Confession, Art. 34.

54. Heidelberg Catechism, Lord's Day 21.

The Meaning and Scope of Baptism

Geoffrey W. Bromiley

I. THE MEANING OF BAPTISM

The fact of baptism and its general nature and administration do not give rise to any particular problems or disagreements. From the very first the disciples of Jesus clearly baptized in some form parallel to the baptism of John (John 4:1-2). The risen Jesus, when giving them his final commission, told them to preach the gospel, to make disciples, and to baptize them into the name of the Father, the Son, and the Holy Spirit (Matt. 28:19). The apostles baptized the first converts on the day of Pentecost (Acts 2:38, 41), and since then baptism has always been, with very few exceptions, the initiatory rite of discipleship. Baptism in the name of Christ is mentioned in Acts (10:48; 19:5), and although this has given rise to considerable discussion, no significant deviation has been found in it. Through the centuries variations have also appeared with regard to the precise formula, mode, and especially the

Reprinted from *Children of Promise* (Grand Rapids: William B. Eerdmans, 1979), pp. 27-37; 77-90.

subjects of baptism. These variations have led to heated controversies; nevertheless, they have had little effect on the fact of baptism. For the most part — to accept the terminology of the Vincentian canon — baptism has been practiced in a valid and recognizable form always, everywhere, and by all.

If, however, we turn from the fact and the general character of baptism to its meaning and purpose, the matter is not so clear. On the one hand there have been those who invest the sacrament with an almost magical quality. For them the rite was divinely instituted as a means of entry both into the church and also into salvation. With the Holy Spirit, water serves as an agent of regeneration and of the infusion of virtues. If it is correctly administered and there are no impediments of insincerity, unbelief, or impenitence, as there can rarely be in infants, baptism is a guarantee, because it is an instrument, of internal cleansing, justification, and renewal. Hence the baptized person, at least at the moment of baptism, can be sure of eternal salvation. Equally, of course, the omission of baptism entails a serious risk — indeed, the virtual certainty of eternal perdition except where omission is made good by the spiritual baptism of perfect conversion or the bloody baptism of martyrdom. On this view no problem of infant baptism arises. The significance of baptism lies in its instrumental function. The instrument is not meant for adults alone. To extend this necessary and efficacious instrument to all qualified infants is a simple act of obedience, service, and charity.

This is one view, but we need not spend unnecessary time on it. To be sure, a measure of real truth underlies it. Christ undoubtedly instituted baptism, and with the word and the Lord's Supper it may rightly be described as a means of grace. At least, many evangelical Christians accept this definition. Nevertheless, its interpretation as an almost automatic instrument for the infusing of grace finds little or no support either in the teaching and practice of the New Testament or in the anticipatory signs and types of the Old. The only possible verse that can be adduced for this understanding is John 3:5, and even if water is meant literally here, the saying does not tell us anything about its mechanical functioning. In Acts, baptism is said to be for the remission of sins, but again nothing is said about its serving as an automatic instrument. The Epistles do not say a great deal about baptism. This is strange in any case but especially so if it was intended, and operated, as an indispensable agent of salvation. Paul, indeed, dismisses it in almost cavalier fashion in 1 Corinthians 1:13-17, although his main point is that no importance ought to be attached to the human minister, as some misguided people apparently thought at Corinth. Titus 3:5 again links baptism with regeneration, but the particular mode of this relationship is not specified. 1 Peter 3:21, in contrast, seems to make it very plain that the external act does not in and of itself entail or effect the internal work. It needs a good deal of speculative inference then, and a certain blindness to the general trend of biblical teaching, to derive this extreme understanding from the Scriptures.

The opposite extreme seems at first to be much more convincing. The thesis here is that baptism serves not as the instrument of something that is done for us, on us, or in us but as a sign of something that we ourselves do. By this public act, in which we openly express our repentance from sin and profess our faith in Jesus Christ, we signify the turning away from the old life of sin and the entry into new life in Christ in whom we believe. The chief significance of the rite, then, is as an attestation of repentance and faith. Its purpose is to offer an opportunity for a public statement and, as it were, enactment of renunciation and renewal. From this standpoint it also has the significance of a test as the first step of Christian obedience. Similarly, it can be viewed as a pledge or commitment to continue in the life of discipleship now entered. If all this is true, then patently it makes no sense that baptism be given to infants. Whatever their covenant status, they cannot make a conscious personal decision or a personal confession of faith. Hence baptism as the enactment of such a decision and confession cannot have any meaning or serve any useful purpose for them. Indeed, when they grow older, it might even confuse them into thinking that a personal decision and confession are not demanded of them. Baptism, then, should be withheld until the time comes when, with their conversion and individual commitment, it can have proper significance and serve its true purpose.

It seems that various passages from Scripture can be adduced in favor of this view of baptism as a confession of faith. Even in the Old Testament we find circumcision linked to faith. As Paul puts it, Abraham's circumcision was the seal of the righteousness of the faith he possessed while yet uncircumcised. When we look at Acts it is clear that adult converts made either a confession of faith or gave some sign of faith prior to their baptism. The Ethiopian eunuch provides an excellent example (except for the textual uncertainty of

8:37) when, in answer to Philip's challenge, he first testifies to his belief in Jesus as the Son of God and is then baptized. The very symbolism of the sacrament as vividly brought out by Paul in Romans 6 lays a certain stress on this aspect. Baptism is the believer's burial with Jesus and subsequent rising again to the new life of the risen Lord. The truth in the association of baptism and faith has always been recognized by all churches. From the very first the baptismal liturgies found a place for the confession of faith as an essential part of the administration. Even when infants are baptized, this element is not left out. The parents or sponsors must make a confession of faith either in their own names or vicariously in that of the child, which comes to much the same thing.

While all this is true and good, one must not leap hastily to the conclusion that it settles the matter. It is still worth investigating whether in the New Testament baptism is in fact constituted and administered solely or even primarily as an act or enactment of the personal faith and confession of the candidate. Where do we learn that this is the meaning and purpose of baptism? In what Scripture do we read that when adult converts are baptized on confession of faith they are baptized in the first instance for this confession or as an active sign of their personal decision for Christ? Where do we find any reference to baptism as a first step of obedience or as a pledge of ongoing discipleship? No one will deny that a close and necessary connection exists, and ought to exist, between baptism and faith or baptism and confession. Where adult converts out of paganism are baptized, as in the primary evangelism of all the churches, it is necessary and right that baptism and personal faith go hand in hand. Where the children of professing Christians are baptized, it is no less necessary and right that a confession of faith be made, for the sign of the covenant is to be given only to those children belonging to the covenant in virtue of the

confessed faith of their parent or parents. It is one thing, however, to say that the confession of faith must be included in baptism as an integral part of it. It is quite another to think or state that this confession constitutes the meaning and purpose of baptism.

When we investigate the matter in Scripture we find that the situation is very different. In fact we ought to be warned at the outset by the very character of the baptismal sign. In contrast to the Lord's Supper, it is an act in which the recipient has a passive, not an active role. Even adult converts do not baptize as they take, eat, or drink. They are baptized. They do not do something for or to themselves. Something is done for, to, and on them. When we turn to the relevant passages in Scripture, we find that this is not accidental, for baptism is not related primarily to what we do, to our faith, or to our decision or confession of faith, but to that which is done for us, to that on which our faith is set. In this again baptism corresponds to circumcision. Paul, as we have seen, undoubtedly links circumcision and faith, yet he does not call circumcision an enactment or expression of faith. He calls it a seal. Moreover, it is not strictly a seal of faith, but a seal of the righteousness of faith (Rom. 4:11). Nor is faith itself the righteousness. According to the whole argument of the first part of Romans, righteousness is a gift and work of God reckoned on account of faith (cf. Rom. 3:2). It is here that we begin to see the element of truth that unfortunately undergoes distortion in exaggerated sacramentalist and quasimagical ideas of baptism.

In relation to baptism, surely the first thing to strike us is the emphasis placed not so much on the person baptized as on the one into whose name he or she is baptized. The words of institution in Matthew 28:19 tell us that baptism is to be into the name of the Father, the Son, and the Holy Spirit. In the Acts accounts we read of baptisms in the name of Jesus Christ, which implies the whole Trinity (e.g., Acts

2:38). Paul disclaims the importance of the human minister only to enhance the one into whose name we are all baptized (1 Cor. 1:12-15). All this means that baptism does not primarily summon either ourselves or others to look at us and our faith and confession of faith but rather invites both us and others to look first at the One who is the object of our faith and whose gracious work we acknowledge when we confess our faith. To be sure, faith has an indispensable role. Nevertheless salvation does not lie in our faith. Peter clearly proclaims that salvation lies in the name of Jesus Christ (Acts 4:12), and baptism, as a sign of the gospel like the Supper, was instituted not to witness to our own name as though we were the first thing but to witness to the name and act of God into which we are caught up in faith. It is our baptism and confession of Christ only because it is Christ's baptizing and confession of us. Baptism finds its basic and central meaning as a sign and proclamation of the work of God whereby the righteousness of faith is sealed to us. It has only secondary and derivative meaning as the confession of our own faith and conversion.

It might be suggested, perhaps, that too much is being read into the mention of the triune name (as if one could ever read in too much when God is mentioned). In reply to this possible objection we will look further in an attempt to see for and to what we are baptized when we are baptized into the name of the Father, Son, and Holy Spirit. Once again it quickly appears that in the New Testament the connection of baptism is not with what *we* do, with our conversion or confession, but with what *God* does for and in us in Jesus Christ and by the Holy Spirit — the forgiveness of sins and regeneration. In Acts 2:38, Peter urges those who are "cut to the heart" to repent and be baptized in the name of Christ for the remission of their sins. Similarly, when Ananias summons Paul to be baptized, he is no doubt as concerned about his faith as Peter is about

repentance; however, the accent falls elsewhere: "arise, and be baptized, and wash away thy sins, calling on the name of the Lord" (Acts 22:16). Again, in John 3:5, if the reference is indeed to water baptism, as seems likely enough, baptism is not linked at all to the believer's action but to regeneration through the ministry of the Holy Spirit. The same holds true in Titus 3:5, which establishes a parallel link between baptism and regeneration in the context of the life-giving work of the Holy Spirit.

Now it is evident that neither the forgiveness of sins nor regeneration is or can be a human work or even a human possibility. We can and must do certain things for ourselves within the totality of God's saving work. We are told to repent, call on the name of the Lord, believe, confess our faith, and receive forgiveness and renewal. We have to do these things if salvation is to be ours, and we have to do them even if only enabled by virtue of what God does. Forgiveness and regeneration, however, are very plainly the work of God, which we cannot and should not try to do. "Who can forgive sins but God only?" (Mark 2:7). The Pharisees were quite right when they put this accusing question before Jesus. They were wrong in failing to see that in Jesus they were dealing with God. Similarly, the new birth is not of blood, nor of the will of humans, nor of the will of the flesh, but of God (John 1:13). If we are to be born again, we must be born from above, born of the Spirit (John 3:3, 6). This means, however, that if baptism is primarily for remission and regeneration, it does not focus on our necessary but secondary and derivative action, faith and the confession of faith. Rather, it focuses on the indispensable, primary, and originative action of God, the divine work of reconciliation and renewal. Baptism declares, signifies, and seals not what I do but what God has done, does, and will do for me.

The above is true even in the passage in Romans 6 that draws the inference of the believer's mortification and renewal. We will come back to this later, yet we may note already that the central message of these verses, and that to which our baptism testifies, is the death, burial, and resurrection of Jesus Christ already enacted on our behalf. Only on this basis, in and with this work, is there even the possibility, let alone the reality, of our own death, burial, and rising again. The primary stress in this passage falls on the same point as in the other verses dealing with baptism. We are not just directed to ourselves and to our own faith and confession of faith or to our own dying to the old life and rising again to the new life. We are directed to God and to what God has done for us in Jesus Christ, to what he does and will do for us and in us by the Holy Spirit. Only in this context and on this basis can we think of the necessary response of faith and of personal entry into God's reconciling and regenerating work.

Surely, then, we are forced to the conclusion that baptism is primarily a sign or seal of God's own work. Saying this, however, is simply another way of saying that it is a sign or seal of the covenant and its fulfillment in Jesus Christ. God's reconciling and regenerating work constitutes the fulfillment of the promise that lies at the heart of the covenant and of all God's dealings with his covenant people. From the very beginning the covenant carried with it the creation of a redeemed and renewed people, at first restricted in the main to a single nation but then broadened to embrace all nations. The fulfillment of the covenant in and with the death and resurrection of Jesus Christ means that the word of promise has been succeeded by the word of accomplishment, and the Old Testament signs of anticipation have been succeeded by the New Testament signs of recollection. If this is so, then it is no less perverse to treat baptism as the sign of personal faith than to treat circumcision as the sign of the faith of Abraham. Indeed, if this is possible, it is even more perverse. It is false to the New Testament and destroys the whole balance of the Christian

gospel and the Christian life. It substitutes an anthropocentric meaning for the theocentric meaning. It puts the "I" and its decision in the place of God and his decision. It gives the primacy and honor to humans and their work and not as it should to God and God's work. It gives this human work an apparent importance of its own in independence of Jesus Christ and the atonement and the Holy Spirit and regeneration. It finds the critical point in our turning to God rather than God's turning to us and God's work in turning us to God. In other words, it turns the gospel upside down. In so doing it misses the real meaning and purpose of the gospel ordinance or sacrament.

By its very nature baptism is calculated to drive home the personal application of the divine work. The same was true of circumcision. Like circumcision, however, it does so only as it proclaims the divine work which is the work of the covenant fulfilled in Jesus Christ by the Holy Spirit.

II. THE SCOPE OF BAPTISM

Baptism declares the inward regenerative operation of the Holy Spirit which makes us conformable to Jesus Christ. In its full compass this operation includes endowment with gifts and graces for the service of God, for a life of identification with Jesus Christ will naturally and necessarily be a life of service as was the life of Jesus. Basically, however, it consists in the movement of death and rising again as participation in the death and rising again of Christ. Applied to us, death and rising again mean remission of sins and regeneration, with both of which baptism is expressly connected in the New Testament. The remission of sins is the canceling of the old life of sin, and regeneration is the beginning of the new and eternal life of righteousness. In the power of the Holy Spirit, therefore, we are inserted or initiated into Christ's crucifixion and resurrection, so that we personally, in and with the company of all believers, die to sin and rise again to righteousness in enjoyment of the benefits of Christ's work of vicarious reconciliation.

Now when we consult Holy Scripture we find that this work of initiation or insertion is not presented merely as the work of a moment. It may certainly be understood as a single act, but one with three successive stages. Dying and rising again with Christ cannot be identified wholly or exclusively with any one of these stages. In particular, it cannot be identified wholly and exclusively with an isolated experience of conversion, important though this undoubtedly is in creating all things new. Dying and rising again with Christ is a whole process of renewal or new creation, and at every point this process is the work of the Holy Spirit as the Spirit identifies us with Jesus Christ. A common pattern runs through the whole process which shows that it is a unified work — the pattern of dying and renewal so clearly declared in baptism. In its witness to the reconciling work of God the Son and the regenerating work of God the Holy Spirit, baptism is the sign and seal of the total fulfillment of the election of God the Father and is also a summons to the baptized to enter into the totality of the divine activity. Baptism tells us what has been done, what is being done, and what will be done for us and in us. God has elected us and reconciled us and is now refashioning us in the image of Christ. Baptism also tells us in the power of the Spirit what we are to do in response. "Be ye reconciled to God" (2 Cor. 5:20). "Be imitators of me, as I am of Christ" (1 Cor. 11:1, RSV).

Now obviously the actual moment of new birth, which finds its counterpart in conversion or the coming to faith, forms the first stage of identification with Jesus Christ. At this first stage the old and sinful self is replaced by the new and righteous self which is born of the Spirit. In terms of conversion, this means a turning away from self in repentance and a turning to Jesus Christ in faith. This stage of regeneration or conversion has all the significance of a beginning, and in this case has a special significance as God's work, for in a sense it already includes the whole. Even when viewed from the standpoint of the believer, it is the entry into a finished work of reconciliation and regeneration. The end, therefore, is given to us with the beginning. Once we are in Jesus Christ by repentance and faith, we can say with confidence, though not, of course, with self-boasting, that we are justified (Rom. 5:1), that we are risen (Col. 3:3), that we are a new creation (2 Cor. 5:17), and that we have eternal life (John 3:36). For, as we read in Hebrews 11:1, "faith is the substance of things hoped for, the evidence of things not seen."

Because conversion, or the moment of new birth, has this very special significance, a very strong connection exists between it and baptism. We must be careful, however, not to understand or state this connection in the wrong way. Baptism, as we have noted, is not primarily the witness, sign, or seal of my own consciousness and confession of repentance and faith; rather, it is first and foremost the witness, sign, and seal of what the Father elected for me, of what the Son did in my place, and of what the Spirit is doing in and to me. Conversion has to be seen, then, in its proper context. Its significance lies in the fact that it is a fulfillment of the election of the Father, an identification with the reconciling death and resurrection of the Son, and a first outworking of the regenerative operation of the Holy Spirit which carries with it the assurance of the continuation and completion of this work and a summons to its ongoing expression in a lifelong identification with Christ.

How does this work out in relation to the baptized? Adults converted from paganism or unbelief are baptized as they profess their faith in the first step of identification — the moment of the new birth. Before this they cannot be baptized: they are outside the sphere of the word and the Spirit. They have no desire for baptism, and it has no meaning for them. But now that they have heard and received the gospel promises, now that the Holy Spirit has done in them the work that leads to repentance and faith, and now that a beginning has been made of participation in Christ, baptism takes on meaning as a testimony, seal, and confirmation. It bears witness to what they do, but it also shows them that their actions have a meaning deeper than just that of a human decision or a change of religious belief and practice. In repentance and faith there is fulfilled the regeneration in us that will bring to personal completion the electing and reconciling work of God for us.

The situation differs with the children of confessing Christians. From the very beginning they are in the sphere of the word and Spirit, and the prayer of parents and congregation is made for them. They are not necessarily converted, and baptism itself will not convert them, but the gospel promises are before them, and every reason exists to believe that the Holy Spirit has begun his work within them. They thus receive baptism as a sign and seal of the divine election, reconciliation, and regeneration. As they grow older, they may come quickly to individual repentance and faith. On the other hand, they may move away for a period, or perhaps forever. But baptism is always there, bearing its witness to the will of the Father, the work of the Son, and the ministry of the Spirit. The church's proclamation tells them what they are to do. They are to die and rise again with Christ in personal repentance and faith and are to begin the outworking of their renewal in conversion. In this personal application, conversion is now the first objective. Baptism has now an evangelistic office as an adjunct of the word. It tells those who are baptized as children that it will find actualization in them only as the first stage of the Spirit's

work is reached and they come to repentance and faith. When they do so, it again serves as a necessary reminder and reassurance that this is not just a human decision but a deep work of God. Until they do, however, it is a continual pointer to the act that they must perform as those within the sphere of the Holy Spirit. As an act that has been performed on them, baptism, like the gospel message they have been taught, is something that they may ignore and forget in resistance to the Spirit's ministry and the church's prayer and plea. But if they do ignore and forget it, it will witness against them on the day of judgment. God made his elective covenant with them, Christ accomplished his vicarious work of reconciliation for them, and the Holy Spirit willed to perform regenerative ministry in them, but like Esau they despised their birthright, exchanging it for a mess of pottage.

Conversion, then, is the first step. It has special importance as such. In isolation, however, it is in no sense the end or the totality of the Spirit's work of conforming us to the death and resurrection of Christ. In no sense does it exhaust the meaning of baptism from the standpoint of the regenerative ministry of the Spirit. The new birth, like natural birth, has its own significance, but not apart from the life into which one is born. Regeneration in the sense of actual entry into the new life in Christ forms part of the entire process of renewal that continues throughout the whole period of the Christian's life on earth. Conversion as the first turning is a necessary beginning, yet it carries with it the ongoing process of turning from sin and turning to Christ, of putting off the old person and putting on the new (Eph. 4:22-24), which is the special meaning of the Christian life. Here again we have to identify with Christ in his death and resurrection. This process is a continual dying to sin and rising again to righteousness on the basis of Christ's vicarious act of reconciliation and in the power of the regenerative and re-creative ministry of the Holy Spirit.

The Epistles in particular are full of this theme. Thus we are told that "if ye through the Spirit do mortify the deeds of the body, ye shall live" (Rom. 8:13). We are not to be "conformed to this world" but "transformed by the renewing of our mind" (Rom. 12:2). Again, we are to "put off concerning the former conversation the old man," to be "renewed in the spirit of our mind," and to "put on the new man, which after God is created in righteousness and true holiness" (Eph. 4:22-24). The goal of the Christian life is to know Christ, "and the power of his resurrection, and the fellowship of his sufferings, being made conformable unto his death" (Phil. 3:10). We must work out the putting off of the old self and the putting on of the new in the mortification of "our members which are upon the earth" (Col. 3:5). This will take place in sufferings as well as in self-discipline, and we can rejoice that "though our outward man perish, yet the inward man is renewed day by day" (2 Cor. 4:16). Naturally this message can be understood in its full range and depth only in the light of the death and resurrection of Christ on our behalf. Nevertheless, it is securely rooted in Christ's own teaching: "if any man will come after me, let him deny himself" (Matt. 16:24), or again, "whosoever he be of you that forsaketh not all that he hath, he cannot be my disciple" (Luke 14:33), or even perhaps, "if thy hand offend thee, cut if off" (Mark 9:43).

What is the relation of all this to baptism? There is, of course, an implicit connection. Baptism bears witness to the death and resurrection of Christ into which we are to enter not only in repentance and faith but also in daily mortification and renewal. This implicit connection is made explicit, however, in the great baptismal passage in Romans 6, where Paul introduces the thought of baptismal death and resurrection as a summons to its outworking in Christian conduct. The apostle's argument seems to be as follows. Baptism into Jesus Christ is baptism into his death and burial for

us. In him we are already dead and buried. Accepting this fact in penitence and faith, we know that our old self is crucified with Christ so that the body of sin might be destroyed. With this knowledge we are thus challenged to reckon ourselves to be dead indeed to sin and alive to God, not yielding our members as instruments of unrighteousness to sin but yielding ourselves to God as those who are alive from the dead and our members as instruments of righteousness to God. In other words, baptism, as the attestation of our death and resurrection in and with Christ, carries a reference to the whole life of the Christian. If it is an evangelistic summons to children born in the covenant sphere of the word and Spirit, to them and to converted adults as well it has ethical significance as a significatory spur to ongoing mortification and renewal.

Again, however, baptism must not be construed as the sign of a purely human decision and work. It was here, perhaps, that the Anabaptists lost their way. No one bore brighter or more consistent witness to the fact that baptism is an initiation into discipleship, into a way of life that carries with it suffering and renewal. Yet they deduced from this that no one ought to be baptized without a steadfast determination and commitment to take up this course of life and to pursue it to the end. Their emphasis tended to fall on the human aspect. Mortification and renewal, however, are more than a venture in human ethics. They are the continuation of the regenerating or re-creative ministry of the Holy Spirit. Christians themselves, of course, are engaged in this work. We cannot escape or minimize the personal reference. The Holy Spirit will not and does not deal with us as automatons here any more than when he brings us to individual repentance and faith. Nevertheless, this work of mortification and renewal is not a possibility or achievement of our own. We are engaged in it only because Jesus Christ has already done it for us and the Holy Spirit is doing it in us. As Paul puts it, it is because we are already dead in Christ that we are to mortify our members. In Galatians 5:16-18, and especially in Romans 8 and Philippians, he makes it plain that this working out of salvation in ethical reconstruction is through the Holy Spirit: "if ye through the Spirit do mortify the deeds of the body, ye shall live" (Rom. 8:13); "it is God which worketh in you both to will and to do of his good pleasure" (Phil. 2:13).

For our part, we learn from the sacrament of baptism what this work of the Spirit is and what identification with Christ means for us in terms of daily life and service. Whether we are baptized as infants or adults makes little difference at this stage. The meaning and message of baptism are the same. None of us can claim that witness is given in baptism to the actual achievement of the ongoing work of baptism in personal life. At most, the subjective side can consist only in a commitment to its future fulfillment. In this pledge only, not in an actual performance, can a right to baptism be sought. For all of us, baptism is in this respect an assurance that our sanctification is a fact accomplished vicariously in Jesus Christ and that its outworking in our lives is to become a present reality in the renewing operation of the Holy Spirit. For all of us, too, baptism is here a summons to be what we are, to enter more and more into the fullness of identification with Christ in his death and resurrection, which in terms of its actualization in daily life and conduct is an ongoing process and thus has always a future as well as a past and present reference.

Nor is this the closing stage. Birth leads on through growth to fullness or maturity. Beyond conversion and ongoing sanctification lies the completion of the Christian life when we enter into the full actuality of the new life in Christ which is even now our true reality and calling. Again, and this time totally and finally, we are in the sphere of identification with Christ in his death and resurrection. On the basis of Christ's vicarious work of recon-

ciliation and in the strength of the Spirit's sovereign ministry of regeneration, we will ultimately be dead in the body and resurrected in a new and spiritual body to the fullness of the new creation and eternal life in Christ.

The New Testament is full of references to this eschatological dimension. In Romans 8, for example, Paul moves from a consideration of the present work of the Spirit to the hoped for and assured redemption: "ourselves also, which have the firstfruits of the Spirit, even we ourselves groan within ourselves, waiting for the adoption, to wit, the redemption of our body" (v. 23). Or again, in 1 Corinthians 15 he speaks at large of the final destiny of Christ's people when this corruptible must put on incorruption and this mortal immortality (vv. 53-54).

Ephesians 1:13-14 also points ahead to the redemption of the purchased possession. Hebrews 11:35 describes it as one of the functions of faith to look forward to a better resurrection. Peter, too, reminds his readers of "an inheritance incorruptible, and that fadeth not away, reserved in heaven for you, who are kept by the power of God through faith unto salvation ready to be revealed in the last time" (1 Pet. 1:4-5). This witness undoubtedly goes back to the teaching of Christ himself when he spoke so clearly of our redemption at his coming again (Luke 21:28) and also of the resurrection of the dead, which is not at all excluded or replaced by the present possession of eternal life (John 6:39-40).

The implied relation to baptism hardly needs to be indicated, for again the theme is that of death and resurrection, the basis is the vicarious dying and rising again of Christ, and the power is that of the life-giving Spirit, who does for us here what we patently cannot do for ourselves, both enabling us to die in the Lord and also raising us up again to eternal life in the spiritual body. Here again, however, there are one or two more explicit references. One of them is the obscure saying in 1 Corinthians

15:29. Probably the exact meaning of this statement will always be something of a mystery. Nevertheless, although commentators differ widely in their detailed suggestions, there can be little disagreement on one point. Baptism arises in this passage because of a definite connection that it bears in some way to physical dissolution and resurrection. In baptism we see both death and rising again. The saying in Ephesians 1:13 is ambivalent as well, for not every exegete would accept a reference to baptism. It seems difficult, however, to perceive how sealing with the Holy Spirit can be anything else, or, if it is, what that something else is. If the reference is to baptism, or to the work of the Holy Spirit which is the thing signified in baptism, then the general thought is similar to that of Romans 8: God will complete the work which God has begun in us. Hence the outward sign and seal of that work declares not only the first installment but also the final redemption of which it is the pledge.

The linking of baptism with the resurrection is significant. It means that baptism, like the Lord's Supper, is given as a sign for the period between the accomplishment of our salvation in Christ's representative death and resurrection and his coming again, when we who have died in the physical body shall be raised again in the new spiritual body. Baptism has a backward look to the vicarious death and resurrection of Christ and a forward look to his triumphant coming again with his transformed and risen people. Between these, it carries a present reference to our identification with Christ in faith and sanctification which is the particular outworking in the intervening days of grace.

The fact that baptism has this forward-looking aspect means, of course, that whether we be baptized as infants or as adults, the personal application cannot be fulfilled nor the work of the Spirit completed prior to the administration of the sacrament. This completion or fulfillment must wait until the faith of conversion gives way to the sight of resurrection. Baptism is a sign the significance of which can

never be exhausted in this life. It speaks to us of the new birth as our initial entry into Christ and his work on our behalf. It speaks to us of lifelong renewal as our ongoing identification with Christ and his substitutionary dying and rising again. It also speaks to us of the resurrection as our definitive participation in Christ and the death and resurrection that he underwent vicariously for us.

This baptismal reference to the resurrection as our final entry into Christ and the new life in him helps us to see and grasp more clearly two important truths that have constantly presented themselves to us in the course of this study. The first is that baptism must not be self-centeredly treated as primarily the witness to some decision or activity of our own. Apart from hastening our dissolution — if that is any help! — there is indeed no contribution that we can make, whether by commitment or by action, to our being raised again from the dead. Here is a sovereign and miraculous act of the Creator Spirit for which we can only wait, for which we can only pray, and in which we can only trust. In relation to conversion and sanctification, the temptation can easily arise to allow what we do to play the central role, as though regeneration and ongoing renewal were a human possibility for which no more than a little cooperation of God with our own will and action were required. In relation to the resurrection from the dead, however, this temptation can find no foothold except among those who foolishly try to transform the kingdom of Christ into an ultimate earthly utopia, and even then the past and present generations can have no hope of participation except by the contribution they might make to it. The granting of resurrection life is solely and exclusively a divine possibility and prerogative. To be sure, the resurrection will be mine, worked out in terms of my personal self. In this it resembles conversion and sanctification. But again, it is my resurrection only on the basis of the resurrection of Christ for me, not on the basis of any inherent quality in me nor of any merit or achievement, not even in conversion or sanctification. It is also my resurrection only in the power of the regenerative and life-giving Spirit, not in the power of any inherent potential nor of any activity or contribution of my own, not even in the life of faith and love and hope. The activity that baptism signifies and seals is first, last, solely, and supremely the activity of the electing Father, the reconciling Son, and the regenerating Spirit.

The second truth is that not one of us can say, "I have a right to baptism because the work of which it speaks has already been fulfilled in me, and I am thus declaring that here and now I am identified in this way with Jesus Christ." Whether we be baptized in infancy or on profession of faith, there is in fact no time when we can say that baptism refers simply to some past or present experience in our own life and that it has meaning and value solely or primarily as a witness to that experience. As a sign of the regenerating, renewing, and resurrecting work of the Holy Spirit, it always has a wider as well as a narrower time reference. It begins with Christ's first coming before our present life, and it ends with his coming again after our present life. Thus we begin with Christ's death and resurrection for us, and we end with our own death and resurrection with him at the last day. Our attainment of this end is the creative work of the Holy Spirit which is declared to us in baptism and which has its initial outworking in conversion and the ongoing movement of renewal. Only when the end has been attained can we say that by the work of the Spirit we have fully entered into the baptism of Christ. But then the thing signified will be present in its totality and the sign and its testimony will no longer be needed.

The Lord's Supper in the Reformed Confessions

Brian A. Gerrish

It would be no great surprise if the classical Reformed confessions of the sixteenth and seventeenth centuries were found to contain a variety of eucharistic theologies. The confessions are both numerous and in origin diverse,[1] and it is common knowledge that the Reformed theologians of Switzerland were at first divided among themselves on the meaning of the Lord's Supper. Two types of eucharistic theology developed among them, with Zwingli and Calvin furnishing the respective models. What one might expect, in view of the mixed parentage of the Reformed church, is the coexistence of two independent eucharistic traditions, or a merging of the two, or perhaps the eventual triumph of one over the other. In actual fact, the evidence is not so simple: it seems to call for the distinguishing of yet a third eucharistic type, of which

Reprinted from *The Old Protestantism and the New* (Edinburgh: T. & T. Clark, 1982), pp. 118-30; previously published in *Theology Today* 23 (1966): 224-43.

Bullinger's Second Helvetic Confession may serve as the model. It is not claimed that these three types need be mutually exclusive, nor that each coincides completely with the thought of the Reformer who provides the confessional model. A full historical inquiry, which would take into account the nonconfessional writings of the Reformers and the eucharistic controversy as a whole, is not here attempted. It is suggested only that careful analysis of the confessions themselves invites the triple distinction.

I.

The assumption still lingers, in the minds of their friends and their foes alike, that the differences between Zwingli's and Calvin's views on the Lord's Supper are not fundamental. Certainly, Calvin did share a number of Zwingli's eucharistic ideas. Nevertheless, the fact is that they represent two different types of eucharistic theology.

A number of Zwingli's writings may be considered confessional or quasiconfessional in character.[2] Without attempting, for the moment, to define the notion of a "confession," I shall simply take account of the documents from Zwingli's hand that are included in one or more of the major collections of Reformed confessions. The earliest of these documents, Zwingli's Sixty-Seven Articles of 1523,[3] is tense, vigorous, and in tone polemical — a kind of Swiss Ninety-Five Theses. It does not contain a full or careful presentation on the Lord's Supper. Nonetheless, two basic notions are already present in this, the earliest Reformed confession: the Lord's Supper is both a memorial and a pledge. Christ offered himself up once and for all as an abiding satisfaction for sins. It follows that the mass is not a sacrifice but a commemoration (widergedächtnüss) of the sacrifice once offered on the cross and a pledge (sicherung) of the redemption made manifest by Christ (Art. 18).

In the *Short and Christian Introduction*[4] of the same year, Zwingli again assails the sacrifice of the Roman mass and insists that Christ's "ordinance" is rather a commemoration and preaching of his one sacrifice upon the cross: not the breaking of the bread but his death was his sacrifice. All we can now offer to God is ourselves, not Christ. We cannot sacrifice Christ, but we can commemorate the sacrifice of Christ, who has left us "a certain visible sign of his flesh and blood." Hence Christ called the Supper not a sacrifice or mass but a testament and memorial. Nevertheless, Zwingli freely uses the traditional terms "sacrament" and "food of the soul,"[5] and he even speaks of "feeding believers with the body and blood of Christ" and "eating and drinking [niessen] the body and blood."[6] Apparently, his motives are pedagogic: he is plainly anxious to avoid offense to tender consciences, and his argument seems to be that *the people* have always believed the right thing about the Lord's Supper — that it is the food

of their souls — despite the efforts of *the priests* to deceive them with the doctrine of the sacrificial mass.

Any possibility of interpreting this language in a "Lutheran" sense is ruled out in the *Fidei Ratio*[7] of 1530, Zwingli's "Augsburg confession," addressed to the Emperor Charles V. Here Zwingli bluntly repudiates the entire notion of the means of grace. The grace or pardon of God is given solely by the Spirit, who needs no vehicle; the sacraments merely testify in public that grace has been received in private. Thus in baptism testimony is given to the church[8] that grace has been exercised on those to whom the sacrament is given. A sacrament, in short, is a sign of past grace, of pardon consummated: it is *factae gratiae signum*. More precisely, it is a kind of picture or image (figura, exemplum) of the invisible grace God has given, a similitude (analogia) of what has been done through the Holy Spirit. Hence the washing of baptism signifies that by God's goodness we have been gathered into the fellowship of the church, which worships its Lord by purity of life.[9] The sacraments visibly associate with the church those who have previously been received into it invisibly.

It is no surprise, then, that when Zwingli turns to the Lord's Supper (or "eucharist," as he prefers to say), he uses realistic language in a consciously figurative sense, for by this definition of a sacrament he has already ruled out any possibility of treating the signs as a vehicle by which Christ's body might be communicated (Art. 8). That the true body of Christ is present to faith (fidei contemplatione) means that, while the worshipers thank God for God's benefits in the Son, everything Christ did in the flesh becomes *as if (velut)* present to them. A plain No is therefore addressed to the papists and "certain who look back to the fleshpots of Egypt": the natural body of Christ is not present in the Supper essentially and really, not masticated with the mouth and teeth.

Obviously, then, despite his liberal use of

the high sacramental terminology, Zwingli has not moved beyond the position of the Sixty-Seven Articles. It is made plain that realistic-sounding language about Christ's body is to be considered figurative or metonymous. To "distribute the body and blood in the Supper," for example, means to distribute the elements, which are signs of the body and blood.[10] The key notion remains that of a memorial; the idea of a "pledge," on the other hand, recedes into the background.[11] But a third idea is added, that of a public confession which identifies a person with the Christian community. Aside from this third factor, the main contribution of the *Fidei Ratio* is to make more explicit Zwingli's understanding of sacramental language, and he believes that he derives his understanding from the fathers. The teaching of the fathers was "not that sacramental eating could cleanse the soul, but faith in God through Jesus Christ, the spiritual eating, of which the external [eating] is a symbol and figure [*symbolum et adumbratio*]." Zwingli displays a tendency, which becomes universal in Reformed thinking, to elaborate the symbolism of the sacramental elements and actions. "Just as bread sustains the body and wine enlivens and exhilarates it, so the fact that God gave us his Son confirms the soul and makes it certain of his mercy; and it revives the mind that the sins which consumed it have been extinguished by Christ's blood." We may say, then, that this fondness for symbolism is a fourth aspect of Zwingli's confessional writing on the Lord's Supper. But it is not just an ingredient like the other three; it is the overarching theory of sacramental language. The three basic ingredients are thankful recollection, the reassurance of faith, and union with the church. And where in the world, asks Zwingli, can that be better found than in the celebration of the sacraments? This is what the elements "say" to Zwingli (his own expression): they proclaim that salvation is from God, they exercise our faith, and they draw us together in a common

confession. In other words, they have to do with our threefold relationship to God, self, and neighbor.[12]

In general, the *Fidei Expositio* (1531)[13] moves along the same lines. Zwingli's symbolic interpretation of the sacrament is developed in the direction of a kind of parallelism. In the Lord's Supper the spiritual feeding upon Christ by faith is symbolized by an outward eating of the bread: "You do inwardly what you enact outwardly." An inward spiritual occurrence is symbolically represented by a parallel outward and physical occurrence. The relation between the two occurrences is not causal, as though the outward eating gave rise to the inward; Zwingli has nothing more to say about it than simply that the outward represents the inward.[14]

The *Fidei Expositio* also heightens the emphasis on the corporate aspect of the sacrament by giving an ecclesiological interpretation to the "body of Christ":[15] in the eucharist we have to do with the ecclesial, not only the natural, body of Christ. This is an aspect of Zwingli's eucharistic thinking that has been strongly emphasized of late (notably by Julius Schweizer and Jaques Courvoisier).[16] I have no doubt about its theological importance, but its role in Zwingli's confessional writings is not especially prominent. The discussions on the Lord's Supper are mainly interested — though possibly for polemical reasons — in Christ's natural body, and even where Zwingli interprets "not discerning the body" ecclesiologically, he also interprets it christologically in the same sentence.[17]

At neither of these points — "parallelism" and the "ecclesial body" — does the *Fidei Expositio* add anything substantially new to the *Fidei Ratio*. It develops and undergirds what we have already noted in the earlier work; to be precise, it develops the aspect of Zwingli's symbolism and undergirds the aspect of identification with the Christian community through a public testimony.

II.

The editors of the *Corpus Reformatorum* included ten writings under the heading "confessions" in their edition of Calvin's works.[18] But the only one of the ten that has established a place among the Reformed confessions is the French Confession, of which Calvin was not strictly the author. Some of the astonishing omissions from the standard collections can perhaps be explained.[19] But the neglect of one of Calvin's confessions remains (to me) a mystery: the excellent Confession of Faith he wrote in his closing years (1562) for the Reformed Christians of France. I shall make occasional reference to this confession, but I shall use as my main Calvin source the Geneva Catechism. Though the Catechism does not appear among the ten confessions in the *Corpus Reformatorum*, it is selected as Calvin's chief contribution in three major editions of Reformed symbols.[20]

The resemblance of Calvin's sacramental ideas to those of Zwingli is striking, and it is not surprising that the two positions have been judged substantially the same. What I have disentangled as the three ingredients of Zwingli's position all reappear in Calvin. In general, Calvin views the sacraments as pledges of God's goodwill toward us, which represent his spiritual benefits (Q. 310). This is their primary function. They also serve as "badges of our profession," by which we identify ourselves with the Christian church (Q. 362). Here, then, are two of the fundamental Zwinglian ideas. Least in evidence is the notion of the Supper as a commemoration; but this also is perhaps implicit in the affirmation that the Lord's Supper "sends us back to [Christ's] death" (Q. 349). Finally, like Zwingli, Calvin has a fondness for elaborating the details of sacramental symbolism. The pouring of water pictures both cleansing from sin and the drowning of the old Adam (Qq. 325-26). Eating and drinking picture the sustenance and exhilaration we receive from Christ's body and blood (Q. 341).

What, then, justifies us in speaking of two types of eucharistic theology? The answer lies in the fact that Zwingli and Calvin held two totally different views of religious symbolism. Because the nature of the symbolical is not simply a fourth ingredient but the total determinant of sacramental theology, it follows that even the verbal agreements of Zwingli and Calvin are totally qualified and may conceal actual disagreement. Hence, though both can detect the same "analogies" in baptism and the Lord's Supper, the disagreement between the two men is more fundamental than their agreements and puts Calvin on Luther's side of the line, not Zwingli's. For in Calvin's view it is the nature of the sacraments to cause and communicate *(apporter et communiquer)* what they signify.[21] On baptism Calvin says, "it is a figure in such fashion that the truth is joined with [*simul annexa;* Fr. *conioincte avec*]. God does not deceive us when he promises us his gifts. It is certain, therefore, that forgiveness of sins and newness of life are offered us in baptism and received by us" (Q. 328). Similarly, in the Lord's Supper the benefits of Christ are not just signified but given (Fr. *données*), so that he makes us participate in his substance (Q. 353). The Confession of 1562 is just as strongly worded: "through the signs of the bread and wine our Lord Jesus presents to us his body and blood." The Supper is addressed both to the wicked and to the good, "to offer Jesus Christ to all without discrimination." The Lord Jesus "vivifies us with the proper substance of his body." "He does not fail to make us partakers of the substance of his body and blood."[22] And so on.

Such passages make it obvious why Calvin, without dismissing it, cannot make much out of Zwingli's favorite notion of commemoration: the focal point of his sacramental theology lies elsewhere — in the notion of the means of grace, a notion Zwingli had rejected.

The two Reformers were both careful to make a distinction between the sign and the thing signified, and for the same reason: to avoid the merging of sign and reality in Roman Catholicism and Lutheranism. But this cannot obscure their complete disagreement over the nature of religious symbols. For Zwingli, symbolism is what enables him to use realistic language without meaning it realistically. For Calvin, symbolism is what assures him that he receives the body of Christ without believing in a localized presence of the body in the elements. No one, Zwingli tells us, can speak so grandly of the sacraments as to give him offense, provided the symbolical is taken for what it is, and no more. Let signs be signs! "If [the sacraments] bestowed the thing or were the thing, they would be things and not a sacrament or sign."[23] Calvin agrees that the sacraments cannot be both signs and the things signified. But his position is still, in effect, the exact opposite of Zwingli's: *because* a sacrament is a sign, *therefore* it bestows what it signifies. More correctly, because sacraments are divinely appointed signs, and God does not lie, therefore the Spirit uses them to confer what they symbolize.[24]

III.

In the next three sections it is not my intention to subject the Reformed confessions to detailed examination but to ask of the major confessions which eucharistic type they seem to follow. And the point of division is whether their central thought on the Lord's Supper is commemoration or communication.

Of the Swiss confessions, the First Helvetic Confession of 1536, a team product of the Reformed theologians, deserves to be mentioned first.[25] It shows plainly that what I have labeled the "Calvinistic type" of eucharistic theology is older than Calvin himself. The sacraments are signs, but not "mere empty signs" (Art. 20). They consist in "signs and essential things" (Latin, "they consist of signs and things at the same time"). In other words, the thing signified is inseparably bound up with the sacramental sign. In the Lord's Supper, the thing signified is the communion (*communicatio*) of the body and blood, the salvation won on the cross, and forgiveness of sins, which are received in faith as the signs are received corporeally. It is, indeed, *through* the signs that the Lord offers his body and blood — that is, himself — to his people (Art. 22). The signs convey and offer the spiritual things that they signify. As with Calvin, so in the first Helvetic Confession, the echoes of Zwinglian ideas are unmistakable. But at the decisive point Zwingli is left behind. The sacrament of the Lord's Supper does not *only* symbolize, commemorate, move us to joyful thanksgiving, and bind us in loyalty to the head and members of the church: it is also the means by which God gives what he promises.

It comes, then, as something of a surprise to turn to the Geneva Confession of the same year (1536) and find an explanation of the Lord's Supper that does not move beyond Zwingli. No doubt it *could* be interpreted Calvinistically, but its language does not *require* such an interpretation. The sacraments are said to represent, but it is not said that they give. It is hard to believe that Calvin even approved the statement, let alone wrote it, and it is significant that the latest research is inclined to attribute the Geneva Confession to Farel. Nevertheless, Calvin did not disapprove of the confession, and it was his desire that the Genevan citizens should be herded into the Cathedral of St. Pierre, lined up by the police, and obliged to confess under oath that this was their faith (July 1537).[26]

Heinrich Bullinger demonstrated in 1545 that Zwinglianism was still very much alive. His Zurich Confession,[27] provoked by renewed Lutheran attacks on the Swiss, defiantly asserts that remembering is the "real chief part and purpose" of the Supper. He who believes *has* eaten Christ's body, for eating is believing. Believers therefore bring Christ *to* the Supper in their hearts; they do not receive him *in* the Supper. Of course, it is possible that unbelievers may be present at the Supper, and they may certainly receive Christ there — that is, they may become believers. But the saving events themselves are present only in the believing imagination *(Eynbildung)*.

By the time Bullinger wrote the Second Helvetic Confession (probably in 1561), the Zurich Consensus had already closed the gap between the two eucharistic theologies. Schaff's description of the Second Helvetic Confession as "the last and the best of the Zwinglian family" needs some qualification.[28] In the Zurich Consensus[29] the favorite Zwinglian terminology was liberally employed and Calvin trod softly in the introduction of non-Zwinglian ideas.[30] The consensus did not say all Calvin liked to say about the sacraments, only what he was not prepared to omit. But enough was said to put it beyond all doubt that Bullinger had moved beyond his teacher. God truly offers *(praestat)* what the sacraments symbolize (Art. 8). The reality is not separated from the signs, but Christ is received with his spiritual gifts (Art. 9). And so on.

That Bullinger did not consent to such expressions merely for a political accommodation with Geneva is proved by the use of similar language in the Second Helvetic Confession,[31] in which he taught a sacramental union of sign and reality (Art. 19). And yet in some passages (Art. 21) Bullinger seems to be thinking in terms of a symbolic parallelism: outwardly we eat the bread, while inwardly *at the same time* we also feed upon Christ's body. (In Latin, the connection is denoted by the words *intus interim*: "meanwhile, inside.")[32] This, of course, does take us beyond Zwingli, whose characteristic tense is the past, not the present. In Zwingli's view, the elements call to

mind something that has happened: Christ's body *was* broken, we *have* turned to him in faith.[33] And yet Bullinger's parallelism is not Calvin's position either, for it lacks the use of instrumental expressions: the outward event does not convey or cause or give rise to inward event, but merely indicates that it is going on.

Perhaps, then, the original distinction between a Zwinglian and a Calvinistic type of eucharistic theology is not adequate for classifying the Reformed confessions. Is there, in fact, also a third type of Reformed eucharist, of which Bullinger's Second Helvetic Confession serves as the model? I advance this suggestion at this point as a hypothesis, to be tested by other Reformed confessions.

IV.

My hypothesis seems to me to be confirmed by the three main Continental Reformed confessions that originated outside of Switzerland: the French and Belgic Confessions and the Heidelberg Catechism. The French Confession of 1559, though not from Calvin's own hand, is for the most part a faithful summary of his theology, especially his sacramental theology.[34] The two sacraments are not empty signs, nor yet do they possess any intrinsic power; they are instruments employed by God to strengthen faith (Art. 34) and to give us Jesus Christ (Art. 37). God signifies nothing to us in vain (Art. 34). In both sacraments he gives us really and efficaciously (Lat. *efficaciter*) what he there represents to us, and with the sign is joined the true possession of what is signified (Art. 37).

The Belgic Confession (1561) was closely modeled on the French Confession, which in some articles it simply amplifies. On the sacraments, however, I would classify it as only semi-Calvinist. The statement on the sacraments in general (Art. 33) seems to follow the

French Confession, but the article on baptism looks rather to Zwingli and Bullinger, and the article on the Lord's Supper then reverts to Calvinism.[35] If this is a correct reading of the Belgic Confession, then we have to make a further observation on the sacramental theology of the Reformed confessions: not only are different theological types represented in the *corpus confessionum* as a whole but there may also be strange combinations within a single confession. However, on the Lord's Supper itself the Belgic Confession does not seem to differ from the French model: "this feast is a spiritual meal in which Christ communicates himself to us . . . nourishing our poor souls by the eating of his flesh" (Art. 35).

The Heidelberg Catechism (1563)[36] shows a subtle variation from Calvin's Geneva Catechism at the very beginning of its presentation on the sacraments: it asks not how Christ communicates himself to us (cf. Geneva Cat., Q. 309) but how we obtain faith (Heidelberg Cat., Q. 65). This is not, I think, a trivial distinction but a quite fundamental one: the Heidelberg Catechism is apparently shy about the notion of sacramental means. Despite the contrary judgments of Schaff and Müller, it does not seem to me that the catechism teaches a full Calvinistic doctrine of the sacraments.[37] The treatment is highly didactic and intellectualistic: the sacraments confirm faith, seal the promise, help us to understand, point us to the cross, remind and assure us, testify to us, and so on. The characteristic formula is *"so gewiss . . . so gewiss"*: as certainly as I am washed with water and eat the bread, so certain can I be that Christ's blood cleanses me from sin and his body nourishes my soul. Of course, the sacraments do not merely inform us that forgiveness is like washing, believing like eating; they also assure us that we really are washed from our sins and united with Christ's body. The broken bread of the Lord's Supper does not only point back to the body broken on the cross but also means that by the same broken

body I am continually fed. The signs are also pledges. The catechism explicitly teaches a communion with the body of Christ, and, like Calvin, makes the Holy Spirit the bond of union between Christ's body in heaven and ourselves on earth. But the elements do not convey this union; they remind us that we have it independently of the sacraments. Hence those who should come to the table are those who trust that their sins are (already!) forgiven and desire to strengthen their faith and improve their life. The overall verdict on the catechism must be, then, that its sacramental theology owes more to Zwingli and particularly to Bullinger than to Calvin.

V.

Finally, I would wish to argue along the same lines in interpreting the British Reformed confessions: if my triple distinction is used as the measure, the results are again very mixed. Whether or not the Anglican Thirty-Nine Articles (1563-71)[38] belong among the Reformed confessions, I would classify their teaching on the Lord's Supper as cautiously Calvinistic. Zwinglianism is plainly ruled out, and the focal point is the *communicatio corporis*: the body of Christ is "given, taken, and eaten in the Supper, only after an heavenly and spiritual manner" (Art. 28). This could, of course, be read as parallelism; it is at least ambiguous, and neither on the sacraments in general nor on the other sacrament do the articles say unambiguously that through the signs God gives what they signify.[39] The definition of a sacrament in the Anglican Catechism (1662),[40] on the other hand, expresses Calvin's intention exactly: a sacrament is "an outward and visible sign of an inward and spiritual grace given to us, ordained by Christ himself, as a means whereby we receive the same, and a pledge to assure us thereof." Taken in conjunction with this definition of a sacrament, the statement on the Lord's Supper must also be judged faithfully Calvinistic.

Curiously enough, the Westminster Confession's[41] teaching on the sacraments (1647) is not so plainly Calvinistic as the teaching of the Anglican Catechism; and the confession comes as close to symbolic parallelism as do the Thirty-Nine Articles. Since the aim of the Westminster divines was to produce a more strictly Calvinist confession than the Thirty-Nine Articles, their lack of clarity in the area of sacramental theology is surprising. The Calvinistic intention of their teaching on the sacraments has to be gleaned from incidental phrases that presuppose the instrumental view.[42] In itself, the article on the Lord's Supper invites the parallelistic interpretation of the sacramental union: "worthy receivers, outwardly partaking of the visible elements in this sacrament, do *then also* inwardly . . . feed upon Christ crucified" (Art. 29, §7). Indeed, the statement that Christ's body is present "to faith" could be understood in a purely Zwinglian sense.

If the hesitance of the Westminster Confession is surprising, even more surprising is the fact that the teaching of the two Westminster catechisms[43] does not fully coincide with that of the confession. Perhaps the difference may be traced to the catechetical structure, which treats Word and sacraments as answers to the question of what the outward means are by which Christ communicates to us the benefits of his mediation (L.C., Q. 154). The sacraments are effectual means of salvation (Q. 161), which exhibit Christ's benefits (Q. 162) and by means of which the benefits are communicated to us (Q. 154). Hence when the catechisms speak of feeding upon the body of Christ, they must surely mean a spiritual feeding that is effected through the outward eating of the bread. Although much of what the confession says on the Lord's Supper is simply repeated in the catechisms, they set it in a clearer light by treating it explicitly under the rubric of the means whereby Christ communicates himself to his people.

That the idea of Christ's self-communication was the heart of the matter for the Westminster divines is demonstrated by comparing the two catechisms. The Larger Catechism lists five functions of a sacrament (Q. 162) and four or five functions of the Lord's Supper (Q. 168). In the interests of brevity, the Shorter Catechism restricts itself precisely to those functions that go beyond Zwingli's or Bullinger's eucharistic types, and particularly to the function of communicating Christ and his benefits (S.C., Qq. 92, 96). The notions of a testimony to our thankfulness, our engagement to God, and our mutual fellowship with one another are simply omitted. The point could hardly be more forcefully made that, although these notions belong to the full presentation of Reformed teaching on the eucharist, they lie close to the perimeter and can, if necessary, be cut out. The essential part of the sacrament is the divine gift conveyed by it, not the church's profession of its faith or love, nor even the church's "affectionate meditation" upon Calvary (L.C., Q. 174). One is astonished at the effectiveness with which the Shorter Catechism puts to flight the oppressive, introspective spirit of the Puritan that broods over the Larger Catechism. In the Larger Catechism generous attention is given to the inward state of the Christian before (Qq. 171-73), during (Q. 174), and after (Q. 175) the sacrament. (Especially formidable is the exhortation to examine ourselves after as well as before the sacrament: "the duty of Christians after they have received the Sacrament of the Lord's Supper, is seriously to consider how they have behaved themselves in it, and with what success" [!]). In the Shorter Catechism, on the other hand, the objective gift of grace, not the subjective operations of grace, holds the center.[44]

I close this section by pointing out that the Scottish church was particularly emphatic in its adherence to the "high Calvinistic" view of the sacraments. In Scotland the Westminster

Standards superseded the native Scots Confession (1560),[45] which affirmed the full Calvinistic doctrine of the Lord's Supper in strikingly realistic language. It has indeed been said that the sacramental affirmations of the Scots Confession can lay claim to a validity that is trans-confessional: not just *reformiert* but *reformatorisch.* "Here in fact," writes Paul Jacobs, "the Reformed and the Lutheran concerns are woven together in a new affirmation."[46] I do not share that verdict, but find it significant that such a verdict has been given.[47]

VI.

The conclusion to this survey of the Reformed confessions is plain. The judgment that Calvin's eucharistic teaching "must be regarded as the orthodox Reformed doctrine" oversimplifies the evidence.[48] In actual fact, Zwingli's view continued to find its way into the confessions even after Calvin's emergence as foremost leader of the Reformed church, and Bullinger's Second Helvetic Confession exhibits a third eucharistic type. There seem to be, then, three doctrines of the eucharist in the Reformed confessions, which we may label "symbolic memorialism," "symbolic parallelism," and "symbolic instrumentalism."

Nevertheless, the major Reformed confessions do not display three equally vigorous and wholly exclusive eucharistic traditions. The characteristic Zwinglian view is represented only in the minor confessions. (Zwingli's own great confessional works, the *Fidei Ratio* and *Fide Expositio,* never attained symbolic authority and ought strictly to be excluded from the *corpus confessionum.*) The view contained in Bullinger's Second Helvetic Confession, on the other hand, appears in several other important statements, including the most respected of the German-language confessions.[49] And yet it is not so much anti-Calvinistic as

timidly Calvinistic: *all* the leading confessions place the emphasis on communication rather than commemoration, but *some* reflect a certain shyness toward the idea of the means of grace. Perhaps this hesitancy does owe something to Zwingli. Yet the real division in the Reformed confessions is not Zwingli versus Calvin but, so to speak, "Franciscan" Calvinists versus "Thomistic" Calvinists. For while the major confessions generally insist (against Zwingli) on a sacramental union between the sign and the thing signified, they are not agreed on the nature of the union. Communion with Christ actually takes place in the Lord's Supper and is the focal point of interest. But is the communion given *simultaneously with* the elements (a kind of "Franciscan" interpretation) or *through* the elements (a "Thomistic" interpretation)? The difference is perhaps just a "school" dispute.[50]

Why did the Calvinists — of both varieties — refuse to follow Zwingli's lead into symbolic memorialism? The answer to this question attests to a fundamental bond between Roman Catholics, Lutherans, and the Reformed. The Roman Catholic controversialist John Eck may be given the credit for spotting the weakness in Zwingli's sacramental theology. He laughs at Zwingli's claim to be the hammer of the Anabaptists, since he was in fact the founder of the sect.[51] "How near is Zwingli now to the Anabaptists whom nevertheless . . . he torments to death . . . and tortures limb by limb." This is not merely unfounded maneuvering to implicate Zwingli in the guilt of the Anabaptists. Zwingli's sacramental theology really does point the way to the denial of infant baptism and to the interpretation of a sacrament as an act of public confession. Against this, Eck makes the same fundamental claim as Luther and Calvin: a sacrament is a sign not of past grace only but of present grace.

It would, I think, be unjust to Zwingli to explain his theology as the product of a philosophical bias. That the Spirit needs no vehicle, least of all a material vehicle, is certainly one of his reasons for rejecting the old concept of the means of grace. But he was also motivated by what we may perhaps anachronistically call a "Barthian" dread of putting God at humanity's disposal. If grace were bound up with the sacraments, they would profit and renew whenever they were celebrated. The clergy would then have infallible power to grant or withhold salvation. Indeed, they would have the fearful power to sell God at a higher price than Judas asked. Zwingli is therefore speaking as reformer and pastor in his protest against abuses in sacramental theology and practice: Do not buy what you possess already! The sacrament is simply a public testimony that you do indeed possess what God has given freely. Zwingli's sacramental theology sounds persistently the joyful note of possession: the "image" of Christ in the eucharist, like the ring the husband gives to his wife, is a perpetual reminder to the church that he is wholly ours in all that he is.[52]

Zwingli is by no means to be underestimated. He held the same gospel as Luther or Calvin, and he wanted the evangelical eucharist to give cultic expression to the evangelical faith. Nevertheless, it does make a profound difference that for Zwingli the Lord's Supper was an act of thanksgiving for the gospel, whereas for Luther and Calvin it was a concrete offer of the gospel. The gift of Christ lies, for Zwingli, in the past, as does the gift of faith, and accordingly it is the Christian believer or the Christian community that is the subject of the present sacramental action: *we* give thanks, *we* make confession before others. Calvin, by contrast, held that the living Christ is the subject, not merely the author, of the sacrament, and that he gives himself here and now.

Bullinger's position, as represented in the Second Helvetic Confession, avoids some of the pitfalls of Zwinglianism. For Bullinger, as for Calvin, Christ is the one who gives, not only gave; and we are to receive, not only to remember that he once gave. But critics have always found something arbitrary and irrational about what I have nicknamed the "Franciscan" way of speaking. Grace, on this view, bypasses human understanding: by some mysterious divine arrangement, grace is given at the same time as the sacrament is administered *(concomitatur!)*. On the strictly Calvinistic ("Thomistic") view, God really works by means of symbols *(significando causant!)*.

It is probably clear enough already what I intend by putting Calvin and Luther together against Zwingli. I have tried to draw the line at a different place than the Lutherans have traditionally selected. The test questions concerning the *manducatio oralis* and the *manducatio indignorum* have simply been ignored in my presentation. If *they* are allowed to define the boundaries, then Calvin stands opposed to both Zwingli *and* Luther, since he teaches that the body of Christ is given to all but received only by faith. In drawing the line elsewhere, I do not believe that I am simply exercising the theologian's right to draw lines anywhere he or she pleases. My line-drawing is historically conditioned. It is an attempt to answer the question of *why* the Lutherans made the *manducatio indignorum* the test question. Obviously, I must be excused for not dealing with the historical problem at any length. But it seems to me that what Luther himself was fighting for — especially in his magnificent work *Against the Heavenly Prophets* (1525) — was precisely the gift character of the Lord's Supper. Luther was shocked at Carlstadt's view, which, he thought, turned the blessed sacrament into a devotional exercise. Instead of receiving the crucified and risen Lord, who offered himself with the broken bread and poured-out wine, Carlstadt strove to focus his thoughts upon Jesus of Nazareth suffering on the cross. As Luther saw it, nothing less than the gospel was at stake, as in the controversy over the Roman mass. Christ gives himself to us in the sacrament; but some presumed to offer him to God, and others turned to their devotions. Both made the gift of God into a human work. Whether these accusations are well founded or not, the heart of Luther's own position seems clear: the sacrament is a gift, and the gift is Jesus Christ. If that is what was dearest to Luther in his reverence for the sacrament, then the Calvinist confessions are on Luther's side of the line.[53]

NOTES

1. The most comprehensive collection of Reformed confessions is *Die Bekenntnisschriften der reformierten Kirche: In authentischen Texten mit geschichtlicher Einleitung und Register,* ed. E. F. Karl Müller (Leipzig: A. Deichert [Georg Böhme], 1903). Other important collections are *Collectio confessionum in ecclesiis reformatis publicatarum,* ed. H. A. Niemeyer (Leipzig: Julius Klinkhardt, 1840); Philip Schaff, *Bibliotheca Symbolica Ecclesiae Universalis: The Creeds of Christendom, with a History and Critical Notes,* 6th ed., 3 vols., ed. David S. Schaff (New York: Harper, 1931); *Bekenntnisschriften und Kirchenordnungen der nach Gottes Wort reformierten Kirche,* ed. Wilhelm Niesel (Zollikon-Zurich: Evangelischer Verlag, 1938). I abbreviate these four works, respectively, as M, N, S, and Ns. Where a satisfactory text is available in M, I do not give duplicate references to the other editions, though I have checked them for variants. I give my own translations of the Continental European confessions, but the most important ones will also be found in *Reformed Confessions of the Sixteenth Century,* ed. Arthur C. Cochrane (Philadelphia: Westminster Press, 1966), and, wherever possible, I mention English versions of sources *not* found in this useful collection. As far as I have been able to ascertain, it is not possible to assemble a specific bibliography on exactly the theme of the present chapter, and I refer to the more general literature only as occasion arises. For a discussion of confessional sources and secondary literature in general, I may refer to *The Faith of Christendom: A Source Book of Creeds and Confessions,* ed. Brian A. Gerrish (Cleveland: World Publishing, 1963); further remarks on the Reformed confessions are made in my article "The Confessional Heritage of the Reformed Church," *McCormick Quarterly* 19 (1966): 120-34.

2. They are as follows: *Syben und sechzig Artickel und meynungen,* 1523 (given by M, N, and S); *Ein kurtze Christenliche inleitung,* 1523 (M only); *Fidei ratio,* 1530 (M, N); *Christianae fidei brevis et clara expositio,* 1531/36 (N only). Of these four, only the second was ever published with official — i.e., "symbolic" authority. Zwingli also had a hand in revising *Die zehen [Berner] Schlussreden* of 1528 (M, N, and S), but the draft was by Berthold Haller and Francis Kolb. Throughout this chapter, I give shortened titles for documents that often carried very long-winded ones; it is by short titles that most of the confessions are generally known. Both the *Fidei ratio* ("account of the faith") and the *Fidei expositio* were translated in the second volume of *The Latin Works and the Correspondence of Huldreich Zwingli,* 3 vols., ed. S. M. Jackson, W. J. Hinke, and C. N. Heller (New York: G. P. Putnam's Sons, 1912; Philadelphia: Heidelberg Press, 1922, 1929).

A fresh translation of the *Fidei expositio* appeared in *Zwingli and Bullinger,* Library of Christian Classics, vol. 24, ed. and trans. G. W. Bromiley (Philadelphia: Westminster Press, 1953). I know of no English version of the *Kurtze inleitung.*

3. M, pp. 1-6 (German).

4. M, pp. 7-29 (German).

5. M, p. 29, l. 7; p. 26, l. 25; p. 28, l. 15.

6. M, p. 29, l. 10; p. 29, l. 14. Presumably the statement that the mass has another purpose than eating and drinking the body and blood of Christ (M, p. 26, l. 19) refers to the Roman mass.

7. M, pp. 79-94 (Latin).

8. The English translation in the *Latin Works* has "the Church certifies that grace has been given" (2: 47). But the Latin text (M, p. 87, l. 12) reads *Ecclesiae testatur.*

9. This does not really fit too well with Zwingli's point of view, since holy living in the church strictly lies in the future for the baptismal candidate.

10. Art. 10 (M, p. 92, l. 19).

11. What confirms and certifies is rather God's gift of his Son (M, p. 91, l. 25). Sacramental eating is but a symbol of faith in Christ. Nevertheless, in his Letter to the Princes (1530), in which he defends himself against Eck, Zwingli comes surprisingly close to Luther and Calvin, arguing that the sacraments do in fact arouse, support, and restore faith (*Latin Works,* 2: 113, 116).

12. The most important passage for Zwingli's idea of symbolism (from which the quotation is taken) occurs in his discussion of the Fathers (M, p. 91, ll. 18ff.). The three ingredients within this symbolic framework are explicitly brought together in Zwingli's Letter to the Princes (*Latin Works,* 2: 116-17). He adds that it is strictly the Spirit who works all these things in us; and, if he so chooses, he can do so without the external instruments.

13. N, pp. 36-77 (Latin).

14. See the entire section entitled "Praesentia corporis Christi in Coena" (N, pp. 44-50). Zwingli distinguished three ways of eating the body of Christ: naturally (which he rejects), spiritually (which he identifies with faith), and sacramentally (which is spiritual eating *adiuncto sacramento*). He denies, of course, that the sacraments can give faith, save in the sub-Christian sense of *fides historica,* but he admits that they may — especially the eucharist — help faith by engaging the attention of all five senses. See the section entitled "Quae sacramentorum virtus" (N, pp. 50-53).

15. This appears in two separate contexts: on the condemnation of the unworthy (unbelievers dishonor the church because their participation in the sacrament is a

false testimony to faith), and on the sacramental symbolism (which has a secondary "analogy," in addition to the idea of nourishment, in the fact that the one loaf is made up of many grains). See N, pp. 48, §67; p. 73, §171 (from the Zurich order of service); p. 51, §78; pp. 52-53, §82. In the last of these passages, the thought of dishonoring (failing to "discern"!) the body is linked with the interpretation of a *sacramentum* as an oath of allegiance: the unbeliever who participates in the sacrament is a traitor *(perfidus)*.

16. Schweizer, *Reformierte Abendmahlsgestaltung in der Schau Zwinglis* (Basel: F. Reinhardt, 1954); Courvoisier, *Zwingli: A Reformed Theologian* (Richmond: John Knox Press, 1963), pp. 74ff.

17. N, p. 53, §82.

18. *Ioannis Calvini Opera quae supersunt omnia* (hereafter abbreviated C.O.), 59 vols. (vols. 29-87 of *Corpus Reformatum*), ed Guilielmus Baum, Eduardus Cunitz, and Eduardus Reuss (Brunswick: Schwetsche, 1963-1900), 9: 693-778. The list could be extended. It omits the Brief Confession translated in Calvin, *Tracts and Treatises*, 3 vols., trans. Henry Beveridge (1844-51; reprint, Grand Rapids: William B. Eerdmans, 1958), 2: 130ff., and the Geneva Consensus of 1552 (on predestination), which is included in Niemeyer's collection, pp. 218-310.

19. Of the ten confessions in C.O., all four major collections give the French Confession (1559), and Müller adds the Geneva Confession and Lausanne Articles (both 1536). Of the remainder, four are restricted to a particular doctrine (the Trinity [1537], the eucharist [1537], predestination [undated], and the ministry [undated]), and two form a family group with the French Confession (the Paris Confession [1557] and the Scholars' Confession [1559]).

20. I refer to the *Catechismus ecclesiae Genevensis* (1545) by the question number (in parenthesis). My translations are from the Latin text (M, pp. 117-53), but I have compared the Latin with the French text (Ns, pp. 3-41), from which I have derived the numbering of the questions. The Latin catechism is translated in *Tracts and Treatises*, 2: 33-94, and *Calvin: Theological Treatises*, Library of Christian Classics, vol. 22, trans. and ed. J. K. S. Reid (Philadelphia: Westminster Press, 1954), pp. 88-139. An English version of the French catechism (1541) will be found in *The School of Faith: The Catechisms of the Reformed Church*, ed. Thomas F. Torrance (London: James Clarke, 1959), pp. 5-65.

21. *Confession à presenter à l'Empereur* (1562), C.O. 9: 764 (I know of no English translation). Cf. the scholastic formula "efficiunt quod figurant."

22. C.O. 9: 768, 769, 770-71.

23. This interpretation of Zwingli gathers together his arguments against Eck (*Latin Works*, 2: 117, 118, 122, 124).

24. See especially the Geneva Catechism, Qq. 312, 328, and 353.

25. *Confessio helvetica prior*, M, pp. 101-9 (German); S, 3: 211-32 (German and Latin). With the First Helvetic Confession may be compared the Tetrapolitan Confession (1530) and the Basel Confession (1534). All

three think of the eucharist as an actual giving of the body and blood, not simply a representation of the body once given. See M, p. 72, l. 20; p. 97, l. 22.

26. *Confession de foy de Genève*, C.O. 9: 693-700. And yet the very next year the three Genevan ministers Farel, Calvin, and Viret prepared a forthright affirmation of eucharistic feeding on the substance of the Lord's body and blood: *Confessio de eucharistia* (1537), C.O. 9: 711-12. Interestingly enough, the Strasbourg ministers Martin Bucer and Wolfgang Capito subscribed to this brief confession — one year *after* the Wittenberg Concord. There is a translation in *Calvin: Theological Treatises*, pp. 168-69.

27. *Warhaffte Bekanntnuss der dieneren der kirchen zu Zürych*, M, pp. 153-59 (German, extracts only; untranslated). It was Luther's *Kurzes Bekenntnis vom heiligen Sakrament* (1544) that provoked Bullinger into this truculent response. Later, he gave his approval to the *Confessio rhaetica* (1552), which likewise does not seem to move beyond Zwinglian ideas (M, pp. 163-70, Latin; untranslated).

28. Schaff, *The Creeds of Christendom*, 1: 390.

29. *Consensus Tigurinus*, M, pp. 159-63 (Latin); trans. in *Tracts and Treatises*, 2: 212-20.

30. For example, it is made abundantly clear that the sacraments have no sacral efficacy in themselves, and for this reason the medieval *sacramenta conferunt gratiam* is denied (Arts. 12, 13, 17). But this is said not to denude the sacraments but to reserve the *agendi facultas* for God, who uses them in freedom *(ubi visum est)* as his instruments (Art. 13). The phrase *ubi visum est* says no more than the Lutheran *ubi et quando visum est Deo* (Augsburg Confession, Art. 5); and even the criticism of Scholasticism is a little specious, seeing that for Thomas, too, the instrumental causality of the sacraments does not alter the fact that the principal cause of grace is God alone (*Summa Theologiae*, III, Q. 62, art. 1). See further the Geneva Catechism, Q. 312.

31. *Confessio helvetica posterior* (1566), M, pp. 170-221 (Latin).

32. M, p. 210, l. 28. A similar passage occurs at M, p. 211, l. 10, but it uses everyday eating as a general analogy to spiritual eating and has no specific reference to the Lord's Supper (cf. John 6).

33. In characterizing parallelism as Bullinger's typical contribution, I do not, of course, overlook the fact that Zwingli in some passages seems to anticipate him, apparently transcending his customary retrospective direction. Moreover, my concern here is only with the confessional sources.

34. *Confessio gallicana*, M, pp. 221-32 (French); N, pp. 329-39 (Latin). The French Confession needs to be read as a whole. Certain passages, if taken in isolation, could be given a parallelistic interpretation. A particular difficulty appears in Article 27, which seems to say that the thing signified in the Lord's Supper is not the body or communion with the body but the *fact* that the body nourishes the soul. How, then, does God give us really and efficaciously what he signifies?

35. I have used the French version of the *Confessio belgica* in S, 3: 383-436, in preference to the later Latin version (M, pp. 233-49). Even the general article on the sacraments (33) does not say unambiguously that God gives what he represents; it could be read to mean that by the sacraments God works faith. This would go further than Zwingli, but it stops short of Calvin. One can only speculate why baptism is interpreted in terms of enlistment and parallelistic representation (Art. 34). Perhaps the hint is to be sought in the statement (Art. 35) that the Word of the gospel is the instrument of regeneration — and therefore (may one add?) baptism cannot be. It may also be pointed out that one section of the article on the Lord's Supper could, if taken out of context, be interpreted parallelistically: the phrase *aussi véritablement . . . aussi vraiment* is echoed by the Heidelberg Catechisms's *so gewiss . . . so gewiss.*

36. *Der Heidelberger Katechismus,* M, pp. 682-719 (German). My exposition uses the entire section on the sacraments (Qq. 65-85).

37. S, 1: 543; M, p. iii.

38. M, pp. 505-22 (Latin); S, 3: 487-516 (Latin and English).

39. Article 25 does not make clear *what* God works through the sacraments, but the answer seems to be that God strengthens faith. Article 26 speaks of four effects brought about through the instrumentality of baptism, but regeneration (of which baptism is the sign) is not among them, unless regeneration is taken ecclesiologically as engrafting into the church.

40. The Catechism dates from 1549, but it underwent several changes before its definitive form of 1662. The section on the sacraments was added by Bishop Overall in response to a request made by the Puritans at the Hampton Court Conference (1604). At the Savoy Conference (1661) the Puritans objected in vain to the first three questions, which touch on baptism. The idea that sponsors can make vicarious vows and promises reappears in the questions devoted directly to baptism (M, pp. 522-25).

41. M, pp. 542-612 (English and Latin). The connecting link between the Thirty-Nine Articles and Westminster was the Irish Articles (1615) of Archbishop Ussher, which incorporate the predestinarian Lambeth Articles (1595) and yet move away from Calvin on the sacraments. Irish Article 89, on baptism, excludes the instrumental language of the Thirty-Nine Articles, and Article 94, on the Lord's Supper, develops the sacramental symbolism into a parallelism of two "parts," one outward and the other inward. The texts are in M, pp. 525-26 (the Lambeth Articles, in Latin) and pp. 526-39 (the Irish Articles, in English).

42. The expression "Grace which is exhibited [*exhibetur*] in or by the Sacraments" (Art. 27, §3; cf. §5) means more than "displayed"; the word *conferred* seems to be used as a synonym. The Latin commonly means "to hold forth" or "to present." Note also the expressions "Efficacy of Baptism" (Art. 28, §5) and "the Grace promised is not only offered, but really exhibited and conferred" (§6).

43. Larger Catechism (hereafter abbreviated L.C.) in M, pp. 612-43 (Latin); *The School of Faith,* pp. 185-234 (English). Shorter Catechism (hereafter abbreviated S.C.) in M, pp. 643-52 (English).

44. On the other hand, the Shorter Catechism persists in ranking *prayer* with the Word and sacraments as a means of grace, as does the Larger Catechism — a rather questionable arrangement. And perhaps both catechisms say too much about Christ's "benefits," although this is not intended to distract attention from his person (cf. L.C., Qq. 165, 170, 176).

45. I have used the texts in Ns, pp. 82-117 (Scots and Latin). M, pp. 249-63, gives the Latin only.

46. *Das Schottische Bekenntnis: Reife Frucht reformierten Glaubens* (Witten/Ruhr: Luther-Verlag, 1960), p. 36. The fact that Danish Lutherans and Scottish Presbyterians practice intercommunion lends support to his thesis. But why speak of "conscious appropriation of Lutheran confessions" to account for Scottish emphasis on eating the body? Why not seek the model in the French or other Calvinistic confessions?

47. There is no space here to discuss the interesting Scottish catechisms, which were virtually superseded by the Westminster catechisms. I should judge that they cover the entire spectrum of eucharistic types, from pure Zwinglian (e.g., *The Little Catechism,* 1556) to high Calvinist (e.g., John Craig's Catechism, 1581). These documents can be found in *The School of Faith.*

48. S, 1: 456. Parallelism does not seem to have been a problem for Schaff, as it is in contemporary German discussions. That the distinction between parallelism and instrumentalism was not made a point of controversy within the confessions themselves is apparent from the Declaration of Thorn (1645), which uses both types of language (N, pp. 681-82).

49. Walter Kreck's claim that the eucharistic teaching of the Heidelberg Catechism cannot be adequately characterized as a "parallelism of two processes divorced from each other" may of course be granted if the qualifying phrase *(voneinander getrennten)* means simply "unrelated." See Kreck, "Das Ergebnis des Abendmahlsgesprächs in reformierter Sicht," in *Zur Lehre vom heiligen Abendmahl: Bericht über das Abendmahlsgespräch der evangelischen Kirche in Deutschland 1947-1957 und Erläuterungen seines Ergebnisses,* ed. G. Niemeier (Munich: Chr. Kaiser Verlag, 1961), p. 43. Cf. Paul Jacobs, *Theologie reformierter Bekenntnisschriften in Grundzügen* (Neukirchen: Neukirchener Verlag, 1959), p. 112. In a fascinating debate of mid-nineteenth-century America, John W. Nevin dismissed as absurd Charles Hodge's view that the Heidelberg Catechism was not purely Calvinistic in its doctrine of the sacraments. But the dividing lines were drawn differently by Hodge than by my own presentation in this chapter. See Brian A. Gerrish, *Tradition and the Modern World: Reformed Theology in the Nineteenth Century* (Chicago: University of Chicago Press, 1978), pp. 60-65. The same holds good for the Dutch discussions of the Heidelberg Catechism reported by G. P. Hartvelt in *Verum Corpus: Een studie over*

een centraal hoofdstuk uit de avondmaalsleer van Calvijn (Delft: W. D. Meinema, 1960), pp. 195-201. Here, as in the debate between Nevin and Hodge, the focal question is whether Calvin's distinctive idea of sacramental nourishment with the substance of Christ's body and blood — the "life-giving flesh" — is maintained in the Reformed creeds. My own question is about the nature of sacramental signs. But the questions are not unrelated. And the fact that others, starting from a different point of inquiry, have seen the Heidelberg Catechism as more the work of Bullinger's spirit than Calvin's lends some added weight to my argument.

50. On the contrast in sacramental theory between Thomas on the one side and Bonaventure and Scotus on the other, see, for instance, Reinhold Seeberg, *Text-Book of the History of Doctrines*, 2 vols., trans. Charles E. Hay (Grand Rapids: Baker Book, 1954), 2: 126-27. It is, of course, not my intention to deny that there are instructive differences between Calvin and Thomas: in sacramental theology, as in other dogmatic themes, Thomas invites the image of a causal sequence, in which the effect of the divine activity is imparted to, and resides in, its object, whereas Calvin thinks in terms of the ever-present activity of God. But Calvin's retention of instrumental language seems to me to be of some theological importance just because of these differences. The interesting question is whether such language is open to revision along what I take to be distinctively Reformation lines — that is, whether one can speak of an instrumentality of signs or symbols that are understood strictly as conveyers of meaning (of "the Word"). Naturally, this line of reflection has pre-Reformation roots that run all the way back to Augustine. It would be out of place to discuss them here. I should make clear, however, that there are scholars who in effect change the partnership I have proposed and hold that Calvin's sacramental theology not only resembles but was influenced by the Scotist tradition. A clear and succinct statement of this alleged Scotist affinity in Calvin will be found, for instance, in François Wendel, *Calvin: The Origins and Development of His Religious Thought*, trans. Philip Mairet (London: Collins, 1963), pp. 344-45. It is not to be denied that if we move beyond the confessional documents, traces of parallelism can be found in Calvin (e.g., in the *Institutes of the Christian Religion*, 4.14.17, 17.5). But I believe that I have sufficiently documented his instrumental language here and elsewhere to warrant the conclusion that it would be mistaken to sum up his eucharistic theology in parallelistic terms as Niesel, for instance, has done in *Calvins Lehre vom heiligen Abendmahl im Lichte seiner letzten Antwort an Westphal*, Forschungen zur Geschichte und Lehre des Protestantismus, vol. 3, 2d ed. (Munich: Chr. Kaiser Verlag, 1935), pp. 67-68.

51. See *Latin Works*, 2: 82-83.

52. *Latin Works*, 2: 113, 118.

53. Luther's *Wider die himmlischen Propheten, von den Bildern und Sakrament* (1525) will be found in the *Weimarer Ausgabe*, vol. 18, and (translated) in *Luther's Works*, vol. 40; see esp. W.A. 18.136-67, 196-98, 202-4; L.W., 40: 146-47, 207-8, 212-14. It must be admitted that the theological insight of these passages is not matched by a charitable spirit, and the same holds only a little less for Luther's earlier critique of the Roman sacrifice of the mass, *De captivitate Babylonica ecclesiae praeludium* (1520) (W.A. 6.519-21; L.W. 36: 46-48). With the first of the citations from the work against Carlstadt compare (and contrast!) Calvin, *Institutes*, 2.5.5.

A Theology of the Lord's Supper from the Perspective of the Reformed Tradition

Robert M. Shelton

That there has been in recent years a revival of interest in sacramental theology among Protestants in general and in the Reformed tradition in particular is not difficult to document. For some this has meant a "rediscovery" of the sacraments as a part of their religious tradition and a desire to understand the meaning of the sacraments for their Christian lives. For others the revived interest has resulted in more serious participation in the sacraments and a yearning to see them become a more integral part of the church's worship and faith.

Here in the United States, the churches of the Reformed tradition with which I am most familiar — the Presbyterian denominations — have demonstrated renewed interest in the sacraments in a number of ways. Study papers dealing with the nature and meaning of baptism and the Lord's Supper have been legion. Theological statements dealing with the two sacra-

ments have been formulated. Questions concerning the mode of baptism, the proper recipients of baptism, and the appropriateness of "renewal baptism" have all been addressed in various ways. With respect to the Lord's Supper, the frequency of celebration has increased significantly, some contending for weekly communion in keeping with the earliest position in the Reformed tradition. Other matters, such as who is to partake of the Lord's Supper (baptized children, unbaptized children, unbaptized adults, etc.) and in what context the sacrament of the Lord's Supper is to be celebrated, have been the topics of extensive discussion and debate. Most, if not all, Presbyterian denominations have produced official statements with regard to such concerns or are in the process of doing so.

Yet it is not clear that these denominational statements and such practices as more frequent communion have resulted in the sacraments having more meaning for the members of those denominations. Indeed, many in our churches today seem to know less about

Reprinted from *Reformed Liturgy and Music* 16 (Winter 1982): 3-11.

exactly what they are doing or why they are doing it than our grandparents did, and this primarily because we have not worked through any adequate theology of the sacraments. Interestingly enough, much of the discussion that bears on a theology of the sacraments is focused instead on issues that in the first instance are psychological or sociological in nature rather than issues that develop directly out of a theology of the sacraments. What is needed is a great deal of hard theological thinking with respect to the sacraments — their nature, meaning, and function in the community of faith. Moreover, this thinking needs to go on at the level of the local congregation, and it needs to take place among clergy and laity, involving as much as possible all members of our churches. This is not a plea for some sort of exercise in "pooling our ignorance" in the name of "doing theology"; rather, what is envisaged are serious discussions among Christian folk who have prepared themselves by reading and study to participate responsibly in theological discussions.

It is for the purpose of stimulating and furthering such discussions among congregations in the Reformed tradition that this paper is sent forth. Certainly it would be presumptuous for me to attempt to set forth a theology of the Lord's Supper and claim that it was some definitive word on the subject. I am convinced that no one person can do that, for the Reformed tradition, as many of us are learning, is broader, if not more eclectic, than is often thought. Moreover, even if a person were judged competent to produce such a definitive statement, I am convinced it would prove not very useful at this juncture. What is needed is more theological exploration among Christian people today in the whole area of sacramental theology so that we can discover what is at stake for the people of God in the sacraments and how we can best understand and communicate that in our day. We may discover, for example, that while many of our traditional approaches to the understanding of the sacraments are not wrong, they are not helpful for our times and in our situations. Others may have found such thoughts and approaches helpful and useful, but we do not. In this regard, a friend of mine has suggested that "many approaches in matters of theology are neither 'true' nor 'false,' rather they are 'helpful' or 'less helpful,' the degree of helpfulness depending on a certain community and situation."[1]

What follows then are notions that in my judgment are fundamental to a theology of the Lord's Supper from the perspective of the Reformed tradition. It is important to keep in mind in reflecting upon the sacraments that while some theological affirmations can be made for both baptism and the Lord's Supper, not everything can be said of one that can be said of the other. There are certainly similarities between the two because they are both sacraments, but there are also differences because they function differently vis-à-vis the community of faith. The theological ideas set forth here obtain particularly for the sacrament of the Lord's Supper.

I. THE REAL OR TRUE PRESENCE OF JESUS CHRIST

It is interesting to observe that while a belief in the real or true presence of Jesus Christ in the Lord's Supper is critical for all the traditional theological statements in the Reformed tradition regarding the sacrament, this fact is not at all well known among members of the Reformed Churches, including both clergy and laity. Many in the Reformed churches assume that the doctrine of the real presence of Jesus Christ in the Lord's Supper is uniquely Roman Catholic and that it has never had a place in their own tradition. (It is hoped many of us Protestants are getting over our prejudices against Roman Catholic theology, particularly with respect to the Roman Catholic doctrines of the church and the sacraments, and are open to learning much that the Roman Catholic tradition has to teach us.) Of course, there are important differences between the doctrine of the real presence as it is held, set forth, and developed in the Roman Catholic and Reformed traditions, but both hold that belief in the real presence of Jesus Christ in the Lord's Supper is fundamental. Furthermore, as the late Scottish theologian Donald M. Baillie once pointed out, if we are to take issue with our Roman Catholic friends with respect to their belief about the real presence, we surely do not want to do so "because they believe too much"; we must not be "content with a smaller, poorer belief."[2] What we should contend for is a belief as rich and meaningful and perhaps even more helpful and useful than theirs.

One cannot read John Calvin, the father of Reformed theology, without being struck, if not overwhelmed, by the prominence that the real or true presence of Jesus Christ has in his theological statements regarding the Lord's Supper. Frequently Calvin asserts that in the Lord's Supper Christ himself is exhibited or manifested. In his *Institutes* he writes:

> I say then, that in the mystery of the Supper, by the symbols of bread and wine, Christ, his body and his blood, are truly exhibited to us, that in them he fulfilled all obedience, in order to procure righteousness for us — first that we might become one body with him; and secondly, that being made partakers of his substance, we might feel the result of this fact in the participation of all his blessings.[3]

Moreover, the "matter" or substance of the Lord's Supper Calvin identifies as "Christ, with his death and resurrection" (*Inst.*, 4.17.11). In the sacred supper, "Christ offers himself to us with all his blessings" and "exhibits his presence in a special manner" (*Inst.*, 4.17.5, 30).

Nothing short of true and full communion with the crucified and risen Christ is what is at stake for Calvin in the sacrament. It is not too much to claim that he, like many theologians before him, believed that salvation is tied to participation in this sacrament. In addressing the issue of our salvation and the Lord's Supper, Calvin declares that "Christ is the only food of our soul, and therefore, our heavenly Father invites us to him, that, refreshed by communion with him, we may ever and anon gather new vigor until we reach the heavenly immortality" (*Inst.*, 4.17.1). Elsewhere in a similar vein he makes the point thus:

> [Christ] is offered by the promises, not that we may stop short at the sight or mere knowledge of him, but that we may enjoy true communion with him. And, indeed, I see not how any one can expect to have redemption and righteousness in the cross of Christ, and life in his death, without trusting first of all to true communion with Christ himself. (*Inst.*, 4.17.11)

Clearly in Calvin's view Christ offers himself to believers in the Lord's Supper, and in the Supper they find true communion with Jesus Christ. Christ's presence is authentically manifested and exhibited; Christ is truly present and is presented to us anew.

Those therefore who have read Calvin with care are not surprised to find that the Westminster Confession states that those who partake of the "visible elements in this sacrament" do "really and indeed . . . receive and feed upon Christ crucified, and all benefits of his death" and further that the "body and blood of Christ" are really, albeit spiritually, present (chap. 31, par. 7).

Such statements, and other similar material that could be cited, make it clear that any responsible discussion of the Lord's Supper in the Reformed tradition will have to take thought for what is at stake in the notion of the real presence of the crucified and risen Jesus Christ in this sacrament. The only issue, as

Calvin himself declares, has to do with the mode of Christ's presence in the sacrament. On this subject Calvin writes extensively, but he is more precise and much clearer when he is stating what he does not mean than what he does mean. Perhaps that will prove to be true for most of us too, but that does not relieve us of the need to attempt to articulate what we can affirm about the real presence of Christ. Nor is it either unimportant or insignificant to state what we do not mean.

For instance, Calvin states emphatically that he does not mean by the real presence of Christ that Jesus Christ is "locally present" in the sense that his body could be "taken into the hand, and chewed by the teeth and swallowed by the throat" (*Inst.*, 4.17.12). On the other hand, he writes, "they are greatly mistaken in imagining that there is no presence of the flesh of Christ in the Supper, unless it is placed in the bread" (*Inst.*, 4.17.31).

For Calvin it was important to affirm that while Christ truly offers himself to us in the Lord's Supper, "there is no necessity to bring Christ on the earth that he may be connected with us" (*Inst.*, 4.17.31) — that is, have true communion with us. To insist on such as that, Calvin contends, is to fail to understand a part of the work of the Holy Spirit. The Holy Spirit "truly unites things separated by space" (*Inst.*, 4.17.10) and makes possible by faith what our minds cannot completely comprehend — namely, that through the power and work of the Holy Spirit "that sacred communion of flesh and blood by which Christ transcends his life into us" (*Inst.*, 4.17.10) is attested and sealed in the Lord's Supper. In order to make this notion clearer to his readers, Calvin uses an interesting analogy. He likens the receiving of life and power and sustenance from the ascended Christ to the manner in which we receive energy, power, and life-sustaining force from the sun. Just as the sun remains far removed from us in space and is never locally present but still makes immediately available

to all on the earth its warmth, power, and energy, so Christ's body remains in heaven but the Spirit of Christ unites us to him and makes available to us, like the rays of the sun, everything that Christ has and is.

Calvin was quick to acknowledge that the mode of Christ's presence can never be grasped fully by our minds but can be apprehended only in faith. He himself wrote concerning his own understanding of the mode of Christ's presence in the sacrament that "should any one ask me as to the mode, I will not be ashamed to confess that it is too high a mystery either for my mind to comprehend or my words to express; and to speak more plainly, I rather feel than understand it" (*Inst.*, 4.17.32). What was of critical importance for Calvin, however, was that those of us who come to the table have no doubt that Christ bids us "take, eat, and drink his body and blood under the symbols of the bread and wine" (*Inst.*, 4.17.32) and that Christ truly gives and we receive.

Yet perhaps some of Calvin's most helpful thoughts with respect to the mode of Christ's presence are in the form of statements suggesting what is appropriate and what is inappropriate when thinking about the mode of Christ's presence in the Lord's Supper.

> The presence of Christ in the Supper we must hold to be such as neither affixes him to the element of bread, nor encloses him in bread, nor circumscribes him in any way (this would obviously detract from his celestial glory); and it must, moreover, be such as neither divests him of his just dimensions, nor dissevers him by differences of place, nor assigns to him a body of boundless dimensions diffused through heaven and earth. All these things are clearly repugnant to his true human nature. Let us never allow ourselves to lose sight of the two restrictions. First, let there be nothing derogatory to the heavenly glory of Christ. This happens whenever he is brought under the corruptible elements of this world, or is affixed to any earthly creatures. Secondly, let no property be assigned to his body inconsistent with his

human nature. This is done when it is either said to be infinite, or made to occupy a variety of places at the same time. But when these absurdities are discarded, I willingly admit anything which helps to express the true and substantial communion of the body and blood of the Lord. (*Inst.*, 4.17.19)

While not everything Calvin says about the mode of Christ's presence in the Lord's Supper may prove helpful, we could do much worse than be guided in our discussions about the mode of Christ's real presence in the Lord's Supper by his parameters.

What other helps do we have in exploring the meaning of the real presence of Jesus Christ in the Lord's Supper? Well, over the years perhaps the phrase most frequently used in the Reformed tradition has been "spiritual presence." The Westminster Confession emphatically declares that Christ is truly present in the elements and is truly received by those partaking, "yet not carnally and corporally, but spiritually" (chap. 31, par. 7). The insistence is that while Christ's presence is not physical in nature it is no less a real and vital presence, as if it were a physical presence.

But what does all this mean? What does "spiritual presence" connote? How can we speak about it in our day and so obtain even richer meaning for our participation in the sacrament? The aforementioned Scottish theologian Donald M. Baillie has suggested that one way to talk about the spiritual presence is in terms of the personal. Baillie asserts that God's presence can never be properly understood in terms of "local" or "spatial" presence, that this is indeed a very unhelpful approach to understanding his presence. More useful, in Baillie's view, is thinking of God's presence in terms of a personal relationship that can and does transcend time and space and is therefore a spiritual relationship.[4]

Baillie's writing in this whole area and the thoughts of others have led me at times to attempt to draw upon my own human experi-

ence to understand how a notion of the spiritual presence can be nonetheless real and vital for us when it is predicated upon a deep personal relationship. When my daughter was about three years old, she became quite ill with a serious viral respiratory infection. Her temperature rose rapidly and became so high that it brought on convulsions. She had to be hospitalized. In those days at that particular hospital you were not allowed to stay in the room with small children. My wife and I could see her only during visiting hours.

For several days her doctors were unsuccessful in finding any way to combat the virus, and she hovered between life and death before taking a turn for the better as eventually her own immune system successfully destroyed the infection.

During one of those days when she was on the critical list, I attended a ministers' meeting where there were present in the same room with me approximately twenty ministers, with whom I had a variety of relationships. As the meeting progressed, I was aware that my mind, my spirit, my entire self was preoccupied with Tammy and her condition. In those moments my daughter was far more "present" with me than all the ministers in that room. Her presence was indeed far more *real.* Why? Primarily because of the depth of the personal relationship I had with her.

Now, I am keenly aware how inappropriate it would be to say that the spiritual presence of Jesus Christ in the sacrament of the Lord's Supper is like that. No human analogy can adequately serve to show what the relationship of the risen Lord is to believers in the sacrament. But it may prove helpful in bringing us to some affirmations we can and want to make concerning the real presence of Jesus Christ in the Lord's Supper.

Those of us in the Reformed tradition are under strong obligation to honor the notion of the real presence of Christ in the Lord's Supper. How will we do that? Certainly not without some understanding of what has historically been at stake in such a theological belief. I suggest further that it is helpful to talk in terms of the personal relationship that makes possible a presence which is deep, besetting, and penetrating. Finally, we will never be able to speak of a "real presence" that no longer involves mystery. Rather we must affirm the mystery and celebrate it, knowing full well that to encounter Christ in any significant way is to be plunged into mystery that always transcends our complete understanding.

II. THE AFFINITY BETWEEN THE SYMBOLS AND THE REALITY

All the Reformed theological statements concerning the sacrament of the Lord's Supper of which I am aware take care to distinguish between the reality of the sacrament and the outward signs or symbols — the visible elements of bread and wine. The Westminster divines set it down in classical form, as follows:

> The outward elements in this sacrament, duly set apart to the uses ordained by Christ, have such relation to him crucified, as that truly, yet sacramentally only, they are sometimes called by the name of the things they represent, to wit, the body and blood of Christ; albeit, in substance and nature, they still remain truly, and only, bread and wine, as they were before. (Chap. 31, par. 5)

As one would imagine, the Confession is struggling to summarize Calvin's thoughts regarding the particular issue of the relation of the body and blood of Christ to the bread and wine in the sacrament. Moreover, it is obvious that something of what Calvin and Westminster are about is to refute the Roman Catholic doctrine of transubstantiation as it was at that time widely understood. But Calvin was interested in more than that, and we should be also. Cal-

vin was intent on making clear that the sacrament of the Lord's Supper consists of two things — the elements and the substance in the sacrament — each critical to the sacrament, but each always distinguishable from the other. So he asserted that "the sacred mystery of the supper consists of two things — the corporeal signs, which presented to the eye, represent invisible things in a manner adapted to our weak capacity, and the spiritual truth, which is at once figured and exhibited by the signs" (*Inst.*, 4.17.11). Calvin was very much influenced in his thinking by the writing of Augustine, whom he cites having repeatedly made the distinction between the sacrament and the matter of the sacrament. Following Augustine further, Calvin wants to make certain that what belongs to the sign or symbols is never transferred to the reality of the sacrament, which is Christ himself and his benefits, and furthermore that what belongs to the substance of the sacrament, what Calvin calls "spiritual truth," is never transferred to the symbols.

Yet it would not be fair to leave it at that. The symbols are never simply incidental to the sacrament so that we may regard them as being of no importance. They are never empty symbols and we are not permitted, as someone else has put it, to reduce the symbols to mere "memory aids." Westminster speaks of the elements being "sacramentally" the body and blood of Christ. This is language borrowed from Calvin, who declared that "the bread is called body in a sacramental manner" (*Inst.*, 4.17.20). Just what is meant by "sacramental manner" is never made completely clear, but Calvin does go on to assert that there is an affinity between that which is exhibited in the elements and the signs themselves, so that it is appropriate to give the name of that which is signified to the signs.

For Calvin the argument appears to be that Christ chose bread and wine to be the symbols of his body and blood, or his death and resurrection, which for Calvin constituted the substance of the sacrament. Therefore, when the bread and wine are held forth in the sacrament, Christ and his benefits are exhibited, because the reality is truly joined to the sign.

This issue is, of course, of paramount importance for Calvin's understanding of a sacrament, and it is likewise crucial for most theologians in the Reformed tradition when they write about the sacraments. "We must [never]," writes Calvin, "by setting too little value on the signs, dissever them from their meanings to which they are in some degree annexed" (*Inst.*, 4.17.5).

One way to state the matter is to say that the outward elements of bread and wine have received a new value by Christ's institution. They have become signs, or visible, external elements, which God has commanded Christians to use in order that they might be sure and confident of the promises offered in Christ. In such a manner Calvin argues that God makes the bow in the cloud as a sacrament to Noah and the tree in the garden as a sacrament to Adam and Eve. In a very interesting passage Calvin writes that "the tree was previously a tree, and the bow a bow; but when they were inscribed with the word of God, a new form was given to them: they began to be what they previously were not" (*Inst.*, 4.14.18). They became sacraments, and Calvin was certain that God also could have made the stars, the sun, the earth, and stones sacraments if God had inscribed God's word on them as in the case of the rainbow, which Calvin reminds us is a witness to this day of the covenant God made with Noah.

The same inscribing of God's word is true for the elements of bread and wine. So true is this that there is no reason to doubt that whenever we see the symbols of bread and wine we can be certain and be persuaded that the spiritual truth being signified is also present. It is not that it *could* be the case that the matter signified is exhibited or manifested, or that *sometimes* it is and *sometimes* it isn't, but that

for those who partake of the elements in faith, it is true that what is signified is present.

Yet the distinction between the substance of the sacrament and the symbols remains. For the nonbeliever, or the person devoid of faith, the symbols remain empty and useless elements. The affinity between the reality and the elements is not such that to partake of them under any circumstances is to receive the reality. The reality is apprehended by faith; without faith the signs remain mere signs for those who partake.

Clearly in the Reformed tradition the sacraments depend on the word for their efficacy. There is no sacrament without an antecedent promise is the way it is traditionally put. And certainly the sacraments do not offer us any grace or mercy not offered in the word. Indeed, it is not inconsistent with the Reformed tradition to speak of a sacrament as a visible word. But Calvin states that in comparison to the word, sacraments "have this peculiarity, that they represent promises to the life, as if painted in a picture" (*Inst.*, 4.14.5). The sacraments are a very graphic way of presenting God's promises, and because we human beings are corporeal, we need that which is material as a testimony or pledge of God's grace. In that sense the sacraments represent God's condescending to our need in the same way that God took on the form of a physical human being to make his grace real and active in our world and in our lives.

To explore the sacrament of the Lord's Supper from the viewpoint of the Reformed tradition involves us in thinking about the manner in which the reality exhibited in the bread and wine is affixed to the bread and wine. Certainly they remain distinguishable, and yet by virtue of God's own choice they are connected so that in a real sense we do not have one without the other.

How then will we talk of the affinity between the elements and the reality? Does Calvin's notion that the sacraments are like a painted picture help? Or can we say that in the elements of bread and wine we see, feel, taste, and touch the promises of God? Or is the often-used image of a seal helpful? Whatever approach we find helpful, the Reformed tradition insists that we take seriously the affinity between the two, but never to the extent that as partakers we stop with the physical, corporeal elements themselves, so as to venerate them; we must look at them and beyond them in order to be redeemed and shaped by the power of Jesus Christ made available to us in eating the bread and drinking the wine.

III. THE NOURISHING AND SUSTAINING OF THE CHRISTIAN LIFE

Those living the Christian life never outgrow certain essential needs. To count ourselves numbered among the people God is not to claim that we are sufficient unto ourselves or that all our needs have been met and we no longer need strength and power from beyond ourselves. Indeed, the opposite is true: membership in the Christian community has as one of its basic expressions the awareness that as human beings we are needy and always will be. We look to Christ to supply us with the strength, forgiveness, grace, and mercy we need to live lives as obedient disciples.

A friend of mine who is no longer active in any part of the Christian movement but who was baptized appropriately as an infant said once to me, "I simply could not go on living what I regarded as a hypocritical life. I was a baptized member of the church, but I was not able to live the life of a Christian as I understood the shape of that life. And I never seemed to change or grow in my life as a Christian."

Admittedly there are numerous factors to which one would need to give consideration in dealing with such a person, but I think that a proper approach to and participation in the Lord's Supper would be a key to rectifying what had gone wrong. And I wonder if those persons who do not place the sacrament of the Lord's Supper at the center of their lives are not in serious danger always of leading dissatisfying lives, because they fail to depend upon and be strengthened by Christ and his saving, redemptive power.

I certainly grant that Christians are nourished and sustained through hearing the word, and I recognize that there is nothing in the Lord's Supper added to what God offers in the word. Nonetheless I regard the Lord's Supper as a valuable and needed part of the Christian pilgrimage without which the Christian life can too easily become misshapen, if not abortive. Calvin is on target when he declares that our faith is "slender and weak" and needs to be "propped up on every side" lest it be shaken, waver, and even fall. He contends that the sacrament "does not so much confirm [God's] word as establish us in the faith of it" (*Inst.*, 4.14.3). It was that sort of experience of being established in his faith that was lacking for my friend, and it is also lacking for many others.

Can anything function more effectively in that regard than the Lord's Supper appropriately celebrated? There at the table we realize powerfully that Christ is our host and that he is for us. And there we realize that what we desperately need he offers — judgment, mercy, forgiveness, strength. There, too, we are keenly aware that the one who meets us at the holy place is the risen Lord who gave his life that we may have life. And there at the table we can hardly miss the truth that what the living Christ offers us is a gift freely given. We cannot earn it; we do not deserve it. It is a graphic portrayal of the gospel. It certainly possesses the power to sustain us and nourish us.

I know of no other place where all people stand on equal footing except at the table of the Lord. Everywhere else there are those who are more powerful than others, those who are more popular than others, those who are more evil than others. But at the communion table we are all the same: we are all beggars, standing with our hands open, needing to receive. We make no claims; we exhibit our need.

Calvin makes the point over and over that once God has received us, God does not abandon us but acts out the role of a kind and loving parent, "providing for our maintenance during the whole course of our lives" (*Inst.*, 4.17.1). Having begotten us through his word, Calvin asseverates, God "performs the office of a provident parent, in continually supplying the food by which he may sustain and preserve us" (*Inst.*, 4.17.1).

This provision contains much of what is indispensable in Calvin's view of the Lord's Supper. Throughout his writing about this sacrament he stresses repeatedly the idea of Jesus Christ as the bread of life, from John 6. And Christ as the bread of life offers himself anew to his people. "That Christ is the bread of life by which believers are nourished unto eternal life," Calvin opines, "no man is so utterly devoid of religion as not to acknowledge" (4.17.5). Furthermore, Calvin makes much of the fact that this nourishment of believers, or this feeding on Christ as the bread of life, is not simply a matter of believing in Christ or knowledge about Christ. No, it is a more sublime and more encompassing notion than that. Calvin's own words are too forceful to miss: "for as it is not the sight but the eating of bread that gives nourishment to the body, so the soul must partake of Christ truly and thoroughly, that by his energy it may grow up into spiritual life" (*Inst.*, 4.17.5). It is undeniable that Calvin gives special force and prominence to the flesh and blood of Christ in his theological position, arguing that we have no life unless we eat Christ's flesh and drink his blood. Yet, as we have already seen, this does not mean that the bread and wine *become* the body and blood of Christ.

However we may be inclined to agree or disagree with Calvin's way of putting the matter, and whether or not we find the approach of Calvin helpful or unhelpful, we still have to grant that the relationship he envisages between Christ and the believer in the sacrament of the Lord's Supper is a dynamic relationship whereby those who encounter Christ truly and thoroughly in this sacrament are nourished, empowered, strengthened, and assured. Can we be content to settle for less? Should we?

The Westminster Larger Catechism is certainly in keeping with Calvin's view when in providing an answer to the question "What is the Lord's Supper?" it suggests that those who communicate worthily "feed upon [Christ's] body and blood to their spiritual nourishment" (Q. 168). Here again the sacrament is viewed primarily as nourishment — nourishment necessary for our lives as Christians.

Most of us who stand within the Reformed tradition would be inclined to be critical of the Anglo-Catholic woman who is reported to have said that "she simply *lived* on her weekly communion and could not get on without it." But what is there in the Reformed tradition that calls that idea into question? Does not our tradition, carefully examined, instead point us in the direction of the very thing the woman was declaring — namely, that we need the nourishment and power that is made available by Christ in this sacrament.

It is here, I think, that we need to focus much of our attention in discussing the matter of the frequency of celebrating the Lord's Supper. Simply to pound the table and say that Calvin advocated weekly communion will hardly settle the issue; nor will it suffice to point out that it was the central act of Christian worship from the very beginning of the Christian movement. Rather, we need to understand the nature of Christian worship. Once it becomes clear to us that in the Lord's Supper Christ offers himself to us as our crucified and risen Lord in a manner that is necessary and useful for our Christian lives, as well as necessary and useful for what we are about in Christian worship, then it will be difficult to keep from affirming Calvin's position that it is appropriate that the Lord's Supper be "dispensed to the Church very frequently, *at least once a week*" (*Inst.*, 4.17.43).

P. T. Forsyth, in his useful book *The Church and the Sacraments,* strongly contends that in order for anything to be sacramental it must involve an act or action that is real. Consequently he maintains that in the Lord's Supper, as was true in his view also for the original Last Supper, it is not the elements that are most critical for the sacrament but the actions of breaking and pouring. His central point with respect to the Lord's Supper is that it has to do with an act, an action. Something happens! Something is done with power! Christ's great act of redemption and victorious resurrection is made available to the participants. He declares of the sacrament of the Lord's Supper that "it does not simply point to the thing signified, nor suggest it, but conveys it, has it within it, brings it with it, gives it, does something, is really sacramental."[5]

As we explore the theology of the Lord's Supper in our day, we in the Reformed family are surely constrained to think clear and useful thoughts about the nourishment and sustaining power integral to that sacrament. We can never settle for a theology of the Lord's Supper that views the sacrament as primarily a memorial or a commemoration. It is more. It is a gift from God that is active and powerful, a gift that when apprehended in faith helps preserve us and sustain us. It is not too much to state, as one in the Reformed tradition has put it, that "the sacrament of the Lord's Supper is indeed a means of grace, an instrument of salvation."[6]

IV. PERSONAL FAITH AND THE LORD'S SUPPER

Traditionally in the Reformed tradition, personal faith has been viewed as touching almost all aspects of the Lord's Supper as a sacrament. Calvin believed that every part of the sacrament ought to relate to faith. Certainly it has been seen as a determining factor in establishing a person's worthiness to partake of the sacrament. "That worthiness which is commanded by God," wrote Calvin, "consists especially in faith, which places all things in Christ, nothing in ourselves" (*Inst.*, 4.17.42). Worthiness can never be established by ourselves: "if we are to seek our worthiness from ourselves, it is all over with us; only despair and fatal ruin await us" (*Inst.*, 4.17.41). Instead, proper worthiness is arrived at by realizing that we never can be worthy in ourselves. Presenting ourselves to God and offering him our own sinfulness and weakness in order that God may make us worthy is the only worthiness we can bring to God. Our worthiness is found by putting our trust in God and relying in faith upon God's mercy. Without the faith, there can be no worthiness.

Moreover, it is not some "perfection of faith" that is called for; indeed, in Calvin's view, if perfection of faith were possible, it would render the sacrament superfluous. The sacrament was not instituted for those of perfect faith; it was instituted for the weak and needy, the imperfect and sinful. Such are the conditions of all human beings, and we can never rise above such imperfections. The sacrament is therefore for sinners and guilty human beings.

Personal faith then is the basis for establishing our worthiness. Somewhat paradoxically it is through this sacrament that personal faith is deepened and shaped. Previously it has been stated that this sacrament both presupposes personal faith and also assists and evokes faith. The sacrament contributes to our faith. It does this by presenting to us evidence of God's grace, a seal of God's promises.

Again, personal faith is an active force in apprehending the benefits conveyed in the sacrament. The sacraments do not confer God's gifts upon us, with no regard for personal faith.

Indeed they "confer nothing, and avail nothing, if not received in faith" (*Inst.,* 4.14.17). That which is offered by Christ in this sacrament is received in faith, and there is always a distinction to be made between Christ's offering grace and power and our receiving them. Receiving what Christ offers is determined by personal faith. Calvin put the matter this way: "I deny that men carry away more from the sacrament than they collect in the vessel of faith" (*Inst.,* 4.17.33). Certainly the unrepentant and those who fail to put their trust in God do not receive the grace offered to them, but through faith that which is offered is truly and fully received. And that personal faith, through which we receive, itself is a gift of God.

It seems to me that it would be profitable for us Presbyterians today to set the discussion of "admitting baptized children to the table" in the context of the issue of personal faith and the Lord's Supper. From the standpoint of sacramental theology it is hardly appropriate to ask "Can baptized children appropriately come to the table of our Lord?" There is no way for an answer to that question to be propounded from the position of sacramental theology. A question to which we can respond is "Can a person who possesses no personal faith appropriately come to the table?" The answer from the position of the Reformed tradition appears to be that it is inappropriate for such a person, be that person a baptized child or a baptized adult, to come to the Lord's table. But can a child have personal faith? Can a child trust God? I am convinced a child can. Is personal faith primarily a matter of advanced intellect or chronological age? I think not. It is rather a matter of one's intent, one's reliance, one's confidence, and one's hope. In all these matters children are hardly excluded and may prove in some sense exemplary. And it just may be that in the matter of faith children can lead us. It could be that in recognizing that children can have personal faith we will broaden and deepen our own understanding of faith.

V. THE CORPORATE NATURE OF THE SACRAMENT

Just a word about the corporate nature of the sacrament. In the Reformed tradition the sacrament of the Lord's Supper, as is true also for baptism, is a sacrament of the church. The sacrament is never merely a matter between the individual and God, even in the area of faith. The sacrament is in the first instance an act of faith on the part of the whole church, the corporate body of believers. We are never free to reduce the sacrament to our individual "experience" with Christ. Christ offers himself to us through the church, and as a part of that community of faith we partake and receive. The sacrament is never ours; it is one of the marks of the church. The sacrament does not exist apart from the church, and it is partly through the sacraments that the church is identified and defined.

In stressing the corporate nature of the Lord's Supper, the Reformed tradition has consistently emphasized the note of fellowship in the celebration of the sacrament. No private celebration is permitted. Only judicatories can authorize the observance of the Lord's Supper. The sacrament is administered ordinarily as a part of corporate worship, and no other setting is envisaged. The sacrament is offered to all believers. Actually, some argue that the primary contribution of the Reformed tradition to sacramental theology is the significance it assigns to the corporate nature of the event.

* * * * *

I have attempted to set forth what I regard as critical or fundamental notions that have strongly shaped the theology of the Lord's Supper in the Reformed tradition. What I have written certainly does not exhaust the Reformed view of the Lord's Supper. No one can do that.

It is my hope that in organizing the Reformed view of the Lord's Supper around these fundamental points I will motivate others to think through the issues related to the matters highlighted and to engage in extensive discussions about them. The tradition we are privileged to continue and to add to is a noble one indeed. It is a tradition that enables a person to attest to the following:

> Pious souls can derive great confidence and delight from [the Lord's Supper], as being a testimony that they form one body with Christ, so that everything which is his they may call their own. Hence it follows, that we can confidently assure ourselves, that eternal life, of which he himself is the heir, is ours, and that the kingdom of heaven, into which he has entered, can no more be taken from us than from him; on the other hand, that we cannot be condemned for our sins, from the guilt of which he absolves us, seeing he has been pleased that these should be imputed to himself as if they were his own. This is the wondrous exchange made by his boundless goodness. Having become with us the Son of Man, he has made us with himself sons of God. By his own descent to the earth he has prepared our ascent to heaven. Having received our mortality, he has bestowed on us his immortality. Having undertaken our weakness, he has made us strong in his strength. Having submitted to our poverty, he has transferred to us his riches. Having taken upon himself the burden of unrighteousness with which we were oppressed, he has clothed us with his righteousness. (*Inst.*, 4.17.2)

What a testimony the Lord's Supper is! It is unquestionably an event of grace!

NOTES

1. Dietrich Ritschl, *Concerning Christ* (Richmond, Tex.: Well-Spring Center, 1980), p. 8.

2. Baillie, *The Theology of the Sacraments* (New York: Scribner's, 1957), p. 93.

3. Calvin, *Institutes of the Christian Religion*, trans. Henry Beveridge (1854; reprint, Grand Rapids: William B. Eerdmans, 1957), 4.17.11. Subsequent references to this work will be made parenthetically in the text.

4. Baillie, *The Theology of the Sacraments*, pp. 97-99.

5. Forsyth, *The Church and the Sacraments* (London: Independent Press, 1947), p. 233.

6. Baillie, *The Theology of the Sacraments*, pp. 101-2.

LITURGICAL DIMENSIONS

The context in which the word and sacraments take shape in the church is worship. The Reformed tradition has emphasized worship as a supreme purpose for Christian existence and has highlighted the praise and glory of God as the "chief end" of humanity as a whole. The essays constituting the "Liturgical Dimensions" of these major themes in the Reformed tradition present varied facets of the church's understandings of what happens in Christian worship theologically and liturgically, how worship is integrally linked with justice, the nature of Christian preaching, and a theology of Christian marriage from a Reformed perspective as an important liturgical action of the church.

"The Reformed Liturgy" is the subject of a vigorous essay by Nicholas Wolterstorff in which he probes for the genius of the Reformed liturgy, its inner intention, and its contribution to "the mosaic of the liturgies of Christendom." Wolterstorff calls for renewed liturgical attention in Reformed churches and a recovery of the proper worship dimension of the liturgy, since "liturgy is divine and human *interaction*."

"Reflections on Liturgy and Worship in the Reformed Tradition" by LindaJo McKim provides a number of theses that briefly outline some of the key features of Reformed worship as they emerged from the thought of the early Reformed theologians. These reflections serve as a way of refocusing on Reformed roots of Christian worship. They also raise the important issue of how these emphases are being observed or neglected in contemporary Reformed churches.

The theological connection between "Worship and Justice" is captured in a second essay by Nicholas Wolterstorff. Because we are united with our fellow human beings in mirroring God's glory, we are to treat others with justice. In worship, we celebrate God's glory too. So worship and justice are justly joined as two ways of acknowledging God's glory. Put this way, it is clear that, as Wolterstorff points out, "to worship and not practice justice is to worship inauthentically . . . and to practice justice and not worship is to practice justice inauthentically." This perspective, grounded in Calvin's thought, joins together what has often been torn asunder.

As Calvin's definition of the church indicates, one of the essential motifs of the Reformed tradition has been its stress on preaching. Reformed preaching has always been regarded as the primary way by which the gospel of Jesus Christ is communicated to the world. In today's world, the place of preaching is often up for grabs and the question of why preachers preach is one with which all Christians must grapple. David Buttrick presents "A Brief Theology of Preaching" as a way of answering that question. He grounds preaching as a solidly theological activity: "preaching is the 'word of God' in that it participates in God's purpose, is initiated by Christ, and is supported by the spirit with community in the world." For the preacher this means that "year in, year out, preaching is terror and gladness."

One of the most frequent liturgical actions of the church is the celebration of Christian marriage. Since it is so central and so attended by ceremony, it is important to reflect on the theological grounding of this liturgical act. In "Toward a Theology of Christian Marriage," Shirley Guthrie provides a definition of Christian marriage and comments on it. He concludes with "a reminder and warning" that sets the theology of marriage within the Christian view of humanity itself.

Week in and week out for Reformed Christians, some of the most visible and perhaps most immediately meaningful aspects of their tradition are its liturgical dimensions. These worship and liturgical actions are rooted in the church's theology, and, conversely, the church's theology emerges from its worship and liturgical practices. In this interplay and mutual relationship, both the church's worship and theology are enriched.

The Reformed Liturgy

Nicholas Wolterstorff

What is the genius of the Reformed liturgy? What is its inner intention? What does it contribute to the mosaic of the liturgies of Christendom?

My question assumes that the Reformed liturgy does have a genius, a coherent controlling idea, an inner intention. More precisely, I assume that the Reformed liturgy has a coherent controlling idea *if* it remains in significant continuity with the liturgical theology and practice of the original Swiss Reformers. For I grant that in the course of history the genius has often been obscured and even lost.

There are those who disagree with my assumption. They see in Reformed liturgy no "genius" at all but only an incoherent and misguided falling away from the genius of the Roman Catholic liturgy. They see in the liturgical reconstructions of the Swiss Reformers only a slicing out from the Roman Mass of what was judged objectionable, leaving behind a graveyard of bleached liturgical bones. They do not discern the enfleshing of a new vision of the nature of the church and of what it does and ought to do in its gatherings.

To inquire into the genius of the Reformed liturgy is thus to enter a polemic in which the very existence of the object of inquiry is under dispute. No one questions that the Orthodox liturgy has a genius. Few question that the Roman Catholic liturgy has its own genius. Probably most would accord the same dignity to the Lutheran and Anglican liturgies. But the Reformed liturgy raises doubts. I shall of course do what I can to quiet those doubts.

Each liturgy with a genius not only has its own peculiar glories but its own peculiar failings and dangers. One of the peculiar dangers of the Reformed liturgy is that it tempts its practitioners into indifference toward reflection on liturgy — even into aversion. Seminaries in the tradition spend months and years teaching their students the theory and practice of preaching; they dispose of liturgy in a week or so. Congregations in the tradition institute elaborate educational schemes for teaching their members about the Scriptures, about theology, about social issues, about missions; liturgy they are more likely than not to overlook entirely. And those in the tradition who do become liturgical scholars must practice their scholarship on the side. The pattern is too per-

273

vasive to be accidental, especially in view of the fact that the Reformed tradition neglects neither the practice of liturgy nor the pursuit of learning. Though it values liturgy and learning, it places no value on liturgical learning. Only when we have uncovered the genius of Reformed liturgy will we be in a position to understand this strange obliviousness, this perplexing aversion.

A consequence to be addressed immediately is that members of the Reformed tradition are unlikely to read this or any other essay on liturgy — indeed, less likely to read this one. A discussion of the Orthodox liturgy might be tempting to satisfy one's taste for the exotic. One on the Roman liturgy might be appealing to satisfy one's taste for the controversial; one remembers yet the Catholic neighbor who in distress remarked that when English came in, all the mystery went out. But a discussion of the Reformed liturgy will seem — well, like the endeavor of some Romanizer. A Reformed person will often not even think of the Reformed churches as having liturgy. The reason for that lies partly in the word *liturgy* itself: it has little currency in the Reformed tradition. So a word should be said about that at once.

As almost every book on liturgy points out, the English word "liturgy" is simply the transliteration of the Greek word λειτουργία *(leitourgia)*. In classical Greek the word was used to refer to a service performed by an individual for the benefit of the public, usually at his own expense.[1] For example, if a warship had to be outfitted, sometimes, instead of taxing the citizenry as a whole, officials invited a wealthy individual to do the outfitting as a personal contribution to the public. Such a public service was a liturgy, and the person performing it, a liturgete *(leitourgos)*.

Etymologically the word *leitourgia* comes from two Greek words, *leitos* and *ergon,* meaning, respectively, "of the people" and "action." In numerous books on liturgy it is said, accordingly, that the word originally meant *action of the people.* And often nowadays an argument for more participation of the people in the church's liturgy is based on this claim. It is said that for something to be liturgy, it must be action of the people and not action of a few priests or pastors. But the word *leitourgia* never did mean action of the people. It meant action *for the benefit of* the people. A liturgy was a type of public service.

In the Septuagint translation of the Old Testament, the word *leitourgia* was regularly borrowed from its Greek civic use and applied, by metaphorical extension, to the kind of service rendered by the priests in the temple.[2] Apparently this was the best that could be done with the language of the day in translating the cultic language of the Old Testament into Greek. This metaphorical extension was continued in rabbinic usage of New Testament times and in the New Testament itself.[3] For example, in Luke 1:23 we read of the priest Zechariah that "when his time of liturgy was ended, he went to his home" (cf. Heb. 9:21; 10:11).

It is only a small step from speaking of the cultic acts of the temple priest as (his) liturgy to speaking of what transpires in the Christian assemblies as liturgy, or service. Eventually such usage became common, and it is in that sense that I shall be using the word. Whether the New Testament itself ever uses the word in this particular sense is not entirely clear, however. Possibly that is the sense in which it is used in Acts 13:2, where it is said of the people in the church at Antioch that "they were performing their liturgy to the Lord and fasting." More customary in the New Testament is the extension of the usage of the word to one and another kind of *noncultic* service rendered by someone to someone else. In Philippians 2:30, for example, we hear of the liturgy of the Philippians to Paul; in Hebrews 8:6, of the liturgy of Christ; and in 2 Corinthians 9:12 the financial gift of the Corinthians to other churches is described as "the ministry of this liturgy."

We in the Reformed churches regularly speak of what transpires in our assemblies as a *service*. We ask when the service will begin, how long it will take, and so forth. In place of the word *service* we could use the word *liturgy* and mean exactly the same thing. The Reformed liturgy is the Reformed service. So of course the Reformed churches have liturgy. The Reformed liturgy is what takes place in the Reformed assemblies, understood as a service to someone by someone. Who is served, and who serves, will eventually become clear.

Sometimes it is said that what goes on in the gatherings of certain Christians is *more* liturgical than what goes on in those of others. The gatherings of Catholics, Orthodox, Lutherans, and Anglicans are said to be more liturgical than those of Baptists and Plymouth Brethren, with those of the Reformed somewhere in between. When *liturgical* is used in this sense, it refers to ceremonies, symbols, fixed responses of the people, and the like. There is nothing wrong with this use of the word, but it is not the sense in which I shall be using it, nor is it the sense in which it is used in contemporary liturgical scholarship. A liturgy is a "divine service." And what transpires when Plymouth Brethren assemble is as much a divine service as what transpires when Orthodox assemble.

The question remains: Why bother? Why bother to reflect on the Reformed liturgy? Specifically, why should *Reformed* people bother to reflect on their "divine services"? I have already hinted that a full answer to this question presupposes a grasp of the genius of the Reformed liturgy. But once it is seen that the Reformed liturgy is just the Reformed church service, then already the propriety of liturgical reflection begins to show itself. In our age, the liturgy in all Reformed congregations has undergone striking changes. Many people have the sense of losing their way; others want yet more radical changes. Surely the only way to find our path in this situation is to reflect

seriously on what we are doing, and what we should be doing, in liturgy. There is another reason: over and over, the person studying the liturgy experiences illumination. "So *that* is what I was doing all these years!" "So *that* is why we do that!" "So *that* is where that comes from!" Liturgical reflection enhances the church's self-understanding.

I have been reflecting on one feature of the situation in which people from the Reformed tradition find themselves as they discuss liturgy: their own tradition is overwhelmingly indifferent to such discussions. Not indifferent to liturgy, let's be clear: indifferent to *discussion* of liturgy. Before we plunge into our topic, I want to call attention to one more feature of the situation in which we find ourselves — this, unlike the other, a relatively new feature.

During the last quarter century or so a most remarkable thing has happened: all the mainline traditions of Christendom, with the exception of the Orthodox and the Anabaptist, have engaged in liturgical reform. And even more striking: all the liturgies recommended are virtually identical in structure. Indeed, they are closely similar even in content. There is an emerging liturgical coalescence. If one laid side-by-side the new Catholic, Presbyterian, Reformed, Lutheran, Anglican, Methodist, and other liturgies, the coalescence would be obvious and striking. Once again we can walk into each other's churches and feel at home. The unity of the church has been made concrete: it is there before our eyes and ears.

The person who has not participated in this development will quite naturally suspect that liturgical scholars from these various traditions have been looking over each other's shoulders and copying what they saw. There has been some of that. But the basic dynamic of coalescence has not been that at all. In our century we have once again become acquainted with the liturgy of the church around A.D. 200 — after it had settled in and before it had become encrusted. All the liturgical reform commissions have felt compelled to return to the structure of the liturgy of that time, enriched by a few additions from later Catholicism and later Protestantism. In my judgment we must regard this emergent coalescence as nothing less than the work of the Spirit.

Not only has coalescence emerged around liturgical practice. After decades of discussion, a remarkable and gratifying convergence has also emerged in liturgical *theology,* represented most recently by the document of the World Council of Churches entitled *Baptism, Eucharist and Ministry (BEM).* To anyone with a knowledge of the various traditions of liturgical reflection who scrutinizes the eucharistic section of this document, it will be evident that this is not a statement of one tradition to which the others have acquiesced; it is a statement to which the various traditions have all contributed their insights. The road ahead has proved to be not the road to Geneva, nor to Canterbury, nor to Augsburg, nor to Rome, nor to Constantinople but to a new city under construction. On that road, those from Constantinople come bearing their gifts and are met by those from Rome bearing theirs, by those from Geneva bearing theirs, and so on.

As we in the Reformed tradition today reflect on our liturgy, we must do so in the context of a vivid awareness of these ecumenical developments to which we ourselves have contributed. We must do so in the awareness of convergence and coalescence in liturgical theory and practice. Of course the degree of such must not be exaggerated. Though the coalescence in official liturgies is truly remarkable, it is not the custom of Reformed and Presbyterian denominations to *order* their congregations to institute new liturgies. Accordingly, the coalescence is more evident at top official levels than in the actual practice of congregations. Furthermore, at some points the convergence around the *BEM* document was achieved by deciding that certain controversial

topics could appropriately be avoided, and at others, by choosing language to which all could agree while interpreting it differently.

Nonetheless the degree of coming together is remarkable and gratifying. And it raises the question of whether the day for discussions about the genius of the Reformed liturgy is not over. Historians can still inquire into the genius of one and another liturgical tradition. But for us, whose eye is on shaping practice, is it not time to inquire into the genius of the *Christian* liturgy and drop all parochial inquiries? If we are genuinely to receive the work of the Spirit among us over the last twenty-five years, is it not time to put behind us all these divergent traditions of liturgical practice and theology and together participate in the liturgy of the one holy catholic church?

The divergence of our liturgical traditions was, of course, an enormous obstacle that had to be overcome if convergence was to come about. These traditions emerged from the breakup of unity and, once formed, served as strong barriers to its recovery. Yet it is evident to anyone following the recent developments that these divergent traditions have not only served the negative function of being obstacles but also the positive function of enriching the whole church. Especially after Vatican II, we who are Reformed find ourselves once again able to enter sympathetically into the liturgical practice and theology of the Roman Church; much of what we find there enriches us. Many Catholics have made it clear that they experience the same thing in our churches. We have together discovered that each of our traditions in its odyssey through history has learned and preserved something of value that the other never knew, or that it forgot. *Forgetfulness* of our traditions would have been an insuperable obstacle to attaining the point at which we have now arrived. But are we not now beyond all that? Is it not time to speak just of the *Christian* liturgy?

I think not. My reason is twofold. For one thing, the convergence is not yet complete.

Baptism, Eucharist and Ministry is indeed a remarkable achievement — or better, a remarkable gift of the Spirit. Yet, as I have already remarked, the convergence that it undeniably represents was achieved at some points by avoiding disagreements. I think this means that the interaction of traditions from which new and better insights emerge is not yet finished. The word that the Reformed tradition wishes to deliver to the others has not yet been completely spoken, nor heard; no doubt the word that the other traditions wish to deliver to the Reformed has also not yet been completely spoken, nor heard.

I have a second reason as well. I remarked that if one laid side-by-side the new liturgies, the coalescence of structure and even of content would be striking. Yet if one looked just a bit longer at this array of new liturgies, one would also shortly sense that the ecumenical structure has acquired, in each tradition, a somewhat different character. The actual liturgy of a given denomination today is the outcome of a subtle interplay between its own liturgical tradition and the dynamic of ecumenical catholicity. The question is whether that is legitimate. As we who are Reformed search for the path ahead, is it legitimate for us to allow the genius of our own tradition to interact with the dynamics of catholicity?

I myself can come to no other conclusion than that it is. For one thing, I have an abhorrence of flat undifferentiated uniformity. But perhaps that is only an aesthetic preference with no more importance than that. More important is that until the great traditions of Christendom wither away, we will each come to the liturgy with our identity determined by one of these traditions. The gospel does not ask of us that that identity be sacrificed. It asks that it be purified, even transcended and relativized, but not suppressed. The Corinthian church did things differently from the Jerusalem church. We have all come to acknowledge that the liturgy must not suppress but rather express our

ethnic identities. Must our religious identities be treated differently? Must not a liturgy be pastoral as well as catholic?

So there remains a place for two sorts of liturgical discussions: those that probe the genius of one and another liturgical tradition in the awareness of an emerging liturgical convergence, and those that probe the genius of the Christian liturgy in the light of divergent liturgical traditions.

* * * * *

The Reformed liturgy is the Reformed service. And the service — what is that? Fundamentally, a sequence of actions. Any liturgy whatever is a sequence of actions. The visual, architectural, and auditory setting within which a liturgy occurs may well have liturgical *significance*, but the liturgy itself is a sequence of *things done*. All the historical disputes about liturgy are disputes over the actions to be performed, over the sequence in which they are to be performed, and over the interpretation of the actions and the sequence.

The Swiss Reformers had a new vision of what is to be done in the liturgy and how it is to be understood. They put their vision into practice, and in doing so brought about the most radical liturgical reform that the Christian church has ever known. The liturgical reform of Vatican II is an immensely important, but distant, second.

I stress the fact that it was a reform. The Reformers saw it as a reform. They did not see themselves as beginning over. And of course they did not reform everything. This means that there is no hope of truly understanding Reformed liturgy without knowing something of the liturgy it sought to reform. All too often Protestants regard ancient and medieval Christianity as not belonging to them. That would be true only if Protestantism had really begun over, shucking off all influence except that of the Bible itself. The truth is that the liturgy of the medieval and of the ancient church is as much our parentage as it is the parentage of the Catholic and the Orthodox. I shall of course have to be ruthlessly selective in describing the liturgy the Reformers reformed.

The earliest indication we have of a complete Christian liturgy comes to us from Justin the Martyr, apparently as a description of the liturgy of Rome around A.D. 150. We have no reason to think that the liturgy was substantially different elsewhere. "On the day named after the sun," says Justin, "all who live in city or countryside assemble."[4] The service opened with someone reading the writings of the apostles and prophets "for as long as time permits." There was, thus, no "opening service" and no "penitential rite" — or at least none significant enough for Justin to mention; the service began straightaway with the reading of Scripture. So far as we can tell, this is how things continued to go in most places for a couple of centuries. When the reading was finished, the "presider" addressed the people in a sermon or homily, exhorting them "to imitate the splendid things" they had heard.

The people's intercessory prayers followed upon this "service of the Word." Describing a liturgy that began with baptism, Justin says, "we offer prayers in common for ourselves, for him who has just been enlightened, and for all men everywhere." As throughout the early church, the people stood for their prayers, presumably with hands raised, and responded with "Amen."

After the prayers the people greeted each other with a kiss. Following this, they celebrated the eucharist, or Lord's Supper. Bread and a cup of wine mixed with water were brought to the presider. The presider took them and offered an extemporaneous prayer "glorifying the Father of the universe through the name of the Son and of the Holy Spirit," uttering "a lengthy thanksgiving (eucharist) because the Father has judged us worthy of these gifts." After the people had spoken their assent with an "Amen," the gifts over which thanksgiving had been spoken were distributed by the deacons.

For the purposes of our discussion, a number of things are worth remarking about this early liturgy — keeping in mind that there may well have been minor elements of the service that Justin neglected to mention. Perhaps the most important thing to note is that the service had two main parts, the service of the word, consisting of the reading of Scripture and a sermon, and the service of the eucharist, with the intercessory prayers forming a bridge between the two. Since I shall want to make several references to this structure of word/sacrament, it will be convenient to call it *the enduring structure.* I call it that because, so far as we know, the main Sunday service of the Christian church in all times and places (except for certain sects) invariably included these two components until in Holy Week in 1525 in his church in Zurich, Zwingli pulled them apart and in place of one service with two main high points instituted two distinct services, a Scripture-sermon service and a Lord's Supper service, with the latter held just four times a year. It must be granted that in the intervening years the service of the word was often truncated by the omission of the sermon. It must also be granted that the people often did not participate in the enduring structure: they did not receive the gifts of bread and wine. And since the language of the whole liturgy was often in a tongue they did not understand, they did not participate in the prayers and did not understand the Scriptures. These are important points: what the people actually did and understood did not exhibit the enduring structure. Yet the other point is just as important: from Justin to Zwingli, the enduring structure was always objectively there, even if only in what the clergy did.

Equally important in the liturgy described by Justin was that there was as yet no significant "divide" between clergy and people.

There was, indeed, an appointed presider. But the extent to which Justin refers to the *people* as the subject or object of the actions is striking: *we* pray, *we* eat, *we* greet one another, *we* say "Amen," the presider exhorts *us*.

And how was the eucharist understood? Well, as the Greek word itself suggests (*eucharisteo* = to give thanks), the overarching context was that of thanksgiving. The eucharist was an act of *thanksgiving* for creation and redemption.[5] But it was also a *doing in memorial:* in obedience to Christ's command, the eucharist was performed as a memorial, remembrance, *anamnesis,* of Christ's passion (*First Apology,* 66). "The bread which our Christ gave us," says Justin, "we offer in remembrance of the body which he assumed for the sake of those who believe in him," and "the cup which he taught us to offer in the Eucharist" we give "in commemoration of his blood" (*First Apology,* 70).[6] It was thirdly an act of *fellowship:* everyone shared in the gifts, even those absent to whom the deacons carried the bread and wine. And fourthly, it was understood as a *sacrifice,* in fulfillment of Malachi's prophecy of the pure sacrifice of the Gentiles (*Dialogue with Trypho* 41; Mal. 1:10-12).

Giving thanks, doing in memorial, fellowshiping, presenting an offering — all these are elements of our devotion addressed to God. But Justin also saw the eucharist as a gracious act of God toward us. We are nourished and transformed by the eating and drinking, for "through the word of prayer that comes from him, the food over which the eucharist has been spoken becomes the flesh and blood of the incarnate Jesus" (*First Apology,* 66).[7]

We do not know the contents of the prayer offered over the gifts in the churches Justin knew, other than that it was an extemporaneous prayer of thanksgiving for creation and redemption. By great good fortune, however, we have a model for such a prayer from about sixty-five years later, set down for us by Hippolytus, bishop in the church of Rome. Since this prayer has been enormously influential on twentieth-century liturgical renewal, it is worth taking a moment to look at it.[8]

The prayer is introduced with the ancient dialogue between presider and people:

— The Lord be with you!
    And with your spirit!

— Let us lift up our hearts.
    They are turned to the Lord.

— Let us give thanks to the Lord!
    It is right and just!

Then comes the expression of thanks for creation and redemption, very christologically oriented in Hippolytus's model:

We give you thanks, O God,
    through your beloved Child Jesus Christ,
    whom you have sent us in the last days
    as Savior, Redeemer, and Messenger of
        your will.
He is your Word, inseparable from you,
    through whom you have created everything
    and in whom you find your delight.

You sent him from heaven
    into the womb of a Virgin.
He was conceived and became flesh,
    he manifested himself as your Son,
    born of the Spirit and the Virgin.

He did your will,
    and, to win for you a holy people,
    he stretched out his hands in suffering
    to rescue from suffering
    those who believe in you.

Following this comes the account of the institution of the eucharist at Christ's last supper:

When he was about to surrender himself to
        voluntary suffering
    in order to destroy death,
    to break the devil's chains,

to tread hell underfoot,
to pour out his light upon the just,
to establish the covenant
and manifest his resurrection,
he took bread,
he gave you thanks and said:
"Take, eat, this is my body
which is poured out for you."
In like manner for the cup, he said:
"This is my blood
which is poured out for you.
When you do this,
do [it] in memory of me."

Immediately following these words of institution came the *anamnesis* — the declaration that the people were indeed doing this as a memorial in obedience to Christ's command:

Remembering therefore your death
and your resurrection,
we offer you the bread and the wine,
we thank you for having judged us worthy
to stand before you and serve you.

Then came what was eventually called the *epiclesis* — a call for the Spirit to make the offering effective:

And we pray you to send your Holy Spirit
on the offering of your holy Church,
to bring together in unity
all those who receive it.
May they be filled with the Holy Spirit
who strengthens their faith in the truth.
May we be able thus to praise and glorify
    you
through your child Jesus Christ.

The prayer closed with a doxology:

Through him glory to you and honor,
to the Father and the Son, with the Holy
    Spirit,
in your holy Church,
now and for ever and ever!
Amen.

Here, in Justin and Hippolytus, we have what Lucien Deiss has appropriately called the "springtime of the liturgy."

The liturgy as the Reformers knew it in central Europe of the early sixteenth century was profoundly different. The enduring structure was still there — in what the priests did. The basic structure of the eucharistic prayer of Hippolytus was still there — discernible if one knew beforehand what to look for. But across the intervening centuries the liturgy as a whole had been radically altered.

The difference in the *phenomena* of the liturgy would have struck one first: how it looked, how it sounded, how it was done was all different. The people no longer spoke; priests and choir alone voiced any words. The people no longer understood what the presider said: Latin endured in the liturgy when the people understood not a word of it. The prayers were recited inaudibly by the priest, whereas in Justin's church the prayers were very much "of the people." The people communicated only infrequently, whereas in Justin's church the people as a whole regularly received the bread and wine. To these and many other such phenomena the Reformers reacted intensely. But the documents of the day make it clear that they did not see these phenomena as a random clutter of corruptions. They saw them as the expression of a coherent controlling idea. It was that controlling idea that caught the brunt of their fire.[9]

What was that idea? What was that inner intention that shaped the whole? It's important to realize, in the first place, that by the time of the Reformation almost all the emphasis of the liturgy had been shifted over to its eucharistic component. Justin's liturgy was nicely balanced between word and sacrament. It was a bi-focal service. But gradually the liturgy was tilted, so that already in the early Middle Ages the first half of the liturgy had lost its independent significance and was understood merely as preparation for the eucharist. Aquinas says, for example, that "the celebration of this mystery" of the eucharist is preceded by a certain preparation "in order that we may perform worthily that which follows after" (*Summa Theologica*, III, Q. 83, art. 4, resp.).[10] And then, under the heading of *preparation*, he discusses everything that precedes "the celebration of the mystery." Reformed and Presbyterian liturgists regularly joke about their clerical colleagues who speak of what precedes the sermon as "preliminaries." In a wholly similar manner, many Catholic writers to this day speak of what precedes the eucharist in the liturgy as the *fore*-mass.

How, then, was the eucharist understood and experienced? I suggest that we can understand the medieval liturgy only if we turn to the distinction between clergy and laity. Thereby hangs a tale, of course — the tale of the clericalization of the church. The most obvious feature of this was the introduction of church offices with hierarchical differentiations of authority among them and with the laity at the bottom. But that was only a surface manifestation of the deep dynamics. Gradually the idea developed that the liturgy is something the clergy do on behalf of the people. Of course they also make the liturgy *available* to the people in one way and another. But God has assigned the performance of the liturgy to the clergy; this is their work. As the great Catholic liturgical scholar J. A. Jungmann puts it, "the people were religious, and they came to the services. Even when they were present, however, the liturgy was for the clergy. . . . The role of the laity was to all intents and purposes that of a spectator."[11]

At the heart of what God has assigned to the clergy is the celebration of the sacraments — preeminently, the sacrament of the eucharist. How, then, were the sacraments understood? What was meant when it was said of the eucharist that it was a *sacrament*? Gradually consensus emerged around the idea that a sacrament is something that both symbolizes and conveys a gift of divine grace. It effects

the grace that it signifies. We read in the *Doctrine of the Seven Sacraments* of the Council of Florence (1438-45), for example, that the sacraments of the Old Testament "did not cause grace, but foreshadowed the grace that was to be bestowed solely through the passion of Christ. Our sacraments, however, not only contain grace, but also confer it on those who receive them worthily."[12]

If we are to grasp the sacramental theology of the medievals, we must in turn understand their notion of *grace*. Probably they never lost sight of the New Testament notion of grace as the graciousness of God toward us in Jesus Christ. Yet that way of thinking was far from prominent. Grace came to be thought of less as the attitude of God toward us and more as something which gets "infused" into the person. Aquinas, for example, speaks of grace as a "quality of the soul" of the human person. (*ST*, II/I, Q. 110, arts. 2-4) This quality of soul is the source of the spiritual life. It is the wellspring of the theological virtues of faith, hope, and charity, which in turn are the source of meritorious works. In a word, grace "is the principle of meritorious works through the medium of virtues" (*ST*, II/I, 110, art. 4, ad 1).[13] The spiritual life that has been weakened and ravaged by sin is restored and strengthened by an infusion of grace. And this infusion of grace is caused by the sacraments when they are received by someone who does not consciously place mortal sin in the way of their reception.

Aquinas firmly insists that we must understand him literally when he says that *the sacraments* cause grace. It is not God who directly causes the grace. God does not use the occasion or the means of the reception of bread and wine to infuse grace; rather, by virtue of God's original institution of the sacrament, the bread and the wine *themselves* cause the infusion of grace: they now have these new causal powers, in addition to their ordinary power of nourishing. God is content to remain in the background. Some people contend, says Aquinas, that the sacraments "are the cause of grace not by their own operation, but in so far as God causes grace in the soul when the sacraments are employed." But if that were so, he says, they would be mere signs of grace, not also instrumental causes thereof. "The sacraments of the New Law cause grace: for they are instituted by God to be employed for the purpose of causing grace" (*ST*, III, Q. 62, art. 1, resp.; see also Q. 62, art. 4, resp.). Naturally the sacraments differ from each other somewhat as to the specific type of grace bestowed. The eucharist bestows the forgiveness of sins[14] and the strengthening of faith, hope, and charity — all this in proportion to the "devotion and fervor" of the person involved (see *ST*, III, Q. 62, art. 5; Q. 64, arts. 1, 5; Q. 79, arts. 3-8).

Of course the sacraments' infusion of grace into the human being occurs only under certain conditions. The medieval church uniformly insisted that those conditions do not include the piety of the priest. The sacraments are not effective *ex opere operantis*, through the activity of the performer; they are effective *ex opere operato*, through the deed performed. The sacrament infuses grace into the soul if it is actually performed and if the recipient does not interpose the obstacle of consciously being in mortal sin.[15] Under normal conditions the sacraments can be performed only by duly ordained persons. But whether or not the ordained person actually performs the sacrament depends not on his personal piety but on whether he has the *intention* "of doing what the church does" — along with whether the requisite *matter* and the requisite *form* (words) are present. "If any one of these is lacking," said the Council of Florence, "the sacrament is not effected."[16]

To us in the Reformed tradition, and to those in the Orthodox, it is surprising that the medievals, when reflecting on what was needed for the effective working of the sacraments, did not at once focus attention on the active presence of the Spirit.[17] In fact they did

not. They became immersed in questions of validity. Juridical issues began to enter deep into the life of the church, and the *epiclesis* of the Spirit, so prominent in the eucharistic prayer of Hippolytus, disappeared from the mass.

No doubt it was in good measure the resistance to Pelagianism that determined the insistence that the sacraments are effective by virtue of the thing done rather than the person doing it. Yet as that fine contemporary Catholic scholar Godfrey Diekmann remarks,

> by the time of the Reformation, the thoroughly sound principle that sacraments effect what they signify . . . had fallen victim, certainly in the popular understanding, to the very pelagianism which it had tried to overcome. Sacraments had come to mean almost automatic dispensers of grace. They were viewed as *things*, valuable and powerful more or less in their own right, as actions to be performed by man guaranteeing him salvation. The line between this and superstition or magic was thin indeed. A good and needed principle had become so stressed that it had largely lost its roots and matrix. It had clearly become too isolated from its intrinsic and essential relation to *faith* so that, until quite recently — I would say until twenty years ago — it was a commonplace to speak of Catholics believing that they were saved by sacraments, whereas Protestants held that man was saved by faith.[18]

It is easy to see how this understanding of the sacraments contributed to the deep clericalization of the church's life. The priest was a dispenser of grace. Inasmuch as he stood in the apostolic succession, Christ's authority had been handed down to him. He was, as it were, an extension of Christ. His ordination assures us that, if the other conditions are satisfied, his performance of the ritual of the eucharist brings it about that the bread and wine infuse grace into those who interpose no obstacle to its reception.[19] The "doctrine of the *ex opere operato*, though pointing chiefly to the objective working of God, carries with it the ideas of *priestly and episcopal power:* where that power is lacking, the objective sacrament cannot be performed. In this sense, the doctrine serves not simply to point to the objective action of God, but also to anchor that action in the activity of his chosen instruments, the priests and bishops of the church. The channels of the divine grace cannot be by-passed!"[20]

Some have argued — with considerable plausibility, I think — that the origins of this deep clericalization are to be found way back in the disposition of the Arian controversy by the Council of Nicea. Arius, remember, held that Christ was subordinate to God the Father. In rejecting this teaching, the Council of Nicea stressed the divinity of the Son, holding that he was of one substance with the Father. No similar emphasis was placed on his humanity. This, says Diekmann,

> weakened disastrously the understanding of the fuller implications of his true humanity, especially in terms of the mediatorship of the man-God, our high priest and brother, who leads us in prayer and worship to the Father. Liturgically this emphasis on Christ's transcendence inexorably led to many of the practices that became dominant in Christian worship during a thousand years or more. In fact some of them are still with us in our own day. To cite a few: the clericalization of the church itself, and the clericalization of its worship; the consequent undermining of the doctrine of the general priesthood and the practical disappearance of lay participation; the infrequent reception of Communion; the proliferation and excesses of worship of Mary and the saints, who in practical Christian devotion, if not in doctrinal principle, often substituted for, instead of illustrated, the absolutely unique mediatorship of Christ.[21]

As one of the accompaniments of the clericalization that originated in Nicea, Diekmann here cites the phenomenon of the infrequency of lay communion in the medieval church.

Laypeople began to think of the sacrament as too holy for them to receive except on those rare occasions when they were at a high pitch of piety and rectitude.[22] Yet if we are to understand medieval liturgical piety and, in particular, to see what replaced the reception of the eucharist in the piety of the people, we must recognize that the Nicene emphasis on the "distance" of Christ was in tension with a (perhaps compensatory) development in the opposite direction. I have in mind the increasingly realistic understanding of the way in which Christ is present in the sacrament. The Western medievals did not merely place the eucharist under the general category of sacrament; they went on to say that the bread and wine, upon consecration by the priest, are altered in substance into the body and blood of Christ so that Christ becomes bodily present before us.

In the mid-800s, Ratramnus, a monk from the monastery of Corbie in France, affirmed in his response to the highly realistic views of his fellow monk Radbertus, that though a change occurs in the eucharist whereby the bread and the wine become the body and blood of Christ, nonetheless "there is a difference between the spiritual flesh which is consumed in the mouth of the faithful and the spiritual blood which is daily presented to believers to drink, and the flesh which was crucified and the blood which was poured out."[23]

Ratramnus held that "the elements 'become' Christ's flesh and blood in the sense that he gives nourishment through them, because 'under the cover of material things the divine power secretly dispenses salvation to those who faithfully receive them.' "[24] In short, Ratramnus's understanding of the *mutatio* that takes place in the eucharist remains within the category of sacrament — the bread and wine become instruments of the grace they signify.

Some two hundred years later, Berengarius of Tours affirmed the same view. But times had changed, and after years of controversy he was forced in 1059, and again in 1079, to recant and sign documents in which were affirmed the very views he had been attacking. In 1059 he signed the following statement:

> I Berengarius . . . anathematise every heresy, especially that of which I have been accused, which attempts to argue that the bread and wine which are placed on the altar are after consecration solely a sacrament and not the true body and blood of our Lord Jesus Christ. . . . I agree . . . that the bread and the wine . . . are not merely a sacrament, but also the true body and blood of our Lord Jesus Christ; and that they are sensibly — not merely in a sacrament, but in truth — handled by the hands of the priests and broken and crushed by the teeth of the faithful.[25]

This very clearly indicates that in the eucharist we have something more than a sacrament. But it does not say how the bread and wine of the eucharist are related to the original body and blood of Christ. On this, Berengarius was forced in 1079 to declare that

> I Berengarius believe . . . that the bread and wine which are placed on the altar are substantially changed through the mystery of the sacred prayer and the words of our Redeemer into the true and proper and lifegiving flesh and blood of Jesus Christ our Lord, and that after consecration they are the true body of Christ which was born of the Virgin . . . and the true blood of Christ which flowed from his side; and this not only through the sign and power of a sacrament, but in the authenticity of their own nature and in the truth of their own substance.[26]

Thus it was that the doctrine of transubstantiation officially entered the theology of the church. The *substance* of the bread and wine are changed into the *substance* of the body and blood of Christ, while the ordinary breadly qualities ("accidents") remain. Though the appearance (species) of bread and wine is retained, the bread has in fact been transubstantiated into the very body of Christ, and the wine

into his blood. Christ is bodily present, though it doesn't *appear* that he is. It appears that we still have only ordinary bread and wine. The doctrine was given its decisive formulation at Trent, where we read that "by the consecration of the bread and of the wine a conversion is made of the whole substance of the bread into the substance of the body of Christ our Lord, and of the whole substance of the wine into the substance of his blood; which conversion is, by the holy Catholic Church, suitably and properly called Transubstantiation."[27] In the eucharist, under the appearance of bread and wine, we are confronted with the objective bodily presence of the Lord himself, making this the supreme sacrament and the summit of the church's devotion.

It was perhaps inevitable that this highly realistic understanding of Christ's presence in the sacrament, when coupled with the sense of Christ's awesomeness inspired by Nicea, would result in a displacement of the focus of the sacrament. In Justin's church at Rome it was the actual reception by the people of the bread and wine that constituted the culminating point of the eucharist. In medieval sacramental theology and practice, the high point became instead that moment of consecration at which the bread and wine are changed into Christ's body and blood. Aquinas is unequivocal: "the sacrament of the Eucharist is completed in the very consecration of the matter, whereas the other sacraments are completed in the application of the matter for the sanctifying of the individual" (*ST*, III, Q. 73, art. 1, ad 3).[28] An ironic consequence of medieval sacramental theology is that it becomes a secondary matter whether or not the eucharist functions sacramentally. That Christ becomes bodily present is primary: presence displaces sacrament.

Though the two categories of *sacrament* and *presence-upon-transubstantiation* were prominent in the theorizing of the theologians about the eucharist, they were not prominent in the liturgy of the mass itself. They did not determine the structure of that with which the worshiper was confronted. At a certain point, upon the elevation of a wafer, the worshiper would have heard the words *hoc est corpus meum* — "this is my body." Every medieval thought that Christ became bodily present at this point. Later in the liturgy the priest would have asked of God that those who take part in the eucharist "be filled with every grace and heavenly blessing." Every medieval familiar with the words and familiar with currents of thought in the church would have understood this as the prayer that the ritual be sacramentally effective. But the shape of the medieval eucharist as a whole was determined by something else. The eucharist was shaped as *our* approach to God.

The eucharist was, for one thing, our *thanksgiving* to God. In that respect the continuity with the ancient church had not been broken. It was also our *intercession* with God. The intercessions that in the ancient church had occurred between Scripture/sermon and eucharist had by now been severely truncated and moved down into the eucharistic component. But above all, the eucharist was our *offering (oblatio)* or *sacrifice (hostia, sacrificium)* to God, for sin. What shaped the medieval liturgy more powerfully than anything else was the conviction that on our behalf the priest offers to God a sacrifice for sin.

In the mass as approved by Trent, for example, the priest prays that God will "accept this unblemished sacrificial offering [*hostiam*] which I, thy unworthy servant, make to thee, living and true God, for my countless sins, offences, and neglects, and on behalf of all who are present here."[29] Shortly after this he says that "we offer thee, Lord, the chalice of salvation." And right after that he prays that "our sacrifice [*sacrificium*] be so offered in thy sight this day that it may please thee." Immediately after that in turn he asks God to "bless these sacrificial gifts" *(hoc sacrificium)*. Again, he

asks God to "accept the offering [*oblationem*] we here make to thee in memory of the passion, resurrection, and ascension of our Lord." And he says, "pray, brethren, that my sacrifice [*sacrificium*] and yours may find acceptance with God the almighty Father," to which the response of his assistant is, "may the Lord accept the sacrifice [*sacrificium*] at your hands." After words of thanksgiving he says, "and so, through Jesus Christ, thy Son, our Lord, we humbly pray and beseech thee, most gracious Father, to accept and bless these offerings, these gifts, these holy, unblemished sacrificial gifts [*sacrificia*]." He says that "we thy servants, and with us thy whole household, make this peace-offering [*oblationem*] which we entreat thee to accept." And he goes on to pray, "make this offering [*oblationem*] wholly blessed, a thing consecrated and approved." We offer, he says, "to thy sovereign majesty, out of the gifts thou hast bestowed upon us, a sacrifice [*hostiam*] that is pure, holy, and unblemished." And he asks God to accept this sacrifice as he accepted Abraham's and Melchizedek's. The point is clear: the language of the eucharist was overwhelmingly the language of sacrifice.

Furthermore, the language was such that it would have been very surprising indeed if the typical layperson had not thought that Christ was sacrificed again for our sins in the eucharist — a view to which the Reformers were of course unrelenting in their opposition. In fairness to our medieval predecessors, however, we must say that many theologians among them were also firmly opposed to such a view.[30] They insisted that the eucharist is not a repetition of the sacrifice of Christ but a memorial, a recalling, an *anamnesis* of it. Though the Christ once sacrificed on Calvary for our sins is bodily present in the eucharist, he is not bodily sacrificed. Trent declared that "in this divine sacrifice which is celebrated in the mass, that same Christ is contained and immolated in an unbloody manner who once offered himself in a bloody manner on the altar of the cross."[31] Admittedly the language here is compatible with the view that the sacrifice of Christ is repeated in the eucharist in such a manner that no blood is shed. But the main line of interpretation was not that. Rather, when sacrifice is understood in the sense that Christ was sacrificed on the cross, then Christ's sacrifice is never repeated. In the eucharist, Christ is sacrificed only in the derivative sense that his (bloody) sacrifice on the cross is (unbloodily) memorialized.[32]

But if this had wholly exhausted the medieval understanding of the eucharist as a sacrifice, the Reformers would have had no trouble with it. Trent is emphatic that there is more:

> If anyone saith, that in the mass a true and proper sacrifice is not offered to God, . . . let him be anathema.

> If anyone saith that the sacrifice of the mass is only a sacrifice of praise and of thanksgiving; or, that it is a bare commemoration of the sacrifice consummated on the Cross, but not a propitiatory sacrifice; or, that it profits him only who receives; and that it ought not to be offered for the living and the dead for sins, pains, satisfactions, and other necessities: let him be anathema.[33]

In the eucharist we do not merely present Christ's sacrifice to the Father: we ourselves make a sacrifice. And the sacrifice we make is not just a sacrifice of praise and thanksgiving — the Reformers were happy to affirm that the eucharist is a sacrifice of that sort. It is, said Trent, a sacrifice of propitiation whereby satisfaction is made for our sins.[34] The medievals regularly insisted that our human actions are a sacrifice obtaining forgiveness of sins only because of the work of Christ. But given that work of Christ as basis, the performance by the priest of the ritual of the eucharist makes satisfaction to God, and thus obtains forgiveness of sins, in proportion to the faith and devotion of the priest or of those on whose behalf he makes the sacrifice.

And what, finally, did the laity do while the liturgy was being performed on their behalf, with or without their understanding and apprehension? What was their mode of participation in the liturgy? Let us review. The emphasis of the liturgy was entirely on the eucharist. Everything that preceded the eucharist was understood as preparation. Further, the preparation was entirely in a language the laity did not understand; indeed, it was entirely concealed from their hearing by its inaudibility and from their sight by large screens ("rood-screens"). As Jungmann notes, "even the readings were considered now as a merely symbolic proclaiming of the Word of God. Indeed, it was already an established tradition that in most cases the reader did not face the people."[35] As to the eucharist itself, the language was overwhelmingly that of sacrifice. But the laity did not themselves make a sacrifice of propitiation for their sins; the sacrifice was made on their behalf by the priest. And though they could indeed receive the wafer (not the wine), the impression was clearly conveyed that this was unimportant. Or rather, they were warned about the dangers of reception: this holy bread and wine must be handled with extreme care lest crumbs or drops fall to the floor, and must be received worthily or the recipient was placed in sin. In short, the objective structure of the liturgy was that of the priest on behalf of the people presenting to God a sacrifice for sins, accompanied by thanksgiving and intercession; about this it was believed that if the priest did it validly, Christ became bodily present under the appearance of the bread and wine. The moment in which *that* happened was the high point of the liturgy.

So once again our question: What did the laity do while the priest performed the liturgy? If we keep in mind the insistence that the bread and wine are transubstantiated into Christ's body and blood so the Christ becomes bodily present, the answer will not be hard to surmise: *adoration*. Adoration of the Christ who is bodily present under the appearance of bread and wine became for the laity the central liturgical act — or better, perhaps, it became their accompaniment to the liturgy. Let us listen once more to Jungmann:

> by the end of the Middle Ages . . . the faithful had become silent. . . . Because the faithful no longer wanted to communicate or dared to (the clergy did not encourage frequent reception, to put it mildly), they wanted to see the sacred Host. From gazing at the sacred Species, they hoped for blessing and help in their earthly needs as well as salvation for their souls. . . . We can therefore attribute a certain pious eucharistic movement to the late Middle Ages. But its goal was not *celebrating* the Eucharist, or communicating more frequently, but looking at the Blessed Sacrament and venerating it.[36]

My suggestion, in short, is that the medieval Western liturgy was a liturgy in which, to an extraordinary degree, the action of God in the liturgy was lost from view. The actions were all human. The priest addressed God. The priest brought about Christ's bodily, but static, presence. The laity adored Christ under the bread-like and wine-like appearances. The reception of the consecrated bread from the hands of the priest caused an infusion of grace in the communicants. But where in all this was God, the living active God? The bread infuses the grace it signifies. The consecration by the priest effects Christ's bodily presence. But God as agent is nowhere in view. And what was the point of it all? "Hearing Mass was reduced to a matter of securing favors from God," says Jungmann.[37]

* * * * *

What, now, was the response of the Reformers to this liturgy and its theology? What did they propose and institute in its place? What became for them, in theory and in practice, the controlling idea of the liturgy? Of course we cannot here immerse ourselves in Reformation debates over sacrifice, real presence, and the like. Our eye must remain on the liturgy. We shall have to confine ourselves to saying only enough to make clear the new vision of what it is that ought to occur in the gatherings of the church. And need I mention that underlying everything the Reformers said was their conviction that the liturgy is the work of the whole people of God? Liturgy is no longer the work of priests on our behalf.

Let me approach my suggestion by considering, first, what they said concerning the Scripture/sermon component of the liturgy. Of course everybody knows that the Reformers stressed the importance of the sermon. But we want to dig beneath this phenomenon to ask why. What was the new idea of which this was a manifestation?

Notice first that the Reformers *recovered* the Scripture/sermon component of the liturgy. Their "innovation" at this point was to return to the practice of the ancient church. We saw that in Justin's church at Rome there was a nice balance between word and sacrament — a balance not just in the objective liturgy but in the people's experience of the liturgy. We also saw that in the medieval church that balance was lost. The Scriptures were read inaudibly in an alien tongue, the sermon all but disappeared, and in theory and practice the entire service of the word lost its inherent significance and was treated merely as preparation for eucharist. The Reformers recovered the audible reading of Scripture, in the language of the people, with a sermonic explication and application thereof.

How did they understand this reading of Scripture and preaching of sermon? What was the idea behind it? To begin, we must recall that the Reformed churches were inclined to see the reading of Scripture and the sermonic explication and application thereof as a single liturgical unit — "one inseparable element which Calvin called 'the incomparable treasure of the church.' "[38] More specifically the Scriptures were read as basis for the preaching. Reading served preaching. To understand why that was so and how, in turn, the Reformers understood preaching, we can do no better than listen to Calvin. Just as God in Old Testament times, says Calvin, was

> not content with the law alone, but added priests as interpreters from whose lips the people might ask its true meaning, so today he not only desires us to be attentive to its reading, but also appoints instructors to help us by their effort. This is doubly useful. On the one hand, he proves our obedience by a very good test when we hear his ministers speaking just as if he himself spoke. On the other, he also provides for our weakness in that he prefers to address us in human fashion through interpreters in order to draw us to himself, rather than to thunder at us and drive us away. . . . Among the many excellent gifts with which God has adorned the human race, it is a singular privilege that he deigns to consecrate to himself the mouths and tongues of men in order that his voice may resound in them.[39]

God's voice resounds in the mouth and tongue of the preacher so that hearing the minister preach is like hearing God himself speak. God "uses the ministry of men to declare openly his will to us by mouth," says Calvin, "as a sort of delegated work, not by transferring to them his right and honor, but only that through their mouths he may do his own work — just as a workman uses a tool to do his work."[40] Through the sovereign action of the Spirit, the minister speaks the Word of God — not in the weak sense that he now reflects on the anciently spoken word of God, but in the radical sense that by way of his now speaking, God now speaks. The reading in the church of the anciently spoken word of God provides the basis for the here-and-now speech of God to God's people. The sermon is "sacramental" of the speech of God — not of the static presence of God but of God's *very speaking*. As the Second Helvetic Confession puts it, "when this

Word of God is now preached in the church by preachers lawfully called, we believe that the very Word of God is preached, and received of the faithful."[41]

Often it is said that the churches of the Reformation have no sacramental consciousness. The truth is that the Calvinistic wing of the Reformed tradition, and the confessional documents of the tradition as a whole, exhibit an intensely sacramental consciousness, more than is typical of such as the Roman and Anglican traditions. Part of this "more" pertains to the sermon. More than any other traditions of Christendom, the churches of the Reformation — Reformed, but Lutheran as well — have emphasized that by way of church proclamation, God acts graciously toward God's people. An irony of the traditional polemics on these matters is that often those most critical of the Reformed churches for their supposed lack of sacramental consciousness were themselves the most resistant to granting any "sacramental" status to church proclamation. Why that should be is something I cannot here explore, beyond suggesting that it was in part because their own sacramentalism was more a sacramentalism of God's static presence than of God's active doing.

It is interesting in this regard to glance at the *Constitution on the Sacred Liturgy* of Vatican II.[42] The Reformers would be profoundly heartened by the emphatic way in which the *Constitution* speaks of the liturgy as one of the central occasions in the life of the church when God speaks to us: "Christ is always present in his Church, especially in her liturgical celebrations. . . . He is present in his word, since it is he himself who speaks when the holy scriptures are read in the Church" (par. 7). "In the liturgy God speaks to his people and Christ is still proclaiming his gospel. And the people reply to God both by song and prayer" (par. 33). The Reformers would also be heartened by Vatican II's insistence on the importance of the sermon: "by means of the homily the mysteries of the faith and the guiding principles of the Christian life are expounded from the sacred text during the course of the liturgical year. The homily, therefore, is to be highly esteemed as part of the liturgy itself. In fact at those Masses which are celebrated on Sundays and holidays of obligation, with the people assisting, it should not be omitted except for a serious reason" (par. 52).[43] Yet in spite of its insistence on the importance of the sermon, Vatican II refrains from saying that God speaks by way of ministerial proclamation. The sermon (homily) is not yet understood "sacramentally."

Consider, by contrast, how the great Swiss Reformed liturgical scholar Jean-Jacques von Allmen speaks of the sermon. The word of God, he says, is communicated verbally in the liturgy in three different ways: (1) in the pronouncement of greeting, absolution, and benediction; (2) in the reading of Holy Scripture; and (3) in the sermon. Von Allmen calls this last the "prophetic proclamation" of the word of God, and he asks, "What is the difference between this proclamation of the Word and the others?" His answer is that there is a twofold difference.

> Firstly, in the hands of God, the sermon is a basic means by which there takes place a direct prophetic intervention in the life of the faithful and of the Church, with the object of consoling, setting to rights, reforming, questioning. . . . The second difference is that preaching . . . introduces into the service an element of witness-bearing. In so doing it expresses one of the deepest mysteries of the love of God: If God gives Himself to us, it is to enter into the depth of our being and invite us to disclose Him to the world, clothed with our flesh.[44]

In short, by way of the sermon God speaks directly *to the contemporary situation of the church by means of one of its contemporary members*. In those two features lies the uniqueness of this mode of God's speech.

Those who are hesitant to ascribe to the sermon so "sacramental" a status as did the Reformers will usually focus on the deficiencies of sermons and the shortcomings of preachers. The answer of the Reformers to this objection is structurally the same as that given by the medieval church to the suggestion that the efficacy of the sacrament depends on the holiness of the priest: God uses fallible human material to accomplish God's ends. We are to look to "the Word itself which is preached," says the Second Helvetic Confession, "not the minister that preaches; who, although he be evil and a sinner, nevertheless the Word of God abides true and good."[45] To this Calvin adds that "this is the best and most useful exercise in humility, when [God] accustoms us to obey his Word, even though it be preached through men like us and sometimes even by those of lower worth than we. If he spoke from heaven, it would not be surprising if his sacred oracles were to be reverently received without delay by the ears and minds of all. . . . But when a puny man risen from the dust speaks in God's name, at this point we best evidence our piety and obedience toward God if we show ourselves teachable toward his minister, although he excells us in nothing."[46] Thus, "those who think the authority of the Word is dragged down by the baseness of the men called to teach it disclose their own ungratefulness."[47]

I have been calling attention to the Reformed insistence that God speaks by way of the liturgical action of reading and explicating Scripture, as indeed God speaks in the reading of the law and the pronouncement of greeting, absolution, and benediction. In listening to church proclamation, we hear God speaking. To say no more than this, however, is to focus too exclusively on the objective side of the matter. The Reformers were just as emphatic in their insistence that we must receive this speech of God in humility and faith and that its effectiveness depends on the work of the Spirit. It can be said, indeed, that it was the Swiss Reformers who brought the Spirit back into the Western liturgy, thus allying themselves with the East. As Hughes Oliphant Old remarks, "for Calvin it was not the words of the Bible printed in a book, but the Bible proclaimed by a preacher under the power of the Holy Spirit and received through the inner testimony of the Holy Spirit by the faithful with obedience which was the Word of God."[48] Thus it was that the Reformed churches introduced into their liturgies the "prayer of illumination" before Scripture and sermon. It was their deep conviction that there is no true preaching and no right hearing without *epiclesis*. The example of such a prayer that comes to us from the Strassburg liturgy of Martin Bucer is among the earliest:

> Almighty, gracious Father, forasmuch as our whole salvation depends upon our true understanding of the holy Word, grant to all of us that our hearts, being freed from worldly affairs, may hear and apprehend thy holy Word with all diligence and faith, that we may rightly understand thy gracious will, cherish it, and live by it with all earnestness, to thy praise and honor; through our Lord Jesus Christ.[49]

Another example, in which the prayer for right hearing by the people is combined with a prayer for right speaking by the preacher, comes to us from the Palatinate:

> Open now the mouth of Thy servant, and fill it with Thy wisdom and knowledge, that he may boldly proclaim Thy Word in all its purity. Prepare our hearts to receive it, to understand it, and to preserve it. Inscribe Thy law, as Thou hast promised, upon the tablets of our heart, and give us the desire and the strength to walk in the ways of Thy precepts, to the praise and glory of Thy name, and to the edification of the Church.[50]

Already we have before us all the materials necessary for a grasp of the controlling idea of the Reformed liturgy. But let me postpone for just a moment my formulation of that idea in order to look at one additional revelatory phenomenon. Chapter 18 of book 4 of Calvin's *Institutes* is a sustained attack on the mass as it was understood and practiced in central Europe in his time. As what he calls the "crowning point" of his discussion, Calvin says that whereas "the Supper itself is a gift of God, which ought to have been received with thanksgiving[,] the sacrifice of the Mass is represented as paying a price to God, which he should receive by way of satisfaction. There is as much difference between this sacrifice and the sacrament of the Supper as there is between giving and receiving." The Lord has "given us a Table at which to feast, not an altar upon which to offer a victim; he has not consecrated priests to offer sacrifice, but ministers to distribute the sacred banquet."[51]

To fully grasp what Calvin is saying here, it is important to realize that though he adamantly denies that the eucharist is a sacrifice of propitiation for sin, he repeatedly insists that it is a sacrifice of praise and thanksgiving. "The Lord's Supper cannot be without a sacrifice of this kind," he says, "in which, while we proclaim his death and give thanks, we do nothing but offer a sacrifice of praise."[52] Yet the fundamental structure of the eucharist for Calvin is not sacrifice but sacrament — God acting and we receiving, rather than we acting and God receiving. And just as in the case of proclamation, God's action must be received in faith and applied by the Spirit.[53] That is why the eucharistic portions of Calvin's Strassburg and Geneva liturgies open with a prayer for faithful receiving.[54]

By now the point will be clear. The liturgy as the Reformers understood and practiced it consists of God acting and us responding through the work of the Spirit. Between the medievals and the Reformers a deep alteration in the understanding of God occurred, from the static, immutable, impassive Unmoved Mover of Aristotelianized theology to the living acting God of the Scriptures. The Reformers saw the liturgy as *God's action and our faithful recep-*

tion of that action. The governing idea of the Reformed liturgy is thus twofold: the conviction that to participate in the liturgy is to enter the sphere of God acting, not just of God's presence, plus the conviction that we are to appropriate God's action in faith and gratitude through the work of the Spirit. What Anglicans and Catholics construe as the "subjectivizing" of the liturgy by the Reformers is rather the liturgical expression of the passionate conviction that we are not to hold God's actions at arm's length but appropriate them into our innermost being.[55] The liturgy is a meeting between God and God's people, a meeting in which both parties act, but in which God initiates and we respond. Once we see this as the controlling idea, then vast stretches of the phenomena of the Reformed liturgy fall quickly into place.

Of course we must keep in mind that it is not only in the liturgy that we are confronted with God acting in love toward us. The liturgy is the *continuation* of God's action in the world, and, in turn, God's action in the world is the *continuation* of God's action in the liturgy. In the liturgy we respond in praise and thanksgiving to God's actions in general. So, too, our response in the liturgy to God's action is not our only response. Our response in the liturgy is a *continuation* of our response in daily life, and, in turn, our response in daily life is a *continuation* of our response in the liturgy. It should be added that from the beginning it has been characteristic of the Reformed churches to insist that our response of working in the world is not inferior to our response of worshiping in church. Work and worship are but different modes of obedient gratitude.

This new vision of the liturgy was part and parcel of a yet more fundamental change between the medievals and the Reformers. The fundamental goal of human existence for the medievals was the happiness that is to be found in the contemplation of God. God was for them the supreme good, luring all humanity toward contemplation of God's self. The fundamental goal of human existence for the Reformers was obedient gratitude to God for God's actions of beneficence toward us. The medieval Christian longed for the full vision of God. The Reformed Christian longed for the full coming of the kingdom of God. The medieval Christian sought to approach God — the eternal immutable Unmoved Mover. The Reformed Christian sought to respond to the acting God. The Roman tradition tried to *see* God; the Reformed, to *hear* God. Their contrasting liturgies are manifestations of these contrasting visions of what it is that we and God have to do with each other.[56]

I am not forgetting the fact that deep in the Reformed tradition is a debate between its Zwinglian and its Calvinian branches on the nature of the sacraments, and specifically on the Lord's Supper. Rather, if I am right in my suggestion about the controlling idea of the Reformed liturgy, that debate is now illuminated for us. Zwingli regarded the eucharist as one facet of our *reception* of God's actions. Calvin, while also insisting on that dimension, saw the Lord's Supper primarily as one mode of God's *action.*

Christ, said Zwingli, "having sacrificed himself once, is to all eternity a certain and valid sacrifice for the sins of all the faithful. Therefore the mass is not a sacrifice, but is a remembrance of the sacrifice and assurance of the salvation which Christ has given us."[57] Accordingly, Zwingli says in the preface to his liturgy for the Lord's Supper that "this memorial is a thanksgiving and a rejoicing before Almighty God for the benefit which He has manifested to us through His Son; and whoever appears at this feast, meal or thanksgiving bears witness that he belongs to those who believe that they are redeemed by the death and blood of our Lord Jesus Christ."[58] Zwingli's liturgy for the Lord's Supper opens then with a prayer for the right performance of our service of praise:

O Almighty, Eternal God, whom all creatures rightly honor, worship and praise as their Lord, Creator and Father: grant us poor sinners that with real constancy and faith we may perform thy praise and thanksgiving, which thine only begotten Son, our Lord and Savior Jesus Christ, hath commanded the faithful to do in memory of His death; through the same Jesus Christ, thy son, our Lord, who liveth and reigneth with thee in unity with the Holy Spirit, God for ever and ever. Amen.[59]

A similar prayer, offered just before the communion itself, speaks of faithful living as well as faithful praising: "Grant also that we may live as purely as becometh thy body, thy family and thy children, so that even the unbelieving may learn to recognize thy name and glory."[60]

Calvin's thought was more complex and subtle. By way of the celebration of the sacrament, says Calvin, we do indeed present a memorial of Christ's sacrifice in praise and thanksgiving. So too we attest our faith and pledge ourselves to love the members of Christ's body. But something else happens as well, and it is this something else that is most important: *God acts*. For one thing, God seals (attests, confirms) the promises made to us in Jesus Christ. This God really does, here and now. Here and now God says: "my promises are 'for real.'" Calvin's point, let it be noted, is not that the bread and wine are signs and seals of God's promises. His point is that God acts here and now, affirming that his promises are for real.

One does not grasp the core of Calvin's thought until one sees that throughout his entire liturgical and sacramental theology runs the passionate concern to keep before us *the acting God*. In the sacrament, "it is God alone who acts by his Spirit. When he uses the instrumentality of the sacraments, he neither infuses his own virtue into them nor derogates in any respect from the effectual working of his Spirit, but in adaptation to our weakness, uses them as helps; in such manner, however, that the whole power of acting remains with him

alone."[61] It comes as no surprise, then, to learn that Calvin resisted all adoration focused on the bread and wine. "The command given us is not to adore, but to take and eat." "Let us not be fascinated," he says in his eucharistic liturgy, "by these earthly and corruptible elements which we see with our eyes and touch with our hands, seeking Him there as though He were enclosed in the bread or wine." Instead, "let us lift our spirits and hearts on high where Jesus Christ is in the glory of His Father."[62] As Kilian McDonnell puts it, for Calvin "the Eucharist is never an object, but a personal instrument."[63]

But God does not only put the seal of authentication on God's promises by way of the celebration of the sacraments — the central promise in the case of the Lord's Supper being God's promise that we shall be mystically united with the flesh and blood of the Son. God also through God's Spirit *effectuates* this promise, so that, if we approach the Supper in faith, our faith will be nourished and strengthened and thereby our unity with Christ in his humanity deepened.[64] In "the sacred mystery of the Supper," says Calvin, God "inwardly fulfills what he outwardly designates."[65] On

receiving the sacrament in faith, according to the ordinance of the Lord, we are truly made partakers of the proper substance of the body and blood of Jesus Christ. How that is done some may deduce better and explain more clearly than others. Be that as it may, on the one hand, in order to exclude all carnal fancies, we must raise our hearts upwards to heaven, not thinking that our Lord Jesus is so debased as to be enclosed under some corruptible elements; and, on the other hand, not to impair the efficacy of this holy ordinance, we must hold that it is made effectual by the secret and miraculous power of God, and that the Spirit of God is the bond of participation, this being the reason why it is called spiritual.[66]

Thus in Calvin's Geneva liturgy, the eucharist component begins with this prayer:

And as our Lord Jesus Christ has not only offered His body and blood once on the Cross for the remission of our sins, but also desires to impart them to us as our nourishment unto everlasting life, grant us this grace: that we may receive at His hands such a great benefit and gift with true sincerity of heart and with ardent zeal. In steadfast faith may we receive His body and blood, yea Christ Himself entire, who being true God and true man, is verily the holy bread of heaven which gives us life.[67]

The contrast to Zwingli's opening prayer could not be more stark. Here we pray that we may receive worthily what God has to give us. There we prayed that we might rightly perform our praise to God. It is ironic, indeed, that in his understanding of the fundamental structure of the eucharist, Zwingli is allied with the medievals against Calvin!

Far and away the majority of the confessional documents of the Reformed churches sided with Calvin rather than with Zwingli on this issue of the nature of the sacraments. The Heidelberg Catechism is somewhat guarded in its Calvinism, and the Lord's Supper liturgy that comes to us from the Palatinate is even more so. But the Second Helvetic Confession, the Belgic Confession, and the Scots Confession of 1560 are all unabashedly and articulatedly Calvinian. The sacraments, says the Scots Confession, were

> instituted by God . . . to exercise the faith of his children, and, by participation of the same sacraments, to seal in their hearts the assurance of his promise, and of that most blessed conjunction, union and society, which the elect have with their Head, Jesus Christ. And thus we utterly damn the vanity of they that affirm sacraments to be nothing else but naked and bare signs. No, we assuredly believe . . . that in the Supper rightly used, Christ Jesus is so joined with us, that he becomes very nourishment and food of our souls. Not that we imagine any transubstantiation of bread into Christ's body, and of wine into his natural blood . . . but this union and conjunction, which we have with the body and blood of Christ Jesus in the right use of the sacraments, wrought by operation of the Holy Ghost, who by true faith carries us above all things that are visible, carnal and earthly, and makes us to feed upon the body and blood of Christ Jesus, which was once broken and shed for us, which now is in heaven and appears in the presence of his Father for us. . . . So that we confess, and undoubtedly believe, that the faithful, in the right use of the Lord's Table, do so eat the body and drink the blood of the Lord Jesus, that he remains in them and them in him. . . . And therefore, whosoever slanders us, as that we affirm or believe sacraments to be naked and bare signs, do injury unto us, and speaks against the manifest truth.[68]

None of the Reformed confessions can match the ringing aggressiveness of this passage. The Belgic Confession, however, does give us the finest brief formula for the Calvinian understanding of the sacraments. In Article 35 we read that God "works in us all that He represents to us by these holy signs."[69] There it is in a nutshell! Aquinas's formula, remember, was that in a sacrament the sign effects the grace that it signifies. For the medievals it was the sign that did the signifying and the sign that effected the infusion of grace. Here in the Confession of the Reformed churches of the Lowlands it is *God* who represents to us the promises and *God* who effectuates in us what is promised — by way of these sacramental signs. To say it once again, to participate in the liturgy is to be confronted with the acting God — or better, with *God acting*.

Consonant with this emphasis on God as active in the sacrament, confirming the promise to unite us more closely with Christ and thereby effectuating that very promise by strengthening us in faith, is Calvin's sharp criticism of the Roman Church for its infrequency of lay communion. "What we have so far said of the Sacrament," he remarks, "abundantly shows that it was not ordained to be received only once a year — and that, too, perfunctorily, as now is the usual custom."[70] "Plainly this custom which enjoins us to take communion once a year is a veritable invention of the devil. . . . It should have been done far differently: the Lord's Table should have been spread at least once a week for the assembly of Christians. . . . None is indeed to be forcibly compelled, but all are to be urged and aroused; also the inertia of indolent people is to be rebuked. All, like hungry men, should flock to such a bounteous repast."[71]

Zwingli, as we all know, felt differently about the matter. In the Holy Week of 1525 he took the momentous step of destroying the enduring shape of the liturgy by pulling apart its two high points of word and sacrament and disposing them into two separate services, a preaching service and a Lord's Supper service, and specifying that the Lord's Supper service be held four times a year and the preaching service forty-eight times. Though I am not aware that Zwingli ever stated explicitly why he did this, we can make some rather solid guesses. For one thing, it solved a pressing pastoral problem. Along with all the Reformers, Zwingli was persuaded that the Supper culminated not at the point of consecration by the minister but at the point of actual communicating by the people. Yet the people in his parish were deeply set in their centuries-old habit of communicating just once a year. What was he to do? Keep the enduring structure and conduct the liturgy on just a few occasions in the year? Hardly. His solution, not at all unreasonable in his circumstances, was to celebrate the Lord's Supper less frequently while maintaining the Scripture reading, sermon, and prayers each Sunday. And it is not inappropriate to observe that quarterly participation in the Lord's Supper by the people was in fact an *increase* for most of them from their previous practice. It should also be noted that Zwingli's solution was a way of coping with the general concern of the Reformers over the lack of discipline in the late medieval church: the table could now easily be fenced without driving those lax in discipline away from the services of the church in general.

Yet one does not hear from Zwingli any words of regret over his solution. His constant repetition, in his discussions on the sacraments, of the statement from John's Gospel that "the flesh profiteth nothing" makes one suspect that such things as bread and wine meant little to him; the meditative reception of the *words* of Scripture and sermon was for him the core of the liturgy. Then too, once he had concluded that the Lord's Supper was only an expression of our reception of God's action, not also an instrument thereof, the issue of the frequency of this mode of response that best serves the life of the church became purely pragmatic. (Yet it is not evident that even when the eucharist is construed as just a mode of our response to God, infrequency of celebration is called for. Why should we not celebrate weekly this commemoration, festival, or celebration of our redemption, as Zwingli calls it? In fact, in one passage Zwingli explicitly says that the church would find much benefit in frequent communion.)[72]

One might also seek to play down the momentousness of Zwingli's recourse. It may be said that if we just look at the *objective* liturgy as conducted by the priests, then it is true that (apart from certain sects) the word/sacrament structure endured in all places on all Sundays until Holy Week of 1525 in the Grossmunster in Zurich. But if we look at the liturgy as experienced and appropriated by the people, then it is evident that by Zwingli's time the enduring structure had broken down almost everywhere for almost everyone and in several different ways. The structure had *not* endured. When regarded from this angle, Zwingli's strategy was more restorative than radically innovative. He *recovered* Scripture and sermon for the people. He *recovered* the reception of bread and wine at each celebration of the Supper for the people. He *increased* the frequency of such reception so that it was closer to what it had once been.

All these points are worth keeping in mind. Yet the fact remains that in its *consequences,* Zwingli's step was momentous. And we should remember that though Calvin was presumably aware of whatever justification Zwingli pleaded, yet he endured in the conservative policy of trying to preserve the enduring structure while urging weekly communion. The momentousness of Zwingli's step is to be seen in the fact that most people in the Reformed churches came to see his solution not as an emergency device to be abolished when the emergency passed but as the right and normal way of doing things. Over Calvin's protests, they came to see it as right and normal to pull apart word and sacrament. They came to see it as right and normal to celebrate the Supper of our Lord just four times a year. In almost all Reformed confessions, the sacramental theology of Calvin prevailed. In almost all Reformed congregations, the liturgical practice of Zwingli won out. And so it is that, in spite of the sacramental theology of the Reformed churches and in spite of Calvin's strong preference regarding practice, the Reformed liturgy became a liturgy in which the sermon assumed looming prominence. The Reformed service became a preaching service — except for those four times a year when it was a Lord's Supper service. Whereas the medievals tilted Justin's nicely balanced bi-focal service way over toward the eucharist, the Reformed now tilted it almost all the way toward the sermon. Calvin's theological victory was overwhelmed by Zwingli's liturgical victory.

There is, in my judgment, no more fundamental liturgical issue facing the Reformed churches today than this ancient dispute within the tradition over the place in the liturgy of the eucharist: ought the liturgy of the Reformed churches to exhibit the enduring structure of word and sacrament, and ought the people of God to eat the Supper weekly? Or is it appro-

priate to keep word and sacrament in separate services and to celebrate the Lord's Supper only infrequently? Like all liturgical issues, this dispute raises a pastoral issue: Does it serve the health of the church to celebrate the Supper infrequently? And like all liturgical issues this dispute raises a theological issue: Was Calvin right in teaching that, by way of the celebration of the Lord's Supper, God acts toward us in love and we respond to God in faith, or was Zwingli right in teaching that the Lord's Supper is no more than an expression of our response to God's action? Karl Barth's words about this issue are worth meditating on:

> We do not any longer even realize that a service without sacraments is one which is outwardly incomplete. As a rule we hold such outwardly incomplete services as if it were perfectly natural to do so. What right have we to do that? We may ask the Roman Catholic church why she celebrates mass without preaching or without proper preaching, but we are asked ourselves what right we have to do what we do. Is there not a pressing danger that by omitting the natural beginning and end of a true service the services we hold are incomplete inwardly and in essence as well? Would the sermon not be delivered and listened to quite differently and would we not offer thanks during the service quite differently, if everything outwardly and visibly began with baptism and moved towards the Lord Supper? Why do the numerous movements and attempts to bring the liturgy of the Reformed church up to date . . . prove without exception so unfruitful? Is it not just because they do not fix their attention on this fundamental defect, the incompleteness of our usual service, i.e. its lack of sacraments?[73]

To understand why the Reformed liturgy acquired the character it did over the centuries, we must take note of one other feature present there at the beginning. I have said that the genius of the Reformed understanding of the liturgy is that in the liturgy God acts in love toward us and by the actions of the Spirit we receive God's actions in faith and gratitude. Yet from its very beginnings the Reformed liturgy exhibited the curious feature that whereas the people were frequently and lengthily exhorted to receive God's actions with praise and thanksgiving and adoration, they were given scant opportunity themselves to do so in the liturgy; there was more exhortation to thanksgiving than giving of thanks. This violates everything that the Reformers said about the liturgy. Yet clearly something in their mentality was here coming to expression. In the liturgical documents and theology of the Reformed churches there is a passionate concern that we not allow our recital of God's actions to remain "out there somewhere" but that we appropriate them in faith and gratitude. Surely *expressions* of praise and gratitude are the appropriate implementation of this vision. Yet the hortatory tone overwhelmed the worshipful.

The point could be made concrete with many examples; let me take just one. Earlier I explained that the Reformed churches introduced the prayer for illumination before the reading and preaching, as an epicletic prayer for the presence of the Spirit so that right speaking and right hearing might occur.[74] I think that we in the Reformed churches should treasure this part of our tradition. It is gratifying to see that in the new liturgies of churches of the Reformed tradition, new prayers of illumination are being composed. But it must also be noted that the Reformers accompanied their introduction of the prayer for illumination with the sweeping away of all those ancient signs of devotion that surrounded the reading of Scripture. Gone are the Alleluia's, gone the "Thanks be to God," gone the "Glory to you, O Lord," gone the "Praise to you, O Christ," gone the "gradual" psalm of response — and of course, gone any such action as kissing the book. But is it not strange that we should pray God for right hearing of the word while suppressing all expression of praise and gratitude *for* that word?[75]

An important exception must be made to my claim that the Reformed churches have interiorized our reception of God's actions in the liturgy, depriving that reception of adequate liturgical expression. From the very beginning, one of the hallmarks of the Reformed churches has been the vigorous singing by the people of psalms and hymns. We all know how the young Calvin in his church in Strassburg commissioned the translation of psalms and their musical settings. The resultant set of so-called Genevan psalms is one of the great musical treasures of the Christian church; it is painful to see that people of the Reformed churches today know almost nothing of this jewel of their tradition. Furthermore, we know how the early Reformers understood the liturgical function of this singing by the people. Hughes Oliphant Old puts it well:

> in the early Reformed worship, the singing of hymns — but more especially the singing of psalms — was understood first of all as the praise of the Church to its Lord. It is in no way dependent upon the preaching or secondary to the preaching. Nor is it to be understood as the frame in which the properly liturgical action is set. Praise is an essential action of the liturgy. Praise has its own unique function in the liturgy just as preaching or communion does. It is not, of course, that any of the elements of the service of worship are independent on each other. They are all of course interrelated. The point is, rather, that the singing of hymns and psalms of praise and thanksgiving is, and has always been, a central element in Biblical worship. . . . Psalmody is not primarily thematic, decorative, or didactic, but doxological. The great care which the early Reformed church paid to the development of psalmody was motivated by a desire to re-emphasize the doxological nature of the liturgy.[76]

Yet it must in all honesty be granted that over the centuries this function of the congregation's singing has all too often been lost from view. Too seldom is it seen as the people's response of praise to God's actions toward us. As Old notes,

> it is often understood as a decoration of the service of worship, a way of achieving splendor, or perhaps as the means of giving the bitter pill of religion the chocolate coating of either culture or entertainment. At other times it has been understood as a way of achieving "audience participation" or a means of getting the people to respond to the preaching or praying of the pastor. At still other times it has been understood as being primarily a means of expressing the theme of the sermon or the "Christian year," making it a pedagogical device.[77]

If I am right that over the years the Reformed churches have not adequately developed the worship dimension of the liturgy, allowing the proclamation dimension to overwhelm the worship dimension, so that in the liturgy proclamation must be received in inwardness, then I think we have the clue to very much indeed of how Reformed people think about and practice their liturgy — especially when this suppression of the worship dimension coincides with the not-unrelated phenomenon of infrequent celebration of the Supper.[78]

For one thing, this explains the tendency of Reformed people to think of the liturgy as purely instrumental for their work in the world. If participation in the liturgy is understood as being in the presence of God speaking to us, but if within the liturgy itself little opportunity is given to respond to this speech of God in praise and adoration, and if furthermore God's nourishing of us through the sacrament is allowed to recede from prominence, then it will be almost inevitable that we will think of our *work in the world* as the totality of our appropriate outward response to God's action in the liturgy. Where else, after all, will our enacted response occur if no opportunity is provided in the liturgy itself? Then, too, people will shortly begin to think that the only really important thing in God's eye is our obedient work in the

world and will begin to think of the liturgy as the issuing of marching orders. They will see the liturgy as motivation and guidance for what really counts — namely, our work in the world. Sunday will be seen as occurring just for the sake of Monday through Saturday. The integrity of *worship* as one mode of our response to God will be lost from view. I indicated earlier that in their beginnings the Reformed churches insisted that work is not inferior to worship. In their latter days, they have often assumed that worship is inferior to work.

I must say emphatically that these remarks are not meant to play down the importance of our work in the world as a response to God's action in the liturgy. Indeed, one of the great merits of the liturgical thought of the Reformed churches is that, from the very beginning, they saw the liturgy as stretching out from the church into the world. There is a moving passage in Calvin that is appropriately cited here:

> the Lord also intended the Supper to be a kind of exhortation for us, which can more forcefully than any other means quicken and inspire us both to purity and holiness of life, and to love, peace, and concord. For the Lord so communicates his body to us there that he is made completely one with us and we with him. Now, since he has only one body, of which he makes us all partakers, it is necessary that all of us also be made one body by such participation. The bread shown in the Sacrament represents this unity. As it is made of many grains so mixed together that one cannot be distinguished from another, so it is fitting that in the same way we should be joined and bound together by such great agreement of minds that no sort of disagreement or division may intrude. . . . We shall benefit very much from the Sacrament if this thought is impressed and engraved upon our minds: that none of the brethren can be injured, despised, rejected, abused, or in any way offended by us, without at the same time, injuring, despising, and abusing Christ by the wrongs we do; that we cannot disagree with our brethren without at the same

time disagreeing with Christ; that we cannot love Christ without loving him in the brethren; that we ought to take the same care of our brethren's bodies as we take of our own; for they are members of our body; and that, as no part of our body is touched by any feeling of pain which is not spread among all the rest, so we ought not to allow a brother to be affected by any evil, without being touched with compassion for him.[79]

I have been suggesting that the tendency of Reformed people to regard the liturgy as purely instrumental to our work in the world is a consequence of the stifling of the liturgy's worship dimension. Perhaps also the liturgical shyness of Reformed people of which I spoke earlier is a consequence of this development. If the function of the liturgy is to enable us to hear the speech of God, and if it is only our work in the world that God wants as our enacted response to his speech, then it will indeed seem odd to pay much attention to the liturgy. We will focus instead on our work in the world — and on training students to preach.

Perhaps the artistic impoverishment and aesthetic starkness so characteristic of Reformed liturgy is a natural consequence of this development. As I put it in another context,

it is not difficult to predict what will happen when proclamation, centered in the sermon, becomes the overwhelmingly dominant action of the liturgy: all that might distract our attention will be stripped away, up to the point where the congregation sits in silence, lined up in rows in a well-lit white box, listening. That this stark removal of the world can yield, at its best, the awesome sense of transcendence, I do not deny. There is good reason why those great mystical paintings in contemporary art — Rothko, Motherwell, Barnet Newmen — are so nearly empty. But how much of what it is to be human is thereby set aside! How much of life is suppressed! By contrast, where proclamation is not allowed to overwhelm the liturgy, where the dimension of *worship* is given

its rightful place, there the richness of life will put in its appearance. There color and gesture and movement and peace and sound will enter as vehicles of praise and gratitude.[80]

Calvin himself says that he does not mean "to condemn the ceremonies which are subservient to decency and public order and increase the reverence for the sacrament, provided they are sober and suitable."[81] Yet his emphasis fell on the fact that ceremonies can *obstruct* proclamation and true worship, not on the fact that they can *contribute*.

Finally, perhaps

what also results from the suppression of the worship dimension of liturgy is the seriousness, the sobriety, the absence of joy so characteristic of the traditional Reformed liturgy and so contrary to the spirit of the divine rest and people's liberation that we are intended to mirror. When proclamation overwhelms worship in the liturgy, then I think we must expect joy to be diminished. It's true, indeed, that proclamation itself should be received in joy. The Orthodox liturgy manages to do so: in a quite marvelous way it surrounds the reading of the scriptures with expressions of joyful devotion. . . . Yet experience seems to teach that unless the worship dimension receives due emphasis throughout the liturgy, proclamation will be received with a form of ethical seriousness that excludes joy.[82]

There are of course many important liturgical issues facing the Reformed churches today. One, is that in so many congregations the liturgy is helter-skelter. There is no rational sequence to it. It's just an assemblage of items, arranged for psychological effect, or perhaps strung out with no rationale at all. Another issue is that far too seldom do people understand the nature of the liturgical act that they are performing. Its structure and meaning and function are obscured from them. But I have been suggesting that of all the issues we face, there are two that loom up from our tradition above all others. One is our practice of celebrating the Supper of our Lord only infrequently — a practice thoroughly out of accord with Calvin's expressed wishes and with the sacramental theology of our confessional documents. The other is our suppression of the worship dimension of the liturgy relative to hortatory address and inwardness. To engage in the liturgy is indeed to enter the sphere of God's action. On that the Swiss Reformers were right; let us not lose sight of what they saw. But to engage in the liturgy is also to enter the sphere of our worship. Liturgy is divine and human *inter*action.

In conclusion, I come back to one of the points made near the beginning. After Vatican II, and after the emergence of liturgical convergence, we live in a situation profoundly different from that of the Reformers. I have explained the genius of the Reformed liturgy by contrasting it with that of the Roman liturgy as the Reformers knew it in central Europe in the early sixteenth century. But we would bear terribly false witness against our Roman Catholic brothers and sisters if we believed that their liturgical thought and practice remain what it was then. It has changed profoundly, and the net effect of the change has been to bring them much closer to what the Reformers were calling for. We must recognize this new situation and acknowledge it with gratitude. I do not say that the *Constitution of the Sacred Liturgy* of Vatican II could in its entirety have been written by the Reformers, but I do contend that, if confronted with it and with the new Roman liturgy, Calvin's response would be, "On this basis, we can talk."

But let us not assume that all the movement must be in our direction. Those two great liturgical issues on which we in the Reformed churches must reflect — on these issues the Roman tradition does better today than we do. We have something to learn. The new city of liturgy that is abuilding needs bricks from all of us.

NOTES

1. Cf. Liddell and Scott, *Greek-English Lexicon*, 26th edition (abridged): "*leitourgia*, a public service: — at Athens a liturgy, i.e., a burdensome public office or charge, which the richer citizens discharged at their own expense, properly in rotation, but also voluntarily or by appointment."

2. See George Morrish, *A Concordance of the Septuagint* (Grand Rapids: Zondervan, 1979), p. 152.

3. See William F. Arndt and F. Wilbur Gingrich, *A Greek-English Lexicon of the New Testament and Other Early Christian Literature* (Chicago: University of Chicago Press, 1965), p. 472. A helpful discussion on the concept of liturgy, including the etymology of the word, can be found in "Liturgy: The Divine Service of the Church," chapter 6 of Richard Paquier's *The Dynamics of Worship* (Philadelphia, Fortress Press; 1967). Chapter 7 of this work, "Worship: The Service of the Community," is also valuable.

4. Justin's description of the liturgy is to be found in his *First Apology*, 65-67. The translation is from Lucien Deiss, *Springtime of the Liturgy* (Collegeville, Minn.: Liturgical Press, 1979).

5. See Justin's *Dialogue with Trypho the Jew*, 41: we "thank God for having created the world, and everything in it, for the sake of mankind, and for having saved us from the sin in which we were born, and for the total destruction of the powers and principalities of evil through Him who suffered in accordance with His will" (*Saint Justin Martyr*, Fathers of the Church, trans. T. B. Falls (Washington: Catholic University Press, 1965).

6. Translation from Falls, *Saint Justin Martyr*.

7. Translation from Deiss, *Springtime of the Liturgy*.

8. All the quotations from Hippolytus are from his *Apostolic Tradition*, in the translation of Lucien Deiss in *Springtime of the Liturgy*.

9. Consider, for example, this passage from Luther's *Pagan Servitude of the Church*: "The third shackle imposed upon this sacrament is by far the most wicked abuse of all. The result of it is that there is no belief more widely accepted in the church today, or one of greater force, than that the mass is a good work and a sacrifice. And this abuse has brought in its train innumerable other abuses; and these, when faith in the sacrament has completely died away, turn the holy sacrament into mere merchandise, a market, and a business run for profit. This is the origin of the special feasts, the confraternities, intercessions, merits, anniversaries, and memorial days" (cited by Alasdair I. C. Heron in *Table and Tradition* [Philadelphia: Westminster Press, 1983], p. 113; I know of no better comparison between the medieval Roman and the Reformation understandings of the eucharist than that to be found in Heron's book).

10. For the references to Aquinas's *Summa Theologica* (hereafter abbreviated *ST*), I shall be using the translation of the Fathers of the Dominican Province (New York: Benzinger Bros., 1947).

11. Jungmann, "Liturgy on the Eve of the Reformation," *Worship* 33 (1959): 508.

12. From *Creeds of the Church*, 3d ed., ed. John H. Leith (Atlanta: John Knox Press, 1982), p. 60. In the sixth of the thirteen canons on the sacraments approved by the Council of Trent we read, now with the Protestant polemic in view, that "if anyone saith, that the sacraments of the New law do not contain the grace which they signify; or, that they do not confer that grace on those who do not place an obstacle thereunto; as though they were merely outward signs of grace or justice received through faith, and certain marks of the Christian profession whereby believers are distinguished among men from unbelievers: let him be anathema" (Seventh Session [3 March 1547], Decree on the Sacraments, in Philip Schaff, *The Creeds of Christendom*, vol. 2 [New York: Harper, 1919], pp. 120-21). Cf. Aquinas, *ST*, III, Q. 62, art. 1, ad 1: "the sacraments of the New Law are both cause and signs. Hence, too, is it that, to use the common expression, *they effect what they signify*." And in III, Q. 79, art. 7, resp.: the eucharist "has the nature of a sacrament inasmuch as invisible grace is bestowed in this sacrament under a visible species." As Heron remarks, the heart of medieval liturgical theology was "the description and definition of a sacrament as a cause of *grace*, in which grace is contained and by which it is objectively conferred. The idea of grace came to occupy a position of remarkable centrality in medieval theology and combined with the Aristotelian conception of causality to construct the very core of their sacramental teaching" (*Table and Tradition*, p. 80).

13. Cf. *ST*, II/I, Q. 109, art. 9, resp.: grace "is a habitual gift whereby corrupted human nature is healed, and after being healed is lifted up so as to work deeds meritorious of everlasting life, which excells the capability of nature." Aquinas adds that grace is also God's moving of the soul to act, normally by way of the causal processes of nature.

14. Hence it is that Trent says (Seventh Session [3 March 1547], Decree on the Sacrament, Canon IV): "If any one saith, that the sacraments of the New Law are not necessary unto Salvation, but superfluous; and that, without them, or without the desire thereof, men obtain of God, through faith alone, the grace of justification . . . : let him be anathema" (Schaff, *The Creeds of Christendom*, 2: 120).

15. Cf. *ST*, III, Q. 79, art. 3, resp.: "whoever is conscious of mortal sin, has within him an obstacle to receiving the effect of this sacrament. . . . He cannot be united with Christ, which is the effect of this sacrament." Furthermore, "whoever receives this sacrament, expresses thereby that he is made one with Christ, and incorporated in His members; and this is done by living faith, which no one has who is in mortal sin. And therefore it is manifest that whoever receives this sacrament while in mortal sin, is guilty of lying to this sacrament, and consequently of sacrilege . . . and therefore he sins mortally" (*ST*, III, Q. 80, art.

4, resp.). In short, the person who receives the sacrament when consciously in mortal sin, which includes absence of faith, does not receive grace (does not "eat the flesh" of Christ). Indeed, to receive the sacrament in that state is itself a mortal sin. All others do in fact receive grace (do in fact "eat the flesh" of Christ), in proportion to their fervor and devotion. Faith and charity unite us by a spiritual union with Christ (*ST*, III, Q. 82, art. 1, ad 2) and with his mystical body, the church. Such union is a prerequisite of actually receiving Christ in his flesh and blood in the eucharist.

16. *Creeds of the Church*, p. 61.

17. John Calvin, for example, writes that "the sacraments properly fulfill their office only when the Spirit, that inward teacher, comes to them, by whose power alone hearts are penetrated and affections moved and our souls opened for the sacraments to enter in. If the Spirit be lacking, the sacraments can accomplish nothing more in our minds than the splendor of the sun shining upon blind eyes, or a voice sounding in deaf ears. Therefore, I make such a division between Spirit and sacraments that the power to act rests with the former, and the ministry alone is left to the latter — a ministry empty and trifling, apart from the action of the Spirit, but charged with great effect when the Spirit works within and manifests his power" (*Institutes of the Christian Religion*, Library of Christian Classics, vols. 20-21, ed. John T. McNeill, trans. Ford Lewis Battles [Philadelphia: Fortress Press, 1960], 4.14.9).

18. Diekmann, "Celebrating the Word," in *Celebrating the Word*, ed. James Schmeiser (Toronto: Anglican Book Centre, 1977), pp. 4-5. Cf. Kilian McDonnell's discussion of "ritual Pelagianism" in *John Calvin, the Church, and the Eucharist* (Princeton: Princeton University Press, 1967), pp. 134-36.

19. Cf. Aquinas: "the priest consecrates this sacrament not by his own power, but as the minister of Christ, in Whose person he consecrates this sacrament. But from the fact of being wicked he does not cease to be Christ's minister; because our Lord has good and wicked ministers or servants. . . . Consequently, a man can be Christ's minister even though he be not one of the just. And this belongs to Christ's excellence, Whom, as the true God, things both good and evil serve, since they are ordained by His providence for His glory. Hence it is evident that priests, even though they be not godly, but sinners, can consecrate the Eucharist" (*ST*, III, Q. 82, art. 5, resp.).

20. Heron, *Table and Tradition*, p. 91.

21. Diekmann, "Celebrating the Word," pp. 2-3.

22. J. A. Jungmann makes the same point in *The Early Liturgy* (Notre Dame, Ind.: University of Notre Dame Press, 1977), pp. 197-98.

23. Retramnus, quoted by Heron in *Table and Tradition*, pp. 93-94.

24. Heron, *Table and Tradition*, p. 94.

25. Berengarius, quoted by Heron in *Table and Tradition*, pp. 94-95.

26. Berengarius, quoted by Heron in *Table and Tradition*, p. 95.

27. Chap. 4 of the Decree concerning the Eucharist (Thirteenth Session [11 Oct. 1551]), in Schaff, *The Creeds of Christendom,* 2: 130.

28. Admittedly there is a tension in Aquinas's thought at this point, for he also says that "this sacrament is both a sacrifice and a sacrament; it has the nature of a sacrifice inasmuch as it is offered up; and it has the nature of a sacrament inasmuch as it is received" (*ST,* III, Q. 79, art. 5, resp.). "Receiving is of the very nature of the sacrament" (*ST,* III, Q. 79, art. 7, ad 3). Yet he never backs off his insistence that "this sacrament is completed in the consecration of the matter, and not in the use, to which the dispensing belongs" (*ST,* III, Q. 82, art. 3, obj. 2). Though the eucharist is a sacrament, it is, qua eucharist, "completed" even if, on a given occasion, it does not *function* sacramentally. Even if its potential for infusing grace goes unrealized on a given occasion, even if it does not in fact sacramentally nourish the people of God, yet it is complete if transubstantiation occurs and Christ's bodily presence is accomplished. It might be thought that Aquinas's way of reliving the tension in his thought at this point was to hold that the *priest's* receiving of the elements fulfills the eucharist as sacrament. He does in fact say that the priest must receive. But it is striking that he bases this insistence not on the sacramental nature of the eucharist but on its sacrificial character! (*ST,* III, Q. 82, art. 4, resp.). It seems that the eucharist is inherently a sacrifice but only functionally a sacrament. That is why I suggest in the text that, in Aquinas's thought, the eucharist is complete even if it does not *function* as a sacrament.

29. Translation from *Liturgies of the Western Church,* ed. Bard Thompson (Cleveland: World Publishing, 1965).

30. Gregory Dix, who is ever one to defend the Roman tradition where it can be defended, says that even the theologians felt themselves drawn — and allowed themselves to *be* drawn — to the view that the priest sacrifices Christ afresh at every eucharist. Though they said it was not a *new* sacrifice, yet they also said that Christ's sacrifice was repeated. See Dix, *Shape of the Liturgy* (New York: Seabury Press, 1983), p. 623.

31. Twenty-Second Session (17 Sept. 1562), chap. 2, in Schaff, *The Creeds of Christendom,* 2: 179.

32. Cf. Aquinas: the eucharist "has the nature of a sacrifice inasmuch as in this sacrament Christ's Passion is represented, whereby Christ *offered Himself a Victim to God*" (*ST,* III, Q. 79, art. 7, resp.). See also *ST,* III, Q. 83, art. 1, resp.: "the celebration of this sacrament is called a sacrifice . . . first, because, as Augustine says . . . , the *images of things are called by the names of the things whereof they are the images.* . . . But, as was said above . . . , the celebration of this sacrament is an image representing Christ's Passion, which is His true sacrifice. Accordingly the celebration of this sacrament is called Christ's sacrifice."

33. Canons I and III of Doctrine on the Sacrifice of the Mass (Twenty-Second Session, 17 Sept. 1562), in Schaff, *The Creeds of Christendom,* 2: 184-85. See also chapter 3 of the same decree, p. 179.

34. The fundamental thought behind Trent on this point was stated clearly by Aquinas. The eucharist, he says, "has the effect of a sacrament in the recipient, and the effect of a sacrifice in the offerer, or in them for whom it is offered. . . . In so far as it is a sacrifice, it has a satisfactory power, i.e., power to make satisfaction. Yet in satisfaction the affection of the offerer is weighted rather than the quantity of the offering. . . . Therefore, although this offering suffices of its own quantity to satisfy for all punishment, yet it becomes satisfactory for those for whom it is offered, or even for the offerers, according to the measure of their devotion" (*ST,* III, Q. 79, art. 5, resp.). Cf. *ST,* III, Q. 82, art. 4, resp.: "whoever offers a sacrifice must be a sharer in the sacrifice, because the outward sacrifice he offers is a sign of the inner sacrifice whereby he offers himself to God." See also *ST,* III, Q. 79, art. 7, ad 3: "the oblation of the sacrifice is multiplied in the several masses, and therefore the effect of the sacrifice of the sacrament is multiplied."

35. Jungmann, "Liturgy on the Eve of the Reformation," p. 508.

36. In Jungmann, "Liturgy on the Eve of the Reformation," pp. 509-11. Cf. Gregory Dix: "in the primitive conception the consecration by the celebrant's prayer is subordinate to the whole eucharistic action as an essential part to the whole. In the medieval devotional conception the whole eucharistic action (carried on by the priest alone) is simply a means to bring about the consecration, for the purpose of individual adoration by each person present" (*The Shape of the Liturgy,* p. 621). Trent defends veneration of "the Blessed Sacrament" in chap. 5 and Canon VI of the Decree concerning the Most Holy Sacrament of the Eucharist (Thirteenth Session, 11 Oct. 1551). Cranmer describes the actual practice of this veneration in sardonic words: "What made the people to run from their seats to the altar, and from altar to altar, and from sacring (as they called it) to sacring, peeping, tooting and gazing at that thing which they saw? What moved the priests to lift up the sacrament so high over their heads? Or the people to say to the priest 'Hold up! Hold up!'; or one man to say to another 'Stoop down before'; or to say 'This day have I seen my Maker'; and 'I cannot be quiet except I see my Maker once a day'? What was the cause of all these, and that as well the priest and the people so devoutly did knock and kneel at every sight of the sacrament, but that they worshipped that visible thing which they saw with their eyes and took it for very God?" (quoted by Dix in *The Shape of the Liturgy,* p. 620).

37. Jungmann, "Liturgy on the Eve of the Reformation," p. 511.

38. *Liturgies of the Western Church,* p. 191. Compare Howard Hageman: the point of view of the Reformers "might be summarized by saying, 'no reading without preaching and no preaching without reading.' The Word of God, primarily and finally the Word made flesh, is not only the written Word between the covers of the Bible. Moreover, there were times when the Reformers came perilously close to saying that the Bible was not the Word

of the Lord until it was made to come loose from the page, speaking to this people in this time and in this place" ("Conducting the Liturgy of the Word," in *Celebrating the Word*, p. 68).

39. *Institutes*, 4.1.5.

40. *Institutes*, 4.3.1.

41. In *Creeds of the Church*, p. 133.

42. Quotations are taken from *Documents of Vatican II*, ed. Austin P. Flannery (Grand Rapids: William B. Eerdmans, 1975).

43. See also par. 35 of the *Constitution;* and pars. 41-42 of chap. 2 of *General Instruction on the Roman Missal* (26 March 1970). The excellent pamphlet, *Fulfilled in Your Hearing: The Homily in the Sunday Assembly*, published by the Bishops' Committee on Priestly Life and Ministry of the National Conference of Catholic Bishops is also important in this regard. The pamphlet opens with these words: " 'The primary duty of priests is the proclamation of the Gospel of God to all.' These clear, straightforward words of the Second Vatican Council (*Decree on the Ministry and Life of Priests*, #4) may still come as something of a surprise to us. We might more spontaneously think that the primary duty of priests is the celebration of the Church's sacraments, or the pastoral care of the People of God, or the leadership of a Christian community. Yet, the words of the document are clear: the proclamation of the Gospel is primary." They then go on to remark that " 'proclamation' can cover a wide variety of activities in the church. . . . But a key moment in the proclamation of the Gospel is preaching." But do they view preaching sacramentally? Well, they certainly come close. "The person who preaches in the context of the liturgical assembly," they say, "is thus a mediator, representing both the community and the Lord" (p. 7).

44. Von Allmen, *Worship: Its Theology and Practice* (London: Lutterworth Press, 1965), p. 143. Cf. Howard Hageman: "as I understand the Reformation in its concept of the celebration of the Word it was not academic; it was virtually sacramental. I've often wondered why the Reformation was apparently afraid of its own logic and refused to speak of the sacrament of the Word, when in celebrating the Word we are dealing, if I may use the term, with a kind of transubstantiation. The words of a human being are mortal with all of his limitations, indigestion, quarrels with his wife and upset attitude; yet his words, by the power of the Holy Spirit, are transformed into the Word of the Lord, that effective force by which recreation and new life take place" (*Pulpit and Table*, pp. 62-63).

45. Chap. 1, in *Creeds of the Church*, p. 133.

46. *Institutes*, 4.3.1.

47. *Institutes*, 4.1.5.

48. Old, *The Patristic Roots of Reformed Worship* (Zürich: Theologischer Verlag, 1975), p. 213. Cf. Calvin: "that the Word may not beat your ears in vain, . . . the Spirit shows us that . . . it is God speaking to us, softening the stubbornness of our heart, and composing it to that obedience which it owes the Word of the Lord" (*Institutes*, 4.14.10).

49. Bucer, in *Liturgies of the Western Church*, p. 170.

50. From the translation in the *Psalter Hymnal* of the Christian Reformed Church.

51. *Institutes*, 4.18.7, 12. Cf. Calvin in his "Short Treatise on the Lord's Supper": "the common opinion approved by all their doctors and prelates is, that by hearing Mass, and causing it to be said, they perform a service meriting grace and righteousness before God. We say, that to derive benefit from the Supper it is not necessary to bring any thing of our own to merit what we ask. We have only to receive in faith the grace which is there presented to us" (in *Tracts and Treatises on the Doctrine and Worship of the Church*, by John Calvin, vol. 2, ed. Henry Beveridge and Thomas F. Torrance [Grand Rapids: William B. Eerdmans, 1958], p. 184).

52. *Institutes*, 4.18.17. See also *Institutes*, 4.18.13, 16.

53. As to the need for reception of the sacrament in faith, see par. 17 of the "Mutual Consent in regard to the Sacraments" between the churches of Zurich and Geneva (1554): "by this doctrine is overthrown that fiction of the sophists which teaches that the sacraments confer grace on all who do not interpose the obstacle of mortal sin. For besides that in the sacraments nothing is received except by faith, we must also hold that the grace of God is by no means so annexed to them that who so receives the sign also gains possession of the thing" (*Tracts and Treatises on the Doctrine and Worship of the Church*, p. 217). This may be compared to the eighth of the canons from the Decree on the Sacraments issued by Trent in its seventh session (3 March 1547): "If any one saith, that by the said sacraments of the New Law grace is not conferred through the act performed, but that faith alone in the divine promise suffices for the obtaining of grace, let him be anathema." Concerning the Spirit as the one who effectuates the benefits of the sacrament in us, consider, from an abundance of passages, this brief one from the *Institutes*: "the sacraments profit not a whit without the power of the Holy Spirit" (4.14.9).

54. See *Liturgies of the Western Church*, pp. 202, 204. Cf. Kilian McDonnell: "Calvin's great ecclesiological concern was to build a theology of the church which is marked by a pervading inwardness and interiority, an interiority which finds its roots in Christology and Pneumatology, and finds its simplest expression in the union with Christ. This was Calvin's answer to the divinization of ecclesiasticism and sacramentalism, to ritualism and ritual Pelagianism. . . . To attain this inwardness, all initiative must be ascribed to the sovereign God. . . . There is no ecclesiology possible apart from this interior union which Christ in the Holy Spirit effects. The essence of the church grows directly out of our being grafted into Christ, which is the work of the Holy Spirit" (*John Calvin, the Church, and the Eucharist*, pp. 181-82).

55. According to Kilian McDonnell, to "dismiss either Calvin or the reformation as mere subjectivism . . . would be the cheapest burlesque of what Calvin and the reformers stood for"; in fact, the Reformers turned away from "what can be called a raging objectivism" (*John Calvin, the Church, and the Eucharist*, p. 38).

56. In first chapter of *Until Justice and Peace Embrace* (Grand Rapids: William B. Eerdmans, 1983) I try to show that those two contrasting visions of what we and God have to do with each other also led to two very different understandings of our social obligations. A point made by William Bouwsma is also of great importance: "Something else about the traditional conception of knowing must be recognized if we are to grasp what was occurring in Calvin's time, namely that knowing was mostly understood as analogous to, perhaps even a rarefied kind of, *seeing*. . . . This bias for the visible and palpable had significantly shaped medieval theology and spirituality. We can discern it in the insistence on a visible church and the visibility of the sacraments. It is apparent also in the use of images, in the words of a thirteenth-century monk (John of Genoa), 'to excite feelings of devotion, these being aroused more effectively by things seen than by things heard.' . . . And since, by analogy, the highest kind of intellectual [attainment] was conceived as a process in which the eye of the mind beholds its object by the light of reason, it should not be surprising that Thomas Aquinas and Dante represented the ultimate religious experience as a beatific *vision*" ("Calvin and the Renaissance Crisis of Knowing," *Calvin Theological Journal* 17 [Nov. 1982]: 192). Calvin's "participation in the crisis of knowing is . . . revealed in his frequent expression of a preference for the ear over the eye as the primary human instrument for knowing, a major departure from the traditional position. He made the point most often in connection with religious knowledge, sometimes metaphorically, as when he suggested the value of *blindness* in compelling us to listen to God's voice. We see, he also remarked, only *after* we hear; because 'mute visions are cold.' . . . God always *speaks* to us" (p. 204).

57. Item 18 from Zwingli's "Sixty-Seven Conclusions," cited by Heron in *Table and Tradition*, p. 115.

58. Zwingli, "Action or Use of the Lord's Supper," in *Liturgies of the Western Church*, p. 150. Cf. his larger statement in *On the Lord's Supper* (1526): Christ "himself instituted a remembrance of that deliverance by which he redeemed the whole world, that we might never forget that for our sakes he exposed his body to the ignominy of death, and not merely that we might not forget it in our hearts, but that we might publicly attest it with praise and thanksgiving, joining together for the greater magnifying and proclaiming of the matter in the eating and drinking of the sacrament of his sacred passion, which is a representation of Christ's giving of his body and shedding of his blood for our sakes" (*Zwingli and Bullinger*, Library of Christian Classics, vol. 24, trans. Geoffrey W. Bromiley [London: SCM Press, 1953], p. 234).

59. Zwingli, "Action or Use of the Lord's Supper," p. 151.

60. Zwingli, "Action or Use of the Lord's Supper," p. 154.

61. Calvin, in par. 12 of "Mutual Consent in regard to the Sacraments," p. 216. See also *Institutes*, 4.14.14, 16-17. The finest discussion of Calvin's view of the eucharist is to be found in McDonnell's *John Calvin, the Church, and the Eucharist*.

62. *Liturgies of the Western Church*, p. 207.

63. McDonnell, *John Calvin, the Church, and the Eucharist*, p. 167.

64. Cf. Calvin: "inasmuch as faith is confirmed and increased by the sacraments, the gifts of God are confirmed in us, and thus Christ in a manner grows in us and we in him" ("Mutual Consent in regard to the Sacraments," par. 19). How this latter occurs, says Calvin, is a deep inexpressible mystery. See his eloquent passage in the *Institutes*, 4.17.7.

65. *Institutes*, 4.17.5.

66. Calvin, par. 60 of the "Short Treatise on the Supper of Our Lord," pp. 197-98. Cf. *Institutes*, 4.17.10.

67. *Liturgies of the Western Church*, p. 202.

68. In Schaff, *The Creeds of Christendom*, 3: 468-70. In view of what I have been saying in the text, it is indeed, as Kilian McDonnell says (*John Calvin, the Church, and the Eucharist*, p. 186n.), "painful and embarrassing to find a scholar of Gregory Dix's stature" saying such things as this about the eucharistic views of the Reformers: "Since the passion is wholly in the past, the church now can only enter into it purely mentally, by *remembering* and imagining it. There is for them, therefore, no real sacrifice whatever in the eucharist. The external rite is at the most an acted memorial, *reminding* use of something no longer present. There is nothing but a 'figurative' meaning in such phrases as 'to eat the Body and drink the Blood' of Christ which are, as Cranmer so often insisted, no longer here but in heaven. At the most we are then especially moved by the tokens or pledges of a redemption achieved centuries ago to rejoice and believe that we *have been* redeemed long ago on Calvary, and to renew our allegiance and gratitude to our Redeemer. We have 'communion' with Him when we take the bread and wine as He bade us do 'in remembrance' of Him, because the mere obedience stimulates devout emotions and aspirations, and thus deepens our purely mental union with Him which we have by conscious faith. All that constitutes the eucharistic action on this view is the individual's reception of the bread and wine. But this is only a 'token.' The real eucharistic action (if 'action' is not a misleading term) takes place mentally, in the isolated secrecy of the individual's mind. The eucharistic action is thereby altogether deprived of its old corporate significance; it is practically abolished even as a corporate act. The external action must be done by each man for himself; the real eucharistic action goes on separately, even if simultaneously, within each man's mind" (*The Shape of the Liturgy*, pp. 623-24). One can imagine what the Scots would say about this incredible misrepresentation of their position. Dix's representation of Calvin's views (pp. 632-33) is if anything even worse; as McDonnell observes, it is mistaken on almost every point. Fundamentally what is going on here, I think, is that Dix is unquestioningly continuing the tradition of the nineteenth-century Anglo-Catholic interpretation of the Reformation.

Perhaps it is worth quoting some passages from Calvin's "Short Treatise" to make totally clear his "realism" concerning the eucharist. "It is necessary, first of all, that [Christ] be given us in the Supper, in order that the things which we have mentioned may be truly accomplished in us. For this reason, I am wont to say, that the substance of the sacraments is the Lord Jesus, and the efficacy of them the grace and blessings which we have by his means. . . . It is necessary, then, that the substance should be conjoined with [the signs], otherwise nothing would be firm or certain. . . . All the benefit which we should seek in the Supper is annihilated if Jesus Christ be not there given to us as the substance and foundation of all. That being fixed, we will confess, without doubt, that to deny that a true communication of Jesus Christ is presented to us in the Supper, is to render this holy sacrament frivolous and useless — an execrable blasphemy unfit to be listened to. . . . Moreover, if the reason for communicating with Jesus Christ is to have part and portion in all the graces which he purchased for us by his death, the thing requisite must be not only to be partakers of his Spirit, but also to participate in his humanity, in which he rendered all obedience to God his Father. . . . Thus it is with the communion which we have in the body and blood of the Lord Jesus. It is a spiritual mystery which can neither be seen by the eye nor comprehended by the human understanding. It is therefore figured to us by visible signs, according as our weakness requires, in such manner, nevertheless, that it is not a bare figure but is combined with the reality and substance. It is with good reason then that the bread is called the body, since it not only represents but also presents it to us. . . . Thus, as a brief definition of this utility of the Supper, we may say, that Jesus Christ is there offered to us in order that we may possess him."

69. I quote from the translation in the *Psalter Hymnal* of the Christian Reformed Church.

70. *Institutes*, 4.17.44.

71. *Institutes*, 4.17.46.

72. See Zwingli, *Commentary on True and False Religion*, ed. S. M. Jackson and C. N. Heller (Durham, N.C.: Labyrinth Press, 1981), p. 248.

73. Karl Barth, *The Knowledge of God and the Service of God* (London: Hodder & Stoughton, 1938), pp. 211-12.

74. Though there was no prayer for illumination in the Roman mass (there was a prayer for worthy reading of the gospel), there is such a prayer in the Orthodox liturgy of John Chrysostom: "Illumine our hearts, merciful Master, with the pure and unfading light of our knowledge of Thee, and open the eyes of our mind to comprehend fully the message of Thy Gospel. And instill in us feared respect for Thy blessed commandments, that, having conquered the desires of the flesh, we may take part in the life of the Spirit, and do all the things that are pleasing to Thee."

75. Of course this particular suppression of the expression of gratitude is connected with the fact that the Reformed churches have generally seen the church reading of Scripture as ancillary to the preaching of the sermon. For a vigorous protest against this practice, see von Allmen, *Worship: Its Theology and Practice*, pp. 131-33. On the matter of *how* to "celebrate" the word, Howard Hageman says some wise and helpful things in "Conducting the Liturgy of the Word." Also worth reading is the French Reformed scholar Richard Paquier's *Dynamics of Worship*, chap. 4: "Word and Sacrament."

76. Old, *The Patristic Roots of Reformed Worship*, pp. 253-54.

77. Old, *The Patristic Roots of Reformed Worship*, p. 253.

78. The two best histories of Reformed liturgy are Hageman's *Pulpit and Table* and James Hastings Nichols's *Corporate Worship in the Reformed Tradition* (Philadelphia: Westminster Press, 1968).

79. *Institutes*, 4.17.38.

80. Wolterstorff, *Until Justice and Peace Embrace*, p. 159.

81. Calvin, "Short Treatise on the Supper of Our Lord," par. 50.

82. Wolterstorff, *Until Justice and Peace Embrace*, pp. 159-60.

Reflections on Liturgy and Worship in the Reformed Tradition

LindaJo H. McKim

Reformation worship practices were not intended as innovations but as a restoration of the ancient Christian balance of word and sacrament. The Reformers sought to bring back into the religious foreground a spiritual realism, a firsthand relation of the person to God. The elaborate ritual system of the later Middle Ages had obscured the personal for all but spiritual specialists.

The Reformers made, and their successor churches continue to make, great contributions to the worship experience. The following reflections are meant to highlight some of the most important dimensions of Reformed understandings of liturgy and worship.

I. PRIMACY OF THE WORD

John Calvin, among others, saw the word as primary to the worship of God. He believed Christ made three demands of the worshiping community: to preach the word, to offer public prayers, and to celebrate the sacraments. The fact that Calvin considered the preaching of the word as the first essential of the worship experience is evident in the life of the church in Geneva, where three parishes held fifteen services weekly, all containing sermons.

Martin Bucer, to whom Calvin is most indebted for his liturgical ideas, suggests in *Grund und Ursach* that the first principle of liturgical recovery is adherence to "the clear and plain declarations of Holy Scripture." Bucer held that the Bible envelops the word of God and is to be authoritatively applied. He emphasized that only when the word goes forth to the church and the church makes its response can true worship occur. In Zurich, Zwingli emphasized the preached word as the apex of the service. The prayers, lessons, responses, creeds, and commandments are "simply the Congregation's way to the Word, and then the way back from the Word and out into life with the Word." He saw preaching of the word not as part of the liturgy, an action to which salvation is bound, but as bound to salvation itself as the work of God spoken to humanity. Scripture is the Word of God itself, and the interpretation and proclamation of the Scripture are not to be separated from it.

Martin Luther noted that the gospel originally had not been a book but sermons, testimonies of the apostolic faith. Those who continue the apostolic preaching are messengers by whom God's revelation is conveyed to all humanity. Luther held that the preached word is as much a revelation as the Scriptures themselves.

With the Reformation came the renewal of preaching. It has been suggested this was the greatest preaching revival in Christian church history. The Reformers, strongly indebted to those of the German humanist movement who attempted to reform the worship from within the Roman tradition, soon realized that a more radical reform movement was required. They expanded the practice of preaching still further and gave it new functions and character. In most Reformed churches there were two or three sermons on the Lord's Day and several throughout the week. The church was hungry for the word preached. Modern parishioners would be startled both by the length and solidity of sermons and the quantity desired by the congregation.

The preached word was so closely identified with the reading of Scripture that Reformed churches considered it one liturgical act. The reading of Scripture was immediately followed by its exposition and was not separated from it by any element of the liturgy. The reading and preaching of Scripture were preceded by a prayer for illumination to God's Holy Spirit asking for the Spirit to bring to light God's word to the congregation.

II. PRECEDENTS OF THE EARLY CHURCH

The Reformers looked back to the precedents of the church when searching for a right way

to worship God. It has been argued that Zwingli's concern for the primacy of Scripture and his rejection of the sacrifice of the mass derived from his knowledge of the works of Augustine, Cyril of Alexandria, Gregory of Nazianzus, Gregory of Nyssa, Jerome, and Origen. There is no doubt that Zwingli loved books. His personal library contained over three hundred volumes from these theologians, many of which have been found to be filled with Zwingli's own handwritten remarks and marginal notes. In addition, Zwingli had all the resources of a particularly rich monastery library. Through a study of his notes on the Pauline epistles, scholars have found that he relied heavily upon Ambrosiaster, Jerome, and Origen, as well as Augustine, Rufinus, Basil, Cyprian, and Cyril of Alexandria.

The Reformer Oecolampadius indexed the works of Jerome and edited Chrysostom's writings. Bucer had a substantial knowledge of the pastoral literature of the early church; he embraced the exegetical school of Alexandria and procured Erasmus's editions of the writings of the early church theologians.

John Calvin stated that Reformed liturgy conformed to the practice of the ancient church, in contrast to the practices of the Roman Church of his day, which he believed contradicted the practices of the patristic church. Calvin claimed that his worship structure was closer to that of Gregory, Basil, Chrysostom, Augustine, Ambrose, and Cyprian than was the sixteenth-century Roman mass. As proof of his sincerity, we need only mention the title of his service book *The Forms of Prayers according to the Custom of the Early Church.* Worship leaders of the early church opposed luxurious worship. Some even forbade the painting of images of Christ and the saints on the walls of the church. They spoke out against withholding the cup from the faithful, making laws for fasting, and requiring celibacy for priests. The Reformers also opposed these customs. But the most important area in which the Reformers looked to history for guidance was the liturgy itself. Both the early church and the Reformers showed a primary concern for the proclamation of the word, the prayer for illumination, the invocation, the prayer of confession, the prayer of intercession, and the celebration of the Lord's Supper.

III. THE PLACE OF THE SACRAMENTS

Though they exhibited differences in their language and orders of worship, the Reformers had a common belief that a service of worship must contain the preaching of the word, prayers of the people, and the sacrament of the Lord's Supper.

Zwingli held that prophecy accompanied the reading of the Scriptures. He gathered together ministers, canons, and students. They read the Scriptures together from various translations. Someone would read from the Vulgate, another from the Hebrew, and others from the Septuagint. One would present a Latin meditation in preparation for the sermon, and another would deliver the text of the sermon in German. The result of this daily ritual was the Zurich translation of the Bible. Perhaps the city's greatest contribution to the Reformation was this emphasis on the Bible, along with the rediscovery of the biblical concept of covenant.

The Lord's Supper was a vital issue for Zwingli. He believed the sacrament was important as a sign of reconciliation already accomplished in the cross of Christ. One remarkable feature of Zwingli's service was the location of the general confession after the sermon, just prior to the final blessing, with no absolution: the congregation received forgiveness and then confessed its sin. Zwingli believed that if faith existed, then absolution was also present. There was no need to make

people certain that their sins were forgiven, since the experience of faith alone offered that certainty, and only God dispenses faith.

Calvin differed from Zwingli. He emphasized the Lord's Supper as the norm for Christian worship. Those who argue that he wished to replace sacramental worship with a preaching service have misunderstood his work and ignored what he taught. Calvin had two aims: to restore the Lord's Supper to its early simplicity, celebrated weekly, and, within this service, to restore Scripture to the authoritative place it had had in the ancient rites. To Calvin the means of grace were twofold, consisting of both word and sacrament. Ministry was a ministry of both word and sacrament. A minister's task was not only to preach and instruct but also to celebrate the Lord's Supper every week and encourage the people to observe the sacrament of communion weekly as well. Prayer became the church's response to the word. Intercessions were spoken for all those in authority as well for all sorts and conditions of humanity. A paraphrase of the Lord's Prayer was recited.

IV. PEOPLE'S FELLOWSHIP

The sacrament of the Lord's Supper was meant to emphasize the communion of the people with God and Christ by the Holy Spirit in the context of communion with one another rather that the resacrificing of Christ as on the altar of the Roman mass.

Luther's conception of the Lord's Supper centered on the fellowship of Christians in and with the living Lord. Fellowship involved belief in the real presence of Christ, which could be realized only when the worshiper received communion. Luther rejected the medieval view of the sacrifice of the mass. He interpreted the idea of sacrifice as an offering up of ourselves in fellowship with Christ rather than as a repetition of the sacrificial death of Christ.

Zwingli protested Luther's sacramental realism on the grounds of his own christology. He held that the Lord's Supper was a sign of the reconciliation already accomplished on the cross. The troubled soul was comforted not through the sacrament but through the atoning work of Christ. Zwingli asserted that Christ's body is present in the Supper to the eye of faith only but that his natural body is not present; indeed, he rejected the latter as contrary to the word of God. Yet he granted that a sort of transubstantiation occurs — in the extent to which the congregation is changed into the body of Christ by means of the sacrament.

Calvin held that the manual acts of breaking bread and pouring wine symbolized the death of Christ, which called for a commensurate death of the human ego. Before Christ suffered, he instituted the sacrament in his last earthly meal. It was Christ's will that in memory of his profound love, demonstrated by his death for human sins, the church partake of the same bread and drink of the same cup without discrimination, as Christ's sacrifice was for all humanity without discrimination.

V. PEOPLE'S PARTICIPATION

The return to the vernacular in worship was an attempt to include the worshiping community, the church, in the worship experience. Calvin believed that people should participate in worship intelligently and that they cannot do so without fully understanding the language being used. He further believed that the worshiping community had been denied its baptismal rights because its people could not understand the language. The church members had to be nurtured to exercise their rights and, insofar as possible, to understand and participate in the sung and spoken prayers of the service.

VI. PSALMS RECLAIMED

The Reformers attempted to reclaim the Psalms and other Scriptures — Calvin through metrical singing, and Zwingli through antiphonal reading.

All the major Reformers rejected some of the church music of their time, and, with the exception of the Lutheran tradition, they sought to return the sung text of the liturgy to the simplicity of Scripture. These Reformers maintained that music should carry the text of the prayers, not distract from them. It was even proposed at the Council of Trent to eliminate music in worship altogether, but only Zwingli did so. He attempted to replace music with antiphonal recitations of the Psalms and Canticles in his German liturgy of 1525. This reform was short-lived, however; the magistrates in Zurich instructed the clergy to take over the people's part, and by 1595 even Zurich followed the general Reformed prescription of singing psalms set to meter (metrical psalmody).

Martin Bucer, a follower of Zwingli, seemed to use some Lutheran ideas in his 1537 Liturgy of Strassburg. For a time he retained the *Kyries* and *Gloria in excelsis,* but he later replaced them with psalms and hymns.

When John Calvin went to Geneva, he too restricted music in worship. Like Zwingli, Calvin initially had no music in worship. But after visiting Strassburg, he set several psalms to the metrical French tunes of Mathews Greitu and Wolfgang Dachstein. He thought these new psalm settings would be a welcome alternative to the "cold tones" of the Genevan worship. Calvin's views on the place of music in worship are stated in the prefaces to the 1542 and 1545 Psalters. He assessed music as the first gift of God for recreation. Music had the power to enter the heart like wine poured into a vessel, with good or evil effects. He considered singing in worship to be an act of prayer in which the music carried the text and did not distract from it. To ensure that this remained the case, he established some conditions. The musical setting had to be simple enough for the congregation to sing (the congregation was no longer displaced by trained personnel), and the psalms were to be sung in unison without accompaniment. (Calvin has been most criticized for discarding the choir; his followers even went so far as to remove the organs from their churches.) He resisted any attempt to make the sung parts of the liturgy more pleasing or aesthetically interesting than the spoken.

Calvin's practice influenced the Anglican Church and the early free-church movement in both England and America, and it still persists in some places today. It has been suggested that the metrical psalmody of the Reformed movement stands as one of the two most notable liturgical exploitations of the Psalter in Christian history, the other being the chanted psalmody of the Benedictines.

VII. PERVASIVE INFLUENCES

No Reformed service existed in and of itself, but each was influenced by other existing services. For instance, Calvin detested what he termed the "monkeying" of the medieval mass, and his standard became the corporate worship service in the German rite of Strassburg. He preferred not to dwell on the fact that the Strassburg rite might have been derived from the mass but rather chose to believe that the work of Schwarz and Bucer conformed to the practice of the primitive church. Calvin altered Bucer's worship design here and there, reducing the number of variants and adding a recitation of the Decalogue.

In 1523 Zwingli began his own attempt to reform the mass. He kept the first part of the mass intact, simplified the lectionary, removed the propers (parts of the mass that vary according to the liturgical calendar), and insisted that the Scripture lessons and sermon be given in the vernacular. By 1525 he had begun using Sargant's *Manale Curatorum* (1502) as a basis for his liturgy.

VIII. POST-REFORMATION TRENDS

The generations following the Reformation brought with them a strong antiliturgical movement that all but removed the reading of Scripture and symbolism from worship. This trend was evidenced most clearly in Elizabethan England. The Queen felt that four sermons a year were plenty, and she directed Archbishop Hooker to construct the liturgy accordingly. Hooker justified the practice with the assertion that the bare reading of Scripture is as effective a presentation of the word of God as preaching. Of course the Puritans objected. They demanded that preaching be reestablished as the norm for worship, but they were unsuccessful.

In Scotland there was also an antiliturgical movement, evidenced in the Westminster Assembly documents. *The Directory for Worship,* for instance, is not a liturgy or service book but a manual for worship leaders. The essentials of worship, according to the Directory, are the reading and exposition of Scripture. A chapter from each Testament was to be read, followed by an expository sermon. There were also guidelines for the minister's prayers, including an opening call to worship, a prayer of adoration and confession, and an invocation. A psalm was to be either read or sung following the Scripture readings. The Directory suggested that prayers of thanksgiving be said after the sermon. The Scots also preferred intercessions after the sermon, followed by the Lord's Prayer.

With the Enlightenment era came a new emphasis on the liturgy. The "Reformed theologians" Turretin, Pictet, and Ostervald were assigned the task of revising the Calvinist liturgies. They watered down the idea of original sin and called into question the need for redemption or the divinity of Christ. Osterwald was very influential in the revision. He eliminated free prayer and tried to reintroduce the Scripture into the main worship service. He also eliminated the sermon from the daily service. The sacraments became sacred ceremonies performed out of obedience. Confirmation took on a more important role than baptism, and the Lord's Supper was less frequently celebrated. Thus the centrality of word and sacrament as a basis for all worship was undermined.

For those churches in which the Lord's Supper was not celebrated weekly there was to be a preparatory service. By the eighteenth century, the Scots kirks no longer adhered to the *Directory for Worship*, and the Lord's Supper all but ceased to be celebrated. It has been asserted that in forty-five years following the Westminster Assembly, Glasgow celebrated communion only eight times. Despite the changes, the Reformed tradition has sought to maintain a high regard for the biblical materials, an awe-filled reverence toward the sacraments, and a fully responsible personal existence before God.

IX. PRESENT PRACTICES

Worship in much of Protestantism during the twentieth century has reflected less its Reformation roots than the influences of the antiliturgical movements that followed the Reformers by a generation or more. With the movements of pietism and evangelicalism, the liturgy of Protestant churches took a turn, however. Hymns have replaced psalms, and extemporaneous prayers have replaced written prayers. In some contexts the Lord's Prayer has fallen into almost complete disuse, while the sermon and Scripture readings have been downplayed. Much of the emphasis in worship has turned to the individual and a conversion experience. Revivalism has flourished and education has waned.

X. REFORMED WORSHIP

The forms of worship of the temple and synagogue influenced the early church in its worship practices. A Reformation principle was to reestablish the worship practices of the early church. Thus it is possible to conclude that the worship of the temple and synagogue as filtered through the practices of the early church influenced the Reformers as well. It should be noted that there has been an attempt on the part of many churches within the Reformed tradition to reclaim the principles of the Reformation through more frequent celebration of the Lord's Supper, the reading of more Scripture in worship, a renewed emphasis on the expository sermon, prayers of intercession after the proclamation of the Word, and the singing of metrical psalms.

BIBLIOGRAPHY

Davies, Horton. *The Worship of the English Puritans.* Nashville: Abingdon Press, 1957.

Hustad, Donald P. *Jubilate! Church Music in the Evangelical Tradition.* Carol Stream, Ill.: Hope, 1981.

Locher, Gottrfied W. *Zwingli's Thought: New Perspectives.* Leiden: E. J. Brill, 1981.

Maxwell, William D. *A History of Worship in the Church of Scotland.* London: Oxford University Press, 1955.

Nichols, James Hastings. *Corporate Worship in the Reformed Tradition.* Philadelphia: Westminster Press, 1968.

Old, Hughes Oliphant. *The Patristic Roots of Reformed Worship.* Zürich: Theologischen Verlag, 1975.

Thompson, Bard. *Liturgies of the Western Church.* New York: World Publishing, 1962.

Underhill, Evelyn. *Worship.* 1936; reprint, New York: Harper, 1957.

Worship and Justice

Nicholas Wolterstorff

Deep in the Reformed understanding of the liturgy is the conviction that to participate in the liturgy is to enter the sphere of God acting redemptively. It is not just to enter the sphere of *God's presence,* though certainly it is that; nor is it just to enter the sphere of *the God who acts,* though it is also that. It is to enter the sphere of *God here-and-now acting.* In the Lord's Supper, Christ is not just present among us, but, through the Spirit, God actively unites us more closely to Christ-in-his-humanity by way of the sharing of bread and wine. In the reading of Scripture and the preaching of the sermon, not only do we hear what God said millennia ago, but God speaks to us here and now by way of the words uttered. And in the greeting, in the benediction, in the law, in the declaration of pardon, God gives to us here and now God's word of grace and God's light for our path.

When comparing this understanding of the liturgy with others, one is tempted to say there

has never been a more sacramental understanding of the liturgy than this classical Reformed understanding. One is tempted to say that though the Eastern Orthodox, Roman, Lutheran, and Anglican traditions join with the Reformed in understanding the Lord's Supper sacramentally, they, with the exception of the Lutheran, do not characteristically understand the sermon thus. They shy away from acknowledging that the preaching of the word *is* the word of God — that *praedicatio verbum dei est verbum dei.* For them, a sermon is a "mere sign." But to summarize the difference in that way would not quite be accurate; it would be to misstate, even to understate, the difference. For a sacrament, on the traditional understanding, consists of some material element that effects the grace it signifies. The Reformed tradition says something much stronger: that in the liturgy we are confronted with sacraments. After all, the efficacy of a sacrament, as traditionally understood, is fully compatible with God's present inactivity. The Reformed tradition insists that to participate in the liturgy is not so much to enter the sphere of grace-efficacious material as to enter the sphere of

Reprinted from *Reformed Liturgy and Music* 19 (Spring 1985): 67-71.

God here and now acting by way of material. The Reformed understanding of the liturgy is thus more than sacramental. It is, to coin a word, a *theourgonic* understanding (from the Greek for God, *theos,* and action, *ergon*).

One of the connections between liturgy, thus understood, and justice is that, *when God is allowed to say to us in the liturgy what God wants to say to us, God speaks often of justice.* God asks of us that we struggle for justice in the world. We must admit that our liturgies often muffle this word of the Lord. Yet we know from the great prophetic literature of the Bible that justice is God's abiding will. Justice is more than human: it is sacred. Injustice is desecration. We take in hand, for example, the book of the shepherd-prophet Amos, and we hear not Amos's opinion but rather Amos's report of what God said to him: "let justice roll down like waters, and righteousness like an ever-flowing stream." The struggle for justice is the struggle for the embodiment of holiness in our world. Authentic liturgy confronts us with God here and now saying to us: Seek justice.

This point has become more or less familiar to all of us from contemporary discussion about liturgy and justice. Accordingly, though it is of profound importance, I wish on this occasion to probe a different connection between liturgy and justice. To participate in the liturgy is not only to *enter* the sphere of God's redemptive action; it is also, for members of that community that acknowledges Jesus Christ as Lord, to *respond* to that action. Naturally we respond to that action throughout the week, but there are also actions of response that have their home right within the celebration of the liturgy: adoration, praise, thanksgiving, confession, blessing, intercession. Such actions as these are the actions of *worship,* properly speaking. It is to the deep connection between worship and justice that I wish on this occasion to speak. The connection between proclamation and justice has be-

come familiar to all of us. The connection between worship and justice has almost eluded our attention. In probing this connection I shall be making special use of some of Calvin's meditations on the image of God in the human person.[1]

THE GROUND OF JUSTICE

In our contemporary world there are basically two theories as the ground, or basis, of justice. One is the utilitarian theory of such thinkers as John Stuart Mill: the struggle for justice is crucial to the pursuit of a happy society — the greatest happiness of the greatest number. The main alternative to this utilitarian theory is the Kantian theory. Kant argued that since the utilitarian theory is based on what as a matter of empirical fact makes us happy, an implication of the theory is that justice is in principle dispensable. If we human beings changed in significant ways with respect to what makes us happy, justice would no longer be an obligation. But that is mistaken, says Kant. It cannot be that we might no longer be obligated to give others their due. Justice must indeed be grounded in our nature, but it must be grounded in our unchangeable, transcendental nature. It is grounded in the unalterable fact that we are free agents. No matter how much our circumstances may buffet us, it is always available to us to *choose* how we shall live. At the core of being a person is *will* — *free* will. And the demand to act justly is at bottom just one of the dictates of our nature as autonomous agents. We are to act in accord with the inescapable fact that we are capable of acting freely on principles. Anyone who fails to act justly is failing to act in accord with his or her nature, and, conversely, anyone who acts in accord with his or her nature will act justly.

Now in the Christian tradition, as I have already indicated, a profoundly different answer is regularly given: *justice is grounded in the will of God.* A fascinating feature of Calvin's thought, however, is that though he shares fully in that tradition, when he urges his readers and listeners to act justly and charitably toward their fellow human beings, he regularly appeals not to the will of God but rather to the fact that human beings are made in the image of God. Thus he appeals to our nature, as do Mill and Kant — though of course he understands that nature very differently. Let me quote a passage in which the point is made repetitively and insistently:

> The Lord commands all men without exception "to do good." Yet the great part of them are most unworthy if they be judged by their own merit. But here Scripture helps in the best way when it teaches that we are not to consider what men merit of themselves but to look upon the image of God in all men, to which we owe all honor and love. However, it is among members of the household of faith that this same image is more carefully to be noted, in so far as it has been renewed and restored through the Spirit of Christ. Therefore, whatever man you meet who needs your aid, you have no reason to refuse to help him. Say, "He is a stranger"; but the Lord has given him a mark that ought to be familiar to you, by virtue of the fact that he forbids you to despise your own flesh. Say, "He is contemptible and worthless"; but the Lord shows him to be one to whom he has deigned to give the beauty of his image. Say that you owe nothing for any service of his; but God, as it were, has put him in his own place in order that you may recognize toward him the many and great benefits with which God has bound you to himself. Say that he does not deserve even your least effort for his sake; but the image of God, which recommends him to you, is worthy of your giving yourself and all your possessions. Now if he has not only deserved no good at your hand, but has also provoked you by unjust acts and curses, not even this is just reason why you should cease to embrace him in love and to perform the duties of love on his behalf. You will say, "He has deserved

something far different of me." Yet what has the Lord deserved? . . . It is that we remember not to consider men's evil intention but to look upon the image of God in them, which cancels and effaces their transgressions, and with its beauty and dignity allures us to love and embrace them.[2]

For Calvin, the demands of justice and the demands of charity are grounded in the fact that *to be a human being is to be a living icon of God* and, as such, to bear a dignity beyond the roles that we inhabit and beyond the ends that we pursue.

But what is the pattern of Calvin's thought here? In what way are we images or icons of God? Calvin was fond of using the metaphor of a mirror: to be human is to mirror God. But in what respects do we mirror God? And how exactly are the demands of justice and of charity grounded in this mirroring? Clearly Calvin's thought is that to abuse the mirror is to abuse that which it mirrors — to abuse a human being is to abuse God. But why is this? Why is the perpetration of injustice a mode of wounding God? Why is the struggle for justice a mode of loving and adoring God?

IMAGE, JUSTICE, AND GOD'S DELIGHT

Two biblical passages seem to have been decisive in shaping Calvin's thought here. One was Genesis 9:5b-6, which in the Jerusalem Bible runs as follows:

> I will demand an account of every man's life from his fellow men.
>
>> He who sheds man's blood,
>> shall have his blood shed by man,
>> for in the image of God
>> man was made.

A direct connection is here drawn between our proper treatment of our fellow human beings and their status as icons of God. Calvin's commentary on the passage is illuminating:

> Men are indeed unworthy of God's care, if respect be had only to themselves; but since they bear the image of God engraven on them, He deems himself violated in their person. Thus, although they have nothing of their own by which they obtain the favor of God, he looks upon his own gifts in them, and is thereby excited to love and to care for them. This doctrine, however, is to be carefully observed, that no one can be injurious to his brother without wounding God himself. Were this doctrine deeply fixed in our minds, we should be much more reluctant than we are to inflict injuries.[3]

The thought is striking: God beholds what God has made. God observes that God's human creatures are icons of God's own self. God observes that they mirror God, that they image God, that they are likenesses of God. In this God delights. This grounds God's love. God delights indeed in all God's works. But human beings are singled out from other creatures in that in them God's own perfections are mirrored. Accordingly, to abuse one of our fellows is to abuse one of those creatures who above all give God delight. It is true, indeed, that the demand for justice is grounded in our nature — specifically, in the fact that to be human is to be a creature standing in that special relation to God of mirroring. It would be better, though, to say that the demands of justice lie in God, and not most fundamentally in God's will but in God's sorrow and in God's joy, in God's suffering and in God's delight. To treat unjustly one of these creatures in whom God experiences the delight of finding God mirrored is to bring sorrow to God. To wound God's beloved is to wound God. Conversely, to treat such a creature with justice and charity is to delight God. "God Himself, looking on men as formed in His own image, regards them with such love and honor that He Himself feels wounded and outraged in the persons of those who are the victims of human cruelty and wickedness."[4]

Admittedly, Calvin does not say in his commentary on Genesis 9 that what delights God in looking upon us human creatures is our *likeness* to God. Rather, he says that what delights God is the presence of "His own gifts in" us. But that Calvin sees likeness to God as central in God's gifts to us is abundantly evident from other passages. " 'So man was created in the image of God'; in him the Creator himself willed that his own glory be seen as in a mirror" (*Inst.*, 2.12.6). "God looks upon Himself, as one might say, and beholds Himself in men as in a mirror."[5] "God's children are pleasing and lovable to him, since he sees in them the marks and features of his own countenance. . . . Wherever God contemplates his own face, he both rightly loves it and holds it in honor" (*Inst.*, 3.17.5).

UNIVERSALITY OF IMAGE

The other passage which especially shaped Calvin's thoughts on image and justice, and to which he repeatedly appealed, is the command in Isaiah 58:7d, "not to hide yourself from your own flesh." To understand the import of this command we must look at the entirety of v. 7, and indeed, at v. 6 as well:

> Is not this the fast that I choose;
>> to loose the bonds of wickedness,
>> to undo the thongs of the yoke,
> to let the oppressed go free,
>> and to break every yoke?
> Is it not to share your bread with the hungry,
>> and bring the homeless poor into your house;
> when you see the naked, to cover him,
>> and not to hide yourself from your own flesh?

In his commentary on this passage, Calvin says (in part) that

> it is not enough to abstain from acts of injustice, if you refuse your assistance to the needy. . . .

By commanding them to "break bread to the hungry," God intended to take away every excuse from covetous and greedy men, who allege that they have a right to keep possession of that which is their own. . . . And indeed, this is the dictate of common sense, that the hungry are deprived of their just right, if their hunger is not relieved. . . . At length he concludes — *And that you hide not yourself from your own flesh.* Here we ought to observe the term *flesh,* by which he means all men universally, not a single one of whom we can behold, without seeing, as in a mirror, "our own flesh." It is therefore a proof of the greatest inhumanity, to despise those in whom we are constrained to recognize our own likeness.[6]

In other passages Calvin makes the same point even more strikingly:

we cannot but behold our own face as it were in a glass in the person that is poor and despised . . . though he were the furthest stranger in the world. Let a Moor or a Barbarian come among us, and yet inasmuch as he is a man, he brings with him a looking glass wherein we may see that he is our brother and neighbor.[7]

Once again the thought is striking. All of us human beings are images and icons of God. All of us mirror God. By virtue of that fact we exist in profound unity with each other: to see another human being is to see another creature who delights God by mirroring God. There can be no more profound kinship among God's creatures than this. Furthermore, each of us mirrors God in the same respects — though as we shall shortly see, some do so more, some less. Thereby we also, in a derivative way, resemble each other. One could say that we mirror each other. In looking at you and at me, God finds God's own self mirrored. Accordingly, in my looking at you I also discern, once my eyes have been opened, that you mirror God — and more, I discern that you mirror me. I discern myself as in a mirror. I discern a family likeness. Thus to fail to practice the requirements of justice toward one's fellow

human beings is not only to bring suffering to God but to fail in the duties of kinship, and thereby to act with "the greatest inhumanity."

It is especially important that we recognize that the duties of justice pertain *irrevocably* to all human beings. For mirroring God is at the core of what it is to be a human being; one cannot be a human being and fail to mirror God. Though a person's mirroring of God can be painfully distorted and blurred, it cannot be eliminated.

Should anyone object, that this divine image has been obliterated, the solution is easy; first, there yet exists some remnant of it, so that man is possessed of no small dignity; and, secondly, the Celestial Creator himself, however corrupted man may be, still keeps in view the end of his original creation; and according to his example, we ought to consider for what end he created men, and what excellence he has bestowed upon them above the rest of living things.[8]

There is nothing that can happen to a human being, and there is nothing that a human being can do, to bring it about that the requirements of justice and of charity no longer pertain to him or her.

WHAT DO WE IMAGE?

But wherein lies our iconicity? In what respects do we mirror God back to God, and then to us? Calvin offers two rules of thumb for answering this question. In the first place, our iconicity is to be discerned in that which differentiates us from other creatures: "the likeness of God extends to the whole excellence by which man's nature towers over all the kinds of living creatures" (*Inst.,* 1.15.4) And second, we must keep in mind that our likeness to God can be increased and diminished. Indeed, the fundamental goal of our human existence is to become as like God as possible — or, to use the language of the Orthodox tradition, to become as divinized as possible. And what would a human being's full likeness to God be like? The answer to that question we apprehend in Jesus Christ, who is "the express image of the Father."

When we follow these two rules of thumb, of looking at our uniqueness and of looking at Jesus Christ, we learn one thing, that we are like God in being creatures of understanding, and that the more our understanding expands — especially our understanding of God — the more we become like God. We learn also that we are like God in being creatures who can govern our affections and thereby our actions, and that the more our heart is upright, the more like God we become. These two are, for Calvin, the principal resemblances, but there are others as well. In our (mandated) governance of creation is to be seen a mirroring of God's governance, and in our formation of communities is to be seen a mirroring of the perfect community of the Trinity. No doubt some of us today would wish to add that we mirror God in our creativity.

Back, though, to our understanding of mind and uprightness of heart. In no human being, says Calvin, are these entirely absent. No human being fails to mirror God in these respects; in all there is some understanding and some goodness. It is for this reason, then, that whenever we come across a human being we are to act in accord with the fact that we have come across an icon of the Holy One in whom God finds delight.

One last turn: not only does the recognition of the iconicity of our fellows require the practice of justice, but in practicing justice, *we ourselves* become like God. Our own imaging is enhanced. To acknowledge God's icon in one's fellow is to enhance one's own iconicity. *For God is just.* The practice of justice is an indispensable means to that goal of becoming like God. In some of the early Greek Fathers one also finds profound reflections on the sig-

nificance of the mysterious biblical word that we are made in the image of God. In answer to the question as to how we can enhance that image in us, the Greek Fathers always said: by contemplation. Calvin agreed with them on that, but he added something else of profound importance. We also enhance our imaging by the practice of justice. The practice of injustice not only brings sorrow to God and violates our bonds of kinship but also prolongs our alienation from our true end.

WORSHIP AND JUSTICE

By now the connection of worship to justice will be evident. It is because our fellow human beings are joined irrevocably with us in mirroring God's glory, especially God's wisdom and goodness, that we are to treat them with justice. But also it is God's glory, including God's wisdom and goodness, that grounds our worship with praise and adoration and blessing and thanksgiving. Worship and justice are thus joined in being two ways of acknowledging God's glory. So united are they, that to worship and not practice justice is to worship inauthentically, or in blindness to God's glory mirrored in human creatures, and to practice justice and not worship is to practice justice inauthentically, or in blindness to God's glory all about us.

I close with one of the ancient prayers of the eucharist, a portion of the anaphora from the Coptic liturgy of St. Mark, in which the glory of God's wisdom, power, and goodness is praised:

> it is truly fitting and right, holy and suitable, and profitable to our souls, Master, Lord, God, Father Almighty, to praise you, to hymn you, to give thanks to you, to confess you night and day with unhushed lips, and unsilenced heart; you who have made heaven and what is in heaven, the earth and what is on earth, seas, springs, rivers, lakes and all that is in them; you

who made man according to your own image and likeness. You made everything through your wisdom, the true light, your only Son, our Lord and God and Savior, Jesus Christ, through whom with him and the Holy Spirit we give thanks to you and offer this reasonable and bloodless service, which all the nations offer you, from sunrise to sunset, from south to north, for your name is great among all the nations, and in every place incense is offered to your holy name and a pure sacrifice, a sacrifice and offering.[9]

NOTES

1. The best treatment of Calvin's reflections on the image of God is to be found in chaps. 3-6 of Thomas F. Torrance, *Calvin's Doctrine of Man* (London: Lutterworth Press, 1952). The best treatment of Calvin's reflections on the social import of the image of God is to be found in Ronald S. Wallace, *Calvin's Doctrine of the Christian Life* (Edinburgh: Oliver & Boyd, 1959), especially part 3, chaps. 1 and 5.

2. Calvin, *Institutes of the Christian Religion*, Library of Christian Classics, vols. 20-21, ed. John T. McNeill, trans. Ford Lewis Battles (Philadelphia: Westminster Press, 1960), 3.7.6. Subsequent references to this work will be made parenthetically in the text.

3. Calvin's *Commentary on Genesis*, trans. John King (Grand Rapids: Baker Book, 1979).

4. Paraphrase of a point made by Calvin in his sermon on Deut. 4:39-43, in Wallace, *Calvin's Doctrine of the Christian Life*, p. 149.

5. Calvin, sermon on Job 10:7, cited by Torrance in *Calvin's Doctrine of Man*, p. 39.

6. From Calvin's *Commentary on Isaiah*, trans. William Pringle (Grand Rapids: William B. Eerdmans, 1948). I have changed the "thou's" in the translation to "you's."

7. Sermon on Gal. 6:9-11, cited by Wallace in *Calvin's Doctrine of the Christian Life*, p. 150.

8. Calvin, commentary on Gen. 9:6.

9. *Prayers of the Eucharist: Early and Reformed*, trans. R. C. Jasper and G. J. Cuming (New York: Oxford University Press, 1980), p. 48.

A Brief Theology of Preaching

David Buttrick

In a comic strip, a frock-coated parson is asked a question, "Why do preachers preach?" The minister scratches his head: "Hmmmmmm," he says. Then, he opens his mouth to answer but "Duhhhh" comes out. Finally, in the last panel of the comic strip, he wanders off with a giant question mark over his head. The giant question mark — "Why do preachers preach?" — hangs over all ministers.

There is no obvious social justification for preaching; people today do not sense that they have to have preaching in the same way that they must have an automobile or the services of a family physician. From a social perspective, preaching may be superfluous — unless we are eager to buy into a Durkheimian view of religion and society. Reasons for preaching can be found only in faith. So, though we may enjoy the sweet freedoms of a superfluous vocation, in faith let us struggle with the question "Why do preachers preach?" On the basis of theological reflection we can say the following.

Reprinted from *Homiletic: Mores and Structures* (Philadelphia: Fortress, 1987), pp. 449-59.

1. *Our preaching, commissioned by the resurrection, is a continuation of the preaching of Jesus Christ.*

According to Scripture, "Jesus came preaching." He announced an imminent kingdom of God and urged people to repent and believe in the gospel. Jesus declared God's new age and called for faith, faith with courage to change. We begin by remembering a Jewish preacher, Jesus of Nazareth.

Almost immediately, Jesus constituted a symbolic community, twelve disciples, who as "fishers" were to share his declarative ministry. So we have Jesus Christ-in-community preaching. Arguments over which came first and, therefore, which has primacy, gospel or church, are chicken-egg disputes. They are irrelevant. God's Word, spoken, constitutes community, for God's Word always takes flesh. What is primary is neither gospel nor church but Jesus Christ, who has created both a word-community and a community-word. The community that Jesus Christ called together was not significantly religious. Jesus handed out no moral placement tests, searched no incipient spirituality, required no sense of priestly vocation; humanity seemed to be the only qualification. We must not view the disciples romantically; they were not humble — fishermen in those days were successful entrepreneurs; they were not outcasts — Levi was the only tax collector in the bunch; they were not single-minded in their response to Christ's call — the sons of Zebedee had their eyes on a main chance. Jesus Christ constituted a symbolic human community and became Jesus Christ-in-community preaching.

The resurrection of Jesus Christ, following his cruel and unusual death, shoved the community into the world and gave the community life. Almost all resurrection accounts include a "Go tell!" commissioning of the community. The community was commissioned to continue Christ's preaching, now unquestionably validated by resurrection. The kingdom *was,* the new age *had begun,* because, though judged, condemned, and crucified, Christ had risen. Resurrection certified the truth of Christ's message and, more, established Christ, Living Symbol, as a part of the message. In essence, we have a gospel with a story line — the kingdom is come, the new age has dawned — and within the gospel, the Living Symbol, Jesus Christ, who reveals God-toward-us. Story and symbol are dimensions of *one* gospel. The community understood itself to be a witness to the resurrection, commissioned to extend the preaching of Christ in the world.

The resurrection also gave the community salvific new life. Joined to Jesus Christ, the community had passed through death, burial, and resurrection. They were judged by Christ's death (had they not betrayed, denied, and deserted him?) but were forgiven by his risen presence with them. They were liberated from the burden of law, for Christ, condemned under the law, was risen! They were free to live as a sign of the kingdom because, with resurrection, the new age had clearly begun. Thus, the community understood itself as a *being-saved* new humanity in the world. The evident new life

they shared confirmed and interpreted the gospel they preached. The resurrection of Jesus Christ was also a resurrection of Jesus Christ-in-community; the early Christians knew that they had passed from death to life.

We continue the preaching of Jesus Christ as witnesses to the resurrection. However, the figure of Jesus Christ, Living Symbol, has not nudged to one side the message he preached, the message of the kingdom of God. This issue is crucial. Theological liberalism preached a "horizontal" gospel: it wrapped up the message of the kingdom in a bundle of social idealism. Neo-orthodoxy, reacting to liberalism, embraced a "vertical" gospel which, to some extent, oriented "repent and believe" toward Christ alone. But these options are not two different gospels between which we must choose. The Living Symbol, Jesus Christ, does not obliterate the message of the kingdom that he declared. Likewise, the message of the kingdom may not be preached without reference to the reality of Christ risen. There is one gospel that Jesus Christ declared and in which he lives! So we are a joined-to-Jesus Christ community, given life by resurrection, which continues the preaching of Jesus in the world.

2. *In our preaching, Christ continues to speak to the church, and through the church to the world.* In this respect, preaching is grace: "I speak, yet, not I; Christ speaks through me."

Events generate language. Perhaps it would be better to say that events are linguistic explosions; they generate conversations that spread through the world, through time and space. Thus, events continue as generated conversations. For example, "the War between the States" continues as phrases generated by the Civil War still function in familiar usage. Think of phrases — "Fourscore and seven years ago . . . ," "Damn Yankees," "Carpetbagger," and (scribbled on a bourbon bottle) "Rebel Yell" — but think also of symbols: from a hushed Lincoln Memorial to a Mississippi cheerleader draped in Confederate flags, singing not so sweetly of a South that "will rise again." Of course, language can die out or be modified so as to mean differently. Thus, probably (and happily) the language of the Confederacy will fade away, if, eventually, there is no sense of "Southern" identity alive. Therefore, what is astonishing about the language of the gospel is its *duration.* Though the language of the gospel is modified, age on age, it continues. Think of sermons (at least a million a week), of religious publishing, of gospel music, of banners and stained-glass and other Christian works of art. We must assume that the gospel continues because the living reality of being-saved in the world persists, and because mysterious Presence-in-Absence still impinges on human consciousness. The gospel continues because the Living Symbol, Jesus Christ, does interpret being-saved and still discloses the interior of the Mystery of God-with-us. Preaching is the preaching of Jesus Christ because it opens to us salvific new life and discloses the reality of God-toward-us.

Christian preaching not only reveals but continues the work of Christ by calling, liberating, and forming a new humanity. The functions of preaching, then, continue the work of Christ who gathered a people to himself and, by death and resurrection, set them free for new life in the world. We have seen that words are not merely tokens of exchange but that they mediate reality, bring reality into being. Christ, the mediator, brought to us God's astonishing love and created a community for God-love. Likewise, our preaching words continue Christ's own work of revelation and redemption in the world.

The mystery of preaching is thus a mystery of grace. By the Spirit, Christ speaks through us, a broken, risen community. Note that the rationale for preaching is not institutional. We do not preach so the church may survive or gain members or triumph in the world. Primarily we preach so Christ may use

our words in a salvific work, revealing and redeeming. The church may well be a sign of redemption, but the church per se is not the *end* of redemption or the reason for our speaking. Preaching, therefore, is a spiritual discipline in which we offer our best words to Christ. No wonder that as preachers we are even on guard against our own ego trips, our self-righteous moralisms, and our whoop-de-do church-boosting impulses. The burden of preaching should send us scurrying to Scripture, to the study of theology, and to an earnest gleeful life of prayer. On the other hand, there is wonderful freedom for preachers in the mystery of grace: "I, yet, not I!" In Christ, the burden of preaching is light.

3. The purpose of preaching is the purpose of God in Christ — namely, the reconciliation of the world.

In Jesus Christ we see the mysterious Love of God reaching out with spectacular modesty to the human world. "God loved the world so much," sings the Gospel of John, "that [God] gave the only Son . . . *not* to condemn the world, *but* so the world could be saved." By "saved," the Scriptures envision a new social reality in communion with God, a social reality in which forgiven people are free for love and may live together as family of God. Such a vision may run counter to notions of personal salvation that rescue individuals from a deathward world for eternal life hereafter, but they also run counter to optimism regarding human potential and social progress, because, after all, *God* must save. The notion of reconciliation also opposes any preaching that, out of lust for orthodoxy, is divisive and will not declare the hope of full human *community* with God. In Scripture, salvation seems to be understood in terms of the Great Commandment. Salvation is reconciliation in which we are free for love of God and neighbors. Thus, God's purpose — however, whenever, wherever — must be conceived as communion with a reconciled world.

The purpose of preaching, broadly considered, is nothing less than the saving purpose of God.

Preaching is liberation. We speak to set people free. Human beings, particularly today, see themselves in bondage, and rightly so. Certainly we are all psychologically bound by sedimentations of the past that still exert a terrifying sway over us; we enact ourselves regressively, we self-destruct over guilts, we depressively rehearse ancient rancors, we reel in dizzy angst, and so on. Moreover, we sense that we live enslaved in a world dominated by principalities and powers, systems of thought and action to which we conform in order to ensure our social acceptance. The social and psychological structures in which we live are bondage to sin and estrangement from God. Therefore, to be reconciled, we will have to be set free from bondage. We will not debate which form of bondage is primary — psychological or social: such debate would be fruitless. There can be no redemption of the self without a liberation of the social world, and no redemption of the social world without release from the self's inner bondage. All we are saying is that preaching, as it shares God's saving purpose, will be a liberating word.

Preaching has a time. Preaching is a conversation generated by the event of Jesus Christ that will continue until Christ's redemptive work is done, a consummation symbolized by his second coming. Though preaching has continued down through many centuries, it is nonetheless an *interim* activity. We preach between the event of Jesus Christ and the fulfillment of God's purpose in Christ. The use of the term *interim* may connote a static waiting period determined by the resiliency of sin and the fortunate patience of God. By *interim*, though, we intend a time filled with the activity of God shaping salvation. The promise of God's future is already acting on our present, is exerting a plotting power over present events — denouement is unfolding even now. Thus, preaching does not hand out the offer of salvation based on past events in a *static* present time. True preaching includes a celebration of God's promise which is *now* happening among us. "Now," says Paul with remarkable enthusiasm, "Now is the day of salvation!"

4. *Preaching evokes response: The response to preaching is a response to Christ, and is, properly, faith and repentance.*

In the preaching of Jesus, the terms *repent* and *believe* should not be understood as a fixed sequence, two steps in a rigid *ordo salutis*. Repentance and faith are facets of the same reality. Faith in mercy is repentant, and repentance has a faith in mercy. So let us realize that faith and repentance are not steps in a pilgrimage of soul — *first* you repent and *then* you believe; rather they interface — we repent into faith, and in faith we repent.

Moreover, let us remember that when Jesus urged people to "repent and believe," he did so in view of an impending kingdom of God, a new social reality in the world. Thus repentance and believing may not be regarded as motions of the soul detached from social reality or even motions of the soul in relation to Christ alone. The message of the kingdom and a call for response belong together: we believe not merely in Jesus but in Jesus Christ as inaugurator of the kingdom. Therefore faith is best understood as entrance into a new order of life and a concomitant turning from an old order (repentance) through Jesus Christ.

Our response to the gospel is made possible by the gospel. As Paul observes, "faith comes from hearing" (Rom. 10:17). Elsewhere, in addressing the blither-headed Galatians, Paul remarks that the Spirit is given via "faith-hearing" of a preached gospel. At minimum we may say that response to the gospel is made possible by gospel preaching. We must not separate Word and Spirit: the Word of preaching (by the Spirit) sets us free to respond to the Word (by the Spirit). Now, we must be cautious. We are not saying that the *way* the gospel is preached will determine response, for example, in conversion. The church has leaped into all kinds of inspirational hokum, not to mention evangelistic manipulation, trying to effect conversion. ("As the choir sings, 'Just as I Am,' raise your hands. . . . Yes, I see you, and you, and you!") If the church has not gone in for hokum, it frequently has designed sermons in a conversionist pattern: first, lay on a heavy sense of guilt, and then, when the congregation quivers in despair, hand out a carrot-on-a-stick Jesus with mercy. Such strategies, including emotional climaxes, threats of coming wrath, last-chance gospels, and the like, border on manipulation and are a denial of our freedom for God. Rightly, preaching sets us free by announcing the new era in Christ and declaring mercy. Preaching is essentially a *good* news that liberates (see the careful contrast drawn in Rom. 1:17-18).

Preaching may also be met with what the Bible terms "hardness of heart." No matter how winsome in style or generous in promise, preaching can be met with fierce opposition. People may oppose the good news because they have overinvested in "this present age" and are afraid they will lose what they have — power, possessions, prestige. They are, of course, quite correct: they probably will! Not surprisingly, affluent, power-structure people may have much difficulty in even hearing the gospel. (Church growth is not likely to occur among the "haves.") Opposition to the gospel may also come from those who have "gotten themselves together" psychologically and, thus, fear they may lose themselves in the new order of the gospel. Again, they are probably quite perceptive. Psychological togetherness these days may well mean adjustment to forms of social self-approval. The two fears — social loss and psychological loss — are both related to "things as they are" being threatened by the new order of the gospel. The usual shibboleth that people refuse the gospel because they are self-righteous and therefore will not admit their

sin and repent is too facile. The gospel may be heard as an assault on cherished values, on life goals, on political and psychological stabilities. When Paul reaches for an explanation of why folks refuse the gospel, he snarls that "the god of this world has blinded the minds of the unbelievers," and he is no doubt quite correct.

Because preachers preach, they may become targets for a refusal of the gospel. We must be very careful, however: preachers may deserve rebuke by being arrogant, obtuse, assertive, or self-righteous. (We preachers may not be all that lovable!) We must examine our gospel by the measure of apostolic preaching to be sure that we are preaching gospel and not merely hyperventilating in our pulpits in some irritating way. Nevertheless, refusal of the gospel should not surprise us. If we do preach good news of a new order in Christ Jesus, it will be received gladly by some (usually those who are broken) but may be rejected by others (usually those who are "together" and have "made it big"). We should not be startled if the gospel is refused, falls on deaf ears, or even provokes angry "yuppie" oppositions.

Preaching in America during the last quarter of the twentieth century may be difficult indeed. America is powerful, affluent, and as a nation is obviously trying to hold onto itself in the world. Thus, a gospel of God's new order will scarcely be well received, particularly by established, and often quite conservative, Protestant communities. In American history the rise of national power has been paralleled by the rise of a Protestant establishment. Will an established order take kindly to the disestablishing message of the gospel? Preaching in America may well be very difficult! Is it any wonder, then, that we have often truncated the gospel? We have preached "repent and believe" as an appeal to personal salvation but frequently neglected to announce the "kingdom of God is at hand." Or we may preach Christ crucified as a sufficient atonement for sin but not mention Christ as the inauguration of God's new age. The gospel does imply a relinquishing of power, position, and even of psychological togetherness. People, American people, may well reject the gospel that announces an end to "this present age."

When some Christians assert that the gospel requires of us a decision or perhaps, more often, a decision for Jesus, they are recognizing the confrontational character of the gospel. If, in fact, the gospel does call us to live in God's new social order, then it is bound to involve a world-conversation, some "letting go" and "deciding for," a profound alteration in our understanding of ourselves. They may also be recognizing a setting free within the gospel which may be expressed decisively. The obvious problem with the notion of a decision is that, overstated, it can undercut the conviction that we are saved by grace and overlook the formative power of the gospel preached. When in retrospect we view our decisions of faith, we stumble on grace at every turn. We heard the gospel preached, and it changed our minds. We were in the presence of a being-saved community which, to some extent, displayed the new age. The notion of decision may never be put forth at the expense of the gospel or as a denigration of the Spirit with community. What the idea of decision does is to underscore the radical revision of world that the gospel truly involves.

We have said that response to the gospel can take the shape of a response to preaching and even of a response to the preacher. For those to whom the gospel is liberation, preaching may be a Word of God, the voice of the living Christ. Those who refuse the gospel preached may sense that on some deep, terrifying level they have hardened and have shut out the Word of God. In this regard, it may be true to say that preaching can harden opposition and drive structures of sin more deeply into resistant people. What preachers may *not* expect (but often fantasize about) is widespread approval of their preaching or even public praise. If people are grateful for a liberating word we have spoken, we may never lay claim to their approval, since ultimately we affirm "the grace of our Lord Jesus Christ." For preachers, preaching is a no-win situation. We can never greet opposition as sure evidence of sin without first examining our own thoroughly mixed motivations, our lack of love, and our strident self-aggrandizements; and we can never bask in praise as if we are anything more than mediators, the servants of grace. Though we can take no credit and, indeed, must accept our share of blame, there are compensations. Because we are preachers, we are afforded the gladness of exploring the gospel week after week and thus coming to know the Mystery of God through Jesus Christ. Gain enough!

5. Preaching is the "Word of God" in that it participates in God's purpose, is initiated by Christ, and is supported by the Spirit with community in the world.

When we affirm that preaching is the "Word of God," we must be careful. Obviously, a great deal of pulpit arrogance has been tossed off by preachers who, without reservation, have equated their voices with the voice of God. But, as the apostles in the book of Acts were quick to admit, we are only human, and we speak with human voices. We are frequently scared, fuzzy-headed, lazy, supercilious, and downright nonsensical. Who was it that suggested that the proper liturgical garb for preaching had to be a clown suit? We are emphatically human, and we speak human words. Preaching must be described as a human activity that draws on human understanding and employs human homiletic skills that can be learned. Thus, though we preach knee-deep in grace, we can claim no status for our words. Gratitude, wonderment, a sense of inadequacy — all are preferable to status claims, particularly status claims for the words we speak.

On the other hand, preachers should not

lose track of mysteries in preaching, so that they regard sermons as human works of art or eloquence. Once more, we must modestly claim that preaching *is* "the Word of God." We may be two-legged little human beings, but we stand before the mysterious Presence-in-Absence and, through Christ, mediate understandings of God to a being-saved community in a most mysterious world. Good heavens, what a vocation! Though we are quite aware of our humanness, nevertheless, by faith we preach as if we were means of grace, which we are! We believe that through our words God reaches out, claims, converts, and saves because we continue the preaching of Jesus Christ. So our ministerial vocation is peculiar. We are chronically bemused by our obvious inadequacy, our demonstrable humanity (we can live without the notion that we are professionals!) and, at the same time, staggered by being *chosen* to preach. Christ transfers preaching to us and gives grace to our speaking, so that, odd as it may seem, our sermons are the Word of God to human communities.

In suggesting that we preach the Word of God, we must sidestep a spiritualist position. The Spirit with our spirits does not by some God-magic hand us words to speak. Grace does not bypass humanity. The Spirit, as Luther claimed, is a matter of faith, not a self-evident experience or some sort of overwhelming God-feeling. When preachers have flat Sundays, as every preacher does, and begin boring themselves with their own sermons, it is not a sign of the Spirit's absence; the preacher merely may be underprepared (or overprepared), weary, sexually frustrated, or goodness knows what. Likewise, when words seem to tumble from our lips, spinning in wild flights of poetic wonder, it is not a sign of the Spirit's presence; we may be feeling good and thus be both free and fanciful. The presence of the Spirit is not self-evident but it is, indeed, an article of faith — of *homiletic* faith. Wherever there is faith in Jesus Christ, the Spirit is with community and with speakers to

community. While the Spirit may give homiletic gifts, courage, wisdom, and even a certain transparency of spirit to preaching, we cannot identify the Spirit with particular rhetoric or particular moments in preaching. The Spirit labors as much in our struggles as in our spontaneities. As Paul suggested, the test of the Spirit in connection with preaching is the edification of the Christian community.

Again, if we say that preaching is or does the "Word of God," we must not argue from a fundamentalist position. The repetition of Scripture, or even the careful interpretation of Scripture, does not guarantee that preaching will be Word of God. To go further, reiterations of the biblical worldview or rehearsals of biblical event over against our more modern worldview will not ensure that preaching is Word of God. To so argue would be to insist that by *works* of fidelity we can take charge of God's Word. No, God is free even from our fidelities! So, let us be willing to say baldly that it is possible to preach the Word of God without so much as mentioning Scripture. Preachers will receive Scripture as a gift of grace, and they will delight in Scripture, study Scripture, live with Scripture so as to be grasped by the God revealed in Jesus Christ. Furthermore, preachers may indeed wish to preach from Scripture as they interpret things of God to a being-saved community in the world. But we must not say that preaching from Scripture is requisite for sermons to be the Word of God. An authority model descending from God to Christ to Scripture to sermon could lead to a terrifying arrogance that not only contradicts gospel but destroys preaching. The little white tabs that dangle from some preachers' necks are said to symbolize the two tablets of the law (a good reason to toss them away). If Scripture should become the *law* of preaching, then preaching will no longer be the Word of God.

A further caveat: we must not dally with a notion that the preacher's character is the

"Word of God." Popular conviction seems to suggest that the minister's Christian personality somehow speaks through sermons so that, no matter how inept the sermon, people are drawn to God. All things considered, we should endorse loving, pious, generous ministers, but we should *not* argue that character speaks louder than words. Even when the notion is buttressed by an Aristotelian appeal to *ethos,* it is still theologically impossible. What the position does is undercut preaching altogether, so that what we say is devalued in the light of who we are. The Second Helvetic Confession rightly insists that we hear the Word of God through the lips of sinful preachers because, after all, what else is there! Just as the Catholic doctrine of *ex opere* was originally framed to protect against the idea that the character of a priest could determine the efficacy of a sacrament, so as preachers (along with the Reformers) we must affirm a kind of *ex opere* of the Word. Our character does not preach. What is more, our character does not determine the gospel or the efficacy of the gospel. Admittedly, we might conceive a preacher who was such an evident "stinker" as to bring public ridicule to the gospel, but even obvious moral turpitude and scandal could not mean that the gospel would not be preached so as to convert, liberate, and save. Yes, most ministers as they preach will be preaching to themselves and, as a result, will wish to bring their broken lives into God's new age. The gospel, however, is always greater than preachers of the gospel —

thank God. As text for our discussion, we recall a truly offensive Christian writer who, when asked why his character was not sweeter, replied, "My God, think what I would have been without Jesus Christ!" The fact is, all preachers serve Christ in brokenness, trusting in grace alone. The Pietist error, in both conservative and liberal communities, has endorsed personality-cult preaching ("Truth through Personality") to the detriment of the gospel. We ourselves are never Word of God.

So, what are we thrown back on? We are flung back on a confidence in the gospel, trust in the grace of God, and prayer for the Spirit with us. Our words are human, and they will not cease to be human; we will work on them just as we work at many human activities, taking pleasure in craft and drawing on intelligence. And we will do our homework like good children of God. Nevertheless, insofar as our words are instigated by Jesus Christ, serve God's salvific purpose, and are ratified by the Spirit with a being-saved community, *they are Word of God.* We speak as we live in mysteries of grace. There is a kind of secret astonishment to preaching: we work hard, we study, we explore the Mystery of God-love and, then — with the naivete of a trusting child, or the desperation of broken people who have to speak of wholeness, or both — we cast ourselves on grace alone. What else? We have been *chosen* to speak God's own Word. No wonder, year in, year out, preaching is terror and gladness.

Toward a Theology of Christian Marriage

Shirley C. Guthrie Jr.

It is obvious that a short article like this cannot provide even a complete outline of a
biblical and theological understanding of
Christian marriage. In what follows I intend
only to propose a brief definition and make
some comments on it that I hope will suggest
some insights, raise some questions, and perhaps stir up some objections that lead readers
to further biblical and theological reflection on
their own. (Those who are familiar with Karl
Barth's extended discussion of marriage in
Church Dogmatics, III/4, pp. 181-240, will recognize how much I have depended on him —
and where at some critical points I have gone
my own way, sometimes in opposition to him.)

> *Christian marriage is a life partnership based
> on mutual human love in faithfulness to God,
> confirmed and witnessed too by a wedding
> ceremony, and sustained by dependence on
> God's forgiving and enabling grace in Jesus
> Christ.*

Reprinted from *Reformed Liturgy and Music* 20
(Summer 1986): 125-28.

A LIFE PARTNERSHIP

The Old Testament speaks of Yahweh as the
husband of Israel. The New Testament speaks
of Christ as the bridegroom of his bride the
church. It is no accident, then, that Christians
think of marriage as a partnership that reflects
the covenant relationship between God and the
people of God. We must, of course, remember
that we can think only of an analogy here in
which there are differences as well as similarities. God's covenant with us is based on the
perfect love, infallible wisdom, and unwavering faithfulness of God, whereas all human
covenants are made between human beings
whose love is imperfect, whose wisdom is
limited, and whose faithfulness is always uncertain. Moreover, the "marriage" between
God and the people of God is a relationship
between a superior divine "husband" and an
inferior human "wife," whereas the marriage
between a man and a woman is a relationship
between two human beings who are equally
created in the image of God (Gen. 1:27) and
for whom all the traditional barriers between
"superior" males and "inferior" females are

broken down and negated in Jesus Christ (Gal. 3:28). Nevertheless, despite such differences, the biblical analogy between God's covenant relationship with the people of God and the covenant relationship between married partners does help us to understand some essential characteristics of a Christian marriage.

1. As God enters freely and gladly into covenant with the people of God and wills them freely and gladly to enter into covenant with him, so it is with a Christian marriage. *A Christian marriage is a partnership in which both partners freely and gladly decide to marry* and are not forced to do so by an external necessity, such as the expectations or demands of parents, social convention, or the church, or by any internal necessity, such as the need to escape loneliness, be married rather than single, have children, and so forth.

2. God makes covenant with the people of God simply because God loves them for their own sake. And God desires them to enter into the covenant relationship simply out of gratitude for who God is, not in order to guarantee their own happiness, power, wealth, or success. So it is with a Christian marriage. *For Christians, marriage exists for its own sake,* not as a means to some other goal such as the satisfaction of sexual needs, the joys and benefits of parenthood, the advancement of the husband's or wife's professional interests, the establishment of a comfortable and beautiful "nest," or any other goal for which marriage partners may use or let themselves be used rather than loving the other for the other's sake.

3. As God wills and enables us in the covenant relationship to be the free, particular human beings God created us to be, so *a Christian marriage is one in which the partners respect, affirm, and encourage the freedom and "otherness" of the other.* In a Christian marriage there can be no expectation or demand that one partner think exactly like the other, have exactly the same tastes, enjoy and do the same things, or in any other way lose

his or her individuality to become a copy, servant, or tool of the other. A Christian marriage is one in which there is mutually freeing, mutually enriching fellowship of two people who affirm (even when they cannot always approve of) the *differences* between them.

4. God is a faithful covenant partner in bad times as well as in good, in sickness as in health, in sadness and failure as in happiness and success, in death as in life. Even when the covenant people are faithless, God remains faithful. Even when they do not deserve God's love, God still loves them and does not reject them. So it is with a Christian marriage. *Christians enter into marriage with the intention and commitment to remain married* not just so long as things go well, so long as it is convenient, so long as it is self-fulfilling and mutually satisfying, so long as the partner is faithful and worthy and deserving — but "until death do us part."

Unlike God and like other fallible, sinful human beings, Christians may make a mistake when they choose their partner. They may sometimes come to the conclusion that their marriage is not and cannot become a true life partnership at all. They may divorce. But a Christian marriage is one in which both partners intend and will a *permanent* partnership, not a temporary or experimental one qualified by any kind of openly expressed or secretly held "if" or "but" or "so long as" escape clause.

5. From God's side the covenant relationship is perfect and final from the very beginning. But from the side of the people of God this perfection is always a hope for the future which they can move toward only slowly, with many setbacks and new beginnings. So it is with a Christian marriage. *A Christian marriage is both a gift and a task.* It is the gift of God to God's human creatures, a gift to be thankfully and joyfully received by them. But it is also a task to be diligently and continually worked at. There are no "perfect marriages." There are at best only life partnerships that

continually and slowly grow in love, commitment, and understanding as the partners work together to *become* truly married.

LIFE PARTNERSHIP BASED ON HUMAN LOVE AND FAITHFULNESS TO GOD

Both things are essential:

1. *Human love.* Christian marriage is based on the love of two people for each other. It is more than just a loving relationship; it is a full life-partnership such as we have described. But the basis of this life partnership is the love of the partners for one another. This love is their free and glad eagerness to live together in mutual openness to see and be seen without withholding anything from one another, to speak honestly and listen attentively, to help and let themselves be helped. It is also love that includes the mutual erotic-sexual desire for each other that Christians and the church have alternately despised and romanticized, underemphasized and overemphasized. While Christian marriage is far more than erotic love, it joyfully and gratefully includes it. For God has created us male and female with physical-sexual needs and has said that this aspect of God's creation, too, is "very good."

2. *Faithfulness to God.* While marriage is the good gift of God, and while Christians will thank God for their partner, God does not make a marriage; two people do. Nevertheless, Christians decide to marry, as they make all other important decisions, seeking to know God's will for what is best for them and other people, seeking God's blessing on their decisions, and seeking God's help in fulfilling their commitments. As they commit their actions, responsibilities, and goals in other areas of life to thankful service of God, so they commit also all their actions, responsibilities, and goals as married people.

This "religious" side of a Christian's decision to marry or stay married does not automatically exclude marriage between a Christian and a non-Christian, or between two people whose Christian faith and commitment are radically different. But it should lead them to consider carefully whether their highest values and deepest commitments might not be so opposed that a genuine life partnership is impossible for them.

LIFE PARTNERSHIP ANNOUNCED AND CONFIRMED BY A WEDDING

A wedding is far more than the civil or religious legalizing of sexual intercourse many consider it to be. But it is also far less than the magical moment a previously unmarried couple suddenly become a married couple, as others consider it to be. It is the public announcement and confirmation of a life partnership that should have begun *before* the wedding ceremony (whether or not the couple has been "sexually active") and will be fulfilled only over a long period of time *after* the wedding.

In order to understand the significance of the wedding, it is important first of all to make a clear distinction between the wedding and "being married." Two people may be legally joined during a civil or ecclesiastical ceremony and yet fail to realize or be on the way toward realizing the life partnership that is a true marriage. (A couple may, therefore, sometimes rightly decide that divorce means not the dissolution of marriage but the acknowledgment that theirs never has been, or is no longer, or cannot become a true marriage.) On the other hand, the full life partnership that is a true marriage could be genuine without the benefit of a civil or religious wedding ceremony. The wedding is only an outward witness and help to the commitment of two people to become married partners.

The distinction between marriage and a wedding does not mean that the wedding is dispensable. As public announcement and confirmation, external witness and help, it is very important if not absolutely essential. This becomes clear as soon as we consider the fact that marriage is never a purely private relationship between two individuals. Each of them is ordinarily a member of a smaller or larger family, and what they do and can become both influences and is influenced by both families for good or ill. Moreover, both partners are also members of a larger society the health, stability, and future of which is helped or hurt by the ordered or disordered, responsible or irresponsible lives of its citizens. Finally, if the couple to be married are Christians, they are members also of a Christian community and are both nurtured by and responsible to that community. Marriage is thus a social and communal matter, not just a private and personal matter, and a wedding is the public recognition, acceptance, and commitment to this fact.

A Christian wedding is one in which all three of these social contexts are recognized and respected.

1. *The familial context.* A Christian wedding is one that takes place, so far as it is possible, in consultation with both families, with their approval and with their participation. So to include both families is on the one hand an expression of the couple's respect for and responsibility to their families ("Honor your father and your mother"), and on the other hand an expression of the families' recognition of a broadening of their family circle. This familial context is so important that couples (especially younger couples) have good reason to consider carefully whether they should marry, and whether their marriage can succeed, when either of their families has strong objections or reservations.

2. *The legal context.* A Christian wedding is one that takes place in connection with the state's demand for the official civil authoriza-

tion, performance, and certification of marriage. It is the couple's public acknowledgment of the fact that Christians, too, are members of a larger society and that they respect the claims it has on them as well as the rights and privileges it gives them.

The questionable American custom of allowing the clergy to act also as representatives of the state confuses the civil and religious aspect of the wedding ceremony and obscures the significance of both. Would we not make both its civil and its religious significance clearer if, as in other parts of the world, all couples were married first by a representative of the state, and Christians then went to the church for a specifically and uniquely Christian ceremony?

3. *The ecclesiastical context.* When a couple asks a minister to conduct their wedding, they signify that they have decided to form a life partnership before God, asking God's blessing and help as they set out to keep the promises they make to each other. Their wedding is also an event in the life of the church. On the one hand, it signifies the couple's intention to live out their partnership in the Christian community, counting on its support and help and pledging themselves to participate in its life and mission. On the other hand, a wedding performed by a minister also signifies the community's reception of the couple as a married couple into its midst, pledging its support and help, and expecting their participation in its life and mission. (When, therefore, a couple is married in a church which is not their local church, or by a minister who will not be their minister, notice should be sent to the church to which they do or will belong.)

This threefold social implication of the wedding exposes what may be most questionable about the practice of "living together" without being "officially married." The greatest danger of this practice is not the illicit sexual activity it involves. It may not even be the fact that the formation of a genuine partnership is seriously impeded by a temporary and provisional relationship in which there is no commitment or promised faithfulness on either side. *The greatest danger may be the isolated* and *self-centered individualism involved in ignoring or rejecting the benefits and claims of family, society, and church.* The result is not only that these "institutions" suffer but that individuals and couples self-destructively deny their own humanity, which by definition is humanity fulfilled in community.

PARTNERSHIP SUSTAINED BY DEPENDENCE ON THE FORGIVING AND ENABLING GRACE OF GOD

We have suggested that the full life partnership that is Christian marriage is both a gift and a task. As task it is a goal toward which Christian couples slowly and often painfully move as long as they live together, never arriving but always on the way. But our last word about Christian marriage, like that about all other aspects of Christian life, must be a word not about the task but about the promises of God that go with it. The promise is that Christian couples do not have to struggle toward the goal alone, dependent only on their own good intentions and efforts. They may depend and count on God's forgiving and enabling grace in Jesus Christ.

Partly because of their limited human wisdom and understanding, and partly because of their sinfulness, even in the best marriages, husbands and wives (not to mention parents and children) hurt one another, fail one another, offend and betray one another in all kinds of ways — conscious and unconscious. But a Christian marriage is one in which husbands and wives count on, pray for, and claim the forgiving and accepting grace of God for themselves and for their partner, despite what has

been said and done or not said and done on both sides. And experiencing the grace of God for themselves inevitably awakens in them the desire and ability to forgive as they have been forgiven. When Jesus taught us to pray "forgive us our debts as we forgive our debtors," he was not only speaking to married couples about their marriages, but the prayer is applicable also to them as they pray about their partnership.

But God's grace in Jesus Christ is not only grace that forgives and accepts us as we are and leads us to forgive and accepts others just as they are; it is also enabling grace that gives us the ability to change and grow, make new beginnings, and move toward a new humanity. That is true also of God's grace in the lives of married couples. A Christian marriage is one in which husbands and wives count on, pray for, and claim the grace of God that sets them free — free *from* everything that separates and alienates them from one another and from their own true humanity, and free *for* one another and therefore for their own true humanity. The promise of this enabling grace of God is not the promise that husbands and wives will ever become perfect partners with a perfect marriage. It is the promise of the enabling grace of God that goes with them, guides them, sustains and helps them *on their way* toward the full life partnership that is a true Christian marriage.

A REMINDER AND WARNING

Marriage is a very great gift and a very great task that God gives to some human beings. But it is not the only or necessarily even the most important gift and task. Human beings can be genuinely and fully human, truly self-fulfilled and faithful to God, without being married. Jesus, the one truly and completely God-pleasing human being who has ever lived, was not married. He was, as we say, "single." It is very important that we remember this when we talk and think about marriage. There are many people who never marry because they cannot or do not choose or feel called to marry, and many who have lost their mate through divorce or death. We must be very careful that we do not become so preoccupied with married people that by attitude, word, or action, in practice if not in theory, we exclude unmarried people from the human race and the Christian community. We must be very careful not to talk so exclusively about the gifts and tasks of married people that we forget about the different but equally great gifts and tasks that are given to those who are not married. We must be very careful to remember and gratefully acknowledge that the forgiving grace of God also accepts single people just as they are, that the enabling grace of God goes with them on their particular way too. What is important, above all, is not that people be married and not single, but that married or single they find themselves as they love God with all their heart, mind, and soul, and their neighbors as themselves.

MISSIOLOGICAL MOTIFS

The Reformed tradition at its best has had a passionate regard for the mission of the church in a comprehensive sense. Individually speaking, one's whole life is committed to God and one lives out that commitment in history through the use of the gifts God has granted. The corporate church uses the resources it has been granted to do the work of ministry in the name of Jesus Christ. To do this effectively, the church's ministry needs to be organized. Thus in the Reformed tradition the structure and polity of the church have been of major importance. As John Leith has noted, "God is concerned about the church's organized life and wills for it to exist in particular ways even though these ways may be diverse and impossible to define precisely. Church organization is never merely functional or a matter of human convenience."[1] The polity of the church serves to enable the spread of the gospel in both word and deed. So Reformed churches are concerned with evangelism and with the spread of the gospel throughout the cultures and societies in which the churches minister.

The essays in this section reflect particular dimensions of the aspects sketched above. It would be impossible to document fully the range of mission and ministry in Reformed churches. But the following pieces indicate some of the foundational themes that provide the impetus and sustenance for Reformed missiological understandings.

In a real sense, "mission" begins with a sense of calling or vocation. The essay by Donald McKim entitled "The 'Call' in the Reformed Tradition" considers the personal aspect of the concept of vocation in Reformed thought.

In a piece entitled "The Offices of Elders and Deacons in the Classical Reformed Tradition," Elsie McKee examines Calvin's thought closely to indicate the nature and uniqueness of the Reformed offices of elder and deacon. This study has special relevance for contemporary Reformed churches, in which the nature of the ministry of church officers is being widely discussed.

If the polity of the church enables the gospel the church proclaims, it is important to have an understanding of how the Reformed tradition has regarded evangelism. Robert Paul provides this in "Reformed Churches and Evangelism: Historical Background," which sets the issue of evangelism in the context of Reformed ecclesiology and the ecumenical relationships of the Reformed churches. He concludes with seven basic insights that helpfully relate the history on this issue to the modern context.

In "A Reformed Perspective on the Mission of the Church in Society," Donald McKim explores the relationships of Reformed theological doctrines to the work of the church in its culture. He indicates how the doctrines of creation, election, kingdom, vocation, and stewardship have direct implications for the mission of the church and its ministry, how theology is thus related directly to human life, and how theological support for the breadth and depth of Reformed involvement in society is provided. Without a sense that what the church does through the whole fabric of societal structures is grounded in its essential theological beliefs, its basic integrity and its ability to enlist members to carry out societal tasks will be impaired.

NOTES

1. Leith, *Introduction to the Reformed Tradition* (Atlanta: John Knox Press, 1977), p. 137. See further chap. 5 of this work, entitled "Polity and the Reformed Tradition."

The "Call" in the Reformed Tradition

Donald K. McKim

One of the key topics in Reformed theology and the Reformed tradition is the doctrine of the "call." As with all such topics, there is more here than meets the eye (or the ear). That is to say, the doctrine of the call is tied quite closely to many other theological topics. It is related to such doctrines as those of the church, ministry, ordination, and election. It touches upon one's views of sacraments, church polity, mission, and much more. In May 1970, the 182nd General Assembly of the United Presbyterian Church in the USA received the interim report of a Special Committee on the Theology of the Call. This was published as a booklet for study entitled "Model for Ministry."[1] This helpful study raises significant questions and touches on many of the issues involved in the theology of the call. The following essay takes up a more modest task. I will work toward a basic definition of what is involved in the "call of God" and try to construct that definition in light of our biblical and theological understandings in the Reformed tradition.

I. GOD'S CALL IN JESUS CHRIST: THE BIBLICAL DATA

The New Testament verb for "to call" is *kalein* (καλεῖν); the related noun is *klēsis* (κλῆσις), meaning "call" or "calling." The term "to call" is used quite frequently in the New Testament, especially in the Gospel of Luke and in Acts. *Kalein* means to call in the sense of "to invite" or "to summon." The corresponding Hebrew word in the Old Testament, *qara* (קָרָא) has the same sense.

But in both the Old Testament *qara* and the New Testament *kalein* we sense that there is much more going on than merely the acts of calling or inviting. Here we have ordinary words that take on a special significance, even a technical meaning. This is seen especially in certain passages in the Gospels and in the letters of Paul, where the term "to call" has a special theological sense.

In the New Testament, it is often stated that it is God or Jesus Christ who calls. And they call people to many things, to many ex-

335

periences. Jesus called his disciples (Matt. 4:21//Mark 1:20). Jesus said he came to call sinners rather than the righteous (Matt. 9:13//Mark 2:17//Luke 5:32). Paul often writes that God calls people to God or calls them to enjoy the blessings of salvation. We read in Romans 8:30, for instance, that "those whom [God] predestined he also called; and those whom he called he also justified. In Romans 9:24, God calls "not from the Jews only but also from the Gentiles" to form a people. And then Paul quotes from Hosea: "Those who were not my people I will call 'my people'" (Rom. 9:25; Hos. 2:23). Christians are said to be "called into the fellowship" of God's Son, Jesus Christ our Lord (1 Cor. 1:9). God has called us to "peace" (1 Cor. 7:15), "not for uncleanness, but in holiness" (1 Thess. 4:7), and into God's kingdom (1 Thess. 2:12). In Hebrews those called are said to receive "the promised eternal inheritance" (9:15) as Abraham received an inheritance when he was "called to go out to a place which he was to receive" and did so by faith (11:8). In 1 Peter 2:9 God is said to call "a chosen race, a royal priesthood, a holy nation, God's own people . . . out of darkness into his marvelous light." Yet the author indicates that this calling also includes suffering, just as Jesus Christ himself suffered (1 Pet. 2:20). But the promise is given that "after you have suffered a little while, the God of all grace, who has called you to his eternal glory in Christ, will himself restore, establish, and strengthen you" (1 Pet. 5:10).

In these New Testament passages, with their occasional flashbacks to Old Testament images, we find God in Jesus Christ calling men and women. God in Christ is always the subject. God issues the call, the invitation, the summons. It remains for humans to respond. As we examine these contexts in the Scriptures where the "calling" pictures occur, we find that the response God seeks to the call is faith. This was the initial response of Jesus' disciples, who "left all and followed him" (see Luke 5:11

etc.). This was the response of the apostle Paul who in Romans 1:1 and 1 Corinthians 1:1 refers to himself as one "called to be an apostle" of Christ Jesus, as one who responded by faith to a living encounter with the risen Christ. And this response of faith was evoked in thousands upon thousands from the days of the early church to the present day. To be called is to hear the voice of God in Jesus Christ and to respond to that voice — to respond to that voice in faith. Like Abraham of old, or the disciples and the anonymous Christians of the past, we respond to the call in faith, not knowing where we are to go.

II. TO ALL WHO BELIEVE TO BE CHRISTIAN

From this quick treatment of some of the biblical data comes a point of significance for us in considering particularly the doctrine of the "call" in Reformed Theology. The point is this: "God's call is to all who believe to be Christian." This is perhaps the fundamental insight about the doctrine of the call that can help us understand all the marvelous diversities of the "calls" of God with which we are familiar. The insight is that at the very heart of what the Scriptures mean as they speak of God's call is the basic experience that God's call is to all who believe to be Christian — that is, God's call first and foremost is a call to salvation in Jesus Christ. This is the conclusion, for example, of the article on *kaleō* in Kittel's *Theological Dictionary of the New Testament*. Karl Ludwig Schmidt asserts that "in the New Testament καλεῖν [to call] is a technical term for the process of salvation." He proceeds to say that "on the basis of this conclusion we may and must assume that there is an element of technical usage even in passages where it is not obvious."[2]

It was this basic theological insight that began the Special Committee's report to the

General Assembly: "there is one call of God to all the people of the earth, to the whole Church, and to every member of the Church, to the one ministry of God's word and work in Jesus Christ."[3] There is one call of God, and that is to all people in Jesus Christ. It is a call or invitation to be involved in salvation, a call to all who believe to be Christian. This is first and foremost. It is what some of the older Reformed theologians and confessional documents speak of as "effectual calling." As the Westminster Shorter Catechism defines it, effectual calling is "the work of God's Spirit, whereby, convincing us of our sin and misery, enlightening our minds in the knowledge of Christ, and renewing our wills, he doth persuade and enable us to embrace Jesus Christ, freely offered to us in the gospel."[4] God calls us to salvation in Christ Jesus. Writing in the Reformed tradition nearly three hundred years after Westminster, Karl Barth summarized this insight as follows:

> in the New Testament κλῆσις always means quite unambiguously the divine calling, i.e., the act of the call of God issued in Jesus Christ by which a man is transplanted into his new state as a Christian, is made a participant in the promise (Eph. 1[18]; 4[4]) bound up with this new state, and assumes the duty (Eph. 4[1]; 2 Pet. 1[18]) corresponding to this state. This calling is holy (2 Tim. 1[9]). It is heavenly (Heb. 3[1]). It comes, therefore, from above (Phil. 3[14]).[5]

From this insight, Reformed theology has gone on to discern that the *ground* of our calling is in our election as God's people — that is, as the church. Our calling is grounded in election. Election is the presupposition of our calling; our calling is the historical realization of our election.[6] As Barth said, for Calvin, "vocation [calling] and election are indissolubly co-ordinated. Election looks forward to the future event of vocation; vocation backward to election."[7] To put this closer to the language of the New Testament, "Christians are ἐκλεκτοί [elected] and therefore κλητοί [called]. They

are κλητοί [called] because they are ἐκλεκτοί [elected]. And on the basis of both election and vocation, they are ἅγιοι [holy] and πιστοί [faithful]."[8] The apostle Paul anchored his calling to be both a Christian and an apostle in his election by God (Rom. 1:1; 1 Cor. 1:1; cf. Gal. 1:15). Romans 8:28 and 8:30 connect predestination and calling in the same ways. What this means, quite simply, is that we do not choose God; God chooses us, God calls us to the joys and benefits and obligations of salvation in Jesus Christ.

This is the one thing that unites us all, that weaves together all the diverse tapestries of the lives we live. We are all, together, called by God. Here is the common thread that runs through all our stories. No matter who we are, where we have come from, or what we have been through, we have each responded in faith to one and the same call by God in Jesus Christ. "Come, follow me," says Jesus. And so we have. And so we will. God issues the same call to all of us: woman/man, rich/poor, black/Hispanic/Native American/Asian/white — the same call is heard no matter what our gender, our race, or our economic location. God in Jesus Christ by the work of the Holy Spirit calls us all to rejoice in our election, in our participation in the body of Christ, the church, and to enter into the life of faith and salvation. This is what unites us: our common call as Christians, grounded in the election of God.

So God calls all who believe to be Christians. The *ground* of God's call is election. The *goal* of God's call is that we be united with Christ in salvation. Again, in the Westminster Confession of Faith, the goal of calling is "grace and salvation by Jesus Christ" (6.056), or, more simply, to "truly come to Christ" (6.059). The Shorter Catechism says that the goal is to "partake of justification, adoption, sanctification, and the several benefits which, in this life, do either accompany or flow from them" (7.032). As we will see, this is not all there is to the eventual fulfillment of our call, but it is part of the common thread that unites us. We all participate — and participate equally — in the benefits and joys of salvation that our union with Jesus Christ makes possible. There are no second-class Christians, nor any Christians who receive an additional call that makes them "just a little bit better" than other called Christians. It is true that the Reformed tradition has put some special emphasis on the calling to "word and sacrament," to the office of pastor in the church, but it is a perversion of the tradition and a diversion from the New Testament if we conclude from this that preachers, evangelists, or missionaries (or even seminary professors!) are somehow blessed by a special calling that puts them head and shoulders above the rest of the called body of Christ. The clergy/laity distinction was unknown to the New Testament church. We turn a fatal corner if we somehow elevate one calling over another or multiply the one call of God in Jesus Christ into two by thinking that the *goal* of Christian calling is somehow this unique kind of Christian existence to be lived only by those with an extra, "special" call. No, the benefits of salvation that our faithful response to God's call brings us are the same for us all. Of course they take different shapes, move us into different ministries. But both the *ground* and the *goal* of the Christian life are the same for all who believe: election by God in Christ, union with Christ, and the joys of Christ's benefits. In this all Christians stand as one. So we can say God's call in Jesus Christ is to all who believe to be Christian. "To be Christian" — that is our primary identity as the called of God — not some other designation such as pastor, teacher, or even "Reformed"! God's call in Jesus Christ is to all who believe to be Christian.

III. IN ALL WE DO

Then we can expand our definition to go on to say that "God's call in Jesus Christ is to all who

believe to be Christian *in all we do.* "In all we do." With this we are drawn to consider both the *locus* and the *focus* of what we do as Christians who have responded in faith to the call of God.

The locus means what our place, our base of operations, is. How does our primary identity as Christians, united with Christ, take practical shape in this world? Where do we come from in the living out of our callings?

Clearly, in the Reformed tradition, our locus or base of operation is the Christian church. The Second Helvetic Confession defines the church as "an assembly of the faithful called or gathered out of the world; a communion . . . of all saints, namely, of those who truly know and rightly worship and serve the true God in Christ" (chap. 18; 5.125). The Greek word translated in the New Testament as "church," ἐκκλησία, is derived from ἐκκαλεῖν *(ekkalein),* "to call forth" or ἔκκλητος *(ekklētos),* "called forth." The church becomes then, those (that assembly) who have been called forth.[9] The church is people, not property or buildings.

With this as background, the locus of our calling is the church in the sense to which the Confession of 1967 refers when it speaks of "God's reconciling work in Jesus Christ and the mission of reconciliation to which he has called his church" (9.06). The church in turn is said to call people "to be reconciled to God and to one another" (9.07).

As we live out the one call that comes to us in Jesus Christ, working for reconciliation — and also for such things as justice, peace, evangelism, the elimination of poverty, hunger, sexism, and all else that tries to strangle the gospel — as we work on these things, as called Christians in the Reformed tradition, we work together, corporately with others in the church of God. This does not mean we will work only in the church, or only with others who are Christians, or even only on those issues with which the church is currently dealing. Our callings do not limit us in these ways. Rather our callings give us a source, a base, a fellowship, a communion, if you will, from which our own understandings and actions can take shape and find power. We work as called Christians with ecclesial identities, ecclesial agendas — identities and agendas formed and molded and launched into action through the help and support of brothers and sisters in Christ in the fellowship of the Holy Spirit, in the church. This entails dialogue. It entails sharing. It entails suffering and struggling together. But the church is the gift of God's grace where our callings can gain their bearings, where we can be corrected and adjusted, even redirected. All this happens through the fellowship of love into which God has called us as Christians. This is why, historically, ordination to the ministry of word and sacrament has always involved as an essential ingredient a "call" to a specific work or ministry. There must be the recognition of how one's own working out of his or her call to salvation in Jesus Christ fits into the broader framework of the Christian church and its overall ministry. We are not called alone, and we are not called to be alone. We live out our calling in Christ in the midst of the company of saints which is likewise committed.

If the locus of our call is the church, the focus of our call should be our vocations. As we continue to develop, our vocations point us to the thought that "God's call in Jesus Christ is to all who believe to be Christian in all we do." "In all we do" includes our vocations.

Vocation comes from the Latin word *vocatio,* meaning "a calling" in the sense of an invitation, or court summons. *Vocatio* is used in the Latin Vulgate to translate all instances of the New Testament Greek word for "calling," *klēsis.* This has some significance in light of how we understand the term *vocation* today and how that understanding has developed historically and theologically.

We have discussed the calling of God in Christ to be Christian. We sometimes use the term *vocation* as a synonym of *call,* though more often we use it in a narrower sense to refer to a definite area of one's occupation. The term *vocation* is not found in the Reformed creeds in *The Book of Confessions,* but it did play a strong role in the thought of Martin Luther. His translation of 1 Corinthians 7:20 is particularly important in this regard. In the Revised Standard Version the verse reads, "every one should remain in the state in which he was called"; the King James Version reads "let every man abide in the same calling wherein he was called." Luther translated the term *klēsis* here with the German *Beruf,* meaning "vocation," "profession," "occupation." He took this to mean that one should recognize one's own job or position as one's "calling" by God and should remain in it. One should remain in one's job and serve God faithfully and obediently in that vocation. This became the teaching of the Augsburg Confession of 1530 (Arts. 16 and 27) and so passed on to our modern usage.

At the time of the Reformation, this was a tremendous breakthrough. Prior to the Reformation, the New Testament sense of *klēsis* as one's calling as a Christian was understood. But gradually this understanding changed, and the term was associated with the call for a Christian to undertake a monastic life. One's "calling" or "vocation" was associated with admission to a monastic order and a transition to a new, special, "religious" life. *Vocatio* came to mean only this unique "calling" — hence the cleavage between monks and ordinary Christians at the time of the Reformation.

With Luther, the focus shifted from the church to the individual Christian in the sense that he viewed every Christian as having a vocation or calling. Each was called to whatever station of life he or she occupied. The clergy/laity distinction was not eradicated in Protestantism, but the new focus on vocation as one's calling in daily life did center attention on each person's duty and opportunity to play a significant part in the overall kingdom of God.[10] Max Weber said that in the Reformation

> one thing was unquestionably new: the valuation of fulfilment of duty in worldly affairs as the highest form which the moral activity of the individual could assume. This it was which inevitably gave every-day worldly activity a religious significance, and which first created the conception of a calling in this sense.[11]

According to Weber, this led to the view that sees "the fulfillment of secular duties as alone the way to please God, and hence the belief that 'every legitimate calling has exactly the same worth in the sight of God.'"[12]

There are some problems with Luther's view here. On exegetical grounds, this more narrow, technical sense of *vocation* as one's job or profession is surely not what Paul had in mind in writing to the Corinthians. There he is most concerned with the state one was in when becoming a Christian. The issues revolve around circumcision or uncircumcision, slavery or freedom. An even greater problem lies in the fact that Luther never tells us how we are to ascertain our vocation or determine the specific shape of our obedience and activity for life. In sixteenth-century society, with its strong notions of hierarchy and authority, Luther assumed we would all find our places or our callings, basically, by where our niches were in society. Our "superiors" — our parents or others somehow set in authority over us — would let us know where we belong.[13] Once we find our niche, we are to serve God actively and obediently within it. This may have worked in Luther's sixteenth-century context, but it does not work as easily as that today. So Luther helps in stressing that the divine call is to everyone, but we need more basic insights to help us work out our "callings" today.

When we turn to Calvin, we find him urging that each of us should look to our calling to give the basis for our "life's actions." God knows, said Calvin "with what great restlessness human nature flames, with what fickleness it is borne hither and thither, how its ambition longs to embrace various things at once. Therefore, lest through our stupidity and rashness everything be turned topsy-turvy, he has appointed duties for each man in his particular ways of life."[14] These various kinds of livings are "callings." They function, said Calvin, as "a sort of sentry post" so that the Christian "may not heedlessly wander about throughout life." They can give purpose and stability. But Calvin saw too that while particular vacations or occupations can provide stars by which to steer our ships, they need not be seen as fixed stars or immutable. In commenting on 1 Corinthians 7:20, Calvin wrote (as Barth says Luther could never have done) that "it would be asking far too much, if a tailor were not permitted to learn another trade, or a merchant to change to farming."[15] God can call us to various ways of service at various times. It need not be that the credo for our "vocations" — here in the sense of our occupations or professions — be like that in the old advertisements for electric ovens: "set it and forget it." We need not necessarily believe that we will serve God in only one profession or one occupation or one vocation throughout our lifetime. God may indeed have other things in store! There is the old story of the young man from the farm who became a preacher. After several years of discouraging results, he returned home. His father asked him why he decided to be a preacher in the first place. The young man answered that he'd had a dream and saw the letters "P. C." in the skies and he knew from then on he was supposed to "Preach Christ." But his mother said, "Son, perhaps that 'P. C.' really meant 'Plant Corn.'" God may call us to preach Christ *or* plant corn!

But what we're moving toward here is a view of vocation that stresses what is most essential. In one sense our vocation is our job, our occupation, what we do. But in a larger, more comprehensive sense, our vocation is what we are. It is our past, our present, our future. It is what we already bring with us when we hear and respond in faith to that one call, that call by God in Jesus Christ to salvation. God uses our abilities, our talents, our gifts. But our vocation is ourselves and our responsibilities where we are when God's call claims us. As Barth puts it, "the divine calling comes from above into all these and other human spheres, cutting diagonally across them. Thus the New Testament *klēsis* has nothing to do with the divine confirmation of these spheres as such, nor with the direction to enter such a sphere or more particularly to enter a special sphere of work."

Barth's purpose here is to remind us, as have both Luther and Calvin, that we can respond to the call of God and serve God in our callings wherever we are, in whatever sphere we are at work. In his own exegesis of the 1 Corinthians 7:20 passage, Barth points out that each is to obey the calling as it has come to that person — whether as circumcised or uncircumcised, free or slave. The Christian must always be true not to the state but to the calling within that state — as a responsible person with a unique background and history. It is not important whether one is circumcised or uncircumcised, says Barth, and he adds parenthetically that "we could surely expand these thoughts as follows": a person is not called to be a doctor, a lawyer, a carpenter, plumber, or a banker, nor is it important that the person be one or the other of these. Then, returning to the main text, Barth emphasizes that "what counts is the keeping of the commandments of God," the obedience one must render — no matter what condition or state one is in when the call to salvation comes.[16] We meet and respond to God in Christ where we are.

So the real locus of vocation goes much further beyond *merely* what *we* do in our occupations as pastors, laypersons, teachers, administrators. Our vocation is to be Christians in all we are, in all we do. For we are much

more, as human beings, than merely our professions, important as they may be. We live as relational individuals, related to many, many people in complex networks of human communities. Should we not see our vocations as extending into all these arenas? Should we not see ourselves comprehensively as people called by God to involvement in all these fibers of human life and bring ourselves as Christians to them all? Yes, we should. We may feel the call of God leading us to vocational changes throughout life. We may have felt the call of God leading us specifically to theological education and perhaps then to specific ministries in the church. These are valid. In fact, they are tremendously important. They can serve as our "sentry-posts" to keep us from aimlessly wandering. But our whole identities as persons and as Christians are not wrapped up solely in what we do for a living — whether we are conscious of doing it "for God" or not. Our identity springs from our salvation in Jesus Christ, our response to the one call of God to be Christian in *all* we do, in all we are, in the church and in the world.

IV. IN SERVICE TO THIS WORLD

To complete our description of the "call" in the Reformed tradition, there is one final phrase we should add: "God's call in Jesus Christ is to all who believe to be Christian in all we do in service to this world." "In service to this world" — that is in one sense the final goal or end of our calling. We are united with Jesus Christ through justification, sanctification, and reconciliation, but the goal of our calling does not stop there. This union with Christ must make a difference *to* us and *in* us: it must lead us to action. The "theological benefits" of which the Reformed creeds and confessions speak have inseparably connected with them this outward thrust to meaningful action. As

Arthur C. Cochrane wrote regarding our participation in the benefits of Christ's work, this is

> only one side of the goal of calling. To be a Christian is to be called to serve, to mission, to be sent into the world, to be a witness, to take up one's cross and to suffer for Christ, to confess by Word and deed, by one's whole existence, what Christ has done, does and will do for all men; in short, it is to be called to be a minister of God's Word and deed.[17]

We minister to the world by our service to the world in Jesus Christ.

This is one part of our definition of the call that needs very little comment. The call to the service of God in Jesus Christ in this world is a point of unity for all of us. Despite diversities of every type, we have all responded to the same God, the same Jesus Christ, by the work of the same Holy Spirit, and now are launched out to put flesh on our calls in service to Christ in this world. We all, each of us, will write the definition of what this service means as we live out our calls. Whether in the ministry of word and sacrament, in teaching, specialized ministries, administration — whatever and wherever — the common thread of service to God in Christ ties us together.

Our Reformed Confessions use such phrases as "word and witness" and "mission and ministry" to give some handles on these various ways of serving. The Confession of 1967 in particular makes it clear in teaching that the church and its members are called to be sent into the world (9.31). God's work of reconciliation in Christ includes the sending of the church. One cannot be reconciled to God without being sent into the world — sent with "God's message of reconciliation" that has been "entrusted" to the church (9.31).[18] Then the Confession goes on to show how the church is both "gathered in corporate life" and "dispersed in society" for the sake of "word and witness," "mission and ministry."

All of us have our own history behind us and our futures in the church in front of us. We are charged with finding new and creative ways of witnessing and serving in ministry in the years ahead. Our ministries need always to reflect the one essential ministry — the ministry of Jesus Christ, who "loved us and gave himself for us" (Gal. 2:20). We need to view our mission as the church in this world in its most comprehensive sense: to provide for human need throughout this planet, to meet both physical and spiritual needs, to establish justice, love mercy, promote peace — all this and so much more. In both word and witness we preach and serve Jesus Christ.

How will all this be done? How can it be done? We know that we cannot rely on human momentum alone. We know the tasks before us are staggering. None of us alone can make even the slightest ultimate impact. Yet the good news is that we do not have to "go it alone." Indeed, the good news is that God does not "go it alone." God cuts *us* in on the action! God calls us — to salvation in Jesus Christ. God calls us as the church to be part of God's work in whatever we do in this world. The call of God is to service. But how we live out that call — and this is where the excitement really is — how we live out God's call is up for grabs. God's call permits us to be flexible, to be mobile, to be fully open to the leadings of the Spirit. In the church we can celebrate the dazzling diversities and the pluralities of the vocations of our sisters and brothers. We can rejoice in the exciting, meaningful ways that others "in Christ" are living out their call to salvation and service. We can live as anticipatory people, as people standing on tiptoe, eager to see what or where God is calling us to next. The world is open. The world is waiting. In word and witness, mission and ministry, the possibilities for God's work in Jesus Christ are limitless. Yet we, limited as we are, are blessed with the grace of God's call to be all we can be as God's people and to live out our vocations in whatever directions we are led. That is real excitement. It can be real joy. It can also be suffering and struggle. But we do not struggle alone. The One who calls us is faithful. The electing God will see us through.

So we rejoice in God's call to us. We live confidently, creatively, and expectantly to see how God will use us as a people who seek above all else to do God's will. For, "God's call in Jesus Christ is to all who believe to be Christian in all we do in service to this world." And to God be "glory in the church and in Christ Jesus to all generations, for ever and ever. Amen" (Eph. 3:20-21).

NOTES

1. *Model for Ministry: A Report for Study Issued by the General Assembly Special Committee on the Theology of the Call,* ed. Lewis S. Mudge (Philadelphia: Office of the General Assembly of the United Presbyterian Church in the United States of America, 1970).

2. Schmidt, καλέω, in *Theologial Dictionary of the New Testament,* 10 vols., ed. Gerhard Kittel, trans. Geoffrey W. Bromiley (Grand Rapids: William B. Eerdmans, 1964-76), 3: 489; hereafter *TDNT.*

3. *Model for Ministry,* p. 15.

4. *The Book of Confessions* (Philadelphia: Office of the General Assembly of the United Presbyterian Church in the United States of America, 1967), 7.031. Subsequent references to documents in *The Book of Confessions* will be cited parenthetically in the text.

5. Barth, *Church Dogmatics,* 4 vols., ed. Geoffrey W. Bromiley and Thomas F. Torrance (Edinburgh: T. & T. Clark, 1936-69), III/4: 600.

6. See Arthur C. Cochrane, "The Doctrine of the Call in the Constitution of the United Presbyterian Church in the United States of America (1968-1969)," Appendix I in *Model for Ministry,* p. 38.

7. Barth, *Church Dogmatics,* IV/3.2: 484.

8. Barth, *Church Dogmatics,* IV/3.2: 484-85.

9. See Hans Schwarz, *The Christian Church* (Minneapolis: Augsburg, 1982), p. 20. Cf. *TDNT,* 3: 501ff.

10. See Barth's discussion of vocation in *Church Dogmatics,* III/4: 595-647, especially pp. 600-607.

11. Max Weber, *The Protestant Ethic and the Spirit of Capitalism,* trans. Talcott Parsons (New York: Scribner's, 1958), p. 80.

12. Weber, *The Protestant Ethic and the Spirit of Capitalism,* p. 81.

13. See Barth, *Church Dogmatics,* III/4: 645.

14. Calvin, *Institutes of the Christian Religion,* Library of Christian Classics, vols. 20-21, ed. John T. McNeill, trans. Ford Lewis Battles (Philadelphia: Westminster Press, 1960), 3.10.6. Subsequent references to this work will be made parenthetically in the text.

15. Calvin, *The First Epistle of Paul the Apostle to the Corinthians,* Calvin's New Testament Commentaries, ed. David W. and Thomas F. Torrance, trans. John W. Fraser (Grand Rapids: William B. Eerdmans, 1960), p. 153.

16. Barth, *Church Dogmatics,* III/4: 605.

17. Cochrane, "The Doctrine of the Call," p. 43.

18. See *Model for Ministry,* pp. 49-50.

The Offices of Elders and Deacons in the Classical Reformed Tradition

Elsie Anne McKee

The classical Calvinist Reformed teaching on the ministries of the church traditionally named four offices. A sketch of this theory of a plurality of ecclesiastical ministries is the appropriate context for a discussion of the nature and uniqueness of the Reformed offices of elders and deacons.[1]

I.

Neither a plurality of ecclesiastical ministries nor the list of particular ministerial functions elevated to the status of individual offices is unique to Calvinist Reformed theology. What is distinctive about the ecclesiology of this branch of Protestantism is the shape, character, and basis of authority of the doctrine of the ministries believed to be necessary for the church to be the church. To grasp the special character of Calvinist Reformed teaching, it is necessary to see how a plurality of ministers, and ministerial functions, were understood in the pre-Calvinist tradition, both Roman Catholic and Protestant.

First of all, a plurality of ministers may be consistent with a single idea of ministerial character. There was a long tradition of teaching that there are several offices of sacramental ministry in the church. Bishops, priests, deacons, and the minor "holy orders" of the medieval Roman Catholic church were different in rank and function, but all were concerned with "ecclesiastical" duties, and in theory the seven ranks were a progression upward in the same kind of religious vocation.

A plurality of ministers means something somewhat different, however, if the character of ministry is more broadly defined. The apparent innovation in Protestant theology was a revision of the idea of the holy. One result of this breaking down of the sacred-profane dichotomy was the (re)introduction of the idea that ecclesiastical ministries might include temporal functions such as the administration of money, charity. Put another way, a plurality of ministers became a matter of argument only when, because of the teaching on justification by faith alone, nonsacramental services or "temporal" duties such as poor relief came to be regarded as properly "religious" vocations. According to Protestant theology, the administration of charity is a ministry having its own raison d'être. It is a function seen as an end in itself and not merely, as in medieval Roman Catholic teaching, as a subordinate part of a sacramental minister's properly spiritual task.

Recognizing a nonsacramental function as holy can lead to a redefining of the people who may appropriately be considered as candidates for ministry. In Roman Catholic theology, all functions perceived as related to the administration of sacramental grace were exercised by clergy and clergy alone. Although moral oversight, the exercise of discipline, is not strictly a sacramental function, except in the extent to which it may lead to exclusion from the sacraments, this religious duty had traditionally been reserved only for ordained "clergy," especially bishops. In accordance with their belief in the priesthood of believers, Protestants denied any essential differences among Christians. They therefore affirmed that laypersons are also ministers not only in private life but also in the leadership of the Christian community. As a consequence, many Protestants cheerfully assigned some nonsacramental roles of religious leadership to the Christian civil rulers, the preeminent laymen of the church. The most critical of the religious functions accorded to or shared with lay leaders was the authority to discipline. This was also the most controversial point of the Protestant revision of the doctrine of the ministry because it took power from one group and gave it to another.

Implicit or explicit theories were developed by Protestants to explain the new conception of a plurality of ecclesiastical ministries. Especially among German-speaking Protestants, all lay ministries, including discipline and poor relief, were given to the Christian magistracy. With or without an explicit theory of plural ministries, what might be called the "pastor and prince" pair fulfilled the necessary functions of ecclesiastical leadership. Thus most Protestant churches in Christian societies revised the traditional view of the character and functions of ministry. Their plurality of ministers and ministries included "clergy" (pastors) for the preaching of the word and administration of the sacraments and "laity" (princely ministers) for all other religious duties, especially moral oversight and poor relief.

Calvinist Reformed were clearly Protestant, but they were Protestant with an interesting twist. The Reformed tradition shared the general Protestant view of the Bible as the whole authority for doctrine, of course, but went beyond Lutherans in believing that Scripture also provides the *bene esse* for church order. Zwinglian and Calvinist Reformed did not agree, however, on the places where prescriptions for church order should be found in the Bible. For Zwinglians, the Old Testament was as influential as the New, while Calvinists maintained that only the New Testament is a proper model for the Christian church order. Thus Zwinglians regarded church and Christian society as coterminous, on the pattern of the holy people of Israel. Calvinist Reformed, however, believed that the Old Testament and New Testament churches had certain differences with regard to their political relationships with the surrounding society. In effect, basing their polity on the New Testament, Calvinists refused on principle to identify ecclesiastical and civil societies in the Christian era, and thus they also insisted on distinguishing ecclesiastical and civil offices, even in a Christian society.

Therefore, when Calvinists combined the common Protestant view of a plurality of ministers and ministries with the study of traditional lists of New Testament ministries (e.g., Eph. 4:11; 1 Cor. 12:28; Rom. 12:6-8), the result was the development of an explicit theory of ministry that included two lay ecclesiastical offices distinct from the similar functions that all Protestants expected of Christian princes. For Calvinist Reformed, the lay Christian ministries of discipline and charity are understood as biblically based offices of the church as church. The church's elders and deacons may cooperate with Christian rulers who are also concerned for the moral and physical well-being of their people, but the ecclesiastical offices are not dependent on any civil power for their existence, and they may function equally well in a "disestablished" context.[2]

The classical Calvinist Reformed teaching of four ecclesiastical offices — pastor, teacher, elder, and deacon — is therefore not innovative in affirming a plurality of ministries or including previously unknown functions. It is unique in that it insists that two of the four offices are "permanent lay ecclesiastical" ministries based on the permanently valid model of the New Testament church.

The uniqueness of the Calvinist Reformed plural ministry theory may be usefully summarized by explaining the several ways the word *permanent* applies to the "lay ecclesiastical" leaders. The offices of elders and deacons are permanent in the sense that they are distinct from each of the other offices and not simply steps to a sacramental ministry — which is to say, the eldership and diaconate are permanently necessary and distinct lay ministries that must not be absorbed into the functions of the pastorate or priesthood. The offices of elders and deacons are also permanent in the sense that, because they were established by Christ's Spirit, their functions must continue in the church as church, even in a society where Christian rulers may exercise similar religious duties of poor relief and moral restraint — which is to say, the eldership and diaconate are permanently ecclesiastical, necessary to the life of the church in any context, friendly or hostile, because they are based on a biblical order that needs no civil support.

An examination of the offices of elders and deacons is therefore worthwhile as an ex-

ploration of one of the most distinctive features of Calvinist Reformed ecclesiology.

II.

The office of elders, of lay Christians elected to share with pastors the moral oversight of the congregation, is one of the most important and controversial aspects of the Calvinist Reformed doctrine of ministry. Before turning to the theological discussion, a brief look at the disputed political context is appropriate.

The Reformed teaching on the elders was a bone of contention from the beginning because the civil authorities of the sixteenth century were eager to control the moral life of their society and resented any claims for ecclesiastical autonomy in the critical sphere of discipline.[3] Protestant rulers who were happy to support the new theological reforms in the shape of Lutheran or Zwinglian "pastor and prince" cooperation were much more resistant to the Calvinist demand for an independent church discipline. The struggle to vindicate and implement a degree of ecclesiastical autonomy in discipline began with Johannes Oecolampadius in Basel and continued with Martin Bucer in Strasbourg. Neither Reformer was markedly successful in persuading his city to allow ecclesiastical autonomy. Their ideas, however, were taken up by their younger colleague John Calvin, who devoted most of his life to winning acknowledgment of the church's right to exercise a moral censorship distinct from civil control. One might ask why Calvinist Reformed leaders were not content to follow the usual German Protestant pattern of trust in the Christian magistracy, and an investigation of the theological understanding of the office of elders is one important source for answering this question.

In the classical formulation found in Calvin's *Institutes of the Christian Religion*, elders are one kind of presbyter, lay officers elected from the congregation to share with the pastors in the exercise of ecclesiastical discipline. Objecting to any monarchical or clerical monopoly, Calvin insisted on leadership by a group, some of whom must be laity.

> Governors [1 Cor. 12:28] were, I believe, elders chosen from the people, who were charged with the censure of morals and the exercise of discipline along with the bishops. For one cannot otherwise interpret his statement, "Let him who rules act with diligence" [Rom. 12:8]. Each church, therefore, had from its beginning a senate, chosen from godly, grave, and holy men, which had jurisdiction over the correcting of faults. Of it we shall speak later. Now experience itself makes clear that this sort of order was not confined to one age. Therefore, this office of government is necessary for all ages.[4]

The cross-reference Calvin supplies here leads the reader to the longer passage that completes this brief definition. This second paragraph also explains in part the reasons for distinguishing between civil and ecclesiastical societies.

> There remains the third part of ecclesiastical power, the most important in a well-ordered state. This . . . consists in jurisdiction. But the whole jurisdiction of the church pertains to the discipline of morals. . . . For as no city or township can function without magistrate and polity, so the church of God . . . needs a spiritual polity. This is, however, quite distinct from the civil polity, yet does not hinder or threaten it but rather greatly helps and furthers it. Therefore, this power of jurisdiction will be nothing, in short, but an order framed for the preservation of the spiritual polity.
>
> For this purpose courts of judgment were established in the church from the beginning to deal with the censure of morals, to investigate vices, and to be charged with the exercise of the office of the keys. Paul designates this order in his letter to the Corinthians when he mentions offices of ruling [1 Cor. 12:28]. Likewise,

in Romans, when he says, "Let him who rules, rule with diligence" [Rom. 12:8, paraphrase]. For he is not addressing magistrates (not any of whom were then Christians), but those who were joined with the pastors in the spiritual rule of the church. In the letter to Timothy, also, he distinguishes two kinds of presbyters: those who labor in the Word, and those who do not carry on the preaching of the Word yet rule well [1 Tim. 5:17]. By this latter sort he doubtless means those who were appointed to supervise morals and to use the whole power of the keys.

> For this power of which we speak depends entirely upon the keys which, in the eighteenth chapter of Matthew, Christ gave to the church. There he commands that those who are contemptuous of private warnings be severely warned in the name of the people; but if they persist in their stubbornness, he teaches that they should be cut off from the believers' fellowship [Matt. 18:15-18].[5]

Several key points about the elders' office are apparent in these two critical paragraphs. Organized logically, these may be listed as the question of function (discipline), the agency for that function (the elders), and the authority for this teaching (Scripture).

The starting point is the function, discipline. Almost all Christian communities have agreed that some form of ecclesiastical moral oversight or censure is necessary, and most have based this conviction on Matthew 18:15-18. In affirming the importance of ecclesiastical censures, therefore, Calvin simply shared a venerable Christian tradition.[6]

Despite agreement on the biblical and practical need for discipline, however, different Christians have designated different agents to carry out this task. Roman Catholics restricted the exercise of moral oversight to the clergy, especially to bishops. All Protestants, on the other hand, insisted that laity must also be involved in discipline on the grounds that Matthew 18:17 assigns jurisdiction to the "church," and the clergy alone do not constitute the church. Some Protestants — especially certain

Anabaptists — interpreted "church" more broadly as all (male) members of the congregation, but most Protestants and many Anabaptists were content to recognize the church as properly represented by its responsible elders. For Lutherans and Zwinglians, the Christian rulers were the appropriate lay representatives for ecclesiastical discipline. Calvinists, on the other hand, maintained that the church elders are in theory distinct from civil rulers because, unlike ancient Israel, the New Testament church did not rely on princes but organized its polity separately from the surrounding civil society.[7]

The argument concerning the relationship of ecclesiastical and civil leaders in discipline points to the third factor raised by Calvin's definition of the office of elders, that of the authority for this teaching. Calvinist Reformed thinkers held not only that the function of discipline itself is established by Scripture but also that the agents of this moral oversight logically must also have been mentioned somewhere in the New Testament. Calvin appeals to three verses — Romans 12:8, 1 Corinthians 12:28, and 1 Timothy 5:17 — as Paul's references to the "council of elders" who represented the church in Matthew 18:17.

Before condemning the Genevan Reformer's ecclesiology as a case of exegesis, it is useful to examine the context of interpretation of the texts to which he refers. Although to modern eyes Calvin's appeal to these verses may seem peculiar, if not completely wrong, the exegetical histories of these verses reveal how much of the content of the Reformer's thought was common to the tradition. Medieval and early Protestant commentators often identified the rulers in Romans 12:8 and the governors in 1 Corinthians 12:28 with clergy and/or ecclesiastical discipline. Calvin selected from and developed the historical explanations of these phrases, making something new of the tradition, more by the way he interrelated the verses than by any addition to the content. The

same thing is true about the most curious aspect of the Timothy verse, the "double presbyterate," which greatly distresses contemporary biblical scholars. Although he uses it in a new way, here again Calvin in fact copied this idea with only slight modification from earlier commentators, Roman Catholic and Protestant alike.[8]

What distressed Calvin's contemporaries about his teaching on the office of elders was not his exegesis but his theology. Lay participation in discipline was inconceivable to Roman Catholics, and ecclesiastical autonomy was unnecessary and inappropriate in the eyes of Protestants who believed in the divine calling of the Christian ruler as God's lieutenant for ecclesiastical leadership in all practical (nonsacramental) matters. The Calvinist Reformed office of elder seemed an incomprehensible hybrid: a "lay ecclesiastical" ministry of discipline, in the Christian society but not of it. For Calvinists, however, a council of lay Christian representatives of the congregation, whose role was to share moral oversight with the pastor(s), was simply the proper application of New Testament church order to the contemporary ecclesiastical scene.

III.

The office of deacon is usually seen as the second major "lay ecclesiastical" ministry of the Calvinist church, though in some respects it may be regarded as prior to the office of elder. Like all Protestants, Calvin recognized diaconal poor relief as a ministry of the New Testament church, and he referred to this diaconate in the earliest edition of the *Institutes*, sometime before clearly defining the ministry of elders. For Calvin, as for other Protestants, deacons are the church's ministers for the exercise of charity, the care of the poor and sick. They are those Christian leaders charged with temporal care for the neighbor in order to leave the presbyters free for the ministry of word and sacraments. Deacons are not proto-priests but carry out a ministry of temporal care that is permanently necessary in the church.

Before examining the theological teaching, it is useful to sketch the social-historical context of Calvin's doctrine of the diaconate.[9] The sixteenth century was a period of increasing or at least much-accelerated change and reform in the sphere of social welfare. Traditional ecclesiastical oversight of charity was being challenged by city magistrates and territorial princes, and new, more rational and centralized organization accompanied this (usually successful) bid for civil control of poor relief.

In Geneva the new pattern of care for the needy was established before Calvin's arrival, but the Reformer claimed that the two kinds of city poor relief administrators were ecclesiastical deacons. This was almost exactly analogous to his claims for lay elders of discipline. Both elders and deacons were understood theologically as first and necessarily ecclesiastical and only secondarily and incidentally civil offices. In practice, for a variety of reasons, Calvin focused the struggle for ecclesiastical autonomy on the issue of discipline, so the fact that he regarded civil poor relief administrators as ecclesiastical deacons did not lead to conflict in sixteenth-century Geneva. Modern scholars, however, have debated the validity of Calvin's claim to base the diaconate on Scripture. They argue logically that it appears that in significant ways, especially in the twofold organization of poor relief personnel, the social welfare movement influenced the Reformer rather than the other way around. What then was Calvin's teaching about the diaconate, and how did it develop?

In the Calvinist Reformed doctrine of the church, deacons are understood as a permanent ecclesiastical ministry of care for the poor and sick, exercised by elected laymen and laywomen on the model of the New Testament church. In parallel with the earlier discussion of the office of elders, three key points about the diaconate may be noted. The function, always with Calvin the primary issue, is the expression of *caritas,* the love of the neighbor. The agents are deacons, men and women, and the authoritative basis for the teaching is Scripture.

The larger theological context for the ministry of deacons is the function of *caritas,* a summary of the second table of the law in Reformed thought.[10] Worship of God and love of the neighbor are the fundamental expressions of the famous Calvinist third use of the law as a guide for regenerate behavior. These two things, worship and love, are required of all believers, but certain individuals are called by God and elected by the church to exercise these ministries in a public and official way. The deacons are the church's ministers for the necessary service of the neighbor, the *caritas* that must flow out of any right adoration of God.

Although the Calvinist Reformed diaconate developed special and distinctive traits, the substance of the teaching was shared with all Protestants.[11] Rejecting the medieval definition of diaconal duties as sacramental or liturgical, Protestants believed that deacons should be charged with temporal care for the needy neighbor. This ministry is not a step to the priesthood but a calling in its own right. Calvin was following unanimous Protestant tradition when he based this ministry of charity on 1 Timothy 3:8-13 and especially on Acts 6:1-6. A passage from the 1536 edition of the *Institutes* expresses clearly this common Protestant view.

> The origin, ordination, and office of the deacons are described by Luke in The Acts [Acts 6:3]. . . . This was the office of deacons, to attend to the care of the poor and minister to them; from this they took their name. For they are so called, as ministers. Then Luke added an account of their institution. Those they had chosen, he says, they ordained in the presence

of the apostles: praying, they laid their hands upon them [Acts 6:6]. Would that the church today had such deacons, and appointed them by such a ceremony. . . . Paul also speaks of the deacons: he wishes them to be modest, not double-tongued, not wine-bibbers, not pursuing filthy gain, well established in the faith [1 Tim. 3:8-9], husbands of one wife, governing their households and children well [1 Tim. 3:12]. But what likeness to this is there in the deacons which these men devise? . . . They say that it is the office of their deacons "to assist the priests; to minister in everything done in the sacraments."[12]

Calvin added some distinctive characteristics to the generally accepted Protestant understanding of the diaconate. One of these was the insistence that deacons are a ministry of the church as church that should be distinguished though not necessarily separated from the civil poor relief system. The implicit argument for this is similar to that for the independence of elders: the early church did not rely on the magistracy, and therefore the latter cannot be considered in any sense necessary for the right functioning of ecclesiastical charity. Explicitly, however, Calvin maintains that the permanence of Luke's model is assured by the command of Paul to Timothy; the election of the seven in the church by the church was intended as an enduring pattern for church order. Calvin also encouraged the cooperation of the Christian ruler, of course, and both "established" (city administered) and "disestablished" (refugee) diaconates existed in Geneva.[13]

The second distinctive feature of the Calvinist diaconate was the inclusion of women as a kind of subordinate deacon, on the New Testament model of the "deacon" Phoebe (Rom. 16:1-2) and the widows (1 Tim. 5:9-10).

The care of the poor was entrusted to the deacons. However, two kinds are mentioned in the letter to the Romans: "He that gives, let him do it with simplicity; . . . he that shows mercy,

with cheerfulness" [Rom. 12:8]. Since it is certain that Paul is speaking of the public office of the church, there must have been two distinct grades. Unless my judgment deceive me, in the first clause he designates the deacons who distribute the alms. But the second refers to those who had devoted themselves to the care of the poor and sick. Of this sort were the widows whom Paul mentions to Timothy [1 Tim. 5-10]. Women could fill no other public office than to devote themselves to the care of the poor. If we accept this (as it must be accepted), there will be two kinds of deacons: one to serve the church in administering the affairs of the poor; the other, in caring for the poor themselves. But even though the term διαϰονία itself has a wider application, Scripture specifically designates as deacons those whom the church has appointed to distribute alms and take care of the poor.[14]

This passage includes a curious reference to Romans 12:8, one of the three verses that support a plurality of ministries, which Calvin here understands as linking the two kinds of deacons. Given the importance of Scripture as the basic authority for the doctrine of the diaconate, it is worthwhile to examine somewhat more closely the controversial passages to which Calvin appealed: Romans 12:8, 1 Timothy 5:9-10, and (implicitly) Romans 16:1-2.[15]

Many scholars have regarded Calvin's use of Romans 12:8 as pure eisegesis, probably influenced by social or political expediency, but in fact it may well have been theologically inspired eisegesis.[16] The sixteenth century had great difficulty with the idea of women in roles of ecclesiastical leadership, but Calvin was forced to explain why in Romans 16:1-2 Paul calls a woman, Phoebe, a "deacon." In addition, as a Protestant he had to reinterpret 1 Timothy 5:9-10 to exclude the traditional medieval use of this text to support women's vows of celibacy. Calvin knew that in addition to Ephesians 4:11 and 1 Corinthians 12:28, the Romans 12:6-8 pericope was commonly understood to indicate a plurality of New Testament ministers. Therefore it was natural for him to introduce the two "diaconal" phrases of Romans 12:8 to explain the connection between the women: Phoebe and her widow colleagues, and the male administrators of Acts 6 and 1 Timothy 3. Although the twentieth century may see his discussion of Romans 12:8, Phoebe, and the widows as more creative than convincing, Calvin's development of the interpretation of these verses had clear basis in the exegetical tradition. It also proved persuasive to many contemporaries and successors, even among those who did not accept the theology or church order that he believed Scripture had established.

Thus, in the case of the diaconate as well as in the development of the office of elders, Calvin's exegesis as such appears to have presented few difficulties for his contemporaries; again, it was his *theology* that was not universally acceptable to his age. However, since he did not actively press for women deacons, and since the struggle for ecclesiastical autonomy was focused on the exercise of discipline rather than poor relief, Calvin's teaching on the diaconate encountered less opposition than his doctrine of the eldership.

Although for practical reasons it has received less attention than the office of discipline, the diaconal office of charity, of care for the neighbor, is clearly critical in the Calvinist Reformed theory of the ministry. In some ways the diaconate is in fact more central, if not more important, to Reformed ecclesiology than the office of elder. In Calvin's doctrine of the church the diaconate is not simply an isolated aspect of church order but, when it is understood in the larger context of the golden rule, the third use of the law, it forms a concrete practical expression of the texture of the whole theology. A permanent lay ecclesiastical ministry of care for the temporal needs of God's people, which distressed traditional Roman Catholics because of its lay character and the elevation of a temporal function to an ordained

ministry and which annoyed German Protestants (and civil rulers!) because of its claim to autonomous ecclesiastical status, constitutes an aspect of Calvinist ecclesiology that continues to be important to the church today.

IV.

The history of the Reformed doctrine of the ministry since the sixteenth century has manifested a number of developments and changes which the twentieth-century church has begun to reexamine in the interests of contemporary renewal.

Calvinist teaching spread both in theory and in practice. The plural ministry theory, including the offices of elders and deacons, was widely adopted in Calvinist Reformed church orders in the sixteenth and seventeenth centuries. For many years, most Reformed and some non-Reformed exegetes who discussed the various biblical texts that Calvin understood to support the different offices often followed the Genevan Reformer's interpretation in their commentaries. Frequently Reformed theologians also used Calvin's exegesis in their polemical writings.[17]

In addition to church orders, commentaries, and controversial treatises, Calvin's teaching on the ministry found practical implementation. In the sixteenth and seventeenth centuries, most churches influenced by Calvinist Reformed thought also instituted at least the offices of pastor, elder, and deacon and occasionally the separate office of teacher. In some places, implementation went even beyond Genevan practice. Although Calvin himself regretted the lack of widow-deacons in Geneva, he had not insisted on this institution. Nonetheless, a few Reformed churches, such as those in the Rhineland (at the synod of Wesel) and some of the early English Separatists in Leiden, did in fact establish this second kind of female deacon to care for the sick and poor of the community.[18]

Over the centuries, Calvin's ideal pattern of church order underwent a number of changes, however.[19] The office of the few women deacons was soon discontinued, probably because of male fears of women's usurpation of leadership. The duties of elders and deacons, although plainly distinguished in theory (and in Genevan practice), became less precisely divided in some Reformed churches (e.g., among the Huguenots). By the late seventeenth century, some congregationalist (Puritan) churches had discontinued the office of elder, reassigning the disciplinary role to the pastors and communicant members together. Other churches, especially in North America, were sometimes constituted without elders or, more frequently, without deacons, although the duties of these ministries were not necessarily neglected when the offices fell into disuse. In the late eighteenth and especially in the nineteenth and twentieth centuries, voluntary societies that had no precise connection with church order often took up the diaconal concerns of the church. In other places, the ecclesiastical offices of elders and deacons were maintained but could not always carry out their roles effectively in the context of modern industrial society and the religious pluralism and individualism characteristic of a secular world.

The twentieth-century ecumenical movement and the renewal of concern for the doctrine of the church have brought to the fore again a consideration of the offices of ecclesiastical leadership. The section of the World Council of Churches' *Baptism, Eucharist and Ministry* document that deals with the office of deacon is one of the least satisfactory parts of the ministry section of this epochal effort at Christian convergence.[20] Moreover, this ecumenical statement makes no mention of the office of elders as it is known in the Reformed tradition. Questions about both of these points have been raised in responses from some of the World Council member churches, but answers or solutions are not yet at hand.[21]

While it is obvious that sixteenth-century interpretations of the church's ministry are only a part of a much longer history and cannot and should not simply be transferred to the twentieth century, it may perhaps be useful for contemporary Reformed Christians to consider what their heritage might have to contribute to the ecumenical dialogue. The classical Calvinist Reformed doctrine on the ministry of elders and deacons, "permanent lay ecclesiastical" offices of moral guidance and social concern for the neighbor, may yet have a role to play in shaping the church's behavior and service to the Lord in the world.

NOTES

1. This article is a very brief summary of material developed at length in several monographs on John Calvin's doctrine of the ministry. In the interest of conserving space, almost all references to secondary literature are therefore omitted here, though a few English-language publications are mentioned by way of example. The reader is asked to consult the bibliographies and notes of the monographs for surveys of historiography and other matters. The two major sources used are Elsie Anne McKee, *John Calvin on the Diaconate and Liturgical Almsgiving* (Geneva: Droz, 1984), hereafter cited as *John Calvin;* and Elsie Anne McKee, *Elders and the Plural Ministry: the Role of Exegetical History in Illuminating John Calvin's Theology* (Geneva: Droz, 1988), hereafter cited as *Elders and the Plural Ministry*.

2. For various discussions of the Calvinist teaching on a plurality of ministries, see McKee, *John Calvin,* pp.

133-36, and McKee, *Elders and the Plural Ministry,* part 2, chap. 7 and esp. chap. 8.

3. The whole question of ecclesiastical-civil relationships in discipline is thorny and controverted, and the bibliography is enormous. It is perhaps useful to point out a few sources for the Calvinist Reformed developments, however. A general discussion of the Protestant context can be found in John Tonkin, *The Church and the Secular Order in Reformation Thought* (New York: Columbia University Press, 1971). A recent treatment of Calvin's political thought can be found in Harro Höpfl, *The Christian Polity of John Calvin* (Cambridge: Cambridge University Press, 1982). Older but still excellent is the survey of Reformed practice and thought in John T. McNeill, *The History and Character of Calvinism* (Oxford: Oxford University Press, 1954). For Genevan practices, see Robert M. Kingdon, "The Control of Morals by the

Earliest Calvinists," in *Renaissance, Reformation, Resurgence*, ed. Peter De Klerk (Grand Rapids: Calvin Theological Seminary, 1976), pp. 95-106; "The Control of Morals in Calvin's Geneva," in *The Social History of the Reformation*, ed. L. P. Zophy (Columbus: Ohio State University Press, 1972), pp. 3-16. See also notes in chap. 1 of McKee, *Elders and the Plural Ministry*.

4. Calvin, *Institutes of the Christian Religion*, Library of Christian Classics, vols. 20-21, ed. John T. McNeill, trans. Ford Lewis Battles (Philadelphia: Westminster, 1960), 4.3.8. Original text in *Johannis Calvini Opera Selecta*, 5 vols., ed. P. Barth, W. Niesel, and D. Scheuner (Munich: Kaiser, 1926-52), 5: 50, ll. 21-28; in subsequent references, this work will be cited as *OS*.

5. Calvin, *Institutes*, 4.11.1; *OS*, 5: 195, ll. 3-31. Calvin first mentions the "council of elders" in the 1539 edition of the *Institutes* (4.20.4), in the context of discussing civil authority.

6. See McKee, *Elders and the Plural Ministry*, pp. 34-37; and "Calvin, Discipline, and Exegesis: Matt. 18:17 and 1 Cor. 5:3-5 in the Sixteenth Century" (Paper delivered at the Third International Conference on Sixteenth Century Exegesis, Geneva, September 1988).

7. Calvin held that Jewish ceremonial and judicial laws are not to be imposed on Christian societies (*Inst.*, 4.20.14, 1536 ed.). He argued against the Zwinglians' desire to turn discipline over to the magistracy (*Inst.*, 4.11.3-5, 1543 ed.). See further McKee, *Elders and the Plural Ministry*, pp. 30, 52ff., *et passim* concerning the Zwinglian effort to read the New Testament through the Old, especially using 2 Chron. 19:6ff. to interpret Rom. 12:8.

8. For exegetical histories of the three verses, see chaps. 2-4 of McKee, *Elders and the Plural Ministry*.

9. For discussion of social welfare reform and the historiography of the debate, see chap. 4 of McKee, *John Calvin*.

10. See chap. 10 of McKee, *John Calvin*.

11. For exegetical histories and a general discussion, see McKee, *John Calvin*, chaps. 6-7 *et passim*.

12. Calvin, *Institution of the Christian Religion* (1536), ed. Ford Lewis Battles (Atlanta: John Knox, 1975), p. 235; *OS*, 1: 218-19.

13. See McKee, *John Calvin*, pp. 106-13, 155-56.

14. Calvin, *Institutes*, 4.3.9, p. 1061. OS, vol. 5, pp. 50-51. Calvin's theory on women in church leadership was probably somewhat less severe than his practice. See Jane Dempsey Douglass, *Women, Freedom, and Calvin* (Philadelphia: Westminster, 1985).

15. For full exegetical histories, see chaps. 8-9 of McKee, *John Calvin*.

16. For a discussion of the argument, see Elsie Anne McKee, "Calvin's Exegesis of Rom. 12:8 — Social, Accidental, or Theological?" *Calvin Theological Journal*, April 1988, pp. 6-18.

17. See McKee, *John Calvin*, pp. 169ff., 197ff., 217ff.; and *Elders and the Plural Ministry*, pp. 55ff., 78ff., 103ff. See also notes in chap. 6 of Elsie Anne McKee, *Diakonia in the Classical Reformed Tradition and Today* (Grand Rapids: William B. Eerdmans, 1989). Both text and notes are intended as only a *very* brief summary of the post–sixteenth-century period. The intent is merely to offer a sketch of some features of the postclassical Reformed teaching on the offices of elders and deacons.

18. McKee, *John Calvin*, pp. 220-21; *Diakonia*, chap. 6.

19. See chap. 6 of McKee, *Diakonia*.

20. See *Baptism, Eucharist and Ministry* (Geneva: World Council of Churches, 1982), pars. 24 and 31 and the commentary on 31, pp. 25, 27.

21. See the discussion of answers in chap. 6 of McKee, *Diakonia*. Many Protestant churches, including some not usually considered Reformed, raise questions about the diaconate. The eldership is naturally more a concern of the Reformed tradition. The list of those who raise the question of the eldership includes the Church of Scotland, the United Reformed Church in the United Kingdom, the Presbyterian Church of Wales, the Presbyterian Church in Ireland, and the Covenanted Baptist Churches in Wales.

Reformed Churches and Evangelism: Historical Background

Robert S. Paul

I.

The dilemma that modern Reformed Christians may feel regarding evangelism is probably shared by members in all the mainline Protestant denominations. It is of no recent origin, for it dates from the time of the Reformation itself and from the time when Christians in the West thought that the evangelical task of the church had already been accomplished by the creation of European Christendom. From the first, the dilemma has been intimately related both to Reformed ecclesiology and the ecumenical relationships of the Reformed churches.

1. Like most of his contemporaries, Calvin believed that practically all the world that was to be saved had already been evangelized, and although he was ready to concede that God might still on occasion raise up an order of evangelists where they were needed, he clearly inferred that this would not happen very frequently.[1] Therefore, with other Reformers of that period, in exegeting Ephesians 4:11-13, he held that the first three offices mentioned in relation to the church — apostles, prophets, and evangelists — were only occasional offices and that the time of their great activity had passed with the apostolic age. For this reason, he held that, of the offices listed by Paul, "only these last two have an ordinary office in the church" (*Inst.*, 4.3.4). Therefore the only permanent officers of the church were pastors and teachers, to which, by reference to other passages, he also added elders and deacons (*Inst.*, 4.3.4-9).

This understanding of the ministry of the local church had repercussions throughout Reformed ecclesiology and particularly in relation to the debate between Presbyterians and Congregationalists in the Westminster Assembly.[2] Both sides in that Reformed dispute were, of course, anxious to cite whatever authorities they could in support of their own

Reprinted from *Austin Seminary Bulletin* 100 (April 1985): 15-23.

polity and also to seek endorsement for their church government from the other Reformed churches. The Presbyterians of the Assembly, led by the commissioners from the Church of Scotland, were particularly anxious to enlist the support of European theologians for their church government, while the Congregationalists appealed to their Puritan colleagues in New England. One of the Scots commissioners, the Reverend Robert Baillie of the University of Glasgow, spent most of his time trying to win the support of European theologians. He was able to persuade the Dutch theologian William Apollonius, pastor of the church at Middelburg, to write a series of questions to the New Englanders that were eventually answered (in Latin) by John Norton of Ipswich, Massachusetts. This reply was the *Responsio,* or, to give it its English title, *The Answer.*

In this book Norton quotes the questions that Apollonius raised, at the heading of each chapter, and then proceeds to his answer in terms of New England ecclesiology. The particular chapter that relates to our subject is chapter 8, "Of Power of the Minister as Evangelist." Apollonius's question runs as follows:

> Is the end and effect of the work of the ecclesiastical ministry only the confirmation of those who are already converted and true church members, so that ministers of churches are not more obliged by virtue of their ecclesiastical function to convert the straying souls of such as live in the world and in sin out of church communion, than are all other believers endowed with the gifts of the Holy Spirit by the common duty of Christian love? Do they never convert any by virtue of their ecclesiastical ministry except by chance?[3]

It should be remembered that the situation of the parish churches in New England was radically different from that of the churches in Europe. The former had already had to engage in evangelism among the native "Indians" who had never heard the gospel, work pioneered by John Eliot and Thomas Shepard. The Puritan

ministers also had to face the issue by reason of the almost constant influx of English immigrants during the 1630s. Norton's response was that

> the end and effect of the ecclesiastical ministry is not only the confirmation and edification of those who are already converted and are true church members, but by virtue of their ecclesiastical function ministers of churches are obliged to convert the straying souls of such as live in the world and in sin out of church communion. Their obligation to do so is far greater than that of any of the rest of the faithful endowed with the gifts of the Holy Spirit and bound by the common duty of Christian love. And when by virtue of their ecclesiastical ministry (divine grace cooperating) they make converts, the conversion is an effect of their ecclesiastical ministry as such and is not by chance.[4]

Norton was even more explicit when he declared that

> a light shining from a candlestick illumines more than the candlestick.
>
> In our judgment, therefore, ministers by virtue of their church office are ministers to every creature as occasion offers. They are the ordinary external means of making salvation effective to the elect in every mode, not only by the conversion of the not yet converted by also by confirmation and edification of those who have already been converted.[5]

It should be clear from these quotations that Reformed ecclesiology would have to deal with the issue of evangelism as soon as it freed itself from the assumptions of an already converted society in Europe, as the extent and challenge of the non-Christian world became more obvious through the explorations of the eighteenth and nineteenth centuries, and as Western society itself became more urbanized and complicated. In this connection it is worth noting that J. C. Hoekendijk interpreted Reformed ecclesiology wholly in terms of evangelism and mission and suggested that, in order to have an adequate understanding of the church and its mission, we must rid ourselves of assumptions inherited from a Christianized society (Christendom).[6]

2. A further legacy from this period that may be even more important for our understanding of evangelism arises from the basic appeal of all Reformed churches to biblical authority.

From the first, Calvinists insisted that Scripture must be given its plain, rational meaning.[7] But if Calvin insisted upon the essential importance of the Holy Spirit for the interpretation of the Scriptures (*Inst.*, 1.9.2-3), he also insisted on the God-given gift of human reason (*Inst.*, 1.3.3, 2.2.12-17), which he regarded as the direct work of the Holy Spirit (*Inst.*, 2.2.16). The earliest history of the Reformed churches shows that in the interpretation of scriptural authority a tension often arose between the interpretation of the Holy Spirit to individual Christian experience and what the Holy Spirit reveals through human reason — the authority of the heart and the authority of the head. These two individualistic answers to the authority problem were kept in proper relationship by holding both within the corporate discipline and testimony of the church. But at the end of the seventeenth century, Reformed doctrines of the church began to erode, and all ecclesiastical polities were under pressure. Individual interpretations of the head (leading to rationalism) or of the heart (leading to pietism) tended to take over. As a result, the Reformed churches of the eighteenth century were liable to fly to one or the other of these extremes. This is important for our subject because they held very different views of the church's mission and of the way in which the churches should approach evangelism. I suggest, therefore, that this is the context in which later disputes between "Old Lights" and "New Lights" in both the first and the second Great Awakenings should be understood — the tendency of Reformed Christians to move into either an essentially rationalistic attitude or else into an emotional pietism.

II.

This tendency to reduce Christian church membership to either a rational or an emotional base was not limited to Presbyterian churches. The Congregationalists of New England had experienced the tension at the time of the Halfway Covenant,[8] and it was at the center of George Whitefield's growing estrangement from the Anglican Church. As Sydney Ahlstrom has noted,

> before he died, this "Grand Itinerant" . . . put a more permanent mark on the Great Awakening and on American evangelical religion in general than any other single colonial figure. In filling this great role, however, he had to defy the Anglican establishments in virtually every colony; he was excoriated by the SPG [Society for the Propagation of the Gospel] missionaries who carried on the chief work of the Church of England in America. Both sought to win souls, rekindle piety, and plant churches, but they worked at opposite ends of the British religious spectrum. Perhaps the greatest irony lies in the fact that, whereas Whitefield's zeal led most of all to the strengthening of Congregational, Baptist, and Presbyterian churches, the SPG developed a clergy and constituency so fervently Anglican that its work was decimated by the Revolution and the exodus of the Loyalists.[9]

Ahlstrom indicates that much the same tension affected the German Reformed when they arrived in America.[10] It may be important in writing of evangelism in relation to Reformed churches to recognize that this is another of our problems in the twentieth century that should be addressed ecumenically.

For the Reformed churches generally, the issue of evangelism came to a head at the time of the Great Awakening, and particularly in the literary battle between Jonathan Edwards and Charles Chauncy. It led Edwards to write his *Treatise on the Religious Affections,* and it stimulated Chauncy to launch a major attack on what he felt were the evil results of emotionalism in the Great Awakening. In a sermon based on 1 Corinthians 14:37 entitled "Enthusiasm Described and Caution'd Against" (1742), he declared that

> in nothing does the enthusiasm of these persons discover it self more, than in the disregard they express to the Dictates of reason. They are above the force of argument, beyond conviction from a calm and sober address to their understandings. As for them, they are distinguished persons; GOD himself speaks inwardly and immediately to their souls.[11]

Chauncy insisted that the best way to "try such spirits" was to test their conformity with Scripture. Look to the Bible, he said, "to point you to a rule by which you may judge of persons, whether they are enthusiasts, meer pretenders to the immediate guidance and influence of the SPIRIT."[12] He also insisted — against the exclusivism and strictures that New Lights were uttering against the regular ministry — that the message must be consistent with the rule of charity: "Tho' I speak, says the apostle, with the tongues of men and of angels, and have not charity, I am become as sounding brass, or a tinkling cymbal."[13]

Edwards, of course, was just as insistent that the results of the Great Awakening should be consistent with the Bible, and he excused the physical excesses as the irrepressible expressions of those under deep conviction of sin. He concluded that "the work that is now carried on in the Land, is the Work of God," and he warned his hearers

> for the future not to oppose it, or say any Thing against it, or any Thing that has so much as an indirect Tendency to bring it into Discredit, lest they should be found to be Opposers of the Holy Ghost. There is no Kind of Sins so hurtful and dangerous to the Souls of Men, as those that are committed against the Holy Ghost.[14]

The issue split both wings of the Reformed churches. New England Congregationalists separated into New Lights and Old Lights, and similar divisions among the Presbyterians of the Middle Atlantic colonies caused tensions in the newly established presbyteries of Philadelphia, New Castle, and Long Island. Sydney Ahlstrom has shown that these tensions were exacerbated by the fact that, under the leadership of Jonathan Dickinson of Elizabethtown, N.J. (who was eventually to become the first president of the College of New Jersey), the New England influence was pronounced, if not dominant, in the early establishment of Presbyterianism, and it produced the tendency to hold less firmly to the Westminster Standards. But in the first years of the eighteenth century, there was a rapid and extensive influx of Scotch-Irish, particularly to the New Castle presbytery, who, under the leadership of John Thompson, insisted on a strict subscription to the Westminster Standards as the basis of Presbyterian orthodoxy.

The churches were brought into concord by the acceptance of the compromise in the Adopting Act of 1729, but the uneasy peace was eventually disrupted when Scotch-Irish frontiersmen were influenced by the preaching of the Tennents in the Great Awakening and, as a result, linked themselves with the more liberal Presbyterians under Dickenson. This led to the ejection of the "Log College" graduates and to the establishment of the "New Side" Synod of New York in 1745 on the basis of the Adopting Act.

III.

But it is a mistake to think that the issue of evangelism in the Great Awakening was concentrated only in the problem of excessive emotionalism. We cannot separate the awakened concern for evangelism from the rising concern for the church's mission to all God's people demonstrated in such things as David Brainerd's mission to the Indians in America, the birth of foreign missions through the *Reveille* among the Reformed in continental Europe (the Basel Mission), and the founding of missionary societies as a result of the evangelical revivals in Britain.

Again we note that the new insights were sometimes viewed as conflicting with traditional orthodoxy and church government. This was expressed in the General Assembly of the Presbyterian Church of Scotland in 1796, when one of the Scottish divines said that he regarded a proposal to start missionary work overseas as thoroughly misguided. "I cannot otherwise consider the enthusiasm on this subject," he said, "than as the effect of sanguine and illusive views, the more dangerous because the object is plausible." One of his colleagues went even further, suggesting that "to spread abroad the knowledge of the Gospel among barbarous and heathen nations seems highly preposterous, in so far as it anticipates, it even reverses, the order of nature."[15]

Fortunately, the evangelical concern demonstrated during the Awakenings was never limited exclusively to the souls of the unconverted. Concern for the spiritual life of individuals, both at home and abroad, led directly to an equal concern for their material necessities. For example, the Great Awakening led to the establishment of a large number of education institutions, such as William Tennent's "Log College" (Princeton University) and Dartmouth College in New England. It has been noted that Eleazar Wheelock, one of the most prominent New Light itinerants in England, "conceived a plan for educating Indian boys so they could spread the gospel effectively to their own people."[16] This educational enterprise was one in which Presbyterians and other Reformed people were particularly involved, and I cannot help feeling that their involvement is at least in part attributable to a theology that insisted on the proper use of the rational faculties.

IV.

The social results of this evangelicalism have never received the attention they deserve. For example, the evangelical revival in England, associated with the names of Whitefield and the Wesleys, was directly related not only to the establishment of foreign and home missionary societies but also to the great movement to emancipate the slaves (William Wilberforce), John Howard's and Elizabeth Fry's prison reform, the regulation of child labor in the factories (the Earl of Shaftesbury), and the establishment of Sunday Schools (Robert Raikes).

Another area that calls for more research is the relationship of evangelistic missions to the beginnings of medical and educational missionary work. Although missions may have sometimes played into the hands of imperial policies, their educational work prepared a generation of younger converts who would agitate for colonial freedom. Very soon after establishing the evangelistic mission, Western missionaries strove to include social services within their total offering to the indigenous peoples. The career of David Livingstone illustrates this fusion between evangelical and social concern. In writing of early missions in India, Kenneth Scott Latourette remarked that "Duff and the Scottish Presbyterians were particularly prominent in introducing Western higher education under Christian auspices."[17] The concern for evangelism and mission, which historically cannot be divided, probably gave to Protestant churches of the West their first glimpse of how the gospel was to be related holistically to all humankind.

Side by side with the problem of excessive emotionalism, which arose out of the experience of evangelical revivals at home, we need to place the social testimony of the evangelicals in the nineteenth century, which arose directly from their contact with human need abroad. This may also suggest something of the ecumenical dimension of the issue as we consider evangelism specifically in relationship to Reformed churches.

In conclusion we may perhaps recognize some of the basic insights about evangelism that arise from our brief survey of Reformed history.

1. We note the importance of both human reason and inward experience in the interpretation of the scriptural norm. We have seen the danger when either of these is appealed to exclusively and without the corporate discipline of the church. In the past, especially during the periods of great religious revival, we have been tempted to concentrate too much on the experiential and to discount the importance of human rationality. But our temptation today may be precisely the opposite — to emphasize rationality at the expense of the inward testimony of the Spirit. If that is the temptation, we should note that it was the Old Lights, those who emphasized the purely rational understanding of Scripture and the Westminster Standards, who fell prey to the cultural rationalism of their age and opened the way to Deism. It would be truer to our history to take our lesson from Calvin and recognize that evangelism should not be separated from ecclesiology and that ecclesiology is the proper context in which the testimonies of rational faculties and religious feelings should be held together.

2. We should underscore the ecumenical and holistic approach to which our history points.

3. These emphases correct the excessive individualism that develops from polarities of "head" or "heart" religion.

4. Indeed, they recognize the need for our churches to take their own corporate (ecclesial) view of salvation with new seriousness.

5. At the same time we realize that a valid ecclesiology must be expressed in ecumenical rather than exclusively denominational terms. We seek to bring people into the church of Jesus Christ, but we can no longer restrict our understanding of "the church" to ourselves or those who define it in precisely our own terms.

6. But the mission should also be holistic in its concern for the whole of life — not simply salvation beyond this life, but also the quality of living made possible to human mortality.

7. There seems to be a growing consensus in the churches of our order against using any methods of evangelism that ignore the individual's responsibility or that are manipulative of human nature.

In sum, our history brings us to the point where we recognize the essential relationship that ecclesiology has to evangelism and the basic biblical insight that the church always points to the kingdom.

NOTES

1. See Calvin, *Institutes of the Christian Religion,* Library of Christian Classics, ed. John T. McNeill, trans. Ford Lewis Battles (Philadelphia: Westminster Press, 1960), 4.3.4. Subsequent references to this work will be made parenthetically in the text.

2. Cf. Robert S. Paul, *The Assembly of the Lord: Politics and Religion in the Westminster Assembly and the 'Grand Debate'* (Edinburgh: T. &. T. Clark, 1985).

3. Norton, *The Answer to the Whole Set of Questions of the Celebrated Mr. William Apollonius, Pastor of the Church of Middelburg,* trans. Douglas Horton (Cambridge: Belknap Press, 1958), p. 108.

4. Norton, *The Answer,* p. 108.

5. Norton, *The Answer,* p. 109.

6. Hoekendijk, *The Church Inside Out,* ed. L. A. Hoedemaker and Pieter Tijmes, trans. Isaac C. Rottenberg (Philadelphia: Westminster Press, 1964).

7. William Perkins wrote that "the Church of Rome maketh 4 senses of the Scriptures: the literall, the allegoricall, tropologicall, and anagogicall. . . . But this her deuice

of the fourefold meaning of the Scripture must be exploded and rejected" ("The Art of Prophesying," in *Works* [1609], p. 737).

8. Cf. Mary M. Currie, "The Puritan Half-Way Covenants," *Austin Seminary Bulletin* [faculty edition] 95 (Oct. 1979): 29ff.

9. Ahlstrom, *A Religious History of the American People* (New Haven: Yale University Press, 1972), p. 229.

10. Ahlstrom, *A Religious History of the American People,* pp. 249-50.

11. Chauncy, as cited by Eugene E. White in *Puritan Rhetoric: The Issue of Emotion in Religion* (Carbondale, Ill.: Southern Illinois University Press, 1972), p. 106.

12. Chauncy, in *Puritan Rhetoric,* p. 107.

13. Chauncy, in *Puritan Rhetoric,* p. 109.

14. Edwards, in a sermon entitled "Distinguishing Marks," based on 1 John 4:1, cited by White in *Puritan Rhetoric,* pp. 97-98.

15. Cited by Alec Vidler in *The Church in an Age of Revolution,* Pelican History of the Church, vol. 5 (Baltimore: Penguin, 1961), pp. 248-49.

16. Ahlstrom, *A Religious History of the American People,* p. 289.

17. Latourette, "The Great Century . . . 1800-1914," in *A History of the Expansion of Christianity,* vol. 6 (London: Eyre & Spottiswode, 1944), p. 190.

A Reformed Perspective on the Mission of the Church in Society

Donald K. McKim

Historically, churches in the Reformed theological tradition have had a passionate concern for their mission in society. This concern has expressed itself in a variety of forms in the many contexts in which Reformed churches have been situated since the sixteenth century. This is not to say that all churches have done all that was possible within their specific fields of influence, but it is to say that, on balance, churches of the Reformed faith have had at their disposal the theological resources from within their own traditions to carry out mission and ministry with integrity and zeal.

We shall illustrate this contention by reference to five themes as they emerge in the writings of John Calvin (1509-1564), the English Puritan William Perkins (1558-1602), and the Dutch theologian Abraham Kuyper (1837-1920).

Reprinted from *Reformed World* 38 (1985): 405-21.

CREATION: THE SOVEREIGNTY OF GOD AND THE SERIOUSNESS OF SIN

The opening thought of the book of Genesis in a sense provides the opening thought for many systems of Reformed theology: "In the beginning God created the heavens and the earth" (Gen. 1:1). This means that God is the sovereign Lord of the universe. As Calvin put it, "God by the power of his Word and Spirit created heaven and earth out of nothing; . . . thereupon he brought forth living beings and inanimate things of every kind."[1]

The Christian doctrine of creation (creation *ex nihilo,* "out of nothing") seeks to honor the biblical affirmations of the power and majesty of God as the One who is the source of all that exists in the universe (see, e.g., Ps. 103:19; Isa. 40:22; Rev. 4:11).[2] Fundamentally, it can be argued that

among the many activities of God, His creative activity is surely the one most essential for our existence. It is through this activity that we are brought into being, and it is this activity, therefore, that establishes our deepest, because our most essential, relation to God: He is our Creator and thus our Lord.[3]

From this basic Christian insight, Reformed theology has put special stress on the meaning and implications of the doctrine of creation. Abraham Kuyper asserted that "the fundamental conception of religion as maintained by Calvinism" is "the confession of the absolute Sovereignty of the Triune God."[4] For "the triune God is the Lord of heaven and earth. On this point Reformed theology has never been in doubt, and this conviction has given a distinctive character to the faith of the Reformed community."[5] The Reformed tradition has often been said to have emphasized "the sovereignty of God" (see *Inst.*, 1.12.1 n. 1), and despite any technical theological debates about the propriety of this term, the basic insight stands: God as Creator implies God as sovereign Lord who has called into existence all that is, including humankind itself.

This view of God's sovereignty over all has been both a great comfort and challenge to Reformed Christians who have contemplated its implications. Calvin urged that the contemplation of God's goodness in the creation should lead us to thankfulness and trust:

> whenever we call God the Creator of heaven and earth, let us at the same time bear in mind that the dispensation of all those things which he has made is in his own hand and power and that we are indeed his children, whom he has received into his faithful protection to nourish and educate. (*Inst.*, 1.14.22)[6]

But William Perkins stated an equal Reformed concern well in a discussion of the "duties" of the doctrine of creation. He listed as one such duty that humanity must "endeavour to perform obedience unto God's word. God is a Creator, and the thing created should in all respects be conformable to his will." Then, drawing on the commercial imagery of his day,

Perkins wrote that "the world is as it were an opened shop, in which God hath set forth unto us his glory and majesty, and the creatures of all kinds be instruments appointed for excellent uses, and specially man for the accomplishment of his will."[7] The creatures of the sovereign God are to be the servants of the sovereign God.

The reason this is such a imperative for the Reformed is that their emphasis on total adherence to the sovereignty of God expressed in creation is conjoined to an equal emphasis on the seriousness of human sin. The good creation has been despoiled and defaced, corrupted and confused by sin. This has affected God's created order including humankind itself. Perkins refers to humans as "traitors and rebels" against their Creator who, instead of giving to God the obedience God requires, have gone their own way and sought their own wills instead of their Creator's will. "God createth man, not that he should do his own will, but God's will."[8] Sin has seriously impaired the relationship of creature and Creator. Ultimately this rupture can be restored only through the work of grace done by Jesus Christ. As Calvin put it, "by his obedience . . . Christ truly acquired and merited grace for us with his Father" (*Inst.*, 2.17.3).

In the Reformed tradition, then, God is supreme over human life. This is part of God's sovereignty over the universe more generally expressed in creation. Absolute allegiance and obedience is due to the Creator. But human sin stands in the way. God must reestablish the relationship of creature with Creator and has done so in Jesus Christ.

Recognition of the sovereignty of God and the seriousness of human sin have led Reformed churches to realize that their mission in society is based fundamentally on the obedience owed to their sovereign Creator. It is a realization that all their efforts on behalf of the gospel of Jesus Christ in whatever forms those efforts take are rooted in this basic obedience that God requires.

At the same time, perceiving sin as a reality that cannot be ignored, the Reformed tradition has recognized all the more the crucial need in this world for its ministry and witness to God in Jesus Christ. The churches of the tradition themselves have been part of the sinful condition to which they seek to minister. But by the grace of God, they have trusted that their obedience to the sovereign Creator, broken as that obedience may be, can nonetheless be used by God for honor, glory, majesty, and praise. So the sovereignty of God and the seriousness of sin are powerful incentives for churches to minister vigorously and zealously in society according to the Reformed faith.

ELECTION: THE PURPOSES OF GOD AND THE PEOPLE OF GOD

Another particular emphasis of the Reformed tradition has been on God's election of a people to serve God. By providence God "governs all events" and has elected or predestined a people to carry out the divine purposes in this world.[9] This people is called the church, and God's relationship with them is sealed by the new covenant in Jesus Christ.[10] Faith is the instrument by which God unites this people to himself (see *Inst.*, 3.2). Christ is the "sole foundation" of the covenant, according to Calvin (*Inst.*, 2.10.4). Its roots reach back into the Old Testament to the covenant made with Abraham (Gen. 12:2-3), through the Sinai covenant (Exod. 20), and to the prophets. Wrote Perkins,

> God had made a covenant with his Church, the tenour whereof is this, I will be thy God, and thou shalt be my people (Jer. 31:33). The covenant is not for a day or an age, or for a thousand years or ages, but is everlasting and without end, so as God's people may say of God for ever, God is our God: and likewise God will say of his Church for evermore, this people is my people.[11]

In Reformed thought, this perception of God's election of a people, the choosing of a corporate body through his covenant in Jesus Christ, has been a powerful spur to action in society. Kuyper points out that for the Reformed, "the Church is a spiritual organism, including heaven and earth, but having at present its center, and the starting-point for its action, not upon earth, but in heaven."[12] The initiative in choosing the covenant people lay with God. People are not chosen by virtue of their merits or because of their own abilities; they are part of the church purely by God's grace. Consequently, their participation in the life and mission of the church in the world is possible only as God continues to uphold them and empower them *by grace*.

This leads to the realization that with the starting point for the church's action "not upon earth, but in heaven," with God, the ultimate outcomes of all labors in the ministry of Jesus Christ belong to God. Calvin saw this as one of the primary benefits of confessing faith in "the communion of saints," the church. He wrote that "even if the whole fabric of the world were overthrown, the church could neither totter nor fall," for "it stands by God's election, and cannot waver or fail any more than his eternal providence can" (*Inst.*, 4.1.3). Reformed thinking holds that the people of God are sustained by the purposes of God. Like Paul, those in the Reformed tradition have emphasized that regardless of who does the "planting" or the "watering" in the ministry of the church, it is always God who "gives the growth" (1 Cor. 3:6). Against all charges that the doctrine of election destroys zeal for an upright life or makes all admonitions meaningless, Calvin insisted (with Augustine) that "godly living" or involvement in the purposes of God is actually the goal of election. And "if election has as its goal holiness of life, it ought rather to arouse and goad us eagerly to set our mind upon it than to serve as a pretext for doing nothing" (*Inst.*, 3.23.12).

Through God's covenant, focused in Christ, the people of God are bound to God. Historically, "the most important vehicle for the widespread influences of the covenant idea in church and society was Covenant (or Federal Theology) and its development by the early seventeenth century Puritans in England and America."[13] For Reformed people who took the covenants found in Scripture seriously, the covenant relationship was not restricted to "the relationship between God and the elect individual. The covenant was also *societal*, for God had shown that he was concerned with the human community."[14] Christians are called to ministry in society as members of the body of Christ. The holy catholic church is the context from which ministry gets its practical starting point. Kuyper noted that "for Calvin, the Church is found in the *confessing individuals themselves*, — not in each individual separately, but in all of them taken together, and united, not as they themselves see fit, but according to the ordinances of Christ."[15] The divine mission of the church issues from Christ himself. The covenant people of God are those corporately joined to carry out that mission in their cultures. They work jointly, in solidarity with one another because their ultimate union is with Christ according to God's gracious election. This gives impetus for the Reformed to ecumenical witness and ministry, to interdenominational action on behalf of Jesus Christ.

KINGDOM: CHRIST THE LORD OF HISTORY

It has been asserted that in his *Institutes,* Calvin expresses "something much more explosive than the dogma of predestination; [the *Institutes* contain] a philosophy of history, a statement of Christian faith in terms of divine purpose."[16]

Calvin was indebted to Augustine (A.D. 354-430) here. In *The City of God,* begun A.D.

413 and completed in 426, Augustine sought to defend Christianity in the face of the destruction of Rome in A.D. 410. He developed the notion of two cities, the city of God and the city of the world, running through history. History now is lived out *sub specie aeternitatis* and will ultimately be consummated in the Last Judgment with the final triumph of God.[17] The establishment of the kingdom of God in history and beyond is seen to be the focus of God's providential activity.

Calvin continued with this theme in his view of the "two kingdoms." "The one we may call the spiritual kingdom," he writes, "the other, the political kingdom" (*Inst.,* 3.19.15). While these two kingdoms are distinct for Calvin, they are not completely separable or antithetical as in Luther. Calvin writes of the civil government that

> this kind of government is distinct from that spiritual and inward Kingdom of Christ, so we must know that they are not at variance. For spiritual government, indeed, is already initiating in us upon earth certain beginnings of the Heavenly Kingdom, and in this mortal and fleeting life affords a certain forecast of an immortal and incorruptible blessedness. Yet civil government has as its appointed end, so long as we live among men, to cherish and protect the outward worship of God, to defend sound doctrine of piety and the position of the church, to adjust our life to the society of men, to form our social behavior to civil righteousness, to reconcile us with one another, and to promote general peace and tranquillity. All of this I admit to be superfluous, if God's Kingdom, such as it is now among us, wipes out the present life. (*Inst.,* 4.20.2)[18]

Calvin's view that the magistracy is ordained by God incorporated the belief that magistrates have God-ordained responsibilities to carry out the appointed tasks of civil government as God's "vicars" and "deputies" (*Inst.,* 4.20.6). Indeed, he suggested that the "image of God" ought to shine in them (*Inst.,* 4.20.24). Thus

Calvin's politics have been said to conjoin a recognition of political reality with a demand that politics be bent to serve a religious purpose.[19]

The contours of history for Calvin, then, are shaped by both "secular" and "spiritual" forces. Yet these are not independent of each other; they are both subsumed under a providential view of history as moving toward its ultimate consummation in the kingdom of God or the kingdom of Christ.[20] Jesus Christ is the Lord of history. The Father has set Christ "over us to exercise his dominion through the Son" (*Inst.,* 2.15.5). This dominion is over all the world, over both "secular" and "spiritual" matters. The kingship of Christ over history means that life itself is all of "one piece," and all of life belongs to God in Christ. "Sacred" and "secular" are not two airtight compartments dividing life into dichotomous spheres. In the church and in the world, humanity bows to the reign of Jesus Christ. Christians in the church seek to be obedient to Christ's rule in history and in the cultural circumstances in which they are set.

Practically, this view of Christ as Lord of history means that Reformed Christians have envisioned no areas of human endeavor or thought as exempt from the reign of Christ. All are valid fields of mission and ministry. This was the burden of Kuyper's *Lectures on Calvinism.* He dealt with the relationship of Calvinism to religion, politics, science, art, and the future after establishing initially that Calvinism is a "life-system." Kuyper argued that Calvinism "demands that all life be consecrated to [God's] service."[21] Particularly, among the Reformed, "instead of monastic flight *from* the world the duty is now emphasized of serving God *in* the world, in every position in life."[22]

All history points toward the final establishment of the kingdom. Christ is the Lord of that kingdom and Lord of the history toward which contemporary events move. With this understanding, no arenas are "out of bounds" as fields of endeavor on behalf of the gospel. H. Richard Niebuhr has classified Augustine, Calvin, and their followers as seeing Christ as "the transformer of culture." The impetus for such a view stems from the conviction that Jesus Christ is Lord of all culture. He commands Christians to labor within their own slices of history, whatever their positions, to carry out the tasks given by God until that day when "at the name of Jesus every knee should bow, in heaven and on earth and under the earth, and every tongue confess that Jesus Christ is Lord, to the glory of God the Father" (Phil. 2:10-11). Jesus Christ is Lord of history.

VOCATION: CALLING TO SERVICE

The summons to participate in the will and work of God in Christ in the midst of human history comes directly to the people of God in Reformed thought. Karl Barth (1886-1968), one of the greatest of the twentieth-century Reformed theologians, underscored this when he wrote that "the command of God does genuinely demand the active life, namely, that man should set his mind on something and accomplish it. It does not allow him to understand and treat his existence as an end in itself."[23] For Barth, "an active life lived in obedience must obviously consist in a correspondence to divine action."[24] Thus the people of God are under an "obligation" to what the Scriptures call "service."[25] To serve God in Jesus Christ is the true freedom of the Christian life since it shows of human life that "its meaning and aim are not to be found simply within creaturely existence."[26] For Barth and his predecessors in the Reformed tradition, "the basic form of the active life of obedience understood and affirmed as service of the cause of God is man's direct or indirect co-operation in the fulfillment of the task of the Christian community."[27]

But as in Reformed thought generally, so specifically here in this "service" rendered by the people of God, the beginning or "calling" comes from God. There is a divine initiative at work. The sovereign, electing Lord at work for the establishment of God's kingdom in Jesus Christ "calls" the people of God into service for this world.

The concept of "vocation" or "calling" (Gr. *klēsis*) is rooted in the New Testament. There, as Barth points out, it

> always means quite unambiguously the divine calling, i.e., the act of the call of God issued in Jesus Christ by which a man is transplanted into his new state as a Christian, is made a participant in the promise (Eph. 1[18], 4[4]) bound up with this new state, and assumes the duty (Eph. 4[1]; 2 Pet. 1[10]) corresponding to this state.[28]

Martin Luther, however, gave the term a distinctive meaning by translating it as *Beruf* ("profession," "occupation") in the German Bible. Max Weber saw in this that in the Reformation

> one thing was unquestionably new: the valuation of fulfilment of duty in worldly affairs as the highest form which the moral activity of the individual could assume. This it was which inevitably gave every-day worldly activity a religious significance, and which first created the conception of a calling in this sense.[29]

Weber said that this led some to view "the fulfillment of secular duties as alone the way to please God, and hence the belief that 'every legitimate calling has exactly the same worth in the sight of God.'"[30]

It has been well noted that in the Reformed tradition, Calvin's doctrine of vocation has two major points of importance. First,

> it is the necessary complement of his doctrine of Election. The doctrine of Election by itself emphasizes a Christian's separation from the world, and can be expounded in such a way

that it presents the Elect as the special favorites of the Almighty. But Vocation shows that there is no Election without responsibility, so that Election is simply the obverse side, the 'Godward side' as it were, of the Christian's calling.[31]

For Calvin, the New Testament concept of the "call" was real. God, through the "inward illumination of his Spirit," causes the preached word to dwell in believers' hearts (*Inst.*, 3.24.8).[32]

Yet God also establishes various "callings" by which human lives are "best ordered." These are the "various kinds of living 'callings' . . . assigned . . . by the Lord as a sort of sentry post so that [Christians] may not heedlessly wander about throughout life" (*Inst.*, 3.10.6).[33] But the service rendered to God as the Christian's duty done through one's occupation or vocation is not for Calvin the *source* of one's election or calling. Rather, the good works are the "fruits of the call" (*Inst.*, 3.14.19).[34] For the people of God, actions done in mission or ministry in the service of Jesus Christ ("good works") are to be regarded by believers as "gifts of God from which they may recognize his goodness and as signs of the calling by which they realize their election" (*Inst.*, 3.14.20). The summons to the service of God in Christ will result in the work of God being done. But serving God through one's occupation — whatever it is — stems from the call of God. The mission accomplished is done from the responsibility of the call by God.

Second, for Calvin, "a Christian's vocation was essentially centered in [the] call to serve God here and now, in this world."[35] This emphasis is struck forcefully by the Puritan Perkins in his "Treatise of the Vocations," an exposition of 1 Corinthians 7:20: "Let every man abide in that calling, wherein he was called." Perkins defines vocation as "a certain kind of life, ordained and imposed on man by God, for the common good."[36] Indeed, says

Perkins, "we must consider the maine end of our lives, and that is, to serve God in the serving of men in the works of our callings."[37] God's pleasure is that humans should be "his instruments, for the good of one another."[38] Then Perkins proceeds to speak of two sorts of "personal callings" that exist in a society: those that are of the "essence and foundation of any societie," such as in the family, as husband or wife, in the commonwealth as magistrate, or in the church as minister or people; and those callings that "serve only for the good, happy, and quiet estate of a society," such as husbandman, merchant, physician, surgeon, lawyer, carpenter, masons, and so forth.[39] Yet regardless of the specific callings, Perkins concludes that there are two "virtues which the word of God requireth of us in the practise of our callings" — namely, "Faith and Love."[40]

Thus it is clear that for Perkins and those who have followed in the Reformed tradition of Calvin, the call to service is a very real and practical summons. It serves to show outwardly in life the interior theological convictions of the people of God as servants of Jesus Christ. Perkins uses the analogy of a clock to show the diversities of human callings and to establish that the author of them all is God:

> In a clocke, made by the arte and handy-worke of man, there be many wheels, and every one hath his seuerall motion, some turne this way, some that way, some go softly, some apace: and they are all ordered by the motion of the watch. Behold here a notable resemblance of Gods speciall providence over mankinde, which is the watch of the great world, allotting to every man his motion and calling: and in that calling, his particular office and function. Therefore it is true that I say that God himself is the author and beginning of callings.[41]

So Reformed Christians in the church are freed to pursue their various callings. But they see those callings as service in the light of the lordship of God in Christ, their election as God's people, and their obedient response to their loving Creator. Thus are they enabled to do the work and will of God in mission through the means or vocations to which they have been called.

STEWARDSHIP: MANAGING GOD'S RESOURCES RESPONSIBLY

One of the most powerful legacies from Old Testament Judaism to the Christian church has been the concept of stewardship. It is found as early as Genesis 1, which speaks of humans in the garden of Eden being told to "fill the earth and subdue it; and have dominion over the fish of the sea and over the birds of the air and over every living thing that moves upon the earth" (Gen. 1:28; cf. 1:26). Humanity is given a measure of power over the resources of this world, yet humans are also reminded of who is ultimately the provider of all these resources: "God said, 'Behold, *I* have given you every plant yielding seed . . . and every tree. . . . And to every beast of the earth, and to every bird of the air, and to everything that creeps on the earth, everything that has the breath of life, I have given every green plant for food'" (Gen. 1:29-30; italics mine). Humans are "over nature but under God."[42] Humans are the "stewards," "overseers," or "managers" of the gifts given.[43]

Appropriations of the stewardship concept in the Reformed churches have been comprehensive at their best. As a contemporary Reformed theologian has put it after speaking of the divorce of religion and secular life that occurred in the Middle Ages with the radical dichotomy between clergy and laity,

> with the coming of the Reformation, all this changed. An effort was made to erase the barrier between clergy and laity, between religion and everyday life. Now householders and

tradespeople were placed at the center of God's purpose. A new concept of Christian citizenship arose, and it could be seen in politics and business as well as in worship and witness. All life now became the arena of God's glory, and every human activity could be related to God's purpose. . . . Stewardship . . . is a synonym for Christian citizenship.[44]

Calvin's personal seal epitomized this comprehensive commitment. It showed a flaming heart in an open hand extended in offering to God with the words "I offer thee my heart, promptly and sincerely."

Comprehensive commitment means the duty to manage the resources of God responsibly, to be good stewards. Reformed views of the church as a basic resource given by God to sustain God's people have stressed this responsibility. They have placed a strong emphasis on polity, the effective government of the church. Reformed Christians have seen this as crucially important because of their "very deep conviction that God calls the Christian to a life of obedience in and through the polity of the church. The ultimate basis for the organized life of the church is not human wisdom but the will of God. The ministry and the polity of the church is God's gift to the church."[45] Thus there is a stewardship to be carried out with regard to the church.

On the personal level, Reformed theology has stressed the importance of the law of God for the best ordering or managing of the Christian life. The law is a gift of God. In it, says Calvin, "a perfect pattern of righteousness stands forth" which is the "one everlasting and unchangeable rule to live by" (*Inst.*, 2.7.13).[46] Rather than espousing a literalist interpretation of the law, however, Calvin stresses the division of the law into two tables and the summary of the law given by Christ in the great commandment — to love God and love our neighbor. Calvin described Jesus Christ as the "best interpreter" of the law (*Inst.*, 2.8.7). Following Calvin in this, the Reformed characteristically

emphasize the "third use" of the law, the view that "the proper purpose of the law" is to "find its place among believers in whose hearts the Spirit of God already lives and reigns" (*Inst.*, 2.7.12). The law can show believers "the pattern for the conduct of life" and the way to "a rightly ordered life" (*Inst.*, 3.6.1), since the law (interpreted by Christ) is "the best instrument for them to learn more thoroughly each day the nature of the Lord's will to which they aspire, and to confirm them in the understanding of it" (2.7.12).[47] Thus to be a good steward of life itself, to manage and oversee it as God intends, one should look to the law for guidance as the law itself looks to and is fulfilled in Christ (see *Inst.*, 2.6.4, n. 11; 2.6.2).

Finally, stewardship means the responsible use of God's resources. Living ethically in the Reformed tradition entails, in part, "an understanding of human life in relation to the powerful Other which requires that all human activity be ordered properly in relation to what can be discerned about the purposes of God."[48] With this sense of responsibility, Reformed Christians have sought to minister in the church and in the world *to* the pressing problems that have been posed in their own cultural contexts. Using their God-given resources, Reformed churches have addressed and ministered to specific issues of injustice, poverty, and oppression as well as to overarching global concerns such as hunger, the environment, and world peace.[49] Their ministering activities have been accompanied as well by the preaching of the gospel of Jesus Christ. Whether it has been in missionary endeavors or in daily or weekly services of divine worship, Reformed churches have stressed the crucial importance of preaching and the spiritual mission of the church in the proclamation of the grace of God in Jesus Christ for salvation.[50] Responsible stewardship in the Reformed tradition impels the church into ministry as "servants of Christ and stewards of the mysteries of God" (1 Cor. 4:1).

CONCLUDING REFLECTIONS ON A REFORMED PERSPECTIVE ON THE MISSION OF THE CHURCH IN SOCIETY

In its "Form of Government," the Presbyterian Church (USA) has identified the "Great Ends of the Church" as follows:

> the proclamation of the gospel for the salvation of humankind; the shelter, nurture, and spiritual fellowship of the children of God; the maintenance of divine worship; the preservation of the truth; the promotion of social righteousness; and the exhibition of the Kingdom of Heaven to the world.[51]

In Reformed thinking, theology is a "practical science." It is not an end in itself. It serves a greater purpose, "the formation of human life and society in conformity to the will of God."[52] Thus it is perfectly appropriate for Reformed churches to see as the end or purpose of the church, the radical involvement of the church in every dimension of mission in society, to the ends of the earth. This mission is rooted in the churches' theology itself. Resources from the churches' best theological reflection serve to undergird and give integrity to the efforts of the millions of men and women of the Reformed faith who have sought to minister actively for the gospel of Jesus Christ through the centuries.

The preceding discussion has elucidated some important themes in Reformed thought. In the Reformed tradition, one lives as a responsible steward, responsibly using the gifts God has given in service, through one's calling. This calling is to ministry in the midst of history and points beyond mere human activity to Jesus Christ, the Lord of history. One ministers not alone but together with other people of God, the church. The church is composed of those who are related to God through the new covenant which is Jesus Christ. The church ministers as the company of the committed. In God's providence the people of God have been chosen by God to do God's will and to seek to carry out God's purposes for this world. Despite the pervasiveness of sin and the failures of the church from a "human point of view," God uses God's people to do God's will as they obey God and acknowledge God's sovereignty over their lives as Creator and Lord.

Thus, in the freedom of the gospel, Reformed Christians and churches seek faithfully to minister and do God's will. Their efforts are carried out not for their own glory but for the greater glory of God, who "by the power at work within us is able to do far more abundantly than all that we ask or think." And to God "be glory in the church and in Christ Jesus to all generations, for ever and ever. Amen" (Eph. 3:20-21).

NOTES

1. Calvin, *Institutes of the Christian Religion*, Library of Christian Classics, vols. 20-21, ed. John T. McNeill, trans. Ford Lewis Battles (Philadelphia: Westminster Press, 1960), 1.14.20. Subsequent references to this work will be made parenthetically in the text.

2. The Nicene Creed captures this thought with the description of God as "Maker of heaven and earth, and of all things visible and invisible." On the Christian doctrine of creation, see Langdon Gilkey, *Maker of Heaven and Earth* (1959; reprint, Garden City, N.Y.: Doubleday, 1965), and the treatments by Reformed theologians such as Karl Barth, *Church Dogmatics*, 4 vols., ed. Geoffrey W. Bromiley and Thomas F. Torrance (Edinburgh: T. & T. Clark, 1936-1969), III/1-4; Emil Brunner, *The Christian Doctrine of Creation and Redemption*, trans. Olive Wyon (Philadel-

phia: Westminster Press, 1952); Otto Weber, *Foundations of Dogmatics*, vol. 1, trans. Darrell L. Guder (Grand Rapids: William B. Eerdmans, 1981), pp. 461-525; Hendrikus Berkhof, *Christian Faith*, trans. Sierd Woudstra (Grand Rapids: William B. Eerdmans, 1979), pp. 149ff.

3. Gilkey, *Maker of Heaven and Earth*, p. 83. The Reformed theologian Donald G. Bloesch has argued that "to affirm God as Creator and Lord also means to affirm the essential goodness of creation and the meaningfulness of history" (*Essentials of Evangelical Theology*, 2 vols. [San Francisco: Harper & Row, 1978], 1: 26).

4. Kuyper, *Lectures on Calvinism* (Grand Rapids: William B. Eerdmans, 1931), p. 46.

5. John H. Leith, *Introduction to the Reformed Tradition* (Atlanta: John Knox Press, 1977), p. 96.

6. The practical significance of this creation doctrine was developed along the same lines by the Scottish Presbyterian James Orr (1844-1913); see Orr, *The Christian View of God and the World*, 8th ed. (New York: Scribner's, 1907), pp. 122ff.

7. Perkins, *Works*, 3 vols. (London: J. Legatt, 1618), 1: 145.

8. Perkins, *Works*, 1: 145.

9. Calvin's discussion of God's providence occurs in *Inst.*, 1.16-17, while election and predestination are dealt with in 3.21-24 in relation to "the way we receive the grace of Christ."

10. See *Inst.*, 2.10, and Perkins, *Works*, 1: 24.

11. Perkins, *Works*, 1: 314.

12. Kuyper, *Lectures on Calvinism*, p. 59.

13. Robert S. Paul, "The Covenant in Church History," *Austin Seminary Bulletin* 96 (March 1981): 38. See also Perry Miller and Jens G. Møller, "The Beginnings of Puritan Covenant Theology," *Journal of Ecclesiastical History* 14 (April 1963): 46-67; and Donald K. McKim, "William Perkins and the Theology of the Covenant," in *Studies of the Church in History: Essays Honoring Robert S. Paul on His Sixty-fifth Birthday* (Allison Park, Pa.: Pickwick Press, 1983), pp. 85-101.

14. Paul, "The Covenant in Church History," p. 42.

15. Kuyper, *Lectures on Calvinism*, p. 62.

16. Lord Eustace Percy, *John Knox* (London: Hodder & Stoughton, 1937), p. 109.

17. Augustine has been called "the father of the Christian philosophy of history." See C. A. Patrides, *The Grand Design of God: The Literary Form of the Christian View of History* (London: Routledge & Kegan Paul, 1972), p. 16. For the Augustinian legacy with respect to history from Calvin to Puritanism, see Donald K. McKim, "The Puritan View of History or Providence 'Without and Within,'" *The Evangelical Quarterly* 52 (October-December 1980): 215-37.

18. In this section Calvin also condemns the detachment from politics advocated by Anabaptists for religious reasons. See Willem Balke, *Calvin and the Anabaptist Radicals*, trans. William Heynen (Grand Rapids: William B. Eerdmans, 1981), pp. 265ff.; and T. F. Torrance, *Kingdom and Church: A Study in the Theology of the Reformation* (Fair Lawn, N.J.: Essential Books, 1956), pp. 158ff. Calvin steered a middle course in his views between Anabaptists on one hand and the principles of Machiavelli on the other. See *Inst.*, 4.20.1 n. 4. For Luther's views, see Paul Althaus, *The Ethics of Martin Luther*, trans. Robert C. Schultz (Philadelphia: Fortress Press, 1972), chap. 4: "The Two Kingdoms and the Two Governments."

19. See Michael Walzer, *The Revolution of the Saints: A Study in the Origins of Radical Politics* (New York: Atheneum, 1974), p. 26. Walzer has explored what he sees as the revolutionary implications of Calvinism's "resistance theory"; see his "Puritanism as a Revolutionary Ideology," *History and Theory* 3 (1964): 59-90.

20. More technically, Calvin sees "the *Regnum Christi* ('kingdom of Christ') as leading up to the all-comprehensive *Regnum Dei* ('kingdom of God') of which it is the anticipation" (Torrance, *Kingdom and Church*, p. 114). This is in reference to 1 Cor. 15:27-28. Cf. G. C. Berkouwer, *The Return of Christ*, ed. Marlin J. Van Elderen, trans. James Van Oosterom (Grand Rapids: William B. Eerdmans, 1972), pp. 431-32; and *Inst.*, 2.14.3, 2.15.5.

21. Kuyper, *Lectures on Calvinism*, p. 53. Cf. Leith, *Introduction to the Reformed Tradition*, chap. 3: "The Ethos of the Reformed Tradition."

22. Kuyper, *Lectures on Calvinism*, p. 30.

23. Barth, *Church Dogmatics*, III/4: 473. Cf. Barth's final lecture fragments for the *Church Dogmatics*, published as *The Christian Life*, trans Geoffrey W. Bromiley (Grand Rapids: Wm. B. Eerdmans, 1981). There, in his exposition of the Lord's Prayer, Barth speaks of "zeal for the honor of God" as "the distinctive Christian passion" (p. 113). This implies an active involvement in the Christian life according to Barth. It means that Christians "cannot come to terms and be satisfied with the status quo" (p. 173).

24. *Church Dogmatics*, III/4: 474. Cf. *The Christian Life*, pp. 263-64, where Barth writes that Christians who live "with a view to the coming kingdom" are "claimed for action in the effort and struggle for human righteousness." Human righteousness is always "imperfect, fragile and highly problematical righteousness," says Barth, yet God commands the struggle for it as a correspondence or analogy of the divine righteousness (see pp. 172ff. and 265-66).

25. *Church Dogmatics*, III/4: 475ff. Thus, the essays presented to Barth on his eightieth birthday were entitled *Service in Christ*. As Torrance writes, "It is highly appropriate that *Diakonia* [service] should be the theme of this tribute to him, for rarely has any theologian so consistently directed his theological work to stimulate and prompt the *diakonia* of the divine mercy as the charge which Christ has laid upon the Church as a whole," *Service in Christ*, eds. James I. McCord and T. H. L. Parker (Grand Rapids: Wm. B. Eerdmans, 1966), p. 16.

26. *Church Dogmatics*, III/4, 478.

27. *Church Dogmatics*, III/4, 483.

28. *Church Dogmatics*, III/4, 600.

29. Weber, *The Protestant Ethic and the Spirit of Capitalism*, trans. Talcott Parsons (New York: Scribner's, 1958), p. 80. There have been many responses to the Weber thesis; see, e.g., the critique by Robert S. Paul, "Weber and Calvinism: The Effects of a 'Calling,'" *Canadian Journal of Theology* 11 (1965): 25-41.

30. Paul, "Weber and Calvinism," p. 30 (citing Weber, *The Protestant Ethic and the Spirit of Capitalism*, p. 81).

31. Paul, "Weber and Calvinism," p. 38.

32. This is the "special" call of God to believers. There is, says Calvin, also a "general call by which God invites all equally to himself through the outward preaching of the word." Cf. Barth, *Church Dogmatics*, III/4: 599.

33. But, as Ronald S. Wallace points out, "Calvin

does not go the length of teaching that if a man is born in one station and calling in life he cannot possibly seek to change it" (*Calvin's Doctrine of the Christian Life* [Grand Rapids: William B. Eerdmans, 1961], p. 154; citing Calvin's commentary on 1 Cor. 7:20).

34. This shows a fundamental error in Weber's views.

35. Paul, "Weber and Calvinism," p. 39.

36. Perkins, *Works*, 1: 750.

37. Perkins, *Works*, 1: 757.

38. Perkins, *Works*, 1: 757.

39. Perkins, *Works*, 1: 758.

40. Perkins, *Works*, 1: 772.

41. Perkins, *Works*, 1: 750.

42. The title of a sermon preached in the Riverside Church in New York City by a preacher in the Reformed tradition, Ernest T. Campbell, and published in his *Locked in a Room with Open Doors* (Waco: Word Books, 1974), pp. 97-104.

43. In biblical usage, the steward (Heb. literally, "man over the house," Gen. 43:19; 44:4; Gr. *oikonomos*, 1 Cor. 4:1; Gal. 4:2; etc.) is "an official who controls the affairs of a large household, overseeing the service at the master's table, directing the household servants, and controlling the household expenses on behalf of the master." In the New Testament, "all Christians are to be stewards of God's mysteries and . . . the Christian concept of stewardship before God involves time, talents, possessions, and self (Luke 12:42; Eph. 3:2)." See *The Interpreter's Dictionary of the Bible*, 4 vols., ed. George A. Buttrick (Nashville: Abingdon Press, 1962), s.v. "Steward, Stewardship."

44. James I. McCord, "Stewardship Is My Life," *A.D.* (October 1976), p. 26.

45. Leith, *Introduction to the Reformed Tradition*, p. 137.

46. Calvin speaks of the law as both the Old Testament Pentateuch and, more specifically, the moral law as comprehended in the Ten Commandments. See I. John Hesselink, "Christ, the Law, and the Christian: An Unexplored Aspect of the Third Use of the Law in Calvin's Theology," in *Reformatio Perennis*, ed. B. A. Gerrish, Pittsburgh Theological Monograph Series, no. 32 (Pittsburgh: Pickwick Press, 1981), p. 15.

47. See Hesselink, "Christ, the Law, and the Christian," pp. 16ff. See also Donald K. McKim, "William Per-

kins and the Christian Life: The Place of the Moral Law in Perkins' Theology," *Evangelical Quarterly* 59 (April 1987): 125-37.

48. James M. Gustafson, *Ethics from a Theocentric Perspective: Theology and Ethics* (Chicago: University of Chicago Press, 1981), p. 164.

49. For particulars on the actions of Reformed churches in ministry, see such denominational histories as Wallace N. Jamison, *The United Presbyterian Story* (Pittsburgh: Geneva Press, 1958); E. T. Thompson, *Presbyterians in the South, 1890-1972*, 3 vols. (Richmond: John Knox Press, 1963-73); and Lefferts A. Loetscher, *A Brief History of the Presbyterians*, 3rd ed. (Philadelphia: Westminster Press, 1978). The actions of twentieth-century Reformed Christians in Germany in opposing Hitler are detailed in Arthur C. Cochrane, *The Church's Confession under Hitler* (Philadelphia: Westminster Press, 1962).

Regarding Reformed responses to topical issues, see Sidney Rooy, "The Stewardship of Gifts in the Universal Church," *Reformed Journal*, February 1979, pp. 16-20, and March 1979, pp. 20-25; Jack B. Rogers, "Philosophy, Theology and Ecology," *Reformed Journal*, January 1974, pp. 15-17; Arthur C. Cochrane, "John Calvin and Nuclear War," *Christian Century*, 4 July 1962, pp. 837-39; *Peacemaking: The Believers' Calling* (New York: Office of the General Assembly of the United Presbyterian Church in the U.S.A., 1980); and Ernest T. Campbell, *Christian Manifesto* (New York: Harper & Row, 1970).

50. On the place of preaching in Reformed thought, see Leith, *Introduction to the Reformed Tradition*, pp. 79-81; Barth, *Church Dogmatics*, I/1, I/2; Bloesch, *Essentials of Evangelical Theology*, vol. 2, chap. 4. The sixteenth-century Reformed theologian Heinrich Bullinger wrote in the Second Helvetic Confession that "the preaching of the Word of God *is* the Word of God." Preaching was also a strong component of Puritanism; see William Haller, *The Rise of Puritanism* (Philadelphia: University of Pennsylvania Press, 1972). For a balanced Reformed approach on evangelism and social concern see Bloesch, *Essentials of Evangelical Theology*, 2: 167-71.

51. *The Book of Order* (New York: Office of the General Assembly of the United Presbyterian Church in the U.S.A., 1981-1982), 33.04.

52. See Leith, *Introduction to the Reformed Tradition*, pp. 106ff.

THEOLOGICAL INTERACTIONS

The Reformed tradition has had a long and rich theological history. It has developed through the centuries as it has tried to listen obediently to God's revelation and understand the message of Scripture in fresh ways. It has also grown through interactions with other traditions and theological positions on significant issues. The essays in the following section show how some contemporary Reformed theologians assess present-day theological trends and movements in light of the Reformed heritage. In some cases they find positive elements to enrich the ongoing life of the tradition; in other cases they reject trends as incompatible with essential insights of Reformed theology. Yet whether ultimate agreements are reached or not, the theological dialogue is crucial. The Reformed tradition can never assume it has finally arrived at all the "right" answers. The future vitality of Reformed theology depends on its willingness to engage contemporary views and its openness to a consideration of theological insights from today's differing voices.

The spirit of this dialogue is modeled in John Hesselink's essay "The Charismatic Movement and the Reformed Tradition." Hesselink finds that certain strains of Reformed theology have placed great emphasis on the person and work of the Holy Spirit and that these emphases provide points of dialogue and contact with charismatic Christians. He also indicates certain reservations about the Pentecostal-charismatic movement, yet concludes that "we need each other."

One of the growing prominent theological views today is process theology. Seeking to put traditional Western theology on a new footing, process thought has significantly reformulated many established Christian perspectives. Donald Bloesch analyzes this movement in "Process Theology and Reformed Theology," comparing process views on authority, God, Christ and salvation, and ethics and spirituality with Reformed positions.

Albert Winn and Jorge Lara-Braud each provide an essay on the relationship of liberation theology to Reformed theology. Starting from different perspectives, the two authors both manage to find positive values as well as questionable elements in the various types of liberation theologies. In the end, their views complement each other and show how varying assessments can be made from within the context of the Reformed tradition.

A serious challenge to the integrity of the Reformed theological tradition arises from the situation of apartheid in South Africa. Pointing to the fact that the tradition in that nation is more than three hundred years old and current-day apartheid practices have been part of the Reformed heritage in that land, Allan Boesak raises the important question of what it means to be black and Reformed in South Africa today in an essay entitled "Black and Reformed: Contradiction or Challenge?" With the passionate zeal of an involved church leader and former president of the World Alliance of Reformed Churches, Boesak makes the troubled and unjust South African situation come alive with poignancy. There black theologians must struggle with the relationship of their oppressed social and political context to a national power structure that also sees itself as standing in the Reformed tradition.

Among the most significant theological voices today are feminist theologians. Cynthia Campbell's essay "Feminist Theologies and the Reformed Tradition," prepared as part of a study entitled *Theologies Written from Feminist Perspectives: An Introductory Study* for the Presbyterian Church (USA), gives an account of criticisms of feminist theologies from the Reformed tradition and also offers feminist responses. She then turns to a consideration of "the contributions that feminist perspectives can make to traditional Reformed ways of understanding both God and the theological enterprise." She concludes that "there may be more common ground between Reformed and feminist perspectives than might at first appear to be the case."

The final essay of this section and of the book is by Alan Sell, a former theological secretary of the World Alliance of Reformed Churches. In "The Reformed Family Today: Some Theological Reflections," Sell draws on his unique vantage point to discuss the diversities of the Reformed traditions and the multifaceted nature of the Reformed family of churches today. He offers provocative suggestions for recovery of the tradition and strategies for Reformed churches concerned with meeting the pressing needs facing them in our time. Sell concludes with the issue of training for the churches' ongoing leadership. He asserts that "few things are more important than the supply of able ministers of the gospel."

As Reformed theology expands its horizons and continues to unfold, theological interactions of the sort discussed in this section, both outside the "family" and within, will continue to be important. The Reformed tradition cannot isolate itself from the fresh concerns and new ideas it has encountered in recent decades. Over time, the perspectives of the tradition's new partners in dialogue may become part of the continually developing Reformed tradition itself. At the same time, the tradition will also maintain its major themes and central insights insofar as these are seen to be theologically grounded in God's revelation in Scripture. Reformed theology and the

Reformed tradition live and breathe through the theologians, writings, and churches of committed believers who will face these challenges. But Reformed Christians will also find substantial and perhaps currently unperceived resources in the Reformed faith. With these, by the power of the Holy Spirit, they can continue witnessing to Jesus Christ to the glory of God.

The Charismatic Movement and the Reformed Tradition

I. John Hesselink

I.

At first it might appear that the Reformed tradition and the approach and theology of the charismatic movement are basically different, if not antithetical, entities. For of all the Protestant tradition, the Reformed has been noted for its emphasis on doctrine and theology as such. The charismatic movement, on the other hand, places great emphasis on experience. The Reformed churches are noted for their theologians, not their "saints" or evangelists. We glory in our confessions and catechisms, solid theology and pure doctrine. Charismatic and Pentecostal groups, on the other hand, boast of healings and ecstatic experiences. Reformed Christians tend to be cerebral, cool, and analytical. Charismatics promote enthusiasm, "letting go," and warm feelings.

Reprinted from *Reformed Review* 28 (Spring 1975): 147-56.

Many of the differences come to focus in divergent views of the church, ministry, and worship. The church, by Reformed definition, exists where the word is preached in its purity, where the sacraments are properly administered, and where discipline is exercised. All of this is rather foreign to the charismatic, who thinks of the church more in terms of an informal fellowship with fluid boundaries and minimal doctrinal requirements. Distinctions between lay and clergy are played down, with with the leaders often being self-appointed and answerable to no higher judicatory. Believers' baptism plays a very important role, but the Lord's Supper appears to receive little attention (except among Catholic charismatics). In the Reformed tradition preaching is exalted, and the ideal is to do everything "decently and in order." (Some people mistakenly think this phrase comes from a Reformed or Presbyterian book of church order! Ironically, it comes from the climax of the apostle Paul's discussion of spiritual gifts in 1 Corinthians 14.) Among charismatics, informal Bible study and unstructured exhortation take the place of more formal preaching, and a premium is placed on informality and spontaneity.

Finally, is there not an irreconcilable barrier in the traditional belief of many Reformed and Presbyterian Christians (particularly ministers) that miracles ceased with the passing of the apostles? By miracles I mean any so-called supernatural manifestations such as speaking in tongues, dramatic healings, prophecy, and the like. In reaction to Roman Catholic claims, Calvin maintained that the "gift of healing, like the rest of the miracles, which the Lord willed to be brought forth for a time, has vanished away in order to make the new preaching of the gospel marvelous forever."[1] Centuries later a staunch American Presbyterian theologian, B. B. Warfield, was still maintaining that miracles ceased with the end of the apostolic age.[2]

In view of all this — and other factors could be cited — it would appear that there is indeed a basic, deep-rooted incompatibility between the Reformed tradition and the charismatic movement, even in its recent, more sophisticated manifestations. But this is only one side of the picture. A case could be made for a fruitful, even fairly natural, relationship between these two, although at certain points there will inevitably be some tension.

II.

It must be conceded at the outset that in many ways the Wesleyan and Baptist traditions are by nature more congenial to a Pentecostal approach or charismatic experiences than the Reformed-Presbyterian. However, the growth and spread of the new Pentecostal-charismatic movement seems to be no respecter of historical traditions or theological emphases. In fact, there appear to be more charismatics among Catholics, Episcopalians, and Lutherans than among Methodists or Baptists, and one of the largest charismatic fellowships can be found among United Presbyterians [now the Presbyterian Church (USA) — ed.]. It might be argued that the charismatic movement flourishes most in denominations or groups that least emphasize personal experience, small groups and sharing, personal witnessing, prayer, and Bible study.

Whether this is true or not, I think a good case can be made for a certain compatibility of these two traditions, at least where both are interpreted according to their best insights and contributions. For the charismatic movement, like the traditional Pentecostal movement, is above all a movement that stresses and magnifies the personality and power of the Holy Spirit. Likewise, the Reformed tradition — at least certain strains of it — has placed great emphasis on the person and work of the Holy Spirit. Not only that; I am convinced that in Reformed theology there is a greater appreciation, deeper understanding, and more comprehensive and balanced presentation of the full power and work of the Holy Spirit than in any other tradition, including the Pentecostal tradition!

In the first place, recall that the mainstream Lutheran-Reformed Reformation was in many ways an effort to recover the freedom, presence, and power of the Holy Spirit. In medieval Roman Catholicism the Spirit, like the whole concept of grace, had become "locked up," in a sense, within an understanding of grace that was dispensed at the behest of the hierarchy. The Reformation was not only a rediscovery of the word and the gospel; it also resulted in an assurance of forgiveness and a peaceful conscience. In other words, through the new outpouring of the Spirit, Christ was more accessible and more real to countless individuals than he had been in centuries. Many of the gifts of the Spirit were experienced in a marvelous new way — not in tongues and healing so much as in wisdom, knowledge, prophecy, discernment, and, above all, faith.

Luther deserves much of the credit for this discovery of the grace of God manifest in Jesus Christ and his Spirit. The Danish Lutheran scholar Regin Prenter even maintains that "the concept of the Holy Spirit completely dominated Luther's theology. In every decisive matter, whether it be the study of Luther's doctrine of justification, of his doctrine of the sacraments, of his ethics, or of any other fundamental teaching, we are forced to take into consideration this concept of the Holy Spirit."[3]

Yet, without detracting from Luther's accomplishment, I would suggest that the title "theologian of the Holy Spirit" belongs more properly to Calvin.[4] This may come as a surprise to many Reformed Christians, who are accustomed to hearing of the sovereignty of God or predestination as being the hallmarks of Calvinism. Granted, this is an aspect of Calvin's theology that has often been overlooked in traditional Calvinism, as a rationalistic orthodoxy has squelched the dynamism of the Reformer's faith and theology. This is not the place to substantiate in detail the thesis that Calvin's theology is above all a theology of the Spirit, but a few points can be mentioned briefly.

1. In his accent on the sovereignty and freedom of God, Calvin wishes to make clear that all that we are and are able to do as Christians is ultimately due to God's grace and is the work of God's Spirit. The Christian life originates in and is continually renewed by the grace and power of the Spirit (*Inst.*, 3.1.3-4).

2. The Spirit of God is also at work in the world, preserving, restoring, guiding, and inspiring. Without this general work of the Spirit, the world would soon be in chaos, and mankind would degenerate into bestiality. All that is good, true, and beautiful — even among pagans and atheists — is due to the Spirit of God (*Inst.*, 2.2.12-20). Calvin also stresses the cosmic dimensions of the Spirit's work in a way rarely found in studies of the Holy Spirit.[5]

3. Calvin's most original and enduring contribution to an evangelical understanding of the nature and authority of Scripture was his doctrine of the internal witness or testimony of the Holy Spirit. This is the keystone of his doctrine of the knowledge of God, the power and authority of the Scriptures, and the efficacy of preaching. Neither the written word nor the proclaimed word has any power or persuasion apart from the secret, inner working and witness of the Spirit (*Inst.*, 1.9.1-3).[6]

4. Calvin develops and views the whole doctrine of the Christian life from the perspective of the Holy Spirit. When he moves from christology in Book 2 of the *Institutes* to soteriology in Book 3, from the objective work of Christ to the subjective application or reception of his benefits, the link or key is the Holy Spirit. For it is by the Spirit that "we come to enjoy Christ and all his benefits"; the Spirit is "the bond by which Christ effectually unites us to himself" (*Inst.*, 3.1.1). Once again we see that apart from the Holy Spirit, all that has been accomplished by the Savior avails nothing.

Calvin proceeds to develop his understanding of the Christian life under the comprehensive category of regeneration.[7] This in itself is significant, for it is expressive of the dominant role the Holy Spirit plays in his theological approach.[8] Whatever the particular aspect of regeneration — calling, conversion, repentance, or justification by faith — Calvin's thought and language are suffused with the reality of the Holy Spirit. Especially noteworthy are his treatments of faith and sanctification. (On the former see the beautiful statements in *Inst.*, 3.2.7-8, 33-36.) In his discussion of faith he rings the changes on the importance of the feeling of full *assurance* (*Inst.*, 3.2.15; cf. 3.2.14, 16), the very thing so earnestly desired by charismatics. Charismatics also ought to have no difficulty in identifying with a key motif in Calvin's doctrine of faith — namely, his beautiful doctrine of the mystical faith-union of the believer with his Lord (*Inst.*, 3.2.24; 11.5, 10).[9]

Moreover, Calvin, no less than Wesley and the Pentecostals, was concerned about *sanctification*.[10] Finally, it should be noted that Calvin is not even averse to using the expression "the leading of the Spirit." In fact, this kind of language is found frequently in his writings (e.g., in *Inst.*, 1.17.3; 2.3.10; 3.20.5; 4.8.13).

This brief overview of some of the pneumatological accents in Calvin's treatment of the Christian life confirms the judgment of Hendrikus Berkhof that "the famous third book of the *Institutes* contains great riches in the field of pneumatology, many of which have not yet been uncovered by Reformed churches."[11]

5. A fifth facet of Calvin's pneumatological emphasis is evident in his doctrine of the church and sacraments. Calvin was a high churchman. He gladly repeated the famous words of the early Church Father Cyprian: "for those to whom God is Father the Church may also be Mother. . . . Away from her bosom one cannot hope for any forgiveness of sins or any salvation" (*Inst.*, 4.1.1, 4). He could say this because he was convinced that the church is "a union of Head (Christ) and members (believers) in love under the Spirit."[12] Here we have an impressive ecclesiology of "inwardness and interiority which finds its roots in Christology and Pneumatology."[13] This description by contemporary Roman Catholic scholar Kilian McDonnell agrees basically with that of a Czech-Austrian Reformed Calvin scholar of a past generation, Joseph Bohatec, who described Calvin's concept of the church as *organic* —that is, a concept of the church as a living organism in which there is a dynamic interplay between Christ the head and the members of his body.[14] More important in view of our present concern is Bohatec's further point that overarching this intimate christocentric view of the church is the sovereignty of the Spirit. He concludes that Calvin's view of the church can accordingly best be described not as a theocracy or christocracy but as a pneumatocracy.[15]

The role of the Holy Spirit in Calvin's doctrine of the sacraments is equally prominent. Again, everything depends on the work of the Holy Spirit: it is "he who brings the graces of God with him, gives a place for the sacraments among us, and makes them bear fruit." They may be "visible signs" of God's grace manifest to us in Christ, but they have no efficacy unless God works in us "by invisible grace through the Holy Spirit" (*Inst.*, 4.14.18).

As in infant baptism (not to mention adult baptism) God in his sovereign freedom begins his work of regeneration and sanctification by his Holy Spirit (*Inst.*, 4.16.17, 18), so also in the Lord's Supper it is by the "secret power of the Holy Spirit" that our hearts are lifted up so that we are truly nourished by the body and blood of our risen Lord who is really present among us. It is the Spirit who "truly unites things separated in space" (*Inst.*, 4.4.17).[16]

So much for Calvin. It is not at all difficult to illustrate Warfield's thesis that Calvin was "the theologian of the Holy Spirit." But then the question arises as to whether the Reformed churches have been aware of and faithful to this magnificent theology of the Holy Spirit developed by Calvin. Unfortunately, the answer, for the most part, has to be No. In the seventeenth century a scholastic orthodoxy on the one hand and a one-sided pietism on the other dealt crippling blows to Calvin's balanced presentation of the work of the Spirit. These two movements were followed in the eighteenth and nineteenth centuries by a liberalism that talked much about "spirit" but which knew little of the biblical understanding of the Holy Spirit.

However, within the Reformed fold there were some notable exceptions. In the Netherlands in the eighteenth century there developed an interesting — some would say an unhealthy — alliance of Reformed orthodoxy with pietism. One of the products of this movement was one of the first great evangelists in the

United States, Theodorus Jacobus Frelinghuysen (1691-1747).[17] One could also include Gilbert Tennent, the Presbyterian revivalist who was influenced by Frelinghuysen, and the leaders of the Great Awakening, Jonathan Edwards and George Whitefield. All of them were Calvinists of a sort, and all were charismatic, if one uses the word in a non-Pentecostal manner.

In nineteenth-century Scotland there were Presbyterian Puritan pastors and theologians who were especially interested in the work of the Spirit and who wrote solid, valuable treatises on this subject. Two whose works have been reprinted recently are James Buchanan (*The Office and Work of the Holy Spirit* [1843]) and Octavius Winslow (*The Work of the Holy Spirit* [1840]). Nor should we omit the important earlier works on this subject by the English Puritan John Owen. (He actually wrote three works on the Holy Spirit, published in 1674, 1682, and 1693.)

On the Dutch Reformed side there has been an impressive, though not consistent, interest in the Holy Spirit.[18] The classic in this field, which has not yet been surpassed, is Abraham Kuyper's monumental work *The Work of the Holy Spirit*, completed in 1888 and published soon thereafter in the United States. This interest in the Holy Spirit by Dutch theologians has continued down to the present. Not well known in the United States but influential in Germany as well as the Netherlands is the theologian O. Noordmans.[19] It is significant that when the well-known Leiden theologian Hendrikus Berkhof was asked to give the Warfield Lectures at Princeton Seminary in 1964, he chose the theme of the Holy Spirit.[20] Then there is the Dutch theologian of the Holy Spirit par excellence, the late A. A. van Ruler of Utrecht.[21]

On the American side we have rather recent significant systematic treatments of this subject by Presbyterians George S. Hendry and Arnold Come.[22] More popular works on the Holy Spirit are legion, but when it comes to serious, comprehensive treatments, B. B. Warfield's judgment made in 1900 still holds — namely, that is only among Calvin's spiritual descendants that the doctrine of the work of the Holy Spirit has received adequate attention — except that we would now have to change the word "only" to "primarily."[23]

I think I have sufficiently well illustrated my thesis that nowhere has there been greater interest in and study of the work of the Spirit than in the Reformed tradition. The classical Pentecostals are late arrivals on the scene and have produced very little in the way of biblical-theological studies of the Holy Spirit. It is true that they can take credit for introducing a new awareness of and appreciation for the gifts ("charismata") of the Holy Spirit, which were largely, though not totally, ignored in the earlier works on the Spirit. But their understanding of the works of the Spirit, even judged by contemporary neo-Pentecostal (or charismatic) standards, was often superficial, one-sided, and bizarre.[24] However, neo-Pentecostals would probably agree with the classical Pentecostals that, whereas the Reformed tradition might claim to be superior in its theological interest in the Holy Spirit, it has shown little practical knowledge or experience of the power of the Spirit, especially as manifested in the extraordinary spiritual gifts.

Here the issue might be joined, but I would like to postpone a final verdict concerning this question until later. I would hope, in any case, that the neo-Pentecostals would not confront us in the Reformed tradition with the old liberal cliche: "what counts is not doctrine but life." This is a superficial, dangerous, and unbiblical dichotomy. Genuine, true doctrine and theology will produce good fruits. Conversely, authentic, wholesome Christian experience can only flourish if it is undergirded by and issues from evangelical truth.

Reformed-Presbyterians may be short on the *experience* of the reality, joy, and fullness of the Spirit. Pentecostals may be lacking in an adequate biblical *understanding* of the work of the Spirit. If so, we need each other and can complement each other. Coexistence, not a hot war — or even a cold one — would appear to me to be a logical and happy response to our situation.

III.

I suspect that some people may be a bit restive about this whole line of reasoning and are not totally convinced of a possible compatibility between these two traditions. It might be judged that my presentation of the data has been rather selective and that I am much too sanguine about the possibilities of a rapprochement between these two seemingly antithetical approaches to the Christian life. I would like, therefore, to call in some witnesses whose names and reputations are far better estab-lished than mine. They are all Reformed-Presbyterian, and they all view the Pentecostal development as not only extremely significant but in a fundamentally positive light.

First, and most surprising perhaps, is the liberal Presbyterian Henry Pitney Van Dusen, former president of Union Seminary in New York. I recall the shock I experienced in reading in the 17 August 1955 issue of *The Christian Century* (pp. 946-48) an article by Van Dusen where he related his positive impressions of the Pentecostal movement on the basis of a trip to the Caribbean Islands. His discovery of the vitality of the 8.5 million Pentecostals there led him to speak of them as representing "a new Reformation" and a new, powerful "third force in Christendom." Later, in 1960, he declared that "the Pentecostal movement . . . is a revolution comparable in importance with the establishment of the original church and with the Protestant Reformation."[25]

One of the first in our tradition to recognize the importance and contributions of this movement, however, was Bishop Lesslie New-

bigin in his book *The Household of God.*[26] Similarly, John Mackay, former president of Princeton Seminary, has also had kind words to say about Pentecostals on various occasions. From a theological standpoint, the most significant observations come from the noted Dutch theologian Hendrikus Berkhof. In the preface to his fine book *The Doctrine of the Holy Spirit,* he notes that "pneumatology is a neglected field of systematic theology."[27] He points out that part of the difficulty is the bad experience the traditional churches have had throughout history with Spirit movements — from the Montanists in the second century to the Anabaptists and Quakers in the sixteenth century and the Pentecostals at the beginning of our century. Words like *enthusiasts, spiritualists, faith healers,* and the like usually evoke negative emotions among most Protestants. The result is an unhappy and sterile alternative.

> On the one hand, we see the established larger churches which are unwilling to focus their attention on the action of the Holy Spirit; in their midst faith is in danger of becoming something intellectual, traditional and institutional. On the other hand, we see the rapidly increasing Pentecostal movements, where the reality of the Spirit is often sought in the emotional, individualistic, and extravagant. Both parts live by the lacks and mistakes of the other, which give them a good pretext not to see their own lacks and mistakes, or the biblical truth represented by the other.[28]

Later, in the substance of his book, he raises the same kind of question. He feels that the revivalists and Pentecostals may well be correct in challenging our traditional analysis of regeneration as having only two aspects — justification and sanctification. They refer to a third aspect, that of the baptism or filling of the Spirit. Berkhof challenges the usual Pentecostal exegesis here, but he attempts to break through the "watertight partition-wall between these two groups" on the grounds that this partition is a detriment to both parties.[29]

I concur with Berkhof and feel that it is high time we dealt with the neo-Pentecostal movement in particular with charity, openness, and a sense of expectation. Too often we — and that includes most mainline Protestant theologians and ministers — have treated this development as a passing phenomenon limited to a lunatic fringe within the church. We have tried to psychologize, sociologize, and theologize it away, recognizing only its dangers and excesses and rejecting the positive challenge, benefits, and blessings it often brings.

We have often hoped it would blow away, but instead it is blowing all over the land. David du Plessis, the well-known Pentecostal leader, reported at a conference on the Holy Spirit held recently in Des Moines, Iowa (sponsored by the United Methodist Church), that there are now ten thousand charismatic pastors within denominations making up the National Christian Council of Churches. That means that almost ten percent of the ministers in ecumenical Protestantism (and Orthodoxy) are part of this movement.[30]

The growth and significance of the neo-Pentecostal movement within American Roman Catholicism is even more striking.[31] (See the June 22, 1973 issue of *Christianity Today*.) Many North Americans may also be unaware of the fact that the churches in Latin America are largely charismatic in character. Emilio Castro, a Methodist pastor and leader in Uruguay, states that "Latin American Protestantism is now made up for the most part of Pentecostal churches,"[32] and that includes the large Presbyterian, Methodist, and Baptist churches as well as the traditional Pentecostal churches.

After having said all these positive things about the charismatic movement, some people might conclude that I am oblivious to its errors and excesses. Not so. I have not only read more than a dozen books by neo-Pentecostal leaders (including the recent fine work by James Jones, *Filled With New Wine* [New York: Harper and Row, 1974]) but have also attended a number of charismatic meetings both in Japan and

North America. I have tried to be as open and sympathetic as possible, and have often been positively impressed by what I witnessed, but I have also found much that is contrived and repetitious, superficial and unbalanced. Scripture was not treated seriously, and what passed for "prophecy" often impressed me as inanities unworthy of the Holy Spirit.

However, far more important than my personal impressions are some deep-seated theological reservations. This is not the place for a full-fledged biblical-theological analysis and critique. That has been provided by such people as Frederick Dale Bruner, James D. G. Dunn, Anthony Hoekema, John Stott, and Bernard Ramm.[33]

My basic reservations are these:

1. There is far too often a failure to take all of Scripture seriously. The result is a truncated gospel.

2. One unfortunate consequence is an inadequate understanding of the Christian life, especially of the whole doctrine of sanctification. Pivotal here is what I feel is the Pentecostal misunderstanding of the so-called baptism in or of the Holy Spirit as something that is subsequent to and distinct from becoming a Christian. It is a personal encounter with Jesus Christ and the concomitant transforming gift of the Spirit that makes a person a Christian. We must be filled with the Spirit again and again, and "stir into flame again the gift already received" (2 Tim. 1:6).

3. My biggest difficulty with the Pentecostal-charismatic movement, in the last analysis, is not that it stresses the work of the Holy Spirit too much, but too little! Its viewpoint is too narrow and myopic. We can learn much from it about the gifts of the Spirit, about power, freedom, and joy in the Spirit. But the charismatic theologians have much to learn from Calvin in particular, and the Reformed tradition in

general, about the Spirit and creation, the relation of the Word and the Spirit, the Spirit and the church and sacraments, the Spirit and tradition, the Spirit and the Christian life. Pentecostal Christians tend to focus on the "individual-spontaneous" aspects of the Spirit's work, whereas traditionalists stress the "continuing collective" manifestations of the Spirit.[34]

Both are necessary — the individual-spontaneous and the continuing-collective. Traditional Protestants, especially in the Reformed tradition, are often lacking in the former area — although many new winds of the Spirit, I trust, have been blowing in the Reformed Church in recent years. Pentecostals tend to be lacking in the latter category. As John Sherrill put it years ago in his best-seller *They Speak with Other Tongues*, the Reformed tradition is strong on order and weak on freedom.[35] The opposite is true of the charismatics. We need each other.

This, in conclusion, is my plea: that we might be as ready to recognize our needs, weaknesses, and practical heresies as we are eager to point out the weaknesses of the charis-matics. *Ecclesia semper reformanda* — by the Word *and* the Spirit. As Presbyterian theologian Lewis Mudge argued in 1963, our creeds and confessions do not do justice to the biblical emphasis on the work of the Holy Spirit, and "the result is that in reading what the Bible says about the Spirit we are blind and deaf."[36]

Many Pentecostals, I am sure, would say Amen to that!

The situation has changed and improved in many ways since Abraham Kuyper wrote the preface to his study of the Holy Spirit. Even so, his closing words are still quite apropos to our situation:

> Even tho we honor the Father and believe on the Son, how little do we live in the Holy Spirit! It even seems to us sometimes that for our sanctification *only*, the Holy Spirit is added accidentally to the great redemptive work.
>
> This is the reason why our thoughts are so little occupied with the Holy Spirit, why in the ministry of the Word He is so little honored, why the people of God when bowed in supplication before the Throne of Grace, make Him so little the object of their adoration. You feel involuntarily that of our piety, which is already small enough. He receives a too scanty portion.[37]

NOTES

1. Calvin, *Institutes of the Christian Religion,* Library of Christian Classics, vols. 20-21, ed. John T. McNeill, trans. Ford Lewis Battles (Philadelphia: Westminster Press, 1960), 4.19.18. Subsequent references to the work will be made parenthetically in the text.

2. See Warfield, *Counterfeit Miracles* (1918; reprint, Edinburgh: Banner of Truth Trust, 1976).

3. Prenter, *Spiritus Creator* (Philadelphia: Muhlenberg Press, 1953), p. ix.

4. I am joined in this judgment by B. B. Warfield, John Mackay, Bernard Ramm, and Werner Krusche, among others. See especially Krusche, *Das Wirken des Heiligen Geistes nach Calvin* (Göttingen: Vandenhoeck & Ruprecht, 1957), p. 12; and Warfield, *Calvin and Augustine* (Philadelphia: Presbyterian & Reformed Publishing, 1956), pp. 21-24, 107.

5. On this, see chap. 2 of Simon van der Linde, *De Leer van den Heiligen Geest bij Calvijn* (Wageningen: H. Veenman, 1943).

6. See also Calvin's commentary of John 14:25-26; Krusche, *Das Wirken des Heiligen Geistes nach Calvin,* pp. 77-78, 206-7; Bernard Ramm, *The Witness of the Spirit* (Grand Rapids: William B. Eerdmans, 1959), chap. 3.

7. In his commentary on John 1:13, Calvin writes that "faith flows from regeneration" and is followed by "newness of life and other gifts of the Holy Spirit."

8. See the fine discussion of this point by Hendrikus Berkhof in *The Doctrine of the Holy Spirit* (Richmond: John Knox Press, 1964), pp. 68-69.

9. Cf. the excellent study by Wilhelm Kolfhaus, *Christusgemeinschaft bei Calvin* (Neukirchen: Neukirchener Verlag, 1939).

10. In terms of accent, Luther could be called the theologian of justification, whereas Calvin is the theologian of sanctification. See Karl Barth, *Church Dogmatics,* 4 vols., ed. Geoffrey W. Bromiley and Thomas F. Torrance (Edinburgh: T. & T. Clark, 1936-1969), IV/2: 509-10.

11. Berkhof, *The Doctrine of the Holy Spirit,* p. 22.

12. Kilian McDonnell, *John Calvin, the Church and the Eucharist* (Princeton: Princeton University Press, 1967), p. 183.

13. McDonnell, *John Calvin, the Church and the Eucharist,* p. 181.

14. See Bohatec, *Calvins Lehre von Staat und Kirche* (Breslau: M. & H. Marcus, 1937), pp. 267-68, 308-9.

15. Bohatec, *Calvins Lehre von Staat und Kirche,* pp. 432-33. Cf. McDonnell, *John Calvin, the Church and the Eucharist,* p. 183.

16. Cf. Joseph Tylenda, "Calvin and Christ's Presence in the Supper — True or Real?" *Scottish Journal of Theology* 27 (Feb. 1974): 72-73.

17. See the superb dissertation by James Tanis, *Dutch Calvinistic Pietism in the Middle Colonies: A Study in the Life and Theology of Theodorus Jacobus Frelinghuysen* (The Hague: Martinus Nijhoff, 1967).

18. The same cannot be said of the German theologians; see B. B. Warfield's lament in his introductory note to the American edition of Abraham Kuyper's *The Work of the Holy Spirit* (1888; reprint, Grand Rapids: William B. Eerdmans, 1946), pp. xxix-xxxii.

19. See, e.g., Noordmans, *Das Evangelium des Geistes* (Zurich: EVZ Verlag, 1960).

20. The lectures have been published in *The Doctrine of the Holy Spirit.*

21. For articles on van Ruler's theology, see *Reformed Review* 26 (Winter 1973).

22. See Hendry, *The Holy Spirit in Christian Theology,* rev. ed. (Philadelphia: Westminster Press, 1965); and Come, *Human Spirit and Holy Spirit* (Philadelphia: Westminster Press, 1959).

23. Warfield, *Calvin and Augustine,* p. xxxiv.

24. See James W. Jones, *Filled with New Wine: The Charismatic Renewal of the Church* (New York: Harper & Row, 1974), pp. 34-35.

25. Van Dusen, quoted by J. Rodman Williams in "The Upsurge of Pentecostalism," *Reformed World* 31 (December 1971): 340.

26. See Newbigin, *The Household of God* (New York: Friendship Press, 1953), pp. 95-96, 122.

27. Berkhof, *The Doctrine of the Holy Spirit,* p. 10.

28. Berkhof, *The Doctrine of the Holy Spirit,* p. 11.

29. Berkhof, *The Doctrine of the Holy Spirit,* p. 85.

30. See *Christian Century,* 30 October 1974, p. 1006.

31. See the 22 June 1973 issue of *Christianity Today.*

32. See *Christian Century,* 27 September 1972, p. 955.

33. See Bruner, *A Theology of the Holy Spirit* (Grand Rapids: William B. Eerdmans, 1970); and Dunn, *Baptism in the Holy Spirit* (London: SCM Press, 1970). The most recent of the studies, Ramm's *Rapping about the Spirit* (Waco, Tex.: Word Books, 1974), is a popular but solid study.

34. See John Stevens Kerr, *The Fire Flares Anew: A Look at the New Pentecostalism* (Philadelphia: Fortress, 1974).

35. Sherrill, *They Speak with Other Tongues* (Old Tappan, N.J.: Fleming H. Revell, 1964), pp. 139-40.

36. Mudge, *One Church: Catholic and Reformed — Toward a Theology for Ecumenical Decision* (Philadelphia: Westminster, 1963), p. 68.

37. Kuyper, *The Work of the Holy Spirit,* pp. xi-xii.

Process Theology and Reformed Theology

Donald G. Bloesch

Process theology is without doubt one of the most vital theological movements in America since the First World War. It has attracted eminent scholars from a variety of Christian traditions, including Roman Catholic, Episcopal, Congregationalist, Methodist, and Presbyterian. Its possible convergence with the newly arising feminist theology could well make it the key theological movement in the English-speaking world in the last part of this century. As one who had the opportunity of studying under some of its leading exponents (Charles Hartshorne, Daniel Day Williams, Bernard Meland), I can testify to its cultural appeal and philosophical profundity.

TWO TYPES OF THEOLOGY

My reason for choosing to compare process thought and Reformed theology is that process thinkers generally see that particular strand of

Reprinted from *Process Theology*, ed. Ronald H. Nash (Grand Rapids: Baker Book, 1987), pp. 35-56.

evangelical theology as their foremost adversary. It is the Augustinian and Calvinist doctrines of the sovereignty of God, the irresistibility of grace, revelation as divine intervention into history, and the shadow of a final, irreversible divine judgment that seem to create special difficulties for process theologians. Just as Augustine and Calvin are considered the *bêtes noires* of the past, so Karl Barth is regarded as the main threat at present. Thomas Aquinas is treated as an adversary but one who can be respected, since his method is basically philosophical (appealing to criteria in nature and experience) rather than theological (calling for submission to a divine revelation). To be sure, there is an undeniable theological side to Thomas as well, and some evangelical theologians — Geoffrey Bromiley, for example — are willing to acknowledge him as basically a theologian of revelation. Yet what makes him attractive to process thinkers is his natural theology. They regard him as a useful foil who can help them to articulate their own position by way of contrast.

Reformed theology has been in eclipse in America ever since Jonathan Edwards (who saw revival as the surprising work of God) was supplanted by Charles Finney (who regarded revival as the result of humanly contrived techniques). Modern evangelicalism is by and large much closer to Finney than to Edwards, just as modern liberal theology is much closer to Schleiermacher, Ritschl, and Bushnell than to the Bible or the Reformation. Neo-Orthodoxy, associated with such names as Karl Barth, Emil Brunner, and Reinhold Niebuhr, succeeded for a time in recovering certain motifs associated with Reformation theology, but the religious academic world today is almost totally engulfed in experientialism and subjectivism.

Process theology fits into the American temperament and culture more than Reformed theology ever could. From the revival period onward, American religion has been experiential and relativistic, and this is true of American philosophy as well. The key figures in modern American religious thought are Emerson, Thoreau, William James, and Walt Whitman (rather than Augustine, Calvin, or Luther), and process theologians readily acknowledge their affinity to this transcendentalist tradition.[1] Instead of upholding the saints of the age-old church, Bernard Meland advocates celebrating the cultural heroes of America's past, including Jefferson, Emerson, Thoreau, Lincoln, and Whitman.[2] Here we see how process theology is admirably adapted to the *Zeitgeist,* the spirit of the times.

Alfred North Whitehead, perhaps the most influential of all process philosophers, had an admiration for Jesus but not for Paul. Like his disciple Charles Hartshorne, he saw much in Buddhism as closer to true religion than the historic Christian faith — including the priority of becoming over being. Two luminaries in Christian tradition for whom he expresses an appreciation are Origen and Erasmus.[3]

When I refer to process theology, I include those renowned representatives of process philosophy — Whitehead, Hartshorne, Teilhard de Chardin, C. Lloyd Morgan, Samuel Alexander, Henri Bergson, Paul Weiss — as well as men and women who consciously seek to relate the process tradition to the heritage of the Christian church — Daniel Day Williams, John Cobb, Norman Pittenger, Marjorie Hewitt Suchocki, Schubert Ogden, David Griffin, Lewis Ford, Paul Sponheim, and Donald Goergen. Henry Nelson Wieman, probably the most creative and innovative of all process theologians, is actually closer to being a philosopher of religion than a theologian. The same can be said for Bernard Meland and Bernard Loomer, and perhaps this is true of all process thinkers. Process theology also includes theologians influenced by the dynamic side of Hegel's thought, including Jürgen Moltmann and Thomas Altizer.

By Reformed theology, I am thinking not of a narrow Calvinism but of that broad theological tradition that seeks continuity with the mainstream Protestant Reformation — Calvin, Luther, and Zwingli. Among the notables in this tradition outside of the Reformation are Zacharias Ursinus, Gisbert Voetius, Philip Schaff, Abraham Kuyper, Herman Bavinck, Benjamin Warfield, P. T. Forsyth, James Denney, Emil Brunner, and Karl Barth.[4] Since I align myself more or less with this venerable tradition, I shall be speaking out of this general perspective in my critique of process theology.[5]

AUTHORITY

The differences between the two types of theology come to light especially in the area of theological methodology and authority. Whereas Reformed theology appeals to an authoritative divine revelation, which is integrally associated with holy Scripture, process thought bases its case on what is experientially accessible and scientifically verifiable. While Reformed theology envisions truth as an event breaking into history from the beyond, process thinkers see truth in terms of the correspondence between sensory perception and empirical reality. Logical consistency together with empirical adequacy is normative for the knowledge of God in process thinking. In Reformed theology, the truth of God is inaccessible to both conception and perception and therefore must be given in an act of divine revelation.[6] God is Wholly Other than what humanity can conceive or imagine (cf. Isa. 55:8, 9; 1 Cor. 2:6-11), though this does not mean that human rationality is totally divorced from divine wisdom, since we are created in God's image. An analogical relation is established between the Word of God and human reason in the illumination of faith, but this does not take away from God's utter transcendence, nor does it underplay the reality of mystery and paradox in Christian faith.

Reformed theology affirms that humanity is separated from God both by ontological fate and by historical guilt. It is primarily because of sin, which clouds the noetic as well as the volitional aspects of our being, that we humans are incapable of rightly perceiving or appreciating the light of God reflected in nature and history. All of us have an inescapable awareness of the living God (through common grace), but only some of us have a saving relationship to this God (through redemptive grace).

In the Reformed understanding, it is not enough to sense the presence of God: we must be awakened by the power of divine grace to the reality of what God has done for us in Christ and then take up the cross and follow Christ in faith and obedience. We must subordinate both our reason and our desires to the claims that God makes upon us in Jesus Christ as we find these in holy Scripture.

Whitehead, by contrast, concludes that "ultimately nothing rests on authority; the final court of appeal is intrinsic reasonableness."[7] "All knowledge," he insists, "is derived from, and verified by, direct intuitive observation."[8] Wieman maintains that valid evidence is the only legitimate ground for accepting a belief,

and "evidence is valid only when it has been gathered and tested by observation, reason and experiment."[9] Hartshorne is more circumspect concerning the power of historical argument and empirical induction to give us ultimate truth; he opts for an intuition that can be validated and confirmed in experience.

Reformed theology in its history has admittedly been guilty of heteronomy — that is, locating authority in an external standard or formula accessible to human understanding and open to human control. At its best, when it speaks of the Bible as the Word of God, it means that the Bible is the source and sign of God's redemptive revelation in Christ, which we never possess, even rationally, but which we can receive through the illumination and empowering of the Spirit.

When Reformed theologians affirm the Bible as the infallible standard for faith and practice, they mean that this original witness to what God has done for us in sacred history participates in the event of revelation by means of the creative and ongoing action of the Spirit. They also confess that the scriptural witness gives an adequate and trustworthy account of his revelation by virtue of its inspiration by the Spirit.

Process theology occasionally uses Scripture because it affords provocative lures that lead us into the promise of the future. Scripture derives its concurrence from the extent to which it tallies with one's self-evident, preconceptual experience. The Bible is a story of humanity's progressive evolving consciousness of the divine presence in human history and nature, which can be confirmed and corrected by the insights provided by the new science and the new philosophy. When comparing the relative dearth of biblical references in process writings to their conspicuous abundance in such seminal Reformed works as Calvin's *Institutes* or Barth's *Church Dogmatics,* one can only conclude that the Bible's authority is not really taken seriously.

DOCTRINE OF GOD

Perhaps nowhere does process theology diverge more from the traditional Christian understanding, and especially the Reformed understanding, than in the area of the doctrine of God. Process theologians are unanimous in asserting that an unwarranted amalgamation of biblical and Hellenistic insights has divorced the God of Christian tradition from historical actuality. They repudiate the position of classical theism in which they think God is equated with a static or completed good that excludes pain, suffering, and anything else indicating deficiency. The doctrine of the impassibility of God is especially the object of their strictures, since it connotes that God, being perfect, cannot suffer, and thus seems to call into question whether God can be meaningfully related to history and humanity.

In the light of modern evolutionary theory, process thinkers have sought to resymbolize God in order to bring the conception of deity into accord with modern sensibilities. According to Whitehead, God is "the Divine Eros," "the Eros of the universe," "the principle of concretion," and "the Ultimate Irrationality." Hartshorne describes God as "Eminent Freedom," "Eternal-Temporal Consciousness," "Personalized Becoming," and "the All-Surpassing One." For Wieman, God is "the Creative Event," "the Creative Process," "the Principle of Integration," "the Directive of History," and "Growth in Qualitative Meaning." Teilhard sees God as "the Divine Energy," "Omega," and "Creative Transformation." Cobb prefers to speak of "a dynamic maximum of possibilities" and "Creative-Responsive Love." Ogden opts for "Creative Becoming," "the eminently relative One," "Pure Unbounded Love," and "Absolute Relatedness."[10] Pittenger's God is the "altogether lovely" and "the Cosmic Lover"; Meland's is "the Creative Event" and "the Creative Passage." Marjorie Suchocki depicts God as the "unification" and "harmonization of all possibilities."[11]

Some process thinkers consider creativity to be more fundamental than God, whom they characterize as simply a privileged agent in the universe (Whitehead, Lewis Ford). Others equate God with the first principle — creativity (Hartshorne, Cobb, Wieman).

Some process thinkers envision God as a person or society of persons (Whitehead, Hartshorne). Others conceive of God as beyond personality, since creativity is prior to personality (Wieman). Even those who view God in personal terms do not really think of God as an absolute individual who reigns over the universe as sovereign Lord (as in Reformed theology); instead, they characterize God as an all-embracing, sympathetic consciousness who tries to influence history by the lure of love rather than rule over history. God is the Cosmic Persuader rather than King and Lord of all creation.

What distinguishes the process view most from the classical Christian view is that God is held to be inseparable from nature. Process thinkers generally take pains to dissociate their position from pantheism, the identification of God with the substance or reality of the world and the reduction of the empirical world to the multiform appearance of a cosmic unity or an overarching idea. Their position is better referred to as panentheism (Hartshorne), the assertion that God encompasses the world and the world is included in God without being identical with God. God is then the soul of the world, and the world is the body of God (Teilhard, Hartshorne). God is the creative force or creative good within the world drawing it toward the eternal ideals of the good, the true, and the beautiful.

God is related to the world as fire to wood. The wood is consumed in the fire, but the fire lives off the wood. What is good and true in the world and in human life is taken up into the life of God, and thereby God is enriched by the world. It is assumed that God needs *some* world in order to be alive and creative;

otherwise God would simply remain an abstraction or principle. Whitehead distinguishes between the primordial nature of God (the idea of God) and God's consequent nature (God's concrete life as a creative force in the world). He also speaks of eternal objects or ideals by which God, as the creative mover in the world, guides and directs the world. Not all process thinkers subscribe to this Platonic vision of a separate world of eternal objects, but they nonetheless speak of the world as moving toward transcendent ideals.

In glaring contradiction to the Reformed view that God created the world out of nothing (*ex nihilo*), process thinkers envisage God as forming the world out of a pre-existent matter (*ex hulas*). God is the unifier and organizer of the world process (Teilhard) rather than an almighty Creator and Lord.

In process theology God does not so much act in history as receive the impressions of history and incorporate them into the divine life. God is a spiritual presence that resides in nature rather than a sovereign Lord who intervenes in history. God moves the world by the magnetic power of the divine beauty and love rather than judging the world by the standards of divine holiness; God is the final cause of the world rather than its formal cause. God empathizes with the world in its sorrow rather than judging the world in its sin. God is a sympathy that soothes much more than a fire that burns.[12]

While the God of classical Christian faith is infinite and personal, the process God is actually finite and potentially infinite. God is suprapersonal rather than personal in a realistic or naive sense. God is characterized not by all-sufficiency and impassibility but by transcendent excellence (Hartshorne). God is not surpassed by any other process or being, but God can and does surpass God's self in the process of striving toward new heights and goals. Process thinkers like to state the issue this way: we much choose between the unchanging and passionless absolute of classical

tradition and the creative surge or creative emergence of modern evolutionary thought.

Reformed theologians would retort that the God of the Bible is not a passionless absolute but absolute love and holiness. God is God in action, not a God who grows. God agonizes over human sin rather than simply empathizing with human suffering. Moreover, God acts to rescue people from sin instead of simply resolving the discords of existence in God's own life. The process God is not a God who is sovereign over the world but a God who can influence the world only by the magnetic attraction of divine beauty and love. No wonder Whitehead describes God as "the poet of the world" rather than its creator.

Anglican theologian Eric Mascall has likened the process view of God's relation to the world to a mutual aid society. This is perhaps a little unfair, since for process thinkers, we owe God our very lives, whereas God depends on us only for enrichment. Moreover, we generally fall short of the ideals to which God beckons us. At the same time, Mascall's metaphor accurately reflects their belief that God and humanity are co-creators and that we contribute to God's perfection just as God contributes to our satisfaction.

Reformed theology affirms a supernatural creationism in which God creates the world out of nothing; the created order is distinct from but entirely dependent on God. Process theology, by contrast, affirms a form of naturalism that envisions God as a creative process within the world or as the creativity that activates the world. British philosopher P. F. Strawson has said that what philosophy can regard as worthy of the veneration formerly directed to God is "the universe." Hartshorne endorses this view, provided that the term *universe* means the all-inclusive reality — the soul as well as the body of the world — and not simply the phenomenal world as such.[13]

Finally, Reformed theology faithful to Christian tradition conceives of God as a Trinity — Father, Son, and Holy Spirit. Even though process theologians sometimes use trinitarian language, their conception is modalistic: God acts in three or more different ways, or there are different aspects of the creative process. Basically God is envisaged as binitarian — as finite (in the concrete aspect) and infinite (in the abstract aspect), as relative and absolute. Whitehead did speak of three natures in God — the primordial, consequent, and superject — but these are not three subjectivities or agencies of consciousness; rather, they represent the ever-continuing cosmic process of God going out of God's self and returning to God's self. In his latest book, Hartshorne portrays God as androgynous or bisexual — with the feminine element predominating.[14] God is both creative and receptive, but God is essentially the receptacle of the world's values. Reformed theology is emphatic that God coexists as a fellowship within the divine self and is not in need of any world for the completion of divine perfection. In process thought, God needs the world out of metaphysical necessity; apart from the world, God is reduced to an empty abstraction.

CHRIST AND SALVATION

Process theologians make a place for Jesus, but basically he is seen not as the Word made flesh but instead as the universal center of psychic convergence, the model of self-realization. Sharply breaking with Christian tradition, they deny that there was just one incomparable incarnation in history — when God became human in Jesus Christ. They argue instead for a universal cosmic incarnation of which Jesus is a supreme manifestation. While some hail Jesus as the perfect embodiment of the ideals of goodness, truth, and beauty, others see him as only one step, albeit a crucial one, in the upward surge of creative evolution. "I do not

think of Jesus as the highest product of the creative process," says Wieman; indeed, "the revelation of God in Christ should never be identified with the man Jesus."[15] Pierre Teilhard de Chardin maintains that Jesus is the bearer and goal of the upward movement of the universe toward the divine. The focus of our attention should not be on the historical Jesus but on the universal Christ, the omega point of evolution, the goal of the evolutionary process.

Process thinkers hold that Jesus is important in the salvific process because in him the power of creative transformation was manifest. In this respect he is the pioneer of our salvation. What rose from the dead, says Wieman, was not the person of Jesus but the life-giving power at work within him which gave the disciples a new horizon of meaning.

Process thinkers are quick to deny many doctrines that are dear to Reformed theology — Jesus as an expiation for sin or as a propitiation of the wrath of God. Such beliefs, they say, belong to a mythological past. Teilhard prefers to speak of "the cross of evolution" instead of the cross of substitution, meaning that Jesus bore the weight of a world in evolution as we also do when we are incorporated into his body.

Salvation involves a growth of qualitative meaning rather than the forgiveness of sins or deliverance from bondage to the powers of darkness. To be saved means to muster the courage to realize one's potential as a bearer of creativity. It is to "enjoy rich harmonies of living, and pour this richness into the one ultimate receptacle of all achievement, the life of God," where it will be forever immortalized in the memory of God.[16]

Whereas Reformed theology envisages a world lost in sin, process theology sees the world as teeming with infinite possibilities. Sin, in this new understanding, is basically a resistance to creativity, a failure to live up to moral ideals. It is stubbornness and resistance to change rather than transgression of a moral law that carries with it the penalty of damnation. Evil is an obstruction rather than a curse that cripples and paralyzes the human race. It is to be traced to a deficiency in understanding and a reluctance to break with the past rather than an inborn lust for power that pits humanity against the living God (as in Reformed theology). It is to be linked with the inertia of nature (Whitehead) or the intractability of matter (Plato).

In the process view, God can mitigate but not eradicate evil, since every new breakthrough into freedom brings with it new possibilities for temptation and sin. The discords of life are transformed in the life of God into a higher unity rather than nailed to the cross as that which God negates; in this sense, what Reformed thinkers regard as evil, process thinkers see as contributing to a higher good.

In the Reformed view, evil signifies an assault on the good, and it must be overcome and defeated rather than altered or transfigured. There is no satisfactory rational explanation for the possibility of evil, but there is a spiritual solution to the presence of evil — the cross and resurrection of Christ, whereby God takes away the sin, guilt, and shame of the world so that all who believe might not perish but have eternal life. This victory over sin is already secured, but it needs to be enacted and fulfilled in concrete human experience.

Following in the tradition of neo-Platonic mysticism, process thinkers see as the ultimate evil not human sin but the "perpetual perishing of time" (Whitehead). In contrast to the mystics, they realize that we cannot escape from time, but they hold that the values of our life can be immortalized in the memory of God.

Process theologians deny the resurrection of the body and, for the most part, the immortality of the soul as well. What is immortal is not the human ego, which is in a constant state of flux, but the ideals that give meaning to human existence and the actions that manifest these ideals. Our good deeds are remembered by God and thus made to serve the ultimate harmony and beauty toward which the world is moving. According to Hartshorne, "the only immortality we need is opportunity, by our joyous and beneficent earthly living, to enrich the divine life, which alone is imperishable and alone is able to appreciate the values we create in all their worth."[17]

Reformed theology envisages the kingdom of God breaking into history but always standing in judgment over history; process thought sees a kingdom of freedom at work in history eventuating in the "christification" of the universe (Teilhard). The idea of progress seems to be an invariable concomitant of the idea of process, though this is not obvious in the work of all process thinkers. Whitehead interprets the history of the world as "the victory of persuasion over force."[18] Wieman believes that "we are passing over one of the great divides of history; possibly it is the last high pass over the top mountain range before we enter the valley of abundance."[19] Yet the march onward and upward is not without tragic interruption. There may be relapses and diversions, though basically the surge of evolution cannot be turned back. Creative evolution will inevitably go forward, even if must pass through much darkness and misery.

ETHICS AND SPIRITUALLY

This optimism concerning the human situation also leaves its imprint in the areas of ethics and spirituality. It is not the corruption of human virtue but the release of human possibilities that engages process thinkers.

Although process theologians speak much about love, they generally have in mind the *eros* of Hellenistic philosophy and religion, not the *agape* of the New Testament. In their view, eros is the love of the good, the true, and the

PROCESS THEOLOGY AND REFORMED THEOLOGY

beautiful. Whitehead even describes God as "the eros of the universe" and "the eternal urge of desire." As Anders Nygren has ably shown, eros is the love that proceeds from emptiness to fullness, whereas agape is the love that proceeds from strength and fullness to emptiness.[20] Eros is self-enriching, while agape is self-denying.

For process thinkers, the primary motivation in both divine and human action is the will to satisfaction. We love others in order to fulfill the deepest yearnings within the self and the universe. This is the ethics of eudaemonism, defended in its classical form by both Plato and Aristotle.

A place is made for altruism, but an altruism in the service of egoism. Our love is directed toward possession of the perfect good. We love others by recognizing the presence of the same God in the depth of their being (Teilhard); consequently, our neighbors are stepping-stones to enrich the life of God and thereby to fulfill ourselves in God (Hartshorne). Our worship of God is a "means to successful living" or an aid in attaining "the supreme good" (Wieman). God, moreover, is motivated to help humanity by a desire to satisfy God's own yearning for fulfillment.

Against this view of love, theology in the Reformation tradition stresses the incompatibility of agape and eros (Luther, Nygren, Barth). God loves us not in order to fulfill God's self (God is already fulfilled) but in order to redeem sinners. We are led to love our neighbors not because we see in them a reflection of the God within us but because we genuinely wish to help them even in their sin. Self-love must be crucified so that love of others may develop and grow. Our love for God is born not out of the desire to possess the greatest good (as in neo-Platonic mysticism and process thought) but out of the joy of knowing that our sins are forgiven.

One of the striking features of process theology is the subordination of ethics to aesthet-

ics. Whitehead asserts that "the real world is good when it is beautiful."[21] Process thinkers are inclined to speak of the holiness of beauty rather than the God of holy love who makes moral demands. This is a God, as Whitehead says, whose love "neither rules, nor is it unmoved; also it is a little oblivious as to morals."[22] How utterly different is the conviction of Calvin and Luther that God sees, knows, and judges every sin!

This aesthetic bent is evident in Hartshorne's remarks on child rearing:

> If I were bringing up a child, I should not start by burdening him with a lot of moral rules. I should begin by trying to help the child see that life can be beautiful and can be lived beautifully. Then I should not need to bother so much about how moral ideas would develop.[23]

Whitehead sees an eternal divine ideal for creation — that of harmony and intensity. It is toward this ideal that all of creation is moving — an ultimate harmony of opposites that will be impressive for the sheer impact of its beauty. While Reformed theology locates the key to peace in reconciliation between God and a fallen humanity, Whitehead regards peace as "primarily a trust in the efficacy of beauty."[24]

Because of their tendency to understand sin as a failure to realize the good rather than as an unfailing proclivity to corrupt the good, process thinkers are inclined to be naive in the area of power politics. Whitehead applauded Chamberlain's accommodation to Hitler at Munich as a promise of better relations between the two countries. Hartshorne advocates a unilateral reduction in our nuclear arsenal in the hope that the Soviet Union will follow our example of common sense. In contradistinction to Reformed theology, process thinkers rest the hope of the world on the persuasive power of reason rather than on the resurrection of Jesus Christ and the outpouring of the Holy Spirit.

In the area of spirituality, scholars in the process tradition regard worship as an adventure into creativity rather than as submission before a holy God who demands loving obedience from God's people. Worship is the celebration of the power of creativity to overcome all obstacles rather than the commemoration of a unique and incomparable event in the past when God in the person of Jesus Christ dealt the death blow to the powers of darkness, the reverberations of which continue to resound throughout history (the Reformed view).

Prayer in the process view is not personal petition to a God who has the power to alter world history but instead an attitude that brings us into contact with the power of creative transformation or the hidden possibilities within ourselves and others. Prayer is meditation on the wonder and joy of living rather than the pouring out of the soul before a merciful and almighty God. In Reformed theology it is not the rhapsody of nature or the exuberance of a creative life but the cross of Christ that is the focal point of spirituality.

Process thinkers do not deny the petitionary dimension in prayer, but they understand petition as basically a formula for self-realization. "As we pray," says Marjorie Suchocki, "we change . . . ourselves in our deepest orientation."[25] Wieman offers this prayer as a model for the believer: "God, quicken every cell of my body, and all the love of my heart, and every impulse of my flesh, to the creativity of beautiful forms of intellectual and artistic achievement."[26] He urges us to repeat this petition until our whole nature "spontaneously expresses itself in artistry." It is therefore not so much a petition as autosuggestion; it is what the New Thought movement would call an "affirmation."

The prayer of praise and thanksgiving is likewise altered in this latest brand of modernism. In Reformed theology we are called to praise and thank God primarily for what has been done for us in Jesus Christ, for the gift of reconciliation and redemption. We also thank God for the good creation and providential care. In process theology we praise God in order to bring ourselves into contact with God's transforming power. We thank God that we can be included in the surge of evolution and celebrate the fact that evolution cannot be defeated or overthrown. In his *Hymn to Matter* Teilhard says, "blessed be you, mighty matter, irresistible march of evolution, reality ever newborn."[27]

Whereas Reformed theology avers that humanity's chief concern should be to glorify God and enjoy God forever (Westminster Shorter Catechism), process theology places the accent on human beings sharing the glory of God in the creative advance into novelty. One process thinker puts it this way: "the work of the church . . . is not to glorify God in the traditional sense, but to enable the individual to fulfill himself by acting wisely and effectively, to find himself through fellowship, and to gain release from inner constraints which render ineffective the flow of creativity."[28]

As might be expected, the traditional goal of missions is radically subverted in favor of "mutual understanding" and "creative interchange."[29] Wieman is not opposed to seeking conversions so long as we are willing to subordinate our limited visions of truth to the higher vision that arises from the encounter between faiths. The religion we should strive for is the one that is most inclusive. To hold uncompromisingly to the particularity of the biblical claims is to raise up an unnecessary impediment to interreligious dialogue.

A BIBLICAL-MODERN SYNTHESIS

Process theology is best understood as an attempted synthesis between biblical and modern thought born out of an apologetic concern to make the gospel credible and palatable to its cultured despisers. This pronounced apologetic thrust is evident in the fervent desire of process theologians to reconcile religion and modern science. It can be seen in their concerted effort to bring into the service of religion such ideas as evolution, relativity, organism, and creativity, all of which are derived from either the natural or social sciences.

Unabashedly capitulating to the cultural pressures around him, Wieman makes clear why the Christian message must be recast in a new mold: "the apologist for religion should present all our most sacred beliefs and programs of action as tentative and experimental. Until he does that he can never make Christianity acceptable to this age."[30]

That process thought signifies an accommodation of the faith to evolutionary naturalism and romanticism is incontrovertible. But it also contains elements of the very same biblical-classical synthesis that it condemns in orthodox theology. Hartshorne in particular believes that we must continue to find points of contact between the Judeo-Christian tradition and classical philosophy if we are to do justice to the search for wisdom in all ages. It can be shown that process thought has a definite affinity to the philosophy of the pre-Socratic Heraclitus, who affirmed the priority of becoming over being. It also has a pronounced Platonic and neo-Platonic cast; indeed, it was Plato who spoke of the world soul as self-moved and interpreted creation as the attempt by God to bring structure and form to chaotic matter in the light of eternal ideas. Aristotle, who envisaged God as the final cause of the world moving the world by the sheer force of attraction, also resonates with the process view. The philosophies of both Whitehead and Hartshorne might be regarded as idealistic as well as naturalistic because of the role of eternal or divine ideals in the evolutionary process.

While it is indisputable that process and Reformed theologies represent two different types of religion, this does not mean that Reformed theologians cannot learn positively from this new adversary of historic Christian faith. On the basis of the doctrine that all people are created in the image of God and that sin can blur but not eradicate this image as well as the doctrine that God's Spirit is at work in the world outside the church preserving the world from chaos, we can detect glimpses of truth in the process position, truth that has sometimes been suppressed in historical orthodoxy. It can be said that in every heresy there is a remnant of orthodoxy, just as in every orthodoxy there is some intimation of heresy. We as evangelical and Reformed theologians need to be aware of our own susceptibility to heresy as well as the accidental wisdom in systems of thought that are obviously heretical.

First, we should acknowledge that the process insistence on the unavoidability of metaphysics in theology and philosophy is valid. Too often theologians have skirted metaphysics and focused only on ethics, soteriology, or spirituality. Because the gospel is a report of the saving deeds of God rather than a worldview as such, some Barthians regard the latter as of little concern. But even though not itself a worldview, does not the gospel carry with it metaphysical implications that distinguish it from the claims of non-Christian religions and philosophies? Whitehead has even declared that neither scientific theory nor method can be divorced from the metaphysics they unconsciously assume.[31]

Furthermore, the insights of the process thinkers on the subject of language and symbolism can be helpful to evangelical theologians. Whitehead rightly recognized that when applied to ultimate reality, "words and phrases must be stretched towards a generality foreign to their ordinary usage."[32] Both Hartshorne and Ogden admit the need for analogical as well as univocal language in the description of God and God's activity in the world. My criticism here is that they relegate the biblical depictions of God to the level of poetry and myth, asserting that philosophical generalizations are closer to literal truth.

Whitehead's stress on the interrelatedness in the world is salutary and indeed may reflect certain themes of his Anglican background. His emphasis on the solidarity of the human race can be useful in clarifying the doctrine of original sin and also the doctrine of the church as the body of Christ.

The process insistence on human dignity and freedom might serve as a welcome antidote to certain strands within Reformed thought that have overemphasized the depravity and helplessness of humanity. The impression is sometimes given in Reformed circles that to glorify God is to reduce humanity to nothing. Irenaeus was closer to the biblical vision when he affirmed that "the glory of God is man full alive." Karl Barth has recaptured the original Calvinist vision that God's glory means the redemption and elevation of humanity. Barth held that even human eros can be redeemed, although it must never be confused with agape, which remains always other-directed.

Finally, we should recognize that there is much truth in the process allegation that orthodox Christian theology has been adversely affected by a synthesis of biblical insights and classical philosophy. The biblical-classical synthesis is discernible not only in the tradition of Christian mysticism but even in the traditions of Reformation and Protestant orthodoxy. The classical idea of perfection as all-sufficiency and completeness has indubitably penetrated Christian thinking and prevented the church through the ages from giving due justice to the biblical idea of God sharing in the pain and suffering of God's people. It has been said that God is impassible, impervious to pain and suffering, and this is why not only the Church Fathers and medieval scholastics but also Calvin and other mainline Reformers insisted that Christ suffered only in his human nature, not in his divine nature. Calvin and Reformed orthodoxy also contend that the biblical descriptions of God "repenting" or "changing his mind" are to be taken metaphori-

cally, not literally. Here again Karl Barth has helped us to reappropriate a neglected side of the biblical tradition.

The principal contrast between Reformed and process theologies is to be found in the area of basic orientation. Reformed theology is unashamedly theocentric. Our goal in life is to glorify God and serve the kingdom of God. Process theology, on the other hand, is essentially anthropocentric. Our goal is to realize our human potential in the service of a better world in which we are included as participants and contributors. We contribute to the enrichment of God, but God also contributes to our enrichment and fulfillment. Wieman put it this way: "God is that in the universe which will yield maximum security and increase of human good when lives are properly adjusted to him."[33] Process theologians would have considerable difficulty in affirming with the early Calvinists in New England that we should be willing to be damned for the glory of God.

The divergences between the two theologies are also glaringly apparent in the area of authority (as we have seen). Reformed theology confesses that God as revealed in Jesus Christ and attested in the Bible has final and unconditional authority for faith and life. Process theology affirms that our authority lies in what can be felt and perceived empirically and what can be tested scientifically. Faith is emptied of cognitive content in the process view: it becomes an open-ended search for truth. In Reformed theology, on the other hand, faith is a steady and certain knowledge of God's promises to us and his beneficence to us.[34]

The fact that process theology locates authority in cultural experience betrays its ideological character. An ideology is here understood as a complex of ideas that appeal more to emotion than to reason and that serve vested interests in society, thereby preventing adherents from perceiving the full reality of the human situation. Democratic liberalism is one such ideology, and it cannot be denied that the process vision of an open universe and its stress on the decisive role of individuals in shaping their own destiny are intimately bound up with the virtues emphasized in liberal democracy: freedom, autonomy, relativity, and pluralism. Indeed, Wieman calls for a new formulation of faith in tune with democracy in which "the guide and standard will be the fullest self-expression and mutual understanding of particular individuals."[35] Hartshorne regards the Calvinist appeal to an infallible divine revelation as compromising "the essential principle of democracy, that none of us is divinely wise, that we all may make mistakes."[36] He complains that to insist on "the classical view of revelation" is to impose "a fearful burden on our democracy."[37] Moreover, the process view that being is to be understood in terms of doing fits in well with such values of the modern technological society as productivity, efficiency, and utility.

In making this kind of criticism, however, we should keep in mind that all theology has an ideological taint, including Reformed theology. The emphasis on predestination and subordination in classical Reformed thought may be partly derived from feudalistic and monarchical ideologies of the past, though this is not to imply that these doctrines do not have biblical roots as well. Christians should at all times endeavor to transcend ideological bias, and we can be partly successful in this task because we are in contact with a God who transcends human culture even while remaining actively at work within it. Yet we should always be circumspect in our claims, especially in the political and social arena, knowing that we are probably more children of our times than prophets to our times.

Process theology represents an excursus religion, calling people out of a past faith orientation into one more in tune with the spirit of the times. Reformed theology, on the other hand, is a confirmatory religion, seeking to maintain continuity with past traditions but endeavoring at the same time to communicate the insights of the past in a fresh way. It is the same faith but phrased in new language, though this new language is a supplement, not a substitute for the original symbolism of Christian tradition — what Barth calls the language of Canaan and the language of Zion. Process theology heralds a new faith, one that is closer both in spirit and in content to the Renaissance and Enlightenment than to the Reformation. Its symbols and metaphors are derived for the most part from physics, biology, and psychology and are to be seen as substitutes for the traditional language of faith.

Nicolas Berdyaev, who is welcomed by process thinkers as an ally in forging a dynamic view of God, contrasts the modern view with the classical one: "the revelation of a suffering and yearning God is higher than the revelation of a God whose sufficiency and satisfaction are in himself."[38] I would have to agree that the modern process conception of a God who shares our suffering is probably closer to the biblical view than the Hellenistic conception of a God who is wholly self-contained, who is removed from temporality and wholly invulnerable. But are these the only alternatives? Much better is the biblical view of God rediscovered though not always maintained in Reformed theology, a view in which God is pictured not as the Unmoved Mover (Aristotle) nor as the creative process but as being in act, the One who decisively enters into history irrevocably altering its course. Such a God changes only in God's ways with humankind, not in innermost being or in overriding will and purpose. God is therefore a God who can be depended upon. Can a God limited in knowledge and deficient in power be depended upon in times of trial and distress? Is such a God even worthy of worship?

At its best, Reformed theology affirms a God who is impassible and omnipotent but who enters into our suffering not to satisfy a yearning for fulfillment (as Berdyaev and process thinkers contend) but out of compassion for a lost human race. This is a God who basically does not need the world because God coexists as a fellowship of love within God's own self. Yet this God chooses freely to relate to the world in order to share the richness of the divine love and mercy; in so doing, God accepts vulnerability to affliction and suffering, which can only touch God where God touches the world — in the person of Jesus Christ. This is a God, moreover, who does not simply empathize with us in our sufferings but who rescues us from pain and suffering through the sacrificial life and death of Jesus Christ and his glorious resurrection from the grave.

Reformed theology insists that in Jesus Christ the whole world has been changed, since God in Christ took upon himself the burden of the world's afflictions, the penalty for human sin. It is not God who needs to be changed (as the process thinkers contend) but fallen humankind, and this change is enacted not through the will to creativity but through the mystery of supernatural regeneration. The hope of humanity rests not on our cooperation with the power of creative transformation but instead on a divine intervention in human history that happened in the past and will happen once more when Jesus Christ comes again to bring in the kingdom that shall have no end.

NOTES

1. Reinhold Niebuhr might also be included in this list except that his impact was restricted primarily to intellectual circles and then only for a brief period — the 1940s and '50s (although his political thought continues to have an influence on the moderate right wing of the political spectrum). His emphasis on tragedy, irony, ambiguity, and the inaccessibility of God represents a foreign intrusion into the American religious scene. It stands in direct opposition to the optimistic, romantic, and Pelagian character of American philosophy and religion, which is reflected in process philosophy and theology, the New Thought movement, and the electronic church movement. Niebuhr is closer to what I have called Reformed theology than to process theology, although he seeks a synthesis of Renaissance and Reformation insights.

Paul Tillich, also worthy of mention, stands closer to the American dream, despite his preoccupation with fate and tragedy. His this-worldly mysticism and ecstatic naturalism reveal an affinity to both process and feminist theologies.

2. Meland, *America's Spiritual Culture* (New York: Harper, 1948), pp. 93, 135.

3. See Whitehead, *Religion in the Making* (New York: Macmillan, 1957), p. 148.

4. I am closer to the theological methodology of Calvin, Kuyper, Forsyth, and Barth than to that of Charles Hodge and Benjamin Warfield. But they all had a common devotion to the glory of God above all else and a zealous adherence to the sovereignty of divine grace.

5. Because this essay is basically a critique of process thought from the perspective of Reformed theology, I shall concentrate on delineating the position of process theologians on various questions and then present what I believe is the proper Reformed alternative. In order to save space, I have refrained from giving substantial corroboration for

my understanding of Reformed theology, but the reader should know that Calvin and Barth are my chief mentors.

6. Heinrich Heppe summarizes the position of Reformed orthodoxy thus: the truth of revelation "is not imparted to man by flesh and blood, but solely by the Spirit of grace, who opens a man's eyes and directs his heart, that he may achieve a certain knowledge of revealed fact" (*Reformed Dogmatics,* trans. G. T. Thomson [Grand Rapids: Baker Book, 1950], p. 7).

7. Whitehead, *Process and Reality* (New York: Macmillan, 1929), p. 63.

8. Whitehead, *Adventures of Ideas* (New York: Macmillan, 1933), p. 228.

9. Henry Nelson Wieman and Regina Westcott-Wieman, *Normative Psychology of Religion* (Westport, Conn.: Greenwood Press, 1971), pp. 114-15.

10. See Schubert Ogden, *The Reality of God and Other Essays* (New York: Harper & Row, 1966), pp. 56-70.

11. Suchocki, *God–Christ–Church: A Practical Guide to Process Theology* (New York: Crossroad, 1982), p. 85.

12. Alan Gragg contends that Hartshorne tries to make a place for this last notion but that he does not develop it sufficiently (*Charles Hartshorne* [Waco, Tex.: Word Books, 1975], p. 112).

13. Hartshorne, *Omnipotence and Other Theological Mistakes* (Albany: State University of New York Press, 1984), p. 123.

14. Hartshorne, *Omnipotence and Other Theological Mistakes,* pp. 59-60.

15. Wieman, in *The Empirical Theology of Henry Nelson Wieman,* ed. Robert W. Bretall (New York: Macmillan, 1963), p. 191.

16. Charles Hartshorne, *The Divine Relativity: A So-*

cial Conception of God (New Haven: Yale University Press, 1948), pp. 127-28.

17. Hartshorne, *Insights and Oversights of Great Thinkers* (Albany: State University of New York Press, 1983), p. 186.

18. Whitehead, *Adventures of Ideas*, p. 31.

19. Wieman, *The Source of Human Good* (Chicago: University of Chicago Press, 1982), p. 52.

20. See Nygren, *Agape and Eros*, trans. Philip S. Watson (Chicago: University of Chicago Press, 1982).

21. Whitehead, *Adventures of Ideas*, p. 345.

22. Whitehead, *Process and Reality*, pp. 520-21.

23. Hartshorne, cited by Norman Pittenger in *The Lure of Divine Love* (New York: Pilgrim Press, 1979), p. 25.

24. Whitehead, *Adventures of Ideas*, p. 367.

25. Suchocki, *God–Christ–Church*, p. 206.

26. Wieman, *The Wrestle of Religion with Truth* (New York: Macmillan, 1927), p. 79.

27. Teilhard, cited by Hans Küng in *Does God Exist?* trans. Edward Quinn (Garden City, N.Y.: Doubleday, 1980), p. 175.

28. Wayne Shuttee, "The Work of the Church," in *The Empirical Theology of Henry Nelson Wieman*, ed. Robert W. Bretall (New York: Macmillan, 1963), p. 220.

29. Wieman, *The Wrestle of Religion with Truth*, p. 169.

30. Wieman, "Wrong Ways to Justify Religion," *Christian Century*, 18 December 1929, p. 1573.

31. Whitehead, *Adventures of Ideas*, p. 198.

32. Whitehead, *Process and Reality*, p. 6.

33. Wieman, *The Wrestle of Religion with Truth*, p. 59.

34. Cf. Calvin: "we shall have a complete definition of faith, if we say, that it is a steady and certain knowledge of the Divine benevolence toward us, which, being founded on the truth of the gratuitous promise in Christ, is both revealed to our minds, and confirmed to our hearts, by the Holy Spirit" (*Institutes of the Christian Religion*, trans. and ed. John Allen [Philadelphia: Presbyterian Board of Christian Education, 1936], 3.2.7).

35. Wieman, *Now We Must Choose* (New York: Macmillan, 1941), p. 174.

36. Hartshorne, *Omnipotence and Other Theological Mistakes*, p. 6.

37. Hartshorne, *Omnipotence and Other Theological Mistakes*, pp. 43, 44.

38. Berdyaev, *Truth and Revelation*, trans. R. M. French (New York: Collier Books, 1962), p. 56.

The Reformed Tradition and Liberation Theology

Albert Curry Winn

It is now clear that the major breakthrough in Christian theology in the last decade has been the explosive emergence of political and liberation theologies. . . . The theological landscape has been irretrievably changed." Those are the words of David Tracy, a Roman Catholic theologian. He gives the liberation theologies a decidedly mixed review but is nonetheless aware of their significance.

Up to this point I have spoken of "theologies" in the plural, because there are clear and evident differences between various types of liberation theology. Latin American liberation theology champions the liberation of the poor from economic oppression. Black liberation theology champions the liberation of black people from racial oppression. Feminist liberation theology champions the liberation of women from sexual oppression. Between these

theologies there are tensions, even jealousies. They are united by the common theme of oppression and the common belief that those who have been oppressed can articulate theologies that are more biblical, more valid, more true than the "traditional" or "dominant" theologies that have been constructed by the oppressors.

In the confines of this brief essay I have chosen to address only Latin American liberation theology, and in particular the arresting work of Gustavo Gutiérrez. I do not mean by this choice to imply that the other liberation theologies are less interesting or important or erudite or significant for our theme of faith and politics. One simply must start somewhere.

I. THE THEMES OF LIBERATION THEOLOGY

What are the principal themes of liberation theology? To attempt a brief answer to that question is a ridiculous effort on its face. Most

Reprinted from *Reformed Faith and Politics*, ed. Ronald H. Stone (Washington: University Press of America, 1983), pp. 77-91.

of us are familiar with the distortion of Calvin's thought that goes under the rubric of "the five points of Calvinism." What we have there is a caricature of a theology far richer and more complex than the "five points" would indicate. Just so, a listing of "five principal themes" of liberation theology may distort that theology's richness and complexity and produce only a caricature.

Let me state my conviction that we are not dealing here with a mere "regional variant" that we can observe comfortably at a distance, as though it were some brilliant butterfly of the Amazon basin with no particular relevance to daily life in North America. Nor are we dealing with "political ideology" or "an ethical reduction of the gospel." We are dealing with a genuine theology. It has its own theological method, gives an account of its own path to truth. It produces its own understanding of God, of Christ, of salvation, of the church, of eschatology. It intends to be, and is, a part of the ongoing dialogue that includes Augustine, Aquinas, Rahner, Bonhoeffer, Barth, Moltmann, the papal encyclicals, and the documents of Vatican II. Above all, it takes Scripture seriously. Biblical references abound. As it is enlightened by the word, it casts fresh light upon the word.

So with profound respect, real trepidation, and a saving, good-natured awareness that all lists of themes result in caricatures, let us proceed to a thematic outline.

1. *God is on the side of the oppressed.* This is first of all a biblical theme. Gutiérrez is keenly aware of the centrality of the exodus event: God is the One who liberated the oppressed slaves in Egypt. Creation and exodus are indissolubly linked, as Deutero-Isaiah makes clear again and again. Creation is the first act of history, human history; and human history is the story of God's liberating action. The exodus begins a long march that culminates in the coming of Christ, who brings new creation and new liberation. In the humane legislation of the Old Testament we see God's "tilt" toward the poor. In the incarnation we see God's solidarity with the oppressed.

To be for the oppressed is to be against the oppressors. Here Gutiérrez cites a plethora of texts from Job, Isaiah, and all the prophets, from Jesus' words in Luke, and from James. The divine indignation is aroused at the cheating of the powerless, the orphans and widows; at fraudulent commerce and exploitation; at the hoarding of lands; at the violence of the ruling classes; at slavery, dishonest courts, unjust taxes, corrupt officials.

This is clear from Scripture. But how can a God who loves all be for some and against others? How can the "universal salvific will" of God, God's purpose to save all, be reconciled with God's own "preferential option for the poor?" Universal love must become concrete, it must embrace some for the sake of all. In the long run, the oppressors can be saved only through the liberation of the oppressed.

2. *In Latin America, oppression is systemic.* It is not enough to describe the crushing poverty of the masses in Latin America. It is not enough to weep in sympathy for their sufferings. The Latin American reality must be analyzed. Such an analysis is human work, human reflection on facts.

The analysis that makes best sense in the Latin American situation is a Marxist analysis. There is a class struggle between those who own and control the means of production and those who own nothing. This is complicated by the dependence of both classes — the poor and the ruling oligarchies — on the great multinational corporations of capitalist North America, the ultimate owners and controllers.

The system is oppressive. It is not enough for religion to transform individuals into persons of goodwill, whether among the poor, the ruling class, or the corporate directors. Persons of goodwill are present in all three groups. But they are trapped in an evil system. Nothing will change until the system is changed.

"Development" is a bankrupt term in Latin America. It stands for efforts to help the Latin American nations "catch up" with the capitalist system in North America and Europe. It is "superversion," change imposed from the top, and it leaves the power of those on top unchallenged. It does not attack the root causes of the evil. At the end of "the decade of development," the Latin American poor were worse off. The underdevelopment of the underdeveloped countries is a direct result of the development of the developed countries.

"Liberation" is the proper term for Latin American aspirations — to be liberated from dependence on the developed nations, to be liberated from the smothering power of the elite ruling circles, to be liberated from the grinding, hopeless poverty of the masses. This calls for "subversion," change imposed from the bottom. Gutiérrez believes that this can come about only through common ownership of the means of production — a socialist state.

Gutiérrez expresses his hope that liberating systemic change, "subversion," can be achieved through the political process, without violence. But he speaks of violence "as a last resort." He does not hesitate to point to Camilo Torres, a Colombian priest who died fighting with the guerrillas, as one of the heroes of liberation theology. There are three levels of violence in Latin America, he says: the violence of the system itself, which kills hundreds of people daily; the violence of the police and armies, accounting for the "disappearance" of those who oppose or are suspected of opposing the ruling regimes; and the violence of the guerrillas, who can tolerate the situation no longer.

3. *To participate in liberation is salvific work.* To engage in the struggle for justice for the poor is to take part in God's great plan of salvation. Here the question of the relationship between faith and political action comes to a head. How is it possible to relate "liberation," which is so thoroughly political, even to the point of violence, with the great spiritual concept of salvation? How can we say that a struggle that is so "horizontal," relating solely to this world, is connected with salvation, which we think of as "vertical," relating to the next world?

Here Gutiérrez analyzes the changes that have taken place in the idea of "salvation" within his own Roman Catholic communion. Salvation used to mean "guaranteeing heaven," and the debate was *quantitative*. For how many could the church, which was the sole repository of salvation, guarantee heaven? What about the salvation of the heathen? Gutiérrez traces the development of such ideas as "general grace" (grace at work in all people, including those outside the church) and "anonymous Christianity" (Christianity beyond the visible frontiers of the church). At length, through a recovery of the teaching of Thomas Aquinas that there is present in every human being an innate desire to see God, and above all through a rediscovery of Paul's teaching that all things were created in, through, and for Christ (Col. 1:16), that all things have been reconciled to God by the blood of the cross (Col. 1:20), and that the grace of God has appeared for the salvation of all human beings (Tit. 2:11), the church has begun to teach in the documents of Vatican II "the universal salvific will of God." This is not, as I understand it, the straightforward universalist teaching that all persons are in fact saved. But it declares that it is God's purpose to save all and that if any are excluded it is by their own choice, not God's. It is closely analogous to Karl Barth's teaching of the election of all human beings in Christ.

With the quantitative question thus solved, Roman Catholic thought has turned to the *qualitative* question. What is the quality of the salvation that God wills for all and that can be obtained beyond the visible boundaries of the church? Gutiérrez repeatedly defines it as communion with God and one's fellow human beings. Sin, then, is not something that cancels the future enjoyment of salvation in heaven; it is what alienates us here and now from our fellow human beings and from God. The overcoming of sin and the restoration of communion becomes a historical, this-worldly project. Heavenly salvation is only the culmination beyond death of what begins here. So it is misguided to distinguish between "salvation history" and "secular history." There is only one history, human history in which God is at work to overcome injustice, to break down all that separates people from God and each other. To participate in the Latin American struggle for liberation, then, is to work along with God in the divine effort to save all people.

At several points Gutiérrez offers a threefold analysis of "liberation." First, there is political liberation, the liberation of oppressed classes from their oppressors, about which I have mainly spoken thus far. Second, there is human liberation, in which human beings begin to assume conscious responsibility for their own destiny, seize the reins of their own evolution, become the creators of a new humanity and a new society. Third, there is liberation from sin, which is the root of all alienation, injustice, and oppression. Unjust situations do not happen by chance; human beings are responsible for them. But this responsibility is not merely individual, private, and interior: it is social, historical fact. Christ dies to liberate us from sin in all its dimensions. Here is a further reason why the term "development" won't do: it dodges the basic issue of sin.

It is clear that if the third level of "liberation" is omitted, we are not dealing with salvation in any full sense of the word. Gutiérrez would argue that if the first level is omitted our notion of salvation is equally truncated!

4. *The church must become the church of the poor.* Neutrality is impossible. Not to side with the poor is to side with those who oppress them. To do nothing and to say nothing is to support the status quo. It is pointless to say that the church should not take sides. It has already taken sides with the rich and powerful. What is needed is the "conversion" of the church, a conversion from the side of the powerful to the side of the powerless.

Through the influence of the liberation theologians, the Latin American bishops at Medellin and again at Puebla declared a "preferential option for the poor." Gutiérrez attempts to spell out what that means. The *gospel* ought to be addressed primarily to the oppressed, remembering that Jesus declared he was sent to preach good news to the poor (Luke 4:18). The voices of the marginalized and dispossessed should be heard in the church; they should take *ownership* and set policy; the owners of this world's goods should no longer be the owners of the gospel. The church should be "the *sacrament* of history" — that is, the place where the liberating grace of God, which is the heart of the historical process, can be seen clearly at work. This means, of course, that oppressive structures within the church must be quickly done away with. The eucharist should be a *celebration* in the church of the liberation that is taking place outside the church walls.

The church's role is *denunciation* and *annunciation*. The church must denounce all the sinful structures that grind down and oppress human beings. Sometimes the church's voice may be the only one that can speak out. The church must announce the coming of God's kingdom, the possibilities of a more just, humane, and sustainable order.

The church must go beyond being "the church of the poor" to become "the poor church." It must surrender its wealth. Its priests and bishops must live in simplicity. It must express in its life solidarity with the poor.

How can the unity of the church be maintained in the midst of the class struggle? Can rich and poor come to the eucharist together? If the church takes the side of the poor will it not drive out the rich? Gutiérrez wrestles with this problem. Is there a real unity to be maintained? Or in a divided world is the unity of the church a myth? Unity is best seen as a gift of God and an achievement of human beings that remains for the future. Only the commitment to the struggle against all that presently alienates and divides people can make the church an authentic sign of unity.

A strange new ecumenical unity is emerging in Latin America. A common understanding of the misery and injustice that abound is binding different communions together more closely and more quickly than all the slow negotiations about faith and order.

5. *Theology is critical reflection on praxis.* As a result of the four convictions discussed above, the liberation theologians feel that they have discovered a new and better way of doing theology. Theology begins with efforts to change the world, echoing Marx's eleventh thesis against Feuerbach: "The important thing is not to understand the world, but to change it." World-changing does not proceed by a set plan where the end is envisioned from the beginning. It proceeds by "praxis." Praxis is a sort of trial-and-error procedure. You try something. Then you reflect on what has happened. Then in the light of what you have learned you try the next thing. Praxis is kin to the "action-reflection model" which is discussed so much nowadays by Christian educators. Theology, then, is not an armchair exercise. It can be done properly only by those already engaged in praxis for the poor.

But theology is *critical* reflection. We do need to understand and criticize our praxis, to examine intelligently what we are doing to change the world. One senses here an indirect parallel to Karl Barth's definition of theology as the church's critical reflection on its preaching. In both cases, theology is not the first thing, but "the second act," as the liberation theologians call it. Theology discerns the positive and negative values in praxis. It makes explicit the faith, hope, and love contained in praxis. It corrects aberrations and one-sided-

ness. It makes the commitment to liberation more evangelical, more authentic, more concrete, and more efficacious.

It does all this "in the light of the Word." Liberation theology does not wish to abandon Scripture. Scripture is not the starting point, because we have read Scripture so long through the eyes of the dominant, oppressing group that justification of the way things are is what we will hear if we begin there. We must come to Scripture out of our struggle to help the poor. They will teach us to read it from "the underside." We will hear it in fresh ways, and in more authentic ways, because Scripture was initially addressed to the oppressed, not to the powerful. This is "the epistemological privilege of the poor."

II. HOW REFORMED THEOLOGY MIGHT BE DEEPENED BY SERIOUS DIALOGUE WITH LIBERATION THEOLOGY

Up to this point we have been trying to set forth liberation theology as fairly, completely, and succinctly as an outsider can. We have been letting it speak for itself, in the form developed by one of its leading Latin American exponents. We have not engaged in any "critical reflection" of our own.

The time for critical reflection has arrived. In this section I will reflect positively on what can be learned from this new theology that exploded onto the theological scene in the past decade. In the next section I will be more negative, emphasizing values in my own tradition that the liberation theologians have neglected to their peril.

First, then, what can we learn from liberation theology? To this question many Presbyterians, if they have read this far, will answer: Nothing! The word *Marxism* triggers in us a completely negative reaction. It stands for atheism, godlessness, tyranny, everything we fear most. It is what many Americans are prepared to combat even at the cost of a nuclear holocaust. How can we "learn" something from a theology that bears so deep a Marxist taint?

The importations from Marxism do indeed need careful theological scrutiny. Regarding some very basic theological flaws I will have strong warnings to issue in the third section of this paper. But some of what Marx said about the oppression of the have-nots by the haves was said much earlier by Jesus and the Hebrew prophets. The fact that Marx repeats these things does not make them false. The basic question about the analysis of the Latin American reality made by the liberation theologians is not whether it is Marxist but whether it is true. In their use of Marxist analysis and in their embrace of the Marxist goal of a classless society, these theologians are clearly neither atheists, godless, nor lovers of tyranny. Reformed Christians should not be so timid and unsure that they fear truth from any quarter.

Other Presbyterians will question whether we have anything to learn because of the taint of violence. This is indeed a vexed and difficult question. But those of us who pay our taxes to support a military system that seeks to uphold our nation's dominance by threatening to annihilate over a hundred million Russians in one thirty-minute salvo can hardly sit in self-righteous judgment over the participation of Camilo Torres in guerrilla warfare as a "last resort." A consistently nonviolent position, applied to ourselves as well as to others, is a Christian option, perhaps *the* Christian option. But so long as we are tainted by violence, let us not refuse to learn from others who are similarly, and perhaps less seriously, tainted.

If we can get beyond these obstacles, we can hear some interesting things from our neighbors to the south.

1. *We can be reminded of our own long history of political involvement.* Those who think it is un-Presbyterian to write their representatives or senators should simply take up a copy of Calvin's *Institutes*. The fundamental document of Reformed theology begins with a political letter, addressed to King Francis I of France. In it, Calvin, who had fled France as a subversive, warns his former sovereign that France is so filled with the fury of wicked persons that there is no place in it for sound doctrine. He speaks of the violence of the established government and the courts, which have condemned, imprisoned, exiled, burned, and exterminated innocent people. He speaks of the lies, frauds, and slanders that have been spread. He expresses the belief that the king has been ill advised and urges him to make his own independent investigation of the facts. He dares to say that a king who in ruling over his realm does not serve God's glory exercises not kingly rule but brigandage. He puts his hope in the strong hand of the Lord which will surely appear in due season, coming forth armed to deliver the poor from their affliction and also to punish their despisers, who now exult with such great assurance.

Those who think it is un-Presbyterian to attend the open meetings of city council should study the constant, unending, exhausting dealings that John Calvin had with the local authorities in Geneva.

Though he never held public office, John Knox was as deeply involved in the politics of Scotland as anyone living; he was the chief political counterforce to Mary, Queen of Scots.

The Westminster Assembly of Divines was appointed and paid by Parliament, in the midst of a civil war between Parliament and King Charles. Its task, to prescribe uniformity of belief, church government, and worship for England, Scotland, and Ireland, was an essential building block in a grand scheme of political unification.

When George III remarked that Cousin America had eloped with a Presbyterian parson, he was not praising the Presbyterian Church for its apolitical stance.

When Presbyterianism divided North and South in these United States, the ostensible issue was highly political: whether loyalty to the federal government should be a requirement for church membership. The underlying issue was even more political: slavery.

There has been an almost schizophrenic split between the rhetoric of Reformed theology and the action of Reformed churches and people. Calvin's rhetoric in his chapter on "Civil Government" is ostensibly antirevolutionary. Leaning on Romans 13, he defends the necessity of civil government and the divine sanction for it. Regardless of the form it takes, Christians should be compliant and obedient to it. He argues at length that obedience is due even to unjust rulers. Christians should not rebel but suffer patiently and trust God to vindicate the right. But, says Calvin, God uses human agents to punish unjust kings, some by an express command, others unwittingly. "The Lord accomplished his work through them alike when he broke the bloody scepters of arrogant kings and when he overturned intolerable governments. Let the princes hear and be afraid."

The last quotation could have been written by a liberation theologian. And the action of American Presbyterians in the American Revolution was based there rather than on the main thrust of Calvin's chapter.

The rhetoric of the Westminster Confession of Faith is decidedly apolitical. The saying most frequently quoted is that synods and councils "are not to intermeddle with civil affairs which concern the commonwealth unless by way of humble petition in cases extraordinary." Yet the Westminster Assembly was sitting at the aegis of a Parliament that finally beheaded a lawfully crowned king, an event that sent shock waves through Europe that extended to the French Revolution and the Russian Revolution.

That Reformed political actions have been at times unwise and at times inexcusably violent is beyond question. But a stance of political apathy, of political noninvolvement, while it may seem to be sanctioned by Reformed rhetoric, is not in accord with Reformed history from the beginning to the present time. When the United Presbyterian Church in the U.S.A. adopted its Book of Confessions, including the Barmen Declaration and the Confession of 1967, it took a bold step to bring Reformed rhetoric into line with Reformed history and tradition.

Liberation theology, with its overtly political stance, can shake us out of our political apathy and remind us what our tradition has been all along.

2. *We can be reminded that Reformed theology was originally a theology of the oppressed.* In the letter to King Francis I referred to above, Calvin says, "what mean and lowly little men we are . . . in men's eyes most despised — if you will the offscouring and refuse of the world, or anything viler that can be named. . . . Some of us are shackled with irons, some beaten with rods, some led about as laughingstocks, some proscribed, some most savagely tortured, some forced to flee. All of us are oppressed by poverty, cursed with dire execrations, wounded by slanders, and treated in most shameful ways."

Geneva was a city crammed with refugees from almost every European land. Money, supplies, and food were short. Survival was a constant problem. When the refugees returned to their homes, they often met with fresh oppression. Such was the case of John Knox and the Scottish refugees. In the preface to the Scots Confession they write, "but such has been the rage of Satan against us . . . that to this day no time has been granted us to clear our consciences, as most gladly we would have done. For how we have been tossed until now the most part of Europe, we suppose, understands."

The burning bush of Exodus 3 figures prominently on most of the seals of the Reformed churches. The church is aflame with persecution, but it is not consumed; it survives. The oppression experienced by the Reformed churches was not primarily economic or racial or sexual; it was plain, straightforward religious oppression.

The Reformed theologians were just as sure as the liberation theologians that God is on the side of the oppressed. That conviction is one root of the strong doctrine of election that is so characteristic of Reformed theology. The oppressed are the elect, and the oppressors are the reprobate. It is one of the ironies of history that in the course of the centuries this became reversed. In many Calvinistic cultures the rich became the elect and the poor became the reprobate; the Scotch-Irish immigrant pioneers were the elect and the Native Americans whose lands they seized were the reprobate; the Calvinist Boers were the elect and the South African blacks were the reprobate; the southern slave owners were the elect and the slaves were the reprobate; the comfortable, educated church members who fill the church on Sunday are the elect and the street people who come for soup on Monday are the reprobate. This is a perversion of primitive Reformed theology. Initially the Reformed church was the church of the poor. It was, as Calvin called it, "the poor little church."

There are Reformed churches that are oppressed today: in places like Czechoslovakia, Taiwan, Korea, LeSotho. In many cases it is because they have exercised a "preferential option for the poor," because they have had a ministry of denunciation and annunciation. I have a notion that Calvin would be more at home in those churches than in the middle-class comfort of our North American Calvinist churches. More important, I suspect Jesus would be too.

3. *We can be helped to take seriously neglected portions of the Bible.* Robert McAfee Brown, perhaps the best North American interpreter of Latin American liberation theology, has remarked more than once on the sort of

canon within the canon utilized by Gutiérrez and his colleagues. There is the exodus, of course — the original record and all the reassessments of its meaning that mark the rest of the Old Testament. There are the prophets, with special weight on such passages as Jeremiah 22:13-16 (to do justice is to know God) and Isaiah 58:6-7 (the true fast is to let the oppressed go free). Then there is Jesus' sermon at Nazareth in Luke 4:16-30 and the picture of the last judgment in Matthew 25:31-46. And don't forget the passage in James 5:1-6 about the wages of the laborers kept back by fraud.

Everyone knows those passages, but they are not really foundational to traditional Reformed theology. When Calvin the commentator dealt with them he spoke as movingly for the poor and the oppressed as Gutiérrez has in anything he has written. For Calvin the widow, the orphan, the plundered poor were "us," not "them" as they are for modern, middle-class Reformed exegetes. But Calvin the theologian founded his system on the Pauline epistles, and that has dictated the shape of Reformed theology ever since.

This can be understood in terms of what Brown calls "the interlocutor." Every theology takes its shape around its questioners and the questions they ask. Calvin's interlocutors were the Roman Catholics on one side and the left-wing Reformers on the other, with second-generation Lutherans nearer the middle. This becomes clear if you look at the index of names in a good edition of the *Institutes*. It begins to account for the table of contents. And finally it explains the index of Scripture references. Calvin was driven to those parts of Scripture that helped him answer his interlocutors.

After the Enlightenment, the interlocutors became the nonbelievers. And this dictated subtle changes in the structure of Reformed theology and in its canon within the canon.

The interlocutors of liberation theology are the nonpersons, the poor and oppressed ones whose humanity and personhood have been denied by the system. It is their questions that dictate the form of liberation theology and drive it to certain Scriptures as foundational.

Should Reformed theology recognize non-persons as interlocutors? The prophets did. Jesus did. It would broaden and deepen our grasp of Scripture to do so.

4. *We can be driven to reconsider the connection between Calvinism and capitalism.* What disturbs many North Americans most about liberation theology is its indictment of capitalism as the root cause of oppression and suffering in Latin America. We react as though someone had uttered blasphemy. That reaction reveals the religious value we tend to give to capitalism. Blasphemy is an irreverent insult to a god. If a charge against capitalism, however reckless or unfounded, strikes me as blasphemous, have I made capitalism a god, an idol?

The material benefits that the capitalist system has brought to most North American Presbyterians are obvious. We live in unprecedented and unparalleled affluence. The source of the affluence may well be primarily the exploitation of the nonrenewable resources of an incredibly rich continent, but those riches could not have been unlocked and delivered to our doors without the aggressive competition that is characteristic of capitalism. Until recently we have been able to believe that the same escalator that carries some to untold riches and power lifted the mass of people at least a few steps higher in income, prosperity, and comfort.

With the vanishing of the frontier and the cultivation of consumer demand that outstrips our resources, things have changed. In a "zero-sum" economy, the rich can grow richer only if the poor grow poorer. Fortunately there are laws that seek to limit and cushion the brutality involved in this competition. But in the international order there are far fewer limiting and cushioning laws and mechanisms. As the rich nations grow richer the poor nations grow poorer in a ruthless, brutal fashion. This is why the underdevelopment of the underdeveloped countries is a direct result of the development of the developed countries.

The capitalist system, which is now so strongly attacked by the liberation theologians, has been closely linked with Calvinism. Max Weber explored this linkage in his famous essay, written early in this century, entitled *The Protestant Ethic and the Spirit of Capitalism.* It has been much criticized as oversimplistic, but a rereading even today reveals its power and insight.

Weber makes a case for Benjamin Franklin as a quintessential capitalist. He quotes the familiar maxims: "Time is money" — any time you are not working is costing you the money you could have made. "Credit is money" — for six pounds a year you may have the use of hundred pounds. "Money can beget money" — he that murders a crown destroys all it might have produced, even scores of crowns.

Here is a working secular religion. The first and greatest commandment is to work as hard as you can as many hours as you can to make as much money as you can. The cardinal sin is waste of either time or money. The monastic, ascetic discipline is that the money thus made is not to be spent on amusement or comfort but straightway invested to beget more money. The cardinal virtues are thrift, industry, prompt payment, keeping contracts — all of which increase your credit and enable you to have the use of the money of others. This religion almost seems designed to achieve the accumulation of capital. We have all known and observed its devotees.

Franklin's father was a Calvinistic Puritan, and Weber contends that Calvinistic Puritanism fathered the secular religion I have described. The great question for Calvinists was "How can I know that I am one of the elect?" Pastoral advice to those tortured by that question was twofold. First, you must consider yourself chosen and beat down all doubts, since doubts betray a lack of faith. Second, you must engage in intense worldly activity to give evidence of your election. Since the making of money is an objective measure of the extent and effectiveness of worldly activity, wealth becomes the most tangible sign of election. Here is the theological root of capitalism. But the theology can be abandoned and you will still have the driving zeal to make money for the sake of making money, without regard to luxury, comfort, or the other things money can buy. It is a contest, a game, and money is the way you keep score. "Enough" is always "more."

It is interesting to compare "the spirit of capitalism," as described by Weber and recognized by us in ourselves and others, with Calvin's own views about money and business. He did regard business as a legitimate way of serving God and working for the greater glory of God. He perceived the circulation of money and goods and services as a concrete form of the communion of the saints. He contended that those engaged in business should aim to help the poor and reduce the gap between the poor and the rich. He thought it would be good to restore the Year of Jubilee, a periodic redistribution of wealth so the gap would never become permanent. This is a far cry from the response of a multinational corporation to a church-sponsored stockholder resolution: "The use to which our products are put is not our concern; the maximization of profit is."

It is not impossible that Calvin would agree with the liberation theologians that capitalism of that stripe is indeed a source of oppression. If Calvinism is the unwitting father of capitalism, is it now called upon to be the corrector of the abuses that have arisen within capitalism?

5. *We can be reminded that praxis, doing the truth, is an old Calvinist custom.* Long before Marx wrote that the important thing is not to understand the world but to change it, Calvin was trying to change Geneva from a brawling, licentious town to a just, humane,

sustainable city, a city ordered according to the word of God. Truth, he believed, is in order to goodness. The successive editions of the *Institutes* that issued from his pen were colored by those efforts, that praxis. He would probably want to turn Gutiérrez's definition around and say that "theology is meditation on the word in the light of praxis." But he would agree that uninvolved, armchair theology is worthless.

III. HOW LIBERATION THEOLOGY MIGHT BE DEEPENED BY SERIOUS DIALOGUE WITH REFORMED THEOLOGY

It is a false humility to assume that because Reformed theology is old and encrusted with tradition it has nothing to contribute to current theological discussion. God bestows gifts on all, even on us. It is part of our obedience to the fifth commandment to honor and value the particular gifts given to our fathers and mothers in faith. So I want to discuss certain aspects of our heritage that the liberation theologians have neglected and that I feel they should not have neglected. One form of love between different parts of the church universal is the duty of serious theological dialogue.

1. *We would remind the liberation theologians that good theology always struggles to be universal.* Calvin's goal in writing the *Institutes* was not to compile a handbook of the peculiarities and special insights of the Reformed churches but to set forth the Christian religion, the faith of the one holy catholic church, what has been believed everywhere, at all times, by all. Every Reformed Confession does the same. Karl Barth wrote his massive *Church Dogmatics* — not Swiss Dogmatics, or Reformed Dogmatics.

The liberation theologians remind us that we cannot really do this. The theology we write is inevitably colored by our time, our situation, our geography, our economics. If we are the oppressors, our theology will unconsciously seek to justify the oppressive status quo. If we are the oppressed, our theology will cry for change and liberation.

This problem was recognized years before the arrival of the liberation theologians by Richard Niebuhr, who wrote eloquently about the relativism that affects physics, philosophy, economics, politics, and theology. In each case, knowledge is conditioned by the situation of the knower. We need to face this, take it seriously, admit it freely.

But should we rejoice in it and glory in it? Or should we struggle against relativism and try to attain such inclusiveness and universality as we can? The liberation theologians have abandoned the attempt for even a measure of universality. They write Latin American theology or black theology or feminist theology. The latter two have even excluded from the conversation those who do not have their particular experience. That is understandable, but it is a cop-out. How can the church be reformed and always reforming if the ongoing dialogue is not open to everybody, and if the central attempt is not to include as many segments of the community of faith as we possibly can?

2. *We would remind the liberation theologians of the reality and pervasiveness of sin.* The Achilles' heel of Marxism is its inadequate doctrine of sin, its unfounded optimism regarding human nature. If only the social order can be changed, if only the proletariat can seize control of the means of production, if only the classless society can come into existence, then greed, lust, selfishness, violence, oppression — all the undesirable aspects of humanity will wither away. Utopia will arrive. That no Marxist state has been able to demonstrate even the first faint beginning of this "withering" process does not seem to diminish the naive optimism of the devoted Marxist.

Gutiérrez seeks to protect himself from this error with a threefold analysis of liberation

in which the third point is liberation from sin. Should that not be the first point?

The main problem, however, lies in the second point: liberation for the self-development of a new humanity. I will quote directly Gutiérrez's still sexist language, because that contributes to the *hubris* that is expressed: "Man, the master of his own destiny"; "liberation from all that limits or keeps man from self-fulfillment"; "liberation from all impediments to the exercise of his freedom"; "man constructs himself"; "man takes hold of the reins of his own destiny"; "man makes himself throughout his own life and throughout history"; "the goal is the creation of a new man."

There is seemingly no sense here of partial depravity, let alone total depravity; no sense of humanity's inability to save itself; no real sense of sin. The New Testament knows of a soaring hope for a new humanity (2 Cor. 5:17). But this is not a self-creation; it is a new creation of God.

The sense of the universality of sin and the vanity of all efforts to re-create ourselves ought not to be used as a defense of the status quo. It is not my intention to argue here that if the masses seize power, they will be just as selfish and greedy as the present ruling elite, and hence we should let things stay as they are. We know they would be sinful. We do not know they would be *as* sinful. In the few test cases we can observe, such as the recapture of political power by blacks in certain counties and cities in the American South, the new rulers have not been on the whole as venal or ruthless as their predecessors. Life would be measurably better if power were overturned in many places in the world. Mary's dream is a good one: "God has put down the mighty from their thrones and exalted those of low degree" (Luke 1:52). But the Magnificat does not speak of "man making himself, seizing the reins of his own evolution." I would like to challenge the legitimacy of such language in Christian theology. If Gutiérrez finds it hard to listen to

Calvin, let him listen to the repeated refrain of Anselm in his own tradition: "Have you considered how weighty sin is?"

3. *We would remind the liberation theologians of the proper place of the word of God.* The word has a place in their definition of theology: critical reflection on praxis in the light of the word. But is this the proper place? In the beginning is the first act: praxis, the trial-and-error process of work for the liberation of the poor. Then comes the second act: critical reflection on what has been happening — in Hegel's phrase, this reflection rises when the sun goes down. Finally comes a third act: "in the light of the word." At length we employ Scripture in order to examine the reflection we have made on the action we have taken. This rises as the moon sets.

Reformed theology is a theology of the word of God. It issues in a church reformed according to the word of God. The word of God has priority in the theological process. Liberation theology correctly warns us that if we come quickly and carelessly to the word we are apt to read it as members of Pharaoh's court, not as enslaved Israel. Thus we should have a "hermeneutical suspicion" about our own hermeneutics. We should acknowledge the "hermeneutical privilege of the poor." We should listen intently and patiently to what the poor find there. But we should also trust the inherent ability of the word to break down prejudices and false readings. It is, after all, "the hammer that breaks rocks in pieces" and "the sword that pierces to the division of soul and spirit." This is true when it is given priority in the theological process, even by those in Pharaoh's court.

The word must guide praxis, not just help us to examine our critical reflections on praxis. The word must guide critical reflection, not just help us to examine it after moonset. The word must be living and active throughout the whole process.

Gutiérrez's practice is better than his theory. His work is studded with references to Scripture. He obviously knows his Bible very well. Why, then, can he not give it a larger place programmatically?

When the dust settles on this confrontation between liberation theology and Reformed theology, what can we say in conclusion? At least this: political neutrality is impossible. While political involvement can be risky and sinful, political noninvolvement is even more risky and sinful. It supports forces that oppress the poor, and God is on the side of the poor.

For centuries the political involvement of the Roman Catholic Church was aimed primarily at defending its privileges as an institution and directing the power of the state to enforce codes of personal morality that the church could not enforce through its own influence. This is not the kind of political involvement that is in line with liberation theology or the best Reformed theology. For Protestant groups to engage in this type of political involvement does not improve it or make it more praiseworthy.

Political involvement on behalf of the oppressed, in solidarity with the poor, will also be tainted with sin, but it bears the sign of grace. It lines up with the long purpose of God. North Americans who choose such involvement may become the opponents of their own class, their own race, their own sex, their own lifestyle, their own government, their own economic system (or at least of the obvious abuses to which it has led). Our cross is not laid down in Latin America, but here. Will we deny ourselves, take up that cross, and follow Christ?

Reflections on Liberation Theology from the Reformed Tradition

Jorge Lara-Braud

Gustavo Gutiérrez has said that Latin American liberation theology desires to contribute to the life and reflection of the universal Christian community. This invitation to dialogue encourages us as members of the Presbyterian Church in the United States [now the Presbyterian Church (USA) — ED.] to listen to liberation theology and then to pose our own questions to the challenge of our Latin American colleagues and to the challenge of U.S. liberation theologies, whether black, feminist, or some other. There are six areas in which the dialogue for us Presbyterians will be especially demanding, even painful.

First we may begin by remembering that the methodological principle of Reformed theology is *ecclesia reformata semper reformanda*, the church reformed and always to be reformed, according to the word of God. Our

---

Reprinted from *What Is Liberation Theology?* (Atlanta: General Assembly Mission Board of the Presbyterian Church [PCUS], 1980), pp. 36-38.

tradition is one that calls for perennial reformation, not unlike what liberation theology calls permanent transformation. The Reformed tradition also recognizes that all theologies are human creations, historically conditioned and subject to correction in the light of God's self-revelation. That revelation is given in Jesus Christ, is mediated in Scripture, and is constantly re-presented to us by the Holy Spirit, who brings us new light on the word. So we can hear liberation theology as stressing again the growing, changing, historically relative character of theology based on revelation.

At the same time, we may raise questions about the tendency to stress ideology in both nonpejorative and pejorative senses. Sometimes it sounds not only as if there is no escaping the relativity of interpretation but also as if there is no true or continuing content to revelation. So ideology in the nonpejorative sense means the relativizing of all doctrine and every ethical principle. For the Reformed tradition, the link between the Bible and human understanding and human action as an expression of faith is considerably more than an ideology and certainly more than a "learning to learn" (Segundo). For us in the Reformed faith, the Bible provides theological principles and ethical paradigms that may not be timeless but that nonetheless withstand the test of time.

Liberation theologians contend that any theology not arising out of "sharing in the sufferings of God in the world" (Bonhoeffer) is ideology in the pejorative sense. Reformed theology has also understood that theology written in books must be written in lives, the truest test of a person's faith being love for the neighbor.[1] The Reformed tradition has also held that believers are called to transform society in accordance with the purpose of God. Calvin wrote that "tyrants and their cruelty cannot be endured without great weariness and sorrow . . . for God hears the cries and groanings of those who cannot bear injustice." At the same time, Reformed theology will call into question the tendency to conceive of any theology but one's own pejoratively as an ideology or to suggest that the situation of the poor and oppressed is somehow free from the taint of sin, selfishness, and loveless disregard for others.

Second, central to the method of liberation theology is the hermeneutical circle. It cannot be denied that such a circle exists, involving the word of God (especially Scripture) in interaction with the life and experience of the believer (and the believing community). We always come to the word from our own experience as well as taking the word to our experience. The liberation theologians, however, do not seem really to have a hermeneutical *circle*, for they talk about the "ideological suspicion" in experience leading to a new system and then to a new exegesis. In actuality they seem to be calling for a theology based more on experience than on the word, which for Reformed theology is an inversion of norms. So, while we are reminded properly by liberation theologians of the inevitable role of experience

against our tendency to naive biblicism, we must also remind them of the need to have experience corrected and transformed by the living word in listening to Scripture.

Third, we may also note some themes common to both liberation theology and Reformed theology: the sovereignty of God over all existence; Jesus Christ as the Savior and the Lord of history; the Holy Spirit as the One who constitutes the church and works within and beyond the church; the triumph of the grace of God in Christ in the forgiveness of sin and the removal of its consequences; the church as a sign of the reality, present and future, of God's new creation, marked by the holiness that is the gift and call of the Spirit to believers and the church. We can rejoice in the new insights into these common convictions that liberation theologians bring us and in the call that comes through their earnestness and their witness to realize these convictions more adequately and truly in our individual lives and our common life as the church.

Fourth, the threefold characterization of liberation as involving human action, as this-worldly, and as intended for all people raises serious challenges to Reformed theology as commonly understood in our church. We have been careful to claim that true liberation is God's work of realizing the kingdom. Perhaps we need to be reminded that it is also our human task to realize the kingdom and that God may use people and movements that do not acknowledge the lordship of Christ to accomplish God's purpose on earth. At the same time we need to remind liberation theology that our ultimate trust and the ultimate power of liberation resides not in human movements or in our power to accomplish good ends but in God.

We also need to be reminded that despite common American orthodox and evangelical attempts to deny it, Reformed faith along with liberation theology has always seen liberation and salvation as transforming life in this world

— providing new life and new conditions of life for persons and societies. To be recalled from an excessive otherworldliness to our expectation and responsibility for this life is at once realistic, biblical, and Reformed. Yet we must recall liberation theologians to the understanding that while utopian visions may enable the translation of biblical understandings into concrete ethical and political action, still every effort toward utopia remains flawed by human sin, every achievement of justice and love is partial, incomplete, and even distorted. Realization of the kingdom in truth and full power lies beyond the present age in which we have only its partial presence and firstfruits at best.

Further, we need to hear that both the power and love of God and the full incarnation and atonement of Jesus Christ imply that the promised liberation is not limited to some favored group but is for all people. Too often we have used our rationalized theology to restrict salvation to some chosen group, to include ourselves and our kind of people and to exclude those who are different. We thus seek to limit God's grace in a way that has no warrant in Scripture, and we limit the power of Christ's atoning work, which extends to all human beings and indeed the whole created order. We are too fearful of what we call "universalism" lest we have nothing of value to offer in evangelism at home and abroad. The fact is that powerful evangelism and authentic mission involve not the giving of something we possess but the announcing of what God has done, is doing, and will do. At the same time, that announcement involves and must never obscure the centrality, sufficiency, and indispensability of Jesus Christ. All liberation and salvation is through him and his work, even when that is hidden and unacknowledged.

A fifth issue is liberation theology's perplexing use of Marxist theory not only to analyze and repudiate capitalism but also to opt for the socialist alternative as a structure more in conformity to the demands of God's king-

dom. The actual socialist societies we know about are uniformly authoritarian, if not totalitarian, with a consequent loss of basic democratic freedoms (as Moltmann underscores in his "Open Letter to Míguez Bonino"). Yet Latin American theologians insist that there are no "third ways"; they leave no room for European-style democratic socialism or for a representative democracy based on a possible but as yet unknown economic democracy. Their faith in the human capacity for good is not matched by the actual record in socialist or capitalist societies, a Calvinist would observe. The Latin American reply is, of course, that socialism has yet to be built, to be indigenized, and even when it does begin, it will be a process of permanent self-correction.

A derivative question from the "instrumental use of Marxism" is really whether it is Marxist theory only that comes to the aid of theology or something beyond theory — Marxist philosophy *as a system*. In the latter case, Reformed theology would question whether the case for a specifically *Christian* theology of liberation can still be made. The recently adopted Confession of Faith of the Reformed Presbyterian Church of Cuba is a case in point. American Calvinists might consider it too much a concession to Marxist socialism to build an account of Christian faith on the notion of God as worker and the human being also as worker. For other Calvinists, certainly for those of Cuba who adopted the Confession, it is the only responsible way to give the account of their faith.

Finally, we are troubled by the ecclesiology of liberation theology, which sees the church in conflictive categories. Here Latin American, black, and feminist theologians alike challenge what we have always understood about the unity and catholicity of the church. Now we are confronted in the interest of a new understanding of holiness and apostolicity in terms of the oppressed and their interests with the demand for struggle and division in the church. That demand seems to deny or destroy the unity and catholicity of the church. Liberation theologians would remind us, however, that the disunity already exists and the catholicity is already denied by the exclusion of persons by class or race or sex. They would remind us further that unity at the expense of justice is neither Christian nor biblical.

In other ways than these, too, we can and shall enter the dialogue with these liberation theologians. If we listen with care, we can, however painfully, shed our innocence as we receive new light from God's word in the struggle with this theology of liberation. And we can in the integrity of our Reformed faith and the power of the Spirit seek to do God's will and thus come to know God's doctrine (John 7:17).

NOTES

1. Calvin, commentary on Habakkuk 2:6, lect. 111.

Black and Reformed: Contradiction or Challenge?

Allan Boesak

The Reformed tradition in South Africa is more than three hundred years old. It was brought here by Dutch Calvinists, who were followed by French Huguenots, and still later by Scottish Presbyterians and Swiss missionaries. When our Khio ancestors were confronted with Christianity for the first time, it was the Reformed expression of it that they experienced. It was this tradition that was to have a lasting impact on the history of South Africa and on the lives of all its citizens. When our ancestors accepted Christianity three centuries ago, they became the members of a Reformed church.

Yet this history is racked with contradictions. The Europeans who claimed this land, who scattered and killed its people, did it in the name of a Christian God whom they prayed to as Reformed Christians. When they introduced slavery and enforced it with the most

vicious forms of dehumanization and violence, it was the Bible read through Reformed eyes and arguments from the Reformed tradition that gave them justification for such acts of violence and human tragedy. The God of the Reformed tradition was the God of slavery, fear, persecution, and death. Yet, for those black Christians this was the God to whom they had to turn for comfort, for justice, for peace.

It was of Reformed Christians that a Dutch pastor of the nineteenth century spoke when he wrote,

> how is it possible that there could be any religious or, let me say, human feeling in persons who force their servants, mostly children of blacks shot dead, to sleep outside without any protection whatsoever in these cold nights, so that these unhappy wretches cover themselves with ashes, thereby inflicting upon themselves terrible burns . . . ? How can there be any religious or even human feeling in persons — big strong men — who beat these children mercilessly with whips at the slightest provocation,

Reprinted from *Black and Reformed* (Maryknoll, N.Y.: Orbis Books, 1984), pp. 83-99.

or even without any reason at all . . . ? God knows, and I myself know, what indescribable injustices occur in these parts! What gruesome ill-treatment, oppression, murder![1]

And yet these were persons who were supposed to be brothers and sisters in Christ, persons who were supposed to form with others the one body of Christ in his church — the Reformed church.

The contradictions did not disappear as time went on. On the contrary, they multiplied. Today, three hundred years later, black Reformed Christians come together to ask what it means to be black and Reformed in South Africa today. It is a question that concerns not only our past but also our present, and it has a direct and fundamental bearing on our future. Indeed, one can also put the question in another way: Does the Reformed tradition have a future in South Africa?

APARTHEID: HERITAGE OF THE REFORMED TRADITION

Today, no less than three centuries ago, being both black and Reformed is an expression of a painful paradox. Reformed Christians have the power in this country, as they did three hundred years ago. Now, as then, they call themselves Christians, and they proudly announce that they stand within the Reformed tradition. Through the power of the gun and sheer trickery they have claimed for themselves 87 percent of this land and they call it "white South Africa." Their avarice and boundless greed have claimed the vast resources and riches of this country. The wealth with which God has blessed this land, the breathtaking natural beauty that is the work of divine artistry, the majestic mountains, the sea, the fertile valleys — on all this is carved out in brazen arrogance: "For whites only." Blacks have come to understand that even though the Bible teaches us that the earth is the Lord's and the fullness thereof, experience has taught us that here the earth belongs to whites.

These Reformed Christians have created a political, economic, and social dispensation that they call apartheid. It is based on racism and white supremacy, on economic exploitation and the misuse of political power. They have made laws that are a perversion of justice and offer no protection for the poor, the weak, and defenseless millions of our land against the power of their oppressors. For the sake of economic privileges that they regard as their right, they deliberately put asunder what God has joined together. They despise the sanctity of marriage and family life when it comes to blacks. They treat the homeless with a callousness and brutality that stun the mind. They detain without trial. They silence the prophetic voices of the nation through arbitrary bannings. They terrorize the innocent. They are prepared to kill children in order to maintain apartheid and white supremacy.

Apartheid is unique. But its uniqueness does not lie in the inherent violence of the system, or in the inevitable brutality without which the system cannot survive, or in the dehumanization and the contempt for black personhood, or even in the tragic alienations and the incredible costs in terms of human dignity and human relationships. No, the uniqueness of apartheid lies in the fact that this system claims to be *based on Christian principles*. It is justified on the basis of the gospel of Jesus Christ. It is in the name of the liberator God and Jesus Christ, the Son of God, that apartheid is perpetuated, and it is Reformed Christians who are responsible for it. Apartheid was born out of the Reformed tradition; it is, in a very real sense, the brainchild of the Dutch Reformed churches. It is Reformed Christians who have split the church on the basis of race and color and who now claim that racially divided churches reflect a true Reformed understanding of the nature of the Christian church.

It is Reformed Christians who have spent years working out the details of apartheid, as a church policy and as a political policy. It is Reformed Christians who have presented this policy to the Afrikaner as the only possible solution, as an expression of the will of God for South Africa, and as being in accord with the gospel and the Reformed tradition. It is Reformed Christians who have created Afrikaner nationalism, equating the Reformed tradition and Afrikaner ideals with the ideals of the kingdom of God. It is they who have devised the theology of apartheid, deliberately distorting the gospel to suit their racist aspirations. They present this policy as a pseudogospel that can be the salvation of all South Africans.

In this uniqueness lies the shame of the Christian church in this country. Apartheid is the grave of the dignity and the credibility of the Reformed tradition.

Today we have reached a state of affairs where many, especially blacks, have come to believe that racism is an inevitable fruit of the Reformed tradition. In the experience of millions of blacks this tradition is responsible for political oppression, economic exploitation, unbridled capitalism, social discrimination, and the total disregard for human dignity that have become the hallmark of South African society.

By the same token, being Reformed is equated with total, uncritical acceptance of the status quo, sinful silence in the face of human suffering, and manipulation of the word of God in order to justify oppression. To be Reformed is to support the intransigence of our present rulers and to expect the unconditional submission of the oppressed.

The anomaly has become more acute than ever. For black Reformed Christians who suffer much under the totalitarian rule of white Reformed Christians, the question is fundamental and decisive. We have reached a point in our history where we can no longer avoid it. Black and Reformed: is this a burden that has to be cast off as soon as possible, or

is it a challenge toward the renewal of church and society? Does the Reformed tradition have a future in South Africa?

A REFORM IN NEED OF REFORM

But we must ask a prior question. Is the Afrikaner version of the Reformed tradition the whole truth? Is the equation of being Reformed with being oppressive and racist justified? In this country, as Douglas Bax has shown, Reformed theology has in many instances become a curious mixture of pietism, German Romanticism and *Volkstheologie,* and the negative aspects of Kuyperianism. Is this acceptable? Is the justification of tyranny Reformed?

Of course, in trying to answer all these questions I must of necessity be brief and selective. My aim here is not to give a detailed assessment of Reformed doctrine but rather to highlight those aspects of the tradition that are especially relevant to us in our situation and that have to be redeemed from the quagmire of political ideology and nationalistic propaganda to which they have fallen victim in South Africa.

The first thing that I should mention, then, is the principle of the supremacy of the word of God that gives life to our words. It is the word of God that shapes life and provides the church with a basis on which to stand. Scripture is the indisputable foundation of the life and witness of the church in the world, and it is the guiding principle for all our actions.

Manipulation of the word of God to suit culture, prejudices, or ideology is alien to the Reformed tradition. But the way in which Reformed Christians in this country have used the Bible to justify black oppression and white privilege, the way in which the gospel has been bypassed in establishing racially divided churches, the way in which Scripture has been used to produce a nationalistic, racist ideology is the very denial of the Reformed belief in the supremacy of Scripture. The word of God is the word that gives life. It cannot at the same time be the justification of the death that comes through oppression and inhumanity. It is the word that speaks to our total human condition and offers salvation that is total, complete. For us today this means that, although the Bible is not a handbook for politics or economics, it nonetheless reveals all we need to know about God's will for the whole of human existence, including our spiritual, political, economic, and social well-being. The church believes that the Bible provides us with the fundamental principles of justice, love, and peace that we in the making of our societies ignore or deny at our own peril. The word of God is the standard for all human actions and holds before us the norms of the kingdom of God.

The kingdom of God is inextricably bound up with the lordship of Jesus Christ — another precious principle for those who adhere to the Reformed tradition. Christ is Lord of all life, even in those situations where his lordship is not readily recognized by willful humans. We believe passionately with Abraham Kuyper that there is not a single inch of life that does not fall under the lordship of Christ. All of life is indivisible, just as God is indivisible, and in all of personal and public life — in politics and economics, sports and art, science and liturgy — the Reformed Christian seeks the lordship of Christ.

Here the Reformed tradition comes so close to the African idea of the wholeness of life that these two should combine to renew the thrust that was brought to Christian life by the followers of Calvin. Reformed piety was *never* intended to include withdrawal from the world. The admonitions of politicians and even (Reformed!) churches to black Christians to "keep out of politics" are not only unbiblical; they are also, as Max Warren has indicated, the "essence of paganism." He quotes a missionary from Uganda as follows:

without realizing it . . . we have drifted back into the old polytheism against which the prophets of the Lord waged their great warfare. The real essence of paganism is that it divides the various concerns of a man's life into compartments. There is one god of the soil; there is another god of the desert. The god of wisdom is quite different from the god of wine. If a man wants to marry he prays at one temple; if he wants to make war, he must take his sacrifice elsewhere.

All this is precisely where the modern paganism of our secular society has brought us today. Certain portions of our life we call religious. Then we are Christians. We use a special language. . . . We call that our Christianity — and there we stop.

We turn to another department of our life called politics. Now we think in quite different terms. Our liturgy is the catchwords of the daily press. Our divine revelation is the nine o'clock news. Our creed is "I believe in democracy." Our incentive is the fear of — we're not sure what. But it certainly is not the fear of the Lord.[2]

This kind of religion is far from the faith that characterized Reformed Christians from the very beginning. Their faith said that Christians were responsible for their world. Their Christianity was what philosopher Nick Wolterstorff has called "world-formative Christianity." As Reformed Christians we see ourselves as human beings who are responsible for the world in which we find ourselves. It is a world made by us, and we are capable of making it different. More than that: we *should* make it different. It *needs* reform. Furthermore, the exercise of that responsibility is part of the discipleship to which the Lord Jesus Christ has called us. It is not an addition to this discipleship but an integral part of it. Doing what we can to reform the social world in which we live is part of our spiritual life.[3]

For us as black Reformed Christians this means that in following Jesus Christ the spiritual experience is never separated from the liberation struggle. In the heart of this process, God is experienced as a Father to whom every effort and every struggle is offered. Our worship of God is what must give direction and content to our action in the world. From God come bravery and courage, truth and justice. Because God raised our Messiah from the dead to demonstrate the truth of his word, God will also give life to those who, in the path of Jesus, give their lives for others.

In South Africa, white Reformed theology has persistently pointed out that we live in the "broken reality" of a fallen world. This is true. But in the theology of apartheid this leads to the acceptance, idealization, and institutionalization of that brokenness and of the kind of apathy that induces Christians to accept sinful realities such as racism.

In true Reformed theology, however, the recognition of the broken, sinful realities of our world becomes the impulse toward reformation and healing. It leads us to understand that human beings do not automatically seek the glory of God and the good of their neighbor. That is why it becomes a Christian's task to work actively for the good of his or her neighbor. In a fallen world, the structures that we create are tainted by sin and will not automatically have a liberating, humanizing effect on human lives. They will therefore have to be changed so that they may serve the humanization of our world. This means that Reformed Christians are called on not to accept the sinful realities of the world but to challenge, to shape, to subvert, and to humanize history until it conforms to the norm of the kingdom of God.

SOCIAL JUSTICE: THE REFORMED TRADITION

What shall we say about the link between South African oppressive society and the Re-

formed tradition? It is necessary that we once again refute the blasphemous claim that apartheid is Christian. We must understand that the Christian character of a government is not proved by good intentions or by the number of times it shouts "Lord, Lord!" It is proved by the care of the poor, the protection of the weak and the needy, the suppression of evil, the punishment of oppressors, the equitable distribution of wealth, power, privileges, and responsibilities. As Calvin says, "the Lord recommends to us . . . that we may, insofar as everyone's resources admit, afford help to the needy, *so that there may not be some in affluence, and others in need.*"[4]

It is tragic that the Reformer's concern for social justice is not reflected in the policies of all those who claim spiritual kinship with him. South African history might have been different if white Reformed Christians in South Africa had taken his word on human solidarity seriously: "The name neighbor extends indiscriminately to every man, because the whole human race is united by a sacred bond of fellowship. . . . To make any person our neighbor, it is enough that he be a man."[5]

In the area of social justice, Reformed belief was expressed magnificently by Abraham Kuyper in a speech to the Christian Social Congress in 1891:

> When rich and poor stand opposed to each other, [Jesus] never takes His place with the wealthier, but always stands with the poorer. He is born in a stable; and while foxes have holes and birds have nests, the Son of Man has nowhere to lay his head. . . . Both the Christ, and also just as much His disciples after Him as the prophets before Him, invariably took sides *against* those who were powerful and living in luxury, and *for* the suffering and oppressed.[6]

Unlike so many rich Calvinists and other Christians who keep on telling the poor that poverty is the will of God, Kuyper refused to believe it:

God has not willed that one should drudge hard and yet have *no bread* for himself and for his family. And still less has God willed that any man with hands to work and a will to work should suffer hunger or be reduced to the beggar's staff just *because* there is no work. If we have "food and clothing" then it is true the holy apostle demands that we should therewith be content. But it can neither nor may ever be excused in us that, while our Father in heaven wills with divine kindness that an abundance of food comes forth from the ground, through *our* guilt this rich bounty should be divided so *unequally* that while one is surfeited with bread, another goes with empty stomach to his pallet, and sometimes must even go without a pallet.[7]

Later, another Reformed theologian, Karl Barth, put it in these words:

The human righteousness required by God and established in obedience — the righteousness which according to Amos 5[24] should pour down as a mighty stream — has necessarily the character of a vindication of right in favour of the threatened innocent, the oppressed poor, widows, orphans and aliens. For this reason, in the relations and events in the life of His people, God always takes His stand unconditionally and passionately on this side and on this side alone: against the lofty and on behalf of the lowly; against those who already enjoy right and privilege and on behalf of those who are denied and deprived of it.[8]

It is in vain that the oppressive system of apartheid and its defenders claim any Reformed legitimation. Rather, the Reformed tradition calls for resistance to so blatantly unjust a government as is the South African.

GOVERNMENT: THE REFORMED TRADITION

For Reformed Christians, government is not "naturally" an enemy. We believe with Calvin that governments are instituted by God for the just and legitimate administration of the world. But note two things. First, the expectation that government is not the enemy of the people must not be read as blind acceptance of any kind of government; it is in fact a crucial criterion for judging the actions of a government. Second, God institutes the authority of government for the *just* and *legitimate* administration of the world. Thus, in order to be able to claim this divine institution and in order to be legitimate, a government has to respond positively to the expectation that Scripture has of it: it is to be a shepherd of the people (Ezek. 34).

In terms of any modern concept of democracy, as well as Calvin's understanding of legitimacy, the South African government is neither just nor legitimate. The Reformed tradition holds that a government should be obeyed because it has the authority instituted by God. But there is always one very important proviso: we obey government *insofar* as its laws and instructions are not in conflict with the word of God. Obedience to earthly authority is only obedience *in God*. On this point John Calvin is clear:

But in that obedience which we have shown to be due to the authority of rulers, we are always to make this exception, indeed, to observe it as primary, that such obedience is never to lead us away from obedience to him, to whose will the desires of all kings ought to be subject, to whose decrees all their commands ought to yield, to whose majesty their scepters ought to be submitted. And how absurd would it be that in satisfying men you should incur the displeasure of him for whose sake you obey men themselves! The Lord, therefore, is King of Kings, who, when he has opened his sacred mouth, must alone be heard, before all and above all men; next to him we are subject to those men who are in authority over us, but only in him. If they command anything against him, let it go unesteemed. And here let us not be concerned about all that dignity which the magistrates [government] possess; for no harm is done to it when it is humbled before that singular and truly supreme power of God.[9]

And Calvin ends with an exhortation to courage and obedience, reminding us that "we have been redeemed by Christ at so great a price as our redemption cost him, so that we should not enslave ourselves to the wicked desire of men — much less be subject to their impiety."[10] Therefore the call is: "We must obey God rather than man."

This was the spirit caught by the Scottish reformation when it formulated article 14 of the *Confessio Scotica:* "[it is our duty] to honor father, mother, princes, rulers, and superior powers: to love them, to support them, yes, to obey their charges *unless repugnant to the Word of God.* To save the lives of the innocent, to repress tyranny, to defend the oppressed" (italics mine).

Commenting on article 25 of the Scottish Confession, Karl Barth says,

> we can afford the state such positive cooperation only when the significance of the state as *service of God* is made clear and credible to us by the state itself, by its attitude and acts, its intervening on behalf of justice, peace, and freedom, and its conduct toward the church. That is the condition which the *Confessio Scotica* is right in constantly laying down. If that condition is not fulfilled, those who administer it make a mockery [of the service of God]. But in that case we can take no share in their responsibility, we cannot further their intentions, we cannot wish to strive with them to attain their aims. We cannot do it under any conditions or on any pretext.[11]

So when Beyers Naudé sides with the poor and the oppressed in South Africa, *he* is the true representative of the Reformed tradition, not those who banned him and sought to bring dishonor to his name.

When the Presbyterian Church of Southern Africa decided to challenge the government on as fundamental an issue as Christian marriage, it was closer to the Reformed tradition than were those who vindicated an unjust law.

It is not the perpetrators of injustice but those who resist it who are the true representatives of the Reformed tradition.

EXIGENCIES OF A BLACK, REFORMED FUTURE

Black Christians who are Reformed have no reason to be ashamed of this tradition. Of course, this is not to say that Reformed Christians have not made mistakes. We know only too well the tendency of those who adhere to this tradition to become self-righteous. We have often exhibited an arrogance that becomes self-sufficiency and gives rise to a tendency toward isolationism, because we feel we do not need anybody else. Think of how the doctrine of election has been used to foster a false sense of superiority and how often it has been coupled with nationalism. Indeed, as Wolterstorff says,

> sometimes one is . . . confronted with that most insufferable of all people, the triumphalist Calvinist, the one who believes that the revolution instituting the holy commonwealth has already occurred and that his or her task is now simply to keep it in place. Of these triumphalist Calvinists the United States and Holland have provided plenty of examples. South Africa today provides them in their purest form.[12]

It is my conviction that the Reformed tradition has a future in this country only if black Reformed Christians are willing to take it up, make it truly their own, and let it once again become what it once was: a champion of the cause of the poor and the oppressed, clinging to the confession of the lordship of Christ and to the supremacy of the word of God. It will have a future when we show an evangelical openness toward the world and toward the worldwide church so that we shall be able to search with others for the attainment of the goals of the kingdom of God in South Africa. I do not mean that we should accept everything in our tradition uncritically; indeed, I believe that black Christians should formulate a Reformed confession for our time and situation in our own words.

Beginning with our own South African situation, we should accept our special responsibility to salvage this tradition from the grip of the mighty and the powerful who have so shamelessly perverted it for their own ends and let it speak once again for God's oppressed and suffering peoples. It is important to declare apartheid to be irreconcilable with the gospel of Jesus Christ, a sin that has to be combated on every level of our lives, a denial of the Reformed tradition, a heresy that is to the everlasting shame of the church of Jesus Christ in the world.

To accept the Reformed confession is more than a formal acknowledgment of doctrine. Churches accepting that confession thereby commit themselves to show through their daily witness and service that the gospel has indeed empowered them to live in this world as the people of God. They also commit themselves to accept in their worship and at the table of the Lord the brothers and sisters who accept and proclaim the lordship of Christ in all areas of life and to work ceaselessly for that justice, love, and shalom that are fundamental to the kingdom of God and the kingly rule of God's Son. Confessional subscription should lead to concrete manifestation in unity of worship and cooperation in the common tasks of the church. In South Africa adherence to the Reformed tradition should be a commitment to combat the evil of apartheid in every area of our lives and to seek liberation, peace, justice, reconciliation, and wholeness for all of God's children in this torn and beloved land.

We must be clear. It is one thing when the rules and laws of unjust and oppressive governments make it impossible for the church to carry out its divine task. But it is quite another thing when churches purposely reject this unity and this struggle, as the white Reformed churches of South Africa have consistently done. Apartheid is not simply a political ideology. Its very existence has depended and still depends on a theological justification by these same white Reformed churches. This, too, is part of our task: in struggling *against* apartheid, we struggle *for* liberation; *against* an oppressive and inhuman ideology but also *for* the sake of the gospel and the integrity of the church of Jesus Christ. Christians and churches purporting to serve the gospel by justifying apartheid on biblical grounds do so only at the risk of blasphemy.

I am also convinced that in this struggle some Reformed expressions of faith, now centuries old, and for many redundant, can provide us with both prophetic clarity and pastoral comfort. Lord's Day 1 of the Heidelberg Catechism asks the question "What is your only comfort in life and death?" The answer is:

> That I, with body and soul, both in life and death, am not my own, but belong to my faithful Savior Jesus Christ; who with His precious blood has fully satisfied for all my sins, and delivered me from all the power of the devil; and so preserves me that without the will of my heavenly Father not a hair can fall from my head; yea, that all things must be subservient to my salvation, wherefore by His Holy Spirit He also assures me of eternal life, and makes me heartily willing and ready, henceforth, to live unto Him.

This is one of the most powerful statements of faith I have ever encountered. In our situation, when black personhood is thoroughly undermined, when our God-given human dignity is being trampled underfoot, when our elderly are uprooted and thrown into the utter desolation of resettlement camps, when even the meager shelter of a plastic sheet is brutally taken away and mothers and their babies are exposed to the merciless winter of the Cape, when young children are terrorized in the early hours of the morning, when the prophetic voices of our youth are teargassed into silence, when the blood of our children flows in the streets of our townships — what *then* is our comfort in life and in death? When we are completely at the mercy of those for whom our humanity does not exist, when our powerlessness against their ruthless rule becomes a pain we can no longer bear, when the stench of our decaying hope chokes us half to death, when the broken lives and silent tears of our aged show the endlessness of our struggle, when the power of the oppressor is arrogantly flaunted in the face of all the world — what *then* is our comfort in life and death? That I, with body and soul, both in life and death, am not my own, but belong to my faithful Savior, who is Jesus the Liberator, Christ the Messiah and *Kyrios,* the Lord.

Is this excessive spiritualization? No, it is not. It is a revolutionary spirituality without which our being Christian in the world is not complete and without which the temptations that are part and parcel of the liberation struggle will prove too much for us. Furthermore, in the situation in which we find ourselves, it is of vital importance that we be able to resist the totalitarian claims of the powers that rule South Africa so harshly. The most frightening aspect of apartheid is the totality of control that the government seeks to exercise over human lives — from the subtle and not-so-subtle propaganda to the harsh, draconian laws designed to ensure the "security" of the country. Apartheid is a false god whose authoritarian audacity allows no room for the essence of meaningful humanity: freedom under God. It is of vital importance that we never forget to whom our ultimate allegiance and obedience are due.

In this country, the government will come to expect more and more unquestioning submission for the sake of "national security." More and more the government will expect the church to participate in its "total strategy." Such participation could only take the form of theological justification of the national security ideology, the sanctification of the militarization of our society, and the motivation of South African soldiers for the "holy war" against communism.[13] The church will be expected to applaud the kind of theology expounded by the state president at the centenary celebrations of the Nederduitse Gereformeerde Sendingkerk in October 1981: "The total onslaught against South Africa is a total onslaught against the kingdom of God."

Furthermore, as the situation of violence and counterviolence develops and the fear among whites that they will lose their over-privileged position grows, the courage of those who seek justice will be challenged.

So the confession that Jesus Christ is Lord of my life is not spiritual escapism. It is a confession with profound implications for the whole of life. It is a fundamental theological affirmation of the place of the Christian in this world, and it firmly sets the limits of the powers of this world. It places us within the best tradition of the Christian church through the ages, opening our eyes and ears to the inspiration of the "great cloud of witnesses on every side of us." It is a reminder, in the midst of the struggle, that our lives have meaning only when they are in the hands of the one who has given his life for the sake of all others. And although he is the Lamb who is slaughtered, for those who call him Lord he is also "Jesus Christ, the faithful witness, the firstborn from the dead, the ruler of the kings of the earth" (Rev. 1:5).

It is comfort, but it is more: it is the quiet, subversive piety that is quite indispensable for authentic Christian participation in the struggle for liberation. And in this struggle I am inspired by the words of article 37 of the Belgic Confession:

> the faithful and elect shall be crowned with glory and honor; and the Son of God will confess their names before God His Father and His elect angels; all tears shall be wiped from their eyes; *and their cause which is now condemned by many judges and magistrates as heretical and impious will then be known to be the cause of the Son of God.*

This is our tradition also, and it is worth fighting for.

NOTES

1. P. Huet, *Het tot der zwarten in Transvaal mededeelingen omtrent slavernij en wreedheden in de zuid-afrikaansche republiek* (Utrecht, 1869), pp. 29-30.

2. Quoted by Warren in *The Christian Mission* (London: SCM Press, 1951), p. 10.

3. For this insight I am dependent on Nicholas Wolterstorff, *Until Justice and Peace Embrace* (Grand Rapids: William B. Eerdmans, 1983).

4. Calvin, quoted by W. Fred Graham in *The Constructive Revolutionary* (Richmond: John Knox Press, 1971), p. 70; italics mine.

5. Calvin, quoted by Graham in *The Constructive Revolutionary,* p. 70.

6. Kuyper, *Christianity and the Class Struggle,* trans. Dirk Jellema (Grand Rapids: Piet Hein, 1950), pp. 27-28, 50.

7. Kuyper, *Christianity and the Class Struggle,* pp. 48-49.

8. Karl Barth, *Church Dogmatics,* 4 vols., ed. Geoffrey W. Bromiley and Thomas F. Torrance (Edinburgh: T. & T. Clark, 1936-1969), II/1: 386.

9. John Calvin, *Institutes of the Christian Religion,* Library of Christian Classics, vols. 20-21, ed. John T. McNeill, trans. Ford Lewis Battles (Philadelphia: Westminster Press, 1960), 4.20.32.

10. Calvin, *Inst.,* 4.20.32.

11. Barth, *The Knowledge of God and the Service of God according to the Teaching of the Reformation* (London: Hodder & Stoughton, 1938), pp. 227-28.

12. Wolterstorff, *Until Justice and Peace Embrace,* p. 21.

13. The thought expressed here is that of Chaplain General the Rev. Van Zyl of the Republic of South Africa.

Feminist Theologies and the Reformed Tradition

Cynthia M. Campbell

CRITICISM OF FEMINIST THEOLOGIES FROM THE REFORMED TRADITION

Is Christianity compatible with feminism? Can one be a Reformed Christian and also a feminist? Many issues are involved in these two questions, and it would be impossible in this space to detail all possible responses. The following issues have been selected for consideration because they seem central both to the Reformed theological tradition and to feminist concerns. The first part of this essay takes up various criticisms of feminist thought from the Reformed theological tradition. The second part surveys responses that might be given by various feminist theologians. The third part of the essays turns to the contribution that feminist approaches might make to those who identify themselves as Reformed or Presbyterian Christians.

Some Reformed theologians have argued that the task of theology is reflection on revelation. From this perspective, the work of the theologian lies in thinking and talking about the implications of God's self-disclosure. It is reflection on Scripture and specifically on Jesus Christ as Scripture bears witness to him. Theology, in this tradition, is not in the first instance reflection on human experience. Experience is not unimportant, but it is quite clearly secondary. As it is often stated, experience is to be interpreted by Scripture and not Scripture by experience.

In light of this position, Reformed theologians criticize the use of experience as a norm or standard of judgment about God when it is made equal or superior to Scripture. Feminist theology, they argue, replaces Scripture as the only norm of God's self-disclosure with human experience. Human experience may be a source of knowledge about God, but it is a

Reprinted from Presbyterian Church (USA) document "Theologies Written from Feminist Perspectives: An Introductory Study," 199th General Assembly (1987).

source, like reason and tradition, that is always judged by Scripture.

Another way of putting this criticism is that in feminist theology there appears to be a danger of replacing theology (talk about God) with anthropology (talk about humanity). When God is made a function of human experience or part of the process of the created order, some wonder whether God, as a reality over against God's creation, continues to exist at all. Further, if God is identified with God's creation (or human experience), there remains no ground from which to criticize human tendencies to sin, idolatry, and oppression. Only a God who is "other" than the human reality can stand in judgment of such perversions as sexism or patriarchy.

At the heart of this criticism is the complaint that feminists have removed the "sovereignty" of God and located God entirely in the realm of human experience. Reformed theologians have long emphasized the idea that God is completely independent of the creation, that all things depend on God while God depends on nothing, and that God is characterized by freedom to act with respect to the creation howsoever God wills. Such views seem to stand in opposition to those feminist views that emphasize the role of humanity as "co-creator" or partner with God. Also, many wonder whether divine freedom is not compromised if God is defined completely in terms of vulnerability or solidarity with human suffering.[1]

A second major criticism from some in the Reformed tradition derives from the insistence that God is self-disclosing and has decisively revealed "himself" as Father, Son, and Holy Spirit. These terms or names for God, it is argued, are neither accidental nor the products of the religious context in which the Scriptures were written and preserved.[2] Rather, these are names in the proper sense that they state the identity of the persons named. God is not simply *called* "Father"; God *is* Father, because God is the Father of the Son, Jesus Christ. Because of our recognition of Jesus as the true Son of God,

we recognize God's relation to him as Father and therefore God's relation to us as "our Father." To replace this language with other terms such as Creator, Redeemer, and Sustainer changes the very nature of God's self-disclosure and thus our understanding of God's relation to us. Moreover, if we were to replace the personal names of God we would risk identifying the persons by their works and ending up with a "modalistic" view of the Trinity. In 1985 the General Assembly of the Presbyterians Church (USA) stated that "the Trinitarian designation, 'Father-Son-Holy Spirit,' is an ancient creedal formula and as such should not be altered."[3]

These critics go on to add that, although the use of these masculine names and masculine pronouns is necessary to a proper naming of God, this usage does not suggest that God is in fact male. God is God, beyond human form and thus beyond gender. Indeed, they argue, the use of feminine pronouns or names for God would introduce sexuality into the concept of God and therefore must be avoided in any other than the most careful metaphorical sense (e.g., he is like a mother). When the names "Father" and "Son" are used for God, these terms are themselves transformed: God is not interpreted by human relationships, but rather these human relations are redefined by the activity and behavior of God.

A third objection centers on feminist views of Jesus Christ. Two questions are central: do feminists really believe in the incarnation, and do they believe that Jesus is rightly named "Redeemer" or "Savior"? Many feminists see Jesus as the representative of the humanity that God intended, but is that the same as saying that in Jesus the reality of God is uniquely disclosed? Clearly, many feminists view Jesus as a "liberator" of broken and oppressed humanity. But some Reformed theologians wonder whether liberation is an adequate translation of "redemption" and whether the notion of atonement or even reconciliation as the act of God has been lost entirely.

A fourth major criticism of the feminist proposal has to do with its suggestions regarding the interpretation of Scripture. As noted above, many feminists begin with a "principle of interpretation" suggesting that those portions of Scripture that affirm the dignity and worth of all persons are "normative" for reading the rest of Scripture and passages that demean or promote the subordination of women are to be regarded as nonauthoritative.

Some Reformed critics maintain that this approach does violence to the nature of Scripture itself. In a distinctive formulation, John Calvin asserted the whole authority of the whole Bible. Old and New Testaments are equally revelatory of God and as a whole constitute God's word to humanity. To set up a principle such as the feminist critique proposes not only places a standard of human judgment over the standard of Scripture but also dilutes what for many is the most traditional way of reading Scripture as itself the word of God. Even among those who recognize that any reading of Scripture is conditioned by the culture of both readers and authors, many claim that feminists read Scripture through the screen of their own ideological convictions rather than reading Scripture itself.

FEMINIST RESPONSES

Feminists who stand within the Reformed tradition themselves raise some of these same questions of other feminists. Reformed feminists respond that many points of criticism are well taken and require serious comment.

With respect to the question of the role of experience as a norm or standard by which theological judgments are made, many, including feminists, would argue that in fact the Reformed tradition has neglected this very important aspect of both religious and theological life. Since the nineteenth century there

has been increasing skepticism in theological circles as to the ability of human beings to speak about God except on the basis of human experience. Even granting the notion of God's self-revelation, revelation can only be received in terms that human beings are capable of understanding. To paraphrase Marshall McLuhan, there is an intrinsic and necessary relation between the medium and the message. To suggest that theological truth can be separated from the people and circumstances in which revelation took place is, among other things, to deny the significance that the incarnation occurred in one very specific place, culture, and time and not any other.

Second, feminists suggest that the Reformed tradition as a biblical tradition must make room not only for the "otherness" of God but for God's presence as well. The God of the Bible is sovereign but also suffers with and for God's people. The prophets display a God who is as infinitely compassionate as God as powerful. To deny that vulnerability or suffering are at the heart of God is to deny the reality of the incarnation and the significance of the cross.

Third, feminists argue that there is a logical fallacy in the argument that God must be referred to with masculine pronouns and names but is not male. If God is really neither male nor female, then names and pronouns that are both masculine and feminine and names that are neither masculine nor feminine must in principle be applicable because all references to God must ultimately be metaphorical or symbolic and not literal. Further, feminists argue that we consider again the power of the symbols we use, especially the symbols for the transcendent or ultimate. Always to name God as male sends a message that feminists suggest Scripture itself would not want to send and does not in fact send.

Fourth, to the question of the interpretation of Scripture, feminists, especially within the Reformed tradition, argue that what they are suggesting is nothing new. Not unlike Rosemary

Radford Ruether and others, both John Calvin and Karl Barth argued that the way to interpret Scripture is by Scripture itself. For them, as for many feminists, the most acceptable means of doing this is by the model of Jesus Christ. It is through the witness and person of Jesus — in Barth's terms, the "Word Incarnate" — that the written word is to be understood.[4]

Building on this view, Reformed feminists suggest that it is precisely on the life and ministry of Jesus that the principle of the full personhood and value of women can be based. Unlike most others in the biblical record or in the culture of his day, Jesus related to women as significant persons. He included them in conversations and at his table; he drew on their experiences for his metaphors of the kingdom. It is to women that the first "apostolic commission" came — namely, to proclaim the event of the resurrection to the rest of the disciples (who not uncharacteristically did not believe the women: see Luke 24:10-11).

Feminists who stand within the Reformed tradition take seriously the criticisms that the tradition raises. They struggle to maintain a balance between the presence of God and the otherness of God. While many wrestle with the ecumenical problems raised by relinquishing traditional language for the Trinity, they urge the tradition to take seriously its own affirmation that God is neither male nor female. With the General Assembly, they affirm that the "church needs to seek new terms which refer to the persons of the Trinity."[5] Finally, they too want to remain faithful to Scripture and argue that it is faithfulness itself that leads to a principle of interpretation that affirms women as created equal with men in the image of God.

THE FEMINIST CONTRIBUTION

Having considered some of the criticisms the Reformed tradition makes of theologies written from feminist perspectives and some responses feminists from within that tradition have offered, we turn now to a consideration of the contributions feminist perspectives can make to traditional Reformed ways of understanding both God and the theological enterprise. These contributions can be grouped into two categories: ways in which feminist perspectives affirm or confirm traditional emphases of Reformed theology and ways in which those perspectives might expand the Reformed tradition.

Despite the criticisms we have noted, there may be more common ground between Reformed and feminist perspectives than might at first appear to be the case. For the purposes of this essay, there are three areas in which these theological systems might make common cause. The first has to do with one of the most distinctive elements of the Reformed tradition: the contention that this tradition, like all theological systems and church organizations, must be "reformed but always being reformed." Theologians and churches claiming their roots in John Calvin have attempted to recognize the incomplete nature of any theological system and the imperfection of any church organization. To this end, the Reformed tradition counsels continual reconsideration of its theology and church life in light of the word of God present both in Scripture and in the life of the church today.

Feminist theologians call the Reformed tradition to return to this basic affirmation and to examine its current theological formulations, its liturgical practice, and its church life in light of what feminists believe Scripture clearly teaches — namely, the full, equal worth and dignity of woman alongside man in both creation and redemption. For many feminists, this notion of "always being reformed" is the most radical theological statement that can be made, because it acknowledges the limitations of any attempt to describe or define the reality of God. In the Reformed tradition, feminists expose all aspects of church life to the strong light of the gospel proclamation of full humanity for all persons.

For feminists, a corollary of this commitment to being continually reformed is the implicit conviction that theological formulations are conditioned by the cultures out of which they come. Feminists suggest that it is precisely Reformed theologians who should be most skeptical of any claim to the "timeless truth" of particular ways of talking either about God or the human condition. The Reformed notion that the faith can and must be confessed anew in each generation implies the limitations of previous confessions in capturing the complete experience of the church's response to God.

In connection with this principle, feminists contend that everyone reads Scripture and interprets Christian tradition from perspectives that are culturally and ideologically conditioned. Thus the question is not whether one confesses the faith with ideological convictions but whether those convictions are made available for public debate and critique. This cultural or ideological influence has both advantages and disadvantages. In the Reformation, criticizing the old way of reading the Bible led to a whole new formulation of the Christian faith. The alteration of a cultural or ideological framework allowed the truth of the gospel to be heard anew. But all ideology and all cultural contexts are limited and must constantly be criticized by other voices and experiences. Thus feminists affirm the need for ongoing reformation and self-criticism as part of the theological process.

A second affirmation that feminists would make of the Reformed tradition follows directly from the first. For Calvin and many of his followers, the most grievous sin was idolatry: the worship of some*thing* other than the one true God. Calvinists have long been scathing in their criticism of other Christians who seem to revere created things (such as theological traditions or liturgical forms) more than God.

Feminists would join that conviction to press the point further. Is it possible that Reformed Christians, like many others, have made an idol of patriarchy? Is it possible that some within the Reformed tradition have made the norm of male leadership into a principle that must not be violated (and thus into a "god")? Is it possible that insisting that God must be called "Father" itself amounts to placing an idol between ourselves and the God who is not literally father or mother? In raising these questions, feminists urge the Reformed tradition to return to its own reforming principle because that principle, as the Reformers so clearly saw, comes out of the very nature of God as beyond what any human can imagine or say.

Finally, feminist theology can join in affirmation of the fundamental principles that undergird Reformed and Presbyterian church government. This system has always been suspicious of creating a "priestly caste" that has authority over the church at large and that is thought to be "better" or "more holy" than the church membership. In recognition of this understanding, Presbyterians have argued that the offices of ministry (of elder, deacon, and minister of the word) are equal in value to the life of the church and that the authority of elders and ministers must always be equal in governing bodies. Further, there is a constitutional suspicion of one-person rule among Presbyterians. The tendency to do everything by committees in fact stems from the conviction that the decision of the group is preferable and less liable to corruption than the decision of an individual acting in isolation from the community.

Such values are clearly in line with feminist concerns about patterns of human community that affirm the equality of all persons and true interdependence. Presbyterian government provides an arena in which to act out the conviction that persons find their true identity in relationships in which all recognize genuine interdependence. This system is a structure that affirms mutuality and connection in ways quite unlike many other denominations or secular organizations. Thus, feminists are likely to find much that can be affirmed about Presbyterian church order when the church is faithful to the values it endorses.

In addition to these affirmations of the Reformed tradition, feminists urge that the Reformed tradition needs to be broadened or expanded. A hallmark of the Reformed tradition is, of course, its emphasis on the sovereignty of God and God's power with respect to the created order. But many have criticized this tradition because it seems to leave no room for human freedom. If grace is irresistible and only those whom God chooses can respond to God, in what sense are human beings free? Feminists and others argue that this emphasis on the sovereignty of God and God's grace ignores those biblical texts that seem clearly to suggest that God values human choice and free will.

Many besides feminists debate whether human beings choose to respond to God or whether even that choice to respond is the gift of God. But feminists argue that to perpetuate the notion that humans do not have the ability to make free choices is related to traditional ways of viewing the male-female relationship. Women have long been stereotyped as weak and passive, in need of someone (some man) to protect or rescue them. This view does injustice to the humanity of women and risks women's complicity in relationships of excessive dependence. What is oppressive in one case, they suggest, is oppressive in the other. To this end, they argue that God's goal is to liberate women and men so that they can respond freely to God and join God as the partners they were created to be in the first place.

The way in which God's sovereignty has been construed also has implications for christology. Feminists contend that Reformed theologians have emphasized the lordship of Christ to the exclusion of the servanthood of Christ. Not only in its confessions and theological statements but in hymns, preaching, and prayer life, Reformed Christians have tended to stress the Christ who reigns in power and who is Lord over all life and all nations. While that theme is clearly represented in Scripture, and while it is an important claim, nevertheless the biblical Jesus is presented more consistently as the one who came "not to be served but to serve and to give his life as a ransom for many" (Mark 10:45). Using the hymn in Philippians, feminists urge that as much emphasis be placed on the notion that Jesus "emptied himself, taking on himself the form of a servant," as is placed on the conclusion that "at the name of Jesus every knee should bow" (Phil. 2:5-11).

Restoring the "servant" image is important for many feminists. However, it is made difficult by the fact that the idea of servanthood has been used to oppress not only women but more generally all those who are economically and racially exploited. Women have been urged to empty themselves for their children, their husbands, male religious leaders, and others. This they have done but often at very great cost to their own identity as persons. If servanthood is to be restored as a viable concept for feminists, the church must begin by affirming the gifts, significance, and worth of women (in particular) who, out of a strong self-affirmation, are called and enabled to serve.

When the servant image for God's manifestation in Christ is regained, God's solidarity with those whom Christ came to serve can be seen more clearly — namely, the poor, the suffering, the excluded, and the oppressed. Here feminists make common cause with other liberation theologians who find in both Old and New Testaments God's particular concern for and solidarity with those who stand outside the boundaries of "good" or religious society. The God who is present as One who serves breaks through barriers to discover what the other needs. God is thereby vulnerable to the reality of human suffering and truly present within it to redeem it.

Rosemary Radford Ruether has suggested the spiritual significance of this affirmation for women by recounting an experience shared in one of her theological seminars. A woman described how she had been attacked one night, dragged into the bushes and raped. The woman thought that the man would kill her, but she regained consciousness later to realize that he had left. As she came to, the woman described having a vision of Jesus hanging on the cross, but his body was that of a woman. The vision filled her with great peace and the knowledge that she would recover. The ability to see Jesus crucified as a woman made real to her the presence of God with all persons who suffer, with all women who are violated, with all children who are abused or starved, with all men who are killed or cast aside.[6]

Finally, feminist theologians suggest that the Reformed tradition be expanded by recalling that God communicates with humanity not simply through "words" or intellectual ideas. As Calvin noted, God accommodates God's self to humanity in ways and means that humans understand and perceive. These include most particularly the sacraments, where words are united with physical elements. In ritual actions, through song and sight, the presence of God and God's grace are made real. The Reformed tradition, in its fear of idolatry, may have removed too quickly those nonverbal means by which people recognize and understand the reality of God. Feminist theology and feminist experience reach out and back into Christian tradition for symbols and liturgies that confront the whole human being with God's self-disclosure.

NOTES

1. Some in the Reformed tradition find these notions equally suspect as they are found in process theology (e.g., in the work of John Cobb, David Griffin, or Majorie Suchocki) and in the work of such Reformed theologians as Jürgen Moltmann (especially in *The Crucified God*).

2. The substance of the criticism can be found in Donald G. Bloesch, *The Battle for the Trinity: The Debate over Inclusive God-Language* (Ann Arbor: Vine Books, 1985).

3. "Definitions and Guidelines on Inclusive Language," Presbyterian Church (USA), 1985.

4. This position can be seen in "Presbyterian Understanding and Use of Holy Scripture," Presbyterian Church (USA).

5. See "Definitions and Guidelines on Inclusive Language."

6. Ruether, "Renewal or New Creation? Feminist Spirituality and Historical Religion," *Harvard Divinity Bulletin,* February-March 1986, p. 7.

The Reformed Family Today: Some Theological Reflections

Alan P. F. Sell

For reasons best known to himself, Donald McKim has asked me to offer some personal comments under the above title. I shall not begin from any supposedly normative definition of "Reformed," for, on almost any proposed definition except the most general (e.g., "the Reformed tradition comprises the heirs of the Zwinglian and Calvinist Reform movements"), any definition would serve only to exclude some who are quite convinced that they (even, in a few cases, that they alone) are Reformed. We must take seriously the variety — theological, historical, methodological, ecclesiological, cultural — that the Reformed family *as we actually experience it* displays. So great is this variety that the patience and charity shown by our dialogue partners of other Christian communions can only be described as exemplary. How often they must wonder with what, precisely, they are dealing when they deal with us! At what point does a "rich diversity" become an unholy muddle? We shall do well to cultivate the distance for which Burns prayed:

O wad some Pow'r the giftie gie us
To see oursels as others see us!

Let us, by an imaginative leap, place ourselves in the position of a friendly observer of our Reformed family. What might such a person expect to find on investigating us? First, one might have some general acquaintance with our classical confessional literature (thereby outshining many of us!), and one might suppose that we all subscribe to the doctrinal positions specified therein. One would be in for a shock! It would appear that subscription to confessional statements has never normally been required of all Reformed church members. In some churches, ministers and elders have been under this necessity (in some ministers only), and latterly the assent is often required in quite general terms. There are some Reformed churches that continue to define themselves by reference to their classical confessions — and these are to be found in many regions of the world, not in one only. But there are more who "honor" their older confessions, and this honoring can vary from general acceptance of content to the most casual acknowledgment that there exist ancient documents within the tradition.

A number of factors have combined to produce this diversity of attitude toward the classical confessions. For example, some confessional statements are nowadays disturbing to many — the anathemas that the First and Second Helvetic and the Belgic Confessions hurl at the Anabaptists come to mind. These have had to be dealt with in the international Mennonite-Reformed dialogue.[1] On the other hand, if our concern is to express our faith today, classical confessions can in places appear too weak. Some feel, for example, that their treatment of the doctrine of creation is inadequate, that in our time we must take much more seriously the ecological threat and the consequent urgency of proper stewardship of the created order. Again, Reformed history is not lacking in examples of those who, like most eighteenth-century English Presbyterians, became "Arian" and then Unitarian, the Westminster Confession notwithstanding;[2] or of those who, like the eighteenth-century English Congregationalists, managed to remain doctrinally orthodox for the most part while making little actual use of their Savoy Declaration of Faith and Order (1658).[3] As for more recent confessions within the Reformed family, these vary greatly in style and type.[4] Some resemble classical confessions in their scope, while others are more in the nature of testimonies upon specific points — such as the need to side with the oppressed and to work for political change. No doubt all of the Reformed affirm the need to relate confessional statements to the Bible — indeed, to subordinate them to it — but there is no one view of the process of achieving that relationship today.

Our friendly observer might well feel bewildered by now; but there is more. "Even if the Reformed adopt somewhat diverse positions vis-à-vis their confessions," one might say, "there must surely be *some* doctrines that are characteristically Reformed and that unite you as a family." It is not that straightforward. Let us, for the sake of argument, suppose that the teaching of Calvin is characteristically Reformed. To approach this teaching is to interpret it, and at once there seem to be many Calvins. Is Calvin the theologian of predestination (in which case some recent Reformed confessions have seriously departed from him)? Is he the theologian of the Holy Spirit? Or of the church? He has been presented in all of these ways, and others. Furthermore, we cannot overlook the fact that, unlike some other Christian communions, the Reformed do employ themselves in hammering our Reformed teaching, and while there is considerable (and some would say providential) common ground — notably in the classical confessions — there are differences of emphasis too. It is thus not surprising that there have been and are numerous squabbles within the family as to who is, or is not, doctrinally "pure." An impartial dictionary describes Karl Barth as "the most influential modern Calvinist theologian"[5] — a description that would be repudiated by some who really know what Calvinism is: they would not deny that Barth was influential, but they would not admit him as a true son of Calvin.[6] There is the further complication that some theologians who are ecclesiastically Reformed are occupied with theology in its existential, process, and manifold contextual expressions, which may but frequently do not owe much to Calvin and his heirs. And, conversely, there are ardent present-day Calvinists within other Christian communions, notably the Anglican and the Baptist. Finally, we cannot fail to observe that there has been marked erosion at the frontiers of some of the traditional doctrinal boundaries. This has enabled the Reformed to unite with Methodists in Canada (1925), Zambia (1965), Australia (1977), and elsewhere, and it has permitted the World Alliance of Reformed Churches and the

World Methodist Council jointly to declare that "the classical doctrinal obstacles [especially those concerning grace and salvation] ought not to be seen as obstacles to unity between Methodists and Reformed."[7]

It would therefore seem that there are not ten or twenty — or even FIVE — doctrines that are Reformed in the sense that they are nobody else's. The Reformers, let us recall, had catholic intentions: they were in quest of a biblically based account of the gospel of God's grace. Thus, if they *emphasized,* as they did, God's sovereignty in creation and redemption; if they *emphasized,* as they did, the priority of the regenerating work of God the Holy Spirit; if they *emphasized,* as they did, the inescapability of the church and the duty of raising the banner of Christ's lordship over the whole of life — then they made these emphases not because they were Reformed but because they were scriptural. They went in quest of catholic truth, and they turned to the Bible to find it.[8]

By now our friendly observer is wondering what could possibly differentiate the Reformed from other Christian communions. Could it be polity? Here again the family is diverse. Both the presbyterial and the congregational polities are represented within the World Alliance of Reformed Churches, and the transconfessionally united churches in membership display yet other governmental characteristics in accordance with their respective heritages. Moreover, both "presbyterian" and "congregational" mean somewhat different things in different places;[9] and while the former polity belongs also to the Methodists, the latter is shared by Baptists and others.

What, then, of worship? Is this the differentiating feature? Hardly. For while there are examples of Reformed liturgies that owe much to the classical directories for public worship, there are many more that have arisen from missionary-borne evangelicalism and that are reproduced by Reformed, Lutherans, Baptists, Methodists, and others alike.

If we look at the Reformed family as it actually exists, then with respect to any possible candidate for distinctiveness to which our friendly observer might point, we should have to explain either that that feature is not ours exclusively or that we manifest it in puzzlingly diverse ways. The traditional boundaries in doctrine and worship are increasingly transgressed, while newer ways of contextualizing the gospel and of worshiping its Lord repudiate (if indeed they are always aware of) older confessional roadblocks.

How ought we to respond to this? Should we endeavor to recall our people to the old paths? Then whose old paths, and how? Or ought we to ask whether the living Lord is challenging us to notice something in the apparent familial confusion by which we are surrounded? Can it be that we are being constrained to see that our unity is not in such "works" as confessional subscription, doctrinal system, polity, or specific forms of worship but in Christ, who transcends them all? If so, this would have important implications for our relations with other Christians — unless, of course, the Reformed intend it to be understood that they alone are in Christ.

Let me immediately guard my flank. I know very well that there are disastrously escapist ways of proclaiming that we are all one in Christ Jesus. If Christians enunciate this truth (and it is true) in some sentimental, spiritual sense, while at the same time manifesting no concern to eradicate those sectarian factors that give the lie to it empirically and that divide the Lord's people at his table, they are verging on the blasphemous. They are, as it were, uprooting the faith from the stuff of history, and for this to happen in a religion that has the incarnation at its heart is, to say the least, paradoxical. I concur with John Whale's whimsical remark that "it would be an Irish result if the only discernible mark of the Church were its invisibility."[10]

Again, I do not wish to be understood as

saying that doctrine, worship, and polity are unimportant and that so long as we are "in Christ" it does not matter what we believe, how we worship, or how we order our churchly life. As a matter of fact, I should like to hear more from Reformed pulpits than I do concerning predestination as *good* news, concerning total depravity as a fact requiring an objective atonement, about the catholicity of the local church, about death (a theme too often confined to funeral services) and resurrection. I could easily extend this list. As for worship, it would be a great advance if in all Reformed places we could take seriously the relation of word and sacrament, to mention but one pressing need. It may appear redundant to remind the Reformed of the importance of polity, for "church lawyers" committees and commissions and (sometimes self-perpetuating) bureaucracies are ubiquitous. But at least we could examine them in the light of the gospel they are intended to serve.

Is it, perhaps, significant that our "friendly observer," when casting around for our differentiating features, did not propose for consideration our methods of church discipline? Have we so lost the idea of discipline under the gospel with a view to the upbuilding of the church for witness and service that the possibility did not occur to the observer?

The conclusion so far is that confronted by the Reformed family's actual variety (nonevaluative term!) on all the points so far raised, and also by the transconfessional processes that have been indicated, we cannot pretend that we are distinguished from all other Christians by any of them. We may thus be helped to grasp that our identity (and that of other Christians) is in Christ, that the church catholic comprises all who are his, and that the pressing questions are "How are we to demolish the sectarian impediments to the expression of this unity?" and "How much confessional, doctrinal, liturgical, and church political tolerance can we muster vis-à-vis others who, *like ourselves,*

have been accepted by *God* just as they are?" How often has the Reformed Christian been given the impression that "doctrinally and emotionally he was to live by grace; but his conduct was to be exactly the same *as if he expected to be justified by works,*"[11] and how often have we conveyed that impression to others?

Precisely because of the multifaceted nature of the Reformed family as it actually exists, it would be foolhardy to wax "prophetic," as if specific injunctions of an universally applicable kind could be enunciated. The diversity within the family is not only doctrinal, ecclesiological, liturgical, and historical; it is linguistic and cultural too. We have to reckon with the fact that churches are at different points in their pilgrimages. It ill behooves one section of the family imperialistically to impose its own sociotheological stances upon another. Thus, for example, in 1987 the United Reformed Church in the United Kingdom (URCUK) celebrated the seventieth anniversary of the ordination of its first woman minister.[12] By contrast, it will be some time before some Reformed churches feel able to take this step, the impediment normally being cultural rather than theological.[13] On the other hand, many churches that are much younger than the traditions that constitute the URCUK have had to witness all through their history in a multifaith context. And consider that if anyone in England had prophesied in 1940 that fifty years on there would be more Muslims in England than Methodists and Baptists together (as there are), he or she would scarcely have been believed.

The very diversity of the Reformed family makes the search for a way of articulating that which we can hold together in a threatened and a divided world the more urgent.[14] However, if prophetic universal prescriptions are out, a few miscellaneous musings, offered tentatively, may be in order.

Can it be that the Reformed family needs to recover what H. H. Farmer used to call "the 'Godness' of God?" We have traditionally proclaimed God as sovereign over all and, sadly, we have sometimes forgotten that it is sovereign *grace* with which we have to do. Here and there "inscrutable will" has all but been substituted for that grace. No wonder the renewed emphasis on God's love came as such a welcome relief to many from the middle of the nineteenth century onward. But if the pendulum should swing so far that we forget that God's love is *holy* love, then we shall have a less than adequate notion of sin, and the atonement will begin to appear redundant. We shall be confirmed in our post-Enlightenment autonomy, our worship will become increasingly anthropocentric, and God will sooner or later become simply a heavenly rubber stamp on policies and programs to which we are committed on strictly nonreligious grounds. Happily, the Orthodox we have always with us, and they will not allow us to overlook the doctrine of the Trinity. But quite apart from our dialogue with them,[15] we should do well to ponder the activity of the triune God as *the* context of Christian theology, by reference to which all our local contextualization is judged.

Can it be that we need to recover our sense of the covenanted family of the church? Under the impact of modern individualism (to which the evangelical emphasis upon "my soul" and the Catholic enthusiasm for "making *my* communion" are not unrelated), and aided and abetted by the increased mobility of many church people, the idea of the visible church as a true congregation of saints has receded. Instead, in some societies, we have the sort of religious consumerism that regards the church as the religious equivalent of a supermarket, from which we take what we desire — or, if we are thwarted, we go to a rival company. Now if consumerism can overtake some local churches, may not the "corporate model" and attendant "professional" notions so consume

some ministers as seriously to undermine the idea of vocation? Although the minister should not be everybody's doormat, there can be a concern for status (measured in terms of the number of degrees held, the size of stipend, the number of church members on the roll, the area covered by the church "plant") that is quite unhealthy. Moreover, I cannot say I was much cheered by an elder who explained that "in our church we now have a called pastor, and a number of contract pastors; and the great thing about the contract pastors is that we can fire them so much more easily." What has happened to the idea of the sanctity of the relation between pastor and people? Do we really wish to exchange the model of the undershepherd of Christ's flock for that of a professionally engaged *individual?*

In some quarters the Reformed have even managed to construe the doctrine of the priesthood of all believers in an individualistic way. Quite apart from the fragmentation of ministry and witness to which this can lead, the hermeneutical price paid can be colossal. We have proclaimed with our lips that we discover the mind of God by the Spirit through the Scripture discerned in fellowship, and then, all too often, we have, so to speak, given the Bible back to the "priest," be he orthodox, fundamentalist, liberal — or even a "prince of the pulpit." This in turn has fostered a spirit of "leaving it to the expert" that is quite out of place in Reformed circles. Not a little inner-Reformed sectarianism has taken root because the ecclesiological locus of hermeneutical activity has been underemphasized: such slogans as "I am of Kuyper," "I am of Old Princeton," and "I am of Van Til" have been church-dividing in our midst. We do not demean the pulpit as the place of gospel proclamation if at the same time we uphold the whole company of believers as a community of biblical interpretation: on the contrary.

Again, has not the individualistic approach adversely affected our understanding of baptism — at least here and there? Almost exactly one hundred years ago the sadly neglected theologian Robert Mackintosh was reflecting upon this point. He regarded both the high (Anglican) churchman and the ranting revivalist as individualists, because to the former the church is the "aggregate of baptized individuals" and to the latter it is the aggregate of converted individuals. His own view, characteristically expressed, was that infant baptism "stands as the one bulwark against the destruction of the Church in favour of the evangelistic committee."[16] The true context of infant baptism — and of believers' baptism too — is the covenant community, and that community is under the obligation of receiving, nurturing, and caring pastorally for all who are by grace grafted into it. Moreover, is there not reason to think that the relation between baptism, nurture, conversion, profession of faith, and admission as a "full" member of the church requires thoughtful attention in our midst — not least in relation to the presence of children at the Lord's Table?

What of the wider expressions of covenant fellowship? Is there work to be done here? Even (or, as I should prefer to say, especially) those of the Reformed tradition who have emphasized the ecclesiology of the gathered church have recognized (when they have behaved themselves!) that their anchorage in the local church is what makes them members of the church catholic. One cannot be a "Christian in general": Christians are earthed saints.[17] But the experience and expression of the catholicity have sometimes left much to be desired. There remains much to be done, for example, in relation to the wider (or, as some would say, the higher) foci of churchly life. Consider national or regional denominations vis-à-vis the question of representation. In some circles the question of representation will be construed as indicating the need to ensure the presence of minority groups on church committees and the like. But what I am thinking of here is the seldom discussed question "How far are the pronouncements of our wider and widest (or higher and highest) assemblies and councils genuinely representative of the mind of the denomination?" Those who attend such councils are to some extent self-selecting — they are retired or able to secure freedom from work — and they usually have access to information and expertise that is not available to most local congregations. We must believe that God the Holy Spirit can address people in church assemblies no less than elsewhere, but the question of the reception of their decisions remains. What seems clear is that if the membership at large cannot identify with those decisions, then rebellion, or more likely apathy (sometimes accompanied by the surly withholding of funds from "them" at the "headquarters"), may ensue.

What then of the global family of Reformed churches? Is there a strong sense of covenant community here? My interpretation of the experience of the World Alliance of Reformed Churches (I cannot speak of the Reformed Ecumenical Synod) is that the situation is mixed. Some member churches of the Alliance feel strong emotional ties to others — and not always only to those with whom they have historic, ecclesiological, missiological, and financial links. Within the constraints of its budget (which are severe) the Alliance can and does provide a forum for converted witness and for theological and other debate. The fact cannot be overlooked, however, that there are those in some member churches who question the continuance of separate Christian world communions. Such voices may on occasion be heard — for example, in one or two of the transconfessionally united churches. No doubt it is somewhat inconvenient for such a church to be in membership with more than one Christian world communion. The reality is, however, that (1) things ecumenical move at different speeds in different places, (2) so long as there exist on the ground churches of the several denominations there will be a need for agencies at all levels to encourage relations between them, and (3) those who have already united have much to share with those of the traditions whence they themselves have come.

But even if the place of the Christian world communions in general, and of the World Alliance of Reformed Churches in particular, be granted, the practical difficulty of involving the grass roots around the world in the international program are formidable. It can even be difficult to secure responses from appropriate church committees and commissions. There are many reasons for this. Some member denominations generate an amazing amount of study material of their own, their regional organizations add still more, and international reports and documents may appear as the most remote and hence the most easily shelvable. Few member churches of the Alliance have the resources of time, money, and people that would be required to study in depth all of the material that actually comes their way. Again, although the Alliance's agenda is set by representatives of the member churches worldwide, it can still happen that some aspects of the program appear remote from the concerns of some local churches. I have heard it said, for example, that international bilateral dialogues between one Christian world communion and another are simply "a Western hobby" — though I should myself hope that attempts to remove the scandal of a divided Lord's Table would be of some interest in all parts of the world. Then there is the practical challenge of rendering international reports into the many languages of the family: some churches can free more resources for this activity than others. At the very least the Alliance is a symbol, and symbols are important. I believe that it is more than a symbol and that many are grateful for the work it does. But we have a good deal to do before we can truly say that all Reformed Christians around the world have a lively sense of membership in a global fellowship of Christ's people.

A small but important step toward fostering international fellowship would be taken if some means could be found of enabling Reformed churches to know more of one another's stories and of the links between them. We have institutes for Reformation studies, denominational historical societies, and such interest groups as the Mercersburg Society, but since cross-fertilization between these is often minimal, opportunities of sharing our stories are lost, and a "tunnel vision" view of the heritage may result. So far as I know, there is nowhere in the world that the several strands of the Reformed heritage — Swiss, Dutch, Scottish, English, Welsh, Kenyan, Korean — are simultaneously studied by scholars working in cooperation. No doubt adverse financial conditions, together with the fact that library and archive resources are scattered over a wide geographical area, will forever prevent the establishment of a permanent base for such an operation. But is an occasionally traveling, regularly corresponding institute of cooperating scholars out of the question?

So to the last piece of miscellaneous musing. Can it be that the Reformed need to give much more urgent attention to the provision of highly trained, ecclesiastically competent personnel? I do not at all wish to sound elitist; I do not say that every minister should pass through exactly the same program of education: there are diversities of gifts; I do not deny that the street preacher who says, "I have never sat at the feet of a theological professor, but I have stood at the foot of the Cross," may have a message from the Lord; and I never forget that when the Puritans extolled a learned ministry they meant, above all, one learned in the things of God. It is simply that I believe that we shall always need some who are highly trained as well as ecclesiastically competent, and I suspect that we may not have enough of them at the moment. For what is the actual situation? Many rapidly growing churches in Africa and Asia cannot produce theological leaders quickly enough to meet the demand. In the West some church memberships are declining, and with them the number of ordinations. Moreover, the average age of ordinands is rising, and increasing numbers are being ordained in their forties and later. We cannot expect that in the normal course of events these (though more than welcome in the ministry) will have the time to become the scholars of the twenty-first century. It is therefore urgent that we identify and nurture academically able younger ordinands.

Again, in some quarters reduced financial support from governments to institutions in which ministers are trained is leaving a sad trail of frozen posts and weakened faculties, while private institutions all too easily succumb to the theological-political predilections of donors and benefactors whether liberal or (perhaps more typically at present) conservative. There has been a laicizing of theological education, and especially of religious studies, that is welcome in itself but that means that many will quite properly acquire their education in theological-religious fields with no church-vocational goal in mind. Within the seminaries there has been a proliferation of "new" disciplines: counseling, church administration, Christian education, ecumenical studies, and many more. This cannot but throw into relief questions concerning course coherence and, especially, depth. Is there not a real possibility that in some institutions we may be giving students so many shallow tastes of so many disciplines that we shall simply inoculate them against those disciplines for life? What is the remedy? Will the Reformed family, with its strong heritage of theological work (now seriously under threat) and its long tradition of "scholar preachers" (now an endangered species), be able to meet the challenge? Will it wish to?

It seems to me (if I may record a conviction rather than simply muse) that few things are more important than the supply of able ministers of the gospel who will declare the good news of God's redeeming grace through clear exposition and well-judged application of the biblical texts; who will view the work of the whole church in a theological perspective; who will care for Christ's flock out of deep theological reflection on the issues and challenges of life and out of prayer; who will relate to other Christians on the ground of that catholicity which insists that in Christ God has made us one body and which therefore shuns sectarianism in all its guises (doctrines of ministerial orders, divergent theological methods, racism, and anything else that would divide those whom Christ has made one); who will testify to Christ's lordship over the whole of life and all creation; who will acknowledge the church's constant need of being reformed by the Spirit through the word; and whose sincere, joyful, and yet imperfect worship of the triune God in this life will be but the prelude to that heavenly praise that will be worthy and know no end. For as long as ministers of this kind are to be nurtured, so long shall we need a nucleus of those able to stimulate, challenge, and resource them.

There are many more theological tasks that those competent will need to undertake. One that arises directly from the earlier part of this chapter may be expressed in question form thus: "How are we to understand theologically the variety in the Reformed family that we actually experience?" One aspect of this question is the matter of the development of doctrine and practice within the church. On what grounds may we say that such developments are worthy or unworthy? It is well known that some assembly politicians are quick to advise their audiences in which way the Spirit is leading — namely, in the direction of the politician's own favored policy. But there must be more to it than that . . .

I was invited to offer some theological reflections on the Reformed family today, and I have attempted to discharge my brief. But even theology needs to be kept in perspective. "The supreme Christian gift is not eternal truth but eternal life, more life, fuller life, godlier life, holier life, a life inspired spiritually from the past but not ruled romantically by the past, ruled rather by perfection."[18] It is no bad thing for the Reformed, whose path has been strewn with intellectual battles within and without, to recall that the Bible says more about letting our light shine than about keeping our pencils sharp. No doubt the Reformed will ever wish to attend to the latter as a means to the former, but let them beware of sharp pencils and dim lights.

NOTES

1. See *Mennonites and Reformed in Dialogue*, ed. H. G. vom Berg, H. Kossen, L. Miller, and L. Vischer (Geneva: World Alliance of Reformed Churches, and Lombard, Ill.: Mennonite World Conference, 1986).

2. See A. P. F. Sell, "Presbyterianism in Eighteenth-Century England: The Doctrinal Dimension," in *Dissenting Thought and the Life of the Churches: Studies in an English Tradition* (Lewiston, N.Y.: Edwin Mellen Press, 1990), chap. 5.

3. See A. P. F. Sell, "Confessing the Faith in English Congregationalism," in *Dissenting Thought and the Life of the Churches*, chap. 1.

4. For a collection of recent confessions, see *Reformed Witness Today*, ed. Lukas Vischer (Bern: Evangelische Arbeitsstelle Oekumene Schweiz, 1982).

5. *The Penguin Dictionary of Religions*, ed. John R. Hinnels (Harmondsworth: Penguin, 1984), p. 76.

6. See, e.g., Cornelius Van Til, *The New Modernism* (1946; reprint, Philadelphia: Presbyterian and Reformed, 1973); and Gordon H. Clark, *Karl Barth's Theological Method* (Philadelphia: Presbyterian and Reformed, 1963).

7. See the report of the international Reformed-Methodist consultation, "Together in God's Grace," *Reformed World* 39 (December 1987): 828. For the traditional positions, see A. P. F. Sell, *The Great Debate: Calvinism, Arminianism and Salvation* (Grand Rapids: Baker Book, 1983).

8. See further, A. P. F. Sell, "The Witness of Reformed Theology and Theologians Today," *Near East School of Theology Theological Review* 7 (1986): 91-106. This is an address originally given at the Collegium Doctorum, Debrecen, Hungary, in August 1985.

9. Consider, for example, the denotation of "elder." See Robert W. Henderson, *Profile of the Eldership* (Geneva: World Alliance of Reformed Churches, 1975).

10. J. S. Whale, *Christian Doctrine* (1941; reprint, London: Collins-Fontana, 1957), p. 134.

11. Robert Mackintosh, "The Insufficiency of Revivalism as a Religious System," in *Essays towards a New Theology* (Glasgow: Maclehose, 1889), p. 8. On Mackintosh, see A. P. F. Sell, *Robert Mackintosh: Theologian of Integrity* (Bern: Peter Lang, 1977).

12. See Elaine Kaye, "Constance Coltman — A Forgotten Pioneer," *Journal of the United Reformed Church History Society* 4 (May 1988): 134-46.

13. See Henny G. Dirks-Blatt, "The Ordination of Women to the Ministry in the Member Churches of the World Alliance of Reformed Churches," *Reformed World* 38 (December 1985): 434-43; 39 (March 1986): 484-95.

14. That the urgency of this quest is not lost upon the World Alliance of Reformed churches may be seen from the theme of its major current study, "Called to Witness to the Gospel Today," from many of its recent publications, and from the theme of its recent General Council (Seoul, 1989): "Who Do You Say That I Am?"

15. The theme of the current international Orthodox-Reformed dialogue is "The Doctrine of the Trinity in the Light of the Nicene-Constantinopolitan Creed."

16. Mackintosh, "The Insufficiency of Revivalism as a Religious System," p. 28. On the previous page he declares that "infant baptism is the great rock of offence to the triumphant revival."

17. See A. P. F. Sell, *Saints: Visible, Orderly and Catholic: The Congregational Idea of the Church* (Geneva: World Alliance of Reformed Churches, 1986).

18. P. T. Forsyth, *Positive Preaching and the Modern Mind* (1907; reprint, London: Independent Press, 1964), p. 208.

Index of Names

Abelard, Peter, 53

Ahlstrom, Sydney, 29, 356

Alexander, Archibald, 51, 59-61

Alexander of Hales, 222

Alexander, Samuel, 387

Altizer, Thomas J. J., 387

Ambrose, 137, 306

Ambrosiaster, 306

Ames, William, 99-100

Anselm of Canterbury, 53, 88, 120, 126, 411

Apollonius, William, 355

Aquinas, Thomas, 6, 53, 58, 66-67, 71-72, 88-89, 171, 222, 258n.50, 280-81, 284, 293, 301n.34, 386, 401-2

Aristotle, 69, 88, 393, 395, 397

Arius, 283

Augustine, 52-53, 55-56, 60-61, 90-91, 96, 117-18, 156, 159, 171, 173, 175, 306, 363-64, 386-87, 401

Aulén, Gustav, 130

Ayer, A. J., 73

Bacon, Francis, 59

Baillie, Donald M., 261, 263

Baillie, Robert, 355

Bainton, Roland H., 10

Ball, John, 100

Barth, Karl, xiv, 3, 6, 14, 62, 78, 87-88, 95, 97, 104, 112, 114-16, 126, 149, 157, 159, 183, 185, 187-89, 191-93, 295, 326, 337, 340-41, 365-66, 386-88, 393, 396-97, 398n.4, 401-2, 404, 409, 421-22, 429, 434

Basil of Caesarea, 306

Bavinck, Herman, 66-67, 72, 149, 163, 165, 226, 387

Bax, Douglas, 418

Baxter, Richard, 100

Bennett, William J., 211

Benoit, Jean-Daniel, 15

Berdyaev, Nicholas, 6, 397

Berengarius of Tours, 283-84

Bergson, Henri, 387

Berkhof, Hendrikus, xiv, 77-78, 103, 380-83

Berkhof, Louis, 88

Berkouwer, G. C., xiv, 78, 127-30, 154n.12, 157, 215

Bernard of Clairvaux, 54

Beza, Theodore, 57-58, 89, 156, 159

Biel, Gabriel, 96-97, 223

Bloch, Ernst, 95

Bloesch, Donald G., 369n.3, 373